R. Gupta's®

IGNOU

Indira Gandhi National Open University

B.Ed

Entrance Test

Previous Years' Papers

(With Answers)

by

RPH Editorial Board

RAMESH PUBLISHING HOUSE, NEW DELHI

Published by

O.P. Gupta *for* Ramesh Publishing House

Admin. Office

12-H, New Daryaganj Road, Opp. Officers' Mess,
New Delhi-110002 ✆ 23275224, 23245124

E-mail: info@rameshpublishinghouse.com
For Online Shopping: www.rameshpublishinghouse.com

Showroom

- Balaji Market, Nai Sarak, Delhi-6 ✆ 23253720, 23282525
- 4457, Nai Sarak, Delhi-6, ✆ 23918938

Book Code: R-1728

ISBN: 978-93-5012-513-7

Price: ₹ 320

Printed at: Deepak Offset, Delhi

CONTENTS

PREVIOUS YEAR PAPERS (SOLVED)

- IGNOU B.Ed. Entrance Test, 2025 1-28
- IGNOU B.Ed. Entrance Test, 2024 1-40
- IGNOU B.Ed. Entrance Test, 2023 1-16
- IGNOU B.Ed. Entrance Test, 2022 1-20
- IGNOU B.Ed. Entrance Test, 2021 1-16
- IGNOU B.Ed. Entrance Test, 2019 1-16
- IGNOU B.Ed. Entrance Test, 2018 1-16
- IGNOU B.Ed. Entrance Test, 2017 1-16
- IGNOU B.Ed. Entrance Test, 2015 1-16
- IGNOU B.Ed. Entrance Test, 2014 1-16
- IGNOU B.Ed. Entrance Test, 2013 17-34
- IGNOU B.Ed. Entrance Test, 2012 35-48
- IGNOU B.Ed. Entrance Test, 2011 49-67
- IGNOU B.Ed. Entrance Test, 2010 68-79
- IGNOU B.Ed. Entrance Test, 2009 80-96
- IGNOU B.Ed. Entrance Test, 2008 97-111
- IGNOU B.Ed. Entrance Test, 2007 112-129
- IGNOU B.Ed. Entrance Test, 2006 130-146
- IGNOU B.Ed. Entrance Test, 2005 147-163
- IGNOU B.Ed. Entrance Test, 2004 164-180

Previous Years' Paper

IGNOU B.Ed. ENTRANCE EXAM 2025

(Exam held on 16-03-2025)

Part-A

Section-I: General English Comprehension

Directions (Qs. No. 1-10): *Read the following passage carefully and choose the most appropriate answer out of the four choices given after each question:*

Bacteriophages (usually referred to simply as phages) are viruses that invade bacteria and seize their genetic material to make copies of themselves. The resulting brood escapes from the bacterium by destroying it. Such viruses are ubiquitous and can even be isolated from wastewater containing human excreta. The human gut contains a large collection of viruses (the phageome), which balances the bacterial microbiome by killing the bad bacteria and allowing good bacteria to thrive. As efficient gene-delivery agents, phages also help bacteria by bringing them new genes. The amazing ingenuity of nature, in this balancing of contending forces in the microbial world, protects us from harm. Across our natural world, phage predation is estimated to destroy one-half of the world's bacteria every 48 hours.

The lower the diversity of the phageome in our bodies, the greater the risk of diseases like inflammatory bowel diseases and colorectal cancer. There are good phages and bad phages. High levels of diversity assure the dominance of good phages. Like the microbiome, phage population is responsive to environmental factors like the composition of our diet, drinking water quality, tobacco and alcohol consumption.

Phages abound in places where bacteria grow–wastewater, garbage, bilge, human and animal excreta. Many countries are now actively hunting for phages, hoping to counter antimicrobial resistance, which is predicted to kill 40 million persons by 2050. India, too, must use its scientific agencies and research institutions to search for friendly phages amidst its vast natural resources of land and water.

1. Phages make copies of genetic material of ....

1. virus
2. bacteria
3. microbe
4. fungus

2. Bacterial microbiome in the gut is balanced by ....

1. phageome
2. virus
3. microbe
4. pH in the gut

3. Bacteriophage destroys ....

1. bacterium
2. fungus
3. worms
4. virus

4. .... deliver new genes to bacteria.

1. Nutrients
2. Pathogen
3. Microbes
4. Phages

5. The amazing ingenuity of nature. Here 'amazing' is the ....

1. adverb
2. verb
3. adjective
4. noun

1. 2 **2.** 1 **3.** 1 **4.** 4 **5.** 3

6. 'Ingenuity of nature' is an example of ....

1. alliteration 2. personification
3. hyperbole 4. metaphor

7. The risk of inflammatory bowel disease can be reduced by ....

1. low level diversity of the phageome
2. high level diversity of good phages
3. low level diversity of microbiome
4. Both 1 and 3

8. Why does the author say that India should search for phages?

1. to fight antimicrobial resistance
2. to fight drug-resistant bacteria
3. to develop antibiotic drugs
4. Both 1 and 2

9. Phages are found in wastewater because of the presence of:

1. virus 2. microbes
3. bacteria 4. Both 1 and 2

10. What is the main theme of the above passage?

1. virtuous viruses 2. drug resistance
3. gut health 4. antibiotics

Section-II: Logical and Analytical Reasoning

Directions (Qs. No. 11-14): *Each of the following questions consists of two pairs of numbers/letter-groups. First pair has a certain relationship Complete the second pair by using the same relationship.*

11. 121 : 1331 :: 441 : ?

1. 1632 2. 8763
3. 9261 4. 9973

12. If $a * b = \dfrac{a+b}{ab}$, then $4 * 1 = ?$

1. 0.80 2. 1.25
3. 0.67 4. 1.75

13. CDE : HIJ :: BCD : ?

1. FGH 2. EFG
3. FGI 4. GHI

14. ACPN : BDQO :: JLYW : ?

1. KMXZ 2. MKZX
3. MKXZ 4. KMZX

Directions (Qs. No. 15-18): *In each of the following questions a number/letter series is given with one term missing. Identify the underlying pattern and complete the series by choosing the correct option.*

15. 1, 2, 3, 6, 4, 5, 6, 15, ...?

1. 7 2. 12
3. 13 4. 21

16. 1, 1, 2, 8, ..., 27.

1. 5 2. 7
3. 3 4. 6

17. AMZ, BLY, CKX, ..., EIV.

1. DIW 2. DJW
3. EJV 4. EKW

18. AMNZ, BLOY, CKPX, ..., EIRV.

1. DJQW 2. DKOW
3. CJQW 4. CKPV

19. If BAT is coded as DCV and CART is coded as ECTV, then SECOND would be coded as:

1. UGFOGE 2. UHFOGE
3. UHEPHE 4. UGEQPE

20. If CARE is coded as ERAC and SCOPE is coded as EPOCS, then SYSTEM would be coded as:

1. METSSY 2. SYSMET
3. METSYS 4. SYSTEM

6. 2	**7.** 2	**8.** 4	**9.** 3	**10.** 1	**11.** 3	**12.** 2	**13.** 4
14. 4	**15.** 1	**16.** 3	**17.** 2	**18.** 1	**19.** *	**20.** 3	

21. If CAR is coded as 105 and DRIVER is coded as 253765, then REVIVE would be coded as:

1. 562736 2. 567637
3. 567376 4. 536752

22. If 35 is written as 8 and 6243 is written as 87, then 453615 would be written as:

1. 766 2. 996
3. 897 4. 985

23. A man walked due east 3 km from his house and then turned left. Then he walked 4 km and stopped. Then he walked the shortest possible distance and reached his house. How far he walked altogether?

1. 14 km 2. 13 km
3. 12 km 4. 10 km

24. You are facing north-east and walk a distance of 12 km. Then, you turn left and walk 5 km. How far are you now from your initial position?

1. 9 km 2. 11 km
3. 13 km 4. 17 km

25. What is the total number of squares hidden in the adjoining figure?

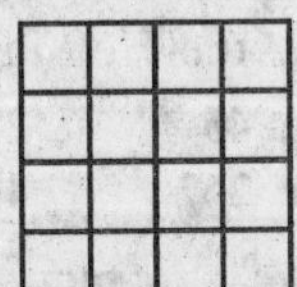

1. 16 2. 24
3. 30 4. 36

26. If Mohan is the brother of the son of Sohan's son, how is Mohan related to Sohan?

1. Nephew 2. Brother
3. Cousin 4. Grandson

27. In an examination 48% students failed in English and 52% failed in Mathematics. If 12% failed in both English and Mathematics, what percentage of students passed in both the subjects?

1. 88% 2. 76%
3. 24% 4. 12%

Directions (Qs. No. 28-30): *Read the following information and answer the questions given below:*

A, B, C, D and E are friends. A is older than B. C is older than B but younger than A. D is younger than E and B. B is older than E.

28. Whose age is between C and E?

1. A 2. B
3. C 4. D

29. Who is of the median age of five?

1. A 2. B
3. C 4. D

30. Who is the eldest of all friends?

1. A 2. B
3. C 4. D

Section-III: Educational and General Awareness

31. Whose teachings inspired the French Revolution?

1. Locke 2. Rousseau
3. Hegel 4. Plato

32. The Rigveda consists of:

1. 1000 hymns 2. 2028 hymns
3. 1028 hymns 4. 1038 hymns

33. Which one of the following nationalist leaders has been described as being radical in politics but conservative on social issues?

1. G. K. Gokhale
2. B. G. Tilak
3. Lala Lajpat Rai
4. Madan Mohan Malviya

21. 3	**22.** 2	**23.** 3	**24.** 3	**25.** 3	**26.** 4	**27.** 4
28. 2	**29.** 2	**30.** 1	**31.** 2	**32.** 3	**33.** 2	

34. Ellora caves were built by:

1. Pallavas 2. Cholas
3. Rashtrakutas 4. Palas

35. Who was called the pioneer of the Panchayati Raj for introducing Local Self-Government in British India?

1. Warren Hastings
2. Lord William Bentinck
3. Lord Canning
4. Lord Ripon

36. Indian Standard Time is the local time of 82.5°E longitude which passes through:

1. Guntur 2. Delhi
3. Prayagraj 4. Kolkata

37. Which country is called the sugar bowl of the world?

1. Cuba 2. India
3. Argentina 4. U.S.A.

38. Which of the following rivers is not a tributary of the Indus?

1. Sutlej 2. Jhelum
3. Bhagirathi 4. Chenab

39. Atmospheric pressure exerted on earth is due to:

1. Rotation of earth
2. Revolution of earth
3. Gravitational pull
4. Uneven heating of earth

40. Which is called the Tiger State in India?

1. Madhya Pradesh
2. Rajasthan
3. Uttar Pradesh
4. Jammu and Kashmir

41. Combination of both face-to-face and technology-mediated instruction is known as:

1. Synchronous learning
2. Blended learning
3. Asynchronous learning
4. Distance learning

42. National Education Policy, 2020 recommends pedagogies which are:

1. Exam-centric 2. Teacher-centric
3. Learner-centric 4. Subject-centric

43. The difference between total revenue and total expenditure is called :

1. Capital deficit 2. Revenue deficit
3. Fiscal deficit 4. Budgetary deficit

44. India is a Federal State because of:

1. Dual Judiciary
2. Dual citizenship prevelent here
3. Share of power between the centre and the states
4. Rigid constitution

45. Money Bill has been defined by the constitution under Article:

1. 109 2. 110
3. 111 4. 112

46. Right to Education Act, 2009 is included in which Article of Indian Constitution?

1. Article 45 2. Article 250
3. Article 252 4. Article 21 (A)

47. Which Section of RTE Act deals with duties of teachers?

1. Section 7 2. Section 11
3. Section 24 4. Section 35

48. Which is the fundamental principle of National Education Policy (NEP, 2020)?

1. Indian Knowledge System (IKS)
2. Multidisciplinary approach of Education
3. Both 1 and 2
4. Establishment of model schools

34. 3	**35.** 4	**36.** 3	**37.** 1	**38.** 3	**39.** 3	**40.** 1	**41.** 2
42. 3	**43.** 4	**44.** 3	**45.** 2	**46.** 4	**47.** 3	**48.** 3	

49. In which of the following Educational Policy/Act of India, Indian sign language for teaching and monitoring is involved?

1. RPWD Act, 2016
2. PWD Act, 1995
3. NPE, 1986
4. NEP, 2020

50. In which year was SWAYAM as a flagship MOOC platform launched in India?

1. 2017 2. 2018
3. 2019 4. 2020

51. Establishment of DIET was the result of one of the recommendations of:

1. National Policy of Education, 1986
2. University Education Commission, 1948-49
3. Secondary Education Commission, 1952-53
4. Education Commission, 1966

52. What is the rank of the earth in the solar system in terms of size?

1. Third 2. Fourth
3. Fifth 4. Sixth

53. "Education makes a man self-sufficient and selfless" is stated in:

1. Samaveda 2. Atharvaveda
3. Yajurveda 4. Rigveda

54. MERUs stands for:

1. Multidisciplinary Education and Research Undertaking
2. Multistage Education and Research Universities
3. Multidisciplinary Education and Research Universities
4. Multilingual Education and Research Universities

55. The age of a tree, in years, can be ascertained by:

1. The number of its annular rings
2. Its weight
3. Its height
4. Length of its root

Section-IV: Teaching-Learning and The School

56. Which of the following levels is called introspective level of teaching?

1. Memory level 2. Understanding level
3. Reflective level 4. Knowledge level

57. Choose the incorrect statement related to teaching and learning:

1. The goal of teaching is to make changes in behaviour.
2. Teaching and learning are interrelated.
3. Teaching and learning should be a matter of sharing and allowing students to construct their knowledge.
4. There is no difference between teaching and training.

58. Effectiveness of teaching has to be judged in terms of:

1. Syllabus coverage
2. Learning outcomes of students
3. Students' attitude
4. Use of multimedia in the classroom

59. Which of the following is not a feature of Academic Bank of Credit?

1. Multidisciplinary academic mobility of students
2. Non-transferable credit
3. Multiple entry and exit options
4. Credit accumulation

49. 1 **50.** 1 **51.** 1 **52.** 3 **53.** 4 **54.** 3 **55.** 1 **56.** 3 **57.** 4 **58.** 2 **59.** 2

60. What is a learning environment?
1. The place students do homework
2. Only the physical atmosphere in a classroom
3. Seating arrangement in a classroom
4. The physical, psychological and instructional atmosphere in a classroom

61. Authoritative administration is based on:
1. Mutual sharing
2. Non-interference
3. Recognition
4. Dictatorship

62. How can a teacher create a positive learning environment with the available space in a classroom?
1. Buy lots of posters
2. Make sure students bring materials from home
3. Create bright, clean and organized space
4. Allow students to use low cost teaching aids

63. Which appropriate verb can be used to make an objective behavioural?
1. To appreciate
2. To know
3. To understand
4. To demonstrate

64. Which type of question has increasing objectivity of marking?
1. Essay type
2. Short paragraph
3. Very short answer type
4. Multiple choice type

65. In which type of questions identifying relationship is possible between two things?
1. True/False item
2. Matching item
3. Multiple choice item
4. Completion item

66. In which register government grants and expenditures are recorded?
1. Shift register
2. Stock register
3. Cash register
4. Contingent register

67. The process of making judgement is:
1. Assessment
2. Measurement
3. Budgeting
4. Evaluation

68. "A class X student is attending a fitness programme besides his regular class hours" is an example of:
1. Formal education
2. Informal education
3. Non-formal education
4. Vocational education

69. Which of the following is not a feature of learning outcome?
1. Learning outcomes should be realistic
2. Learning outcomes should be specific.
3. Learning outcomes should be simple.
4. Learning outcomes should focus on learning process.

70. Which of the following is not related with affective domain?
1. Articulation
2. Responding
3. Valuing
4. Receiving

71. What is the name of the National Assessment Centre as proposed by NEP, 2020?
1. GYAN
2. DIKSHA
3. PARAKH
4. NCFCS

72. What is the age group covered in school education according to NEP, 2020?
1. 3–14
2. 3–18
3. 5–18
4. 6–14

73. **Assertion (A):** Learner-centered approach is one where learner is the centre of all learning.

Reason (R): Students in middle school learn best when asked to reproduce the text as it is.

Choose the correct option:
1. Both (A) and (R) are true.
2. Both (A) and (R) are false.
3. (A) is true but (R) is false.
4. Both (A) and (R) are true and (R) is the correct explanation of (A).

60. 4	**61.** 4	**62.** 3	**63.** 4	**64.** 4	**65.** 2	**66.** 3
67. 4	**68.** 3	**69.** 4	**70.** 1	**71.** 3	**72.** 2	**73.** 3

74. SEDGs stands for:
1. Socio-Economically Divided Groups
2. Socio-Economically Disadvantaged Groups
3. Socio-Educationally Disadvantaged Groups
4. Socio-Economically Degraded Groups

75. In which level of teaching, the learner gets an opportunity to discriminate between positive and negative exemplars of concepts?
1. Understanding level
2. Evaluative level
3. Memory level
4. Reflective level

76. Concept formation is depended upon:
1. Learning
2. Transfer
3. Creativity
4. Imagination

77. The tool of summative evaluation is:
1. Daily assignment
2. Classroom observation
3. Term end test
4. Quizzes

78. Attitudes, values and interests are reflected by:
1. Cognitive Domain
2. Affective Domain
3. Conative Domain
4. Psychomotor Domain

79. Formative evaluation is:
1. Predictive
2. Diagnostic
3. Comprehensive
4. Continuous

80. How does constructivism help students with learning disabilities?
1. Students can isolate concepts in the area in which they are strongest.
2. Students can focus on the behaviour of others and this helps them learn.
3. Students can combine concepts from multiple content areas to help them build knowledge in a weak area.
4. Students can read about concepts in various disciplines to combine learning.

Part-B

Section-V: Subject Competence (i) Science

81. Identify the compound with high melting point:
1. Methane
2. Ethanol
3. Acetic acid
4. Chloroform

82. The correct reactivity series is:
1. Potassium > Magnesium > Lead > Gold
2. Magnesium > Potassium > Lead > Gold
3. Lead > Magnesium > Potassium > Gold
4. Gold > Potassium > Magnesium > Lead

83. The bases changes the colour of red litmus to:
1. white
2. blue
3. black
4. violet

84. $CH_4 + O_2 \rightarrow CO_2 + H_2O$ is a/an:
1. Balanced chemical equation
2. Equation with conserved mass
3. Stoichiometric chemical equation
4. Skeletal chemical equation

74. 2 **75.** 1 **76.** 1 **77.** 3 **78.** 2 **79.** 4 **80.** 3 **81.** 3 **82.** 1 **83.** 2 **84.** 4

85. Which of the following is an olfactor indicator?

1. Iron
2. Gold
3. Nitrogen
4. Phenolphthalein

86. Ethanol is .... in water.

1. Soluble
2. Partially soluble
3. Partially insoluble
4. Insoluble

87. The aerobic respiration takes place in the presence of:

1. Carbon dioxide
2. Nitrogen
3. Oxygen
4. Hydrogen

88. Which of the following is not a part of human excretory system?

1. Septum
2. Kidney
3. Urethra
4. Urinary bladder

89. Many of the involuntary actions are controlled by :

1. Mid brain
2. Hind brain
3. Mid brain and Hind brain
4. Fore brain

90. The growth hormone is secreted by:

1. Testes gland
2. Adrenal gland
3. Thyroid gland
4. Pituitary gland

91. The reproduction of planaria is through:

1. Fission
2. Fragmentation
3. Regeneration
4. Budding

92. "The ratio of sine of angle of incidence to the sine of angle of refraction is a constant for the light of a given colour and for the given pair of media". This law is known as:

1. Hooke's law
2. Snell's law
3. Lenz's law
4. Pascal's law

93. Power (P) of a lens of focal length (f) is given by:

1. $P = 1/f$
2. $P = f$
3. $P = 2f$
4. $P = 3f$

94. A person with hypermetropia can see:

1. Nothing
2. Every object clearly
3. Nearby objects clearly
4. Distant objects clearly

95. Blue colour of the sky is due to:

1. Scattering
2. Dispersion
3. Refraction
4. Interference

96. The SI unit of electric potential difference is:

1. Coulomb (C)
2. Volt (CV)
3. Hertz (Hz)
4. Joule (J)

97. The region around a magnet in which the forces of the magnet can be detected is called:

1. Electric field
2. Electric force
3. Magnetic field
4. Magnetic force

98. During short circuit, the current in the circuit:

1. Abruptly increases
2. Abruptly decreases
3. Slowly increases
4. Slowly decreases

99. The magnetic field produced at a given point increases as the current through the conductor:

1. does not change
2. becomes zero
3. decreases
4. increases

100. Unlike poles of magnets:

1. have no effect on each other
2. spin around each other
3. attract each other
4. repel each other

85. 4	**86.** 1	**87.** 3	**88.** 1	**89.** 3	**90.** 4	**91.** 3	**92.** 2
93. 1	**94.** 4	**95.** 1	**96.** 2	**97.** 3	**98.** 1	**99.** 4	**100.** 3

(ii) Mathematics

101. What number will come in place of '?' ?
45 : 36 :: 63 : ?
1. 71 2. 54
3. 61 4. 64

102. Sam ranks twelfth in a class of 46. What is his rank from the bottom?
1. 33rd 2. 35th
3. 37th 4. 34th

103. The LCM of 22, 54, 108 and 135 is:
1. 5405 2. 5490
3. 5940 4. 5095

104. The sum of smallest four-digit number and greatest three-digit number is:
1. 1999 2. 1989
3. 1900 4. 1909

105. A gardener plants 17956 trees in such a way that there are as many rows as there are trees in a row. The number of trees in a row is:
1. 136 2. 144
3. 134 4. 143

106. The ratio of two numbers is 3 : 4 and their HCF is 4. Their LCM is ....
1. 12 2. 16
3. 24 4. 48

107. The least among the following is:
1. 0.2 2. 1 ÷ 0.2
3. 0.20 4. $(0.20)^2$

108. Solve the following equation for x:
$$\frac{x}{2}+\frac{x}{3}-\frac{x}{4}=1$$
1. 12/7 2. 13/7
3. 7/12 4. 5/12

109. The average of first nine prime numbers is:
1. 9 2. 11
3. $11\frac{1}{9}$ 4. $11\frac{2}{9}$

110. In an examination the candidate must get 80% marks to pass. Candidate who gets 210 marks fails by 50 marks. The maximum marks are:
1. 235 2. 523
3. 325 4. 352

111. A sum of ₹ 12,500 amounts to ₹ 15,500 in 4 years at the rate of simple interest. What is the rate of interest?
1. 3% p.a. 2. 4% p.a.
3. 6% p.a. 4. 5% p.a.

112. The sum of ages of 5 children born at the interval of 3 years each is 50 years. What is the age of youngest child?
1. 4 years 2. 8 years
3. 10 years 4. 12 years

113. 'A' can finish a work in 10 days and 'B' does the same work in 15 days. In how many days, they together will do the same work?
1. 5 days 2. 6 days
3. 8 days 4. 9 days

114. Pipe A can fill a tank in 5 hours, pipe B in 10 hours and pipe C in 30 hours. If all the pipes are open, then the tank will be filled in:
1. 2 hours 2. 2.5 hours
3. 3 hours 4. 3.5 hours

101. 2	**102.** 2	**103.** 3	**104.** 1	**105.** 3	**106.** 4	**107.** 4
108. 1	**109.** 3	**110.** 3	**111.** 3	**112.** 1	**113.** 2	**114.** 3

115. If the price of 6 toys is 264, what will be the price of 5 toys?

1. ₹ 140
2. ₹ 100
3. ₹ 200
4. ₹ 220

116. The value of $\left(7+3\sqrt{5}\right)\left(7-3\sqrt{5}\right)$ is:

1. 4
2. $\sqrt{5}$
3. 2
4. $3\sqrt{5}$

117. If $x^3 - 6x^2 + 12x - 4$ is divided by $x - 2$, the remainder is:

1. 4
2. 0
3. 5
4. 6

118. If $\sqrt{4^n} = 1024$, then the value of n is:

1. 5
2. 8
3. 10
4. 12

119. If the LCM of three numbers is 9570, then their HCF will be:

1. 11
2. 12
3. 19
4. 21

120. The sum of two numbers is 42 and their product is 437, then their difference is:

1. 9
2. 4
3. 18
4. 5

(iii) Social Science

121. Article 21(A) of the constitution of India provides for:

1. Right to Information
2. Right of children to free and compulsory education
3. Equality before law
4. Abolition of untouchability

122. Almatti Dam is located on which of the following rivers?

1. Kaveri river
2. Godavari river
3. Krishna river
4. Mahanadi river

123. Which of the following is the youngest mountains of India?

1. Himalayas
2. Nilgiris
3. Arāvalli
4. Vindhyachal

124. The capital of Pallavas was:

1. Arcat
2. Malkhed
3. Banaras
4. Kanchipuram

125. 'Harshacharita' was written by:

1. Banabhatta
2. Harshavardhana
3. Kanishka
4. Ravikirti

126. Who gave the slogan "Do or Die" during India's freedom struggle?

1. Subhash Chandra Bose
2. Bal Gangadhar Tilak
3. Mahatma Gandhi
4. Lala Lajpat Rai

127. Who founded the Arya Samaj?

1. Bal Gangadhar Tilak
2. Gopal Krishna Gokhale
3. Swami Shraddhanand
4. Swami Dayanand Saraswati

128. Fiscal policy is connected with:

1. Public revenue and expenditure
2. Exports and imports
3. Issue of currency
4. Population control

129. The Gandhi-Irwin Pact was associated with which of the following movements?

1. Civil Disobedience Movement
2. Non-Cooperation Movement
3. Khilafat Movement
4. Quit India Movement

115. 4	**116.** 1	**117.** 1	**118.** 3	**119.** 1	**120.** 2	**121.** 2	**122.** 3
123. 1	**124.** 4	**125.** 1	**126.** 3	**127.** 4	**128.** 1	**129.** 1	

130. When can the members of parliament raise issues of urgent public importance?

1. Adjournment motion
2. Cut-motion
3. Guillotine
4. Zero hour

131. Which is a type of metamorphic rock?

1. Limestone 2. Sandstone
3. Marble 4. Granite

132. Green Revolution is associated with:

1. Milk production
2. Industry
3. Science and Technolgy
4. Agriculture

133. How many fundamental duties were added to the Indian constitution through 42nd Amendment Act of 1976?

1. 9 2. 10
3. 11 4. 12

134. In which State is Kolar Gold Mine situated?

1. Karnataka 2. Madhya Pradesh
3. West Bengal 4. Tamil Nadu

135. Which kind of soil is suitable for cultivation of cotton?

1. Black 2. Red
3. Alluvial 4. Sandy

136. When did the British shift their capital from Calcutta to Delhi?

1. 1914 2. 1911
3. 1909 4. 1905

137. Who had constructed Grand Trunk Road?

1. Shahjahan 2. Jahangir
3. Akbar 4. Shershah Suri

138. Which is the highest mountain peak in India?

1. Kanchenjuga 2. Mount Everest
3. Nanda Devi 4. Annapurna

139. The Red Sea is an example of:

1. Residual structure
2. Faulted structure
3. Folded structure
4. Lava structure

140. Which is the currency of Bhutan?

1. Rupee 2. Dinar
3. Ngultrum 4. Taka

(iv) English

Directions (Qs. No. 141-145): *Choose the word that is nearest in meaning to the underlined word:*

141. The western powers treat the countries of the third world in a callous manner.

1. hate 2. insensitive
3. rude 4. aggressive

142. The thief got a death sentence; that was the verdict of the jury.

1. voice 2. judgement
3. decision 4. outcome

143. White tigers are becoming very rare; in fact almost extinct.

1. distant
2. unwell
3. non-existent
4. visible

144. The girl inadvertently stepped on the toes of her grandmother, who was in great pain.

1. willingly 2. jokingly
3. accidently 4. lovingly

130. 4	**131.** 3	**132.** 4	**133.** 2	**134.** 1	**135.** 1	**136.** 2	**137.** 4
138. 1	**139.** 2	**140.** 3	**141.** 2	**142.** 2	**143.** 3	**144.** 3	

145. Science and religion are two of the most persuasive influences the world has known.

1. powerful 2. capable
3. likely 4. valid

Directions (Qs. No. 146-150): *In the following group of words, only one is correctly spelt. Select the one with the correct spelling:*

146. 1. Alleniate 2. Alienate
3. Allienate 4. Aliennate

147. 1. Buroucracy 2. Bureaucracy
3. Buraucracy 4. Bureaurecy

148. 1. Pedagogy 2. Pedagoguey
3. Pedagogi 4. Paedagogy

149. 1. Curriculum 2. Curiculum
3. Curiculam 4. Cariculum

150. 1. Antrapreneur 2. Enterapreneur
3. Entaraprenur 4. Entrepreneur

Directions (Qs. No. 151-154): *Choose the word that is opposite to meaning to the underlined word:*

151. His progress in his business surprised many.

1. stagnation 2. show
3. speed 4. rise

152. She was optimistic joining a new course in the college close to her house.

1. aesthetic 2. pessimistic
3. agnostic 4. puristic

153. The king had no choice but to abdicate his throne.

1. surrender 2. retain
3. leave 4. retire

154. She emanates power and confidence.

1. show 2. divulge
3. emit 4. conceal

Directions (Qs. No. 155-156): *Pick out the most appropriate word from the given alternatives to complete the sentence:*

155. The .... king would not even spare children from punishment.

1. tyrannical 2. bossy
3. controlling 4. philanthropic

156. You already have an .... personality, we believe you will overcome the crises.

1. anxious 2. ardent
3. extrovert 4. adventurous

Directions (Qs. No. 157-160): *Choose the correct answer:*

157. Which of the following Indian writers got a Nobel Prize for literature in 1913?

1. Shart Chandra
2. Premchand
3. Rabindranath Tagore
4. Bankim Chandra Chatterjee

158. The book 'Train to Pakistan' by Khushwant Singh is about heart-rending stories of:

1. The Partition, 1947
2. The Independence Day
3. The Indian Republic
4. The British Rule

159. 'Romeo and Juliet' is a play written by:

1. William Shakespeare
2. Bernard Shaw
3. John Keats
4. Jane Austen

160. Vikram Seth, the English writer is known for his novel:

1. A Suitable Boy
2. Swamy and Friends
3. Gora
4. Fire on the Ganges

145. 1	**146.** 2	**147.** 2	**148.** 1	**149.** 1	**150.** 4	**151.** 1	**152.** 2
153. 2	**154.** 4	**155.** 1	**156.** 3	**157.** 3	**158.** 1	**159.** 1	**160.** 1

(v) हिन्दी

निर्देश (प्रश्न संख्या 161 से 165 तक): *निम्नलिखित गद्यांश को ध्यानपूर्वक पढ़कर उसके आधार पर पूछे गए प्रश्नों के उत्तर दीजिए।*

समय-चक्र की गति बड़ी अद्भुत है। इसकी गति में अबाधता है। समय का चक्र निरंतर गतिशील रहता है, रूकना इसका धर्म नहीं है। इस संसार की कोई भी वस्तु रूक सकती है, किसी में किसी भी प्रकार का अवरोध उत्पन्न हो सकता है, किन्तु समय की गति अबाध रूप से चलती रहती है, इसमें निरंतरता है। यदि मनुष्य की सम्पत्ति एक बार नष्ट हो जाए तो संभव है परिश्रम, प्रयत्न एवं संघर्ष से वह उसे पुनः प्राप्त कर ले, किंतु बीता हुआ समय पुनः वापस नहीं आ सकता।

समय कभी किसी की प्रतीक्षा नहीं करता। आप चाहें तो समय को व्यर्थ की बातों में नष्ट कर सकते हैं और चाहें तो उसका सदुपयोग कर सकते हैं, जिससे वह आपकी उन्नति में चार चाँद लगा सकता है। समय के सदुपयोग में ही जीवन की सफलता का रहस्य निहित है। संसार में जितने भी महापुरुष हुए हैं, वे सभी समय का सदुपयोग करने के कारण ही इस पद पर पहुँच सके हैं।

161. प्रस्तुत गद्यांश के लिए एक उचित शीर्षक दीजिए :

1. समय और धन
2. पश्चाताप का समय
3. महापुरुषों का जीवन
4. समय का महत्व

162. समय की गति 'अबाध' है, क्योंकि :

1. समय का बहाव स्थिर है।
2. वह निरन्तर चलता रहता है।
3. वह दूसरों की गति बाधित करता है।
4. वह अनिश्चित है।

163. समय और धन में क्या अन्तर है?

1. धन जोड़ा जा सकता है, समय जुड़ता है।
2. धन से लोग धनी होते हैं जबकि समय से नहीं।
3. धन समय के साथ-साथ बढ़ता है।
4. गया हुआ धन लौट सकता है, समय नहीं।

164. मानव की उन्नति में चार चाँद कैसे लग सकता है?

1. समय को व्यर्थ न बिताकर
2. अपनी पूँजी कमाकर
3. समय को वश में करके
4. प्रचार-प्रसार में समय बिताकर

165. महापुरुषों ने समय का उपयोग कैसे किया?

1. काम को आराम-आराम से करके
2. दूसरों से काम कराकर
3. काम को समय पर सम्पन्न करके
4. धन के विषय में सोचते हुए

166. 'अमोल' का तत्सम क्या है?

1. अनमोल 2. अमूल्य
3. अमल 4. अचलस्थ

167. 'तुरंग' का अर्थ है :

1. पृथ्वी 2. आकाश
3. घोड़ा 4. बैल

168. 'कौमुदी' इनमें से किसका पर्यायवाची है?

1. चाँदनी 2. कस्तूरी
3. समुद्र 4. चंदन

169. 'अस्तित्व' का विलोम क्या है?

1. अवरोहण 2. अपसरण
3. अनस्तित्व 4. विकर्षण

170. 'घी' क्या है?

1. स्त्रीलिंग 2. पुल्लिंग
3. दोनों 1 और 2 4. इनमें से कोई नहीं

161. 4 **162.** 2 **163.** 4 **164.** 1 **165.** 3 **166.** 2 **167.** 3 **168.** 1 **169.** 3 **170.** 2

171. 'जिसका वर्णन न हो सके' ऐसे व्यक्ति को कहते हैं?

1. अनिवार्य 2. अनित्य
3. अनिरुद्ध 4. अनिर्वचनीय

172. 'ऐतिहासिक' शब्द में प्रत्यय है :

1. इक 2. सिक
3. क 4. क्

173. 'लड़की ने गीत गाया' में है :

1. कर्म कारक 2. कर्ता कारक
3. संप्रदान कारक 4. संबोधन कारक

174. 'मुनि' का बहुवचन है :

1. मुनियों 2. मुनि लोग
3. मुनि 4. मुनि जन

175. निम्नलिखित में से कौन-सा शब्द उपसर्ग से नहीं बना है?

1. स्वागत 2. प्रतिमूर्ति
3. दुर्घटना 4. स्थिति

176. 'सुनीता' के लेखक हैं :

1. जैनेन्द्र कुमार 2. अज्ञेय
3. यशपाल 4. प्रेमचंद

177. 'हाथ के तोते उड़ जाना' का आशय है :

1. घबरा जाना 2. पछताना
3. दुर्बल होना 4. कल्पना में होना

178. 'अपना काम महाकाम' कहावत का अर्थ है :

1. बिना परिश्रम के सिद्धि
2. अपनी प्रतिष्ठा का ध्यान
3. अपना अभीष्ट सर्वोपरि
4. छोटी वस्तु की रक्षा

179. 'पीपर पात सरिस मन डोला' में कौन-सा अलंकार है?

1. श्लेष 2. यमक
3. अनुप्रास 4. उपमा

180. कौन-से शब्द की वर्तनी अशुद्ध है?

1. काँच 2. बँगला
3. अत्योक्ति 4. दुरवस्था

EXPLANATORY ANSWERS

1. **(2):** Phages are viruses that "invade bacteria and seize their genetic material" to replicate. Therefore, they make copies of the genetic material of bacteria.

2. **(1):** The passage says, "The human gut contains a large collection of viruses (the phageome), which balances the bacterial microbiome by killing the bad bacteria."

   Hence, phageome balances the bacterial microbiome.

3. **(1):** Phages destroy bacteria by replicating within and then bursting them. The phrase "escapes from the bacterium by destroying it" confirms this.

4. **(4):** The passage states, "phages also help bacteria by bringing them new genes", indicating that phages are gene-delivery agents.

5. **(3):** In the phrase "The amazing ingenuity of nature", the word "amazing" qualifies or describes the noun "ingenuity", thus it functions as an adjective.

6. **(2):** "Ingenuity of nature" assigns human-like intelligence or craftiness to nature, which is a personification.

7. **(2):** The passage explains that a higher diversity of phages reduces risk of diseases like inflammatory bowel disease and promotes the dominance of good phages.

171. 4 **172.** 1 **173.** 2 **174.** 3 **175.** 4 **176.** 1 **177.** 1 **178.** 3 **179.** 4 **180.** 3

8. (4): The passage says countries are hunting for phages "hoping to counter antimicrobial resistance", and India must do the same. Fighting drug-resistant bacteria is part of combating antimicrobial resistance.

Hence, both 1 and 2.

9. (3): The passage says phages "abound in places where bacteria grow" such as wastewater. Thus, phages are found there due to the presence of bacteria.

10. (1): The passage focuses on the beneficial role of phages (viruses) in maintaining gut health, combating bacteria, and fighting drug resistance. Hence, the most appropriate theme is virtuous viruses.

11. (3): 121 : 1331 : 441 : ?

$\Rightarrow \quad (11)^2 : (11)^3 :: (21)^2 : (21)^3$

$\Rightarrow \quad 121 : 1331 :: 441 : \boxed{9261}$

$\therefore \quad ? = 9261.$

12. (2): Given, $a * b = \dfrac{a+b}{ab}$

$\therefore \quad 4 * 1 = \dfrac{4+1}{4\times1} = \dfrac{5}{4}$

$= 1.25.$

13. (4): C D E → (+5, +5, +5) → H I J

Similarly, B C D → (+5, +5, +5) → G H I

$\therefore$ CDE : HIJ :: BCD : $\boxed{\text{GHI}}$

$\therefore$? = GHI.

14. (4): A C P N → (+1, +1, +1, +1) → B D Q O

Similarly, J L Y W → (+1, +1, +1, +1) → K M Z X

$\therefore$ ACPN : BDQO :: JLYW : $\boxed{\text{KMZX}}$

$\therefore$? = KMZX.

15. (1):

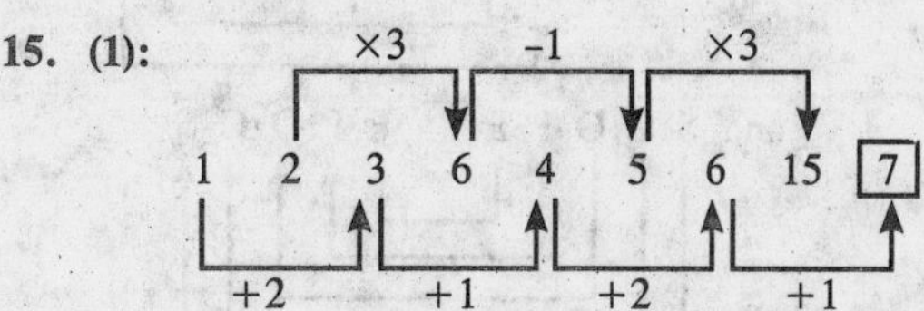

Here, ? = the missing term = 7.

16. (3):

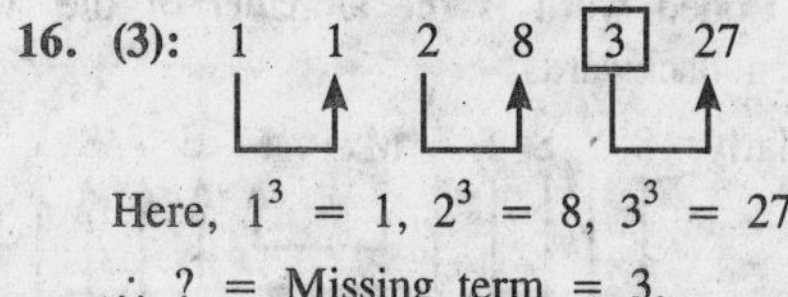

Here, $1^3 = 1,\ 2^3 = 8,\ 3^3 = 27$

$\therefore$? = Missing term = 3.

17. (2):

Here, Missing term = DJW.

18. (1):

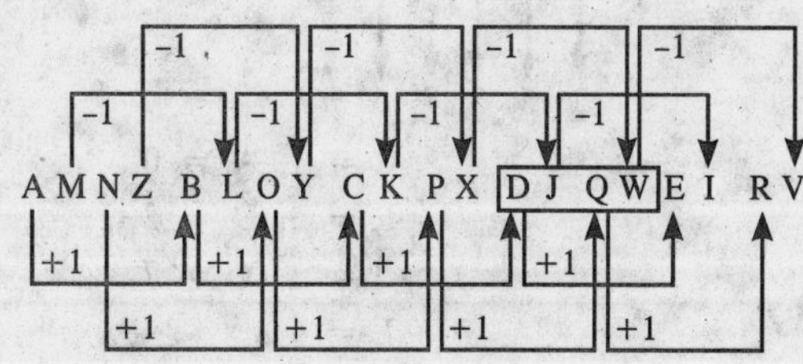

Here, Missing term = DJQW.

19. (*): Given, B A T → (+2, +2, +2) → D C V

and C A R T → (+2, +2, +2, +2) → E C T V

Similarly, S E C O N D → (+2, +2, +2, +2, +2, +2) → U G E Q P F

$\therefore$ SECOND will be coded as UGEQPF.

20. (3): Given, C A R E E R A C

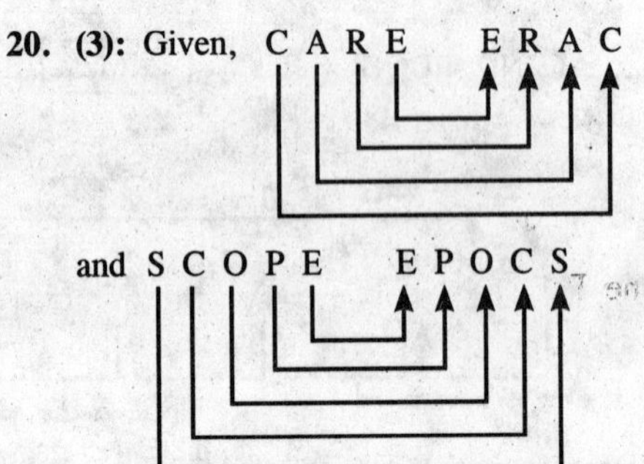

and S C O P E E P O C S

The Coded word is the alphabet of the word written backwards.

Similarly, S Y S T E M M E T S Y S

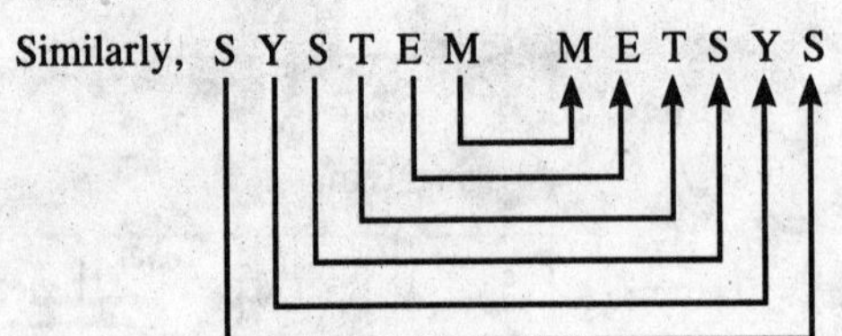

∴ SYSTEM would be coded as METSYS.

21. (3): Given, C A R → 1 0 5

and D R I V E R → 2 5 3 7 6 5

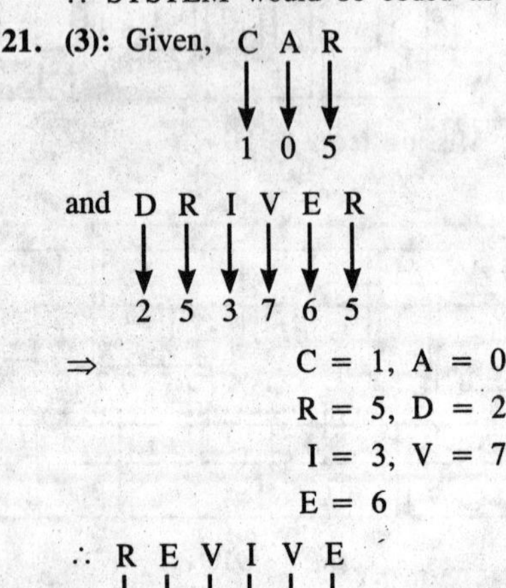

$\Rightarrow$ C = 1, A = 0,
R = 5, D = 2,
I = 3, V = 7,
E = 6

∴ R E V I V E → 5 6 7 3 7 6

∴ REVIVE would be coded as 567376.

22. (2): Given, 35 is written as 8

$\Rightarrow$ $3 + 5 = 8$

and 6243 is written as 87

$\Rightarrow$ $6 + 2 = 8$

$4 + 3 = 7$

Similarly, $4 + 5 = 9$

$3 + 6 = 9$

$1 + 5 = 6$

∴ 453615 would be written as 996.

23. (3): Here, Starting point = H

HA = 3 km

AB = 4 km

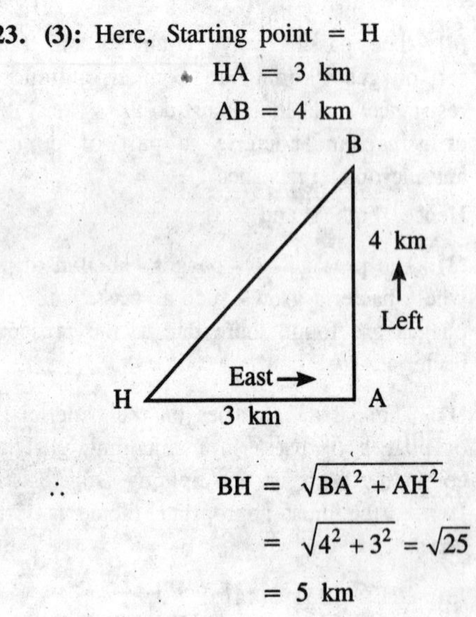

$$\therefore \quad BH = \sqrt{BA^2 + AH^2}$$

$$= \sqrt{4^2 + 3^2} = \sqrt{25}$$

$$= 5 \text{ km}$$

$\Rightarrow$ BH = 5 km

∴ Shortest distance = BH = 5 km

∴ He walked altogether = 3 + 4 + 5 = 12 km.

24. (3): Here, Initial position = 0,

OA = 12 km,

AB = 5 km,

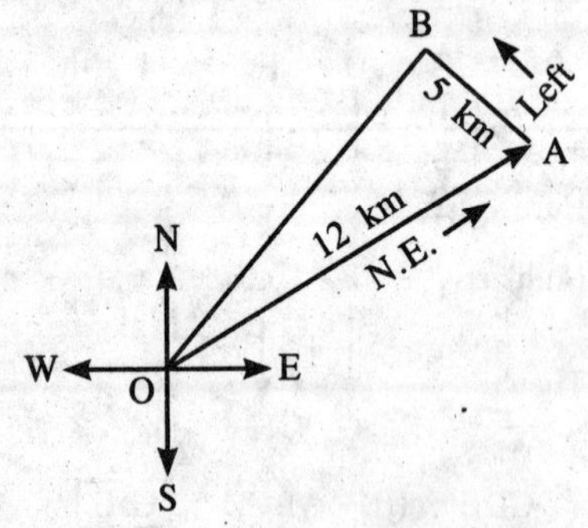

In ΔOAB, $OB = \sqrt{OA^2 + AB^2}$

$$= \sqrt{12^2 + 5^2}$$

$$= \sqrt{144 + 25} = \sqrt{169}$$

$$= 13 \text{ km}$$

$\Rightarrow$ OB = 13 km

∴ You are now 13 km far from your initial position.

25. **(3):** Let squares from given figure:

Then, squares in the figure:
AJET, JKZE, KLFZ, LBMF, TEYU, EZOY, ZFWO, FMNW, UYHV, YOXH, OWGX, WNPG, VHSD, HXRS, XGQR, GPCQ, AKOU, KBNO, UORD, ONCR, JLWY, EFGH, YWQS, TZXV, ZMPX, ALGV, JBPH, TFQD, EMCS, ABCD

∴ The total number of squares hidden in the adjoining figure = 30.

26. **(4):**

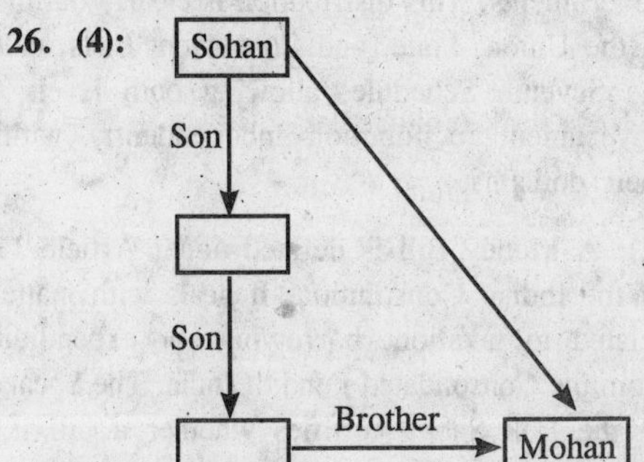

Here, Mohan is the Grandson of Sohan.

27. **(4):** Let A and B be the sets of students who failed in English and Mathematics respectively.

Then, $n(A) = 48\%$

$n(B) = 52$

$n(A \cap B) = 12$.

So, $n(A \cap B) = n(A) + n(B) - n(A \cap B)$

$= 48 + 52 - 12$

$= 100 - 12 = 88$

$\Rightarrow \quad n(A \cap B) = 88$

⇒ Percentage of students failed in both the subject = 88%

∴ Percentage of students passed in both the subject = 100 - 88 = 12%.

For Qs. No. 28-30:

From given information:

A, B, C, D and E are friends

A > C > B > E > D

28. **(2):** B's age is between C and E.

29. **(2):** B is of the median age of five.

30. **(1):** A is the eldest of all five.

31. **(2):** The French Revolution was heavily influenced by the philosophical ideas of Jean-Jacques Rousseau, a prominent Enlightenment thinker. His work The Social Contract argued that legitimate political authority rests on the will of the people and not on divine right or monarchy. His emphasis on equality, liberty, and fraternity deeply resonated with the revolutionaries who sought to overthrow the oppressive monarchy in France.

32. **(3):** The Rigveda, the oldest of the four Vedas in Hindu literature, is composed of 1028 hymns (known as suktas) arranged into ten books called mandalas. These hymns are dedicated to various deities like Agni, Indra, and Soma, and they reflect early Vedic culture, spirituality, and rituals practiced by the Indo-Aryans.

33. **(2):** Bal Gangadhar Tilak was a leading figure in India's national movement known for his assertive and radical political stance. He promoted the slogan "Swaraj is my birthright and I shall have it". However, in social matters, he was conservative, opposing certain reforms like the Age of Consent Bill and supporting orthodox practices, which is why he is described as radical in politics but traditional in social views.

34. **(3):** The Ellora caves, located in Maharashtra, are a UNESCO World Heritage Site that showcases a mix of Hindu, Buddhist, and Jain monuments. The most remarkable among them, the Kailasa Temple, was built during the reign of the Rashtrakuta dynasty (8th century CE). This temple is entirely carved from a single rock and is considered a marvel of ancient Indian rock-cut architecture.

35. **(4):** Lord Ripon, who served as the Viceroy of India from 1880 to 1884, is remembered as the pioneer of local self-government in British India. In 1882, he introduced a resolution advocating democratic decentralization by empowering local bodies like municipalities and rural boards, which laid the groundwork for the later Panchayati Raj system in independent India.

36. (3): Indian Standard Time (IST) is based on the 82.5° east longitude, which passes near Mirzapur, a town in the Prayagraj district of Uttar Pradesh. This central meridian was selected to provide a uniform time across the country, avoiding regional time differences and confusion.

37. (1): Cuba is historically known as the "Sugar Bowl of the World" due to its extensive sugarcane plantations and dominance in sugar production and export during the 18th to 20th centuries. The favorable tropical climate and colonial economic structure helped Cuba become one of the world's top sugar exporters.

38. (3): Among the rivers listed, Bhagirathi is not a tributary of the Indus River. Instead, it is a major source stream of the Ganga River in India, originating from the Gangotri glacier in Uttarakhand.

On the other hand, rivers like Sutlej, Jhelum, and Chenab are all significant tributaries of the Indus system, flowing through India and Pakistan.

39. (3): The atmospheric pressure experienced on Earth's surface is a result of the gravitational pull exerted by the Earth on the atmospheric gases. This gravitational force causes air molecules to be pulled towards the surface, creating a pressure that decreases with altitude.

40. (1): Madhya Pradesh is referred to as the "Tiger State of India" because it hosts the largest population of tigers among all Indian states. With prominent tiger reserves like Kanha, Bandhavgarh, Satpura, and Pench, the state plays a crucial role in India's tiger conservation efforts under Project Tiger.

41. (2): Blended learning refers to a teaching approach that combines face-to-face classroom methods with technology-mediated instruction, such as online modules or digital resources. This model leverages the strengths of both traditional and digital methods to enhance learning effectiveness and flexibility.

42. (3): The National Education Policy (NEP) 2020 emphasizes a learner-centric approach that prioritizes students' interests, curiosity, and understanding over rote learning or exam-driven teaching. It encourages critical thinking, creativity, and experiential learning to make education more holistic and student-friendly.

43. (4): The budgetary deficit is the difference between the total revenue (receipts) and total expenditure of the government. It indicates the amount by which government expenses exceed its income in a fiscal year. It reflects the need for borrowing or adjustments in future financial planning.

44. (3): India is considered a federal state because its Constitution provides for a division of powers between the central government and the state governments. This distribution is clearly outlined in the Union, State, and Concurrent Lists under the Seventh Schedule, allowing both levels of government to function independently within their domains.

45. (2): A Money Bill is defined under Article 110 of the Indian Constitution. It deals with matters related to taxation, borrowing, or expenditure from the Consolidated Fund of India. The Speaker of the Lok Sabha certifies whether a bill is a Money Bill.

46. (4): The Right to Education (RTE) Act, 2009 was enacted to give effect to Article 21(A) of the Constitution, which guarantees free and compulsory education to all children between the ages of 6 to 14 years as a fundamental right.

47. (3): Section 24 of the Right to Education Act lays down the duties of teachers, including maintaining regularity and punctuality, completing curriculum, assessing student performance, and participating in training programs to ensure quality education delivery.

48. (3): The NEP 2020 is grounded in several core principles, notably the Indian Knowledge System (IKS) and a multidisciplinary approach to education. IKS promotes cultural heritage, ethics, and traditional knowledge, while multidisciplinary learning fosters creativity, flexibility, and innovation across subjects.

49. (1): The Rights of Persons with Disabilities (RPWD) Act, 2016 includes provisions for the use of Indian Sign Language (ISL) in education and communication. It promotes inclusive education by mandating accessible teaching and monitoring for children with hearing impairments and other disabilities.

50. (1): SWAYAM (Study Webs of Active–Learning for Young Aspiring Minds), India's premier MOOC platform, was officially launched in 2017 by the Government of India to provide free online education through interactive courses prepared by top institutions like IITs and IIMs.

51. (1): The District Institutes of Education and Training (DIETs) were established based on a key recommendation of the National Policy on Education (NPE), 1986. The goal was to strengthen teacher education and improve the quality of elementary education by creating district-level resource centers for pre-service and in-service training of teachers.

52. (3): In terms of size (diameter and volume), the Earth ranks fifth among the eight planets in the solar system. The largest is Jupiter, followed by Saturn, Uranus, and Neptune. Earth comes next, making it the fifth largest planet.

53. (4): The statement "Education makes a man self-sufficient and selfless" aligns with the values expressed in the Rigveda, which emphasizes wisdom, moral development, and the holistic growth of an individual through learning. The Rigveda lays the foundation for many philosophical ideas in ancient Indian thought, including the role of education in shaping character and promoting self-realization.

54. (3): MERUs stands for Multidisciplinary Education and Research Universities, a concept introduced in the National Education Policy (NEP) 2020. These institutions aim to provide high-quality education and research across disciplines, encouraging innovation and broad-based learning.

55. (1): The age of a tree is determined by counting its annular rings (also known as growth rings) visible in a cross-section of its trunk. Each ring generally represents one year of growth, making it a reliable method to estimate a tree's age.

56. (3): The reflective level of teaching is the introspective or advanced level, where learners critically analyze, evaluate, and apply knowledge to solve complex problems. It promotes higher-order thinking and self-reflection, often used in research and deep learning contexts.

57. (4): There is no difference between teaching and training: This statement is incorrect. Teaching is a broader process aimed at knowledge construction, critical thinking, and intellectual development, while training is more skill-specific and performance-oriented. Therefore, equating the two is inaccurate.

58. (2): The effectiveness of teaching is best judged by the learning outcomes of students, which reflect what they have understood, retained, and can apply. It indicates the real impact of teaching, beyond just syllabus coverage or tools used.

59. (2): The Academic Bank of Credit (ABC) is designed to promote flexibility in higher education by allowing credit accumulation and transfer. Hence, non-transferable credit is not a feature of ABC. Instead, it supports multiple entry-exit points and student mobility.

60. (4): A learning environment encompasses the physical setup, psychological climate, and instructional practices within a classroom. It includes how students feel, interact, and engage with learning materials, making it a holistic concept beyond just physical space.

61. (4): Authoritative administration is rooted in strict control and top-down decision-making, where power is centralized in one individual or authority. It is not based on participation or mutual consensus but rather on issuing commands and expecting compliance, which aligns with the characteristics of a dictatorship.

62. (3): To foster a positive learning environment, a teacher should focus on using the available classroom space effectively by making it well-lit, tidy, and organized. A clean and cheerful space helps students feel comfortable and motivated, improving focus and reducing distractions.

63. (4): In framing behavioural objectives, verbs must reflect observable and measurable actions. "To demonstrate" is suitable because it implies a visible performance or application of knowledge, unlike abstract verbs like "to understand" or "to know", which are difficult to assess directly.

64. (4): Among the given types, multiple-choice questions (MCQs) offer the highest objectivity in marking, as they have clearly defined correct answers and eliminate subjectivity or bias in evaluation. This makes them highly suitable for standardized assessments.

65. (2): Matching questions require students to identify relationships or associations between two sets of items (e.g., terms and definitions). This format is specifically designed to assess the ability to link related concepts, making it ideal for subjects requiring factual associations.

66. (3): A cash register in the context of school or institutional administration is the record where all receipts (grants received) and expenditures (payments made) in cash are entered. It serves as the primary financial register for tracking daily cash flow — including government grants, fees collected, and amounts spent.

67. (4): Evaluation is the comprehensive process of making judgments about a learner's performance or the effectiveness of a program. It includes both assessment (data collection) and measurement (quantification) but goes further by interpreting the results to form decisions.

68. (3): Activities like a student attending a fitness program outside regular school hours are categorized as non-formal education. It is structured and intentional but conducted outside the formal academic system, often catering to specific skills or interests.

69. (4): Learning outcomes are statements of what learners are expected to achieve at the end of an instructional period, hence they focus on results, not the process. Saying they should focus on the process is incorrect, as outcomes must be specific, realistic, and measurable achievements.

70. (1): In Bloom's taxonomy, the affective domain involves attitudes, emotions, and values, with levels such as receiving, responding, and valuing. However, articulation belongs to the psychomotor or higher-order cognitive domains, not the affective. It involves coordinating actions and ideas, not emotions or attitudes.

71. (3): As per the National Education Policy (NEP), 2020, the proposed National Assessment Centre is named PARAKH, which stands for Performance Assessment, Review, and Analysis of Knowledge for Holistic Development. It is intended to set norms, standards, and guidelines for student assessments and evaluate the performance of educational institutions across the country.

72. (2): EP 2020 restructures school education into a 5+3+3+4 system, beginning from age 3 (preschool) to age 18 (end of Grade 12). This structure emphasizes early childhood care and education and covers all stages from foundational to secondary level.

73. (3): The assertion is correct as learner-centered approaches focus on the active role of learners in constructing knowledge. However, the reason is false because rote reproduction of text is a teacher-centric or memory-based approach, not learner-centered. Middle school learners benefit more from inquiry, discussion, and critical engagement rather than memorization.

74. (2): SEDGs as mentioned in NEP 2020 refer to Socio-Economically Disadvantaged Groups, which include marginalized communities based on caste, tribe, gender, disability, and socio-economic status. The policy promotes inclusive practices to ensure equity in access to quality education for these groups.

75. (1): At the understanding level of teaching (according to Bloom's taxonomy and Herbartian approach), learners are encouraged to differentiate between correct and incorrect examples of a concept. This stage involves interpreting and classifying information, which includes identifying positive and negative exemplars.

76. (1): Concept formation is fundamentally rooted in learning through experience, observation, and categorization. It requires the learner to identify common features across different instances, which happens through structured and reflective learning processes.

77. (3): Summative evaluation is conducted at the end of an instructional period (e.g., term-end or annual exams) to measure student achievement against set objectives. Therefore, a term-end test is the most suitable tool for summative assessment.

78. (2): The affective domain in Bloom's taxonomy involves the development of attitudes, values, emotions, and interests. It addresses how learners emotionally engage with the content, which is different from the cognitive (knowledge) and psychomotor (skills) domains.

79. (4): Formative evaluation is a continuous process carried out during the course of learning to monitor student progress and provide feedback. It helps teachers identify areas where learners need support and adjust instruction accordingly.

80. (3): Students can combine concepts from multiple content areas to help them build knowledge in a weak area. Constructivism supports integrated learning, where students draw from various subjects and experiences to build their own understanding. For students with learning disabilities, this approach allows them to leverage strengths in one area to compensate for weaknesses in another, fostering meaningful and personalized learning.

81. (3): Acetic acid (CH_2COOH) has the highest melting point among the given compounds. This is due to its ability to form strong hydrogen bonds, particularly through dimer formation in the solid state.

Methane is a non-polar molecule with very weak van der Waals forces, while ethanol and chloroform have lower melting points compared to acetic acid.

82. (1): Potassium > Magnesium > Lead > Gold: This is the correct reactivity series. Potassium is one of the most reactive metals, followed by magnesium. Lead is less reactive, and gold is one of the least reactive metals. The reactivity series helps predict the ability of a metal to displace another in chemical reactions.

83. (2): A base turns red litmus paper blue. This is a standard test used to identify basic substances. The change occurs due to the increase in hydroxide ion concentration, which affects the dye in the litmus paper.

84. (4): The equation $CH_4 + O_2 \rightarrow CO_2 + H_2O$ is a skeletal (or unbalanced) chemical equation because it does not account for the correct number of atoms of each element on both sides. The balanced version is:

$$CH_4 + 2O_2 \rightarrow CO_2 + 2H_2O$$

85. (4): Phenolphthalein is an olfactory indicator in certain conditions. It can change its smell in acidic and basic media, though it is primarily used as a visual indicator changing from colorless to pink in basic solution. None of the metals or gases listed (iron, gold, nitrogen) serve as olfactory indicators.

86. (1): Ethanol is completely soluble in water because it can form hydrogen bonds with water molecules. Its -OH group interacts well with water, leading to homogeneous mixing.

87. (3): Aerobic respiration is the process in which glucose is broken down in the presence of oxygen, releasing energy in the form of ATP along with carbon dioxide and water. This occurs in most plants, animals, and many microorganisms.

88. (1): The septum is a part of the heart, not the excretory system. The other options—kidney, urethra, urinary bladder—are all components of the human excretory system, responsible for the formation and expulsion of urine.

89. (3): Involuntary actions like breathing and heartbeat are mainly controlled by the hindbrain (especially the medulla), while the midbrain helps regulate reflexes and sensory coordination. Both together play key roles in managing involuntary functions, making option 3 the most accurate.

90. (4): The pituitary gland, often called the "master gland", secretes growth hormone (GH), which stimulates growth and cell reproduction. It is located at the base of the brain and regulates several other endocrine functions as well.

91. (3): Planaria reproduce by regeneration, a process where an organism can regrow its lost body parts. If a planarian is cut into pieces, each piece can regenerate into a complete organism, which is a remarkable form of asexual reproduction.

92. (2): The law that relates the sine of the angle of incidence and refraction is called Snell's law. It governs how light bends when it passes from one medium to another, maintaining the ratio sin(i)/sin(r) = constant.

93. (1): The power (P) of a lens is given by the formula P = 1/f, where f is the focal length in meters. The unit of power is diopter (D). A shorter focal length means a more powerful lens.

94. (4): A person with hypermetropia (farsightedness) can see distant objects clearly, but nearby objects appear blurry. This condition occurs when the image is focused behind the retina.

95. (1): The blue colour of the sky is due to Rayleigh scattering. Molecules in the atmosphere scatter shorter wavelengths of light (blue) more effectively than longer wavelengths (red), making the sky appear blue.

96. (2): The SI unit of electric potential difference is the volt (V). One volt is defined as the potential difference when one joule of work is done to move one coulomb of charge.

97. (3): The area around a magnet where magnetic forces can be detected is called a magnetic field. It is represented by field lines that indicate the direction and strength of the force.

98. (1): During a short circuit, resistance drops drastically, causing the current to increase abruptly. This sudden surge can damage circuits and start fires if not protected by safety devices.

99. (4): The magnetic field around a conductor becomes stronger as the electric current increases. This is a direct relationship, as per Ampere's law.

100. (3): Unlike poles (north and south) of two magnets attract each other, while like poles repel. This is a fundamental property of magnetism.

101. (2): 45 : 36 :: 63 : ?

$\Rightarrow 9 \times 5 : 9 \times 4 :: 9 \times 7 : 9 \times 6$

$\Rightarrow 45 : 36 :: 63 : \boxed{54}$

∴ 54 will come in place of 54.

102. (2): Given, Sam ranks twelfth in a class of 46

∴ His rank from the bottom

$= 46 - 12 + 1$

$=$ 35th.

103. (3):

$22 = 2 \times 11$

$54 = 2 \times 3^3$

$108 = 2^2 \times 3^3$

$135 = 3^3 \times 5$

∴ The LCM of 22, 54, 108 and 135

$= 2^2 \times 3^3 \times 5 \times 11$

$= 4 \times 27 \times 55$

$= 5940.$

104. (1): The sum of smallest four-digit number and greatest three-digit number

$= 1000 + 999$

$= 1999.$

105. (3): The number of trees in a row

$= \sqrt{17956}$

$= 134.$

106. (4): Let the two numbers are $3x$ and $4x$

Then, HCF $= x = 4$ (given)

and LCM $= 3 \times 4x$

$= 12x$

$= 12 \times 4 = 48$

$\Rightarrow$ Their LCM = 48.

107. (4): (1) 0.2

(2) $1 \div 0.2 = \frac{1}{0.2} = \frac{10}{2} = 5$

(3) 0.20

(4) $(0.2)^2 = 0.04$

$\therefore 5 > 0.20 > 0.2 > 0.04$

∴ 0.04 is the least among given options.

108. (1): $\frac{x}{2}+\frac{x}{3}-\frac{x}{4} = 1$

$\Rightarrow \frac{6x+4x-3x}{12} = 1$

$\Rightarrow 7x = 12$

$\Rightarrow x = \frac{12}{7}.$

109. (3): The average of first nine prime number

$= \frac{2+3+5+7+11+13+17+19+23}{9}$

$= \frac{100}{9} = 11\frac{1}{9}.$

110. (3): Let the maximum marks are

Then, $x \times \frac{80}{100} = 210 + 50$

$\Rightarrow x \times \frac{4}{5} = 260$

$\Rightarrow x = 260 \times \frac{5}{4}$

$= 65 \times 5$

$\Rightarrow x = 325.$

111. (3): Simple Interest = A – P

= ₹ 15,500 – ₹ 12,500

= ₹ 3,000

and t = 4 years,

$\therefore$ The rate of interest $= \frac{\text{S.I.} \times 100}{\text{P} \times t}$

$= \frac{3000 \times 100}{12500 \times 4}$

$= \frac{30 \times 25}{125} = 6\%$

$\Rightarrow r = 6\%.$

112. (1): Let the age of youngest child be x years

Then, $x + (x + 3) + (x + 6) + (x + 9) + (x + 12) = 50$

$\Rightarrow 5x + 30 = 50$

$\Rightarrow 5x = 20$

$\Rightarrow x = 4$ years.

113. (2): A's 1 day's work $= \frac{1}{10}$

B's 1 day's work $= \frac{1}{15}$

(A + B)'s 1 day's work $= \frac{1}{10}+\frac{1}{15}$

$= \frac{3+2}{30}$

$= \frac{5}{30} = \frac{1}{6}$

They together will do the same work in 6 days.

114. (3): Part filled by A in 1 hour $= \frac{1}{5}$

Part filled by B in 1 hour $= \frac{1}{10}$

and part filled by C in 1 hour $= \frac{1}{30}$

$\therefore$ Part filled by (A + B + C) in 1 hour

$= \frac{1}{5}+\frac{1}{10}+\frac{1}{30}$

$= \frac{6+3+1}{30}$

$= \frac{10}{30}$

$= \frac{1}{3}$

$\therefore$ The tank will be filled in 3 hours.

115. (4): Given, the price of 6 toys = ₹ 264

$\Rightarrow$ The price of 1 toy $= \frac{264}{6}$

= ₹ 44

$\therefore$ The price of 5 toys = 5 × 44

= ₹ 220.

116. (1): $(7+3\sqrt{5})(7-3\sqrt{5})$

$= (7)^2 - (3\sqrt{5})^2$

$= 49 - 45 = 4.$

117. **(1):** Given, $x^3 - 6x^2 + 12x - 4$ is divided by $(x - 2)$

$$
\begin{array}{r|l|l}
(x-2) & x^3 - 6x^2 + 12x - 4 & (x^2 - 4x + 4) \\
 & x^3 - 2x^2 & \\
 & - \quad + & \\
\hline
 & -4x^2 + 12x - 4 & \\
 & -4x^2 + 8x & \\
 & + \quad - & \\
\hline
 & 4x - 4 & \\
 & 4x - 8 & \\
 & - \quad + & \\
\hline
 & 4 &
\end{array}
$$

Hence, required remainder = 4

118. **(3):** Given, $\sqrt{4^n} = 1024$

$\Rightarrow \quad (4^n)^{1/2} = 32 \times 32$

$\Rightarrow \quad 4^{n/2} = 2^5 \times 2^5$

$\Rightarrow \quad (2^2)^{n/2} = 210$

$\Rightarrow \quad 2^n = 210$

$\Rightarrow \quad n = 10.$

119. **(1):** $\because$ LCM of three numbers = 9570

2	9570
3	4785
5	1595
11	319
29	29
	1

$\therefore$ LCM = $2 \times 3 \times 5 \times 11 \times 29 = 9570$

Numbers, $\mathbf{11} \times 30 = 330$

$\mathbf{11} \times 29 = 319$

$\mathbf{11} \times 1 = 11$

$\therefore$ HCF = 11.

120. **(2):** Let the two numbers be a and b

Then, $a + b = 42$

$ab = 437$

$\because \quad (a - b)^2 = (a + b)^2 - 4ab$

$\therefore \quad (a - b)^2 = (42)^2 - 4 \times 437$

$= 1764 - 1748 = 16$

$\Rightarrow \quad (a - b)^2 = (4)^2$

$\Rightarrow \quad a - b = 4$

$\therefore$ The difference of two number is 4.

121. **(2):** Article 21(A) of the Indian Constitution was inserted by the 86th Constitutional Amendment Act, 2002, and it provides that every child aged 6 to 14 years has the right to free and compulsory education in a manner determined by the State. This article made education a Fundamental Right under Part III of the Constitution and mandates the government to ensure schooling facilities and no denial of education due to financial or social barriers.

122. **(3):** The Almatti Dam is a major dam constructed across the Krishna River in Bagalkot district, Karnataka. It is part of the Upper Krishna Irrigation Project, and its main purpose is irrigation and hydroelectric power generation. The dam plays a significant role in the agricultural development of northern Karnataka and helps regulate water supply to several downstream regions.

123. **(1):** The Himalayas are the youngest mountain range in India and the world, formed approximately 50 million years ago when the Indian tectonic plate collided with the Eurasian plate. This orogenic event led to the upliftment of the Himalayas, which continue to rise slowly due to ongoing tectonic activity. The range includes some of the world's highest peaks, including Mount Everest and Kanchenjunga, and plays a vital role in influencing the climate and river systems of India.

124. **(4):** Kanchipuram, located in modern-day Tamil Nadu, served as the capital city of the Pallava dynasty, which ruled from the 4th to the 9th century CE. It was a major center of temple architecture, learning, and culture during that period. Many significant rock-cut temples and sculptures, including those at Mahabalipuram, were commissioned by the Pallavas, making Kanchipuram a historical hub of South Indian civilization.

125. **(1):** Banabhatta was the court poet of Harshavardhana, and he authored Harshacharita, a detailed Sanskrit biographical account of Harsha's life. The work is notable for its ornate literary style and provides crucial information about the political, social, and cultural conditions of 7th-century India. It is among the earliest historical biographies in Indian literature.

126. **(3):** The slogan "Do or Die" was given by Mahatma Gandhi on 8 August 1942 during the launch of the Quit India Movement at the Bombay session of the All India Congress Committee. This powerful call urged Indians to actively resist British rule and attain complete independence, even at the cost of their lives. It mobilized millions and led to widespread protests and mass arrests, marking one of the most intense phases of India's freedom struggle.

127. **(4):** Swami Dayanand Saraswati, a prominent Hindu reformer, founded the Arya Samaj in 1875 in Mumbai. The movement aimed to revive Vedic ideals and promoted social reforms like the abolition of untouchability, child marriage, and the promotion of widow remarriage. He emphasized Vedic authority, monotheism, and the education of both men and women, making the Arya Samaj a major force in India's socio-religious awakening.

128. **(1):** Fiscal policy refers to the government's use of taxation, public spending, and borrowing to influence the nation's economic health. Managed by the Ministry of Finance, it plays a key role in stimulating economic growth, controlling inflation, and reducing unemployment. The annual Union Budget is the main instrument of fiscal policy in India, outlining planned revenues and expenditures.

129. **(1):** The Gandhi-Irwin Pact, signed in March 1931, was an agreement between Mahatma Gandhi and the then Viceroy, Lord Irwin, during the Civil Disobedience Movement. Under the pact, Gandhi agreed to suspend the movement and attend the Second Round Table Conference, while the British agreed to release political prisoners and withdraw certain ordinances. The pact aimed to create a truce, though many within the Congress were skeptical of its results.

130. **(4):** Zero Hour is an informal parliamentary device in the Indian Parliament that starts immediately after the Question Hour (12 noon) and allows Members of Parliament to raise urgent matters of public importance without prior notice. Though not officially mentioned in the rules of procedure, it is a significant tool for ensuring parliamentary accountability and responsiveness, often used to highlight local or national issues requiring immediate attention.

131. **(3):** Marble is a classic example of a metamorphic rock, formed when limestone undergoes heat and pressure over time deep within the Earth's crust. This process changes the mineral composition and structure of the original rock, giving marble its characteristic hardness and crystalline texture, often used in sculpture and construction.

132. **(4):** The Green Revolution refers to a period during the 1960s and 1970s when agricultural production in India increased dramatically due to the use of high-yielding variety (HYV) seeds, chemical fertilizers, pesticides, and improved irrigation techniques. Led by agricultural scientist M.S. Swaminathan, this revolution focused on crops like wheat and rice, particularly in states like Punjab and Haryana.

133. **(2):** The 42nd Amendment Act of 1976 added 10 Fundamental Duties to the Indian Constitution under Article 51A in Part IV-A. These duties were inspired by the Constitution of the former USSR and aim to promote a sense of responsibility, patriotism, and commitment among Indian citizens. A 11th duty was later added in 2002, bringing the total to 11 now.

134. **(1):** The Kolar Gold Fields (KGF) are located in the Kolar district of Karnataka. Once known for being one of the deepest and oldest gold mines in the world, KGF played a significant role in India's gold production until its closure in 2001 due to unprofitability and environmental concerns.

135. **(1):** Black soil, also known as Regur soil, is ideal for cotton cultivation because of its high moisture retention, clayey nature, and rich mineral content such as lime, iron, and magnesium. This soil is predominantly found in the Deccan Plateau regions including Maharashtra, Madhya Pradesh, and Gujarat.

136. (2): The British shifted their capital from Calcutta (now Kolkata) to Delhi in the year 1911, during the Delhi Durbar held to commemorate the coronation of King George V. Delhi was chosen due to its historical and political significance, as it had been the seat of several earlier empires in India.

137. (4): The historic Grand Trunk Road (GT Road), one of Asia's oldest and longest roads, was expanded and modernized by Sher Shah Suri, the Afghan ruler of the Sur Empire in the 16th century. It connected Chittagong (Bangladesh) to Kabul (Afghanistan) and played a major role in trade, travel, and administration.

138. (1): Kanchenjunga, located in Sikkim, is the highest mountain peak in India, with an elevation of 8,586 meters (28,169 feet). It is the third highest peak in the world after Mount Everest and K2. Mount Everest, although the world's highest, lies in Nepal, not within Indian territory.

139. (2): The Red Sea is a classic example of a faulted structure or rift valley, formed due to divergent tectonic plate movements. The Arabian and African plates are moving apart, causing the Earth's crust to fracture and sink, forming the elongated depression filled with seawater.

140. (3): The official currency of Bhutan is the Ngultrum (BTN). It is pegged to the Indian Rupee (INR) at par, meaning 1 Ngultrum equals 1 Rupee. While Indian Rupees are also accepted in Bhutan, the Ngultrum is issued by the Royal Monetary Authority of Bhutan.

141. (2): The word "callous" means emotionally hardened, unfeeling, or insensitive to others' suffering. So, the word closest in meaning is "insensitive". It refers to a lack of empathy or compassion, particularly in dealing with vulnerable individuals or groups.

142. (2): The word "verdict" refers to the formal decision or judgment given by a jury or judge in a court of law. Hence, the nearest in meaning is "judgement", which is a more general term but fits the context of a legal conclusion.

143. (3): If something is extinct, it means it no longer exists, especially in terms of species that have died out. Therefore, the word "non-existent" accurately conveys the meaning of being gone or no longer living.

144. (3): "Inadvertently" means without intention; accidentally or unknowingly. The correct synonym is "accidently" (a variant spelling of "accidentally"), which matches the context of the girl unintentionally stepping on someone's toes.

145. (1): "Persuasive" in this context refers to having a strong influence or effect on someone's thoughts or behaviour. While it usually implies convincing power, here it refers more broadly to being influential or powerful, making "powerful" the best fit.

146. (2): "Alienate" means to cause someone to feel isolated or estranged, and this is the correct spelling. All other options are incorrect variations.

147. (2): "Bureaucracy" refers to a system of government or management run by departments or officials. Option 2 is correctly spelled; the others contain errors in syllables or vowels.

148. (1): "Pedagogy" is the science or art of teaching and education. This is the standard spelling. Other options are incorrect or archaic spellings.

149. (1): "Curriculum" refers to the set of courses or content offered by an educational institution. This is the correct spelling; others are misspellings.

150. (4): An "Entrepreneur" is someone who starts and runs a business, taking on financial risks. Option 4 is the correct spelling; the rest are incorrect phonetic attempts.

151. (1): The word "progress" means advancement or forward movement, especially in terms of success or development. Its opposite is "stagnation", which implies a lack of growth or movement, often resulting in no improvement or development.

152. (2): "Optimistic" refers to having a positive and hopeful outlook. Its antonym is "pessimistic", which describes someone who expects the worst outcome or has a negative viewpoint about future events.

153. (2): To "abdicate" means to give up or renounce power or a position, especially a throne. The opposite of that is to "retain", which means to keep or hold onto something, in this case, the throne or position of power.

154. (4): The word "emanates" means to radiate or issue forth, often used with qualities like power or light. The opposite is "conceal", which means to hide or suppress something so that it does not show or become evident.

155. (1): The sentence describes a king who punishes even children, suggesting cruel and oppressive behavior. The word "tyrannical" fits best, as it refers to a ruler who uses power unjustly or cruelly. Other options like "bossy" or "controlling" are too mild, and "philanthropic" (charitable) is opposite in tone.

156. (3): An extrovert is someone who is outgoing, confident, and socially active, which aligns with a strong personality capable of handling crises. The sentence implies encouragement based on personality traits, making "extrovert" the most appropriate word.

157. (3): Rabindranath Tagore was awarded the Nobel Prize for Literature in 1913 for his collection "Gitanjali", making him the first non-European to receive this honor. His works are noted for their spiritual depth and lyrical beauty.

158. (1): "Train to Pakistan" by Khushwant Singh is a powerful novel that portrays the horrific events and human suffering during the Partition of India in 1947. It captures the trauma, violence, and loss experienced by people on both sides of the border.

159. (1): "Romeo and Juliet" is a famous tragedy written by William Shakespeare, centered on the doomed love story of two young lovers from feuding families. It remains one of the most well-known plays in world literature.

160. (1): Vikram Seth is best known for his epic novel "A Suitable Boy", a sweeping story set in post-independence India. The novel explores themes of family, politics, and arranged marriage, and is one of the longest novels published in a single volume.

161. (4): गद्यांश में समय की महत्ता, उसकी अबाध गति, और सदुपयोग से मिलने वाली जीवन की सफलता पर बल दिया गया है।

अतः 'समय का महत्व' सबसे उपयुक्त शीर्षक है।

162. (2): गद्यांश में स्पष्ट कहा गया है कि समय का चक्र निरंतर गतिशील रहता है और रुकना उसका धर्म नहीं है। अतः उसकी गति अबाध है क्योंकि वह निरंतर चलता रहता है।

163. (4): गद्यांश में कहा गया है कि मनुष्य की नष्ट हुई सम्पत्ति को प्रयास से फिर पाया जा सकता है, लेकिन बीता हुआ समय लौट कर नहीं आता। इससे स्पष्ट है कि यही मुख्य अंतर है।

164. (1): गद्यांश में कहा गया है कि समय का सदुपयोग करें तो यह उन्नति में चार चाँद लगा सकता है। इसका अर्थ है कि समय को व्यर्थ न गँवाकर इसका सही उपयोग करने से व्यक्ति सफल हो सकता है।

165. (3): महापुरुषों ने समय का सदुपयोग किया, इसलिए वे महान बन सके। इससे स्पष्ट है कि उन्होंने काम को समय पर पूर्ण करके समय का उचित उपयोग किया।

166. (2): 'अमोल' शब्द का तत्सम रूप होता है 'अमूल्य', जिसका अर्थ है–जिसका मूल्य न हो सके या बहुत अधिक मूल्यवान।

167. (3): 'तुरंग' शब्द का अर्थ होता है–घोड़ा। यह एक संस्कृत-निष्ठ शब्द है जो तेज गति से दौड़ने वाले पशु के लिए प्रयुक्त होता है।

168. (1): 'कौमुदी' शब्द का पर्यायवाची है 'चाँदनी'। यह शब्द शरद पूर्णिमा की रात्रि में विशेष रूप से चन्द्रप्रकाश को दर्शाने के लिए प्रयुक्त होता है।

169. (3): 'अस्तित्व' का अर्थ होता है 'होना' या 'वजूद' और उसका विलोम होगा 'अनस्तित्व', जिसका अर्थ है 'न होना' या 'अभाव'।

170. (2): 'घी' शब्द एक पुल्लिंग शब्द है। उदाहरण : यह घी शुद्ध है। अतः इसका लिंग है पुल्लिंग।

171. (4): 'अनिर्वचनीय' का अर्थ होता है–जिसका वर्णन न किया जा सके, यानी जो अवर्णनीय हो। यह शब्द 'निर्वचन' (वर्णन) में 'अन्' उपसर्ग और 'ीय' प्रत्यय जोड़कर बना है।

172. **(1):** 'ऐतिहासिक' शब्द में 'इतिहास' मूल शब्द है और इसमें 'इक' प्रत्यय जुड़कर 'ऐतिहासिक' बना है। यह विशेषण बनाने वाला सामान्य प्रत्यय है।

173. **(2):** वाक्य 'लड़की ने गीत गाया' में 'लड़की ने' कार्य करने वाली है, इसलिए यह कर्ता कारक है। 'ने' कर्ता कारक का चिह्न है।

174. **(3):** 'मुनि' शब्द का बहुवचन रूप भी 'मुनि' ही होता है, विशेषतः संस्कृतनिष्ठ या साहित्यिक हिंदी में। जैसे–'कई मुनि वहाँ एकत्र हुए।' 'मुनियों' प्रयोग तो पदबद्ध रूप (जैसे 'के मुनियों') में होता है, लेकिन सरल बहुवचन में 'मुनि' ही सही है।

175. **(4):** 'स्थिति' शब्द धातु 'स्था' से बना है, इसमें कोई उपसर्ग नहीं है।

जबकि 'स्वागत; (स्व + आगत), 'प्रतिमूर्ति' (प्रति + मूर्ति), और 'दुर्घटना' (दुर् + घटना) उपसर्ग से बने हैं।

176. **(1):** 'सुनीता' उपन्यास के लेखक हैं जैनेन्द्र कुमार, जो हिंदी के प्रमुख मनोवैज्ञानिक कथा लेखक माने जाते हैं।

177. **(1):** 'हाथ के तोते उड़ जाना' मुहावरे का अर्थ है–अचानक घबरा जाना या बहुत डर जाना। यह उस स्थिति को दर्शाता है जब व्यक्ति पूरी तरह स्तब्ध या हक्का-बक्का रह जाता है।

178. **(3):** 'अपना काम महाकाम' का अर्थ है कि व्यक्ति को अपना कार्य सबसे बड़ा लगता है। यह कहावत स्वार्थपूर्ण सोच को भी इंगित करती है।

179. **(4):** पंक्ति 'पीपर पात सरिस मन डोला' में मन की चंचलता की तुलना पीपल के पत्ते से की गई है। 'सरिस' (समान) उपमेय और उपमान को जोड़ता है, इसलिए यह उपमा अलंकार है।

180. **(3):** यहाँ 'अत्योक्ति' शब्द की वर्तनी अशुद्ध है। इसका शुद्ध रूप है–'अत्युक्ति' जिसका अर्थ है–अतिशयोक्ति करना या बढ़ा-चढ़ाकर कहना। अन्य सभी शब्द शुद्ध हैं।

Previous Paper (Solved)

IGNOU B.Ed. ENTRANCE EXAM 2024

(Exam held on 07 January, 2024)

Part-A

Section-I: General English Comprehension

Directions (Qs. No. 1-5): *Read the following passage carefully and choose the best answer out of the four choices given after each question that follow:*

I am concerned about all organized sports activities for children between the ages of six and twelve. The damage I see results from non-contact as well as contact sports, from sports organized locally as well as those organized nationally. Highly organized competitive sports are too often played to adult standards, which are developmentally inappropriate for children and can be both physically and psychologically harmful. Furthermore, because they eliminate many children from organized sports before they are ready to compete, they are actually counterproductive for developing either future players or fans. Finally, because they emphasize competition and winning, they unfortunately provide occasions for some parents and coaches to place their own fantasies and needs ahead of children's welfare.

One readily understandable danger of overly competitive sports is that they entice children into physical actions that are bad for growing bodies. Although the official Little League Website acknowledges that children do risk injury playing baseball, it insists that "severe injuries ... are infrequent," the risk "far less than the risk of riding a skateboard, a bicycle, or even the school bus". Nevertheless, Leonard Koppett in *Sports Illusion, Sports Reality* claims that a twelve-year-old trying to throw a curve ball, for example, may put abnormal strain on developing arm and shoulder muscles, sometimes resulting in lifelong injuries.

Besides physical hazards and anxieties, competitive sports pose psychological dangers for children. Martin Rablovsky, a former sports editor for the *New York Times,* says that in all his years of watching young children play organized sports, he has noticed very few of them smiling. "I've seen children enjoying a spontaneous pre-practice scrimmage become somber and serious when the coach's whistle blows." Rablovsky says. "The spirit of play suddenly disappears, and sports becomes joblike." The primary goal of a professional athlete — winning — is not appropriate for children. Their goals should be having fun, learning, and being with friends. Although winning does add to the fun, too many adults lose sight of what matters and make winning the most important goal. Several studies have shown that when children are asked whether they would rather be warming the bench on a winning team or playing regularly on a losing team, about 90 percent choose the latter.

Winning and losing may be an inevitable part of adult life, but they should not be part of childhood. Too much competition too early in life can affect a child's development. Children are easily influenced, and when they sense that their competence and worth are based on their ability to live up to their parents and coaches high expectations — and on their ability to win — they can become discouraged and depressed.

1. The most appropriate title of the passage could be:
A. Children need to play, not compete
B. All work and no play makes Jack a dull boy
C. Ruining children
D. Cooperation not competition

2. The primary style of the passage is:
A. Argumentative B. Descriptive
C. Historical D. Narrative

3. The main idea of the passage is:
A. Most children are deprived of sports
B. Children who take sports non-seriously are going to be excluded
C. Future competitors may not be nurtured because they are averse to competition
D. The fun of just playing is marred for some children

4. The word 'counterproductive' in para 1 of the passage would mean:
A. worthless B. feeble
C. ineffectual D. hopeless

5. The phrase "... provide occasions for some parents and coaches to place their own fantasies and needs ahead of children's welfare." implies:
A. Parents and coaches impose adult standards on children's sports which is not good for the children.
B. Parents and coaches fulfil their own dreams through their children, which is not beneficial for the children.
C. Frustrated parents and coaches push their children to the extent that it becomes unhealthy.
D. Parents and coaches are essentially bothered about their children not getting eliminated from sports.

6. What does the paragraph 2 not suggest?
A. that playing these rough sports is physically unhealthy for the children
B. children's growth will be stunted if they continue playing these sports
C. children may get numerous injuries and may not be able to play sports
D. children may be made to perform physical actions during playing sports, which may be good for their bodies

7. In paragraph 3, the author suggests that children:
A. don't like to win
B. only like to have fun
C. prefer to play regardless of winning and losing
D. are not serious at that stage of their life

8. The 'psychological dangers' mentioned in para 3 that such children face, could be:
A. caused by unrealistic parents'/coaches' expectations
B. because the children are afraid of play
C. due to lack of respect to parents/coaches
D. caused by immense and unnecessary physical stress

9. In the sentence 'Winning and losing are an inevitable part of adult life ...." winning and losing are examples of:
A. noun B. verb
C. gerund D. participle

10. All the ideas given below in the passage are there except ONE. Pick that sentence:
A. The ability to cooperate is also important for success in life
B. Competitive sports are too selective and only a few children get to participate
C. Winning should not be the most important goal for children
D. Contact sports can be physically hazardous for children

1. A **2.** A **3.** D **4.** C **5.** B **6.** B **7.** C **8.** A **9.** C **10.** B

Section-II: Logical and Analytical Reasoning

Directions (Qs. No. 11-14): *Each of the following questions consists of two pairs of numbers/letter-groups. First pair has a certain relationship. Complete the second pair by using the same relationship.*

11. 169 : 26 :: 361 : ?
A. 66 B. 54
C. 38 D. 27

12. 11 : 122 :: 17 : ?
A. 288 B. 289
C. 290 D. 291

13. CDE : WVU :: KLM : ?
A. ONP B. NOP
C. RPO D. PON

14. ACEG : NPRT :: BDFH : ?
A. PSRT B. OQSU
C. MPRS D. ORSU

Directions (Qs. No. 15-18): *In each of the following questions a number/letter series is given with one term missing. Identify the underlying pattern and complete the series by choosing the correct option.*

15. 31, 37, 41, ?, 47, 53, ______ .
A. 42 B. 43
C. 44 D. 45

16. 17, 26, 35, 44, 53, ?,
A. 58 B. 62
C. 68 D. 72

17. AMZ, BLY, CKX, ______, EIV.
A. DJW B. DHU
C. DKV D. DIV

18. AMZN, BLYO, CKXP, ______, EIVR.
A. DKUX B. DJUV
C. DLXV D. DJWQ

19. If NET is coded as PGV and LEAD is coded as NGCF, then STORM would be coded as:
A. WUSRP B. UVQTO
C. UXRSO D. VUPSP

20. If NO is coded as ON and ARE is coded as ERA, then RAMA would be coded as:
A. MARA B. AMRA
C. ARMA D. AMAR

21. If 234 is coded as 345 and 514 is coded as 625, then 4273 would be coded as:
A. 3162 B. 5384
C. 5172 D. 5372

22. If PEAK is coded as 5236 and PORT is coded as 5147, then ORPAT would be coded as:
A. 45321 B. 53172
C. 23517 D. 14537

23. A man is walking toward east and turns 135° left, and then turns right by 90°. In which direction is he now walking?
A. South-East B. South-West
C. East-West D. North-East

24. A boy cycles north from his house. After moving 8 km, he turns right and moves 6 km. How far is he now from his house?
A. 8 km B. 10 km
C. 12 km D. 14 km

25. What is the order of occurring of the following words in the dictionary?
(*a*) PURE (*b*) PEAR
(*c*) POOR (*d*) POUR
A. (*a*), (*c*), (*b*), (*d*) B. (*b*), (*c*), (*d*), (*a*)
C. (*d*), (*b*), (*c*), (*a*) D. (*a*), (*b*), (*d*), (*c*)

11. C **12.** C **13.** D **14.** B **15.** B **16.** B **17.** A **18.** D **19.** B **20.** D
21. A **22.** D **23.** D **24.** B **25.** B

26. What is the number of triangles hidden in the adjoining figure?

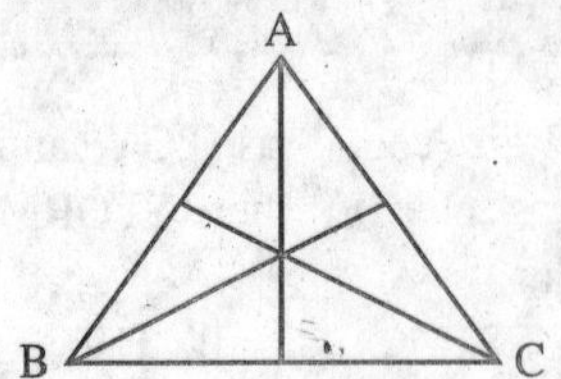

A. 6 B. 8
C. 12 D. 16

27. The average age of 5 boys is 15 years. One more boy joins the group and average age is increased by six months. The age of the new boy is:

A. 17 years B. 18 years
C. 19 years D. 20 years

28. Five books A, B, C, D and E are placed in such a way that A is below D but above B. B is above E and D is below C. Which book is in the middle?

A. A B. B
C. C D. D

29. Find the missing number in the following series:

5376412, 537641, 37641, ______, 764, 76

A. 3764 B. 7641
C. 5376 D. 76412

30. A is the son of the only brother of B's father's wife. How is A related to B?

A. Brother B. Uncle
C. Cousin D. Nephew

Section-III: Educational and General Awareness

31. Who among the following is NOT associated with medicine in ancient India?

A. Sushruta B. Charak
C. Dhanvantri D. Bhaskaracharya

32. Uplift of the backward classes was the main programme of the:

A. Prarthana Sabha
B. Arya Samaj
C. Ramakrishna Mission
D. Satya Shodhak Samaj

33. Which one of the following territories was not affected by the revolt of 1857?

A. Jhansi B. Jagdishpur
C. Chittor D. Lucknow

34. Which of the following is the oldest dynasty in India?

A. Mauryan dynasty
B. Chola dynasty
C. Gupta dynasty
D. Pallava dynasty

35. Which Article of the Indian constitution empowers parliament to make laws for giving effect to international agreement?

A. Article 249 B. Article 250
C. Article 252 D. Article 253

36. The constitution of India borrowed the scheme of Indian Federation from the constitution of:

A. U.S.A. B. Canada
C. Ireland D. U.K.

37. How many schedules are there in the Indian constitution?

A. 11 B. 12
C. 13 D. 14

38. Sarkaria Commission was set up for reviewing the relations between:

A. The Prime Minister and the President
B. Legislature and the Executive
C. Executive and the Judiciary
D. Centre and the States

26. D **27.** B **28.** A **29.** A **30.** A **31.** D **32.** D **33.** C **34.** A **35.** D
36. B **37.** B **38.** D

39. Directive Principles of State Policy are:
A. Justiciable
B. Non-justiciable
C. Quasi-justiciable
D. A fundamental right

40. National Knowledge Commission was headed by:
A. Sam Pitroda B. D.S. Kothari
C. Amartya Sen D. Azim Premji

41. The Indian Independence League was set up by:
A. Rasa Behari Bose
B. S.M. Joshi
C. Jai Prakash Narayan
D. Aruna Asaf Ali

42. Mahatma Gandhi got his inspiration for civil disobedience movement from:
A. Thoreau B. Ruskin
C. Confucius D. Tolstoy

43. When was the ABC scheme launched in India?
A. 2020 B. 2022
C. 2021 D. 2023

44. The variety of coffee largely grown in India is:
A. Old chicks B. Coorgs
C. Arabica D. Kents

45. Which mountain has the oldest rocks in India?
A. The Himalayas
B. The Aravallis
C. The Indo-Gangetic Plain
D. Shivaliks

46. The Himalayan mountain system belongs to which one of the following?
A. Fold mountains B. Volcanic mountains
C. Black mountains D. Aravallis

47. Which of the following is the longest dam in India?
A. Bhakhara Nangal Dam
B. Hirakud Dam
C. Nagarjuna Sagar Dam
D. Tungabhadra Dam

48. What is the full form of MOOCs?
A. Massive Office Online Courses
B. Massive Open Online Courses
C. Modern Online Office Courses
D. Massive Open Offline Courses

49. NEP, 2020 proposes that learning should be:
A. Recall based B. Experiential
C. Textbook centric D. Exam oriented

50. Common salt is obtained from sea water by the process of:
A. Sublimation B. Evaporation
C. Crystallisation D. Filtration

51. The deepest ocean is:
A. Arctic B. Atlantic
C. Pacific D. Indian

52. The aim of National Education Policy, 2020 is to increase the Gross Enrollment Ratio in Higher Education by 2035 to:
A. 50% B. 35%
C. 26.3% D. 40%

53. When was decimal coinage introduced in India?
A. 1950 B. 1957
C. 1947 D. 1960

54. What portion of land in India is covered with forests?
A. 1/5th B. 1/4th
C. 1/3rd D. 2/5th

55. MOOCs is built on the idea of:
A. Group learning
B. Peer learning
C. Web based learning
D. Co-operative learning

39. B	**40.** A	**41.** A	**42.** A	**43.** C	**44.** C	**45.** B	**46.** A	**47.** B	**48.** B
49. B	**50.** B	**51.** C	**52.** A	**53.** B	**54.** B	**55.** C			

Section-IV: Teaching-Learning and The School

56. How a teacher should deal with the individual differences in a classroom?
A. Divide the students based on the mental age
B. Know the strengths and weaknesses of each student
C. Design the curriculum as per the interests, abilities and needs of different students
D. Adopt a single method of teaching

57. What are the classes which cover at 'Secondary' stage according to NEP, 2020?
A. Classes 6 to 9
B. Classes 9 to 12
C. Classes 6 to 8
D. Classes 11 and 12

58. "Same subject should not be kept for two consecutive periods in a timetable".

This statement is related to which of the following principles of timetable construction?
A. Principle of Elasticity
B. Principle of relative importance of subjects
C. Principle of Justice
D. Principle of Variety

59. Which of the following does not affect the learning process of a learner?
A. Motivation
B. Desire for learning
C. Intelligence
D. Social recognition

60. Group dynamics can only be understood by:
A. Reading books
B. Note-taking
C. Collaborative work
D. Self-reflection

61. Which of the following activities is an example of concrete experience?
A. Analogies
B. Field visit
C. Self-thinking
D. Discussion

62. If you want to enhance the ability to observe in children, which of the following would you recommend?
A. Sharpening the senses
B. Developing interest in subject
C. Preparing a model
D. Training mental faculties

63. Which is the apex institution involved in planning and coordination of teacher education in the country?
A. UGC
B. NCTE
C. NCERT
D. RCI

64. Which of the following methods develop cognitive, emotional and physical development in students?
A. Demonstration method
B. Lecture method
C. Play-way method
D. Heuristic method

65. Which of the following ability helps an individual to use different approaches in responding to a stimulus?
A. Fluency
B. Flexibility
C. Originality
D. Elaboration

56. C **57.** B **58.** D **59.** D **60.** C **61.** B **62.** A **63.** B **64.** C **65.** B

66. PARAKH stands for:
A. Performance Assessment Review and Analytical Knowledge for Holistic Development
B. Peer Assessment Review and Analysis of Knowledge for Holistic Development
C. Performance Assessment Review and Analysis of Knowledge for Holistic Development
D. Peer Assessment Retention and Analysis of Knowledge for Holistic Development

67. A teacher engages his/her learners in brainstorming before beginning a new lesson. The purpose behind this is to:
A. energize the learners
B. assess the previous knowledge of learners
C. discipline the learners in the classroom
D. reduce the monotony in the classroom

68. A teacher asks the learners to think of ideas quickly about the topic 'Waste Management' and also ask them to note down their ideas in a notebook. S/he is focusing on:
A. Brainstorming
B. Note-taking
C. Drill
D. Journal writing

69. A teacher analyses the written performance of students of class III and realizes that 80% have not been able to do single digit multiplication correctly. At what phase of teaching, this activity will happen?
A. Pre-teaching phase
B. Introduction phase of teaching
C. Teaching phase
D. Post-teaching phase

70. ABC stands for:
A. Academic, Business and Community
B. Antecedent, Behaviour and Consequence
C. Academic Bank of Credit
D. Accountability Basics and Control

71. The portal which provides national digital infrastructures for teachers is:
A. DIKSHA
B. SHIKSHA
C. GYAN
D. SHAKTI

72. Which of the following is related to the goal of teaching?
A. To ensure participation of students
B. To impart knowledge
C. To bring desirable change in behaviour
D. To provide information

73. In which of the following skills, testing of prior knowledge comes?
A. Skill of introduction
B. Skill of demonstration
C. Skill of stimulus variation
D. Skill of closure

74. Teaching in miniature where it is scaled down in size of the class time and task with focus on a specific teaching skill is known as:
A. Macro-teaching
B. Collaborative teaching
C. Team teaching
D. Micro-teaching

75. Which of the following theories focuses on acquisition of new behaviours and experiences by observing others in the immediate environment?
A. Behavioural theory
B. Social learning theory
C. Cognitive theory
D. Psychosocial theory

76. Which of the following is a tough issue related to school effectiveness?
A. Developing good attitude
B. Style of leadership
C. Developing appropriate skills
D. Policies

66. C **67.** B **68.** A **69.** D **70.** C **71.** A **72.** C **73.** A **74.** D **75.** B **76.** D

77. Which of the following is an objective of organising cultural activities in school?
A. Develop independent thinking
B. Develop skill of comprehension
C. Promote national integration
D. Trace references related to a topic

78. Cumulative record card is an example of:
A. Record of learners
B. Record of teachers
C. Record of all staffs
D. Record of staff meeting

79. Which of the following is not related to professional development of teachers?
A. Mastery of content
B. Knowing recent trends in education
C. Getting high salary
D. Understanding pedagogy

80. Quality of educators who train teachers is related to which quality factor in teaching profession?
A. Context factor B. Process factor
C. Product factor D. Governance factor

Part-B

Section-V: Subject Competence (i) Science

81. Which one of the following would help one to determine a chemical reaction has taken place?
A. Change in state
B. Change in colour
C. Evolution of a gas
D. All of these

82. The most ductile metal is:
A. Gold B. Iron
C. Copper D. Aluminium

83. Galvanisation is the method of protecting steel and iron from rusting by coating them with a thin layer of:
A. Silver B. Zinc
C. Aluminium D. Lead

84. The pH value of acidic solution is:
A. Less than 7 B. Above 7
C. 0 D. 7

85. Most carbon compounds are ________ conductor of electricity.
A. Very good B. Good
C. Poor D. Very poor

86. The structure of ethane is:

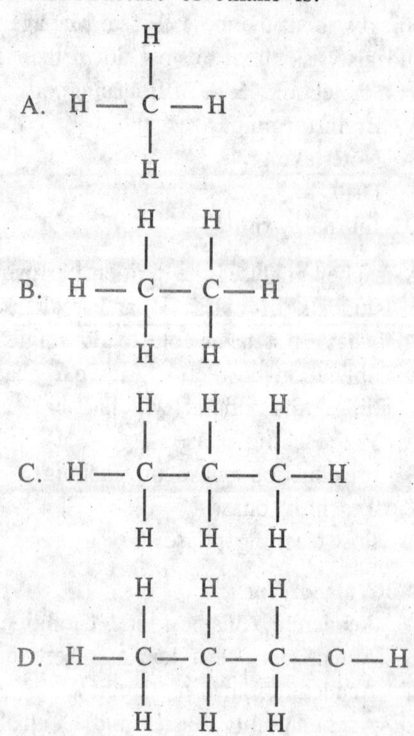

77. C **78.** A **79.** C **80.** B **81.** D **82.** A **83.** B **84.** A **85.** C **86.** B

87. The longest part of the alimentary canal in human beings is:
A. Large intestine
B. Small intestine
C. Oesophagus
D. Liver

88. The loss of water in the form of vapour from the aerial parts of the plant is known as:
A. Transpiration
B. Photosynthesis
C. Respiration
D. Absorption

89. The hormone that regulates blood sugar level is:
A. Testosterone
B. Adrenaline
C. Insulin
D. Growth hormone

90. Which of the following is a plant hormone?
A. Insulin
B. Thyroxin
C. Oestrogen
D. Cytokinin

91. The reproductive parts of a flower are:
A. Petal and Sepal
B. Petal and Stamen
C. Stamen and Pistil
D. Sepal and Pistil

92. The number of pairs of chromosomes in a human body cell is:
A. 46 B. 23
C. 69 D. 92

93. The relationship between the radius of curvature (R) and focal length (F) of a spherical mirror is
A. R = 2F B. R = 3F
C. R = 4F D. R = 5F

94. The nature of the image formed by a concave mirror is virtual and erect, when the object is placed:
A. At infinity
B. At C
D. Between C and F
D. Between P and F

95. A person with _______ can see nearby objects clearly but cannot see distant objects distinctly.
A. Myopia
B. Hypermetropia
C. Far-sightedness
D. Presbyopia

96. Twinkling of a star is duo to ______ of sunlight.
A. Dispersion B. Refraction
C. Diffraction D. Interference

97. The instrument used to measure electric current in a circuit is:
A. Voltmeter B. Altimeter
C. Ammeter D. Anemometer

98. The electric power is given by:
A. $P = VI$ B. $P = \frac{V}{I}$
C. $P = \frac{I}{V}$ D. $P = VR$

99. Who among the following showed that electricity and magnetism are related phenomena?
A. Bohr B. Lorentz
C. Heisenberg D. Oersted

100. The magnetic field inside a current carrying solenoid is:
A. Zero
B. Decreases as one moves towards end
C. Uniform
D. Non-uniform

87. B	88. A	89. C	90. D	91. C	92. A	93. A	94. C	95. A	96. B
97. C	98. A	99. D	100. C						

(ii) Mathematics

101. The sum of the first 40 positive integers divisible by 6 is:
A. 4120 B. 4720
C. 4920 D. 5120

102. Twelve observations are recorded as under:
10, 13, 18, 22, 12, 24, 27, 22, 28, 30, 34, 36
The median is:
A. 22 B. 24
C. 23 D. 27

103. The difference of third and first quartile divided by 2 is known as:
A. Mean Deviation
B. Quartile Deviation
C. Standard Deviation
D. Standard Error

104. When Mean < Median, the curve is:
A. Negatively skewed
B. Positively skewed
C. Frequency curve
D. Normal Probability curve

105. The value of
$(1 + \tan\theta + \sec\theta)(1 + \cot\theta - \operatorname{cosec}\theta)$ is:
A. –1 B. 0
C. 1 D. 2

106. The angle of elevation of the top of the tower from the point on a ground which is 30 m away from the foot of the tower is 30°. The height of the tower is:
A. $10\sqrt{3}$ m B. $\frac{10}{\sqrt{3}}$ m
C. $8\sqrt{3}$ m D. $\frac{8}{\sqrt{3}}$ m

107. Sides of two similar triangles are in the ratio of 4 : 9. The areas of these triangles are in the ratio:
A. 81 : 16 B. 16 : 81
C. 4 : 9 D. 2 : 3

108. Ram and Shyam working separately can do a piece of work in 9 days and 12 days respectively. In how many days the work will be completed if they work together?
A. $5\frac{1}{2}$ days B. $10\frac{1}{2}$ days
C. $7\frac{1}{3}$ days D. $8\frac{2}{3}$ days

109. The marked price of a watch was ₹ 720. A man bought it for ₹ 550.80 after getting two successive discounts. If the first discount was 10%, what percentage discount was the second?
A. 11% B. 13%
C. 14% D. 15%

110. A conical tent 14 metre in diameter and 4.5 metre high is to be erected. How much cloth would it require if the lateral side has to be 6 metre in length?
A. 132 sq. metre B. 180 sq. metre
C. 208 sq. metre B. 120 sq. metre

111. The value, correct to two decimal places of $\frac{0.0343 \times 2.92 \times 49}{146 \times 0.07 \times 4.9}$ is:
A. 0.09 B. 0.10
C. 0.11 D. 0.08

112. A train 108 m long moving at a speed of 50 kmph crosses a train 112 m long coming from opposite direction in 6 seconds. The speed of second train is:
A. 52 kmph B. 62 kmph
C. 72 kmph D. 82 kmph

101. C **102.** C **103.** B **104.** A **105.** D **106.** A **107.** B **108.** A **109.** D **110.** A
111. A **112.** D

113. A student secured 300 marks in an examination with minimum pass marks being 40%. He would have not failed if could secure 20 more marks. The maximum marks for the exam are:

A. 700 B. 750
C. 800 D. 850

114. The capital which will amount to ₹ 1,331 in 5 years at 2% per annum simple interest is:

A. ₹ 1,210 B. ₹ 1,100
C. ₹ 1,300 D. ₹ 1,250

115. The largest number, which exactly divides the sum of the numbers of any number of twin prime, is:

A. 1 B. 2
C. 4 D. 8

116. A man's salary was increased by 20% and then decreased by 15%. The net change is:

A. 2% decrease B. 2% increase
C. 3% increase D. 3% decrease

117. Three years ago the average age of a family of 5 members was 27 years. On the addition of a child into the family, the present average age of family is still 27 years. The present age of the child is:

A. 15 years B. 10 years
C. 11 years D. 12 years

118. There are black and white balls in a bag in the ratio of 3 : 1. If we add 5 black balls and take out 5 white balls, the ratio turns to 5 : 1. Originally the number of white balls in the bag is:

A. 10 B. 15
C. 20 D. 25

119. The age of a father is 4 times the age of his son. Five years later father's age will be 3 times of the age of his son. How old is the father now?

A. 36 years B. 40 years
C. 44 years D. 48 years

120. A two-digit number is below 50. The sum of digits is 13 and difference is 5. The number is:

A. 27 B. 38
C. 49 D. 16

(iii) Social Science

121. Who wrote the book 'A History of British India'?

A. James Mill
B. Rudyard Kipling
C. Robert Orme
D. Fazal Khan Changawi

122. In which year was the first cotton textile mill set up in Bombay?

A. 1834 B. 1844
C. 1854 D. 1864

123. Who was the ruler known as 'Devanampriya' and 'Priyadarshi'?

A. Bindusara B. Ashoka
C. Chandragupta D. Brihadratha

124. In which year was the first National Policy on Education formulated in India?

A. 1967 B. 1968
C. 1969 D. 1970

125. When did the constitution of India come into force?

A. 15th August, 1948
B. 26th November, 1949
C. 5th December, 1949
D. 26th January, 1950

113. C **114.** A **115.** C **116.** B **117.** D **118.** B **119.** B **120.** C **121.** A **122.** C
123. B **124.** B **125.** D

126. The student-teacher ratio at the upper primary level recommended by the RTE Act, 2009 is:
A. 35 : 1 B. 25 : 1
C. 30 : 1 D. 40 : 1

127. Which is the most popular classical dance form of Uttar Pradesh?
A. Kuchipudi B. Bharatnatyam
C. Kathak D. Kathakali

128. Which is the oldest mountain range in India?
A. The Himalayan Range
B. The Aravalli Range
C. The Karakoram Range
D. The Satpura Range

129. The highest peak of Satpura Range is:
A. Gurushikhar B. Pachmarhi
C. Mahendragiri D. Dhupgarh

130. Which of the following is the longest river in Asia?
A. Yangtze B. Ganga
C. Brahmaputra D. Indus

131. Who is the chairperson of the NITI Aayog?
A. Vice-President
B. Prime Minister
C. Finance Minister
D. Home Minister

132. Which is not an Igneous Rock?
A. Basalt B. Halite
C. Dionite D. Granite

133. In the mixed economy:
A. Economic problems are solved by the government departments
B. Economic decisions are made by the private sector and free market.
C. Economic problems are solved by the capitalists.
D. Economic problems are solved by the government and private sectors.

134. In consumption of additional units of good, if the satisfaction level decreases, such situation is called:
A. Diminishing marginal utility
B. Self-interest utility
C. Increasing marginal utility
D. Zero marginal utility

135. The best quantitative method to control inflation in the economy is:
A. Moral suasion
B. Selective credit control
C. Cash reserve ratio
D. Bank rate policy

136. Who was the first Indian ruler whose territory was outside India?
A. Ashoka
B. Kanishka
C. Harshavardhana
D. Chandragupta Maurya

137. Who initiated the Chipko Movement?
A. Gaura Devi B. Suraksha Devi
C. Chandi Bhatt D. Sunderlal Bahuguna

138. When too much money chases too few goods, such inflation is called:
A. Cost-push inflation
B. Demand-pull inflation
C. Built-in inflation
D. Creeping inflation

139. In which year, was Indian Citizenship Act passed?
A. 1955 B. 1952
C. 1950 D. 1949

140. The veto that grants the President of India power to reject a bill passed by the Parliament is:
A. Qualified veto B. Pocket veto
C. Absolute veto D. Suspensive veto

126. A **127.** C **128.** B **129.** D **130.** A **131.** B **132.** B **133.** D **134.** A **135.** C **136.** B **137.** D **138.** B **139.** A **140.** C

(iv) English

Directions (Qs. No. 141-145): *Choose the word that is nearest in meaning to the underlined word:*

141. The Roman Empire was overthrown by Nordic <u>barbarians</u>.
A. rude B. aggressive
C. impolite D. uncivilised

142. The captain <u>bemoans</u> the fact that his team lost again.
A. disagrees B. hates
C. laments D. criticizes

143. Her career reached its <u>zenith</u> in the 1990s.
A. end B. side
C. middle D. pinnacle

144. His <u>ambition</u> is to sail around the world.
A. plan B. roadmap
C. desire D. thought

145. The talks have failed. There seems to be no way out of this <u>impasse</u>.
A. obstacle B. indecision
C. stalemate D. rough patch

Directions (Qs. No. 146-150): *In each of the following group of words, only one of them is correctly spelt. Select the one with the correct spelling:*

146. A. embarrassment B. embarasment
C. embbarrasment D. emmbarasment

147. A. reccomend B. rreccomend
C. recommend D. recomend

148. A. pronunciation B. pronouunciation
C. pronnuouncìation D. prrounciation

149. A. supercede B. supperceed
C. superrcede D. supersede

150. A. amateur B. amature
C. ematurre D. emature

Directions (Qs. No. 151-154): *Choose the word that is opposite in meaning to the underlined word:*

151. The animal body decided to be <u>kind</u> to animals in its vicinity.
A. soft B. happy
C. hard D. cruel

152. The teacher asked the boy to be <u>polite</u>.
A. sad B. rude
C. quiet D. smart

153. His article in the newspaper got <u>adverse</u> comments.
A. intolerable B. harmful
C. favourable D. evil

154. The tourists got an <u>incredulous</u> view of the Taj Mahal in moonlight.
A. believable
B. unlikely
C. shaky
D. laughable

Directions (Qs. No. 155-156): *Pick out the most appropriate word from the given alternatives to complete the sentence:*

155. The baby bird was restless as it was ________.
A. fed B. abandoned
C. rejected D. killed

156. We all agreed after dinner, Shobha had organised a ________ evening.
A. proficient
B. magnificent
C. major
D. big

141. D	**142.** C	**143.** D	**144.** C	**145.** C	**146.** A	**147.** C	**148.** A	**149.** D	**150.** A
151. D	**152.** B	**153.** C	**154.** A	**155.** B	**156.** B				

Directions (Qs. No. 157-160): *Choose the correct answer:*

157. Which of the following novels is written by R.K. Narayan?
A. Malgudi Days
B. The Flight of the Pigeons
C. Train to Pakistan
D. Anand Math

158. The author of the series on 'Harry Potter' is:
A. H.G. Wells B. Roald Dahl
C. J.K. Rowling D. Harry Potter

159. Who is the author of the famous book, 'Alice in Wonderland'?
A. Anita Desai
B. William Shakespeare
C. Lewis Carroll
D. Premchand

160. Ruskin Bond has written the following in the famous Rusty Series:
A. Wings of Fire
B. The Namesake
C. The Room on the Roof
D. The Blue Umbrella

(v) हिन्दी

निर्देश (प्रश्न संख्या 161 से 165 तक): *निम्नलिखित गद्यांश को पढ़कर उसके आधार पर पूछे गए प्रश्नों के उत्तर दीजिए।*

"यदि हमारे वृक्ष स्वस्थ हैं, तो निश्चित मानिए हम भी स्वस्थ हैं। हमें प्राणवायु वृक्षों से ही मिलती है। हम उन्हें कार्बन डाइऑक्साइड देते हैं और वे बदले में हमें ऑक्सीजन देते हैं जो हमारे जीवन की हर क्रिया के लिए आवश्यक है। हमारे स्वास्थ्य का हर बिन्दु ऑक्सीजन की उपलब्धता से अनुप्राणित है, यह वैज्ञानिक प्रामाणिकता है। यदि हम आस-पास खड़े वृक्षों की रक्षा की जिम्मेदारी अपने कंधों पर उठा लें, तो निश्चित मानिए हमने अपने स्वास्थ्य को लंबे समय तक स्वस्थ रखने की गारंटी प्राप्त कर ली है। वृक्षों की रक्षा में ही हमारे जीवन की सुरक्षा का राज छिपा है। कहा जाता है कि एक स्वस्थ मन हजारों सोने के सिंहासनों से कहीं अधिक मूल्यवान होता है क्योंकि स्वस्थ मन ही स्वस्थ देश की रचना करने में समर्थ है। कुत्सित विचारों वाले लोग अपना जीवन तो चला सकते हैं, किन्तु समाज और देश को नहीं चला सकते।

161. गद्यांश का उचित शीर्षक चुनिए :
A. वृक्षों का जीवन
B. जीवन में वृक्षों की महत्ता
C. स्वस्थ समाज का निर्माण
D. वृक्ष और आत्म-निर्भरता

162. हमारा स्वास्थ्य वृक्षों पर निर्भर है, क्योंकि ये :
A. पर्यावरण को शुद्ध रखते हैं।
B. हमें फल देते हैं।
C. प्राणवायु देते हैं
D. छाया देते हैं।

163. हमारे स्वास्थ्य का हर बिन्दु अनुप्राणित है :
A. ऑक्सीजन की उपलब्धता से
B. कार्बन डाइऑक्साइड की उपलब्धता से
C. पेड़-पौधों से
D. श्वासों से

164. हजारों सिंहासनों से कहीं अधिक मूल्यवान है :
A. हमारा जीवन B. एक स्वस्थ मन
C. हरियाली D. स्वस्थ पर्यावरण

165. स्वस्थ रहने की गारंटी है :
A. स्वस्थ देश की रचना
B. दुनिया के समस्त वृक्षों की रक्षा
C. अपना जीवन मर्जी से जीना
D. अपने आस-पास के पेड़ों की रक्षा

166. अव्ययीभाव समास किसमें है?
A. निस्सन्देह B. गंगाजल
C. पुष्प D. सीताराम

157. A **158.** C **159.** C **160.** C **161.** B **162.** C **163.** A **164.** B **165.** D **166.** A

167. 'कोई' विशेषण है :
A. परिमाणवाचक विशेषण
B. गुणवाचक विशेषण
C. सार्वनामिक विशेषण
D. इनमें से कोई नहीं

168. 'काली घटा का घमंड घटा' में अलंकार है :
A. श्लेष अलंकार B. यमक अलंकार
C. अनुप्रास अलंकार D. अर्थालंकार

169. दोहे का उल्टा छंद है :
A. बरवै B. सोरठा
C. रोला D. चौपाई

170. 'आँख' का तत्सम रूप है :
A. लोचन B. चक्षु
C. नेत्र D. अक्षि

171. 'अंगुली' का तद्भव रूप कौन-सा है?
A. अंगुल B. अंगुठा
C. उंगली D. अंगुलीनी

172. 'प' वर्ग का अंतिम व्यंजन है :
A. फ B. म
C. ब D. न

173. 'अक्ल का दुश्मन' मुहावरे का सही अर्थ है :
A. शत्रु
B. मित्र
C. मूर्खता से काम करने वाला
D. समझदार

174. 'जो माँस खाता है' के लिए उपयुक्त शब्द है :
A. हिंसावादी B. सर्वभक्षी
C. सामिष D. निरामिष

175. निम्नलिखित में से देशज शब्द है :
A. किशन B. गड़बड़
C. हिमालय D. परिवार

176. 'आलस्य' शब्द का विशेषण है :
A. आलसी B. आलस्य
C. आलसीपन D. आलस

177. शुद्ध शब्द है :
A. ईतिहासिक B. इतिहासिक
C. अतिहासिक D. ऐतिहासिक

178. देवनागरी लिपि में लिखी जाती है :
A. हिन्दी B. अंग्रेजी
C. पंजाबी D. उर्दू

179. 'अधिकतम' शब्द का विलोम होगा :
A. सर्वाधिक B. न्यूनतम
C. थोड़ा नम D. थोड़ा अधिक

180. 'रंगभूमि' किसकी रचना है?
A. मुंशी प्रेमचन्द B. जयशंकर प्रसाद
C. महादेवी वर्मा D. मोंहन राकेश

EXPLANATORY ANSWERS

1. (A): Children need to play, not compete. The passage argues that overly competitive sports are harmful to children in both physical and psychological ways.

It emphasizes that children should be playing for fun, learning, and being with friends, rather than focusing on winning. Title A accurately reflects this message, while the other titles are less relevant or misleading.

2. (A): The primary style of the passage is argumentative, as it presents a clear viewpoint and supports it with evidence and reasoning. The author expresses concern about organized sports activities for children

167. C **168.** B **169.** B **170.** D **171.** C **172.** B **173.** C **174.** C **175.** B **176.** A
177. D **178.** A **179.** B **180.** A

aged six to twelve, arguing that they are often too competitive and potentially harmful, both physically and psychologically. The passage presents various examples and perspectives to support this argument, such as the risks of physical injury from adult-level competition and the negative impact on children's enjoyment and emotional well-being. Through logical reasoning and examples from experts, the passage aims to persuade the reader of the need to reconsider the approach to children's sports and prioritize their well-being over intense competition.

3. **(D):** The passage emphasizes throughout the harmfulness of overly competitive sports on children due to the pressure to win and meet adult expectations. It highlights the loss of joy and spontaneity that occurs when sports turn into "job-like" activities solely focused on competition. The author specifically quotes Martin Rablovsky observing the seriousness and lack of smiles in young children playing organized sports.

4. **(C):** In the context of the passage, the term "counterproductive" is used to describe the negative consequences of highly competitive organized sports for children aged six to twelve. The author argues that despite intending to foster future players and fans, these sports activities often have the opposite effect. They drive children away from sports due to the pressure to win and the focus on adult standards, ultimately failing to achieve their goals. "Ineffectual" serves as an apt synonym because it encapsulates the idea of these activities not producing the desired outcome of nurturing young athletes and fans, highlighting the failure of the overly competitive approach to organized sports for children.

5. **(B):** The phrase "provide occasions for some parents and coaches to place their fantasies and needs ahead of children's welfare" suggests that some adults involved in children's sports prioritize their own desires and ambitions over the well-being of the children. This implies that parents and coaches may project their own unfulfilled aspirations onto their children, pushing them excessively in pursuit of personal goals rather than considering what is best for the child. The passage indicates a concern that such behavior can have detrimental effects on children, as they may be subjected to undue pressure and expectations that are not in line with their developmental needs or interests. Overall, the phrase highlights the potential negative impact of adults imposing their own agendas onto children's sports experiences.

6. **(B):** Paragraph 2 of the passage primarily suggests that playing rough sports can be physically unhealthy for children, as it highlights the potential risks of injury associated with such activities. It emphasizes that both contact and non-contact sports pose dangers, pointing out that even seemingly innocuous activities like baseball can lead to lifelong injuries if not approached with caution. The paragraph warns against the strain placed on developing muscles, particularly citing the example of a twelve-year-old attempting to throw a curve ball. However, it does not suggest that children's growth will be stunted by continuing to play these sports, nor does it mention that children may be made to perform physical actions during sports that could be beneficial for their bodies. Overall, the focus is on the potential physical harm rather than the overall impact on growth or the potential benefits of physical activity.

7. **(C):** Paragraph 3 suggests that children, at their developmental stage, prioritize playing for the sake of enjoyment and socialization over the outcome of winning or losing.

The author emphasizes that children's primary goal in sports should be to have fun, learn, and spend time with friends rather than focusing solely on winning. By highlighting instances where children overwhelmingly choose playing regularly on a losing team over sitting on the bench of a winning team, the passage illustrates that children inherently value participation and engagement in sports activities over achieving victory. This implies that children are more interested in the process of playing and the camaraderie it brings rather than the competitive aspects of winning or losing. Overall, the paragraph underscores the importance of maintaining a child-centered approach to sports that prioritizes enjoyment and participation over winning at all costs.

8. (A): Paragraph 3 suggests that the psychological dangers faced by children in sports stem from the unrealistic expectations imposed by parents and coaches. The passage highlights how the pressure to win and meet adult standards can lead to children feeling discouraged and depressed. By emphasizing the importance of fun, learning, and socialization in sports, the author implies that children's well-being is compromised when they are pushed to prioritize winning above all else. This suggests that the psychological challenges arise from the undue stress and expectations placed on children by adults in authority positions rather than from any inherent fear of play or lack of respect. Overall, the paragraph underscores the detrimental effects of intense competition and unrealistic demands on children's mental health and emotional development in the context of organized sports.

9. (C): In the sentence "Winning and losing are an inevitable part of adult life", "winning" and "losing" are gerunds. A gerund is a verb form that ends in "-ing" and functions as a noun. For example, in the sentence "Everyone enjoyed Tyler's singing," the word "singing" is a gerund. Gerunds can show action or a state of being. For example, "hiking," "swimming" and "studying" are gerunds that show action, while "refreshing" and "amusing" are gerunds that show a state of being. Gerunds can also be the object of a preposition. For example, "We are thinking about walking in the woods".

10. (B): The passage discusses various concerns regarding organized sports activities for children, emphasizing the negative impact of overly competitive environments. It highlights the physical and psychological risks associated with such activities, including the potential for lifelong injuries from contact sports and the pressure to win at the expense of children's enjoyment and well-being. Additionally, the passage underscores the importance of fostering cooperation and prioritizing fun and learning over winning. While it addresses the hazards of contact sports and the importance of cooperation and de-emphasizing winning, it does not specifically mention the selectivity of competitive sports and the limited participation opportunities for children, making option B the outlier among the given ideas.

11. (C): 169 : 26

$\Rightarrow \quad \sqrt{169} \times 2 = 13 \times 2 = 26$

$\therefore$ 361 : ?

$\Rightarrow \quad \sqrt{361} \times 2 = 19 \times 2 = 38$

Hence, 169 : 26 : : 361 : $\boxed{38}$

Hence, ? = 38.

12. (C): 11 : 122

$\Rightarrow \quad 11 \times 11 + 1 = 121 + 1 = 122$

$\therefore$ 17 : ?

$\Rightarrow \quad 17 \times 17 + 1 = 289 + 1 = 290$

Hence, 11 : 122 : : 17 : $\boxed{290}$.

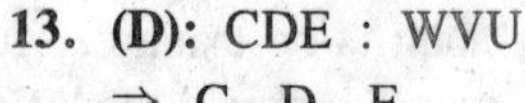

13. (D): CDE : WVU

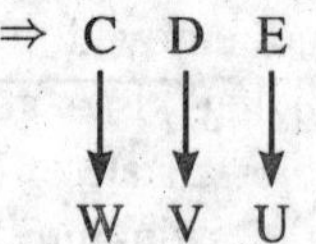

C + W = 26
D + V = 26
E + U = 26

and KLM : ?

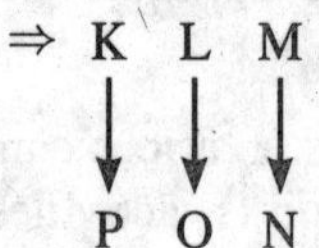

K + P = 27
L + O = 27
M + N = 27

∴ CDE : WVU : : KLM : PON

Here, ? = PON.

14. (B): ACEG : NPRT

⇒ A C E G
+13 +13 +13 +13
N P R T

∴ BDFH : ?

⇒ B D F H
+13 +13 +13 +13
O Q S U

∴ ACEG : NPRT : : BDFH : OQSU

Hence, ? = OQSU

15. (B): 31 37 41 43 47 53
+6 +4 +2 +4 +6

Here, the missing term = 43

16. (B): 17 26 35 44 53 62
+9 +9 +9 +9 +9

Here, ? = the missing term = 62.

17. (A):

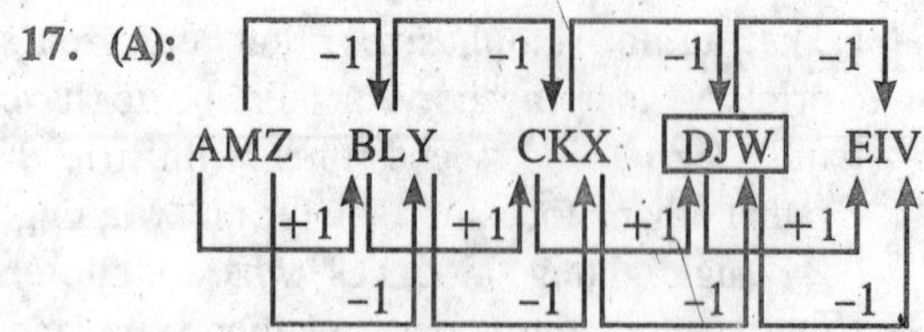

Here, ? = missing term = DJW.

18. (D):

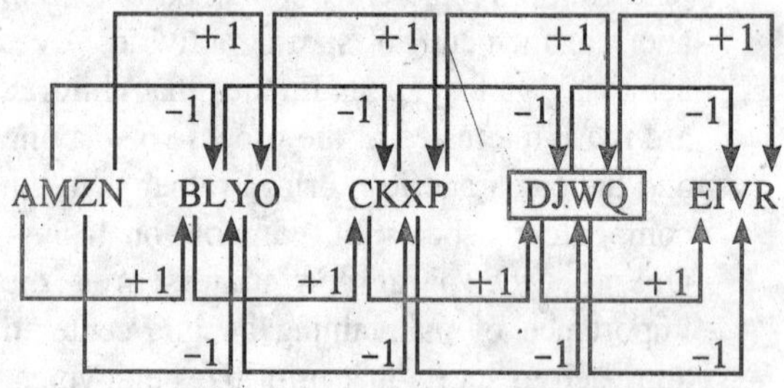

Here, ? = missing term = DJWQ.

19. (B): Given,

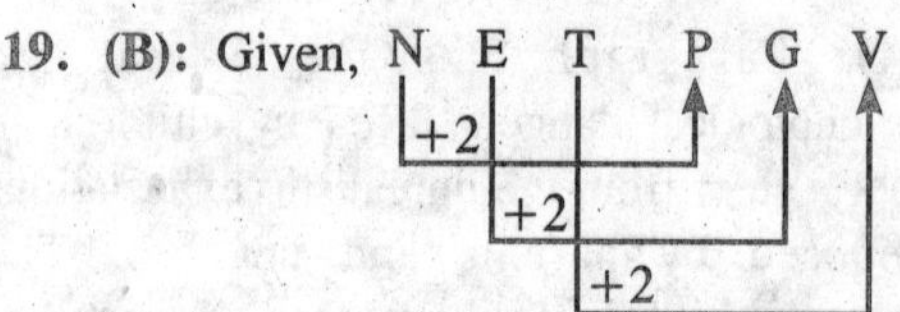

and

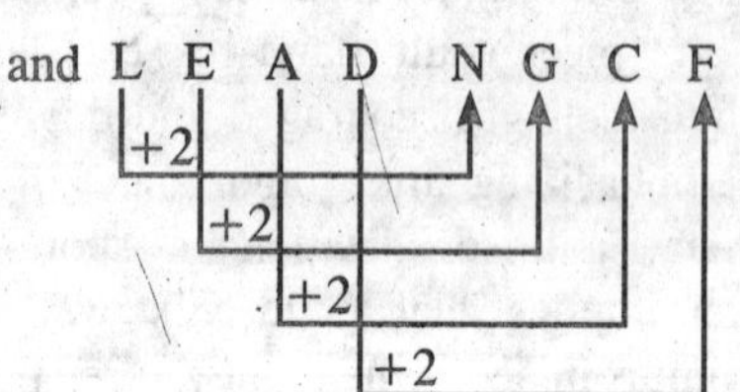

Similarly,

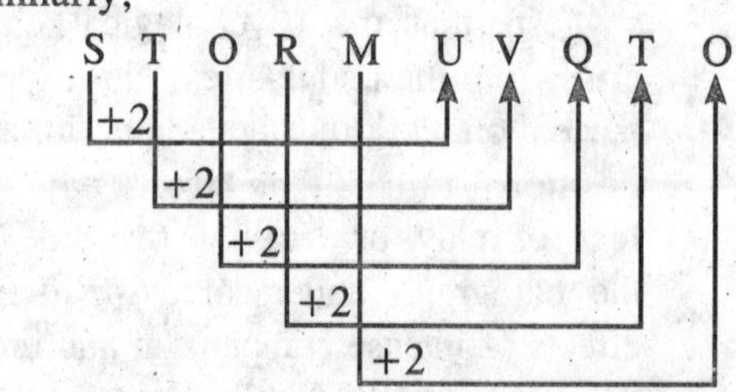

∴ STORM would be coded as UVQTO.

20. (D): Given, NO ⇒ ON

ARE ⇒ ERA (Letters in reverse order)

Similarly, RAMA ⇒ AMAR

∴ RAMA would be coded as AMAR.

21. (A): Given, 234 is coded as 345

$\Rightarrow \quad 345 - 234 = 111$

and 514 is coded as 625

$\Rightarrow \quad 625 - 514 = 111$

Similarly,

$4273 - 1111 = 3162$

$\Rightarrow \quad 4273 - 3162 = 1111$

$\therefore$ 4273 would be coded as 3162.

22. (D): Given, P E A K and P O R T

↓ ↓ ↓ ↓ ↓ ↓ ↓ ↓

5 2 3 6 5 1 4 7

$\Rightarrow$ P = 5, E = 2, A = 3, K = 6,

O = 1, R = 4, T = 7

Similarly, O R P A T

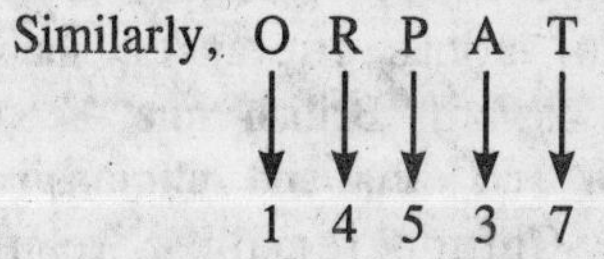

1 4 5 3 7

$\therefore$ ORPAT would be coded as 14537.

23. (D):

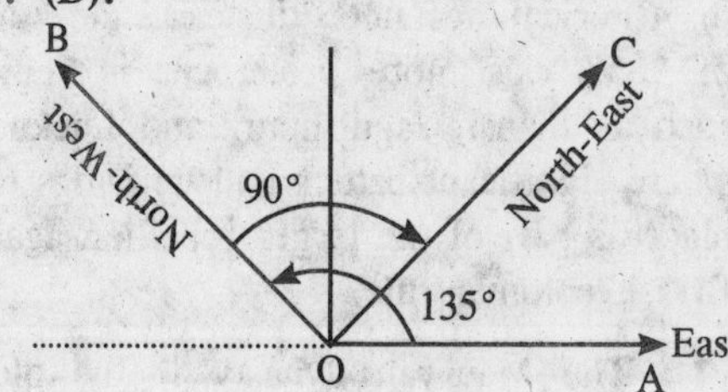

Here, He is now walking in North-East direction.

24. (B): Here, O = Boy's house = Starting Point

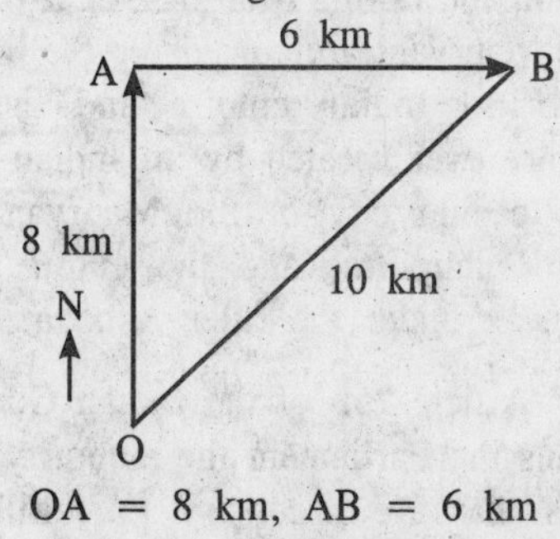

OA = 8 km, AB = 6 km

$\therefore \quad OB = \sqrt{OA^2 + AB^2}$

$= \sqrt{8^2 + 6^2}$

$= \sqrt{64 + 36} = \sqrt{100}$

$= 10$ km

Hence, He (B) is now 10 km far from his house (O).

25. (B): Given words: According to English dictionary,

PEAR → POOR → POUR → PURE

Here, option (B) is correct order.

26. (D): Triangles in the given figure:

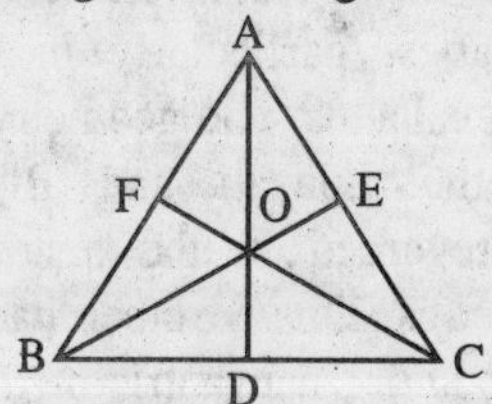

ΔAOF, ΔBOF, ΔBOD, ΔCOD, ΔCOE, ΔAOE, ΔAOB, ΔBOC, ΔAOC, ΔABD, ΔACD, ΔBAE, ΔBCE, ΔCAF, ΔCBF, ΔABC

Hence, total number of triangles in the given figure = 16.

27. (B): Total age of 5 boys

$= 5 \times 15 = 75$ years

and total age of 5 + 1 = 6 boys

$= 6 \times \left(15 + \frac{1}{2}\right)$ years

$= 6 \times \frac{31}{2} = 93$ years

$\therefore$ The age of the new boy

$= 93 - 75 = 18$ years.

28. (A): Given, 5 books are placed in such a way

C

D

A — Middle Book

B

E

Here, Book-A is in the middle.

30. (A):

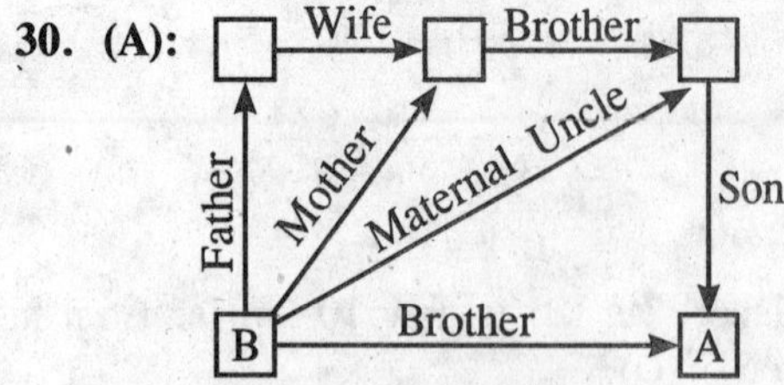

Here, A is the brother of B.

31. (D): Bhaskaracharya is not associated with medicine in ancient India. Bhaskaracharya was a renowned mathematician and astronomer who lived during the 12th century CE. He made significant contributions to mathematics, particularly in the fields of algebra, calculus, and geometry. His works, such as the "Lilavati" and "Bijaganita," are highly regarded in the history of Indian mathematics. On the other hand, Sushruta, Charak, and Dhanvantri are all prominent figures in ancient Indian medicine. Sushruta is considered the author of the "Sushruta Samhita," an ancient Sanskrit text on surgery and medicine, while Charak is known for his work in Ayurveda, particularly in the compilation of the "Charaka Samhita," a foundational text in traditional Indian medicine. Dhanvantri is revered as the god of Ayurveda and is believed to have discovered the science of Ayurveda. Therefore, Bhaskaracharya stands out as the individual not associated with medicine in ancient India.

32. (D): The main program of the Satya Shodhak Samaj was the upliftment of the backward classes. Founded by Jyotirao Phule in the 19th century in Maharashtra, India, the Satya Shodhak Samaj advocated for the rights and social upliftment of marginalized communities such as the lower castes, women, and peasants. Phule, a social reformer and activist, strongly advocated for social equality and the eradication of caste-based discrimination. The Satya Shodhak Samaj aimed to challenge the oppressive caste system prevalent in Indian society at the time by promoting education, encouraging social reform, and providing a platform for the oppressed classes to voice their grievances. Through its various initiatives and campaigns, the Samaj sought to empower the backward classes and create a more just and equitable society.

33. (C): Chittor was not significantly affected by the revolt of 1857. While the rebellion of 1857, also known as the Indian Mutiny or the First War of Independence, spread across various regions of India, Chittor, a historic city in present-day Rajasthan, did not witness major insurgent activities during this period. The revolt primarily erupted in response to various grievances, including resentment towards British rule, economic exploitation, and social and religious issues. However, Chittor remained relatively calm during the uprising, with no notable instances of rebellion or resistance recorded in historical accounts. Instead, the revolt of 1857 was more prominent in regions such as Jhansi, Jagdishpur, and Lucknow, where significant battles and uprisings took place as part of the larger rebellion against British colonial rule.

34. (A): The Mauryan dynasty is the oldest dynasty in India, founded by Chandragupta Maurya and existing from 325–185 BCE. The Mauryan Empire was the first pan-Indian empire, covering most of the Indian region and lasting from 321 BCE–185 BCE. The Mauryans are considered the first major historical Indian empire and the largest empire ever created by an Indian dynasty. The capital city of the Mauryan dynasty was Pataliputra, and the empire reached its peak under the ruler Ashoka.

35. (D): Article 253 of the Indian Constitution grants the Parliament the authority to enact laws that are necessary to fulfill India's obligations under international agreements or treaties. This article provides the legal basis for Parliament to legislate on matters that arise from international treaties or agreements, ensuring that India complies with its international commitments. Essentially, Article 253 enables the integration of international law into the domestic legal framework of India, allowing for the implementation of agreements made with other countries. Through this provision, Parliament has the power to pass laws that align with and enforce the terms of international treaties, thereby facilitating cooperation and adherence to international standards and obligations.

36. (B): The constitution of India drew inspiration for its federal structure from the constitution of Canada. This borrowing is evident in several aspects of India's federal system, including the distribution of powers between the central and state governments, the appointment of governors in the states, and the presence of a bicameral legislature at the national level. Like Canada, India adopted a federal structure that allocates specific powers to both the central government and the state governments while maintaining a degree of autonomy for each. Additionally, India's parliamentary system of government, with a President as the head of state and a Prime Minister as the head of government, reflects influences from the Canadian constitution. Overall, the Indian constitution's federal scheme, influenced by Canada, aims to balance the principles of federalism with the need for a strong central authority, ensuring unity while accommodating diversity within the nation.

37. (B): The Indian Constitution comprises 12 schedules, which provide additional details and information pertaining to various aspects of governance, administration, and other important matters. These schedules cover a wide range of subjects, including the allocation of seats in the Rajya Sabha (the Upper House of Parliament), the emoluments and allowances for various constitutional functionaries, the official languages recognized in different states and Union territories, and the forms of oaths and affirmations for public officeholders. Additionally, the schedules also address issues such as the administration and allocation of tribal areas, the recognition of scheduled castes and tribes, and the provisions for the allocation of seats in the legislative bodies of states and Union territories.

38. (D): The Sarkaria Commission was established to review and examine the relationship between the Centre (the Union Government) and the States (the state governments) in India. Formally known as the Commission on Centre-State Relations, it was constituted in 1983 by the Government of India under the chairmanship of Justice Rajinder Singh Sarkaria. The primary objective of the Sarkaria Commission was to analyze and evaluate the distribution of powers and responsibilities between the central and state governments, as outlined in the Indian Constitution. The commission extensively studied various aspects of Centre-State relations, including fiscal federalism, administrative cooperation, and the role of governors in states. Its recommendations aimed to enhance cooperation and collaboration between the Union and the states while maintaining the federal structure and integrity of the Indian polity.

39. (B): Directive Principles of State Policy (DPSP) are non-justiciable. This means that they cannot be enforced through a court of law. However, they are fundamental in the governance of the country and the state is required to apply them when making laws.

DPSP are ideals that the state should keep in mind when formulating policies and enacting laws. They are affirmative directions, while Fundamental Rights (FRs) are negative or prohibitive in nature. This means that FRs put limitations on the state, while DPSP are not subordinate to FRs. DPSP are not legally binding. This means that a person can appeal to the court of law if their FRs are violated, but people cannot appeal to the court if the government does not implement the DPSP.

40. (A): The National Knowledge Commission (NKC), chaired by Sam Pitroda from 2005 to 2009, was established by Prime Minister Dr. Manmohan Singh in June 2005. This high-level advisory body was tasked with providing policy recommendations aimed at reforming knowledge-related institutions and infrastructure in India. With a mandate to prepare a blueprint for these reforms, the NKC played a crucial role in identifying areas for improvement and proposing strategies to enhance India's knowledge ecosystem. Under Sam Pitroda's leadership, the commission focused on leveraging technology and innovation to drive socio-economic development and foster a culture of knowledge creation and dissemination. By advising the Prime Minister on matters related to education, research, innovation, and information technology, the NKC aimed to contribute to India's progress as a knowledge-driven economy and society.

41. (A): The Indian Independence League was established by Rasa Behari Bose, a revolutionary leader born in West Bengal, during his exile in Japan in 1942. Bose, driven by his fervent desire for Indian independence, founded the league with the aim of collaborating with the Axis powers, particularly Japan, to achieve freedom from British colonial rule. Despite its controversial nature, the league attracted support from some Indians residing in Southeast Asia who harbored disillusionment with British Raj. Bose's leadership of the league was characterized by his long-standing commitment to revolutionary activities, including his involvement in the Ghadar Party and subsequent escape from a death sentence in India. Although he eventually grew disenchanted with the motives of the Japanese, leading to his departure from the league in 1943, his efforts laid the groundwork for Subhash Chandra Bose to assume leadership and continue the league's mission towards Indian independence.

42. (A): Mahatma Gandhi drew inspiration for the civil disobedience movement from the writings of Henry David Thoreau, particularly his essay titled "Civil Disobedience". Thoreau's ideas, advocating for non-violent resistance against unjust laws and government actions, deeply resonated with Gandhi's philosophy of Satyagraha (truth-force) and Ahimsa (non-violence). In "Civil Disobedience," Thoreau argues that individuals have a moral obligation to resist laws that they believe to be unjust, even if it means facing the consequences of disobedience. Gandhi, greatly influenced by Thoreau's principles, adapted and applied them to the Indian independence movement, emphasizing the power of non-violent protest as a means of challenging oppressive colonial rule. Thus, Thoreau's writings played a significant role in shaping Gandhi's approach to civil disobedience and his quest for Indian self-rule.

43. (C): The Academic Bank of Credit (ABC) scheme was launched in July 2021. The scheme was proposed under the National Education Policy (NEP) 2020. The ABC scheme helps students study across higher educational institutions in India by providing them with a platform to access information about all their credits in one place. It also helps faculty manage and check the credits earned by students.

44. (C): Arabica beans are predominant in India's coffee cultivation landscape, constituting over 60% of the country's coffee production. Particularly flourishing in the southern states of Karnataka, Kerala, and Tamil Nadu, Arabica coffee is esteemed for its mild flavor profile and delicate aroma. This variety thrives in the cool, mountainous regions of these states, where conditions are conducive to its cultivation. Arabica coffees delicate nature necessitates meticulous cultivation practices and shade from taller trees to protect it from excessive sun exposure. The cultivation of Arabica beans in India reflects a careful balance of environmental factors and agricultural practices aimed at producing high-quality coffee renowned for its distinctive taste and aroma.

45. (B): The Aravalli Range, stretching across the northwestern part of India, is home to the oldest rocks in the country. These ancient rocks, dating back to over two billion years, form the foundation of the Aravalli Mountains. Comprising mainly of igneous and metamorphic rocks, the Aravallis hold significant geological importance, providing insights into the early history and formation of the Indian subcontinent. Over millions of years, these rocks have undergone various geological processes, including upliftment, erosion, and tectonic activity, shaping the landscape of the region. Despite their age, the Aravalli Range continues to influence the geography, ecology, and socio-economic aspects of the areas they traverse, serving as a natural barrier and a vital watershed for the surrounding regions.

46. (A): The Himalayan mountain system is a type of fold mountain. Fold mountains are the most common type of mountain in the world. They are formed at convergent boundaries due to the collision of two tectonic plates. The Himalayas are considered to be young fold mountains because they have been formed only a few million years ago. The Himalayan mountain range formed as a result of the collision between the Indian Plate and Eurasian Plate, which began 50 million years ago and continues today. The Himalayas stretch through the borders of China, Bhutan, Nepal, India, and Pakistan. They represent the loftiest and one of the most rugged mountain barriers of the world.

47. (B): The Hirakud Dam is the longest dam in India, with a length of 25.79 kilometers. It is also one of the longest dams in the world. The Hirakud Dam is located on the Mahanadi River in the Indian state of Odisha. It is a hydroelectric power plant and historical landmark that helps control floods in the Mahanadi delta.

48. (B): MOOCs stands for Massive Open Online Courses. These are online courses aimed at unlimited participation and open access via the internet. MOOCs typically provide course materials such as lectures, readings, and assignments to a large number of learners, often free of charge. They offer a flexible learning environment where participants can engage with course content at their own pace and from anywhere with an internet connection. MOOCs have gained popularity for their ability to democratize education by providing access to high-quality learning resources to individuals around the world, regardless of geographical location or financial constraints. They are offered by universities, colleges, and online learning platforms, covering a wide range of subjects and disciplines.

49. (B): The National Education Policy (NEP) 2020 proposes that learning should be experiential. This approach emphasizes hands-on, interactive learning experiences that engage students directly in the learning process. Instead of focusing solely on rote memorization or recall-based assessments, experiential learning encourages students to actively participate in activities, experiments, and real-world projects. By engaging with the material in a practical and immersive manner, students can develop a deeper understanding of concepts and enhance critical thinking, problem-solving, and communication skills. The NEP 2020 advocates for integrating experiential learning across all levels of education to foster holistic development and prepare students for the challenges of the 21st century.

50. (B): Common salt is obtained from seawater through the process of evaporation. This process involves allowing seawater to evaporate under controlled conditions, typically in large shallow ponds called salt pans or salt flats. As the seawater evaporates, the water content decreases, leaving behind concentrated brine containing dissolved salts. Over time, as evaporation continues, the concentration of salts increases until the point of saturation is reached, causing salt crystals to form. These salt crystals are then harvested through mechanical means and further processed to obtain refined common salt, also known as table salt. Evaporation is a cost-effective and widely used method for salt production, particularly in regions with access to abundant seawater resources.

51. (C): The Pacific Ocean is the largest and deepest ocean on Earth, covering about one-third of the planet's surface. It contains more than half of the world's free water and is home to more marine species than any other ocean. The Pacific Ocean also provides 70% of the world's fish catch. The Pacific Ocean extends from the Arctic Ocean in the north to the Southern Ocean in the south. It's bordered by Asia and Oceania to the west and the Americas to the east. The Pacific Ocean averages a depth of 4,000 meters (13,000 feet). The Pacific Ocean is important for climate and food security. It's also home to many islands, including American Samoa, Australia, Canada, Chile, China, Colombia, the Cook Islands, and Costa Rica.

52. (A): The National Education Policy (NEP) 2020 aims to significantly increase the Gross Enrollment Ratio (GER) in Higher Education to 50% by 2035. This ambitious goal reflects the policy's emphasis on expanding access to higher education and ensuring that a larger proportion of India's population has the opportunity to pursue advanced studies. By increasing GER to 50%, the NEP 2020 seeks to promote inclusivity and equity in higher education, enabling more individuals, including those from marginalized and underprivileged backgrounds, to access quality higher education institutions. Achieving this target entails implementing a range of strategies, including the establishment of new universities and colleges, the expansion of existing institutions, the adoption of flexible learning pathways, and the promotion of digital technologies to enhance access and affordability.

53. (B): India's coinage became decimal on April 1, 1957, ten years after gaining independence from the British. In the decimal currency system, each unit of currency can be divided into 100 sub-units. India's rupee remained unchanged in value and nomenclature, but was now divided into 100 "Paisa" instead of 16 Annas or 64 Pice. For a short period of time, both decimal and non-decimal coins were in circulation. To distinguish between the two pice coins in circulation, the coins minted between 1957 and 1964 were printed with the legend "Naya Paisa" ("New Paisa"). On June 1, 1964, the term "Naya" was dropped and the denomination was simply called "One paisa".

54. (B): 24.62% of India's geographical area is covered by forests and trees, this would be roughly equivalent to approximately one-fourth of India's land area. This significant portion of land dedicated to forests underscores the crucial role that forests play in India's ecosystem and environment. Forests provide numerous ecological benefits, including biodiversity conservation, carbon sequestration, soil conservation, and water regulation. Additionally, forests support the livelihoods of millions of people, including indigenous communities, by providing essential resources and ecosystem services. Therefore, recognizing the importance of this extensive forest cover, it is imperative to implement robust conservation measures and sustainable forest management practices to safeguard India's forests for current and future generations.

55. (C): MOOCs (Massive Open Online Courses) are built on the idea of web-based learning. These courses leverage internet-based technologies to deliver educational content to a large number of participants simultaneously. Through MOOC platforms, learners can access a wide range of courses covering diverse subjects and disciplines from anywhere with an internet connection. MOOCs typically utilize multimedia elements such as video lectures, interactive quizzes, discussion forums, and downloadable resources to engage learners in the learning process. The web-based nature of MOOCs enables flexibility in terms of access and scheduling, allowing learners to progress through course materials at their own pace and according to their individual preferences.

56. (C): Teachers should strive to design the curriculum in a way that accommodates the diverse interests, abilities, and needs of different students. This approach, known as differentiated instruction, involves tailoring teaching strategies, content, and activities to match the individual learning styles, preferences, and readiness levels of students. By incorporating various instructional methods, providing multiple avenues for learning, and offering opportunities for student choice and autonomy, teachers can effectively address the individual differences present in the classroom. This ensures that all students have the opportunity to engage with the curriculum in meaningful ways and achieve academic success.

57. (B): According to the National Education Policy (NEP) 2020, the secondary stage covers classes 9–12. The secondary stage is divided into two phases, with classes 9–10 in the first phase and classes 11–12 in the second. The secondary stage covers children aged 14–18. The curriculum at the secondary stage is designed to provide students with a comprehensive education that prepares them for higher education, vocational training, or entry into the workforce. It aims to foster critical thinking, problem-solving skills, and subject-specific competencies essential for academic and professional success. Additionally, the secondary stage offers opportunities for students to explore diverse subjects and pursue areas of interest through elective courses or specialized streams, enabling them to develop their talents and aspirations further.

58. (D): The principle of variety in timetable construction aims to prevent monotony and fatigue among students by ensuring diversity in the subjects taught consecutively. This principle recognizes that prolonged focus on a single subject or topic can lead to decreased attention and engagement among students. By alternating subjects and activities, educators can help maintain students' interest and motivation throughout the school day. For example, scheduling different subjects or types of activities in consecutive periods allows students to shift their focus and utilize different cognitive skills, preventing mental fatigue and enhancing overall learning experiences.

59. (D): Social recognition primarily operates as extrinsic motivation, meaning it stems from external sources rather than internal desires. While it can encourage participation and effort in some cases, it doesn't directly influence the cognitive processes involved in learning itself. Learners motivated solely by social recognition may prioritize external validation over genuine interest in the subject matter, potentially hindering their ability to develop a true love of learning or internalize the knowledge they acquire. Additionally, relying solely on external rewards like social recognition may lead to shallow understanding or superficial engagement with the material, as learners may be more focused on meeting others' expectations rather than deepening their own understanding.

60. (C): Group dynamics, the interactions and relationships between members of a group, can best be understood through collaborative work. Engaging in collaborative activities allows individuals to directly experience and observe group dynamics in action. Through participation in group projects, discussions, and problem-solving tasks, individuals can witness how different personalities, communication styles, and leadership approaches influence group functioning and outcomes. Additionally, collaborative work provides opportunities for individuals to actively contribute to and shape group dynamics, fostering a deeper understanding of the factors that drive group behavior. By engaging in collaborative activities, individuals not only gain insight into group dynamics but also develop essential teamwork and interpersonal skills necessary for effective collaboration in various personal, academic, and professional settings.

61. (B): A field visit is an example of a concrete experience, which involves direct, firsthand encounters with real-life situations or phenomena. During a field visit, individuals have the opportunity to engage with the physical environment, observe natural or human-made structures, interact with people, and collect data or information through direct observation. This hands-on approach allows individuals to explore concepts or topics in a tangible and experiential manner, deepening their understanding and facilitating the application of theoretical knowledge to real-world contexts. Field visits provide learners with opportunities to connect theoretical concepts with practical experiences, enhancing their learning outcomes and fostering a deeper appreciation for the subject matter.

62. (A): To enhance the ability to observe in children, sharpening the senses is recommended. This involves stimulating and refining the sensory faculties, including sight, hearing, touch, taste, and smell. By providing opportunities for children to engage in sensory-rich experiences, such as exploring nature, conducting experiments, or participating in hands-on activities, their observational skills can be developed and heightened. Encouraging children to actively use their senses to perceive and interpret the world around them not only enhances their observational abilities but also fosters curiosity, critical thinking, and scientific inquiry. Additionally, exposing children to diverse stimuli and sensory inputs helps expand their perceptual horizons, enabling them to notice details, patterns, and nuances that might otherwise go unnoticed.

Therefore, sharpening the senses serves as a foundational step in nurturing keen observation skills and promoting overall cognitive development in children.

63. (B): The National Council for Teacher Education (NCTE) serves as the apex body responsible for the planning, coordination, and regulation of teacher education programs across India. Established by the Government of India in 1995, the NCTE operates under the National Council for Teacher Education Act, 1993. Its primary objectives include setting and maintaining standards for teacher education, approving teacher education institutions (TEIs) and their programs, promoting research and innovations in teacher education, and ensuring the overall quality and effectiveness of teacher preparation. The NCTE plays a crucial role in shaping the policies and practices related to teacher education, with a focus on enhancing the professional competencies of teachers to meet the evolving needs of the education sector.

64. (C): The play-way method is a learner-friendly method that can help children develop cognitive, emotional, and physical skills. The play-way method is based on psychological principles of development and is considered a suitable method for teaching primary school children. To help children develop emotionally through play, caregivers can provide puzzles, games, and arts and crafts supplies. Creative craft kits can help children express their emotions creatively while also building motor skills. By incorporating games, puzzles, role-playing, storytelling, and other interactive activities into the learning process, the play-way method engages students in hands-on experiences that stimulate their cognitive faculties, encourage creativity, and promote problem-solving skills.

65. (B): Flexibility refers to the ability of an individual to use different approaches in responding to a stimulus. It encompasses adaptability, open-mindedness, and the willingness to consider alternative perspectives or strategies. In cognitive terms, flexibility enables individuals to shift their thinking, problem-solving methods, or behavioral responses depending on the context or demands of a situation. This skill is crucial in various domains, including problem-solving, creativity, decision-making, and interpersonal interactions. Flexibility allows individuals to navigate complexities, overcome obstacles, and effectively adjust their actions or perspectives when faced with new challenges or changing circumstances.

66. (C): PARAKH stands for Performance Assessment, Review, and Analysis of Knowledge for Holistic Development. It was established as a National Assessment Centre in the National Education Policy (NEP) 2020. PARAKH is a body that sets standards, guidelines, and norms for student evaluation and assessment for all recognized school boards in India. The framework emphasizes the importance of a balanced assessment approach that considers both academic achievements and non-academic factors crucial for overall development. Through PARAKH, educators can gain valuable insights into students' strengths, areas for improvement, and individual learning needs, enabling them to tailor instruction and support to promote holistic development effectively.

67. (B): Engaging learners in brainstorming before commencing a new lesson serves the purpose of assessing their previous knowledge. By encouraging students to share their ideas, thoughts, and prior experiences related to the topic at hand, teachers gain valuable insights into the students' existing understanding and misconceptions.

This active participation allows educators to gauge the diversity of knowledge among learners and tailor the upcoming lesson accordingly. Additionally, brainstorming fosters a sense of ownership and engagement among students, as they feel valued for their contributions to the learning process. Moreover, it sets a collaborative tone for the lesson, promoting interaction and peer learning opportunities.

68. (A): The teacher's approach of asking learners to generate ideas quickly about the topic of "Waste Management" and noting down their thoughts in a notebook aligns with the concept of brainstorming. Brainstorming is a creative technique aimed at generating a large number of ideas or solutions to a problem within a short period. By encouraging students to brainstorm, the teacher fosters a collaborative and open environment where learners can freely express their thoughts and ideas without fear of judgment. Additionally, noting down ideas in a notebook helps students organize their thoughts, retain important information, and refer back to their contributions later. This active engagement in brainstorming and note-taking enhances critical thinking, creativity, and problem-solving skills among learners while promoting a deeper understanding of the topic.

69. (D): The activity of analyzing the written performance of students and realizing that 80% have not mastered single-digit multiplication correctly would typically occur during the post-teaching phase. In this phase, the teacher assesses the students' performance after instruction has been delivered. Based on the assessment results, the teacher identifies areas of weakness or misunderstanding and then adjusts their teaching strategies accordingly. In this case, the teacher's analysis of the students' written performance highlights the need for remediation or additional instruction in single-digit multiplication, indicating that this assessment occurred after the teaching phase.

70. (C): Academic Bank of Credit- A bank for academic purposes that offers services such as credit verification, credit accumulation, credit transfer, and authentication of academic awards. Credits earned by students are valid for seven years and can be redeemed at any time.

71. (A): DIKSHA is a portal that serves as a national digital infrastructure for teachers, offering a wide range of educational resources and tools to support teaching and learning. Through DIKSHA, teachers gain access to a vast repository of digital content, including lesson plans, worksheets, interactive simulations, and multimedia resources across various subjects and grade levels. Additionally, the platform provides professional development courses, training modules, and workshops to enhance teachers' pedagogical skills and subject knowledge. DIKSHA also facilitates collaboration and knowledge sharing among educators through discussion forums, communities of practice, and peer-to-peer learning networks.

72. (C): The goal of teaching extends beyond simply imparting knowledge or providing information; it encompasses the broader objective of bringing about desirable changes in behavior among students. While imparting knowledge is an essential aspect of teaching, the ultimate aim is to inspire, motivate, and guide students towards positive behavioral outcomes. Effective teaching involves fostering critical thinking skills, promoting creativity, nurturing social and emotional development, and instilling values such as empathy, integrity, and resilience. By creating engaging learning experiences, fostering a supportive classroom environment, and employing various instructional strategies, teachers strive to empower students to apply their knowledge, skills, and understanding to real-world situations and challenges. Ultimately, the goal of teaching is to equip students with the competencies, attitudes, and values necessary for personal growth, success in academics and beyond, and active participation in society.

73. (A): The skill of introduction is vital for initiating effective learning experiences. It involves capturing learners' attention, establishing relevance, and providing context for the topic being taught. Through a well-crafted introduction, educators can create a positive learning environment and stimulate students' interest and curiosity. Additionally, this skill enables teachers to assess students' prior knowledge and understanding, which informs instructional decisions and helps tailor the lesson to meet learners' needs effectively. A successful introduction sets the stage for meaningful engagement and lays the groundwork for deeper learning throughout the lesson. Therefore, mastering the skill of introduction is essential for facilitating engaging and impactful teaching experiences.

74. (D): Micro-teaching is a pedagogical technique where teaching is conducted on a smaller scale, typically in a controlled environment such as a teacher training institute or workshop. It involves breaking down the teaching process into manageable components and focusing on specific teaching skills or strategies. During micro-teaching sessions, educators deliver short lessons to a small group of peers or students, allowing for focused observation, feedback, and reflection. This approach provides teachers with opportunities to practice and refine their teaching techniques, experiment with different instructional methods, and receive constructive criticism from peers and mentors.

75. (B): Social learning theory focuses on how people learn new behaviors by observing and imitating others. It also considers how people learn from observing rewards and punishments, a process called vicarious reinforcement. Social learning theory goes beyond the idea that learning is the result of direct experience with the environment. It suggests that observation and modeling play a primary role in how and why people learn. Social learning theory expands on traditional behavioral theories, which consider behavior to be governed solely by reinforcements. It places emphasis on the important roles of various internal processes in the learning individual.

76. (D): One tough issue related to school effectiveness revolves around policies. Policies encompass a wide range of regulations, guidelines, and directives that govern various aspects of school operations, curriculum development, resource allocation, and student outcomes. Crafting and implementing effective policies requires careful consideration of diverse stakeholder perspectives, educational research, legal frameworks, and societal needs. Challenges arise in formulating policies that address complex issues such as equity, inclusivity, accountability, and educational quality while navigating political, economic, and social dynamics.

77. (C): Organizing cultural activities in schools serves the objective of promoting national integration. These activities provide a platform for students from diverse cultural backgrounds to come together, celebrate their shared heritage, and appreciate the rich tapestry of cultures that make up the nation. Through participation in cultural events such as festivals, performances, and exhibitions, students develop a sense of unity, respect, and understanding for different cultures, languages, and traditions. These experiences foster a spirit of inclusivity, tolerance, and harmony, contributing to the cultivation of a strong sense of national identity and belonging among students. By celebrating cultural diversity within the school community, cultural activities serve as a catalyst for fostering mutual respect, cooperation, and solidarity, thereby promoting national integration and social cohesion.

78. (A): Cumulative record card is an example of a record of learners. It's a permanent record of a student that includes their educational history, school achievements, attendance, health, test scores, and other related data. Teachers maintain cumulative record cards up to date by entering new information about a student. The card provides a complete picture of a student's educational progress, past achievements, and current standing. Teachers can use cumulative record cards to provide information to parents and teachers. Cumulative record cards can also be called personal data cards or permanent data cards.

79. (C): Professional development of teachers primarily focuses on enhancing their instructional skills, pedagogical knowledge, and overall effectiveness in the classroom. It entails activities such as workshops, seminars, coursework, and collaborative learning experiences aimed at improving teaching practices and student outcomes. While salary may be a motivating factor for some teachers, it is not directly related to professional development in the same way as mastering content knowledge, understanding pedagogy, or staying updated on educational trends. While adequate compensation is essential for attracting and retaining qualified educators, it is not the primary objective of professional development initiatives, which are more focused on enhancing teaching effectiveness and student learning. Therefore, while salary considerations are important for teachers' overall well-being, they are not typically included within the scope of professional development activities.

80. (B): The quality of educators who train teachers is closely linked to the process factor in the teaching profession. This factor encompasses the methods, approaches, and strategies employed by educators to facilitate learning and professional growth among teachers. Educators who train teachers play a pivotal role in shaping teaching practices, pedagogical knowledge, and instructional effectiveness. Their expertise, pedagogical skills, and ability to model effective teaching strategies directly influence the quality of teacher training programs and the subsequent impact on student learning outcomes. By providing mentorship, guidance, and feedback, these educators contribute to the continuous improvement and professional development of teachers, ultimately enhancing the overall quality of education delivery. Thus, the process factor underscores the importance of effective teaching methodologies and instructional practices in teacher training contexts.

81. (D): All of the options listed—change in state, change in color, and evolution of a gas—can indicate that a chemical reaction has occurred. When a chemical reaction takes place, substances may undergo a change in their physical state, such as from solid to liquid, liquid to gas, or vice versa. Additionally, a change in color can suggest the formation of new substances with different chemical properties. Furthermore, the release or absorption of gas during a reaction, known as evolution or production of gas, is a common indicator of chemical change. Therefore, observing any of these changes can provide evidence that a chemical reaction has occurred, helping to determine the occurrence of a chemical transformation.

82. **(A):** Gold is renowned for its exceptional ductility, making it the most ductile metal among the options provided. Ductility refers to a material's ability to deform under tensile stress, such as stretching or being drawn into thin wires, without fracturing. Gold exhibits remarkable ductility, allowing it to be easily drawn into long, thin wires without breaking. This property is highly valued in various industries, including electronics, jewelry making, and dentistry, where gold's malleability and ductility enable intricate designs and precise applications. Its superior ductility, along with other desirable properties like corrosion resistance and conductivity, contributes to gold's widespread use and enduring appeal across diverse fields.

83. **(B):** Galvanization is a process used to protect steel and iron from rusting by applying a thin layer of zinc to their surfaces. This protective coating of zinc acts as a barrier between the metal substrate and the surrounding environment, preventing corrosion by forming a physical barrier and sacrificing itself to protect the underlying metal through a process known as sacrificial protection. Zinc is chosen for galvanization due to its excellent corrosion resistance properties, even in harsh environments. The zinc coating can be applied through various methods such as hot-dip galvanizing, electroplating, or spraying, providing durable protection against rust and extending the lifespan of steel and iron structures, equipment, and components used in various industries.

84. **(A):** The pH value of an acidic solution is less than 7. pH is a measure of the acidity or alkalinity of a solution, ranging from 0 to 14 on the pH scale. A pH value below 7 indicates acidity, with lower pH values indicating stronger acidity. In acidic solutions, there is an abundance of hydrogen ions (H^+), which contribute to the sour taste and corrosive properties commonly associated with acids. These solutions can react with metals, neutralize bases, and turn litmus paper red. Examples of acidic solutions include lemon juice, vinegar, and gastric acid in the stomach. Understanding the pH of a solution is crucial in various fields such as chemistry, biology, and environmental science, as it influences chemical reactions, biological processes, and environmental quality.

85. **(C):** Most carbon compounds are poor conductors of electricity. This is because carbon compounds, such as organic molecules, typically consist of covalent bonds formed by sharing electrons between atoms. In these compounds, electrons are tightly bound within the covalent bonds and do not move freely. As a result, carbon compounds lack the free-moving charged particles (ions or electrons) necessary to conduct electricity. However, there are exceptions to this generalization. For example, certain carbon compounds, such as graphite, can conduct electricity due to the presence of delocalized electrons within their structure. Nonetheless, compared to metallic or ionic compounds, carbon compounds generally exhibit poor electrical conductivity.

87. **(B):** The small intestine is the longest part of the human alimentary canal. It's about 22 feet long, or three and a half times the length of the human body. The small intestine is narrower than the large intestine, but it's the longest section of the digestive tube. The small intestine is the primary digestive organ in the body. It's where most digestion and absorption occurs. The small intestine is divided into three parts: the duodenum, jejunum, and ileum. The ileum absorbs any remaining nutrients that weren't absorbed in the jejunum.

88. (A): Transpiration is the process of water moving through a plant and evaporating from its aerial parts, such as leaves, flowers, and stems. It's a passive process that doesn't require the plant to expend any energy. Transpiration occurs when plants absorb liquid water from the soil and release water vapour into the air from their leaves. The water is warmed by the sun and turns into vapour, passing out through the aerial parts, mostly on the underside of the leaf surface.

89. (C): The hormone that regulates blood sugar levels is insulin. Produced by the pancreas, insulin plays a crucial role in maintaining glucose homeostasis in the body. When blood sugar levels rise after a meal, insulin is released into the bloodstream, prompting cells in the liver, muscle, and fat tissues to absorb glucose for energy or storage. This process helps to lower blood sugar levels, preventing hyperglycemia. Conversely, when blood sugar levels drop, insulin secretion decreases, allowing the release of stored glucose into the bloodstream to maintain optimal levels.

90. (D): The plant hormone among the options provided is Cytokinin. Unlike insulin, thyroxin, and estrogen, which are hormones, found in animals, cytokinins are a class of plant hormones involved in various physiological processes in plants, including cell division, shoot and root growth, and responses to environmental stimuli. These hormones play a crucial role in regulating plant growth, development, and adaptation to changing conditions.

91. (C): The reproductive parts of a flower are Stamen and Pistil. Petals and sepals are considered the non-reproductive parts of a flower, while stamens and pistils are directly involved in the reproductive process. Stamens are the male reproductive organs, consisting of the filament and anther, where pollen is produced. The pistil, also known as the carpel, is the female reproductive organ, consisting of the stigma, style, and ovary, where ovules are produced.

92. (B): The number of pairs of chromosomes in a human body cell is 23. This includes 22 pairs of autosomes (non-sex chromosomes) and one pair of sex chromosomes, totaling 46 chromosomes in all. Each parent contributes one chromosome to each pair, resulting in 23 chromosomes from each parent, hence making a total of 46 chromosomes.

93. (A): The relationship between the radius of curvature (R) and the focal length (F) of a spherical mirror is R=2F. This relationship holds true for both concave and convex spherical mirrors, where the radius of curvature is twice the focal length. In other words, the distance from the center of curvature to the mirror's surface is twice the distance from the focal point to the mirror's surface.

94. (C): When an object is positioned between the center of curvature (C) and the focal point (F) of a concave mirror, a virtual and erect image is produced. This occurs because the light rays diverging from the object are reflected by the mirror and appear to converge behind it, creating an image that cannot be projected onto a screen. Instead, the observer perceives the image as if it were located behind the mirror, hence virtual. Additionally, the image is upright, or erect, relative to the object's orientation, further emphasizing its virtual nature.

95. (A): Myopia, also known as nearsightedness, is a refractive error of the eye where distant objects appear blurred while close objects can be seen clearly. This condition occurs when the eyeball is too long or the cornea is too curved, causing light rays to focus in front of the retina instead of directly on it. As a result, distant objects are not properly focused on the retina, leading to blurred vision. However, nearby objects can still be seen clearly because the focal point falls in front of the retina, allowing for sharp focus.

96. (B): The twinkling of a star occurs due to the refraction of starlight as it passes through the Earth's atmosphere. When starlight enters the Earth's atmosphere, it encounters different layers of air with varying densities and temperatures. These variations cause the light to bend or refract continuously as it travels towards the observer on the ground. As a result, the apparent position of the star appears to fluctuate slightly, causing it to appear as if it is twinkling. This phenomenon is similar to the way a straw appears to bend when partially submerged in water due to the change in the speed of light as it moves from one medium (air) to another (water).

97. (C): The instrument used to measure electric current in a circuit is an ammeter. An ammeter is connected in series with the circuit to measure the current. It's usually low resistance so it doesn't cause a significant voltage drop in the circuit. The SI unit for measuring electric current is the ampere (A), which is equal to a flow of one coulomb of charge per second. An ammeter consists of two small pieces of soft iron. One is attached to the coil and the other is attached to the pointer. When the soft iron attached to the coil becomes magnetized, it causes either attraction or repulsion of the other piece of soft iron which then rotates proportionally.

98. (A): The electric power (P) in a circuit can be calculated using the formula: P=VI where V represents the voltage (in volts) and I represents the current (in amperes). This formula indicates that power is the product of voltage and current.

99. (D): Hans Christian Oersted (1777-1851) was the first to suggest a connection between electricity and magnetism. In 1820, the Danish physicist and chemist discovered that a compass needle deflects when placed near a wire carrying an electric current. This provided the first empirical evidence of a connection between electric and magnetic phenomena. At the time, most scientists believed electricity and magnetism were not related. However, there were some reasons to think there might be a connection. For example, it had long been known that a compass could reverse polarity when struck by lightning. Oersted's discovery led to the discovery that electric currents create magnetic fields.

100. (C): When an electric current passes through a solenoid, it creates a magnetic field inside the solenoid. This magnetic field is characterized by its uniformity, meaning that the magnetic field strength is consistent at all points within the solenoid. This uniformity arises from the arrangement of the wire coils in the solenoid, which ensures that the magnetic field lines are parallel and evenly distributed throughout the interior space. As a result, the magnetic field inside the solenoid remains constant regardless of the position of the observation point, providing a stable and predictable magnetic environment for various applications such as electromagnets and magnetic sensors.

101. (C): Let S_{40} = The sum of first 40 positive integer divisible by 6

$\therefore a = 6, d = 6, n = 40$

$$\because \quad S_n = \frac{n}{2}[2a + (n-1)d]$$

$$S_{40} = \frac{40}{2}[2 \times 6 + (40-1) \times 6]$$

$$= \frac{40}{2} \times 6\,[2 + 39]$$

$$= 20 \times 6\ [41]$$

$$\Rightarrow \quad S_{40} = 120 \times 41 = 4920.$$

102. (C): Arranging 12 observation in ascending order: 10, 12, 13, 18, 22, 22, 24, 27, 28, 30, 34, 36

$$n = 12 \text{ (even)}$$

$$\therefore \text{ Median} = \frac{1}{2}\left[\frac{n}{2}\text{th term} + \left(\frac{n}{2}+1\right)\text{th term}\right]$$

$$= \frac{1}{2}[\text{6th term} + \text{7th term}]$$

$$= \frac{1}{2}[22+24] = \frac{46}{2} = 23$$

Hence, required Median = 23.

105. (D): $(1+\tan\theta+\sec\theta)(1+\cot\theta-\operatorname{cosec}\theta)$

$$= \left(1+\frac{\sin\theta}{\cos\theta}+\frac{1}{\cos\theta}\right)\left(1+\frac{\cos\theta}{\sin\theta}-\frac{1}{\sin\theta}\right)$$

$$= \left(\frac{\cos\theta+\sin\theta+1}{\cos\theta}\right)\left(\frac{\sin\theta+\cos\theta-1}{\sin\theta}\right)$$

$$= \frac{(\sin\theta+\cos\theta+1)(\sin\theta+\cos\theta-1)}{\sin\theta\cos\theta}$$

$$= \frac{(\sin\theta+\cos\theta)^2-1^2}{\sin\theta\cos\theta}$$

$$= \frac{\sin^2\theta+\cos^2\theta+2\sin\theta\cos\theta-1}{\sin\theta\cos\theta}$$

$$= \frac{1+2\sin\theta\cos\theta-1}{\sin\theta\cos\theta} = \frac{2\sin\theta\cos\theta}{\sin\theta\cos\theta} = 2.$$

106. (A): Let AB be a tower

and BC = 30 m

$\angle ACB = 30°$

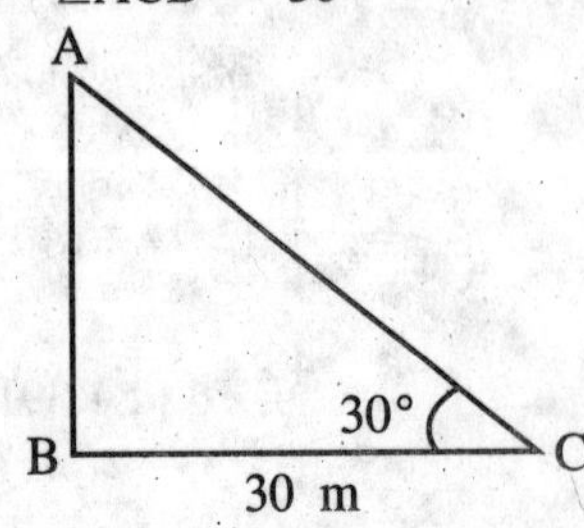

In Δ ABC,

$$\tan 30° = \frac{AB}{BC}$$

$$\Rightarrow \quad \frac{1}{\sqrt{3}} = \frac{AB}{30}$$

$$\Rightarrow \quad AB = \frac{30}{\sqrt{3}} = 10\sqrt{3}$$

Hence, the height of the tower = $10\sqrt{3}$ m.

107. (B): $\because$ The ratio of the area of two similar triangle is equal to the ratio of square of its corresponding sides.

$\therefore$ The areas of these triangles are in the ratio $\Rightarrow 4^2 : 9^2 = 16 : 81$.

108. (A): Ram's 1 day's work = $\frac{1}{9}$

and Shyam's 1 day's work = $\frac{1}{12}$

$\therefore$ (Ram + Shyam)'s 1 day's work

$$= \frac{1}{9}+\frac{1}{12} = \frac{4+3}{36} = \frac{7}{36}$$

Hence, working together they will complete the work in

$$\frac{36}{7} = 5\frac{1}{7} \text{ days.}$$

109. (D): Let the second discount was x%

Then, $720 \times \frac{100-10}{100} \times \frac{100-x}{100} = 550.80$

$$\Rightarrow \quad 720 \times \frac{90}{100} \times \frac{100-x}{100} = 550.80$$

$$\Rightarrow \quad 72 \times 9 \times (100-x) = 55080$$

$$\Rightarrow \quad 100 - x = \frac{55080}{72 \times 9}$$

$$\Rightarrow \quad 100 - x = 85$$

$$\Rightarrow \quad x = 100 - 85 = 15\%$$

$$\Rightarrow \quad x = 15\%.$$

110. (A): Here, $r = \frac{14}{2} = 7$ m

$h = 4.5$ m,

$l = 6$ m

$\therefore$ Lateral surface area of a conical tent

$= \pi rl$

$= \frac{22}{7} \times 7 \times 6$

$= 132$ sq. m.

Hence, required cloth = 132 sq. metre.

111. (A): $\frac{0.0343 \times 2.92 \times 49}{146 \times 0.07 \times 4.9}$

$= \frac{0.0343 \times 292 \times 10}{146 \times 7 \times 1}$

$= \frac{0.343 \times 2}{7} = \frac{0.7 \times 0.7 \times 0.7 \times 2}{7}$

$= 0.49 \times 0.2 = .098 = 0.09.$

112. (D): Let the speed of second train is x km/h

Then, relative speed of trains

$= (50 + x)$ km/h

$\therefore \quad \frac{108 + 112}{(50 + x) \times \frac{5}{18}} = 6$

$\Rightarrow \quad 220 = (50 + x) \times \frac{5}{3}$

$\Rightarrow \quad 660 = 250 + 5x$

$\Rightarrow \quad 5x = 410$

$\Rightarrow \quad x = 82$ kmph

Hence, the speed of second train is 82 kmph.

113. (C): Let maximum marks for the exam are x

Then, $x \times \frac{40}{100} = (300 + 20)$

$\Rightarrow \quad x \times \frac{2}{5} = 320$

$\Rightarrow \quad x = 160 \times 5$

$\Rightarrow \quad x = 800.$

114. (A): $\because$ Amount $= \text{P} + \frac{\text{P}rt}{100}$

$\therefore \quad 1331 = \text{P} + \frac{\text{P} \times 2 \times 5}{100}$

$\Rightarrow \quad 1331 = \frac{110\text{P}}{100}$

$\Rightarrow \quad \text{P} = 1331 \times \frac{10}{11} = 121 \times 10$

$\Rightarrow \quad \text{P} = 1210.$

116. (B): Let A Man's salary = ₹ 100

Then, New salary

$= ₹\ 100 \times \frac{120}{100} \times \frac{85}{100}$

$= 6 \times \frac{85}{5}$

$= 6 \times 17$

$= ₹\ 102$

Hence, the net change is 2% increase.

117. (D): 3 years ago the total age of a family of 5 members = 27 × 5 = 135 years

$\therefore$ Present age of a family of 5 members

$= 135 + 3 \times 5$

$= 135 + 15 = 150$ years

And present age of a family of 6 members

$= 27 \times 6 = 162$

Hence, the present age of the child

$= 162 - 150 = 12$ years.

118. (B): Let the black and white balls in a bag are $3x$ and x.

Then, $(3x + 5) : (x - 5) = 5 : 1$

$\Rightarrow 1(3x + 5) = 5(x - 5)$

$\Rightarrow \quad 3x + 5 = 5x - 25$

$\Rightarrow \quad 5x - 3x = 5 + 25$

$\Rightarrow \quad 2x = 30$

$\Rightarrow \quad x = 15$

$\therefore$ Originally the number of white balls in the bag is 15.

119. (B): Let the age of son is x years then the age of father is $4x$ years,

5 years later,

$$4x + 5 = 3(x + 5)$$
$$\Rightarrow \quad 4x + 5 = 3x + 15$$
$$\Rightarrow \quad 4x - 3x = 15 - 5$$
$$\Rightarrow \quad x = 10$$

Hence, father's age $= 4x = 4 \times 10$
$= 40$ years.

120. (C): Let the unit's digit be x and ten's digit be y

Then, the two-digit number is $10y + x$

Now, $x + y = 13$ ...(*i*)

and $x - y = 5$ ...(*ii*)

From solving (*i*) and (*ii*), we get,

$$x = 9 \text{ and } y = 4$$

Hence, the number

$$= 10y + x$$
$$= 10 \times 4 + 9 = 49.$$

121. (A): The book "A History of British India" was written by James Mill. He was a British historian, economist, political theorist, and philosopher, known for his influential works on British colonialism and Indian history. Published in 1817, Mill's book provided a comprehensive overview of British rule in India, focusing on political, economic, and social aspects of colonial administration. His work played a significant role in shaping British perceptions of India and colonial policies during the 19th century.

122. (C): The first cotton textile mill in Bombay, India was established in 1854. The mill, named the Bombay Spinning and Weaving Company, was established by Cowaszee Nanabhoy Davar and his associates on July 7, 1854. The mill began production on February 7, 1856. The Bombay Spinning and Weaving Company was the first steam-powered cotton mill in Asia. The mill marked the beginning of the industrial revolution in India, which was slow at first. The expansion of modern cotton mills didn't begin until the 1870s and 1880s.

123. (B): The ruler known as 'Devanampriya' and 'Priyadarshi' was Ashoka, the third emperor of the Maurya dynasty. Ashoka, also referred to as Ashoka the Great, is renowned for his conversion to Buddhism after the Kalinga War and his subsequent efforts to spread the teachings of Buddhism throughout his empire. He adopted the titles 'Devanampriya' and 'Priyadarshi,' which signify his devotion to the Gods and his desire to be beloved by his subjects, respectively.

124. (B): The first National Policy on Education in India, formulated in 1968, marked a significant milestone in the country's educational landscape. Aimed at addressing the diverse educational needs of the nation, it laid down comprehensive guidelines and objectives to improve the quality and accessibility of education. Key highlights of the policy included the promotion of universal elementary education, expansion of vocational and technical training, enhancement of adult education programs, and the establishment of educational institutions catering to diverse needs.

125. (D): The Constitution of India came into force on January 26, 1950. The Constituent Assembly of India adopted the Constitution on November 26, 1949. This day is celebrated as Constitution Day or National Law Day. The Constituent Assembly first met in December 1946, and by November 1949, the draft constitution was approved.

126. (A): The Right of Children to Free and Compulsory Education (RTE) Act, 2009 states that the student-teacher ratio (PTR) for upper primary schools should be 35:1. The PTR is the number of students per teacher, which is calculated by dividing the total number of teachers by the number of students. Research suggests that lower student-teacher ratios and smaller class sizes can help student achievement.

127. **(C):** The most popular classical dance form of Uttar Pradesh is Kathak. Kathak has its roots in northern India and is known for its intricate footwork, graceful movements, and expressive storytelling through hand gestures, facial expressions, and body movements. It originated in the temples of north India and later evolved into a sophisticated dance form under the patronage of Mughal rulers. Kathak is characterized by its rhythmic compositions (tukras and tihais), pirouettes (chakkars), and intricate rhythmic footwork (tatkar). It remains a prominent and revered classical dance form in Uttar Pradesh and throughout India.

128. **(B):** The oldest mountain range in India is the Aravalli Range. Stretching across the states of Gujarat, Rajasthan, Haryana, and Delhi, the Aravalli Range is one of the oldest fold mountain ranges in the world, with geological formations dating back millions of years. It runs approximately 800 kilometers in length from southwest to northeast. While not as high as the Himalayas, the Aravalli Range has significant cultural, ecological, and geological importance.

129. **(D):** Dhupgarh, the highest peak of the Satpura Range, rises majestically in the Pachmarhi region of Madhya Pradesh, India. Standing at an elevation of approximately 1,350 meters (4,429 feet) above sea level, it offers visitors panoramic vistas of the picturesque landscape below. Renowned for its tranquil ambiance and stunning natural surroundings, Dhupgarh attracts tourists and nature enthusiasts alike who come to admire its scenic beauty and revel in the tranquility of its surroundings. Whether it's witnessing the awe-inspiring sunrise or soaking in the serene atmosphere, a visit to Dhupgarh promises a rejuvenating experience amidst the captivating charm of the Satpura Range.

130. **(A):** The Yangtze River, known as Chang Jiang in Chinese, is the longest river in Asia and the third-longest in the world. Stretching approximately 6,300 kilometers (3,917 miles) from its source in the Tanggula Mountains of western China to its mouth at the East China Sea near Shanghai, the Yangtze plays a vital role in the cultural, economic, and ecological landscape of China. It serves as a major transportation route, providing access to inland cities and facilitating trade. Moreover, the river basin supports diverse ecosystems and is home to numerous species of plants and animals. Additionally, the Yangtze has historically been an essential part of Chinese civilization, influencing agriculture, industry, and human settlement along its course.

131. **(B):** The Prime Minister of India serves as the chairperson of NITI Aayog, which stands for National Institution for Transforming India. NITI Aayog is a policy think tank of the Government of India that aims to facilitate and guide the country's development by formulating strategic and long-term policies. Established in 2015, NITI Aayog replaced the Planning Commission and operates with a focus on cooperative federalism, innovation, and fostering economic growth. Under the leadership of the Prime Minister, NITI Aayog plays a crucial role in shaping India's developmental agenda and fostering sustainable and inclusive growth across various sectors of the economy.

132. **(B):** Igneous rocks are formed through the cooling and solidification of magma or lava. Basalt and granite are two common examples of igneous rocks. Basalt typically forms from lava flows on the Earth's surface and is characterized by its fine-grained texture and dark color. Granite, on the other hand, forms from the slow cooling of magma beneath the Earth's surface and is known for its coarse-grained texture and light-colored appearance. These rocks provide valuable insights into Earth's geological history and processes, reflecting the conditions under which they were formed. Halite, however, is a type of sedimentary rock formed from the precipitation of minerals from evaporating water bodies, making it distinct from igneous rocks like basalt and granite.

133. (D): In a mixed economy, economic decisions are made by both the private sector and the government. This economic system combines elements of both capitalism, where the private sector dominates economic activities, and socialism, where the government plays a significant role in managing the economy. In a mixed economy, the private sector operates businesses and makes production and consumption decisions based on market forces such as supply and demand. However, the government also intervenes to regulate certain industries, provide public goods and services, and implement policies to address social welfare and economic stability. Therefore, economic problems in a mixed economy are typically solved through a combination of efforts from both the government and the private sector.

134. (A): Diminishing marginal utility refers to the economic principle that states as a consumer consumes more units of a good or service, the additional satisfaction or utility derived from each successive unit tends to decrease. This concept is rooted in the idea that individuals typically fulfill their most pressing needs first, so as they consume more of a particular good, its marginal utility diminishes. In practical terms, this means that consumers are willing to pay less for additional units of a good as they acquire more of it, reflecting a decrease in the perceived value or satisfaction gained from each additional unit consumed.

135. (C): The best quantitative method to control inflation in the economy is the use of the cash reserve ratio (CRR). CRR refers to the portion of total deposits that banks are required to keep with the central bank in the form of reserves. By increasing the CRR, the central bank reduces the amount of money available for lending, thereby curbing excess liquidity in the economy. This helps in controlling inflation by reducing aggregate demand and preventing excessive growth in prices. While other methods like moral suasion, selective credit control, and the bank rate policy are also used to influence credit availability and interest rates, adjusting the CRR directly impacts the money supply, making it a potent tool for inflation control.

136. (B): Kanishka, a significant figure in Indian history, was the first Indian ruler whose territory extended beyond the Indian subcontinent. He was the emperor of the Kushan Empire, which encompassed regions in present-day Afghanistan, Pakistan, parts of Central Asia, and northern India. Kanishka's reign, which began around the 1st century CE, marked a period of cultural and economic prosperity, as well as significant developments in art, trade, and religion. His empire served as a crucial link between East and West, facilitating the exchange of ideas, goods, and cultures along the Silk Road. Kanishka's support for Buddhism and his patronage of Buddhist art and architecture further contributed to his enduring legacy in the region.

137. (D): Sunderlal Bahuguna is considered the leader of the Chipko movement. The movement began in 1973 in the village of Mandal in the Chamoli district of

Uttarakhand, India. The movement was non-violent and aimed to stop the commercial felling of trees. The Chipko movement started when villagers, including women, organized themselves into smaller groups to stand up against commercial logging operations. Villagers embraced trees to prevent logging, and when their appeals were denied, the government canceled the company's logging permit.

138. (B): When too much money chases too few goods, the resulting inflation is referred to as "Demand-pull inflation". This type of inflation occurs when the demand for goods and services exceeds their supply in the economy, leading to upward pressure on prices. It often arises due to factors such as increased consumer spending, expansionary fiscal or monetary policies, or supply shortages. Demand-pull inflation can result in a rise in the general price level and decreased purchasing power of money.

139. (A): The Indian Citizenship Act was passed in 1955. This legislation defined who could be considered a citizen of India and laid out the process by which citizenship could be acquired, terminated, or revoked. The act established various provisions regarding citizenship, including citizenship by birth, descent, registration, or naturalization. It also delineated the rights and privileges of Indian citizens, as well as the obligations and duties associated with citizenship.

140. (C): The veto that grants the President of India the power to reject a bill passed by Parliament is the "Absolute veto." This authority allows the President to refuse to give assent to a bill, effectively preventing it from becoming law. The absolute veto is the power of the President to withhold assent to a bill. The President can only exercise an absolute veto once for a bill. The President can either give or withhold assent to a Money Bill. However, the President cannot return a Money Bill to the House for reconsideration.

141. (D): "Barbarians" refers to groups of people considered uncivilized or primitive by the standards of the dominant civilization, often used pejoratively to denote foreign or non-native peoples. The term originated from ancient Greece, where it was used to describe anyone who did not speak Greek and therefore sounded like they were saying "bar-bar" rather than recognizable language.

142. (C): laments- "Laments" expresses the captain's deep sadness and regret over the team's loss. While "disagrees" implies opposition, "hates" is too strong, and "criticizes" suggests blame rather than sadness.

143. (D): pinnacle- "Zenith" means the highest point or peak. "End" suggests conclusion, "side" doesn't convey the idea of achievement, and "middle" implies the opposite of peak.

144. (C): desire- "Ambition" refers to a strong desire or goal, not a specific plan or thought. "Roadmap" implies a detailed plan, which isn't necessarily present in ambition.

145. (C): stalemate- "Impasse" refers to a situation where no progress is possible, similar to a stalemate in a game or conflict. "Obstacle" suggests a specific hurdle, "indecision" implies lack of commitment, and "rough patch" suggests a temporary difficulty.

151. (D): cruel- While all the options have negative connotations, "cruel" directly opposes "kind" by signifying a tendency to inflict pain or suffering. "Soft" and "happy" don't capture the opposite of kindness, while "hard" is irrelevant to the context.

152. (B): rude- "Rude" is the antonym of "polite," as it describes someone lacking manners or respect. "Sad" doesn't express the opposite behavior, "quiet" can be polite, and "smart" is unrelated to politeness.

153. (C): favourable- "Favourable" means positive or supportive, the opposite of "adverse" which signifies disapproval or criticism. "Intolerable" implies something too extreme to bear, "harmful" suggests causing damage, and "evil" carries a stronger negative connotation.

154. (A): believable- "Incredulous" means something difficult to believe, so its opposite is "believable" which suggests something readily accepted as true. "Unlikely" implies something improbable, "shaky" doesn't convey the opposite meaning, and "laughable" suggests something funny rather than believable.

157. (A): "Malgudi Days" is a captivating novel written by R.K. Narayan, depicting the charming and whimsical tales set in the fictional town of Malgudi. It was first published in 1943. The book is a collection of 32 stories, all set in the fictional town of Malgudi, located in South India. Each of the stories portrays a facet of life in Malgudi, from the everyday lives of ordinary people to the more fantastical and magical. Each story within the novel offers a glimpse into the humor, pathos, and intricacies of life in Malgudi, leaving a lasting impression on readers with its timeless themes and universal appeal.

158. (C): J.K. Rowling is the brilliant author behind the beloved "Harry Potter" series, which has captivated millions of readers worldwide. Through her imaginative storytelling and masterful world-building, Rowling created a magical universe filled with wizards, witches, and enchanting creatures, centered around the young wizard Harry Potter and his adventures at Hogwarts School of Witchcraft and Wizardry. Harry Potter and his friends, Hermione Granger and Ron Weasley, who are students at Hogwarts School of Witchcraft and Wizardry. The seven books in the series were published between 1997 and 2007 and have been translated into 85 languages. They have sold more than 600 million copies worldwide, making them the best-selling book series in history.

159. (C): "Alice in Wonderland" was penned by the renowned author Lewis Carroll. Published in 1865, this timeless classic follows the whimsical adventures of a young girl named Alice who falls down a rabbit hole into a fantastical world filled with peculiar creatures and nonsensical events. Carroll's vivid imagination and mastery of wordplay bring to life a rich tapestry of characters and settings, ranging from the enigmatic Cheshire Cat to the tyrannical Queen of Hearts. Through Alice's journey, Carroll explores themes of identity, logic, and the absurdities of adult society, captivating readers of all ages with its blend of fantasy, humor, and profound philosophical undertones.

160. (C): In the famous Rusty Series, Ruskin Bond introduces readers to the endearing character of Rusty, a young Anglo-Indian boy navigating the complexities of adolescence and life in India. "The Room on the Roof". the first novel in the series, follows Rusty's journey as he rebels against the constraints of his guardian and embarks on a quest for independence and belonging. Set against the backdrop of Dehradun, India, Bond intricately weaves together themes of friendship, love, and self-discovery, capturing the essence of youth and the allure of adventure. Through Rusty's experiences, Bond offers readers a poignant and nostalgic glimpse into the idyllic landscapes and cultural tapestry of post-colonial India, earning acclaim for his evocative storytelling and vivid characterizations in this beloved series.

Previous Paper (Solved)

IGNOU B.Ed. ENTRANCE EXAM 2023*

PART-A

Section-I : General English Comprehension

Directions (Qs. Nos. 1-10): *Read the following passage carefully and choose the best answer out of the four choices given after each question that follows:*

The best way to learn is to teach. This is the message emerging from experiments in several schools in which teenage pupils who have problems at school themselves are tutoring younger children—with remarkable results for both sides.

According to American research, pupil-tutoring wins 'hands down' over computerized instruction and American teachers say that no other recent innovation has proved so consistently successful.

Now the idea is spreading in Britain. Throughout this term, a group of 14-year-olds at Trinity Comprehensive have been spending an hour a week helping children at a nearby primary school with their reading. The younger children read aloud to their tutors and then play word games with them.

All the 14-year-olds have some of their own lessons in a special unit for children who have difficulties at school. Though their intelligence is around average, most of them have fallen behind on reading, writing and maths and, in some cases this has led to truancy or bad behaviour in class.

Jean Bond, who is running the special unit, says that the main benefit of tutoring is that it improves the adolescents' self-esteem. "The younger children come rushing up every time and welcome them. It makes the tutors feel important whereas, in normal school lessons, they often feel inadequate. Everyone benefits. The older children need practice in reading but, if they had to do it in their own classes, they would say it was kids' stuff and be worried about losing face. The younger children get individual attention from very patient people. The tutors are struggling at school themselves so, when the younger ones can't learn, they know exactly why."

The tutors agree. "When I was little, I used to skive and say I couldn't do things when I really could," says Mark Gregor. "The boy I've been teaching does the same. He says he can't read a page of his book so I tell him that, if he does do it, we can play a game. That works."

Jean Bond, who describes pupil tutoring as an 'educational conjuring trick', has run two previous experiments. In one, six persistent truants, aged 15 upwards, tutored 12 slow-learning infants in reading and maths. None of the six played truant from any of the tutoring sessions. "The degree of concentration they showed while working with their tutees was remarkable for pupils who had previously shown little ability to concentrate on anything related to school work for any period of time," says Bond. The tutors became 'reliable, conscientious, caring individuals'.

Their own reading, previously mechanical and monotonous, became far more expressive as a result of reading stories aloud to infants. Their view of education, which they had previously dismissed as 'crap' and 'a waste of time', was transformed. They became firmly resolved to teach their own children to read before starting school because, as one of them put it, 'if they go for a job and they can't write, they're not going to employ you, are they?' The tutors also became more sympathetic to their own teacher's difficulties, because they were frustrated themselves when the infants mucked about.

* Exam held on 08 January, 2023.

1. According to the writer, the tutors wouldn't normally practice reading in class because:

A. they would find it humiliating.
B. they wouldn't be able to concentrate.
C. their teachers wouldn't consider it necessary.
D. their teachers would get impatient with them.

2. The main reason that the tutors make such successful teachers seems to be that:

A. they enjoy being the centre of attraction.
B. they can relate to their pupils' problems.
C. they are never strict with their pupils.
D. their pupils enjoy playing games with them.

3. The phrase, "it improves the adolescents' sense of self-esteem" suggests that the teenagers:

A. feel more self-confident.
B. sense of worth improves.
C. fell more welcome.
D. feel proud of their abilities.

4. Pupil tutoring is described as 'an educational conjuring trick' because:

A. no one understands why it works so well.
B. it has caught the attention of the media.
C. educational authorities are suspicious of it.
D. it is a simple idea with extraordinary results.

5. One of the important results of the Trinity experiment seems to have been that the tutors:

A. learnt to overcome their fear of reading.
B. improved their own ability to speak.
C. came to see the importance of the writing skill.
D. learnt to love their pupils.

6. The tutors "became more sympathetic to their own teacher's difficulties ______" because:

A. they valued the efforts and patience of their teachers.
B. they realized that reading is a difficult skill to teach.
C. they understood the feelings of their teachers when their own pupils misbehaved.
D. they understood that teaching-learning is a difficult process.

7. In the sentence "Their own reading, previously mechanical and monotonous ______", 'mechanical' and 'monotonous' are:

A. verbs B. adjectives
C. adverbs D. nouns

8. The most appropriate title for this passage would be:

A. Teenage teachers
B. Truant children
C. A solution to all problems
D. How to improve reading skills

9. The passage is part of:

A. a report B. an article
C. a narrative D. a proposal

10. Which of the following statements is not correct according to the passage?

A. Both the tutors and pupils showed improvement in their reading skills.
B. The tutors made future plans for their pupils.
C. The tutors feel important when the younger children welcome them.
D. The tutors behaved very patiently with the pupils.

Section-II : Logical and Analytical Reasoning

Directions (Qs. Nos. 11-14): *Each of the following questions consists of two pairs of numbers/letter groups. First pair has a certain relationship. Complete the second pair by using the same relationship:*

11. 12 : 143 :: 2 : ?

A. 1
B. 2
C. 3
D. 4

12. 225 : 14 :: 81 : ?
A. 7 B. 8
C. 9 D. 10

13. ABD : BCE :: NOQ : ?
A. PRS B. ORS
C. PRT D. OPR

14. AZYB : CXWD :: BYXC : ?
A. DWVE B. EXDE
C. DXVE D. CXDE

Directions (Qs. Nos. 15-18): *In each of the following questions, a number/letter series is given with one term missing. Identify the underlying pattern and complete the series by choosing the correct option:*

15. 3, 13, 23, 43, 53, 73, ?, _____
A. 33 B. 83
C. 93 D. 103

16. 5, 10, 20, 35, ?, 80, 110, _____
A. 30 B. 45
C. 55 D. 75

17. BAC, CBD, ?, EDF, FEG, _____
A. CDE B. ACE
C. BDC D. DCE

18. MNAZ, LOBY, KPCX, JQDW, ?, _____
A. HRCW B. IREV
C. ISDV D. HTZX

19. If RATS is coded as STAR and TOPS is coded as SPOT, then SMART would be coded as:
A. STRMS B. RASTM
C. TARMS D. TRAMS

20. If BAR is coded as RAB and REAK is coded as KAER, then SPEAR would be coded as:
A. ARESP B. PARES
C. RAEPS D. PEARS

21. If RACE is coded as 1234 and SPARK is coded as 56217, then SPEAKER would be coded as:
A. 5642741 B. 5424417
C. 6512341 D. 6413542

22. If 1234 is coded as 10 and 3456 is coded as 18, then 5678 would be coded as:
A. 28 B. 26
C. 32 D. 36

23. Kapil is walking North-East, then he turns right. After walking for one minute, he again turns right. In which direction is he now walking?
A. East-South B. North-West
C. South-East D. South-West

24. A man is facing east. He turns 45° clockwise. Then he turns 180° anticlockwise. Which direction does he face now?
A. North-West B. West
C. South D. North-East

25. Which of the following appears first in the dictionary? Select the correct answer:
A. Mountain B. Monument
C. Momentum D. Movement

26. The total number of rectangles hidden in the following figure is:

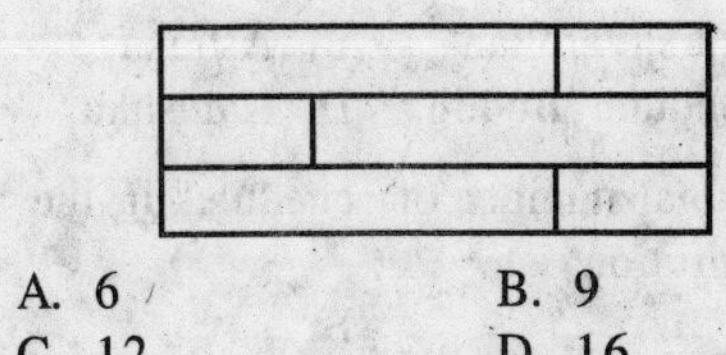

A. 6 B. 9
C. 12 D. 16

27. Of the two brothers elder one is 6 years elder than the younger. After 3 years, the elder one will be twice as old as the younger one then. The present age of younger one is:
A. 3 years B. 4 years
C. 5 years D. 6 years

28. A man is the son of the father of your daughter's mother. What is he to you?
A. Son-in-law B. Brother-in-law
C. Father-in-law D. Maternal Uncle

29. A, B, C, D and E are friends. B is taller than A but shorter than E. B is taller than D, but shorter than C. E is the tallest. Who is at the median height?
A. A B. C
C. D D. B

30. Which of the following names is somehow different from the other three?
A. V.P. Singh B. Chandrashekhar
C. Manmohan Singh D. H.D. Deve Gowda

Section-III : Educational and General Awareness

31. The term 'Epicentre' is associated with:
A. Earthquakes B. Volcanoes
C. Cyclones D. Landslides

32. A review of NPE, 1986, Programme of Action (POA) was done by:
A. National Commission for Teachers
B. Yashpal Committee
C. Ramamurti Committee
D. Hansa Mehta Committee

33. The first open university in India was established in the year:
A. 1961 B. 1982
C. 1985 D. 2001

34. Sarnath Pillar was built by:
A. Harshvardhan B. Ashoka
C. Gautam Buddha D. Kanishka

35. The total number of schedules in the Indian constitution is:
A. 6 B. 14
C. 12 D. 10

36. Which ruler founded the city of Agra?
A. Sikandar Lodi B. Akbar
C. Firoz Tughlaq D. Shahjahan

37. 'A Farewell to Arms' was written by:
A. Ernest Hemingway B. George Orwell
C. J.K. Galbraith D. Gunnar Myrdal

38. Who was the first Vice-Chairman of NITI Aayog?
A. Arvind Panagariya
B. Raghuram Rajan
C. Chandrashekhar Subramaniam
D. Rajiv Kumar

39. Which river crosses the tropic of cancer twice?
A. Narmada B. Tapti
C. Chambal D. Mahi

40. Direct Tax Code in India is related to which of the following?
A. Sales Tax B. Income Tax
C. Excise Duty D. Service Tax

41. Which of the following is not included in the assets of a commercial bank in India?
A. Advances
B. Deposits
C. Investment
D. Money at call and short notice

42. In which Article of the constitution the adult suffrage is recognised?
A. 324 B. 325
C. 326 D. 327

43. The Attorney General of India is appointed by:
A. The Law Minister
B. The President of India
C. The Speaker of the Lok Sabha
D. The Prime Minister

44. The Battle of Buxar was fought in:
A. 1764 B. 1757
C. 1526 D. 1761

45. 'Jaziya' was reimposed during the reign of:
A. Akbar B. Aurangzeb
C. Jahangir D. Humayun

46. India's first ATM was installed by which bank?
A. Citi Bank B. HSBC
C. PNB D. SBI

47. Adhai Din-Ka-Jhonpra at Ajmer was constructed by:
A. Shershah
B. Qutbuddin Aibak
C. Jalaludin Firoz Khilji
D. Balban

48. In which year Tsunami occurred in India?
A. 2005 B. 2004
C. 2006 D. 2007

49. Which of the following is a Kharif crop?
A. Wheat B. Barley
C. Millet D. Mustard

50. Which of the following states of India has the longest coastline?
A. Maharashtra B. Andhra Pradesh
C. Kerala D. Gujarat

51. Who built the Jama Mosque of Delhi?
A. Akbar B. Qutbuddin Aibak
C. Jahangir D. Shahjahan

52. Which of the following temple is not situated at Khajuraho?
A. Parshvanath
B. Vishwanath
C. Kandaria Mahadev
D. Lingraj

53. Selection test for admission to teacher training programme was suggested by:
A. NCTE B. NAAC
C. NPERL D. NCERT

54. International Day of Persons with Disabilities is observed on:
A. 5 December B. 3 December
C. 11 December D. 18 December

55. Which state first adopted the Panchayati Raj System in 1959?
A. Rajasthan B. Karnataka
C. Gujarat D. Punjab

Section-IV : Teaching-Learning and The School

56. According to National Education Policy, 2020, structure of school education will be:
A. 10 + 2 + 3
B. 11 + 2 + 2
C. 5 + 3 + 3 + 4
D. 3 + 3 + 5 + 4

57. In the context of the school, what does CCE stand for?
A. Centres for Continuing Education
B. Continuous and Comprehensive Evaluation
C. Core Committee on Education
D. Committee on Curriculum Evaluation

58. "Students will be able to enumerate the functions of a commercial bank." This objective pertains to:
A. Cognitive domain
B. Affective domain
C. Psychomotor domain
D. Both Cognitive and Affective domain

59. The method which expects students to learn on their own is:
A. Lecture Method
B. Demonstration Method
C. Heuristic Method
D. Lecture-cum-Demonstration Method

60. Which one of the following characteristics does not describe the scientific attitude?
A. Curiosity of knowing things
B. Critical thinking
C. Exploring 'what', 'why' and 'how' of the phenomena
D. Not being openminded

61. Which one of the following statements best indicates the difference between the syllabus and curriculum?
A. Syllabus includes academic subjects only whereas the curriculum deals with the totality of learning experiences.
B. Curriculum is not comprehensive whereas syllabus is.
C. Curriculum is based on the needs of the child whereas syllabus is not.
D. Curriculum is school centric and syllabus is classroom centric.

62. Behaviourism is not described by:
A. Knowledge construction
B. Readiness for learning
C. Learning by trial and error
D. Conditioning

63. "NISHTHA" portal facilitates:
A. In-service training of school teachers
B. Pre-service training of school teachers
C. In-service training of university teachers
D. Pre-service training of university teachers

64. As per cognitivism, learning involves:
A. Trial and error
B. Linking new and old learning
C. Learning within social setting
D. Conditioning

65. A sound recreational activity promotes development of:
A. body only
B. mind only
C. both mind and body
D. neither mind nor body

66. Knowledge explosion in the world today requires a teacher to be:
A. Facilitator of learning
B. Provider of knowledge
C. Creator of knowledge
D. Both creator and provider of knowledge

67. Which of the following is not a co-curricular activity?
A. a quiz in a class
B. a cultural programme
C. reading textbook
D. reading a story book in the school library

68. Instructions in a Distance Education system are commonly imparted through:
A. Personal Contact Programme
B. Printed Study Material
C. Radio
D. Television

69. Which of the following does not hold good for the use of audio-visual aids?
A. use of multiple sense organs
B. creating novality
C. making abstractions concrete
D. making simple concepts complex

70. Jacques Delors report to the UNESCO was titled:
A. International Commission on Education Report
B. Millennium Development Report
C. Learning : The Treasure Within
D. World Declaration on Educa-tion for All

71. For the qualitative improvement of elementary education in India, NPE, 1986 recommended the establishment of:
A. NCERT B. SCERT
C. DIET D. IASE

72. Which teaching method makes learner's participation optimal and proactive?
A. Discussion method
B. Lecture method
C. Demonstration method
D. Lecture-cum-demonstration method

73. Summative evaluation is:
A. assessment while teaching a topic
B. assessment after teaching a topic
C. assessment at the end of a semester
D. assessment after teaching a chapter

74. In a lively classroom situation, it is unlikely that there would be:
A. occasional roars of laughter
B. complete silence
C. frequent teacher-student dialogue
D. discussion among students

75. Teaching should involve:
A. Avoidance of proximity
B. Voice modulation
C. Repetitive pause
D. Fixed posture

76. RCI stands for:
A. Reserve Court of India
B. Rehabilitation Centre of India
C. Reserve Council International
D. Rehabilitation Council of India

77. The approach explaining learning from peers is:
A. Behaviourism
B. Cognitivism
C. Constructivism
D. Social constructivism

78. Research undertaken to solve problems of students in schools is called:
A. Fundamental Research
B. Action Research
C. Applied Research
D. Basic Research

79. Change in attitude pertains to:
A. Cognitive Domain
B. Psychomotor Domain
C. Affective Domain
D. Both Affective and Cognitive Domains

80. Elementary education is a fundamental right under the Article ________ of the Indian Constitution.
A. 15 A B. 20 A
C. 21 A D. 20 B

PART-B

Section-V : (i) Science

81. Which colour of the rainbow has the maximum wavelength?
A. Violet B. Green
C. Yellow D. Red

82. A body moving along the circumference of a circle may have a constant:
A. speed B. velocity
C. momentum D. acceleration

83. A normal eye forms the image of an object on:
A. Iris B. Cornea
C. Retina D. Pupil

84. The instrument used to measure atmospheric pressure is:
A. Thermometer B. Sonometer
C. Barometer D. Hygrometer

85. The density of water is maximum at:
A. –4°C B. 0°C
C. 4°C D. 100°C

86. If weight of a person on earth is W_E and his weight on Moon is W_M, we have:
A. $W_E > W_M$
B. $W_E < W_M$
C. $W_E = W_M$
D. No prediction is possible

87. An organic compound must contain:
A. Hydrogen B. Carbon
C. Oxygen D. Silicon

88. Diamonds are made of:
A. Pure Carbon B. Carbon and Silicon
C. Glass and Silicon D. Pure Silicon

89. On heating white phosphorus it is converted into red phosphorus. If a little Iodine is added the conversion is faster. Here Iodine acts as:
A. Oxidizer B. Catalyst
C. Lubricant D. Detergent

90. Starch can be detected using a drop of iodine. In the presence of starch, iodine:
A. Turns blue
B. Vapourises
C. Becomes colourless
D. Turns black

91. Geiger-Muller counters are instruments for measuring:
A. Time B. X-rays
C. Photons D. Radioactivity

92. Which of the following is not essential for rust to form?
A. Iron B. Water
C. Oxygen D. Carbon dioxide

93. Which of the following is a chemical compound?
A. Copper B. Oxygen
C. Common salt D. Iron

94. All the following organs in the human body are located both on the right and the left sides, except:
A. Kidneys B. Lungs
C. Eyes D. Spleen

95. Typhoid is caused by:
A. Bacteria B. Virus
C. Hormones D. Fungus

96. All living beings have this process:
A. Respiration B. Photosynthesis
C. Breathing D. Transpiration

97. Molybdenum is a:
A. Macronutrient
B. Micronutrient
C. Not a nutrient
D. Compound

98. Cataract is the disease of:
A. Eye B. Ear
C. Lungs D. Heart

99. Of the following types of teeth which one is used for grinding food?
A. Canine
B. Molar
C. Incisor
D. Milk teeth

100. The depletion of ozone layer in the atmosphere is caused by:
A. Nitrous oxide
B. Sulphur dioxide
C. Carbon dioxide
D. Chlorofluorocarbons

Section-V : (ii) Mathematics

101. The sum of the first 15 multiples of 8 is:
A. 760 B. 1060
C. 860 D. 960

102. Twelve observations are recorded as under:
14, 25, 14, 28, 18, 17, 18, 14, 23, 22, 14, 18
The mode is:
A. 14 B. 17
C. 18 D. 22

103. Twenty fifth percentile is the same as:
A. First quartile B. Second quartile
C. Third quartile D. Quartile deviation

104. When Mean > Median, the curve is:
A. Positively skewed
B. Negatively skewed
C. Normal probability curve
D. Frequency curve

105. The value of $9 \sec^2 A - 9 \tan^2 A$ is:
A. 1 B. 0
C. 8 D. 9

106. A tower stands vertically on the ground. From a point on the ground, which is 15 m away from the foot of the tower, the angle of elevation of the top of the tower is 60°. The height of the tower is:
A. $\frac{15}{\sqrt{3}}$ m B. $15\sqrt{3}$ m
C. $\frac{5}{\sqrt{3}}$ m D. $5\sqrt{3}$ m

107. ABC and BDE are two equi-lateral triangles such that D is the mid point of BC. Ratio of the areas of the triangles ABC and BDE is:
A. 4 : 1 B. 1 : 4
C. 1 : 2 D. 2 : 1

108. 16 men or 20 women can do a piece of work in 25 days. In how many days 28 men and 15 women will do the same?
A. 10 days B. $14\frac{2}{7}$ days
C. $18\frac{3}{4}$ days D. $20\frac{1}{3}$ days

109. A coconut merchant finds that the cost price of 2750 coconuts is the same as the selling price of 2500 coconuts. Percentage of gain or loss is:
A. 15% loss B. 15% gain
C. 10% gain D. 10% loss

110. What should be diameter of the wheel if a distance of 5.5 kilometres is to covered in 1750 revolutions?
A. 0.5 metre B. 0.75 metre
C. 1.0 metre D. 1.25 metre

111. The most approximate value of
$3\sqrt{5} - 4\sqrt{3} + 2\sqrt{80} + 2\sqrt{12}$ is:
A. 24 B. 24.5
C. 25.0 D. 24.6

112. The length of a train and that of a platform are equal. If with a speed of 90 kmph the train crosses the platform in one minute, then the length of train (in metres) is:
A. 700 m B. 750 m
C. 800 m D. 850 m

113. A student failed by 30 marks, securing 201 marks. If minimum pass marks are 33%, the maximum marks for the exam is:
A. 700 B. 750
C. 650 D. 600

114. A sum of money amounts to ₹ 1,008 in 2 years and ₹ 1,112 in 3 years. The rate of interest is:
A. 13.5% B. 12%
C. 13% D. 12.5%

115. The median of the following ten numbers is:
14, 32, 24, 18, 29, 15, 13, 27, 26, 31
A. 27 B. 26
C. 24 D. 25

116. A person's salary was increased by 25% and then decreased by some per cent to bring at the previous level. The decrease per cent was:
A. 25% B. 20%
C. 24% D. 18%

117. The average weight of A, B and C is 45 kg. If the average weight of A and B is 40 kg and that of B and C is 43 kg, then the weight of B is:
A. 31 kg B. 41 kg
C. 36 kg D. 38 kg

118. There are two numbers in the ratio of 7 : 4. If 12 is added to the smaller number the ratio becomes 7 : 5. The bigger number is:
A. 48 B. 64
C. 77 D. 84

119. Twelve years ago, a father's age was 2 times the age of his son. Three years later, the ratio of father and son's ages will be 5 : 3. How old is the son now?
A. 38 years B. 40 years
C. 42 years D. 45 years

120. A two-digit number is below 30. Sum of its digits is 10 and difference is 6. The number is:
A. 24 B. 26
C. 28 D. 29

Section-V : (iii) Social Science

121. Who was the first Governor-General of India during the British rule?
A. Lord Mountbatten B. Warren Hastings
C. William Bentinck D. Charles Wood

122. The treaty that ended the First World War was:
A. The treaty of Paris
B. The treaty of Brest-Litovsk
C. The treaty of Versailles
D. The treaty of Nevilly

123. Who was the founder of Brahmo Samaj Movement?
A. Bipin Chandra Pal
B. Bal Gangadhar Tilak
C. Lala Lajpat Rai
D. Raja Ram Mohan Roy

124. Which of the following structures of school education has been recommended by the National Education Policy, 2020?
A. 5 + 3 + 4 + 3 B. 5 + 4 + 3 + 3
C. 4 + 5 + 3 + 3 D. 5 + 3 + 3 + 4

125. When was the constitution of India adopted by the Constituent Assembly?
A. 26 January, 1950
B. 5 December, 1949
C. 26 November, 1949
D. 15 August, 1948

126. Which of the following Articles of the Indian constitution includes the Right of Children to Free and Compulsory Education Act, 2009?
A. Article 21 (A) B. Article 45
C. Article 30 D. Article 29 (1)

127. Which of the following states has Kuchipudi as a classical dance form?
A. Karnataka B. Andhra Pradesh
C. Kerala D. Odisha

128. The Aravalli mountain range stretches across which of the Indian states?
A. Maharashtra, Goa and Karnataka
B. Kerala, Tamil Nadu and Andhra Pradesh
C. Delhi, Haryana, Rajasthan and Gujarat
D. Punjab, Himachal Pradesh and Jammu and Kashmir

129. What soil is the best for the growth of sugarcane?
A. Black soil B. Alluvial soil
C. Red soil D. Loamy soil

130. Which of the following is the longest river in the world?
A. Nile B. Amazon
C. Yangtze D. Ganga

131. Who is called as the 'Father of Sociology'?
A. Karl Marx B. Auguste Comte
C. Max Weber D. Harriet Martineau

132. Which is not a sedimentary rock?
A. Limestone B. Sandstone
C. Granite D. Siltstone

133. The regulation and control of all banks in India is performed by:
A. Central Bank of India
B. State Bank of India
C. Reserve Bank of India
D. Punjab National Bank

134. Which is not an example of the Barter System?
A. Mangoes are exchanged for oranges
B. Tea is exchanged for salt
C. Shoes are exchanged for cloths
D. Purchasing goods as per market rate by exchanging money

135. The book "Das Kapital" by Karl Marx was published in the year:
A. 1867 B. 1877
C. 1887 D. 1897

136. Which of the following battles was fought between Alexander and King Porus in 326 B.C.?
A. Panipat B. Hydaspes
C. Buxar D. Tarain

137. Chipko movement is associated with:
A. Human Rights
B. Milk Production
C. Environmental Conservation
D. Agricultural Production

138. Which of the following Acts introduced provincial autonomy during the British rule?
A. The Government of India Act, 1919
B. The Government of India Act, 1909
C. The Government of India Act, 1858
D. The Government of India Act, 1935

139. Where did the practice of 'Shadow Cabinet' originate?
A. India B. Great Britain
C. U.S.A. D. Italy

140. Hirakud Dam is located on which of the following rivers?
A. Mahanadi B. Kaveri
C. Godavari D. Krishna

Section-V : (iv) English

Directions (Qs. Nos. 141-145): *Choose the word that is nearest in meaning to the underlined word:*

141. Covalent compounds consist of discrete molecules.
A. Concrete B. Grouped
C. Separate D. Convoluted

142. The pearls bought by Anaisha are genuine.
A. Inexpensive B. Attractive
C. Expensive D. Authentic

143. There is not a single word that is redundant in the report.
A. Bombastic B. Unimportant
C. Flowers D. Unnecessary

144. All mail is censored by the government during war time.
A. distributed B. confiscated
C. examined D. supervised

145. The art movie that I watched this evening has put me in expensive mood.
A. cheerful B. reflective
C. confused D. depressed

Directions (Qs. Nos. 146-150): *In each of the following group of words, only one of them is correctly spelt. Select the one with the correct spelling:*

146. A. asending B. ascending
C. acending D. ascanding

147. A. presumptous B. presamptous
C. presumptus D. presamptus

148. A. fasade B. facade C. fasad D. facad

149. A. mundane B. mondane C. mundan D. mondan

150. A. falacy B. fallacy C. falecy D. fallecy

Directions (Qs. Nos. 151-154): *Choose the word that is opposite in meaning to the underlined word:*

151. The Gupta rulers patronised all cultural activities and thus the period came to be called the 'Golden Age' of Indian history.
A. admired B. rejected
C. indulged D. favoured

152. Tilak always advocated the use of indigenous goods.
A. cheap B. native
C. silly D. foreign

153. His timidity led him to trouble.
A. boldness B. arrogance
C. self-assertion D. self-confidence

154. We should not belittle the value of small things.
A. expand B. downplay
C. praise D. scorn

Directions (Qs. Nos. 155 and 156): *Pick out the most appropriate word from the given alternatives to fill in the blank to complete the sentence:*

155. He is too ______ to be deceived easily.
A. strong B. modern
C. kind D. intelligent

156. The police have ______ a complaint against the culprits.
A. entered B. registered
C. noted D. lodged

Directions (Qs. Nos. 157-160): *Choose the correct answer:*

157. The novel 'Jane Eyre' was written by:
A. Charlotte Bronte B. Emily Bronte
C. George Eliot D. Jane Austen

158. The poem 'Ode to the West Wind' was written by:
A. Keats B. Shelley
C. Wordsworth D. Byron

159. The play 'Othello' was written by:
A. Shakespeare B. Bernard Shaw
C. Eugene O'Neil D. Brecht

160. The novel 'Gora' was written by:
A. Tagore B. R.K. Narayan
C. Anita Desai D. Khushwant Singh

Section-V : (v) हिन्दी

निर्देश (प्रश्न संख्या 161 से 165): *निम्नलिखित गद्यांश को ध्यानपूर्वक पढ़कर उसके आधार पर पूछे गए प्रश्नों के उत्तर दीजिए :*

निर्लिप्त रहकर दूसरों का गला काटने वालों से लिप्त रहकर दूसरों की भलाई करने वाले कहीं अच्छे होते हैं। क्षात्रधर्म का संबंध लोकरक्षा से है। अतः वह जनता के सम्पूर्ण जीवन को स्पर्श करने वाला है। कोई राजा होगा तो अपने घर का होगा .... इससे बढ़कर झूठी बात शायद ही कोई हो। झूठे खिताबों द्वारा यह कभी सच नहीं की जा सकती। क्षात्र जीवन के इतना व्यापक होने के कारण ही हमारे मुख्य अवतार राम और कृष्ण क्षत्रिय हैं।

कर्म-सौंदर्य की योजना जितने रूपों में क्षात्र जीवन में संभव है, उतने रूपों में किसी में नहीं। शक्ति के साथ क्षमा, वैभव के साथ विनय, तेज के साथ कोमलता, पराक्रम के साथ रूप-माधुर्य, प्रताप के साथ कठिन धर्म-पथ का अवलंबन क्षात्रधर्म में ही हो सकता है। इस व्यापार युग में, इस वणिग्धर्म प्रधान युग में क्षात्रधर्म की चर्चा करना शायद पुरानी बातों को याद करना समझा जाए परन्तु आधुनिक व्यापार की अन्याय रक्षा भी शास्त्रों द्वारा ही की जाती है। क्षात्रधर्म का उपयोग समाप्त नहीं हुआ है, केवल धर्म के साथ उसका असहयोग हो गया है।

161. प्रस्तुत गद्यांश के लिए एक उचित शीर्षक दीजिए :
A. क्षात्रधर्म से हानि B. क्षात्रधर्म की महत्ता
C. वणिग्धर्म के दोष D. राम-कृष्ण का व्यक्तित्व

162. क्षात्रधर्म में कौन-सा सौंदर्य अनेक रूपों में दिखाई देता है?
A. धर्म B. अर्थ
C. कर्म D. भलाई

163. वणिग्धर्म किसको कहा गया है?
A. व्यापारी के काम को
B. व्यापारी के सौंदर्य को
C. व्यापार के धन को
D. व्यापारी की सोच को

164. क्षात्रधर्म का संबंध किससे है?
A. जीवरक्षा
B. पशुरक्षा
C. लोकरक्षा
D. झूठे खिताबों से

165. क्षात्रधर्म की चर्चा वणिग्धर्म प्रधान युग में कैसी समझी जाती है?
A. पुरानी बातों को याद करने जैसी
B. सफलता प्रदान करने वाली
C. व्यर्थ की
D. बहुत ही ज्ञानवर्धक

166. सब कुछ जानने वाले को कहते हैं :
A. कृतज्ञ
B. सर्वज्ञ
C. अज्ञ
D. विशेषज्ञ

167. हिन्दी वर्णमाला में अयोगवाह वर्ण कौन-से हैं?
A. अ, आ
B. इ, ई
C. उ, ऊ
D. अं, अः

168. 'ऋजु' का विलोम शब्द कौन-सा है?
A. मृदु
B. वक्र
C. अद्यतन
D. निश्चित

169. कौन-से शब्द की वर्तनी अशुद्ध है?
A. कवियत्री
B. कवयित्री
C. आकलन
D. प्रादुर्भाव

170. जिस वाक्य में 'एक कर्त्ता' और 'एक क्रिया' हो, उसे कहते हैं :
A. संयुक्त वाक्य
B. मिश्र वाक्य
C. सरल वाक्य
D. विकसित वाक्य

171. 'अथ' का विलोम शब्द है :
A. अंत
B. शब्द
C. अर्थ
D. इति

172. किस शब्द में 'आवा' प्रत्यय नहीं है?
A. चढ़ावा
B. दिखावा
C. लावा
D. भुलावा

173. निम्नलिखित शब्दों में से विशेषण कौन-सा शब्द है?
A. सौंदर्य
B. कृतज्ञ
C. व्यक्तित्व
D. बड़प्पन

174. 'अमिय' का पर्यायवाची शब्द है :
A. आम्र
B. सुधा
C. विष
D. मधुप

175. 'ध्रुवस्वामिनी' नाटक के रचनाकार का नाम है :
A. महादेवी वर्मा
B. जयशंकर प्रसाद
C. मुंशी प्रेमचंद
D. मोहन राकेश

176. 'कहाँ राजा भोज कहाँ गंगू तेली' कहावत का अर्थ है?
A. गुण के विरुद्ध नाम होना
B. उच्च और साधारण की तुलना कैसी
C. घर के गुणी व्यक्ति को तुच्छ समझना
D. केवल बाह्य प्रदर्शन

177. 'आँख-कान खुले रखना' मुहावरे का अर्थ है :
A. आँख खोलकर सुनना
B. एक-दूसरे को देखना
C. सचेत रहना
D. होश में रहना

178. 'काली घटा का घमंड घटा' में अलंकार है :
A. श्लेष
B. यमक
C. अनुप्रास
D. अर्थालंकार

179. पुस्तक कौन-सा शब्द है?
A. तद्भव
B. तत्सम
C. विदेशज
D. देशज

180. 'देशभक्ति' में कौन-सा प्रत्यय है?
A. तत्पुरुष समास
B. कर्मधारय समास
C. द्वंद्व समास
D. द्विगु समास

ANSWERS

1. (A) **2.** (B) **3.** (B)
4. (D) **5.** (A) **6.** (C)
7. (B) **8.** (D) **9.** (A)
10. (D)

11. (C): 12 : 143
$\Rightarrow (12)^2 - 1 = 144 - 1 = 143,$
2 : ?
$\Rightarrow (2)^2 - 1 = 4 - 1 = 3$
$\therefore ? = 3$

12. (B): $225 : 14 \Rightarrow \sqrt{225} - 1 = 15 - 1 = 14$

$81 : ? \Rightarrow \sqrt{81} - 1 = 9 - 1 = 8 \therefore ? = 8.$

13. (D) **14. (A)**

15. (C):

+30 +30

3 13 23 43 53 73 [93]

+20 +30 +40

∴ the missing number = 93.

16. (C): 5 10 20 35 [55] 80 110

+5 +10 +15 +20 +25 +30

∴ the missing number = 55.

17. (D):

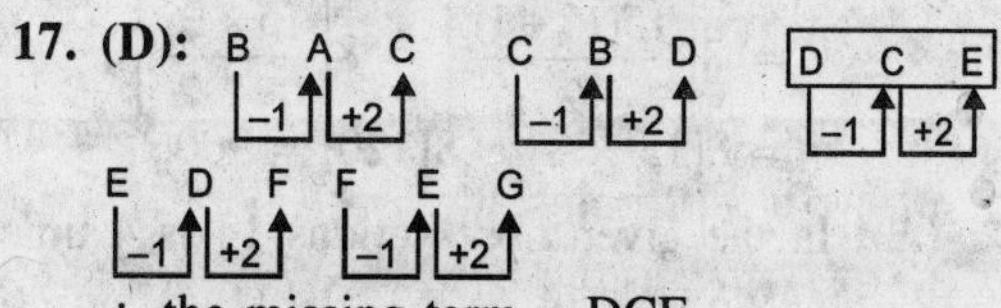

∴ the missing term = DCE.

18. (B): The letters of the word are coded by their represented letters in the reverse series.

C O M E → letters in natural series

X L N V → letters in reverse series

↓ ↓ ↓ ↓

3rd 15th 13th 5th

∴

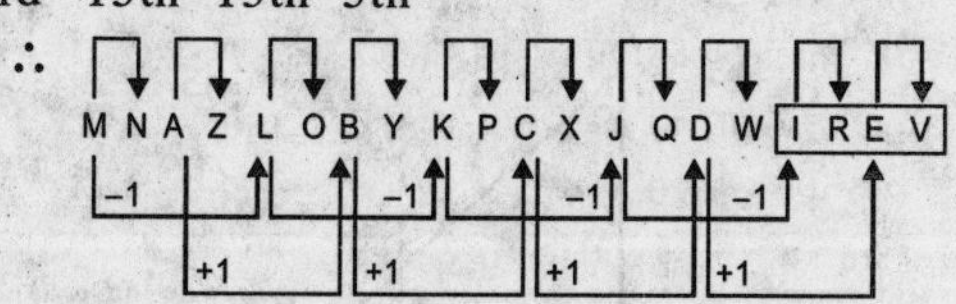

∴ the missing term = IREV.

19. (D): Given,

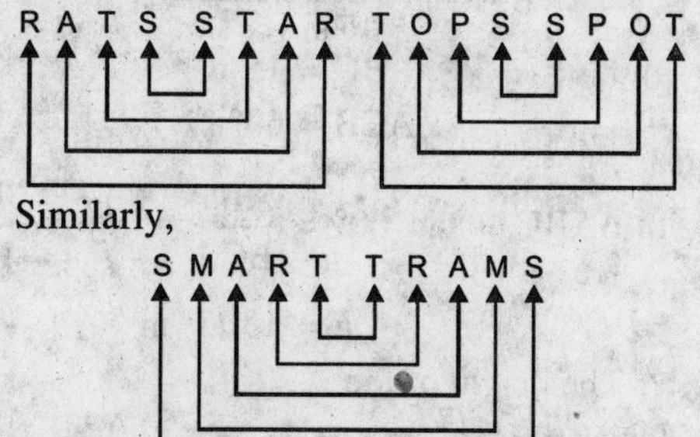

∴ SMART would be coded as TRAMS.

20. (C): Given, BAR ⇒ RAB

REAK ⇒ KAER (Letters written in reverse)

Similarly, SPEAR ⇒ RAEPS

∴ SPEAR would be coded as RAEPS.

21. (A): Given, R A C E

↓ ↓ ↓ ↓

1 2 3 4

and, S P A R K

↓ ↓ ↓ ↓ ↓

5 6 2 1 7

∴ S P E A K E R

↓ ↓ ↓ ↓ ↓ ↓ ↓

5 6 4 2 7 4 1

∴ SPEAKER would be coded as 5642741.

22. (B): Given, 1234 = 10

⇒ 1 + 2 + 3 + 4 = 10

and 3456 = 18

⇒ 3 + 4 + 5 + 6 = 18

Similarly 5678 = ?

⇒ 5 + 6 + 7 + 8 = 26

∴ 5678 would be coded as 26.

23. (D):

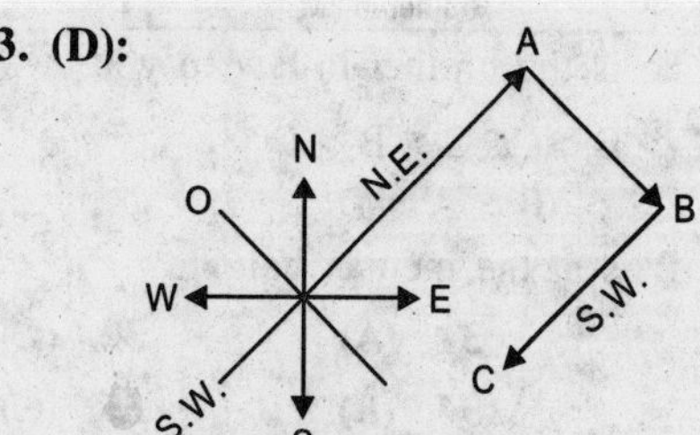

Here, Starting point = O

Finally, he is walking in South-West direction.

24. (A):

N

N.W.

C 180°

W E

A

45°

B

S.E.

S

Here, Starting point = A

Final point = C

Now he is facing in North-West direction.

25. (C): Momentum → Monument → Mountain → Movement.

Momentum appears first in the dictionary.

26. (C)

27. (A): Let the present age of younger is x yrs. then, the present age of elder is $(x + 6)$ yrs. According to question,
After 3 yrs.

$$x + 6 + 3 = 2(x + 3)$$
$$\Rightarrow \quad x + 9 = 2x + 6$$
$$\Rightarrow \quad 2x - x = 9 - 6 \Rightarrow x = 3 \text{ years.}$$

28. (B):

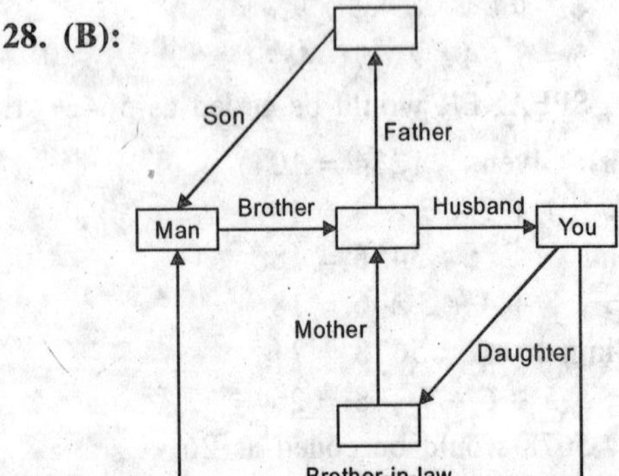

Here, he is the brother-in-law to you.

29. (D): E > B > A, C > B > D
⇒ E > C > B > A > D
Here, B is at the median height.

30. (C)	**31. (A)**	**32. (C)**
33. (B)	**34. (B)**	**35. (C)**
36. (A)	**37. (A)**	**38. (A)**
39. (D)	**40. (B)**	**41. (B)**
42. (C)	**43. (B)**	**44. (A)**
45. (B)	**46. (B)**	**47. (B)**
48. (B)	**49. (C)**	**50. (D)**
51. (D)	**52. (D)**	**53. (A)**
54. (B)	**55. (A)**	**56. (C)**
57. (B)	**58. (D)**	**59. (C)**
60. (D)	**61. (D)**	**62. (A)**
63. (A)	**64. (C)**	**65. (C)**
66. (D)	**67. (C)**	**68. (B)**
69. (D)	**70. (C)**	**71. (C)**
72. (A)	**73. (C)**	**74. (B)**
75. (B)	**76. (D)**	**77. (D)**
78. (B)	**79. (D)**	**80. (C)**
81. (D)	**82. (A)**	**83. (C)**
84. (C)	**85. (C)**	**86. (A)**
87. (B)	**88. (A)**	**89. (B)**
90. (A)	**91. (D)**	**92. (D)**
93. (C)	**94. (D)**	**95. (A)**
96. (A)	**97. (B)**	**98. (A)**
99. (B)	**100. (D)**	

101. (D): [Sum of first n natural numbers $= \frac{n(n+1)}{2}$]

Here, The sum of the first 15 multiples of 8

$$= 8(1 + 2 + 3 + ... + 15)$$
$$= 8\left[\frac{15(15+1)}{2}\right] = 8\left[\frac{15 \times 16}{2}\right]$$
$$= 8[15 \times 8] = 8[120] = 960.$$

102. (A): In the given observations 14 is 4 times
∴ Mode = 14.

103. (A) **104. (A)**

105. (D): $9 \sec^2 A - 9 \tan^2 A$
$= 9(\sec^2 A - \tan^2 A = 9 \times 1 = 9$
$[\because \sec^2 A - \tan^2 A = 1]$

106. (B): Let AB be a tower of height h m.

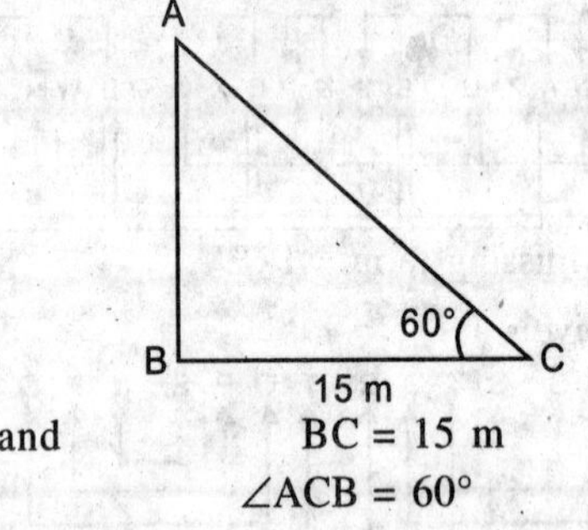

and BC = 15 m
$\angle ACB = 60°$

In ΔABC, $\tan 60° = \frac{AB}{BC} \Rightarrow \sqrt{3} = \frac{h}{15}$

$\Rightarrow \quad h = 15\sqrt{3}$ m

∴ The height of the tower = $15\sqrt{3}$ m.

107. (A): Given, ΔABC and ΔBDE are two equilateral triangles such that D is the mid-point of BC

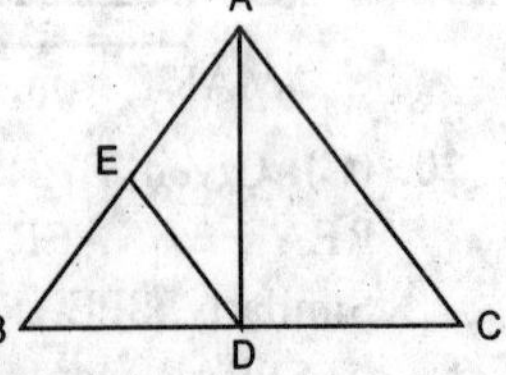

Let side of equilateral $\Delta ABC = x$

then, $BD = \frac{x}{2}$

$\therefore$ side of equilateral $\Delta BDE = \frac{x}{2}$

[$\because$ Area of equilateral triangle $= \frac{\sqrt{3}}{4} \times (\text{side})^2$]

$\therefore$ area (ΔABC) : area (ΔDBC)

$$= \frac{\sqrt{3}}{4}(x)^2 : \frac{\sqrt{3}}{4}\left(\frac{x}{2}\right)^2$$

$$= \frac{\sqrt{3}}{4}x^2 : \frac{\sqrt{3}}{4} \times \frac{x^2}{4} = 1 : \frac{1}{4}$$

$= 4 : 1.$

108. (A): Given, 16 men = 20 women

$\Rightarrow$ 1 men $= \frac{20}{16}$ women $= \frac{5}{4}$ women

$\Rightarrow$ 1 women $= \frac{4}{5}$ men

$\therefore$ 28 men + 15 women

$= 28$ men $+ 15 \times \frac{4}{5}$ men

$= 28$ men + 12 men = 40 men

$\because$ more men, less days $\rightarrow$ Indirect proportion

Men Days

16 : 40 :: x : 25

$\Rightarrow 16 \times 25 = 40 \times x$

$$\Rightarrow \quad x = \frac{16 \times 25}{40} = \frac{16 \times 5}{8}$$

$= 2 \times 5 = 10$

$\therefore$ Required number of days = 10.

109. (C): Let the selling price of 1 coconut is ₹ 1 then, selling price of 2750 coconuts = ₹ 2750 and cost price of 2750 coconuts

= selling price of 2500 coconuts = ₹ 2500

profit = S.P. – C.P.

$\therefore$ gain = 2750 – 2500 = ₹ 250

$$\therefore \quad \text{gain } \% = \frac{\text{gain} \times 100}{\text{C.P.}}$$

$$= \frac{250 \times 100}{2500} = \frac{100}{10} = 10\%.$$

110. (C): Here,

Distance = 5.5 kilometres

= 5.5 × 1000 metres

= 5500 metres

and number of revolutions = 1750

$$\therefore \quad 1 \text{ revolution} = \frac{5500}{1750} = \frac{22}{7} \text{ metre}$$

$$\Rightarrow \quad 2\pi r = \frac{22}{7}$$

$$\Rightarrow \quad 2 \times \frac{22}{7} r = \frac{22}{7}$$

$\Rightarrow$ $2r = 1$ metre

$\Rightarrow$ diameter = 1 metre.

111. (D): $3\sqrt{5} - 4\sqrt{3} + 2\sqrt{80} + 2\sqrt{12}$

$= 3\sqrt{5} - 4\sqrt{3} + 2\sqrt{16 \times 5} + 2\sqrt{4 \times 3}$

$= 3\sqrt{5} - 4\sqrt{3} + 8\sqrt{5} + 4\sqrt{3} = 11\sqrt{5}$

$= 11 \times 2.2360 = 24.59 = 24.6$ (approx)

112. (B): Let the length of a train

= length of a platform = x m

given, speed of train = 90 kmph

$= 90 \times \frac{5}{18}$ mps = 25 mps

$$\because \quad \text{time} = \frac{\text{distance}}{\text{speed}}$$

$$\Rightarrow \quad \frac{x + x}{25} = 1 \text{ minute}$$

$$\Rightarrow \quad \frac{2x}{25} = 60 \text{ seconds}$$

$\Rightarrow$ $2x = 60 \times 25$

$\Rightarrow$ $x = 30 \times 25 = 750$ metres

$\therefore$ the length of train = 750 m.

113. (A): Let the maximum marks for the exam is x

then, $x \times \frac{33}{100} = 201 + 30 \Rightarrow \frac{33x}{100} = 231$

$$\Rightarrow \quad x = \frac{231 \times 100}{33} = 7 \times 100$$

$\Rightarrow$ $x = 700.$

114. (C): According to question

Interest of money in 1 year

= ₹ 1112 – ₹ 1008 = ₹ 104

$\Rightarrow$ Interest of money in 2 years

$= 2 \times 104 = ₹\ 208$

$\therefore$ principal of money in 2 years

$= 1008 - 208 = ₹\ 800$

$\therefore$ The rate of interest

$$= \frac{\text{Interest} \times 100}{p \times t} = \frac{208 \times 100}{800 \times 2} = \frac{26}{2} = 13\%.$$

115. (D): Given, ten numbers in ascending order.
13, 14, 15, 18, 24, 26, 27, 29, 31, 32
Here, number of observations

$n = 10$ (even number)

$$\therefore \text{ Median} = \frac{1}{2}\left[\frac{n}{2}th \text{ term} + \left(\frac{n}{2}+1\right)th \text{ term}\right]$$

$$= \frac{1}{2}[\text{5th term} + \text{6th term}]$$

$$= \frac{1}{2}[24 + 26] = \frac{1}{2} \times 50 = 25.$$

116. (B): The decrease per cent was

$$= \frac{25}{100+25} \times 100 = \frac{25}{125} \times 100 = \frac{1}{5} \times 100 = 20\%.$$

117. (A): The total weight of A, B and C

$= 3 \times 45 = 135$ kg

the total weight of A and B

$= 2 \times 40 = 80$ kg

and the total weight of B and C

$= 2 \times 43 = 86$ kg

$\therefore$ the total weight of A + 2B + C

$= 80 + 86 = 166$ kg

$\therefore$ the weight of B $= 166 - 135 = 31$ kg.

118. (D): Let the two numbers are $7x$ and $4x$

then $\frac{7x}{4x+12} = \frac{7}{5}$

$\Rightarrow \quad 7x \times 5 = 7 \times (4x + 12)$

$\Rightarrow \quad 35x = 28x + 84$

$\Rightarrow \quad 35x - 28x = 84 \Rightarrow 7x = 84$

$\therefore$ The bigger number = 84.

119. (C): Let 12 years ago, father's age was $2x$ years and his son was x year
Then, father's present age = $2x + 12$ years
Son's present age = $x + 12$ years
Now, 3 years later

$(2x + 12) + 3 : (x + 12) + 3 = 5 : 3$

$\Rightarrow (2x + 15) : (x + 15) = 5 : 3$

$\Rightarrow 3(2x + 15) = 5(x + 15)$

$\Rightarrow \quad 6x + 45 = 5x + 75$

$\Rightarrow \quad 6x - 5x = 75 - 45 \Rightarrow x = 30$

$\therefore$ Son's present age $= x + 12$

$= 30 + 12 = 42$ years.

120. (C): Let two digits number is $10y + x$
According to question,

$x + y = 10$ ...(*i*)

and $x - y = 6$ ...(*ii*)

Adding (*i*) and (*ii*)

$2x = 16 \Rightarrow x = 8$

Putting the value of x in (*i*)

$8 + y = 10 \Rightarrow y = 2$

$\therefore$ Number $= 10 \times 2 + 8 = 28$.

121. (C)	**122. (C)**	**123. (D)**
124. (D)	**125. (C)**	**126. (A)**
127. (B)	**128. (C)**	**129. (D)**
130. (A)	**131. (B)**	**132. (C)**
133. (C)	**134. (D)**	**135. (A)**
136. (B)	**137. (C)**	**138. (D)**
139. (B)	**140. (A)**	**141. (C)**
142. (D)	**143. (D)**	**144. (C)**
145. (A)	**146. (B)**	**147. (A)**
148. (B)	**149. (A)**	**150. (B)**
151. (B)	**152. (D)**	**153. (A)**
154. (C)	**155. (D)**	**156. (D)**
157. (A)	**158. (B)**	**159. (A)**
160. (A)	**161. (B)**	**162. (C)**
163. (A)	**164. (C)**	**165. (A)**
166. (B)	**167. (D)**	**168. (B)**
169. (A)	**170. (C)**	**171. (A)**
172. (C)	**173. (B)**	**174. (B)**
175. (B)	**176. (B)**	**177. (C)**
178. (B)	**179. (B)**	**180. (A)**

Previous Paper (Solved)

IGNOU B.Ed. ENTRANCE EXAM 2022*

PART-A

Section-I : General English Comprehension

Directions (Qs. No. 1-10): *Read the following passage carefully and choose the best answer out of the four choices after each question that follows:*

A great deal of discussion continues as to the real extent of global environmental degradation and its implications. What few people challenge, however, is that the renewable natural resources of developing countries are today subject to stresses of unprecedented magnitude. These pressures are brought about, in part, by increased population and the quest for an ever expanding food supply. because the health, nutrition and general well-being of the poor majority are directly dependent on the integrity and productivity of their natural resources, the capability of government to manage them effecting over the long-term becomes of paramount importance.

Developing countries are becoming more aware of the ways in which present and future economic development must build upon a sound and sustainable natural resource base. Some are looking at our long tradition in environmental protection and are receptive to US assistance which recognises the uniqueness of the social and ecological systems in these tropical countries. Developing countries recognise the need to improve their capability to analyse issues and their own natural resource management. Some countries such as Senegal, India, Indonesia, Thailand etc. are now including conservation concerns in their economic development process.

Because so many governments of developing nations have recognised the importance of these issues, the need today is not merely one of raising additional consciousness, but for carefully designed and sharply focussed activities aimed at the establishment of effective resource management reforms that are essential to the achievement of sustainable development.

1. Some developing countries of Asia and Africa have:

A. formulated very ambitious plans of protecting the habitat in their region.

B. laid a great stress on the conservation of natural resources in their educational endeavour.

C. carefully dovetailed environmental conservation with the overall strategies of planned economic development.

D. sought the help of US experts in solving the problems of environmental degradation.

2. Technical know-how developed in the USA:

A. cannot be easily assimilated by the technocrats of developing countries.

B. can be properly utilised on the basis of developing countries being able to launch an in-depth study of their specific problems.

C. can be easily borrowed by the developing countries to solve the problem of environmental degradation.

D. can be very effective in solving the problem of resource management in tropical countries.

3. There has been a pronounced deterioration of habitat all over the globe because of:

A. population explosion

B. unprecedented urbanisation

* Exam held on 08 May, 2022.

C. massive industrialisation in the developing countries
D. large scale deforestation

4. The poor people of the developing world can lead a happy and contented life if:
A. aid flows freely to the developing world.
B. industries based on agriculture are widely developed.
C. economic development takes place within the ambit of conservation of natural resources.
D. there is an assured supply of food and medical care.

5. How much environmental pollution has taken place in the developing and the developed world?
A. There has been a marginal pollution of environment in the developed world and extensive damage in the developing world.
B. There has been a considerable pollution of environment all over the globe.
C. There has been an extensive environmental degradation both in the developed as well as the developing world.
D. The environmental pollution that has taken place all over the globe continues to be a matter of speculation and enquiry.

6. What, according to the passage, is an unquestionable reality today?
A. The renewable natural resources in developing countries are in great danger and on the verge of coming to an end.
B. The renewable natural resources in developed countries will never end.
C. The renewable natural resources all over the world are going to end soon.
D. The renewable natural resources in the developed world will end soon.

7. What is the most important reason for the depletion of natural resources in developing countries?
A. Lack of knowledge
B. Population explosion
C. Life style of people
D. Callousness of their governments

8. What is the most important for the preservation of natural resources?
A. Funding from external sources to manage resources.
B. Advancement in science and technology to manage resources.
C. Awareness of the people to manage resources.
D. Capability of governments to manage resources.

9. Activities aimed at preservation of natural resources is important for:
A. Social Development
B. Sustainable Development
C. Political Development
D. Cultural Development

10. The passage is about:
A. Population Explosion
B. Expanding Food Supply
C. US assistance for managing natural resources
D. Effective resource management for sustainable development

Section-II : Logical and Analytical Reasoning

11. If 4 + 4 = 15 and 6 + 6 = 35, then 8 + 8 = ?
A. 65 B. 63
C. 64 D. 62

12. If SYSTEM is coded as METSYS and FORMER is coded as REMROF, then CARPET would be coded as:
A. PETCAR B. PETRAC
C. TEPRAC D. RACTEP

13. According to the dictionary order, which of the following words will appear last of others?
A. Dress B. Drink
C. Dream D. Drift

14. Gaurav ranks 23rd from the top and 22nd from the bottom in a certain test. How many students appeared in the test?

A. 43 B. 44
C. 45 D. 46

15. In a certain coding system, NAME is coded as 3245 and MINT is coded as 4137, then MITE would be coded as:

A. 4317 B. 4725
C. 4571 D. 4175

16. Which of the following is the next term in the series?

2, 9, 28, 65, ____

A. 99 B. 121
C. 126 D. 145

17. Five books are placed in such a way that book C is above book D, book E is below book A, book D is above book A and book B is below book E. Which book is at the bottom?

A. A B. B
C. C D. D

18. A bag contains equal number of rupee 1, 50 paisa and 25 paisa coins. If the total amount of money in the bag is ₹ 35, what is the number of each type of coins?

A. 15 B. 18
C. 20 D. 25

19. A man walking from north to south turns right at right angle. Again he turns right at right angle. In which direction is he now walking?

A. East B. North
C. South D. West

20. Which of the following pairs of numbers is different from others in some way?

A. 27–57 B. 25–63
C. 18–28 D. 36–96

21. Which of the following numbers will be placed at the blank space in the series?

20, 19, 17, ____, 10, 5

A. 9 B. 11
C. 14 D. 16

22. A woman pointed to a man and said, "His mother is the only daughter of my mother." What is the woman to the man?

A. Niece
B. Sister
C. Daughter
D. Mother

23. Which of the following numbers is different from others in some way?

A. 42 B. 81
C. 121 D. 144

24. If CHDR represents DIES, then SHLD will represent:

A. LIME B. LINE
C. SINE D. TIME

25. Which of the following numbers continues the series?

1, 8, 27, 64, 125, ____?

A. 156 B. 196
C. 216 D. 225

26. EFGH : DEFG :: OPQR : ?

A. PQRS B. QRST
C. MNOP D. NOPQ

27. Which of the following would be the next term in the series?

CE, HJ, MO, RT, ____?

A. WY B. YZ
C. XZ D. UV

28. 'Ignorance' is to 'Education' as 'Disease' is to:

A. Doctor B. Hospital
C. Medicine D. Nurse

29. Which of the following fills the gap in the series?

25, 100, 225, ____, 625

A. 256 B. 324
C. 400 D. 484

30. Which of the following continues the series?

ABD, DEH, HIM, MNS, ___?

A. STZ B. SRY
C. TSR D. TSY

Section-III : Educational and General Awareness

31. 'Story of My Life' was written by:
A. Morarji Desai B. Abdul Kalam
C. Vivekananda D. Tagore

32. The Father of English Poetry was:
A. Geoffery Chaucer
B. Shakespeare
C. Wordsworth
D. Dryden

33. World Water Day is celebrated on:
A. 21st March B. 22nd March
C. 24th March D. 23rd March

34. Who advises the State Government on legal matters?
A. Attorney General
B. Advocate General
C. Chief Justice of High Court
D. Chief Justice of Supreme Court

35. The maximum duration of zero hour in the Lok Sabha is:
A. 30 minutes B. 60 minutes
C. 2 hours D. Indefinite period

36. 'No appeal, No Daleel, No Vakil' perfectly sums up which of the following?
A. Rowlatt Act
B. Non-co-operation Movement
C. Satyagrah
D. Swadesh Movement

37. 'Alice in Wonderland' was written by:
A. George Orwell B. Lewis Carroll
C. Chester Bowls D. Sinclair Lewis

38. The question asked orally after the question hour in the House is called:
A. Supplementary Question
B. Short Notice Question
C. Starred Question
D. Unstarred Question

39. Article 280 of the constitution of India deals with:
A. Finance Commission
B. Information Commission
C. Election Commission
D. Public Service Commission

40. Where is the New Moore island situated?
A. Arab Sagar B. Indian Ocean
C. Bay of Bengal D. Bay of Mannar

41. Sea territory of India extends upto:
A. 4 nautical miles
B. 12 nautical miles
C. 200 nautical miles
D. 400 nautical miles

42. World Economic Forum was founded by:
A. Klaus Schwab B. Paul Krugman
C. Bill Gates D. Peter Thiel

43. Which of the following prepared the draft of Basic Education?
A. Sapru Commission
B. Shiksha Sammelan Wardha
C. Radhakrishnan Commission
D. Zakir Hussain Committee

44. How many inhabited islands are there in Lakshadweep?
A. 17 B. 20
C. 10 D. 15

45. In which of the following historical sites of Haryana did excavation indicate 4500 years old civilization relics?
A. Rakhigarhi B. Siswal
C. Rohtak D. Karnal

46. Who described Bal Gangadhar Tilak as the 'Maker of Modern India'?
A. G.K. Gokhale B. Mahatma Gandhi
C. Jawaharlal Nehru D. B.C. Pal

47. In which year did the Industrial Policy express the concept of a mixed economy for India?
A. 1948 B. 1951
C. 1954 D. 1956

48. Who translated 'Atharvaveda' in Persion during Mughal period?

A. Abdul Hamid Lahori
B. Haji Ibrahim Sarhindi
C. Khathi Khan
D. Malik Muhammad Jayasi

49. The Rigveda consists of:
A. 1028 hymns B. 1000 hymns
C. 2028 hymns D. 1038 hymns

50. Which of the following rivers is called 'Biological Desert'?
A. Brahmaputra
B. Ganga
C. Damodar
D. Yamuna

51. Who is remembered as the pioneer of economic nationalism?
A. Bipin Chandra Paul
B. Gokhale
C. R.C Dutt
D. Madan Mohan Malviya

52. The 15th Pravasi Bhartiya Diwas, 2019 was held in:
A. Lucknow B. Agra
C. Prayagraj D. Varanasi

53. Establishment of DIETs was the result of the recommendation of:
A. Indian Education Commission (1964-66)
B. University Education Commission (1948-49)
C. Secondary Education Commission (1952-53)
D. National Policy on Education (1986)

54. The ruling dynasty in India during Timur's invasion was:
A. Lodhi B. Tughlaq
C. Saiyyad D. Khilji

55. When did Curzon pass the Indian Universities Act?
A. 1901 B. 1902
C. 1903 D. 1904

Section-IV : Teaching-Learning and The School

56. Which of the following is a maxim of teaching?
A. Simple to complex
B. Unknown to known
C. Abstract to concrete
D. Far to near

57. Human Development is determined:
A. by the genetic makeup of the individual.
B. by a complex of inherited and environmental factors.
C. primarily by environmental factors over which the individual has no control.
D. primarily by environmental factor over which the individual has control.

58. Non-formal education means:
A. education obtained through open educational institutions.
B. education obtained through formal schools.
C. education obtained through polytechnics.
D. education obtained in conventional universities.

59. Text-book development at the national level is carried out by:
A. UGC B. NCERT
C. NCTE D. AICTE

60. Which among the following is constructivist approach to teaching-learning?
A. Bloom's Approach
B. 5-E Approach
C. Morrison Approach
D. Herbartian Approach

61. The purpose of National Science Talent Search Scheme is to:
A. conduct an all India examination.
B. identify students for recruitment to scientific posts.
C. identify talented students and nurture their talent.
D. provide uniformity in science teaching.

62. While counseling students, a teacher should:
A. plan to do most of talking
B. establish rapport with students

C. refrain from giving information
D. assume complete responsibility for solving problems

63. In teaching, if noting has been learnt, nothing has been:
A. Taught B. Studied
C. Examined D. Observed

64. Basic requirement for success of lecture method is:
A. use of teaching aids
B. content delivery in a lucid language
C. theme based interaction among participants
D. including a large number of ideas

65. One of the most powerful factors influencing teaching effectiveness is:
A. teacher's gender
B. experience of teachers
C. location of schools
D. teachers' communication skills

66. The best way for providing value education is through:
A. discussions on texts of a particular religion
B. integration of values within subject content
C. religious discourses
D. lectures on values

67. The purpose of continuous and comprehensive evaluation is to:
A. evaluate scholastic and co-scholastic aspects continuously
B. priorities term and examination
C. evaluate mainly scholastic aspects
D. evaluate primarily co-scholastic aspects

68. What is not required for good teaching?
A. Direction B. Diagnosis
C. Remedy D. Teacher's bias

69. Which of the following factors does not impact teaching?
A. Classroom activities that encourage learning
B. Socio-economic background of teachers
C. Learning through experience
D. Teacher's knowledge

70. A good learner is one who:
A. only memorizes
B. is not open-minded
C. does not think divergently
D. thinks critically

71. Instructional aids are used by the teacher to:
A. adhere to educational policies
B. utilise school's resources
C. clarify the concepts
D. ensure discipline

72. CLASS stands for:
A. Complete Literacy and Studies in Schools
B. Computer Literates and Students in Schools
C. Computer Literacy and Students in Schools
D. Centre for Literacy and Studies in Schools

73. The first National Policy on Education following independence was formulated in:
A. 1948 B. 1958
C. 1968 D. 1978

74. Classroom environment should not have:
A. interactivity
B. activity
C. autocracy
D. brainstorming

75. "Spare the rod and spoil the child" gives the message that:
A. punishment the class should be banned
B. corporal punishment is not acceptable
C. undesirable behaviour must be punished
D. positive discipline should be encouraged

76. What is the other name of Yashpal Committee Report?
A. Learning with Burden
B. Learning without Burden
C. Learning with Grace
D. Learning with Progress

77. Choose full form of NCERT:
A. National Coordinator of Educational Resources and Tools
B. National Council of Educational Research and Training
C. National Centre for Educational Research and Training
D. New Centre of Educational Resources and Tools

78. 'Fill in the blanks' with alternatives is which type of question?
A. Open-ended question
B. Objective type question
C. Short answer question
D. Subjective type question

79. Classroom management is ineffective when it is:
A. Autocratic B. Democratic
C. Co-operative D. Participatory

80. The idea of basic education was proposed by:
A. Dr. Zakir Hussain
B. Dr. Rajendra Prasad
C. Mahatma Gandhi
D. Rabindranath Tagore

PART-B

Section-V : (i) Science

81. The effective resistance of the following combination from A to B is:

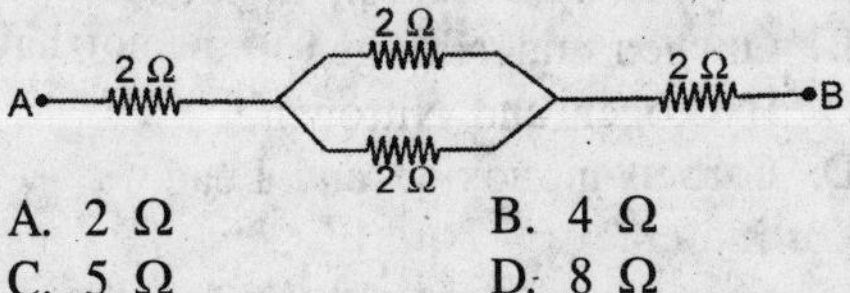

A. 2 Ω B. 4 Ω
C. 5 Ω D. 8 Ω

82. Light year is a unit of:
A. Time B. Distance
C. Density D. Pressure

83. Ice floats in water in a cylinder and the water level is at level A. When the ice melts the water level:
A. will remain unchanged
B. will go up
C. will go down
D. may go up or down

84. An ideal fuse wire should have:
A. a low resistance and low melting point
B. a high resistance and high melting point
C. a low resistance and high melting point
D. a high resistance and low melting point

85. Total internal reflection can take place when light travels from:
A. Air to glass B. Air to water
C. Water to glass D. Glass to air

86. The lightest element in our world is:
A. Hydrogen B. Helium
C. Oxygen D. Chlorine

87. In the upper layers of the earth, that is, in the crust, the most abundant metal is:
A. Iron B. Zinc
C. Aluminium D. Copper

88. The nucleus of Helium is like:
A. An alpha particle
B. A beta particle
C. A gamma particle
D. A proton

89. If a chemical reaction is accompanied by evolution of heat, it is:
A. Exothermic reaction
B. Endothermic reaction
C. Reversible reaction
D. Redox reaction

90. Pressure cooker works on the principle:
A. When the pressure increases the boiling point of water increases.
B. When the pressure increases the boiling point of water decreases.
C. Pressure has no effect on boiling point.
D. Heat and steam does not escape from the cooker.

91. For reducing friction between different parts of machines the following is used:
A. Lubricant B. Detergent
C. Levers D. Catalyst

92. The sugar in the milk in the natural form is called:
A. Glucose B. Sucrose
C. Lactose D. Fructose

93. The following is not an element of the bone:
A. Oxygen
B. Phosphorus
C. Uranium
D. Calcium

94. The following treatment is suggested for a person whose kidneys are not working:
A. Surgical removal of kidneys
B. Radiotherapy
C. Blood transfusion
D. Dialysis

95. If mitochondria are removed from the cell:
A. Nothing happens
B. The cell cannot reproduce
C. Leaves become white
D. Energy metabolism of the cell is reduced

96. The foetal growth is monitored using:
A. X-rays B. Microwaves
C. Ultrasonics D. Ultraviolet rays

97. Viruses need the following for growth:
A. Living host B. Dead host
C. Minerals D. Sugars

98. The following process does not increase the amount of carbon dioxide in the air:
A. Breathing
B. Photosynthesis
C. Petrol burning
D. Decay of vegetation

99. Polio is a disease of the following type:
A. Air-borne B. Water-borne
C. Food-borne D. Bacteria-borne

100. The major pollutants are:
A. Oxygen and Carbon dioxide
B. Oxygen and Nitrogen
C. Hydrogen and Nitrogen
D. Carbon monoxide and Lead

Section-V : (ii) Mathematics

101. Which of the following has the largest numerical value?
A. $\sqrt{10}$ B. $\sqrt{100}$
C. $\frac{1}{\sqrt{0.01}}$ D. $\frac{1}{0.01}$

102. The value of
$$5\frac{1}{2}-\left[2\frac{1}{3}\div\left\{\frac{3}{4}-\frac{1}{2}\left(\frac{2}{3}-\frac{1}{6}+\frac{1}{8}\right)\right\}\right]$$ is:
A. $5\frac{1}{2}$ B. $5\frac{1}{3}$
C. $\frac{1}{6}$ D. $\frac{1}{8}$

103. A batsman scores 448 runs in x innings. In his next innings he is out for 62 and thereby increases his average by 2. The value of x is:
A. 16 B. 18
C. 20 D. 22

104. A's salary is 50% above B's. How much per cent is B's salary below A's?
A. $33\frac{1}{3}\%$ B. 40%
C. 100% D. 150%

105. A producer blends two varieties of tea, one costing ₹ 150 per kg and the other ₹ 200 per kg in the ratio of 7 : 3. He sells the blended variety at ₹ 181.50 per kg. His profit per cent is:
A. 20 B. 15
C. 10 D. 8

106. A tradesman sells his goods at 10% discount on the marked price. What price should he mark on an article that costs him ₹ 900 to gain 10%?
A. ₹ 1,000 B. ₹ 1,100
C. ₹ 1,150 D. ₹ 1,200

107. A sum of ₹ 1,000 invested at 10% per annum compound interest amounts to ₹ 1,331. The period of time is:

A. 2 years B. 3 years
C. 3½ years D. 4 years

108. A person buys a pen costing ₹ 240 on hire purchase basis. He pays ₹ 60 cash down and the rest in 6 monthly instalments of ₹ 32 each. The rate of interest charged by the dealer is:

A. 18% B. 20%
C. 22% D. 24%

109. A plane left 30 minutes later than the scheduled time and in order to reach its destination 1500 km away in time it has to increase its speed by 250 km/hr. from its usual speed. The usual speed of the plane is:

A. 850 km/hr. B. 800 km/hr.
C. 750 km/hr. D. 700 km/hr.

110. If sec θ + tan θ = *m*, then the value of sin θ is:

A. $\frac{m+1}{m-1}$ B. $\frac{m-1}{m+1}$
C. $\frac{m^2+1}{m^2-1}$ D. $\frac{m^2-1}{m^2+1}$

111. The value of

$2\left(\frac{\sin 43°}{\cos 47°}\right)^2 - \frac{\cot 30°}{\tan 60°} - \sqrt{2}\sin 45°$ is:

A. 0 B. 1
C. –1 D. $\sqrt{2}$

112. From a building 60 metres high the angles of depression of the top and bottom of a lamp post are 30° and 60° respectively. The difference of heights between the building and the lamp post is:

A. $20\sqrt{3}$ m B. $\frac{20}{\sqrt{3}}$ m
C. 20 m D. 25 m

113. The length of the sides of a triangle are in the ratio 3 : 4 : 5 and its perimeter is 144 cm. The area of the triangle is:

A. 840 cm² B. 1080 cm²
C. 1440 cm² D. 864 cm²

114. The minute hand of a clock is 12 cm long. The area of the face of the clock described by the minute hand in 35 minutes is:

A. 210 cm² B. 264 cm²
C. 280 cm² D. 285 cm²

115. A metallic cone having base radius 2.1 cm and height 8.4 cm is melted and moulded into a sphere. The radius of the sphere is:

A. 2.1 cm B. 1.05 cm
C. 1.5 cm D. 2 cm

116. Water is flowing at a rate of 15 km/hr through a pipe of diameter 14 cm into a rectangular tank which is 50 m long and 44 m wide. The time in which level of water in the tank will rise by 21 cm is:

A. 1 hour B. 1½ hours
C. 2 hours D. 2½ hours

117. The mode of the following series is 36:

Class Interval	Frequency
0 – 10	8
10 – 20	10
20 – 30	?
30 – 40	16
40 – 50	12
50 – 60	6
60 – 70	7

The missing frequency is:

A. 10 B. 12
C. 8 D. 7

118. What is the probability that an ordinary year as 53 Mondays?

A. $\frac{2}{7}$ B. $\frac{1}{7}$
C. $\frac{7}{53}$ D. $\frac{7}{52}$

119. The sum of all the three-digit natural numbers which are multiples of 7 is:

A. 70336 B. 73306
C. 76033 D. 73360

120. The value of *p* for which the points (–5, 1), (1, *p*) and (4, –2) are collinear is:

A. 2 B. –2
C. 1 D. –1

Section-V : (iii) Social Science

121. In the absence of the President and Vice President who discharges the function of President?
A. Attorney General
B. Chief Justice of India
C. PM of India
D. Advocate General

122. Which of the following institutions can expand and increase the scope of Fundamental Rights in the constitution?
A. High Court
B. Supreme Court
C. National Human Rights Commission
D. State Human Right Commission

123. How many members are there in the Election Commission?
A. 1 B. 2
C. 3 D. 4

124. Panchayati Raj is based on the ideology of:
A. Democratic Decentralization
B. People Participation in Govt.
C. Centralization
D. Community Development

125. The United Nations Organisation was established on:
A. 24th September, 1945
B. 15th July, 1945
C. 24th October, 1945
D. 26th August, 1945

126. The last country to join SAARC was:
A. Sri Lanka B. Bangladesh
C. Maldives D. Afghanistan

127. Which of the following nations adopted an Open Door Policy?
A. China B. Japan
C. U.S.A. D. South Korea

128. The central nodal agency for implementing value support works for commercial crops is:
A. NAFED B. NABARD
C. FCI D. TRIFED

129. Diminishing marginal utility is the basis of:
A. Law of Supply
B. Law of Return
C. Law of Demand
D. Law of Consumption

130. Loss of interest income on funds is an example of:
A. Explicit Cost B. Implicit Cost
C. Marginal Cost D. Direct Cost

131. Who was the leader and inspirer of the Young Bengal Movement of the late 1820s and 1830s?
A. Rasik Krishna Mallic
B. Ramtaru Lahiri
C. Henry Vivian Derozio
D. Pearey Chand Mitra

132. The first Indian ruler who joined the subsidiary alliance was:
A. The Nawab of Awadh
B. The Nizam of Hyderabad
C. Peshwa Baji Rao
D. Jhansi ki Rani

133. The Raja Rani temple is located in:
A. Bhubaneshwar B. Khajuraho
C. Kanchipuram D. Varanasi

134. Which one of the following rivers flows westward?
A. Godavari B. Kaveri
C. Krishna D. Tapti

135. The term "Fani" is associated with:
A. Cyclone B. Rainfall
C. Flood D. Landslide

136. The literacy rate of India in 2011 was:
A. 72.04% B. 73.04%
C. 74.04% D. 75.04%

137. Dualistic economy means existence of:
A. Both industrial and agricultural sectors
B. Both public and private sectors
C. Both socialist and capitalist economies
D. Both foreign and domestic investments

138. Who was the first to unfurl the first Indian National Flag, the parent and precursor of the flag of independent India?
A. Dada Bhai Naoroji
B. Taraknath Das
C. Raja Mahendra Pratap
D. Madam Bhikaji Cama

139. Operation Flood is also known as:
A. Green Revolution
B. White Revolution
C. Blue Revolution
D. Black Revolution

140. In India the Tropic of Cancer passes through how many states?
A. 7 B. 8
C. 6 D. 5

Section-V : (iv) English

Directions (Q. Nos. 141-145): *Choose the word that is nearest in meaning to the underlined word:*

141. Employers like diligent employees.
A. Conscientious B. Obedient
C. Meticulous D. Hardworking

142. The meeting was adjourned after discussion for two hours.
A. Postponed B. Stopped
C. Begun D. Reviewed

143. He is such sham that it is different to get along with him.
A. pretender B. unnatural
C. blunt D. unfair

144. On who despises his colleagues can never be successful.
A. accuses B. ignores
C. hates D. discourages

145. The school took the students of 9th class on a three days' excursion to Goa.
A. trip B. picnic
C. visit D. tournament

Directions (Q. Nos. 146-150): *In each of the following group of words, only one of them is spelt correctly. Select the one with the correct spelling.*

146. A. megnificent B. magnifecent
C. magnificant D. megnifecant

147. A. tanacious B. tenacious
C. tanecious D. tenecious

148. A. consummation B. consumation
C. consammation D. consamation

149. A. menifest B. menifast
C. manifest D. manifast

150. A. posterity B. postarity
C. posterety D. portarety

Directions (Q. Nos. 151-154): *Choose the word that is opposite in meaning to the underlined word:*

151. The criminal was detained by the police.
A. protected B. dismissed
C. released D. deterred

152. His depressing attitude was not liked by anyone.
A. horrifying B. uplifting
C. bewildering D. digressing

153. Feasibility of the project is under study.
A. Unsuitability B. Impracticability
C. Impropriety D. Applicability

154. A mammoth statue overlooked the building.
A. effluent B. tiny
C. huge D. narrow

Directions (Q. Nos. 155 and 156): *Pick out the most appropriate word from the given alternatives and fill in the blanks to complete the sentence:*

155. This book is about a man who ______ his family and went to live in the Himalayas.
A. exited B. deserted
C. banished D. expelled

156. The villagers ______ the death of their leader by keeping all the shops closed.
A. announced B. protested
C. mourned D. consoled

Directions (Q. Nos. 157-160): *Choose the correct answer:*

157. The novel 'Persuasion' was written by:
A. Charlotte Bronte B. Emily Bronte
C. George Eliot D. Jane Austen

158. The poem 'Ode to Nightingale' was written by:
A. Keats B. Shelley
C. Wordsworth D. Bacon

159. The play 'Desire under the Elms' was written by:
A. Shakespeare
B. Bernard Shaw
C. Eugene O'Neill
D. Brecht

160. The novel 'Train to Pakistan' was written by:
A. Tagore B. R.K. Narayan
C. Anita Desai D. Khushwant Singh

Section-V : (v) हिन्दी

निर्देश (प्रश्न संख्या 161 से 165): *निम्नलिखित गद्यांश को ध्यानपूर्वक पढ़कर उसके आधार पर पूछे गए प्रश्नों के उत्तर दीजिए :*

"मनुष्य की विशेषता उसके चरित्र में है। चरित्र के कारण ही एक मनुष्य दूसरे से अधिक सम्मानित समझा जाता है। विद्या का मान तभी होता है जब विद्यावान विनय एवं चरित्र से युक्त हो। विद्या, बल तथा पद होते हुए भी रावण अपने राक्षसी कर्म के कारण निंदनीय रहा। रावण ज्ञानी होते हुए भी सम्मानित नहीं बन पाया। मनुष्य का मूल्य उसके चरित्र में है। विनय, उदारता, सत्यता, धैर्य, वचन प्रतिबद्धता तथा कर्त्तव्यपरायणता ये सब गुण चरित्र में आते हैं।

161. मनुष्य की विशेषता किसमें है?
A. उसके पद में
B. उसके ज्ञान में
C. उसके अच्छे विचारों में
D. उसके चरित्र में

162. मनुष्य सम्मान किस कारण से पाता है?
A. चरित्र के कारण B. पद के कारण
C. शिक्षा के कारण D. विचार के कारण

163. चत्रि में कौन-कौन से गुण आते हैं?
A. अधिक शिक्षित होना
B. सत्यता तथा वचन प्रतिबद्धता
C. अच्छे पद पर आसीन होना तथा धन कमाना
D. आर्थिक रूप से सम्पन्न होना तथा व्यवसाय करना

164. रावण की निंदा क्यों की जाती थी?
A. उसके ज्ञानी होने के कारण
B. वेदों के ज्ञाता होने के कारण
C. राक्षसी कर्मों के कारण
D. सीता हरण के कारण

165. विद्यावान का मान कब होता है?
A. जब वह आर्थिक रूप से सम्पन्न हो।
B. जब वह विनय तथा चरित्र से युक्त हो।
C. जब वह अच्छे पद पर आसीन हो।
D. जब वह उच्च जाति से संबंध रखता हो।

166. 'महात्मा' में कौन-सा समास है?
A. बहुब्रीहि समास B. अव्ययीभाव समास
C. तत्पुरुष समास D. कर्मधारय समास

167. किस शब्द में अनुस्वार के स्थान पर 'ण' लिखा जाता है?
A. पंडित B. पंक्ति
C. पंजा D. पंद्रह

168. कौन-सी भाववाचक संज्ञा है?
A. बचपन B. पानी
C. नदी D. समुद्र

169. 'क्ष' ध्वनि किसके अन्तर्गत आती है?
A. घोष वर्ण B. तालव्य
C. संयुक्त वर्ण D. अघोष वर्ण

170. इनमें से विरामचिह्न नहीं है :
A. अवतरण B. अल्पविराम
C. पूर्णविराम D. विस्मयादि बोधक

171. संज्ञा के भेद हैं :
A. पाँच B. सात
C. आठ D. दस

172. हवा का पर्यायवाची है :
A. तनुज B. बयार
C. आँधी D. तूफान

173. 'पृथ्वीराज रासो' किस काल की रचना है?
A. आदिकाल
B. भक्तिकाल
C. रीतिकाल
D. आधुनिककाल

174. प्रत्यययुक्त शब्द है :
A. आजन्म B. खुशबू
C. इकहरा D. पगड़ी

175. 'ई' और 'इ' किस प्रकार के वर्ण है?
A. दन्तोष्ठ्य B. कण्ठ्य
C. दन्त्य D. तालव्य

176. 'आँखें बिछाना' किस मुहावरे का अर्थ है?
A. धमकी देना B. बहुत इज्जत देना
C. बेइज्जती करना D. आँख बंद कर लेना

177. 'काली घटा का घमंड घटा' में अलंकार है :
A. श्लेष अलंकार B. यमक अलंकार
C. अनुप्रास अलंकार D. अर्थालंकार

178. 'आग' कौन-सा शब्द है?
A. विदेशज B. देशज
C. तद्भव D. तत्सम

179. 'पुस्तक' कौन-सा शब्द है?
A. तद्भव B. तत्सम
C. विदेशज D. देशज

180. निम्नलिखित में से किसके प्रथम तथा तृतीय चरण में 13-13 तथा द्वितीय व चतुर्थ चरण में 11-11 मात्राएँ होती हैं?
A. दोहे में B. चौपाई में
C. सोरठा में D. रोला में

ANSWERS

1. (D) **2.** (D) **3.** (A)
4. (C) **5.** (D) **6.** (A)
7. (B) **8.** (D) **9.** (B)
10. (D)

11. **(B):** $\because$ $4 + 4 = 15$
$\Rightarrow$ $4 \times 4 - 1 = 15$
and $6 + 6 = 35$
$\Rightarrow$ $6 \times 6 - 1 = 35$
Then, $8 + 8 = 63$
$\Rightarrow$ $8 \times 8 - 1 = 63$.

12. **(C):** S Y S T E M is coded as
↓ ↓ ↓ ↓ ↓ ↓
M E T S Y S
and F O R M E R is coded as
↓ ↓ ↓ ↓ ↓ ↓
R E M R O F
Then, C A R P E T would be coded as
↓ ↓ ↓ ↓ ↓ ↓
T E P R A C

13. (A)

14. **(B):** 23 + 21 = 44
Hence, there are 44 students appeared in the test.

15. **(D):** N A M E is coded as
↓ ↓ ↓ ↓
3 2 4 5
and M I N T is coded as
↓ ↓ ↓ ↓
4 1 3 7
Then, M I T E would be coded as
↓ ↓ ↓ ↓
4 1 7 5

16. **(C):** 2 9 28 65 [126]
↓ ↓ ↓ ↓ ↓
$(1)^3+1$ $(2)^3+1$ $(3)^3+1$ $(4)^3+1$ $(5)^3+1$
Hence, 126 will come in the next term in the series.

17. (B):

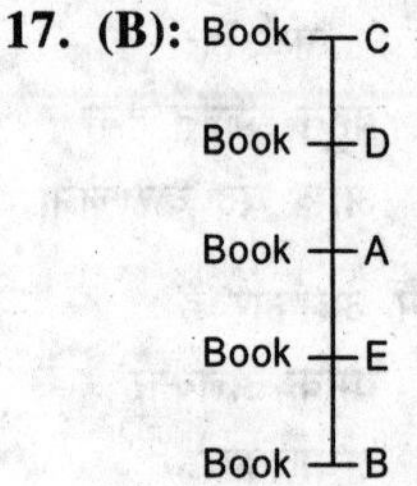

Hence, Book B is at the bottom.

18. (C): Let each type of coins = x

According to the question,

$$x+\frac{x}{2}+\frac{x}{4} = 35 \Rightarrow \frac{4x+2x+x}{4} = 35$$

$$\Rightarrow \quad 7x = 4 \times 35$$

$$\Rightarrow \quad x = \frac{4\times 35}{7} = 20$$

Hence, the number of each type of coins = 20.

19. (B):

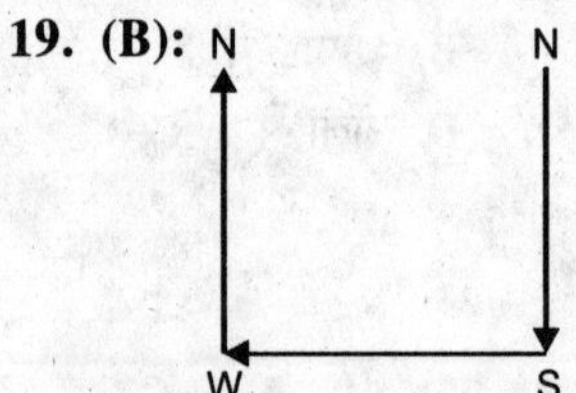

Now, man is walking in North direction.

20. (B): 27 – 57

18 – 28

36 – 96

But 25 – 63 unit digit of both numbers is not same.

Hence, the pair 25 – 63 is different from others.

21. (C):

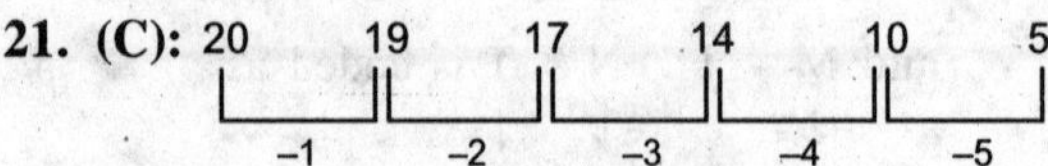

Hence, 14 will come at the blank space in the series.

22. (B):

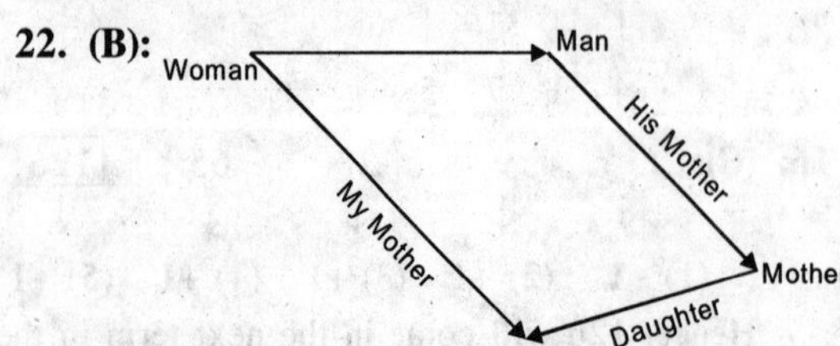

Hence, woman is sister to the man.

23. (A): 42 81 121 144

No any square 9^2 11^2 12^2

Hence, 42 is difference from others.

24. (D):

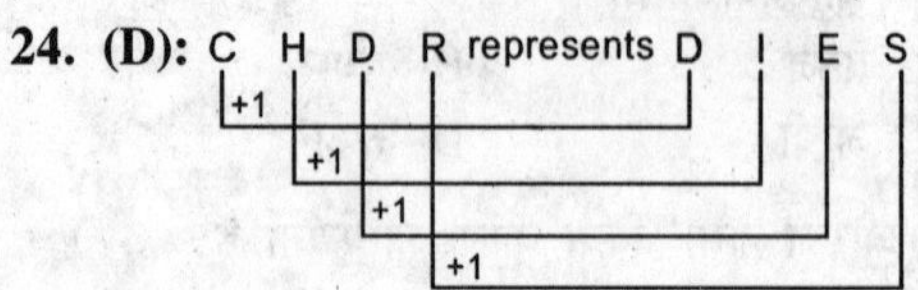

Then

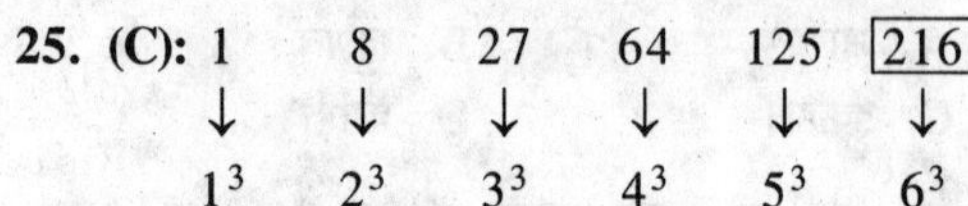

25. (C): 1 8 27 64 125 216

1^3 2^3 3^3 4^3 5^3 6^3

Hence, 216 will come at the place of blank which continues the series.

26. (D):

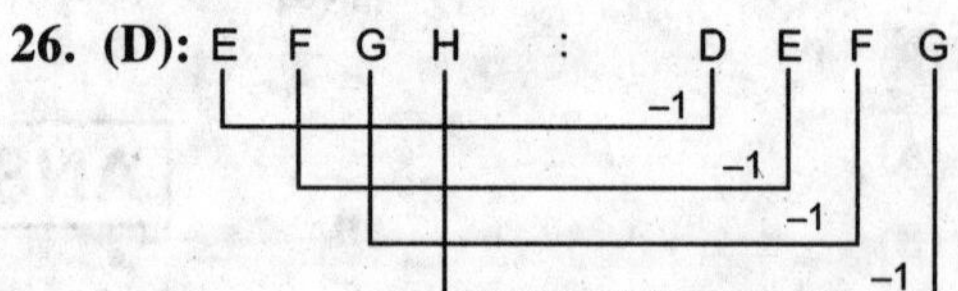

Then,

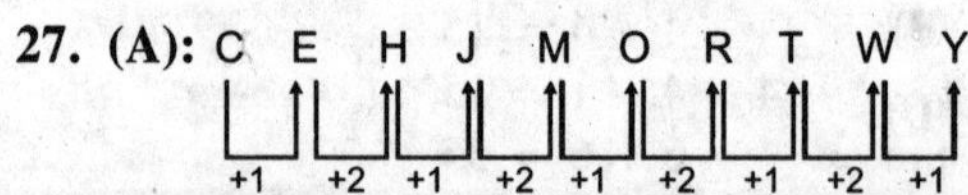

27. (A): C E H J M O R T W Y

+1 +2 +1 +2 +1 +2 +1 +2 +1

hence, WY will come at the place of blank in the series.

28. (C)

29. (C): 25 100 225 400 625

5^2 10^2 15^2 20^2 25^2

Hence, 400 fills the gap in the series.

30. (A):

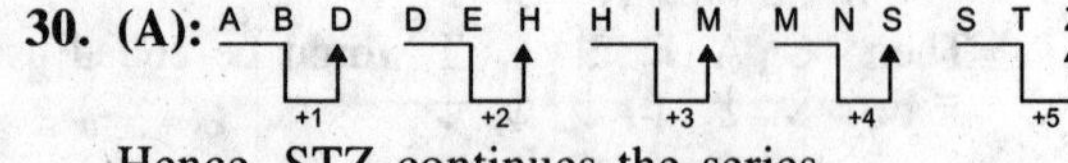

Hence, STZ continues the series.

31. (A)	**32. (A)**	**33. (B)**
34. (B)	**35. (A)**	**36. (A)**
37. (B)	**38. (A)**	**39. (A)**
40. (C)	**41. (B)**	**42. (A)**
43. (D)	**44. (C)**	**45. (A)**
46. (B)	**47. (A)**	**48. (B)**
49. (A)	**50. (C)**	**51. (C)**
52. (D)	**53. (D)**	**54. (B)**
55. (D)	**56. (A)**	**57. (B)**
58. (A)	**59. (B)**	**60. (D)**
61. (C)	**62. (A)**	**63. (A)**
64. (B)	**65. (B)**	**66. (D)**
67. (A)	**68. (D)**	**69. (B)**
70. (D)	**71. (C)**	**72. (C)**
73. (C)	**74. (C)**	**75. (C)**
76. (B)	**77. (B)**	**78. (A)**
79. (A)	**80. (C)**	**81. (C)**
82. (B)	**83. (A)**	**84. (D)**
85. (D)	**86. (A)**	**87. (C)**
88. (A)	**89. (A)**	**90. (A)**
91. (A)	**92. (C)**	**93. (C)**
94. (D)	**95. (D)**	**96. (C)**
97. (A)	**98. (B)**	**99. (B)**
100. (D)		

101. (D): $\frac{1}{0.01} = \frac{1}{\frac{1}{100}} = 100$

Hence, the largest numerical value is $\frac{1}{0.01}$.

102. (C): $5\frac{1}{2} - \left[2\frac{1}{3} \div \left\{\frac{3}{4} - \frac{1}{2}\left(\frac{2}{3} - \frac{1}{6} + \frac{1}{8}\right)\right\}\right]$

$= \frac{11}{2} - \left[\frac{7}{3} \div \left\{\frac{3}{4} - \frac{1}{2}\left(\frac{16-4+3}{24}\right)\right\}\right]$

$= \frac{11}{2} - \left[\frac{7}{3} \div \left\{\frac{3}{4} - \frac{1}{2} \times \frac{15}{24}\right\}\right]$

$= \frac{11}{2} - \left[\frac{7}{3} \div \left\{\frac{3}{4} - \frac{5}{16}\right\}\right]$

$= \frac{11}{2} - \left[\frac{7}{3} \div \left\{\frac{12-5}{16}\right\}\right]$

$= \frac{11}{2} - \left[\frac{7}{3} \div \frac{7}{16}\right] = \frac{11}{2} - \left[\frac{7}{3} \times \frac{16}{7}\right]$

$= \frac{11}{2} - \frac{16}{3} = \frac{33-32}{6} = \frac{1}{6}.$

103. (A): According to the question,

$$\frac{448+62}{x+1} - \frac{448}{x} = 2$$

$$\Rightarrow \frac{510x - 448x - 448}{x(x+1)} = 2$$

$$\Rightarrow 62x - 448 = 2x^2 + 2x$$

$$\Rightarrow 2x^2 - 60x - 448 = 0$$

$$\Rightarrow x^2 - 30x - 224 = 0$$

$$\Rightarrow (x - 16)(x - 14) = 0$$

$$\Rightarrow x = 16 \text{ or } x = 14$$

Hence, the value of $x = 16$.

104. (A): $\because$ A's salary is 50% above B's

$\therefore$ B's salary below A's $= \left(\frac{100 \times x}{100 + x}\right)\%$

$= \left(\frac{100 \times 50}{100 + 50}\right)\%$

$= \left(\frac{100 \times 50}{150}\right)\% = \frac{100}{3}\%$

$= 33\frac{1}{3}\%.$

105. (C): C.P. of 1 kg blended variety

$= \frac{7 \times 150 + 3 \times 200}{10}$

$= \frac{1650}{10} = ₹\ 165$

Profit $= 181.50 - 165 = ₹\ 16.50$

Profit % $= \frac{16.50}{165} \times 100 = 10\%.$

106. (B): $\because$ C.P. = 900

gain = 10%

$\therefore$ S.P. = $\frac{110}{100}\times 900$ = ₹ 990

Now, Discount = 10%

$\therefore$ S.P. = ₹ 90

When S.P. ₹ 90 then M.P. = ₹ 100

When S.P. ₹ 990 then M.P.

= ₹ $\frac{100}{90}\times 990$ = ₹ 1100

Hence, Marked price of the article = ₹ 1100.

107. (B): $A = P\left(1+\frac{r}{100}\right)^t$

$\Rightarrow \quad 1331 = 1000\left(1+\frac{10}{100}\right)^t$

$\Rightarrow \quad \frac{1331}{1000} = \left(1+\frac{10}{100}\right)^t$

$\Rightarrow \quad \left(\frac{11}{10}\right)^3 = \left(1+\frac{10}{100}\right)^t$

$\Rightarrow \quad \left(\frac{11}{10}\right)^3 = \left(\frac{11}{10}\right)^t \Rightarrow t = 3$

Hence, the period of time = 3 years.

108. (*)

109. (C): Let the usual speed of the plane = x km/hr.

According to the question

$$\frac{1500}{x} - \frac{1500}{x+250} = \frac{1}{2}$$

$\Rightarrow \quad \frac{1500(x+250-x)}{x(x+250)} = \frac{1}{2}$

$\Rightarrow \quad 3000 \times 250 = x^2 + 250x$

$\Rightarrow \quad x^2 + 250x - 750000 = 0$

$\Rightarrow x^2 + 1000x - 750x - 750000 = 0$

$\Rightarrow x(x + 1000) - 750(x + 1000) = 0$

$\Rightarrow \quad (x - 750)(x + 1000) = 0$

$\Rightarrow \quad x = 750$ or $x = -1000$

Hence, usual speed of the plane = 750 km/hr.

110. (D): $\because$ $\sec\theta + \tan\theta = m$ ...(*i*)

We know that

$\sec^2\theta - \tan^2\theta = 1$

$\Rightarrow (\sec\theta + \tan\theta)(\sec\theta - \tan\theta) = 1$

$\Rightarrow m(\sec\theta - \tan\theta) = 1$

$\Rightarrow \quad \sec\theta - \tan\theta = \frac{1}{m}$ ...(*ii*)

Adding (*i*) and (*ii*)

$\sec\theta + \tan\theta + \sec\theta - \tan\theta = m+\frac{1}{m}$

$\Rightarrow \quad 2\sec\theta = \left(m+\frac{1}{m}\right)$

$\Rightarrow \quad \sec\theta = \frac{1}{2}\left(m+\frac{1}{m}\right)$

Subtracting (*ii*) from (*i*) then we get

$\tan\theta = \frac{1}{2}\left(m-\frac{1}{m}\right)$

Dividing we get,

$\sin\theta = \frac{m^2-1}{m^2+1}.$

111. (A): $2\left(\frac{\sin 43^\circ}{\cos 47^\circ}\right)^2 - \frac{\cot 30^\circ}{\tan 60^\circ} - \sqrt{2}\sin 45^\circ$

$= 2\left[\frac{\sin 43^\circ}{\sin 43^\circ}\right]^2 - \frac{\sqrt{3}}{\sqrt{3}} - \sqrt{2}\times\frac{1}{\sqrt{2}}$

$= 2 - 1 - 1 = 2 - 2 = 0.$

112. (C):

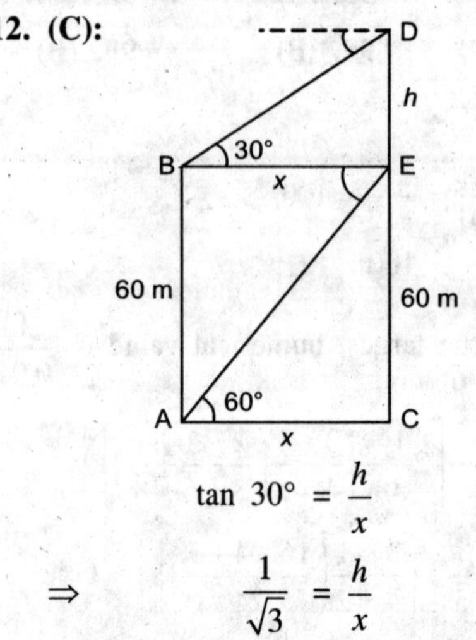

$\tan 30^\circ = \frac{h}{x}$

$\Rightarrow \quad \frac{1}{\sqrt{3}} = \frac{h}{x}$

$$\Rightarrow \quad x = \sqrt{3}h \quad ...(i)$$

$$\tan 60^\circ = \frac{60}{x}$$

$$\Rightarrow \quad \sqrt{3} = \frac{60}{x}$$

$$\Rightarrow \quad \sqrt{3}x = 60^\circ$$

$$\Rightarrow \quad x = \frac{60}{\sqrt{3}} \quad ...(ii)$$

From (*i*) and (*ii*)

$$\sqrt{3}h = \frac{60}{\sqrt{3}}$$

$$\Rightarrow \quad 3h = 60 \Rightarrow h = 20 \text{ m}$$

Hence, required difference

$$= 80 \text{ m} - 60 \text{ m} = 20 \text{ m}.$$

113. **(D):** Let sides of triangle be $3x$, $4x$ and $5x$

According to the question

$$3x + 4x + 5x = 144$$

$$\Rightarrow \quad 12x = 144 \Rightarrow x = 12$$

$\therefore$ Sides are $3 \times 12 = 36$ cm

$4 \times 12 = 48$ cm

and $5 \times 12 = 60$ cm

$$\text{Now,} \quad S = \frac{a+b+c}{2}$$

$$= \frac{36+48+60}{2} = \frac{144}{2} = 72$$

$$\text{Area of triangle} = \sqrt{S(S-a)(S-b)(S-c)}$$

$$= \sqrt{72(72-36)(72-48)(72-60)}$$

$$= \sqrt{72 \times 36 \times 24 \times 12}$$

$$= \sqrt{2 \times 36 \times 36 \times 2 \times 12 \times 12}$$

$$= 36 \times 12 \times 2 = 864 \text{ cm}^2.$$

114. **(B):** In 60 minutes the minute hand makes angle

$$= 360^\circ$$

In 35 minutes the minute hand makes angle

$$= \frac{360}{60} \times 35 = 210^\circ$$

$$\text{Area of sector} = \frac{210}{360} \times \frac{22}{7} \times 12 \times 12$$

$$= 22 \times 12 = 264 \text{ cm}^2$$

Hence, the area of the face of the clock described by the minute hand = 264 cm^2.

115. **(A):** Volume of the cone = Volume of sphere

$$\Rightarrow \frac{1}{3}\pi(2.1)^2 \times 8.4 = \frac{4}{3}\pi r^3$$

$$\Rightarrow \quad \frac{21}{10} \times \frac{21}{10} \times \frac{84}{10} = 4r^3$$

$$\Rightarrow \quad \frac{21 \times 21 \times 21}{10 \times 10 \times 10} = r^3$$

$$\Rightarrow \quad r = \frac{21}{10} = 2.1$$

Hence, the radius of sphere = 2.1 cm.

116. **(C):** Volume of rectangular tank

$$= 50 \times 44 \times \frac{21}{100} \text{ m}^3$$

$$= 22 \times 21 \text{ m}^3$$

Volume of water flowing through a pipe

$$= \frac{22}{7} \times \frac{7}{100} \times \frac{7}{100} \times 15000 \text{ m}^3 \text{ in 1 hr}$$

$$= 11 \times 7 \times 3 \text{ m}^3$$

According to the question

$$11 \times 7 \times 3 \times x = 22 \times 21$$

[Where x = time taken]

$$\Rightarrow \quad x = \frac{22 \times 21}{11 \times 7 \times 3} = 2 \text{ hrs.}$$

Hence, the required time taken = 2 hrs.

117. **(A):** $\text{Mode} = l + \left(\frac{f - f_1}{2f - f_1 - f_2}\right) \times h$

$$\Rightarrow \quad 36 = 30 + \left(\frac{16 - f_1}{32 - f_1 - 12}\right) \times 10$$

$$\Rightarrow \quad 6 = \frac{160 - 10f_1}{20 - f_1}$$

$$\Rightarrow \quad 120 - 6f_1 = 160 - 10f_1$$

$$\Rightarrow \quad 10f_1 - 6f_1 = 160 - 120$$

$$\Rightarrow \quad 4f_1 = 40$$

$$\Rightarrow \quad f_1 = 10$$

Hence, the missing frequency = 10.

118. (B):

119. (A): 105, 112, 119, ..., 994

$$994 = 105 + (n - 1)7$$

$[\because n\text{th term} = a + (n-1)d]$

$$\Rightarrow \quad n = 128$$

$$S_n = \frac{n}{2}\{2a+(n-1)d\}$$

$$= \frac{128}{2}\{2 \times 105 + (128-1) \times 7\}$$

$$= 64\{210 + 889\}$$

$$= 1099 \times 64 = 70366$$

Hence, the sum of all the three digit natural numbers which are multiples of 7 = 70366.

120. (D): Since, points are collinear. Hence, area = 0

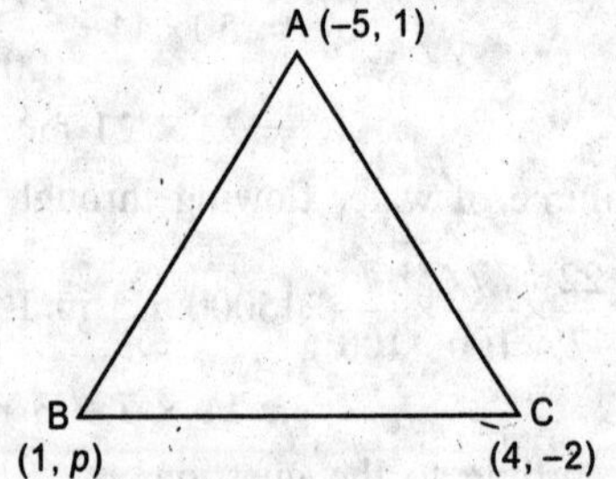

Area of triangle

$$= \frac{1}{2}[x_1(y_2 - y_3)x_2 + (y_3 - y_1) + x_3(y_1 - y_2)]$$

$$0 = \frac{1}{2}[-5(p+2) + 1(-2-1) + 4(1-p)]$$

$$\Rightarrow \quad 0 = [-5p - 10 - 3 + 4 - 4p]$$

$$\Rightarrow \quad 0 = -9p - 9$$

$$\Rightarrow \quad 0 = -9(p + 1)$$

$$\Rightarrow \quad p + 1 = 0$$

$$\Rightarrow \quad p = -1.$$

121. (B)	**122. (B)**	**123. (C)**
124. (A)	**125. (C)**	**126. (D)**
127. (A)	**128. (A)**	**129. (C)**
130. (B)	**131. (C)**	**132. (B)**
133. (A)	**134. (D)**	**135. (A)**
136. (C)	**137. (A)**	**138. (D)**
139. (B)	**140. (B)**	**141. (C)**
142. (A)	**143. (A)**	**144. (C)**
145. (A)	**146. (*)**	**147. (B)**
148. (A)	**149. (C)**	**150. (A)**
151. (C)	**152. (B)**	**153. (B)**
154. (B)	**155. (B)**	**156. (C)**
157. (D)	**158. (A)**	**159. (C)**
160. (D)	**161. (D)**	**162. (A)**
163. (B)	**164. (C)**	**165. (B)**
166. (D)	**167. (A)**	**168. (A)**
169. (C)	**170. (A)**	**171. (A)**
172. (B)	**173. (A)**	**174. (C)**
175. (D)	**176. (B)**	**177. (B)**
178. (C)	**179. (B)**	**180. (A)**

Previous Paper (Solved)

IGNOU B.Ed. ENTRANCE EXAM 2021*

PART-A

Section-I : General English Comprehension

Directions (Qs. No. 1-10): *Read the following passage carefully and choose the best answer out of the four choices given after each question that follows:*

Nature is like business. Business sense dictates that we guard our capital and live from the interest. Nature's capital is the enormous diversity of living things. Without it, we cannot feed ourselves, cure ourselves of illness or provide industry with the raw materials of wealth creation. Professor Edward Wilson of Harvard University, says: "The folly our descendants are least likely to forgive us is the ongoing loss of genetic and species diversity. This will take millions of years to correct."

Only 150 plant species have ever been widely cultivated. Yet over 75,000 edible plants are known in the wild. In a hungry world, with a population growing by 90 million each year, so much wasted potential is tragic. Medicines from the wild are worth around 40 billion dollars a year. Over 5000 species are known to yield chemicals with cancer fighting potential. Scientists currently estimate that the total number of species in the world is between 10-30 million with only around 1.4 million identified.

The web of life is torn when human beings exploit natural resources in short-sighted ways. The trade in tropical hardwoods can destroy whole forests to extract just a few commercially attractive specimens. Bad agricultural practices trigger 24 billion tonnes of top soil erosion a year losing the equivalent of 9 million tonnes of grain output. Cutting this kind of unsuitable exploitation and instituting "sustainable utilization" will help turn the environmental crisis around.

1. Why does the author compare 'nature' to 'business'?
A. Because of the capital depletion in nature and business
B. Because of the similarity with which one should use both
C. Because of the same interest level yield
D. Because of the diversity of the various capital inputs

2. "The folly our descendants are least likely to forgive us"—What is the business equivalent of the folly the author is referring to?
A. Reducing the profit margin
B. Not pumping some money out of profits into the business
C. Eroding the capital base of the business
D. Putting interest on capital back into the business

3. Which of the following statements is ***false*** in the context of the passage?
A. The diversity of plant life is essential for human existence
B. Scientists know the usefulness of most plant specie
C. Chemicals for cancer treatment are available from plants
D. There are around ten times the plant species undiscovered as compared to the discovered ones

4. Which of the following correctly reflects the opinion of the author to take care of hunger in the world?

* Exam held on 11 April, 2021.

A. Increase the number of species of edible plants being cultivated
B. Increase cultivation of the 150 species presently under cultivation
C. Increase the cultivation of medicinal plants
D. Increase the potential of the uncultivated edible plants

5. Which of the following is mentioned as the immediate cause for the destruction of forests?
A. Soil Erosion
B. Destruction of Habitat.
C. Cutting of Trees
D. Bad Agricultural Practices

6. The author gives two examples of 'unsuitable exploitation'. These are:
A. Bad agricultural practices and soil erosion
B. Bad agricultural practices and trade in tropical hardwoods
C. Trade in tropical hardwoods and soil erosion
D. Trade in tropical hardwoods and losing tonnes of grain output

7. The passage is about
A. Business
B. Nature
C. Environmental Crisis
D. Agricultural Practices

8. What, according to the author, is 'environmental crisis'?
A. Trade in tropical hardwoods
B. Bad agricultural practices
C. Soil erosion
D. The ongoing loss of genetic and species diversity

9. Which of the following words is nearly the same in meaning as the words 'wasted' as used in the passage?
A. Consumed B. Squandered
C. Unutilised D. Unprofitable

10. Which of the following words is nearly opposite in meaning to 'cutting' as used in the passage?
A. Uniting B. Avoiding
C. Joining D. Combining

Section-II : Logical and Analytical Reasoning

11. Which of the following is the next term in the series?
PAT, PEN, PIT, PON, ?
A. PET B. POT
C. PUT D. PAN

12. Which of the following continues the series?
2, 4, 6, 9, 12, ?
A. 14 B. 15
C. 16 D. 17

13. Which of the following fills the gap in the series?
25, 49, 81, ?, 169
A. 100 B. 64
C. 121 D.144

14. Rohit said to a girl, "Your mother is the only daughter of my mother-in-law." How is Rohit related to the girl?
A. Father B. Uncle
C. Brother D. Cousin

15. In a code language, STAR is written as RATS, then ROUT will be written as:
A. TOUR B. TORU
C. ROTU D. TUOR

16. In a code language 25 means, 'Green Apple', 35 means 'Red Apple' and 34 means 'Red Cherry'. What is the code for 'Green Chery'?
A. 23 B. 24
C. 34 D. 43

17. Father said to the son, "When you were born, I was of your present age." If the father is 36 years old now, how old was the son 7 years ago?
A. 11 years B. 13 years
C. 15 years D. 17 years

18. A circular coin is placed on a plane surface. How many more coins of the same size can be placed around it so that each touches the central coin and adjacent coins?

A. 4 B. 6
C. 8 D. 10

19. From a starting point, a man moves 3 km north, then turns west and walks 2 km, again turns back and walks 1 km and then moves 5 km towards east. How far is he now from starting point?
A. 5 km B. 8 km
C. 10 km D. 12 km

20. If 3rd of December is Saturday, then the last day of the month would be:
A. Monday B. Saturday
C. Thursday D. Sunday

21. Five houses A to E are in a row. A is to the right of B, E is to the left of C and right of A, and B is to the right of D. Which house is in the middle?
A. D B. C
C. B D. A

22. The medians of a triangle ABC intersect at D. How many triangles are formed in the resulting figures?
A. 18 B. 16
C. 12 D. 8

23. If 6 + 7 is 43 and 5 + 6 is 31, then 4 + 5 is:
A. 9 B. 20
C. 21 D. 25

24. If 213 is written as 6 and 432 is written as 9, then 543 would be written as:
A. 10 B. 11
C. 12 D. 13

25. If order of first 13 English alphabets is reversed, then which letter would ***not*** change its position?
A. E B. F
C. G D. H

26. Which of the following fills the gap in the series?
1, 2, 3, 1, 4, 9, 1, ?, 27
A. 5 B. 6
C. 7 D. 8

27. The population of a town consists of 45% men and 40% women. If the number of children is 30,000, then the total population of the town is:
A. 2 lakhs B. 3 lakhs
C. 4.5 lakhs D. 6 lakhs

28. Which of the following words appears first of all in the dictionary?
A. Compensate B. Compassionate
C. Compression D. Competition

29. Preeti ranks 38th in her class both from top and bottom. How many students are there in the class?
A. 77 B. 76
C. 75 D. 74

30. A square is divided into 16 equal parts by intersecting lines parallel to its sides. How many squares are formed in the resulting figure?
A. 16 B. 28
C. 30 D. 36

Section-III : Educational and General Awareness

31. Kisan Diwas is celebrated on:
A. October 23 B. November 23
C. December 23 D. September 23

32. "A Bunch of Old Letters" was written by:
A. Jawaharlal Nehru B. Mahatma Gandhi
C. Abdul Kalam D. Morarji Desai

33. Who is known as 'Man of Destiny'?
A. Adolf Hitler
B. George Bernard Shaw
C. Napoleon
D. Shakespeare

34. Mission Innovation aims to:
A. accelerate clean energy innovation to address climate change
B. promote indigeous development of Nano Satellites

C. adopt new methods of agriculture
D. adopt new methods of water harvesting

35. Who was the Viceroy at the time of Quit India Movement?
A. Lord Warren Hastings
B. Lord Dalhousie
C. Lord Curzon
D. Lord Linlithgow

36. The 'Red Line campaign' started by India is related to which of the following field?
A. Fencing of India-Pakistan Border
B. Zero open defecation
C. Curb irrational use of antibiotics
D. Zero corruption

37. The Union Budget is presented under which Article of the Constitution of India?
A. 110 B. 111
C. 112 D. 113

38. When was the Indian Post Office Act passed?
A. 1852 B. 1853
C. 1854 D. 1898

39. Which event occurred first in India's Independence struggle?
A. Simon Commission
B. Non-Cooperation Movement
C. Gandhi-Irwin Pact
D. Tripura Adhiveshan of Congress

40. The concept of Public Interest Litigation originated in:
A. UK B. Canada
C. USA D. South Africa

41. The country which levied a tax on WhatsApp and Facebook in the year 2018 is:
A. Uganda B. Zambia
C. Zimbabwe D. Tanzania

42. According to the World Bank, which country remained the top recipient of remittances in 2018?
A. India B. China
C. Mexico D. Philippines

43. The Tropic of Capricorn does ***not*** pass through:
A. Argentina B. Bolivia
C. Brazil D. Chile

44. Similipal Tiger Reserve is situated in the State of:
A. Odisha B. Madhya Pradesh
C. West Bengal D. Karnataka

45. In which State is Silent Valley situated?
A. Tamil Nadu B. Kerala
C. Assam D. Arunachal Pradesh

46. A document called "The Future We Want" relates to which of the following organizations?
A. United Nations Conference of Sustainable Development
B. Global Environment Facility
C. United Nations Framework Convention on Climate Change
D. Convention on Biological Diversity

47. The Spratly Islands are located in which of the following seas?
A. The Caspian Sea
B. The Black Sea
C. The Mediterranean Sea
D. The South China Sea

48. Tapti river originates from which district of Madhya Pradesh?
A. Betul B. Balaghat
C. Chhindwara D. Hoshangabad

49. Which of the following monuments in India is ***not*** a world heritage?
A. Fatehpur Sikri
B. Ajanta and Ellora
C. Khajuraho
D. Jantar Mantar in Delhi

50. 'Life Divine' is written by:
A. Aurobindo Ghosh
B. V.V. Giri
C. Amrita Pritam
D. V.D. Savarkar

51. Which writ is issued by the High Court to the lower courts to stop legal actions?
A. Habeas corpus B. Prohibition
C. Quo warranto D. Certiorari

52. Return of income is submitted under which Section of the Income Tax Act?
A. Section 138(1) B. Section 142(1)
C. Section 139(1) D. Section 129(1)

53. National Knowledge Commission was headed by:
A. Ashok Ganguly B. P. Balaram
C. Sam Pitroda D. Deepak Nayyar

54. Which of the following is the apex body in the area of Teacher Education in India?
A. UGC B. NIEPA
C. NCTE D. NCERT

55. The idea of Four Pillars of Education was suggested by:
A. UNICEF B. UNESCO
C. UNDP D. UNITAR

Section-IV : Teaching-Learning and The School

56. RTE Act, 2009 envisages all children free admission to:
A. Sainik schools
B. Army schools
C. Neighbourhood schools
D. Navodaya schools

57. "Learning Without Burden" is the report submitted by a committee under the chairmanship of:
A. Prof. Amrit Desai
B. Prof. Amrik Singh
C. Prof. Ved Prakash
D. Prof. Yashpal

58. What is the verbal component of a poster?
A. Image B. Caption
C. Graph D. Table

59. Which of the following learner characteristics impacts teaching the most?
A. Prior experience of the learner
B. Educational status of the parents of the learner
C. Peer group of learner
D. Family size from which the learner comes

60. National Education Day is observed on November 11 every year in the memory of:
A. Sarvepalli Radhakrishnan
B. Maulana Abul Kalam Azad
C. Zakir Hussain
D. Mahatma Gandhi

61. Determining the aims of Education is the responsibility of:
(*a*) Parents (*b*) Teachers
(*c*) Students (*d*) Society

Select the correct answer from the codes given below:
A. (*b*) and (*c*)
B. (*b*), (*c*) and (*d*)
C. only (*a*)
D. (*a*), (*b*), (*c*) and (*d*)

62. Immediate outcome of teaching is related to:
A. desirable changes in the behaviour of students.
B. development of personality of students.
C. moral development of students.
D. enhancing employability.

63. Discipline in the class essentially helps to:
A. establish teacher's authority.
B. make children understand that indiscipline is punishable.
C. make classroom activities organised and orderly.
D. adhere to the time-table.

64. Which of the following is ***not*** desirable for effective teaching?
A. Questioning
B. Using teaching aids
C. Following textbook rigidly
D. Encouraging student talk

65. What are the characteristics of Continuous and Comprehensive Evaluation?
(*a*) Multiple tests
(*b*) Criteria-based tests
(*c*) Assessment for learning
(*d*) Assessing scholastic and co-scholastic aspects

Select the correct answer from the codes given below:

A. (*a*), (*b*) and (*d*)
B. (*b*) and (*d*)
C. (*a*), (*b*) and (*c*)
D. (*a*), (*b*), (*c*) and (*d*)

66. Which one of the following statements is correct in the context of multiple choice type questions?

A. These are objective.
B. These are subjective.
C. These do not need appropriate distractors.
D. These do not have a fixed answer.

67. The key component of teacher-student communication during teaching is:

A. Humour
B. Learners' problems
C. Subject content
D. Motivating statements

68. Which among the following is a teacher-centred method?

A. Project B. Lecture
C. Group work D. Brainstorming

69. A teacher as a facilitator is one who:

A. delivers lectures.
B. explains concepts and principles.
C. gives printed notes to students.
D. inspires students to learn.

70. Which one of the following is considered a sign of motivated teaching?

A. Students asking questions
B. Maximum attendance of students
C. Silence in the classroom
D. Students taking notes

71. In the classroom, the teacher sends the message either as words or images. The students are:

A. Encoders B. Decoders
C. Noise eliminators D. Senders

72. CIET stands for:

A. Centre for Integrated Education and Technology
B. Central Institute for Engineering and Technology
C. Central Institute for Educational Technology
D. Centre for Integrated Evaluation Techniques

73. An effective classroom environment has:

A. No teching aids
B. Lively student-teacher interaction
C. Silence
D. Strict discipline

74. In which period did India become a centre of higher learning with Nalanda and Taxila?

A. Chola period
B. Gupta period
C. Harappa Civilization period
D. Mughal period

75. Curriculum is:

A. same as syllabus.
B. content to be taught
C. overall educational activities within and outside the school.
D. only teaching, no other activities.

76. What is the full form of SWAYAM?

A. Study Webs of Active-Learning for Young Aspiring Minds
B. Study Webs for Accustomed Learning for Young Aspiring Minds
C. Study Ways of Active-Learning for Young Aspiring Minds
D. Study Webs of Actual Learning for Young Aspiring Minds

77. Operation Blackboard was launched under National Policy on Education (1986) to:

A. provide schools with adequate number of blackboards.
B. create awareness for using blackboards.
C. provide minimum essential facilities to the schools.
D. use blackboard effectively in the teaching-learning process.

78. Effectiveness of teaching has to be judged in terms of:

A. course coverage.
B. aims of teaching.
C. learning outcomes of students.
D. use of teaching aids in the classroom.

79. Good teaching does ***not*** involve:
A. Guiding
B. Motivating
C. Explaining
D. Encouraging rote learning

80. Project method is based on the principle of:
A. Learning by play-way
B. Learning by doing
C. Learning from teacher
D. Learning from books

PART-B

Section-V : (i) Science

81. Cause of Acid rain is:
A. Release of oxides of Carbon, Nitrogen and Sulphur in the atmosphere due to burning of fossil fuels.
B. Friction among clouds causes electric charges
C. Humidity produces acid vapour
D. Sun heats up the clouds

82. Which of the following is acidic in nature?
A. Common salt solution
B. Pure water
C. Lemon juice
D. Baking soda solution

83. What is the volume of 16 g of oxygen at Standard Temperature and Pressure (S.T.P.)?
A. 22.4 litres B. 11.2 litres
C. 22.4 cm^3 D. 11.2 cm^3

84. Mass number of an element is X and it has 11 electrons. The number of neutrons in it is:
A. X + 11 B. X
C. 11 D. X – 11

85. An example of a chemical change is:
A. Conversion of water into ice
B. Conversion of water into steam
C. Heating of a resistor on passing current
D. Conversion of milk into curd

86. A man is 10 feet away from his image in a plane mirror fixed in a wall. He walks 3 feet towards the mirror. What is the distance between him and his image now?
A. 2 feet B. 3 feet
C. 4 feet D. 6 feet

87. If a ray of light is going from air to glass and angle of incidence is i and angle of refraction is r we have:
A. $i < r$
B. $\sin i = \sin r$
C. $\frac{\sin i}{\sin r} = \text{Constant}$
D. $\sin i \times \sin r = \text{Constant}$

88. Two resistance of two ohms each are joined in parallel. What is the equivalent resistance?
A. 1 ohm B. 2 ohms
C. 3 ohms D. 4 ohms

89. What unbalanced force in Newton (N) will accelerate a 25 kg body from 5 m/s to 10 m/s in 5 seconds?
A. 1 N B. 5 N
C. 25 N D. 50 N

90. Watt is the unit of:
A. Energy B. Work
C. Force D. Power

91. The planet nearest to Earth in our Solar System is:
A. Mercury B. Venus
C. Mars D. Jupiter

92. Alpha particles are:
A. Positively charged
B. Negatively charged
C. Not charged
D. Same as photons

93. Night blindness is caused due to:
A. Deficiency of Vitamin 'A'

B. Deficiency of Vitamin 'B'
C. Deficiency of Vitamin 'C'
D. Excess of Vitamin 'A'

94. Why is a flash of lightning seen before the sound of thunder is heard?
A. Because light travels faster than sound
B. Because light is produced much earlier
C. Because sound is obstructed by clouds
D. Because sound is produced farther away

95. The disease 'Jaundice' is associated with:
A. Eyes B. Lungs
C. Gums D. Liver

96. It is the process by which green plants manufacture food in the form of carbohydrates in the presence of sunlight.
A. Osmosis B. Radioactivity
C. Photosynthesis D. Ecology

97. Which one of the following is ***not*** an essential micronutrient for plants?
A. Zinc B. Copper
C. Boron D. Sodium

98. What is the measure of acidity of a liquid?
A. Boiling Point B. Freezing Point
C. pH D. Density

99. Which one of the following is also known as 'Laughing Gas'?
A. Helium B. Nitrous oxide
C. Nitrogen dioxide D. Nitrogen

100. Respiration involves exchange of:
A. Oxygen and Carbon dioxide
B. Oxygen and Nitrogen
C. Nitrogen and Carbon dioxide
D. Hydrogen and Nitrogen

Section-V : (ii) Mathematics

101. The sum of the odd numbers between 0 and 50 is:
A. 575 B. 625
C. 675 D. 725

102. Ten observations have been arranged in ascending order as under:

29, 32, 48, 50, x, $x + 2$, 72, 78, 84, 95

The median is 63. The value of x is:
A. 60 B. 61
C. 62 D. 64

103. 75th Percentile coincides with:
A. Median B. Mode
C. First Quartile D. Third Quartile

104. Mean, Median and Mode coincide in:
A. Positively skewed curve
B. Negatively skewed curve
C. Normal probability curve
D. Leptokurtic curve

105. The value of sec A(1 – sin A) (sec A + tan A) is:
A. 0 B. 1
C. sin A D. cos A

106. The angle of elevation of the top of a building from the foot of the tower is 30° and the angle of elevation of the top of the tower from the foot of the building is 60°. The tower is 50 m high. The height of the building is:
A. $16\frac{2}{3}$ m B. $16\frac{1}{3}$ m
C. $14\frac{2}{3}$ m D. $14\frac{1}{3}$ m

107. In ΔABC, $AB = 6\sqrt{3}$ cm, $AC = 12$ cm and $BC = 6$ cm. The angle B is:
A. 45° B. 60°
C. 90° D. 120°

108. 8 men can dig a pit in 20 days. If a man works half as much more as a boy, 4 men and 9 boys will dig a similar pit in:
A. 12 days B. 14 days
C. 16 days D. 18 days

109. 12 copies of a book were sold for ₹ 1,800 thereby gaining the cost price of 3 copies. The cost price of a copy is:
A. ₹ 100 B. ₹ 120
C. ₹ 140 D. ₹ 160

110. A wooden box is 110 cm × 90 cm × 40 cm is size. Packets 22 cm in length, 15 cm in breadth and 6 cm in height are to be placed in it. How many of these can be placed in the box?

A. 160 B. 180
C. 200 D. 220

111. The approximate value of:

0.4 × 0.4 + 0.04 × 0.04 + 0.04 is:

A. 0.16 B. 0.20
C. 0.44 D. 0.46

112. Two trains 126 m and 114 m long are running in opposite directions, one at the rate of 30 kmph and another one at 42 kmph. From the moment they meet, the will cross each other in:

A. 13 seconds B. 12 seconds
C. 11 seconds D. 10 seconds

113. A student passed in first division securing 440 marks, but missed distinction marks of 75% by 10 marks. The maximum marks for the exam was:

A. 500 B. 550
C. 700 D. 600

114. A sum of money amounts to ₹ 1,800 in 2 years and ₹ 2,592 in 4 years at a compound interest rate of:

A. 10% B. $12\frac{1}{2}\%$
C. 15% D. 20%

115. The HCF and LCM of two number are 16 and 672 respectively. If one of the numbers is 112, what is the other number?

A. 96 B. 192
C. 80 D. 48

116. A man's salary was decreased by 30% and then increased by 30%. The net change is:

A. 10% increase B. 10% decrease
C. 9% decrease D. 9% increase

117. The average salary of male employees in a firm is ₹ 5,200 and that of female employees is ₹ 4,200. The mean salary of all employees is ₹ 5,000. The percentage of female employees is:

A. 15% B. 20%
C. 25% D. 30%

118. How much would A get if a sum of ₹ 890 is to be divided amongst A, B and C such that A : B is 4 : 5 and B : C is 6 : 7?

A. ₹ 160 B. ₹ 200
C. ₹ 220 D. ₹ 240

119. A father's age is 5 times the age of his daughter. It was 9 times, five years ago. How old is the father now?

A. 45 years B. 50 years
C. 55 years D. 60 years

120. A two-digit number is less than 30. The sum of its digits is 7 and their multiplication product is 10. The number is:

A. 16 B. 24
C. 25 D. 28

Section-V : (iii) Social Science

121. Which of the following periodicals is ***not*** correctly matched with the editor?

A. *Bande Mataram : Aurobindo Ghosh*
B. *Sandhya : Barindra Ghosh*
C. *New India : Bipin Chandra Pal*
D. *Yugantar : Bhupendranath Datta*

122. An instrument used to record the motion of the ground during an earthquake is:

A. Seismometer B. Seismogram
C. Seismology D. Seismograph

123. The idea of 'Directive Principles of State Policy' in the Indian Constitution is taken from the Constitution of:

A. Ireland B. Australia
C. Britain D. USA

124. The idea of "Lokpal" bill is taken from:

A. Britain
B. America
C. Scandinavian countries
D. France

125. Who was the First Woman President of Indian National Congress?
A. Sarojini Naidu
B. Rajkumari Amrita Kaur
C. Annie Besant
D. Vijaya Lakshmi Pandit

126. Mahatma Gandhi gave the title of 'Sardar' to Vallabhbhai Patel for his great organisational skill in the:
A. Kheda Satyagraha
B. Bardoli Satyagraha
C. Salt Satyagraha
D. Champaran Satyagraha

127. Andaman wild pig is an example of:
A. Vulnerable species B. Endemic species
C. Rare species D. Extinct species

128. Which country has the highest productivity of rice?
A. India B. China
C. Sri Lanka D. Banlgadesh

129. The main source of National Income in India is ....
A. Primary Sector B. Secondary Sector
C. Service Sector D. Allied Sector

130. The central banking functions are performed by the:
A. Central Bank of India
B. Reserve Bank of India
C. State Bank of India
D. Punjab National Bank

131. The First Battle of Panipat was in the year:
A. 1520 B. 1526
C. 1530 D. 1535

132. Who was popularly known as the "Parrot of India"?
A. Amir Khusro
B. Khwaja Nasir
C. Parthasarathi Mishra
D. Chand Bardai

133. The Capital of the kingdom of Maharaja Ranjit Singh was:
A. Lahore B. Ambala
C. Patiala D. Amritsar

134. Of the four events mentioned below, which was the last to take place?
A. The Cripps Mission
B. Simla Conference
C. Cabinet Mission Plan
D. The Ratings Mutiny

135. Which dynasty ruled during the years 1206 – 1290 in India?
A. Mauryan dynasty B. Slave dynasty
C. Gupta dynasty D. Chalukya dynasty

136. The organization that negotiates trade agreements between almost all of the nations in the world is:
A. WTO B. UNO
C. UNDP D. IMF

137. The lowest layer of the Earth's atmosphere is:
A. Stratosphere B. Mesosphere
C. Troposphere D. Thermosphere

138. Black soil is most suitable for the cultivation of:
A. Paddy B. Maize
C. Cotton D. Wheat

139. Which of the following rivers is called as Dakshina Ganga?
A. Kaveri B. Krishna
C. Godavari D. Tungabhadra

140. A Public Service Commission was established in India for the first time by:
A. Indian Council Act, 1892
B. The Government of India Act, 1919
C. The Act of 1909
D. The Government of India Act, 1935

Section-V : (iv) English

Directions (Q. Nos. 141-145): *Choose the word that is nearest in meaning to the underlined word.*

141. Being a big businessman, Gita's father is very <u>affluent</u>.
A. Prosperous B. Poor
C. Talkative D. Intelligent

142. The <u>massacre</u> of Kashmiri Pandits in 1990 was tragic.

A. Stabbing
B. Slaughter
C. Murder
D. Genocide

143. The young boys were reprimanded for watching obscene videos.
A. Objectionable
B. Vulgar
C. Displeasing
D. Condemnable

144. He pilfered many precious things from the palace.
A. Destroyed
B. Damaged
C. Stole
D. Snatched

145. Resilience is a desirable human trait.
A. Flexibility
B. Pride
C. Rigidity
D. Joyfulness

Directions (Q. Nos. 146-150): *In each of the following group of words, only one of them is correctly spelt. Select the one with the correct spelling.*

146. A. acomodate
B. accomodate
C. accommodate
D. acommodate

147. A. purtinacious
B. pertinacious
C. purtenacious
D. pertenecious

148. A. perilous
B. parilous
C. perilus
D. parilus

149. A. bleeth
B. blith
C. blithe
D. bleethe

150. A. invidous
B. invidious
C. envidous
D. envidious

Directions (Q. Nos. 151-154): *Choose the word that is opposite in meaning to the underlined word.*

151. He is mystic by nature.
A. spiritual
B. magical
C. visionary
D. worldly

152. The number of words in a dictionary are finite.
A. strange
B. endless
C. indefinite
D. vague

153. He had ample number of days to prepare for the exam.
A. insufficient
B. large
C. small
D. adequate

154. He lived a lavish life:
A. showy
B. rich
C. simple
D. moral

Directions (Q. Nos. 155 and 156): *Pick out the most appropriate word from the given alternatives to fill in the blank to complete the sentence.*

155. The soldiers were instructed to .... restraint and handle the situation peacefully.
A. exercise
B. control
C. prevent
D. enforce

156. Since one cannot read all books, one should be content with making a .... selection.
A. normal
B. standard
C. judicious
D. moderate

Directions (Q. Nos. 157-160): *Choose the correct answer.*

157. The novel 'Wuthering Heights' was written by:
A. Charlotte Bronte
B. Emily Bronte
C. George Eliot
D. Jane Austen

158. The poem 'Daffodils' was written by:
A. Keats
B. Shelley
C. Wordsworth
D. Byron

159. The play 'Man and Superman' was written by:
A. Shakespeare
B. Bernard Shaw
C. Eugene O'Neil
D. Aurobindo Ghosh

160. The novel 'The Guide' was written by:
A. Rabindranath Tagore
B. R.K. Narayan
C. Anita Desai
D. Khushwant Singh

Section-V : (v) हिन्दी

निर्देश (प्रश्न संख्या 161 से 165): *निम्नलिखित गद्यांश को ध्यानपूर्वक पढ़कर उसके आधार पर पूछे गए प्रश्नों के उत्तर दीजिए।*

सच्चे वीर अपने प्रेम के जोर से लोगों को सदा के लिए बाँध देते हैं। वीरता की अभिव्यक्ति कई प्रकार से होती है, कभी लड़ने से, खून बहाने से, तोप तलवार के सामने बलिदान

करने से होती है, तो कभी जीवन के गूढ़ तत्व और सत्य की तलाश में बुद्ध जैसे राजा विरक्त होकर वीर हो जाते हैं। वीरता हमेशा निराली और नई होती है। वीरों को बनाने के कारखाने नहीं होते हैं और वे देवदार वृक्ष की तरह बिना किसी के पानी दिए, बिना दूध पिलाए बढ़ते हैं। जीवन के केन्द्र में निवास करो और सत्य की चट्टान पर दृढ़ता से खड़े हो जाओ। बाहर की सतह छोड़कर जीवन के अंदर की तहों में पहुँचो तब नए रंग खिलेंगे। यही वीरता का संदेश है।

161. इस गद्यांश के लिए उपयुक्त शीर्षक होगा :
A. वीरता संस्मरण B. वीरों का जन्म
C. सच्ची वीरता D. सच्चे वीर

162. वीरता का संदेश क्या है?
A. उद्देश्य के लिए सच्चाई पर चट्टान की तरह अटल रहना।
B. यह संकल्प कि किसी भी तरह युद्ध जीतना है।
C. बुद्ध जैसे राजा की भाँति विरक्त होना।
D. युद्ध में पराजय को स्वीकार कर लेना।

163. 'वीर' शब्द का विलोम क्या है?
A. निर्भीक B. कायर
C. निडर D. जीतना

164. बुद्ध जैसे राजा विरक्त कैसे हो जाते हैं?
A. जीवन के गूढ़ तत्व और सत्य की तलाश में बुद्ध जैसे राजा विरक्त होकर वीर हो जाते हैं।
B. वे झूठ के कारणों की खोज करते हैं।
C. कभी भी सत्यता की खोज नहीं कर पाते।
D. पराजय को स्वीकार करना सत्यता समझ लेते हैं।

165. वीरों की देवदार वृक्ष से तुलना क्यों की गई है?
A. क्योंकि दोनों लम्बे होते हैं
B. क्योंकि दोनों संघर्ष करते हुए बढ़ते हैं।
C. क्योंकि दोनों स्वयं पैदा होते हैं और बिना किसी के पानी पिलाए बढ़ते हैं।
D. दोनों में नए-नए रंग होते हैं।

166. 'म' किस वर्ग का अंतिम व्यंजन है?
A. प वर्ग B. क वर्ग
C. ट वर्ग D. च वर्ग

167. वर्णों के समूह को क्या कहते हैं?
A. संयुक्त शब्द B. वर्णमाला
C. ऊष्म शब्द D. समूह शब्द

168. सप्ताह में कौन-सा समास है?
A. बहुब्रीहि B. तत्पुरुष
C. द्विगु D. कर्मधारय

169. मृत्यु + उपरांत में संधि करने पर कौन-सा शब्द बनता है?
A. मृत्यूपरांत B. मृत्योपरांत
C. मत्र्योपरांत D. मृत्युपर्यन्त

170. आँख शब्द किस शब्द का तद्‌भव रूप है?
A. नेत्र B. चक्षु
C. अक्षि D. लोचन

171. 'फूल' इनमें से कौन-सी संज्ञा है?
A. भाववाचक B. व्यक्तिवाचक
C. समूहवाचक D. जातिवाचक

172. 'मैं' इनमें से कौन-सा पुरुष है?
A. उत्तम पुरुष B. मध्यम पुरुष
C. अन्य पुरुष D. प्रथम पुरुष

173. किस शब्द में उपसर्ग **नहीं** है?
A. प्रभाव B. अपवाद
C. ओढ़ना D. अनुपस्थित

174. अशुद्ध शब्द है :
A. कलश B. पूण्य
C. कल्याण D. शत्रुता

175. इनमें से कौन-सा पद अव्ययी भाव समास है?
A. आचार B. कुशल
C. प्रतिदिन D. चतुर्भुज

176. 'विनयपत्रिका' के रचनाकार हैं :
A. सूरदास B. रहीमदास
C. तुलसीदास D. केशवदास

177. दो वर्णों के मेल से होने वाले विकार को कहते हैं :
A. संधि B. उपसर्ग
C. समास D. प्रत्यय

178. 'आसमान से बातें करना' मुहावरे का अर्थ है :

A. आसमान में उड़कर बातें करना

B. बहुत ऊँचा होना

C. आसमान की ओर देखना

D. ऊँचे सपने देखना

179. 'जलज' किसका पर्यायवाची शब्द है?

A. कमल B. तालाब

C. नदी D. सागर

180. 'जेते तुम तारे तेते नभ में न तारे हैं' में अलंकार है :

A. उपमा B. रूपक

C. यमक D. श्लेष

ANSWERS

1	**2**	**3**	**4**	**5**	**6**	**7**	**8**	**9**	**10**
D	C	B	C	C	B	B	D	C	D
11	**12**	**13**	**14**	**15**	**16**	**17**	**18**	**19**	**20**
C	C	C	A	D	B	A	B	A	B
21	**22**	**23**	**24**	**25**	**26**	**27**	**28**	**29**	**30**
D	B	C	C	C	D	A	B	C	C
31	**32**	**33**	**34**	**35**	**36**	**37**	**38**	**39**	**40**
C	A	C	A	D	C	C	D	B	C
41	**42**	**43**	**44**	**45**	**46**	**47**	**48**	**49**	**50**
A	A	B	A	B	A	D	A	D	A
51	**52**	**53**	**54**	**55**	**56**	**57**	**58**	**59**	**60**
B	C	C	C	B	C	D	B	A	B
61	**62**	**63**	**64**	**65**	**66**	**67**	**68**	**69**	**70**
D	B	C	C	D	A	D	B	D	A
71	**72**	**73**	**74**	**75**	**76**	**77**	**78**	**79**	**80**
B	C	B	B	C	A	C	C	D	B
81	**82**	**83**	**84**	**85**	**86**	**87**	**88**	**89**	**90**
A	C	B	D	D	C	C	A	C	D
91	**92**	**93**	**94**	**95**	**96**	**97**	**98**	**99**	**100**
A	A	A	A	D	C	D	C	B	A
101	**102**	**103**	**104**	**105**	**106**	**107**	**108**	**109**	**110**
B	C	D	C	B	A	C	C	B	C
111	**112**	**113**	**114**	**115**	**116**	**117**	**118**	**119**	**120**
B	B	D	*	A	C	B	D	B	C
121	**122**	**123**	**124**	**125**	**126**	**127**	**128**	**129**	**130**
B	D	A	C	C	B	B	B	C	B
131	**132**	**133**	**134**	**135**	**136**	**137**	**138**	**139**	**140**
B	A	A	C	B	A	C	C	C	B
141	**142**	**143**	**144**	**145**	**146**	**147**	**148**	**149**	**150**
A	D	B	C	A	C	B	A	C	B
151	**152**	**153**	**154**	**155**	**156**	**157**	**158**	**159**	**160**
D	B	A	C	A	C	B	C	B	B
161	**162**	**163**	**164**	**165**	**166**	**167**	**168**	**169**	**170**
C	A	B	A	C	A	B	C	A	C
171	**172**	**173**	**174**	**175**	**176**	**177**	**178**	**179**	**180**
D	A	C	B	C	C	A	B	A	C

EXPLANATORY ANSWERS

11. 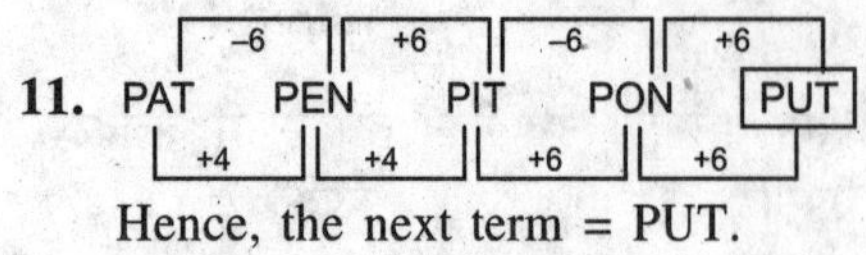

Hence, the next term = PUT.

12. 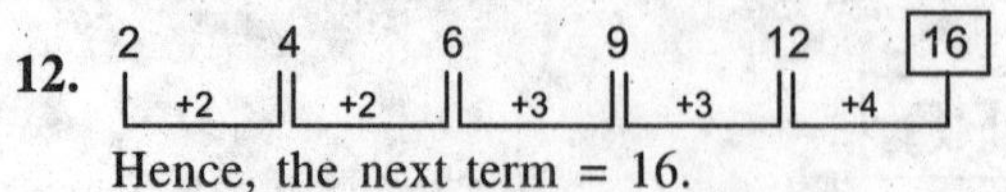

Hence, the next term = 16.

13. 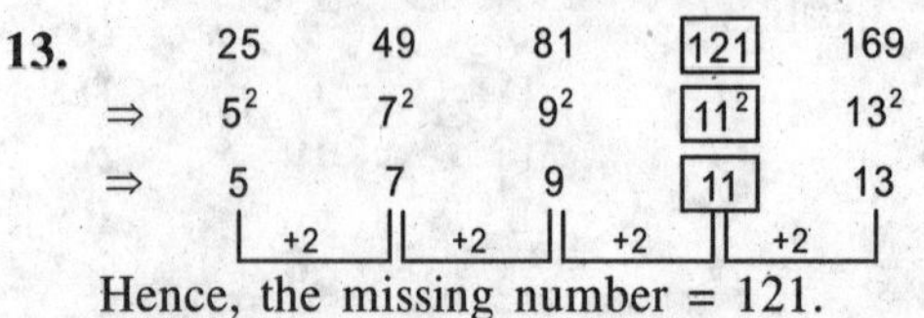

Hence, the missing number = 121.

14. 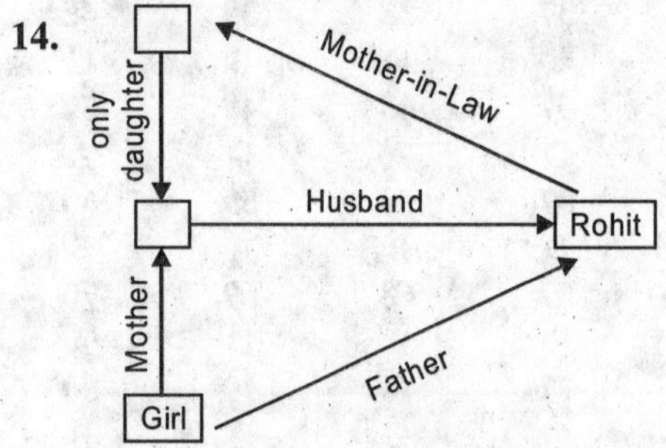

Hence, Rohit is the father of the girl.

15. Given, 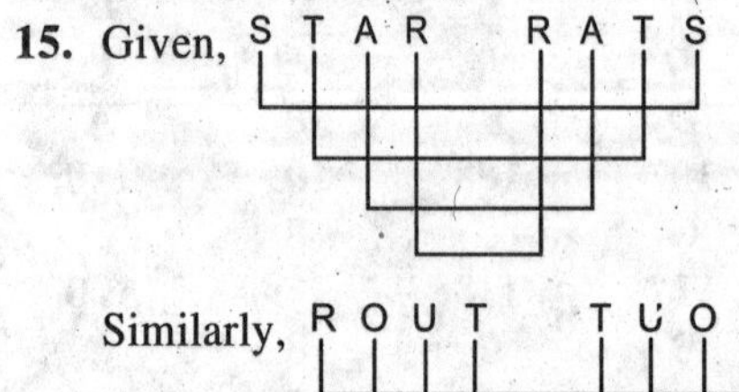

Similarly,

Letters of the word are written in reverse order.
Hence, ROUT will be written as TUOR.

16. Given,

25 means 'Green Apple' ...(*i*)
35 means 'Red Apple' ...(*ii*)
34 means 'Red Cherry' ...(*iii*)

From (*i*) and (*ii*)
5 means 'Apple'

From (*ii*) and (*iii*)
3 means 'Red'

From (*iii*), 4 means 'Cherry'
From (*ii*), 2 means 'Green'
Hence, 'Green Cherry' means '24'.
Hence, 24 is the code for 'Green Cherry'

19. 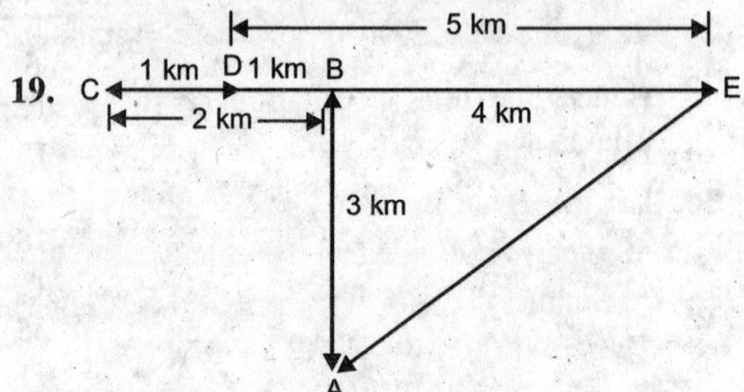

Here, starting point = A,
AB = 3 km, BC = 2 km,
CD = 1 km, DE = 5 km

∴ DB = 1 km

∴ BE = DE − DB = 5 − 1 = 4 km

∵ $(EA)^2 = (BE)^2 + (AB)^2$

∴ $(EA)^2 = 4^2 + 3^2$

⇒ $(EA)^2 = 16 + 9 \Rightarrow (EA)^2 = 25$

⇒ $(EA)^2 = 5^2 \Rightarrow EA = 5$ km

Hence, He is now 5 km from starting point.

20. Given, 3rd December = Saturday
10th Dcember = 17 December
= 24 December
= 31 December = Saturday

Hence, the last day of the month would be Saturday.

22. The number of triangle in the resulting figure:
= 16

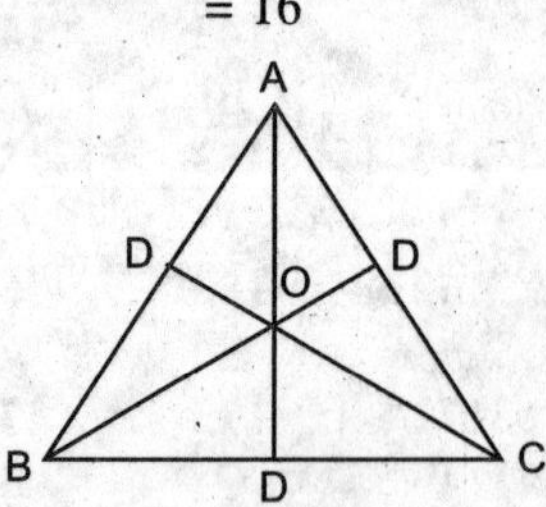

26.

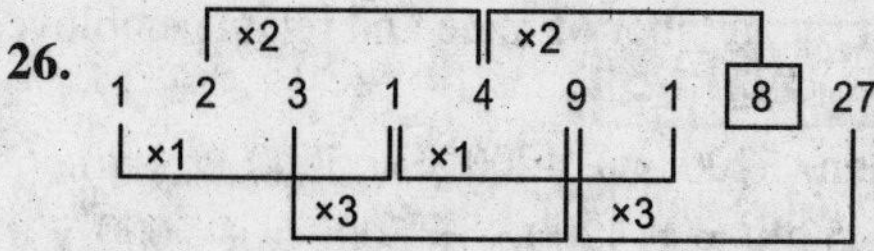

27. Let the population of a town = x
then, the number of children

$$= x \times \frac{100-(45+40)}{100}$$

$\Rightarrow$ $$30{,}000 = x \times \frac{15}{100} \Rightarrow x = 200000$$

Hence, the total population of the town is 2 lakhs.

30. Let the given square = 4 × 4 unit^2
$\because$ square is divided in 16 equal parts
$\therefore$ Smallest square will be 1 × 1 sq. unit
There will be 16 squares of 1 × 1 units
There will be 9 squares of 2 × 2 units
There will be 4 squares of 3 × 3 units
There will be 1 square of 4 × 4 units
Hence, the total number of squares
= 16 + 9 + 4 + 1 = 30

101. Here, $a = 1, d = 2, n = 25$

$\therefore$ $$S_n = \frac{n}{2}[2a+(n-1)d]$$

$\therefore$ $$S_{25} = \frac{25}{2}[2\times1+(25-1)\cdot2$$

$$= \frac{25}{2}\times2[1+24]$$

$$= 25 \times 25 = 625$$

Hence, the sum of odd numbers between 0 and 50 = 625.

102. Given, observations are in ascending order:
29, 32, 48, 50, x, x + 2, 72, 78, 84, 95
Here, n = 10 is an even number

$$\therefore \text{Median} = \frac{1}{2}\left[\frac{n}{2}\text{th term} + \left(\frac{n}{2}+1\right)\text{th term}\right]$$

$\Rightarrow$ $$63 = \frac{1}{2}\ [\text{5th term + 6th term}]$$

$\Rightarrow$ $$63 = \frac{1}{2}\ [x + x + 2]$$

$\Rightarrow$ $$126 = 2x + 2 \Rightarrow 2n = 126 - 2$$

$\Rightarrow$ $$2x = 124 \Rightarrow x = 62$$

105. sec A (1 – sin A) (sec A + tan A)

$$= \sec A\,(1-\sin A)\left(\frac{1}{\cos A}+\frac{\sin A}{\cos A}\right)$$

$$= \sec A(1-\sin A)\frac{(1+\sin A)}{\cos A}$$

$$= \sec A\frac{(1-\sin^2 A)}{\cos A}$$

$$= \sec A\cdot\frac{\cos^2 A}{\cos A} = \sec A\,.\cos A$$

$$= \sec A\cdot\frac{1}{\sec A} = 1$$

106. Let AB be a building and CD be a tower.
CD = 50 m, $\angle$ACB = 30°
and $\angle$DBC = 60°
In ΔDCB

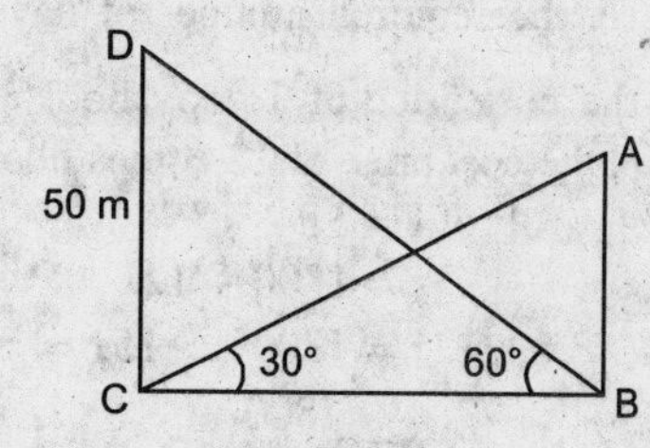

$$\tan 60° = \frac{DC}{CB} \Rightarrow \sqrt{3} = \frac{50}{CB}$$

$\Rightarrow$ $$CB = \frac{50}{\sqrt{3}}\ \text{m}$$

and In ΔABC, $\tan 30° = \frac{AB}{BC} \Rightarrow \frac{1}{\sqrt{3}} = \frac{AB}{\frac{50}{\sqrt{3}}}$

$\Rightarrow$ $$\frac{1}{\sqrt{3}} = \frac{AB\sqrt{3}}{50} \Rightarrow 3AB = 50$$

$\Rightarrow$ $$AB = \frac{50}{3}\ \text{m}$$

Hence, the height of the building

$$AB = 16\frac{2}{3}\ \text{m}$$

107. In ΔABC, $AC^2 = AB^2 + BC^2$

$\Rightarrow \quad 12^2 = (6\sqrt{3})^2 + 6^2$

$\Rightarrow \quad 144 = 108 + 36 \Rightarrow 144 = 144$

Hence, ΔABC is a right angle triangle.

$\therefore \quad \angle B = 90°$

108. Given, 1 man $= \frac{3}{2}$ boy

$\therefore \quad$ 8 men $= 8 \times \frac{3}{2}$ boy $= 12$ boy

and 4 men and 9 boys $= 4 \times \frac{3}{2} + 9$

$= 6 + 9 = 15$ boys

$\because$ More boys, less day $\rightarrow$ Indirect proportional

$\therefore \quad$ boys $\quad$ day

$12 : 15 :: x : 20$

$\Rightarrow \quad 12 \times 20 = 15 \times x$

$\Rightarrow \quad x = \frac{12 \times 20}{15} = \frac{12 \times 4}{3}$

$= 4 \times 4 = 16$ days

Hence, the required number of days = 16.

109. Let the cost price of 1 copy book = ₹ x

Then, the cost price of 12 copies book = ₹ $12x$

$\because \quad$ Profit = SP − CP

$\therefore \quad 3x = 1800 - 12x$

$\Rightarrow \quad 3x + 12x = 1800 \Rightarrow 15x = 1800$

$\Rightarrow \quad x = \frac{1800}{15} \Rightarrow x = 120$

Hence, the cost price of a copy is ₹ 120.

110. The number of packets $= \frac{\text{Volume of box}}{\text{Volume of packet}}$

$= \frac{110 \times 90 \times 40 \text{ cm}^3}{22 \times 15 \times 6 \text{ cm}^3}$

$= \frac{10 \times 6 \times 40}{2 \times 6} = 10 \times 20 = 200$

112. Distance to cover = 126 + 114 = 240 m

and Relative speed = 30 + 42 = 72 kmph

$= 72 \times \frac{5}{18}$ m/s $= 20$ m/s

$\therefore$ Time to cross each other

$= \frac{240}{20} = 12$ seconds

117. Let the number of male and female employees are x and y

Then, $5200x + 4200y = 5000(x + y)$

$\Rightarrow 5200x + 4200y = 5000x + 5000y$

$\Rightarrow 5200x - 5000x = 5000y - 4200y$

$\Rightarrow \quad 200x = 800y$

$\Rightarrow \frac{x}{y} = \frac{4}{1} \Rightarrow x : y = 4 : 1$

$\therefore$ The percentage of female employees

$= \frac{1}{4+1} \times 100 = \frac{1}{5} \times 100$

$= 20\%$

118. Given, $\quad$ Sum = ₹ 890

A : B = 4 : 5 = 24 : 30

and $\quad$ B : C = 6 : 7 = 30 : 35

$\therefore \quad$ A : B : C = 24 : 30 : 35

$\therefore$ A gets money $= 890 \times \frac{24}{24+30+35}$

$= 890 \times \frac{24}{89}$

$= 10 \times 24 =$ ₹ 240

119. Let daughter's age = x years

Then, father's age = $5x$ years

five years ago $9(x - 5) = 5x - 5$

$\Rightarrow \quad 9x - 45 = 5x - 5$

$\Rightarrow \quad 4x = 40$

$\Rightarrow \quad x = 10$

Hence, father's present age = $5x$ = 50 years

120. Let the numbers are x and y

Then, $\quad x + y = 7 \quad$ ...(*i*)

and $\quad xy = 10$

$\because \quad (x - y)^2 = (x + y)^2 - 4xy = 49 - 40$

$(x - y)^2 = 9 = (3)^2$

$\Rightarrow \quad x - y = 3 \quad$ ...(*ii*)

Adding (*i*) and (*ii*),

$2x = 10$

$\Rightarrow \quad x = 5$

From (*i*) $\quad y = 7 - 5 = 2$

Hence, number = 25 (less than 30)

Previous Paper (Solved)

IGNOU B.Ed. ENTRANCE EXAM 2019*

PART-A

Section-I : General English Comprehension

Directions (Qs. No. 1-10): *Read the passage carefully and select the appropriate answers given in front of each question.*

This is a monologue delivered in a 1998 movie. The speaker is about to scatter the ashes of his friend.

"Donny was a good bowler, and a good man. He was one of us. He was a man who loved the outdoors...and bowling, and as a surfer he explored the beaches of Southern California, from La Jolla to Leo Carrillo and ...upto... Pismo. He died, like so many young men of his generation, he died before his time. In your wisdom, Lord, you took him, as you took so many bright, blooming young men at Kheshang, at Hill 364 of Langdoh (battle of Vietnam war).

These young men gave their lives. And so would Donny. Donny who loved bowling. And so, Theodore Donald Karabotsos, in accordance with what we think your dying wishes might well have been, we commit you final mortal remains in the lap of the Pacific Ocean, which you loved so well. Goodnight, sweet prince".

1. The first sentence of the paragraph "Donny was a good bowler, and a good man" is a:
A. Simple Sentence
B. Complex Sentence
C. Compound Sentence
D. Complex-compound Sentence

2. Attitude towards 'bowling' of the narrator better defines:
A. Dishonour B. Respect
C. Disobedience D. Disinterested

3. In this context, the nearest synonym for 'in the lap' in the last sentence, would be:
A. Chest B. Rest
C. Water D. Foam

4. The sentence "died like a young man" shows that:
A. He gave his life while fighting for his country.
B. He committed suicide.
C. He died in adolescence.
D. He was murdered.

5. In the last two sentences, the narrator's expressions can be better considered as:
A. Enraged
B. Confused
C. Encouraged
D. Formal

6. In the above paragraph, the attitude of the narrator towards Donny is mainly:
A. Is of sad companionship.
B. Is without bias.
C. Is of obvious rancour.
D. Is of proudly separation.

7. The reference to Kheshang, Hill 364 of Langdoh in the sentence "By his will, God..." suggests that:
A. Donny was killed in the battle
B. Donny was buried on Hill 364
C. The narrator also lost his friends in these places
D. The narator is remembering these places

* Online Exam conducted by NTA on 27 July, 2019.

8. In this perspective, the sense of line "In your wisdom, Lord....took the youth" is well explained:

A. Excitement B. Flurried
C. Patient D. Ambivalent

9. In the sentence "In your wisodm, Lord ...." the word 'bright' most nearly means:

A. intelligent B. light
C. vivid D. dazzling

10. In the statement "He was a man who loved the outdoors...." the word 'bowling' is a:

A. Verb B. Adjective
C. Gerund D. Noun

Section-II : Logical and Analytical Reasoning

Directions (Qs. No. 11-14): *Study the following information carefully and answer the questions that follow.*

There are six members in a family—A, B, C, D, E and F. C is the sister of F. D is father of A and F is grandson of D. B is brother-in-law of F's mother. E is the daughter of D. There are only two females in the family.

11. Who is the daughter of A and E?

A. C B. E
C. B D. D

12. Who is the mother of F?

A. C B. E
C. A D. B

13. Two female members of the family are:

A. D, E B. A, C
C. C, E D. F, C

14. Who is the uncle of C?

A. D B. A
C. F D. B

Directions (Qs. No. 15-18): *In the following questions a series is being given. Select from the alternatives the correct term to fill in the missing term.*

15. 2, 9, 28, 65, 126, ?

A. 210 B. 215
C. 217 D. 252

16. 15, 32, 67, 138, ?, 568

A. 276 B. 278
C. 280 D. 281

17. 19, 29, 41, 55, ?, 89

A. 69 B. 71
C. 74 D. 76

18. 64, 63, 49, 49, 48, 36, 36, 35, 25, 25, 24, ?

A. 16 B. 18
C. 20 D. 22

19. Find the missing number:

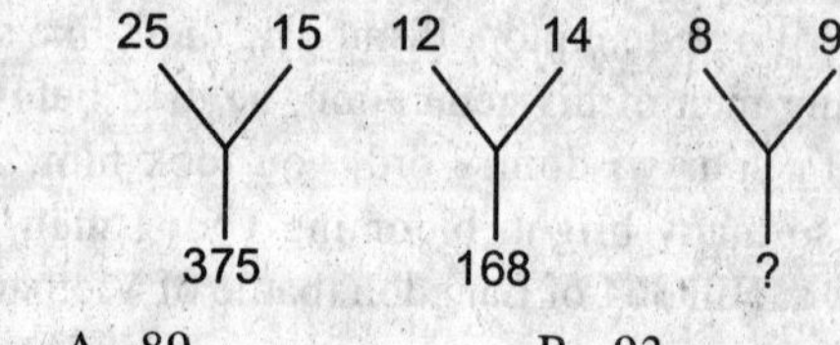

A. 89 B. 93
C. 72 D. 64

20. Which is different from the rest of the three on any basis?

A. Edge B. Corner
C. Tip D. Vertex

21. If OCCUPATION is coded as QEEWRCVKQP, how will PROFESSION be coded?

A. STQHGUUKQP B. RTQHGUUKPQ
C. RTQHGUUKQP D. RTQGHUUKQP

22. If POTENTIAL is coded as 657247314, how will TALENT be coded?

A. 714274 B. 714247
C. 741247 D. 724147

Directions (Qs. No. 23-26): *Study the following passage carefully and answer the questions that follow.*

Mariam, Kunti, Begum, Shilpi and Meera are five friends. Each has six balls. Mariam gave three balls to Shilpi, who gave two balls each to Kunti and Meera. Begum gave four balls to Mariam who in turn gave three each to Kunti and Meera. Kunti gave five balls to Begum and Meera gave four balls to Shilpi.

23. Who possesses the most balls?
A. Begum B. Shilpi
C. Meera D. Kunti

24. How many balls are with Begum?
A. 9 B. 6
C. 8 D. 7

25. How many balls are with Kunti?
A. 6 B. 7
C. 8 D. 9

26. Who has the fewest balls?
A. Begum B. Meera
C. Mariam D. Kunti

Directions (Qs. No. 27-30): *Study the following passage carefully and answer the questions that follow.*

A and B play cricket and tennis. B and D play hockey. A and C play volleyball and tennis. C, D and E play football.

27. Who plays hockey and football?
A. A B. B
C. C D. D

28. Who plays cricket, tennis and volleyball?
A. A B. B
C. C D. D

29. Who plays only football?
A. E B. D
C. C D. B

30. Who plays volleyball and football?
A. A B. B
C. C D. D

Section-III : Educational and General Awareness

31. Where is the headquarter of International Renewable Energy Agency (IRENA)?
A. Tel Aviv City, Israel
B. Paris, France
C. Tehran, Iran
D. Masdar City, United Arab Emirates

32. What is geographically closest to Greater Nicobar?
A. Sumatra B. Borneo
C. Java D. Sri Lanka

33. Which of the following is a multi-level global campaign to spread awareness about the importance of education for girls?
A. Girl's Rising
B. The most important part of our life: Girl
C. Save Girls : Educate Girls
D. Education for Girls

34. Lord Macaulay is related to:
A. By introducing instruction through English medium
B. Military reform
C. End of sati practice
D. Legal disclosure

35. Which of the following is not composed by Sant Tulsidas?
A. Geetawali B. Kavitawali
C. Vinay Patrika D. Sahitya Ratna

36. Which browser is developed by Google?
A. Internet Explorer B. Firefox
C. Safari D. Chrome

37. Who wrote the book "The Coalition Years 1996-2012"?
A. Yashwant Sinha B. P. Chidambaram
C. Pranab Mukherjee D. Sitaram Yechury

38. Parliament approved the National Education Policy in:
A. 1985 B. 1986
C. 1988 D. 1989

39. Which of the following acts was called by Jawaharlal Nehru as "Proclamation Letter of Slavery"?

A. Regulating Act, 1773
B. Pitt's India Act, 1784
C. Government of India Act, 1919
D. Government of India Act, 1935

40. Where is Jog Falls located?
A. On the Tapti river
B. On the Sharavati river
C. On the Kaveri river
D. On the Bhima river

41. In which year did the Sarva Shiksha Abhiyan scheme start?
A. 1999-2000 B. 2000-2001
C. 2001-2002 D. 2002-2003

42. Yashpal Committee Report (1993) is known as:
A. Learning the pleasure within
B. Learning without Burden
C. Learning to Learn
D. Learning to Live Together

43. Who was given the Jnanpith Award for the year 2016?
A. Sankha Ghosh B. Mridula Garg
C. Namvar Singh D. Sankara Kurup

44. National Curriculum Framework was created by NCERT:
A. 2005 B. 2006
C. 2007 D. 2008

45. Which book was written by Swami Dayanand Saraswati?
A. Satyarth Prakash B. Raja Yoga
C. Geetanjali D. Chaturang

46. How can the number of judges in the Supreme Court of India be increased?
A. By the notification of President
B. By Parliamentary law
C. By amending the Constitution of India
D. By a representation of the Supreme Court

47. When did Sukanya Samriddhi Yojana enforce?
A. 2014 B. 2015
C. 2016 D. 2017

48. The main objective of the Hunter Commission (1882) was:
A. Assessing the status of primary education and suggesting improvements
B. Suggesting Police Reforms
C. Examining revolutionary movements in India
D. Translation of Indian literature into English

49. Section '51A' of the Constitution deals with:
A. Fundamental Rights
B. Fundamental Duties
C. Girl education
D. Woman education

50. In which year was the All India Muslim League established?
A. 1905 B. 1904
C. 1907 D. 1906

51. Which region is called the 'rice bowl' of India?
A. North-East Region
B. Kerala and Tamil Nadu
C. Indus-Ganga Plain
D. Krishna-Godavari delta region

52. For which book Viren Dangwal was given the Sahitya Akademi Award?
A. *Syahi Tal*
B. *Esi Duniya mein*
C. *Dushchakra Mein Srasta*
D. *Kal ki Baat*

53. "Jeevan ka Pahiya" is used as a 'Theme' in which of the following?
A. Varli painting B. Thanka painting
C. Manjusha painting D. Kalamkari painting

54. First President of India was:
A. Dr. Radhakrishnan
B. Dr. Zakir Husain
C. Dr. Shankar Dayal Sharma
D. Dr. Rajendra Prasad

55. Recently, the Energy Ganga Project implemented by the Government of India is:
A. Saving Gangai Dolphin in Ganges River
B. Removing water pollution from the Ganges River and conserving the Ganges River
C. Protection of Ganga flood affected plains
D. Providing LPG from pipes to residents

Section-IV : Teaching-Learning and The School

56. The objective of teaching is:
A. Change in behaviour of students in expected direction
B. Complete personality development of students
C. Character building of students
D. Getting selected in a proper job

57. Why should there be discipline in the classroom?
A. Children should feel that it is compulsory.
B. Children should accept the tribunal.
C. Children should understand the importance of organized and systematic work.
D. If they want to become teachers, it will help them.

58. On which channel IGNOU's programs are shown?
A. Mukt channel B. Eklavya channel
C. Gyan channel D. Vyas channel

59. The best definition of education can be:
A. The preparation
B. To acquire knowledge
C. Learning
D. Intellectual freedom

60. Which of the following organizations looks after the quality of teacher education in India?
A. NCTE B. MCI
C. AICTE D. CSIR

61. The dictionary is a:
A. Audio medium
B. Visual medium
C. Print media
D. Audio-Visual medium

62. Which title will be appropriate for the opening of the first day in nursery class?
A. My best friend
B. My neighbourhood
C. My school
D. My family

63. A good teacher is one who:
A. Encourages children for all round development.
B. Helps children to learn their lesson easily.
C. Prepares children to pass the exam.
D. Establishes discipline in the classroom.

64. What will you do if a child does not understand the lesson properly taught in class?
A. Repeat the lesson
B. Students will be asked to read additional books/learning materials.
C. Know the child's prior knowledge
D. Will reread the lesson by choosing examples from the child's background

65. In the perspective of education, socialization means:
A. Building your own social standards
B. To respect elders in society
C. Adaptation and adjustment in social environment
D. Always comply with social standards

66. The most important objective of teaching is:
A. To understand teacher's narrative to children
B. Completing the lesson of your subject
C. Keeping children comfortable during teaching
D. Taking classes regularly

67. Statement 'Men are generally more intelligent than women':
A. is true
B. can be true
C. shows gender differences
D. Perfect for multiple areas of intelligence

68. Which one of the following is not an 'output' device?
A. Keyboard
C. Visual Display Unit
C. Printer
D. Plotter

69. Which of the following is not the main objective of NCERT?

A. To organize pre-service and in-service training of teachers.

B. To act as a nodal institution in achieving the goals of universal elementary education

C. To encourage and coordinate research in the field of school education

D. Developing rules for teacher education programs

70. The purpose of the task is to:

A. Keeping students busy at home

B. Improvement in handwriting

C. Parents' participation in student learning

D. Promotion of self-learning

71. In which state the first Open University was established in India?

A. Andhra Pradesh

B. Delhi

C. Himachal Pradesh

D. Tamil Nadu

72. Which is not a suitable tool for structural assessment?

A. Duty

B. Oral question

B. Terminal examination

D. Question Forum & Puzzle

73. Which of the following is not correct about the school?

A. They are powerful agencies of social change.

B. They are social units of cultural transfer.

C. They are influenced by the social and economic scenario in the country.

D. They are possible means of conflict and separation.

74. What is the biggest benefit of interaction between teachers and fellows?

A. It helps in effective learning.

B. It provides satisfaction to the teacher.

C. It encourages scholars to ask questions.

D. It creates better collective relationships.

75. If a child often quarrels with his siblings, how will you help him as a teacher?

A. You punish him in school

B. Comparing him to others will discourage him

C. Will ask parents to take drastic action

D. By taking him alone find the reason for such behaviour.

76. An effective teaching-aid material has one of the following characteristics/qualities:

A. It looks good.

B. Awakens all departments.

C. Visible to everyone.

D. It is easy to make.

77. What is not desired for a proper teaching-learning environment in the classroom?

A. Autonomy of fellowship

B. Freedom to teacher for innovation

C. Meeting of continuous teacher-parent association

D. Punishment for wrong behaviour

78. An effective classroom environment occurs in:

A. Different types of educational aids

B. Live interaction of student-teacher

C. Torrential silence

D. Excessive discipline

79. Ethical values can be developed effectively in students when teachers:

A. Speaks of sustainable values.

B. He complies himself.

C. Tells the story of great people.

D. Provides reading material.

80. The success of teaching depends on:

A. On advance skills

B. On oral communication skills

C. On children's understanding

D. On children's choice

PART-B

Section-V : (i) Science

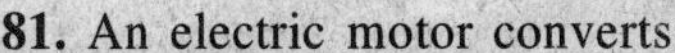

81. An electric motor converts:
A. Electrical energy into heat energy
B. Electrical energy into mechanical energy
C. Mechanical energy into electrical energy
D. Mechanical energy into heat energy

82. The part of DNA that informs a protein, is called:
A. Nucleus
B. Chromosome
C. Modesty
D. Gene

83. Which of the following is a greenhouse gas?
A. Sulphur dioxide B. Nitrogen dioxide
C. Carbon dioxide D. Carbon monoxide

84. Which of the following would be true for highly acidic and highly alkaline solutions?
A. The concentration of hydrogen ion in the solution will be 10^{-7} M
B. The solution will turn litmus into red colour
C. Solutions will be very good conductor of electricity
D. The solutions will release hydrogen by reacting with Mg

85. Which colour of visible light has the lowest frequency?
A. Violet B. Red
B. Yellow D. Green

86. The blood corpuscles that help in blood clotting at the place of injury are:
A. RBC B. WBC
C. Platelets D. Eosinophils

87. The result of the ozone hole is:
A. Green effect house
B. Global warming
C. Acid rain
D. Increase in UV radiation

88. Choose a compound that has an oxidation number of +5 to chlorine.
A. $HClO_4$ B. $HClO_3$
C. $HClO_2$ D. HClO

89. If the focal length of a lens is *f*, the power of the lens will be:
A. $\frac{100}{f(\text{cm})}$ B. $\frac{10}{f(\text{cm})}$
C. $\frac{100}{f(\text{m})}$ D. $\frac{1}{100f(\text{cm})}$

90. Which of the following electronic distributions should have a minimum ionic energy?
A. $1s^2\ 2s^2\ 2p^6\ 3s^2$ B. $1s^2\ 2s^2\ 2p^6\ 3s^1$
C. $1s^2\ 2s^2\ 2p^6$ D. $1s^2\ 2s^2\ 2p^3$

91. Which of the following is not a renewable source of energy?
A. Wind energy
B. Ocean energy
C. Solar energy
D. Fossil energy

92. Which of the following properties is different for neutral atoms of two isotopes of the same element?
A. Atomic number
B. Mass
C. Number of electrons
D. General chemical reaction

93. What percentage of genes does a child get from his father?
A. 25% B. 50%
C. 75% D. 100%

94. Xylem in plants are responsible:
A. For water transport
B. For manure transport
C. For the transport of amino acids
D. For oxygen transport

95. Resistance of metal Conductor:
A. Increases with increase in temperature
B. Decreases with increase in temperature
C. Doesn't change with change in temperature
D. Becomes zero at high temperature

96. Which of the following will form an ionic solution in water?
A. CO_2 B. CCl_4
C. O_2 D. NaI

97. The reason for the movement of food in the esophagus is:
A. Balsamic by saliva
B. Peristalsis
C. Gravitational pull
D. Filtration

98. In which production the biodegraded waste can be used?
A. Manure
B. Biogas
C. Both manure and biogas
D. Neither manure nor biogas

99. In human beings, kidney is part of which system?
A. Nutrition B. Respiration
C. Excretion D. Circulation

100. The fastest depleting natural resources in the world are:
A. Water B. Forest
C. Air D. Sunlight

Section-V : (ii) Mathematics

101. The largest 4-digit number divisible by 15, 25, 40, and 75 will be?
A. 9000 B. 9200
C. 9400 D. 9600

102. How many digits will be in the right of the decimal point in the product of 65.425, and 0.03216?
A. 6 B. 7
C. 8 D. 9

103. 17 pen are sold at ₹ 720, there is a loss equal to the cost price of 5 pens, what is the cost price of one pen?
A. ₹ 43 B. ₹ 60
C. ₹ 55 D. ₹ 34

104. A fruit seller purchases 5 oranges in ₹ 4 then sells 4 oranges in ₹ 5, what is his profit per cent?
A. 50% B. 48.56%
C. 56.25% D. 62.25%

105. If $(5.6)^2 + 5.6p + (3.4)^2$ is a perfect square, then what is the value of p?
A. 3.4 B. 9.0
C. 2.2 D. 6.8

106. If the shadow of a pole is $\sqrt{3}$ times its length, then the angle of elevation towards the sun will be:
A. 30° B. 45°
C. 60° D. 75°

107. How many two-digit prime numbers have 1 as a second digit?
A. 03 B. 04
C. 05 D. 06

108. The total number of prime numbers between 20 and 50 will be:
A. 6 B. 7
C. 8 D. 9

109. The value of $\frac{3.6^2 - 1.4^2}{3.6 - 1.4}$ is:
A. 1.2 B. 3.8
C. 5.0 D. 4.0

110. HCF of two numbers is 5 and LCM is 150. If one number is 25, then the second number will be:
A. 45 B. 40
C. 30 D. 20

111. At 8.30 am, the angle between the minute and the hour hand in a watch will be:
A. 60° B. 70°
C. 75° D. 90°

112. If a shopkeeper gives 5% discount in his sale 3 times continuously, the total discount will be:
A. 15% B. 12.27%
C. 17.74% D. 14.26%

113. A clock starts in the afternoon. The hour needle will be bent at 5.10 pm?
A. 145° B. 155°
C. 160° D. 175°

114. A fruit seller has some oranges. He sold 30% of the oranges, yet he has 245 oranges left. How many oranges did he have in the beginning?
A. 250 B. 300
C. 350 D. 400

115. A 350 m. long train is running at a speed of 45 km/hr. In how much time it will cross 140 m. long platform?
A. 30 seconds B. 40 seconds
C. 45 seconds D. 50 seconds

116. If $\log\frac{a}{b} + \log\frac{b}{a} = \log(a+b)$, then:
A. $a = b$ B. $a + b = 1$
C. $a - b = 0$ D. $a - b = 1$

117. If one number is 10% less than another, which is 10% more than 200, then what is the first number?
A. 190 B. 198
C. 202 D. 218

118. Which of the following represents the ratio of seconds to hours?
A. .00025 B. .00026
C. .00027 D. .00028

119. A train running at a speed of 40 km/hr crosses a post in 18 seconds. The length of the train will be:
A. 180 m B. 200 m
C. 240 m D. 360 m

120. A student gets 240 marks in the examination and is failed with 60 marks, if the maximum marks is 600, then what is the passing percentage?
A. 36% B. 40%
C. 45% D. 50%

Section-V : (iii) Social Science

121. The word 'mansab' is used:
A. A piece of land B. A position
C. An office D. A pay scale

122. The Constitution of India was adopted:
A. By the Governor General
B. By British Parliament
C. By Constituent Assembly
D. By Indian Parliament

123. Excise duty is a tax:
A. On sale of goods
B. On export of goods
C. On the production of goods
D. On import of goods

124. Which of the following is not a fundamental feature of the Indian Constitution?
A. Presidential government
B. Parliamentary government
C. Federal government
D. Freedom of judiciary

125. The Similipal Tiger Reserve is located at:
A. Madhya Pradesh B. Uttarakhand
C. Maharashtra D. Odisha

126. Which state is the largest producer of coal in India?
A. Bihar B. Jharkhand
C. Madhya Pradesh D. Odisha

127. Supernova is a:
A. A dwarf star B. A black hole
C. A meteor D. A dead star

128. Who is called the father of Indian Constitution?
A. B.R. Ambedkar B. Mahatma Gandhi
C. Jawaharlal Nehru D. Vallabhbhai Patel

129. Which of the following Gupta emperors was equally important in war and personal achievements?
A. Chandragupta I B. Chandragupta II
C. Kumargupta I D. Skandagupta

130. Which English Governor General started postage stamps in India?
A. Lord Dalhousie
B. Lord Auckland
C. Lord Canning
D. Lord William Bentinck

131. Where was the Mughal ruler Bahadur Shah II sent as captive by the British?
A. Mendeley jail
B. Andaman and Nicobar
C. Rangoon
D. Hyderabad

132. Members of Rajya Sabha are:
A. Directly elected.
B. Mostly nominated.
C. Both chosen directly and indirectly.
D. Elected by the assembly members.

133. Which section of the constitution has given residuary rights to the Parliament?
A. Section 45 B. Section 21A
C. Section 148 D. Section 360

134. On which river is the Gandhi Sagar Dam built?
A. Narmada B. Chambal
C. Tapti D. Mahanadi

135. The President of the Union of India is conferred with equivalent to which of the following:
A. British Monarch
B. President of America
C. President of Egypt
C. President of Russia

136. Who is the Chairman of Rajya Sabha?
A. Prime Minister
B. Finance Minister
C. Commerce Minister
D. Vice-President of India

137. Who was the last Mughal emperor?
A. Babur
B. Humayun
C. Bahadur Shah Zafar
D. Aurangzeb

138. Which of the following is the longest national highway in the country?
A. National Highway-1
B. National Highway-44
C. National Highway-3
D. National Highway-4

139. Who is considered as the founder of scientific socialism?
A. Rousseau B. Karl Marx
C. Engels D. Lenin

140. India is a ....
A. Social economy
B. Capitalist economy
C. Mixed economy
D. Open economy

Section-V : (iv) English

Directions (Q. Nos. 141-145): *Choose the word that is nearest in meaning to the underlined word.*

141. The treacherous accountant gave away secrets to the rival company.
A. greedy B. perfect
C. faithful D. disloyal

142. The compliant student made sure to compliment her supervisor at every stage.
A. brilliant B. amicable
C. obliging D. faithful

143. The personalities of the twins are as disparate as day and night.
A. dissimilar B. similar
C. common D. incomprehensible

144. Ania is a vociferous defender of labour unions.
A. eloquent B. forceful
C. submissive D. amiable

145. The critic described the painting as insipid.
A. Inspiring B. Uninteresting
C. Significant D. Aesthetic

Directions (Q. Nos. 146-150): *In this group of words, only one word is correctly spelt. Select the one with the correct spelling.*

146. A. Grigarious B. Gregerious C. Gregarious D. Grigerious

147. A. Alleviate B. Allevate C. Aleviate D. Aleeviate

148. A. Transitery B. Transitory C. Transetory D. Transetery

149. A. Erasable B. Erasible C. Erasibal D. Erascible

150. A. Dessonance B. Dissonance C. Desonance D. Disonance

Directions (Q. Nos. 151-154): *Choose the word which is opposite in meaning to the underlined word.*

151. His volatile personality made it difficult to predict his reaction to anything.
A. capricious B. erratic C. fickle D. calm

152. The character Scrooge in 'A Christmas Carol' is a misanthrope.
A. cynic B. philanthropist C. pessimist D. recluse

153. His prodigal son quickly wasted all of his savings.
A. miserly B. extravagant C. lavish D. wasteful

154. Anita has a reputation for veracity, so everyone trusted her.
A. candour B. exactitude C. dishonesty D. fidelity

Directions (Q. Nos. 155 and 156): *Select the word in each group that does not properly belong to it.*

155. A. ardent B. enthusiastic C. passionate D. apathetic

156. A. professional B. lay person C. amateur D. novice

Directions (Q. Nos. 157-160): *Pick out the most appropriate word from the given alternatives to fill in the blank to complete the sentence.*

157. Despite the efforts to _____ the discord between the two fractions, the two groups remained sworn enemies.
A. intensify B. exploit C. assuage D. excite

158. To avoid being _____, the teacher often includes jokes and amusing anecdotes in her lectures.
A. amusing B. complex C. eccentric D. monotonous

159. The mines of the gold rush dug so deeply into the mountain that any more excavation could have had _____ consequences, causing a cave-in or a complete collapse.
A. rigid B. devastating C. alienating D. moderate

160. To properly represent its _____ forms, Manu included, in his paper on the history of renaissance Art, over twenty sections each describing a different style.
A. diverse B. simplest C. identical D. singular

Section-V : (v) हिन्दी

निर्देश (प्रश्न संख्या 161 से 165): *निम्नलिखित गद्यांश को पढ़कर उसके आधार पर पूछे गए प्रश्नों के उत्तर दीजिए।*

"मैं तारीफ ही करूँगा अश्क जी के होशो-हवास की। उन्होंने ममदू के हाथ से एक टार्च ले ली और उसे इधर-उधर घुमाकर वे कुछ देख रहे थे। टार्चों के सैल जवाब दे रहे थे, पर वे इधर-उधर बजरी पर बार-बार रोशनी डालते और कुछ उठाकर अपने ओवरकोट में डाल लेते। बजरी दिखाई देने लगी थी, यह इस बात का सबूत था कि हम ग्लेशियर के पास आ गए थे। हमारी समझ में कुछ नहीं आया था। राकेश अपनी टार्च बुझाकर धीरे-धीरे हँस रहा था। वह शायद बात समझ गया था। तभी ममदू बोला, "साब, रोशनी बचाकर रखना है। अभी बहुत लम्बा रास्ता है। बीच-बीच में दलदल भी पड़ सकता है...।"

"सर्दियों में जमी बर्फ में दबकर कुछ पत्थर बहुत कीमती

बन जाते हैं।'' अश्क जी ने कहा था। राकेश यह सुनकर बेसाख्ता हँस पड़ा था।

हमारे पैर दो-दो मन के हो गए थे। अब उनसे शरीर और कपड़ों का बोझ उठ नहीं पा रहा था। दलदल पार करके हम सुस्ताने लगे थे। मौत की बर्फीली वादी से हम जरूर निकल आए थे पर अंधेरी घाटियों, सतलंजन के मैदान, पानी से भरे खतरनाक कुंडों में जंगली जानवरों के खतरों से अभी हम पार नहीं हुए थे। जैसे-तैसे हम उस जगह पहुँच गए जहाँ घोड़ेवाले को छोड़कर गए थे। आधी रात हो चुकी थी। हमें खत्म हो गया समझकर वे लौट गए थे। रुकने के लिए कोई जगह नहीं थी। ऊपर से बारिश आ गई थी। गनीमत थी कि हम सतलंजन का मैदान पार कर आए थे....अब ऊबड़-खाबड़ रास्ता आ गया था, जिसके नीचे जगह-जगह पानी के कुंड थे। अंधों की तरह सँभल-सँभलकर चलने के अलावा कोई चारा नहीं था। ममदू सब खतरे उठाता हुआ आगे-आगे चल रहा था। उसकी आवाज आ रही थी, 'हिम्मत कर, साहबा! होश साहबा! सँभल के साहबा!' इसी आवाज के सहारे हम चल रहे थे...कहीं कोई रोशनी नहीं, कहीं कोई पगडंडी नहीं, कोई रास्ता नहीं, कोई सहारा नहीं...बस ममदू की आवाज गूँजती। उसी का सिरा पकड़कर हम चलते जा रहे थे। रोशनी की एक झलक के लिए हम तरस रहे थे।

161. गद्य में 'टार्च के सैल जवाब देने' का क्या अर्थ है?
A. टार्च टूटने वाली थी
B. टार्च हाथ से गिरने वाली थी
C. ठण्ड से सैल लगभग जम गए थे
D. टार्च के सैल समाप्त होना

162. प्रस्तुत गद्य में किस प्रहर की चर्चा की गई है?
A. सुबह B. रात्रि
C. संध्या D. आधी रात

163. पैर दो-दो मन के होने का आशय स्पष्ट कीजिए।
A. हार मानना B. बहुत थकना
C. बोझ मानना D. निराश होना

164. इस गद्य में किस मैदान की चर्चा की है?
A. दलदल B. ग्लेशियर
C. अंधेरी घाटी D. सतलंजन का मैदान

165. रात के अंधेरे में लेखक किसके सहारे चल रहा था?
A. पगडंडी के सहारे
B. ममदू के आवाज के सहारे
C. टार्च के सहारे
D. भगवान भरोसे

निर्देश (प्रश्न संख्या 166 से 170): *निम्नलिखित प्रत्येक प्रश्न के चार-चार विकल्प दिए गए हैं। उनमें से सही विकल्प चुनिए।*

166. उपेक्षा का विलोम है :
A. सापेक्ष B. आदर
C. सम्मान D. अपेक्षा

167. चौराहा में कौन-सा समास है?
A. अव्ययीभाव B. कर्मधारय
C. द्विगु D. बहुब्रीहि

168. 'नूतन ब्रह्मचारी' उपन्यास के लेखक हैं :
A. मिश्रबन्धु B. प्रतापनारायण मिश्र
C. जगमोहन सिंह D. बालकृष्ण भट्ट

169. अश्व का पर्यायवाची है :
A. पद्म B. अनंग
C. बाजि D. इन्दीवर

170. पवन में कौन-सी संधि है?
A. दीर्घ B. गुण
C. अयादि D. यण

171. कौन-से वर्णों को व्यंजन तथा स्वर के मध्य का माना जाता है?
A. अनुस्वार B. आयोग वाह
C. उष्म D. अन्तस्थ

172. *चिरंजीव जोरि जुरै, क्यों न स्नेह गंभीर।*
को घटि ये वृषभानुजा, वे हलधर के वीर।।
में अलंकार है :
A. यमक B. दीपक
C. श्लेष D. उत्प्रेक्षा

173. भावुक शब्द का सन्धि विच्छेद है :
A. भव + आवुक B. भाव + उक
C. भौ + उक D. भावु + उक

174. तत्सम शब्द का चयन कीजिए :
A. अश्रु B. पगड़ी
C. कान D. रेडियो

175. मनमाना में समास है :

A. अव्ययीभाव B. कर्मधारय

C. बहुव्रीहि D. द्विगु

176. सर्प में कौन-सा प्रत्यय है?

A. अ B. अर

C. अर्प D. सर्

177. "अंग फूले न समाना" मुहावरे का अर्थ है :

A. बहुत खुश होना

B. अपनी झूठी प्रशंसा करना

C. असम्भव कार्य करना

D. सीने से लगाना

178. 'घी का लड्डू टेढ़ा भी भला' कहावत का अर्थ है :

A. मुँह पर मीठी-मीठी बातें करना

B. योग्य व्यक्ति की आलोचना करना

C. उपयोगी वस्तु का रूप-रंग नहीं देखा जाता

D. सरल स्वभाव का होना

179. अरविंद दर्शन से प्रभावित कवि हैं :

A. प्रसाद B. निराला

C. पंत D. अज्ञेय

180. शुद्ध वर्तनी का चयन कीजिए :

A. मृत्यूंजय B. म्रित्यन्जय

C. मृत्युंजय D. मृत्युन्जय

उत्तरमाला

1	**2**	**3**	**4**	**5**	**6**	**7**	**8**	**9**	**10**
C	B	B	A	D	A	C	C	A	D
11	**12**	**13**	**14**	**15**	**16**	**17**	**18**	**19**	**20**
A	B	C	D	C	D	B	A	C	A
21	**22**	**23**	**24**	**25**	**26**	**27**	**28**	**29**	**30**
C	B	B	D	A	C	D	A	A	C
31	**32**	**33**	**34**	**35**	**36**	**37**	**38**	**39**	**40**
D	A	A	A	D	D	C	B	D	B
41	**42**	**43**	**44**	**45**	**46**	**47**	**48**	**49**	**50**
B	B	A	A	A	B	B	A	B	D
51	**52**	**53**	**54**	**55**	**56**	**57**	**58**	**59**	**60**
D	C	B	D	D	A	C	C	D	A
61	**62**	**63**	**64**	**65**	**66**	**67**	**68**	**69**	**70**
C	D	A	D	C	A	C	A	D	D
71	**72**	**73**	**74**	**75**	**76**	**77**	**78**	**79**	**80**
A	C	D	A	D	B	D	B	B	C
81	**82**	**83**	**84**	**85**	**86**	**87**	**88**	**89**	**90**
B	D	C	C	B	C	D	B	A	B
91	**92**	**93**	**94**	**95**	**96**	**97**	**98**	**99**	**100**
D	B	B	A	A	D	B	C	C	B
101	**102**	**103**	**104**	**105**	**106**	**107**	**108**	**109**	**110**
D	C	B	C	D	A	C	B	C	C
111	**112**	**113**	**114**	**115**	**116**	**117**	**118**	**119**	**120**
C	D	B	C	B	B	B	C or D	B	D
121	**122**	**123**	**124**	**125**	**126**	**127**	**128**	**129**	**130**
B	C	C	A	D	B	D	A	B	A

131	132	133	134	135	136	137	138	139	140
C	D	*	B	A	D	C	B	B	C
141	**142**	**143**	**144**	**145**	**146**	**147**	**148**	**149**	**150**
D	C	A	B	B	C	A	B	A	B
151	**152**	**153**	**154**	**155**	**156**	**157**	**158**	**159**	**160**
D	B	A	C	D	A	C	D	B	A
161	**162**	**163**	**164**	**165**	**166**	**167**	**168**	**169**	**170**
D	D	B	D	B	D	C	D	C	C
171	**172**	**173**	**174**	**175**	**176**	**177**	**178**	**179**	**180**
B	C	C	A	A	A	A	C	C	C

व्याख्यात्मक उत्तर

Qs. No. 11-14:

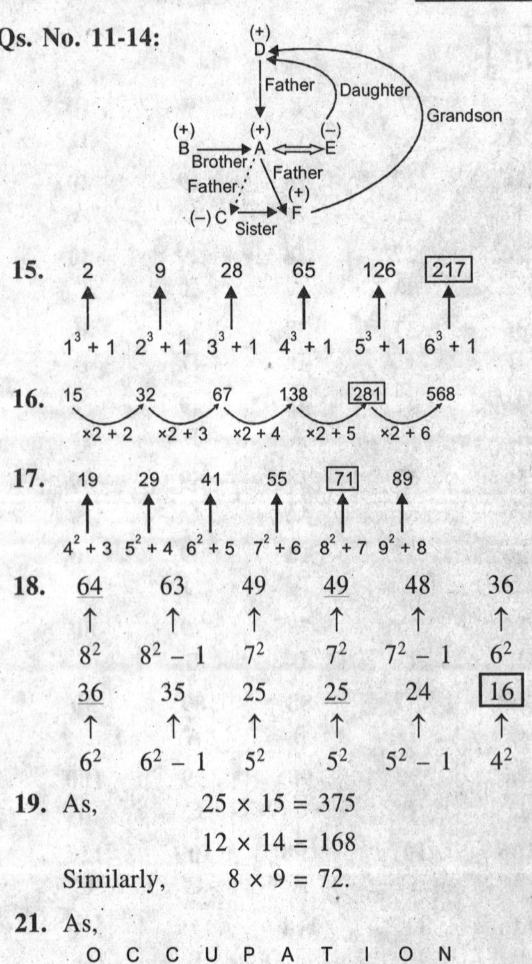

15. 2, 9, 28, 65, 126, [217]

1^3+1, 2^3+1, 3^3+1, 4^3+1, 5^3+1, 6^3+1

16. 15, 32, 67, 138, [281], 568

×2 + 2, ×2 + 3, ×2 + 4, ×2 + 5, ×2 + 6

17. 19, 29, 41, 55, [71], 89

4^2+3, 5^2+4, 6^2+5, 7^2+6, 8^2+7, 9^2+8

18. 64, 63, 49, 49, 48, 36

8^2, 8^2-1, 7^2, 7^2, 7^2-1, 6^2

36, 35, 25, 25, 24, [16]

6^2, 6^2-1, 5^2, 5^2, 5^2-1, 4^2

19. As, 25 × 15 = 375

12 × 14 = 168

Similarly, 8 × 9 = 72.

21. As,

O C C U P A T I O N

+2 +2 +2 +2 +2 +2 +2 +2 +2 +2

Q E E W R C V K Q P

Similarly,

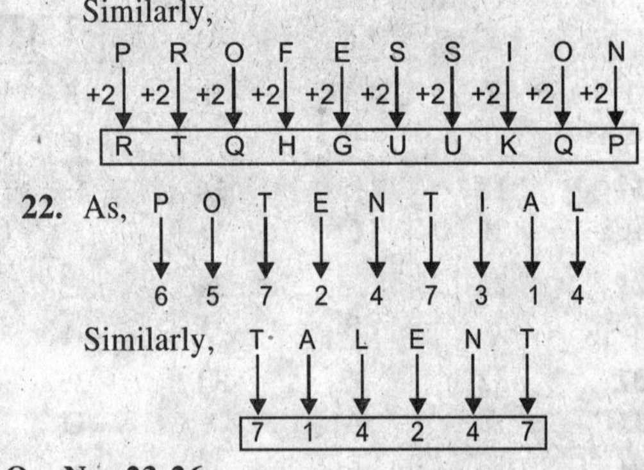

P R O F E S S I O N

+2 +2 +2 +2 +2 +2 +2 +2 +2 +2

R T Q H G U U K Q P

22. As, P O T E N T I A L

6 5 7 2 4 7 3 1 4

Similarly, T A L E N T

7 1 4 2 4 7

Qs. No. 23-26:

	Mariam	Kunti	Begum	Shilpi	Meera
Initially	6	6	6	6	6
Step–1	3	6	6	9	6
Step–2	3	8	6	5	8
Step–3	7	8	2	5	8
Step–4	1	11	2	5	11
Step-5	1	6	7	5	11
Step-6	1	6	7	9	7

Qs. No. 27-30:

	Sports				
Player	**Cricket**	**Tennis**	**Hockey**	**Volleyball**	**Football**
A	✓	✓	×	✓	×
B	✓	✓	✓	×	×
C	×	✓	×	✓	✓
D	×	×	✓	×	✓
E	×	×	×	×	✓

101. LCM (15, 25, 40, 75)

$= 5 \times 5 \times 3 \times 2 \times 2 \times 2 = 600$

5	15,	25,	40,	75
5	3,	5,	8,	15
3	3,	1,	8,	3
2	1,	1,	8,	1
2	1,	1,	4,	1
2	1,	1,	2,	1
	1,	1,	1,	1

$\because$ Largest number of 4 digit = 9999

```
600) 9999 (16
     600
     3999
     3600
      399  ← Remainder
```

$\therefore$ Required Number = 9999 − 399 = 9600.

102. We have, 65.425×0.03216

$= 65425 \times 10^{-3} \times 3216 \times 10^{-5}$

$= (65425 \times 3216) \times 10^{-8}$

Hence, there will be 8 digit after decimal point.

103. Let the cost price of one pen = x

Loss = Cost price of 5 pen = ₹ $5x$

Cost price of 17 pen = $17x$

$\therefore$ Selling price = Cost price − Loss

$17x - 5x = 720$

$12x = 720 \Rightarrow x =$ ₹ 60.

104. Cost price of one orange = ₹ $\frac{4}{5}$

Selling price of one orange = ₹ $\frac{5}{4}$

Required profit %

$= \frac{SP - CP}{CP} \times 100$

$= \frac{\frac{5}{4} - \frac{4}{5}}{\frac{4}{5}} \times 100 = \frac{\left(\frac{9}{20}\right)}{\left(\frac{4}{5}\right)} \times 100 = \frac{9 \times 5}{80} \times 100$

= 56.25%.

105. $(5.6)^2 + 5.6p + (3.4)^2$

$= (5.6)^2 + 2 \times 5.6 \times 3.4 + (3.4)^2$

$= (5.6 + 3.4)^2$

$= (9)^2 = 81$ (Perfect square)

On comparing,

$p = 2 \times 3.4 = 6.8.$

106. Let the height of pillar be = x

Then, length of shadow = $\sqrt{3}x$

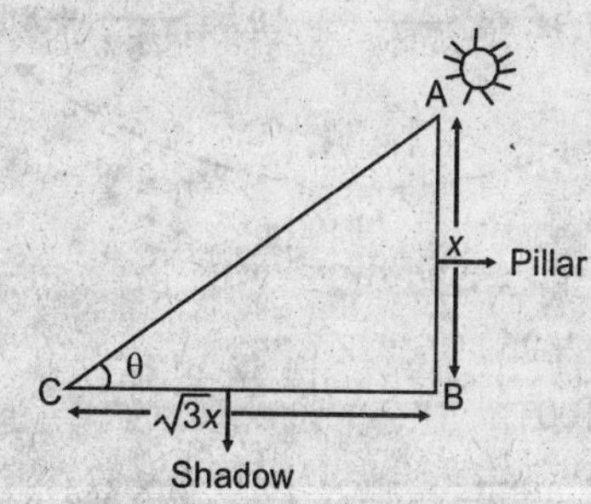

In ΔABC, $\tan\theta = \frac{AB}{BC}$

$\tan\theta = \frac{x}{\sqrt{3}x}$

$\tan\theta = \frac{1}{\sqrt{3}}$

$\tan\theta = \tan 30°$

$\theta = 30°.$

108. Prime Number between 20 and 50 are

23, 29, 31, 37, 41, 43, 47.

109. $\frac{(3.6)^2 - (1.4)^2}{3.6 - 1.4}$

$= \frac{(3.6 + 1.4)(3.6 + 1.4)}{(3.6 - 1.4)}$

$= 3.6 + 1.4 = 5$ [$\because a^2 - b^2 = (a + b)(a - b)$]

110. $\because$ Multiplication of two numbers

= HCF × LCM

25 × Second number = 5 × 150

Second number = $\frac{5 \times 150}{25} = 30.$

111. $\because$ Minute hand is behind hour hand

$\therefore$ Required Angle $= \dfrac{60\text{H} - 11\text{M}}{2}$

$= \dfrac{60 \times 8 - 11 \times 30}{2}$

$= \dfrac{480 - 330}{2} = \dfrac{150}{2} = 75°.$

112. Let Marked price = ₹ 100

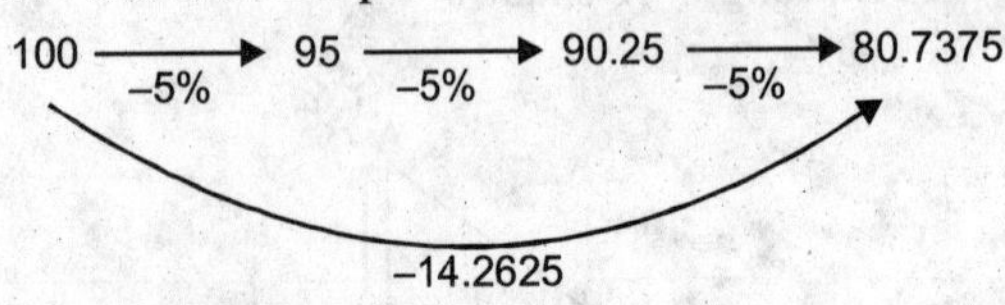

Required single discount

$= \dfrac{14.2625}{100} \times 100 = 14.26.$

113. Total minute till 5 : 10 O'clocks

$= 5 \times 60 + 10 = 310$ minutes

$\because$ Hour hand moves in 1 minute $= \left(\dfrac{1}{2}\right)^\circ$

Hour hand moves in 310 minutes

$= \dfrac{1}{2} \times 310 = 155°.$

114. Let fruit seller had x oranges initially

Oranges left with Fruit seller

$= (100 - 30)\%$ of x

$= 70\%$ of $x = \dfrac{7x}{10}$

According to question, $\dfrac{7x}{10} = 245$

$x = \dfrac{2450}{7} = 350$

Hence, Fruit seller had 350 oranges initially.

115. We have, speed of train = 45 km/h

$= 45 \times \dfrac{5}{18} = \dfrac{25}{2}$ m/s

Total distance travelled = 360 + 140 = 500 m

$\because$ Time $= \dfrac{\text{Distance}}{\text{Speed}} = \dfrac{500}{\left(\dfrac{25}{2}\right)}$

$= 20 \times 2 = 40$ sec.

116. $\log\dfrac{a}{b} + \log\dfrac{b}{a} = \log(a + b)$

$\because$ $\log m + \log n = \log mn$

$\therefore$ $\log\dfrac{a}{b} \times \dfrac{b}{a} = \log(a + b)$

$\log(a + b) = \log 1$

$\log(a + b) = 0$

$\because$ $a + b = e^0$

$a + b = 1.$

117. The number which is 10% more than 200

$= 200 \times 110\% = 220$

Hence, first number $= 220 \times (100 - 10)\%$

$= 220 \times 90\% = 198.$

118. $\because$ 1 hour $= 60 \times 60 = 3600$ seconds

$\therefore$ Required Ratio $= \dfrac{1}{3600}$

$= 0.00027$ or $0.00028.$

119. Speed of train = 40 km/h

$= 40 \times \dfrac{5}{18}$

$= \dfrac{200}{18} = \dfrac{100}{9}$ m/h

$\because$ Length of train = Speed × Time

$= \dfrac{100}{9} \times 18$

$= 200$ m.

120. Passing marks = 240 + 60 = 300

$\therefore$ Required passing percentage

$= \dfrac{300}{600} \times 100 = 50\%.$

Previous Paper (Solved)

IGNOU B.Ed. ENTRANCE EXAM 2018*

PART-A

Section-I : General English Comprehension

Directions (Q. Nos. 1-10): *Read the following passage carefully and choose the best answer out of the four choices given after each question that follows.*

Among the most important themes in the Disney movie 'The Little Mermaid' are those of questioning conventional thinking and pursuing a dream. Not only is Ariel the little memaid, demonstrating original thought (something that many seem to think she is lacking) but she is rebelling against her speciesist father. When Ariel expresses her love for the human prince, King Trident is furious. When Ariel points out angrily that he does not understand her, or even know the man whom she loves, Trident retorts "know him? I don't need to know him! He's a human!" In a very real way, Disney is encouraging children to question preconceived ideas that we may have against a certain group.

Disney also teaches children to pursue what they love. We see that Ariel's love for Prince Eric is more important than all else. In turning to the sea witch, Ursula, for help, Ariel makes a mistake but no true hero or heroine is flawless. Ariel puts herself, her family and all merfolk in danger, but we see that with the help of her prince, she is able to put everything to right.

At the end of the film, when Ursula has forced King Trident to sacrifice his kingdom for his daughter's soul, the sea witch uses out of the water, gigantic and terrifying, wearing the king's crown and holding his magic trident. She laughs evilly and declares that she is the ruler of all mermen and women. "So much for true love!" She screams victoriously. Eric, however, succeeds in piloting the prow of his ship straight through her Belly, vanquishing her. The moral here is that while we all make mistakes, what is truly important is how we right the wrongs we may do to others.

1. Why does the author use parentheses around the comment "Something that many seem to think she is lacking"?
A. to indicate a side comment to the reader
B. to indicate that it is unimportant
C. to indicate a humorous tone
D. to indicate a shift in meaning

2. Ariel's father is called a 'speciesist' because he:
A. does not understand Eric
B. opposes Ariel's love based only on Eric being human
C. is furious
D. is rebelling against preconceived notions

3. Which of the following fictional plot line would best illustrate the assertion "Disney is encouraging children to question pre-conceived ideas that we may have against a certain group"?
A. A movie about the develop-ment of the television
B. A movie that details the honours of war
C. A movie about a girl who overcomes her fear of snakes
D. A movie that documents the travels of a rock band

4. When Ursula says "So much for true love", what does it imply?
A. She is specialist
B. She was hurt in a previous love affair
C. Marriage was unacceptable to her
D. She is mocking true love

* Held on 16-12-2018.

5. In the sentence "Eric, however, succeeds in piloting the prow of his ship straight through her Belly, vanquishing her", what does 'vanquishing' mean?
A. Killing B. Loving
C. Vanishing D. Squashing

6. The author's attitude towards 'The Little Mermaid' is primarily one of:
A. frustration B. stoicism
C. respect D. wonder

7. The author's main point in the passage is:
A. Ariel should not have been allowed to marry Eric
B. 'The Little Mermaid' (film) teaches children to follow their hearts
C. Disney movies teach that love is stronger than hate
D. Only Prince Eric truly understood Ariel

8. 'Prow' of a ship is at the:
A. back B. middle
C. front D. top

9. What was the mistake committed by Ariel?
A. Loving Eric
B. Rebelling against her father
C. Taking Ursula's help
D. Killing Ursula with the help of Eric

10. In the sentence "...... the sea witch rises out of the water, gigantic and terrifying, ...", 'terrifying' is:
A. a gerund B. a participle
C. an adjective D. an adverb

Section-II : Logical and Analytical Reasoning

Directions (Q. Nos. 11-14): *Study the following information carefully and answer the questions that follow.*

There are six members in a family—A, B, C, D, E and F. There are two married couples in the family. B is a businessman and father of E. F is the grandfather of C and is a property dealer. D is grandmother of E and is a housewife. C is the daughter of A. There are one businessman, one property dealer, one lady lecturer, one housewife and two students in the family.

11. What is the profession of A?
A. Housewife B. Lecturer
C. Student D. Business

12. Who is sister of E?
A. C B. D
C. A D. B

13. Which of the following are two married couples?
A. AC and DF B. AB and EF
C. AB and AC D. AB and DF

14. Which of the following is definitely a group of male members?
A. BF B. AB
C. CD D. EF

Directions (Qs. No. 15-18): *In the following questions a series is being given. Select from the alternatives the correct term to fill in the missing term.*

15. 10, 40, __?__, 1920, 19200
A. 80 B. 160
C. 200 D. 240

16. 0, 7, 26, 63, __?__, 215
A. 116 B. 128
C. 124 D. 130

17. 13, 21, 31, 43, 57, 73, __?__.
A. 87 B. 89
C. 91 D. 94

18. 4, 5, 8, 9, 10, 27, 16, 17, 64, 25, 26, __?__
A. 78 B. 94
C. 112 D. 125

19. Find the missing number.

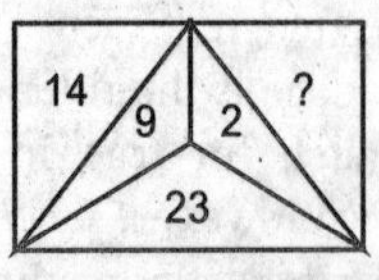

A. 25 B. 21
C. 19 D. 7

20. If EDUCATION is coded as DCTBZSHNM, how will PROMOTION be coded?

A. OQNNLSHNM B. NOQLNSHNM
C. NNOQLSHNM D. OQNLNSHNM

21. If REGISTRATION is coded as 723489719465, then GENERATOR will be coded as:

A. 325721967 B. 352721967
C. 325271967 D. 325917267

22. Which one is different from the other three in some respect?

A. August B. October
C. March D. December

Directions (Q. Nos. 23-26): *Read the paragraph and answer the questions that follow:*

Ira, Vara, Shweta, Pushpa and Saroj are five friends. Each one of them has six balls. Vara gives 3 balls to Pushpa who gives four balls to Saroj. Saroj gives five balls to Shweta who in turn gives four balls to Vara. Vara gives three balls each to Ira and Pushpa.

23. How many balls does Vara have?

A. 2 B. 1
C. 5 D. 6

24. How many balls does Saroj have?

A. 2 B. 4
C. 5 D. 6

25. Who has the minimum number of balls?

A. Ira
B. Pushpa
C. Saroj
D. Vara

26. Who has the maximum number of balls?

A. Ira B. Shweta
C. Saroj D. Vara

Directions (Q. Nos. 27-30): *Read the paragraph and answer the questions that follow.*

A and B play Volleyball and Football. B and D play Tennis, A and C play Hockey and Tennis. C, D and E play Cricket.

27. Who plays Volleyball, Football, Tennis and Hockey?

A. D B. C
C. B D. A

28. Who plays only Cricket?

A. A B. E
C. C D. D

29. Who plays Hockey and Cricket?

A. A B. B
C. C D. D

30. Who plays Tennis and Cricket?

A. A B. B
C. C D. D

Section-III : Educational and General Awareness

31. The recommendations of Shanta Kumar Committee are related to:

A. Restructuring of Food Corporation of India (FCI)
B. Restructuring of Security Exchange Board of India (SEBI)
C. Restructuring of Central Board of Film Certification (CBFC)
D. None of the above

32. The book 'at the Close of the Play' is an autobiography of:

A. Gary Kirsten B. Yuvraj Singh
C. Rahul Dravid D. Ricky Ponting

33. Which of the following is the largest gulf in the world?

A. Gulf of Aden B. Gulf of Guinea
C. Persian Gulf D. Gulf of Mexico

34. Who was the author of the Book "The Indian War of Independence, 1857"?

A. Sir Syed Ahmed Khan
B. V.D. Savarkar
C. S.R. Sharma
D. R.C. Majumdar

35. World Yoga Day is celebrated every year on:

A. 20th June B. 21st June
C. 22nd June D. 23rd June

36. Who abolished the use of Persian as court language and ordered the use of vernacular language?

A. William Bentinck B. Cornwallis
C. Warren Hastings D. John Shore

37. Abdul Kalam Island is located in:

A. Tamil Nadu B. Andhra Pradesh
C. West Bengal D. Odisha

38. In the context of Indian history, the principle of 'Dyarchy' refers to:

A. Division of the Central legislature into two houses
B. Introduction of double Government *i.e.*, Central and State Government
C. Having two sets of rulers; one in London other in Delhi
D. Division of the subjects delegated to the provinces into two categories

39. Which one of the following countries topped the World Happiness Report, 2017 published by United Nations Sustainable Development Solutions Network?

A. India B. Denmark
C. Norway D. USA

40. According to Swachh Survekshan 2017, which city is declared as Cleanest City in India?

A. Vishakhapatnam B. Bhopal
C. Idukki D. Indore

41. Which of the following universities celebrated its Centenary Year in 2017?

A. Allahabad University
B. Patna University
C. Banaras Hindu University
D. Aligarh Muslim University

42. Vidhyanjali Scheme was an initiative of:

A. Ministry of Youth Affairs and Sports
B. Ministry of Science and Technology
C. Ministry of Labour and Employment
D. Ministry of Human Resource Development

43. The first country to implement G.S.T. was:

A. France B. USA
C. Britain D. Japan

44. The objective of Butler Committee of 1927 was to:

A. Defend the Jurisdiction of the Central and Provincial Governments
B. Define the powers of the secretary of State for India
C. Impose censorship on national press
D. Investigate and clarify the relationship between the paramount power and the princess of princely states

45. Right to Education Act was enacted in the year:

A. 2007 B. 2008
C. 2009 D. 2010

46. The statement "Tamsoma Jyotirgamya" was originally mentioned in:

A. Upanishad B. Mahakavya
C. Purana D. Shaddarshan

47. Who built the Khajuraho Temples?

A. Vijayanagar Kings
B. Bahmani Kings
C. Chandel Kings
D. Gupta Kings

48. Hockey India League started in the year:

A. 2010 B. 2011
C. 2013 D. 2012

49. With reference to the economic history of Medieval India, the term 'Araghatta' refers to:

A. Bonded labour
B. Land grants made to military officers
C. Waterwheel used in the irrigation of land
D. Waterland converted to cultivated land

50. The Rashtriya Madhyamik Shiksha Abhiyan (RMSA) Scheme was launched in the year:

A. 2007 B. 2008
C. 2009 D. 2010

51. Mahila Samakhya is a programme which focuses on:

A. Women education
B. Issues of adolescent girls
C. Women empowerment
D. Health issues of rural women

52. Who originally commissioned Sanchi Stupa?
A. Emperor Ashoka
B. Chandragupta Maurya
C. Harshvardhan
D. Kanishka

53. SWAYAM PRABHA channel was launched by MHRD during:
A. 2014 B. 2015
C. 2016 D. 2017

54. The norms and regulations of NCTE for two year B.Ed. programme were notified in the year:
A. 2013 B. 2014
C. 2015 D. 2016

55. Who is awarded Sahitya Academy Prize in Hindi for the year 2016?
A. Prabha Verma B. Geeta Upadhyay
C. Nasira Sharma D. Swaraj Bir

Section-IV : Teaching-Learning and The School

56. The purpose of formative assessment is to:
A. check learner's performance graph
B. grade student's learning outcome
C. accelerate student's learning performance
D. provide feedback to teacher effectiveness

57. Why is teacher training necessary?
A. Helps in acquiring teaching skills
B. In understanding methods of school organisation
C. Upgrading knowledge of content
D. All the above

58. Drama is suitable for teaching:
A. History B. Science
C. Language D. All the above

59. The greatest satisfaction in teaching is:
A. Feeling of love for children
B. A sense of service to mankind
C. A secured monetary gain
D. A sense of contribution to learner's all-round develop-ment

60. Human personality is the result of:
A. Upbringing at home
B. Interaction between heredity and environment
C. Only environment
D. Only heredity

61. Which of the following is an objective type question?
A. Short answer question
B. Open ended question
C. True and False
D. Essay type question

62. Who is regarded as a first teacher of a child?
A. Headmaster
B. Class teacher
C. Mother
D. Tutor

63. A teacher who is not able to draw the attention of her students should:
A. resign from the post
B. find fault in her learners
C. start dictating
D. evaluate her teaching method and improve it

64. Blackboard can be included in which group/ category of teaching aid?
A. Audio aid
B. Visual aid
C. Audio-Visual aid
D. None of these

65. 10+2+3 system of education was recom-mended by:
A. Mudaliar Commission
B. National Policy of Education (1986)
C. Kothari Commission
D. Radhakrishanan Commission

66. For maintaining an effective discipline in the class, the teacher should:
A. allow students to do what they like
B. deal with the students strictly

C. involve the students in interesting activities
D. deal with them politely and firmly

67. Informal education is:
A. Just schooling
B. Lifelong
C. Time bound
D. Pre-planned

68. Mental Health is:
A. Symptoms of maladjustment
B. Harmonious functioning of the total personality
C. Terrible excitement
D. Throwing up temper tantrums

69. Which of the following is mainly concerned with the software aspect of technology?
A. Computer
B. TV set
C. Floppy
D. Scripts

70. The psychological barrier in communication is:
A. noise
B. wrong perception
C. ambiguous words
D. previous knowledge

71. Full form of CABE is:
A. Central Administration Board of Education
B. Central Allied Board of Education
C. Central Advisory Board of Education
D. Central Administrative Board of Education

72. Which of the following is ***not*** a co-curricular activity?
A. organising a quiz
B. participating in a cultural programme organised in the school
C. reading a Journal in the school library
D. deputing a student for drama competition

73. Evaluation ascertains:
A. how far the learning objectives have been achieved
B. the weakness of instructional procedures
C. reinforcement and feedback
D. all of the above

74. Work experience in education means:
A. to inculcate in students right attitude towards work
B. to participate in productive work for living
C. to bridge the gap between school life and real life
D. all of the above

75. If a child is not taking interest in the classroom, the teacher must:
A. give more home assignment
B. report to parents
C. use teaching aids
D. involve students in teaching-learning through interactive activities

76. Maximum participation of students is possible in teaching through:
A. Lecture method
B. Textbook method
C. Discussion method
D. Audio-Video aids

77. A good textbook does ***not*** have the criteria of:
A. learner friendly
B. logical sequencing of content
C. high cost
D. interactive language

78. Slow learners in the class should be:
A. motivated
B. neglected
C. treated sympathetically
D. given easy assignment

79. The worst type of classroom management style is:
A. autocratic
B. democratic
C. co-operative
D. participatory

80. What is best suited source to acquire knowledge systematically?
A. from authority
B. by personal experiences
C. through scientific method
D. by expert opinion

PART-B

Section-V : (i) Science

81. Positive ions are formed from neutral atoms by the loss of:
A. neutrons B. nuclear charge
C. protons D. electrons

82. Which of the following statements is TRUE? Elements in the first column of the Periodic Table
A. are called alkali metals
B. are inert gases
C. have metallic lusture
D. are radioactive in nature

83. Which one of the following properties would a solution have if it is an acid?
A. Solution turns litmus blue.
B. Solution feels slippery.
C. Solution has a hydrogen ion concentration of 10^{-13} M.
D. Solution is a very good conductor of electricity.

84. Which of the electronic configurations given below would you expect for a noble gas?
A. $1s^2\ 2s^2\ 2p^6\ 3s^2$ B. $1s^2\ 2s^2\ 2p^6\ 3s^1$
C. $1s^2\ 2s^2\ 2p^6$ D. $1s^2\ 2s^2\ 2p^5$

85. How many atoms are contained in a mole of sulphuric acid, H_2SO_4?
A. $7 \times 6.02 \times 10^{23}$ atoms/mole
B. $5 \times 6.02 \times 10^{23}$ atoms/mole
C. $3 \times 6.02 \times 10^{23}$ atoms/mole
D. $8 \times 6.02 \times 10^{23}$ atoms/mole

86. What is the power of a convex lens whose focal length is 50 cm?
A. –2 D B. –0.5 D
C. +2 D D. +0.5 D

87. Which of the colours of visible light has minimum wave length?
A. Violet B. Red
C. Yellow D. Green

88. In a metallic conductor, electric current is due to the movement of:
A. ions B. amperes
C. electrons D. protons

89. An electric charge in uniform motion produces:
A. an electric field only
B. a magnetic field only
C. both electric and magnetic fields
D. no such field at all

90. The radiations emitted by a hot furnace are:
A. ultra-violet B. infra-red
C. X-rays D. microwaves

91. Normal blood pressure range (mm Hg) is:
A. 120/80 B. 100/60
C. 140/90 D. 90/50

92. Gastric digestion takes place efficiently in:
A. acidic medium
B. alkaline medium
C. neutral medium
D. highly alkaline medium

93. A doctor advised a person to take an injection of insulin because:
A. his blood pressure was low
B. his heart was beating slowly
C. he was suffering from goitre
D. his sugar level in blood was high

94. Which of the following is a plant hormone?
A. Insulin B. Thyroxine
C. Oestrogen D. Cytokinin

95. If a tall plant is crossed with a dwarf plant, what is this type of cross called?
A. dihybrid B. monohybrid
C. reciprocal D. trihybrid

96. What is the name of the discipline dealing with the study of inheritance?
A. Cytology B. Evolution
C. Genetics D. Morphology

97. Which of the following constitutes a food chain?
A. Grass, wheat and mango
B. Grass, goat and human
C. Goat, cow and elephant
D. Grass, fish and goat

98. The depletion of ozone shield is due to:
A. Chlorofluorocarbons
B. Oxides of nitrogen
C. Methane
D. All of these

99. Which of the following fuel is a fossil fuel?
A. Biogas
B. Biodiesel
C. Coal and Petroleum
D. Nuclear fuel

100. The main aim of conservation and preservation of the environment is to:
A. Preserve the plants
B. Preserve the animals
C. Preserve the fuels
D. Preserve the biodiversity

Section-V : (ii) Mathematics

101. The mean of first n natural numbers is:
A. $\frac{n}{2}$ B. $\frac{n(n+1)}{2}$
C. $\frac{n+2}{2}$ D. $\frac{n+1}{2}$

102. The fifth decile is the same as:
A. Mean B. Median
C. Mode D. Geometric Mean

103. For a positively skewed curve, which of the following is true?
A. Mean > Median B. Median > Mean
C. Mean = Median D. Mode > Mean

104. The 25th percentile coincides with:
A. Mean B. First Quartile
C. Median D. Third Quartile

105. If each side of a rectangle is increased by 20%, its area would increase by:
A. 20% B. 40%
C. 44% D. 56%

106. If the radius of circle is increased by 50%, the area of the circle would increase by:
A. 25% B. 125%
C. 50% D. 75%

107. Anil and Ankur can do a piece of work in 12 days, Ankur and Harish in 15 days. Harish and Anil in 20 days. How much time will Anil alone take to finish the work?
A. 25 days B. 35 days
C. 30 days D. 40 days

108. Which fraction is the largest?
A. $\frac{3}{7}$ B. $\frac{5}{9}$
C. $\frac{5}{11}$ D. $\frac{7}{13}$

109. Which fraction is the smallest?
A. $\frac{5}{6}$ B. $\frac{6}{7}$
C. $\frac{7}{8}$ D. $\frac{8}{9}$

110. What is 5 per cent of 10 per cent of 5?
A. 0.25 B. 0.0125
C. 0.0625 D. 0.025

111. A train moves at the speed of 180 km per hour. The speed of the train per second is:
A. 180 m B. 120 m
C. 90 m D. 50 m

112. A man sells an article for ₹ 20 and earns a profit of 20%. What is the cost price?
A. ₹ 16 B. ₹ 16.66
C. ₹ 15 D. ₹ 15.87

113. A student's score was wrongly entered as 83 instead of 63 which led to increase in average by $\frac{1}{2}$. The number of students in the class is:

A. 35 B. 40
C. 45 D. 50

114. A fruit vender buys oranges at 4 oranges for ₹ 3 and sells them at 3 oranges for ₹ 4. The profit per cent is about:
A. 66 B. 77
C. 88 D. 55

115. A man's speed along the current is 15 km/hr and the speed of the current is 1.5 km/hr. Man's speed against the current is:
A. 12.0 km/hr B. 16.5 km/hr
C. 13.5 km/hr D. 15.5 km/hr

116. Two numbers are in the ratio 2 : 3. If their LCM is 48, then the sum of numbers is:
A. 28 B. 36
C. 40 D. 42

117. What is the greatest possible length which can be used to measure exactly the rods of 8 m, 4 m 20 cm and 12 m 20 cm length?
A. 10 cm B. 15 cm
C. 20 cm D. 25 cm

118. What per cent of a day is the time of 4 hours?
A. 6% B. 33%
C. 16.66% D. 18.87%

119. A student obtained 125 marks but failed by 40 marks. If minimum pass marks are 33%, then the maximum marks for the exam is:
A. 240 B. 360
C. 420 D. 500

120. A man's salary was decreased by 50% and then increased by 50%. The net change is:
A. 25% increase B. 33% increase
C. 25% decrease D. 33% decrease

Section-V : (iii) Social Science

121. The Sikh Khalsa was founded by:
A. Guru Teg Bahadur
B. Guru Nanak
C. Guru Gobind Singh
D. Guru Hargobind

122. Relics of Buddha are preserved in a:
A. Vihara B. Chaitya
C. Stupa D. Monastery

123. Which was the first metal used by man?
A. Copper B. Silver
C. Bronze D. Brass

124. Who among the following attended all the three Round Table Conferences?
A. Madan Mohan Malviya
B. Annie Besant
C. Mahatma Gandhi
D. B.R. Ambedkar

125. Tulsidas was a contemporary of:
A. Babar
B. Akbar
C. Jahangir
D. Shahjahan

126. The study of heavenly bodies is known as:
A. Astrology B. Astronautics
C. Astronomy D. Astrophysics

127. A star which appears blue is:
A. Cooler than the moon
B. Hotter than the sun
C. As hot as the sun
D. Cooler than the sun

128. A sudden fall in the barometric reading indicates:
A. Rain B. Storm
C. Fine weather D. Extreme cold

129. Lunar eclipse is caused when the:
A. Moon comes between the Sun and the Earth
B. Earth comes between the Sun and the Moon
C. Sun comes between the Earth and Moon
D. None of the above

130. Which of the following is the largest river in the world?
A. Nile B. Congo
C. Ganga D. Amazon

131. Who among the following was the constitutional adviser to the Constituent Assembly of India?
A. Dr. B.N. Rau B. Dr. B.R. Ambedkar
C. K.M. Munshi D. M.C. Setalvad

132. The Annual Financial Statement is caused to be laid before both Houses of Parliament by the:
A. President B. Speaker
C. Vice-President D. Finance Minister

133. Which is the highest and final judicial tribunal in respect of the Constitutional of India?
A. Parliament B. President
C. Supreme Court D. Union Cabinet

134. Which of the following rights was described by Dr. B.R. Ambedkar as The Heart and Soul of the Constitution?
A. Right of Freedom of Religion
B. Right to Property
C. Right to Equality
D. Right to Constitutional Remedies

135. Which of the following is ***not*** a source of revenue to the village panchayats?
A. Property Tax B. House Tax
C. Land Tax D. Vehicles Tax

136. Who is called the Father of Economics?
A. Max Muller
B. Karl Marx
C. Adam Smith
D. None of these

137. Green Revolution is associated with _____ .
A. Agriculture
B. Science & Technology
C. Milk Production
D. Industry

138. GDR means:
A. Gross Domestic Ratio
B. Global Depository Receipt
C. Global Development Range
D. Geographically Developed Regions

139. What is Laissez-faire?
A. Mixed Economy
B. Controlled Economy
C. Non-interference of Govern-ment in economic affairs
D. None of the above

140. The Right to Information Act was enacted in the year:
A. 2005 B. 2006
C. 2007 D. 2008

Section-V : (iv) English

Directions (Q. Nos. 141-145): *Choose the word that is nearest in meaning to the underlined word.*

141. The annual meeting of Philosophy Professors was a gathering of the most erudite.
A. experienced B. senior
C. learned D. famous

142. Sarika was so ingenuous that her parents feared that she would be exploited.
A. genius B. clever
C. intelligent D. simple

143. Most of the Snakes are innocuous.
A. harmless B. fast
C. poisonous D. scary

144. The burglar tried to placate the barking dog.
A. hit B. pacify
C. shun D. harm

145. In traditional families, the young venerate their elders.
A. copy B. follow
C. revere D. fear

Directions (Q. Nos. 146-150): *In each of the following group of words, only one of them is correctly spelt. Select the one with the correct spelling.*

146. A. vasillate B. vacilate
C. vasilate D. vacillate

147. A. fluorescence B. flourescence
C. fluroscence D. florscence

148. A. Rapudiate B. Repudiate
C. Repudete D. Repudate

149. A. Pristin B. Prestine
C. Pristine D. Prestin

150. A. Maleable B. Meleable
C. Melleable D. Malleable

Directions (Q. Nos. 151-154): *Choose the word that is opposite in meaning to the underlined word.*

151. Particle physics is an esoteric field of knowledge.
A. Popular B. Abstruse
C. Obscure D. Difficult

152. The life of mayflies seems momentary.
A. Mysterious B. Evanescent
C. Eternal D. Transient

153. The principal was uncompromising on the issue of discipline.
A. Inflexible B. flexible
C. tenacious D. intransigent

154. The store cashier was so lethargic that he always had a long queue in front of him.
A. Apathetic B. Listless
C. Energetic D. Languid

Directions (Q. Nos. 155 and 156): *Select the word in each group that does not belong to it.*

155. A. Loquacious B. Gossipy
C. Verbose D. Amicable

156. A. Unscruplous B. Meticulous
C. Conscientious D. Precise

Directions (Q. Nos. 157-160): *Pick out the most appropriate word from the given alternatives to fill in the blank to complete the sentence.*

157. After Amar betrayed his teammates by giving away their plan to the opposition, they called him _______ .
A. a sycophant B. a traitor
C. an imbecile D. an expert

158. Although Mary receives ______ from critics for her unconventional acting style, she never considers changing to please them.
A. kudos B. appreciation
C. tirades D. empathy

159. Friends often seek Deepika's _______ as she is known for her ability to listen carefully and offer unbiased advice.
A. concern B. empathy
C. attention D. counsel

160. Behavioural theory is _______ in nature as it focuses on observation and direct study of actions.
A. empirical B. didactic
C. theoretical D. obtuse

Section-V : (v) हिन्दी

निर्देश (प्रश्न संख्या 161 से 165): *निम्नलिखित गद्यांश को ध्यानपूर्वक पढ़कर उसके आधार पर पूछे गए प्रश्नों के उत्तर दीजिए।*

"एक ही काम अब शेष था। पर्ण कुटी कैसी बनी है, देर से जानने की इच्छा मुझे हो रही थी। सो बट-दादा के केश पकड़कर फिर नीचे उतरा और पास की एक शिला पर बैठकर निश्चिंत हृदय से अपनी इच्छा तृप्त करने लगा। अपनी वस्तु चाहे कितनी ही साधारण क्यों न हो, पर हमारी आँखें उसे बहुत सुंदर रूप में देखती हैं। यही हाल मेरा था। वास्तव में पर्ण-कुटी चाहे कैसी ही रही हो, मुझे वह सुंदर जान पड़ रही थी। इस पर भी कुशा घास एवं वट वृक्ष के सहयोग से वह पर्णशाला मुझे किसी योगाश्रम की पवित्र कुटी-सी मालूम पड़ी। भयंकर जंगल के बीच सिंह-व्याघ्र आदि से रक्षा करने वाली धरती से पंद्रह फीट की ऊँचाई पर बनी पर्ण-कुटी को देखकर मेरा हृदय पुलकित हो उठा। बट-दादा की अनेक भुजाओं ने उसे चारों तरफ से घेरकर अपनी गोद में सुरक्षित बैठाया हुआ था।

161. पर्ण-कुटी किससे बनी थी?
A. बट-दादा के केश से
B. कुशा घास से
C. पत्ते से
D. बट-दादा की भुजाओं से

162. पर्ण-कुटी कहाँ पर बनाई गई थी?
A. आंगन में
B. बाग में
C. घर में
D. जंगल में

163. लेखक को पर्ण-कुटी सुरक्षित क्यों लगी?
A. क्योंकि यह जंगल में थी।
B. क्योंकि इसे वट वृक्ष की भुजाओं ने चारों ओर से घेर रखा था।
C. क्योंकि यह धरती से पन्द्रह फीट ऊँचाई पर थी।
D. क्योंकि यह कुटी पवित्र-सी मालूम होती थी।

164. लेखक अपनी इच्छा कैसे तृप्त करने लगा?
A. जंगल में घूमकर
B. वट वृक्ष पर बैठकर
C. शिला पर बैठकर पर्णकुटी देखकर
D. झूला-झूल कर

165. ''एक ही काम अब शेष था'' से लेखक का क्या तात्पर्य है?
A. यह जानना कि पर्णकुटी कैसी बनी थी।
B. यह जानना कि पर्णकुटी किससे बनी थी।
C. यह जानना कि पर्णकुटी कैसे बनी थी।
D. यह जानना कि पर्णकुटी कहाँ बनी है।

निर्देश (प्रश्न संख्या 166 से 180): *निम्नलिखित प्रत्येक प्रश्न के चार-चार विकल्प दिए गए हैं। उनमें से सही विकल्प चुनिए।*

166. जिसमें स्वरों का परिवर्तन य्, र्, व में होता है :
A. वृद्धि सन्धि
B. यण सन्धि
C. गुण सन्धि
D. अयादि सन्धि

167. त्रिफला में कौन-सा समास है?
A. द्वन्द्व
B. द्विगु
C. अव्ययीभाव
D. बहुब्रीहि

168. हंस का पर्यायवाची है :
A. पुष्कर
B. मराल
C. महाग्रीव
D. मर्कट

169. 'गूलर का फूल होना' मुहावरे का अर्थ है :
A. बहुत प्रिय होना
B. अवसरवादी होना
C. सदा कुटिल होना
D. दुर्लभ होना

170. 'सहन' में कौन-सा प्रत्यय है?
A. अ
B. अन
C. सह
D. हन

171. अंतस्थ व्यंजन नहीं है :
A. य
B. व
C. ल
D. ह

172. 'पृथ्वीकल्प' किसकी रचना है?
A. गिरिजा कुमार माथुर
B. धूमिल
C. कुमार विकल
D. दुष्यंत कुमार

173. आहार का विलोम है :
A. विहार
B. अनाहार
C. निराहार
D. संहार

174. ''ना सावन सूखा ना भादो हरा'' का क्या अर्थ है?
A. बेकार रहना
B. बारिश न होना
C. सर्वदा एक स्थिति में रहना
D. प्रसिद्ध होना

175. शिल्पगत आधार पर दोहे से उल्टा छन्द है :
A. सोरठा
B. शार्दूल
C. चौपाई
D. कुण्डलिया

176. *'पूत कपूत तो का धन संचय।*
पूत सूपत तो का धन संचय'।।
में अलंकार है :
A. उपमा
B. रूपक
C. भ्रान्तिमान
D. अनुप्रास

177. लिपि का विशेषण है :
A. लिपिबद्ध
B. लिपिक
C. लिपिक कार्य
D. लेखक

178. पुष्पित में प्रत्यय है :
A. इ
B. आइ
C. इत्
D. अ

179. तत्सम शब्द का चयन कीजिए :

A. कोसा B. कुपात्र

C. काहिल D. किसान

180. शुद्ध वर्तनी का चयन कीजिए :

A. परिणिति B. परणति

C. परणिति D. परीणीत

ANSWERS

1	2	3	4	5	6	7	8	9	10
A	B	C	D	D	C	B	C	C	C
11	**12**	**13**	**14**	**15**	**16**	**17**	**18**	**19**	**20**
B	A	D	A	D	C	C	D	B	D
21	**22**	**23**	**24**	**25**	**26**	**27**	**28**	**29**	**30**
C	C	B	C	D	A	D	B	C	D
31	**32**	**33**	**34**	**35**	**36**	**37**	**38**	**39**	**40**
A	D	D	B	B	A	D	A	C	D
41	**42**	**43**	**44**	**45**	**46**	**47**	**48**	**49**	**50**
B	D	A	D	C	A	C	C	C	C
51	**52**	**53**	**54**	**55**	**56**	**57**	**58**	**59**	**60**
A	A	C	B	C	C	D	D	D	B
61	**62**	**63**	**64**	**65**	**66**	**67**	**68**	**69**	**70**
C	C	D	B	B	C	B	B	A	B
71	**72**	**73**	**74**	**75**	**76**	**77**	**78**	**79**	**80**
C	C	D	D	D	C	C	C	D	B
81	**82**	**83**	**84**	**85**	**86**	**87**	**88**	**89**	**90**
D	A	D	C	A	C	A	A	C	B
91	**92**	**93**	**94**	**95**	**96**	**97**	**98**	**99**	**100**
A	A	D	D	B	C	B	A	C	D
101	**102**	**103**	**104**	**105**	**106**	**107**	**108**	**109**	**110**
D	D	A	C	C	B	C	B	A	D
111	**112**	**113**	**114**	**115**	**116**	**117**	**118**	**119**	**120**
D	B	B	B	A	C	C	C	D	C
121	**122**	**123**	**124**	**125**	**126**	**127**	**128**	**129**	**130**
C	C	A	D	B	C	B	B	C	A
131	**132**	**133**	**134**	**135**	**136**	**137**	**138**	**139**	**140**
A	A	C	D	A	C	A	B	C	A
141	**142**	**143**	**144**	**145**	**146**	**147**	**148**	**149**	**150**
C	D	A	B	C	D	A	B	C	D
151	**152**	**153**	**154**	**155**	**156**	**157**	**158**	**159**	**160**
A	C	B	C	D	A	B	C	D	A
161	**162**	**163**	**164**	**165**	**166**	**167**	**168**	**169**	**170**
B	D	B	C	A	B	B	B	D	B
171	**172**	**173**	**174**	**175**	**176**	**177**	**178**	**179**	**180**
D	A	C	C	A	D	A	C	B	A

Explanatory Answers

11-14.

(Property Dealer) F (+) ⟺ D (−) (Housewife)

(Lecturer) A (−) ⟺ B (+) (Businessman)

(Student) C (−) ⟺ E (Student)

11. Profession of A is Lecturer.

12. C is Sister of E.

13. AB and DF.

14. BF.

15. 10 → 40 → **240** → 1920 → 19200

×4, ×6, ×8, ×10

16. 0, 7, 26, 63, **124**, 215

1^3-1, 2^3-1, 3^3-1, 4^3-1, 5^3-1, 6^3-1

17. 13, 21, 31, 43, 57, 73, **91**

+8, +10, +12, +14, +16, +18

+2, +2, +2, +2, +2

18. 4, 5, 8, 9, 10, 27, 16, 17, 64, 25, 26, **125**

2^2, 2^2+1, 2^3, 3^2, 3^2+1, 3^3, 4^2, 4^2+1, 4^3, 5^2, 5^2+1, 5^3

20. As,

E D U C A T I O N

−1 −1 −1 −1 −1 −1 −1 −1 −1

D C T B Z S H N M

Similarly,

P R O M O T I O N

−1 −1 −1 −1 −1 −1 −1 −1 −1

O Q N L N S H N M

21. As,

R E G I S T R A T I O N

↓ ↓ ↓ ↓ ↓ ↓ ↓ ↓ ↓ ↓ ↓ ↓

7 2 3 4 8 9 7 1 9 4 6 5

Similarly,

G E N E R A T O R

↓ ↓ ↓ ↓ ↓ ↓ ↓ ↓ ↓

3 2 5 2 7 1 9 6 7

22. Except (C) March, all others are even number months.

23-26.

Ira (6 Balls) – Vara (6 Balls) – Shweta (6 Balls) – Pushpa (6 Balls) – Saroj (6 Balls)

Vara (6 – 3 = 3 Balls) → Pushpa (6 + 3 = 9 Balls)

Pushpa (9 – 4 = 5 Balls) → Saroj (6 + 4 = 10 Balls)

Saroj (10 – 5 = 5 Balls) → Shweta (6 + 5 = 11 Balls)

Shweta (11 – 4 = 7 Balls) → Vara (3 + 4 = 7 Balls)

Vara (7 – 3 = 4 Balls) → Ira (6 + 3 = 9 Balls)

Vara (4 – 3 = 1 Balls) → Pushpa (5 + 3 = 8 Balls)

23. 1 **24.** 5 **25.** Vara **26.** Ira

27-30.

	Volleyball	Football	Tennis	Hockey	Cricket
A	✔	✔	✔	✔	×
B	✔	✔	✔	×	×
C	×	×	✔	✔	✔
D	×	×	✔	×	✔
E	×	×	×	×	✔

27. A **28.** E **29.** C **30.** D

101. The sum of first n natural numbers

$$= \frac{n(n+1)}{2}$$

$$\therefore \quad \text{Mean} = \frac{\text{sum}}{n} = \frac{n+1}{2}.$$

105. Let, the initial length and Breadth of Rectangles are x and y unit respectively.

∴ Initial Area = xy square unit

$$\text{New length} = 120\% x = \frac{6}{5}x$$

New Breadth = 120%y = $\frac{6}{5}y$

$\therefore$ New Area (A′)

$$= \left(\frac{6}{5}x\right)\left(\frac{6}{5}y\right) = \frac{36}{25}xy$$

% increase in Area

$$= \frac{A' - A}{A} \times 100 = \frac{\frac{36}{25}xy - xy}{xy} \times 100$$

$$= \frac{36-25}{25} \times 100 = 44\%.$$

106. Let, Initial Radius = r

Initial Area (A) = πr^2

New radius = 150%r = $\frac{3}{2}r$

$$\text{New Area (A}') = \pi\left(\frac{3}{2}r\right)^2 = \frac{9}{4}\pi r^2$$

% increase in Area

$$= \frac{A' - A}{A} \times 100 = \frac{\frac{9}{4}\pi r^2 - \pi r^2}{\pi r^2} \times 100$$

$$= \frac{5}{4} \times 100 = 125\%.$$

107. Anil and Ankur's one day work

$$= \frac{1}{12}$$

Ankur and Harish's one day work

$$= \frac{1}{15}$$

Harish and Anil's one day work

$$= \frac{1}{20}$$

2(Anil + Ankur + Harish)'s one day work

$$= \frac{1}{12} + \frac{1}{15} + \frac{1}{20} = \frac{5+4+3}{60} = \frac{12}{60}$$

(Anil + Ankur + Harish)'s one day work

$$= \frac{1}{10}$$

Anil's, one day work

$$= \frac{1}{10} - \frac{1}{15} = \frac{1}{30}$$

$\therefore$ Anil can complete the work in 30 days.

108. A. $\frac{3}{7} = 0.43$ B. $\frac{5}{9} = 0.56$

C. $\frac{5}{11} = 0.45$ D. $\frac{7}{13} = 0.54$

$$\frac{3}{7} < \frac{5}{11} < \frac{7}{13} < \frac{5}{9}$$

$\therefore$ $\frac{5}{9}$ Fraction is the largest.

109. A. $\frac{5}{6} = 0.83$ B. $\frac{6}{7} = 0.86$

C. $\frac{7}{8} = 0.87$ D. $\frac{8}{9} = 0.89$

$$\frac{5}{6} < \frac{6}{7} < \frac{7}{8} < \frac{8}{9}$$

$\therefore$ $\frac{5}{6}$ Fraction is the smallest.

110. (5 × 10%) × 5%

$$= \left(\frac{5 \times 10}{100}\right) \times 5\%$$

$$= \frac{0.5 \times 5}{100} = 0.025.$$

111. Speed = 180 km per hour

$$= 180 \times \frac{5}{18} \text{ m/s}$$

[$\because$ 1 km/hour = $\frac{5}{18}$ m/s]

= 50 m per second.

112. We have,

Selling Price = ₹ 20

Profit = 20%

$\because$ Profit% $= \dfrac{SP - CP}{CP} \times 100$

$20 = \dfrac{20 - CP}{CP} \times 100$

$\dfrac{1}{5} = \dfrac{20 - CP}{CP}$

CP = 100 − 5 CP

6 CP = 100

CP = ₹ 16.66.

113. Let the number of students in the class is x and average of score is y

Then,

$xy - 63 + 83 = x\left(y + \dfrac{1}{2}\right)$

$xy + 20 = xy + 0.5x$

$20 = 0.5x$

$\therefore$ $x = 40$.

114. Cost price of one orange = ₹ $\dfrac{3}{4}$

Selling price of one orange = ₹ $\dfrac{4}{3}$

Profit per cent $= \dfrac{SP - CP}{CP} \times 100$

$= \dfrac{\frac{4}{3} - \frac{3}{4}}{\frac{3}{4}} \times 100 = \dfrac{\frac{7}{12}}{\frac{3}{4}} \times 100$

$= \dfrac{7 \times 4}{12 \times 3} \times 100 = \dfrac{7}{9} \times 100$

$= 77.77\% \approx 77\%$.

115. Let man's and current's speed on still water are x km/hr and y km/hr respectively

Then, $x + y = 15$ km/hr ...(*i*)

and speed of the current (y)

= 1.5 km/hr

$\therefore$ $x = 15 - 1.5 = 13.5$ km/hr

Man's speed against the current

$= x - y$

$= 13.5 - 1.5 = 12$ km/hr.

116. Let, two numbers are $2x$ and $3x$

Then,

LCM $(2x, 3x) = 48$

$6x = 48$

$x = 8$

$\therefore$ Numbers are 16 and 24

Hence, sum of the numbers is 40

$= 16 + 24 = 40$.

117. Greatest possible length

= HCF (8 m, 4 m 20 cm, 12 m 20 cm)

= HCF (800 cm, 420 cm, 1220 cm)

= 20 cm.

118. $\because$ A day = 24 hours

$\therefore$ Required percentage

$= \dfrac{4}{24} \times 100 = 16.66\%$.

119. Let, the maximum marks for the exam was x

Then,

$x \times 33\% = 125 + 40$

$x \times 33\% = 165$

$x = \dfrac{165 \times 100}{33} = 500$.

120. Let, the initial Salary of man

= ₹ 100

Then,

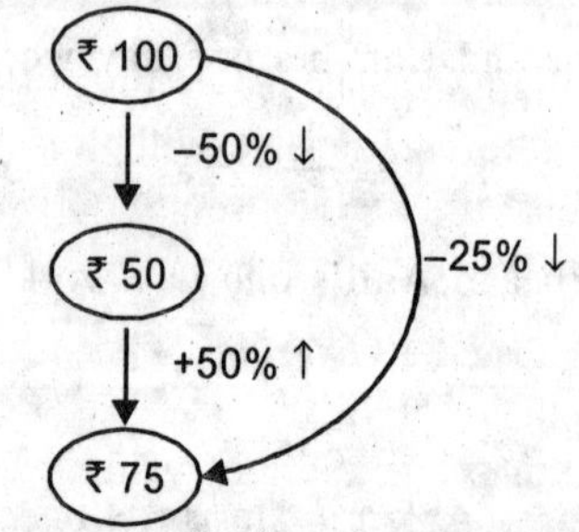

$\therefore$ Net change is 25% decrease.

Previous Paper (Solved)

IGNOU B.Ed. ENTRANCE EXAM 2017*

PART-A

Section-I : General English Comprehension

Directions (Q. Nos. 1-10): *Read the following passage carefully and choose the best answer out of the four choices given after each question that follows.*

White cement is the basic raw material for producing cement tiles and cement paint which are used extensively in building construction. The main consumers of white cement are, therefore, cement tile and cement paint manufacturing units. These consumers, mostly in the small scale sector, are today facing a major crisis because of a significant increase in the price of white cement during a short period. The present annual licensed production capacity of white and grey cement in the country is approximately 3.5 lakh tonnes. The average demand is 2-2.5 tonnes. This means that there is idle capacity to the tune of one lakh tonnes or more. The price rise is, therefore, not a phenomenon arising out of inadequate production capacity but evidently because of artificial scarcity created by the manufacturers in their self-interest.

The main reason for the continuing spurt in cement price is its decontrol. As it is, there is stiff competition in the cement paint and tile manufacturing business. Any further price revision at this stage is bound to have a severe adverse impact on the market conditions. The Government should take adequate steps to ensure that suitable controls are brought in. Else it should allow import of cement.

1. Why is the price of white cement going up?
   A. Because the government is controlling the quota.
   B. Because of export of white cement.
   C. Because of the large usage of white cement.
   D. None of the above

2. Which of the following statements is false according to the passage?
   A. Price rise in white cement would increase the price of cement paint.
   B. White cement is a controlled product.
   C. Increase in price of white cement is not because of production problem.
   D. Price rise in white cement would upset cement tile market.

3. What is the crisis being faced by the cement tile manufacturers as described in the passage?
   A. White cement is priced very low.
   B. White cement is not of good quality.
   C. White cement usage is high.
   D. White cement prices are very high.

4. Which of the following words has the same meaning as the word 'idle' as used in the passage?
   A. Lazy B. Clumsy
   C. Large D. Excess

5. Which of the following is correct according to the passage?
   A. White cement is not used in the manufacture of paint.
   B. White cement forms a minor part of tile manufacturing.
   C. White cement is very important for tile manufacturing.
   D. White cement is used only for making paints.

6. Which of the following words has the same meaning as the word 'artificial' as used in the passage?
   A. Unnatural B. Prolonged
   C. Deliberate D. Practical

*** Held on 24-09-2017.**

7. What is the author's suggestion to bring down prices?
A. Government should control the white cement market.
B. Production capacity should be increased.
C. Usage of white cement in other areas should be reduced.
D. Competition among manufactures of cement paints and tiles should be reduced.

8. Which of the following words has the opposite meaning as the word 'basic' as used in the passage?
A. Vital
B. Unimportant
C. Acidic
D. Last

9. Which of the following is correct according to the passage?
A. Cement production capacity is more than usage.
B. Cement production capacity is less than usage.
C. Cement production capacity is equal to usage.
D. Cement production capacity is twice than usage.

10. What can be presumed from the passage regarding foreign trade in cement?
A. The country is exporting cement at present.
B. The country is importing cement at present.
C. The country is exporting and importing cement at present.
D. The country is neither exporting nor importing cement at present.

Section-II : Logical and Analytical Reasoning

Directions (Q. Nos. 11-14): *Study the following information carefully and answer the questions that follow.*

There are six members M, N, O, P, Q and R in a family. There are two married couples in family; N is the businessman and father of Q; R is the grandfather of O; and is a property dealer; P is the grandmother of Q and is a housewife; O is daughter of M; There are one businessman, one property dealer, one lady lecturer and two students in the family.

11. Who is father in law of M?
A. P B. R
C. N D. O

12. What is the profession of M?
A. Housewife B. Student
C. Lecturer D. Property dealer

13. Who is sister of Q?
A. O B. P
C. M D. N

14. Which of the following are two married couples?
A. MO and QR B. MN and PR
C. PR and OQ D. MN and QR

15. Find the missing number:

	3			8			9	
7	[40]	10	4	[24]	6	5	[?]	4

A. 46 B. 32
C. 20 D. 16

Directions (Qs. No. 16-19): *In the following questions a series is being given select from the alternatives the correct term to fill in the missing term.*

16. 7, 21, 43, __?__, 111, 157, 211
A. 73 B. 71
C. 75 D. 77

17. 6, 24, 60, 114, 186, __?__.
A. 276 B. 290
C. 272 D. 280

18. 7, 13, 21, 31, 43, __?__.
A. 53 B. 55
C. 57 D. 59

19. 3, 15, 35, 63, __?__.
A. 69 B. 79
C. 89 D. 99

20. If PUZZLE is coded as LEPUZZ, then MENTAL will be coded as:
A. ZZOPEM B. ZENSOM
C. ALMENT D. MOSNET

21. If CONFRONTATION is coded as 5931793484693, then TORONTO will be coded as:
A. 4797347 B. 4393743
C. 4898348 D. 4979349

22. Which pair is different in some way from the others in the following?
A. Town - Shandy B. Village - Mall
C. City - Market D. Arcade - Shop

Directions (Q. Nos. 23-26): *Read the paragraph and answer the questions that follow.*

Geeta, Sita, Promila, Bhavana and Nafisa are five friends. Each one of has six balls : Geeta gives 3 balls to Nafisa who gives 4 balls to Promila. Bhavana gives 2 balls to Sita who gives 3 balls to Geeta. Promila gives 4 balls to Bhavana who gives 2 balls each to Nafisa and Geeta.

23. How many balls does Nafisa have?
A. 4 B. 5
C. 6 D. 7

24. How many balls does Sita have?
A. 4 B. 5
C. 6 D. 7

25. Who has the minimum number of balls?
A. Bhavana B. Nafisa
C. Sita D. Promila

26. Who has the maximum number of balls?
A. Promila B. Nafisa
C. Sita D. Geeta

Directions (Q. Nos. 27-30): *Read the paragraph and answer the questions that follow.*

A and B play Cricket and Hockey, B and D play Tennis, A and C play Volley-Ball and Tennis, C and D and E play Football.

27. Who plays Cricket, Hockey and Volley-ball?
A. A B. B
C. C D. D

28. Who plays only Football?
A. A B. B
C. D D. E

29. Who plays Tennis and Football?
A. A B. B
C. C D. D

30. Who plays Volley-ball and Football?
A. A B. B
C. C D. D

Section-III : Educational and General Awareness

31. World Population day is celebrated on:
A. 19 July B. 11 July
C. 15 July D. 17 July

32. Gandhiji made a dramatic bid for temple entry rights for untouchables in the year:
A. 1940 B. 1935
C. 1930 D. 1920

33. National Repository of Open Educational Resources (NROER) is being managed by:
A. IGNOU B. NCERT
C. UGC D. NUEPA

34. Who was the Editor of the Revolutionary Paper 'Bande Matram'?
A. Shyamji Krishan Verma
B. Bhikaji Cama
C. V.D. Savarkar
D. G.D. Savarkar

35. How many Nations had signed the charter of United Nations on 26th June, 1945?
A. 64 B. 61
C. 52 D. 51

36. Who among the following has termed Indian Federalism as "Co-operative Federalism?
A. K.C. Wheare B. Morris Jones
C. Granville Austin D. Jennings

37. By which year, the Union Cabinet on June 17, 2015 has proposed to provide 'Housing for All'?
A. 2030 B. 2025
C. 2022 D. 2018

38. Which country topped the Global Innovation Index (GIL) 2015 that was released on 17 September, 2015?
A. Switzerland B. United Kingdom
C. Sweden D. The Netherlands

39. The United Nations Children's Fund (UNICEF) is head quartered in:
A. Paris (France)
B. Vienna (Austria)
C. New York City (USA)
D. Brussels (Belgium)

40. Which city is hosting the 2016 Olympic games?
A. Seoul B. Barcelona
C. Rio-De-Janerio D. Los Angeles

41. The main objective of 'Sakshar Bharat' is:
A. to promote 'education for all'
B. to promote adult education
C. to promote vocational education
D. to promote education for women

42. Under which article of the Constitution the President of India has been empowered to promulgate ordinance?
A. Article 356 B. Article 360
C. Article 200 D. Article 123

43. Right to Education Act, 2009 is mainly concerned with:
A. Higher Education
B. Elementary Education
C. Secondary Education
D. Higher Secondary Education

44. Who is the author of the Book 'Fundamental Unity of India'?
A. Radhakumud Mukherji
B. Jawaharlal Nehru
C. Rajani Kothari
D. Max Weber

45. In which year state reorganisation commission gave its report on the basis of language?
A. 1953 B. 1954
C. 1955 D. 1956

46. According to United Nations Report released in July 2015, which of the following countries will become the world's most populous country by 2022?
A. India B. China
C. Pakistan D. Bangladesh

47. During September 2015, which of the following countries has published first report written by a 'robot journalist'?
A. Japan B. China
C. Germany D. Switzerland

48. Where did Madam Cama hoist the first tricolour Flag in 1907?
A. London B. Paris
C. Moscow D. Stuttgart

49. Which committee/commission gave its specific recommendations to improve the conditions of Teacher Education in India?
A. Hansa Mehta Committee
B. Radha Krishnan Commission
C. Justice Verma Commission
D. National Knowledge Commission

50. "IEDSS" stands for:
A. International Education for Disadvantaged at Social Stage
B. Integrated Education for Disabled at Secondary Stage
C. Inclusive Education for Disadvantaged at Secondary Stage
D. Inclusive Education for Disabled at Secondary Stage

51. Who among the following shall preside over the joint sitting at two houses of Parliament?
A. President
B. Prime Minister
C. Chairman of Rajya Sabha
D. Speaker of Lok Sabha

52. Which article of the Constitution defines the duties of Chief Minister?
A. 162 B. 164
C. 165 D. 167

53. Light from the Sun reaches earth in:
A. 8 minutes B. 2 minutes
C. 6 minutes D. 4 minutes

54. Which one of the following was the last step in the Gandhian strategy of Satyagraha?
A. Boy-Cott
B. Picketing
C. Fast
D. Strike

55. Finances are distributed between the centre and the state on the recommendation of:
A. Planning Commission
B. Public Accounts Committee
C. Finance Commission
D. National Development Council

Section-IV : Teaching-Learning and The School

56. Determining, the aim of education is the responsibility of:
A. Parents B. Teachers
C. Students D. Society

57. The schools through its programmes help students to:
A. Assimilate culture
B. Protest culture
C. Ignore other cultures
D. Make them cultured

58. To make all students interested in home work, it should be:
A. Of equal level
B. According to the ability of student
C. Only from the book
D. Out of the book

59. Navodaya schools have been established to:
A. Increase number of schools in rural areas
B. Provide good education in rural areas
C. Complete "Sarva Shiksha Abhiyan"
D. Check wastage of education in rural areas

60. The most important quality of an effective teacher is:
A. Deep knowledge about the subject taught
B. A strict disciplinarian
C. Good rap port with the students
D. A good motivator

61. The idea of basic education was propounded by:
A. Dr. Zakir Hussain
B. Dr. Rajendra Prasad
C. Mahatma Gandhi
D. Rabindra Nath Tagore

62. Individual attention is important in Teaching-learning process because:
A. Learners always learn better in group
B. Teacher training programmes prescribed it
C. It offers better opportunities to teachers to discipline each learner
D. Children develop at different rates and learn differently

63. If a child writes with his/her left hand and is comfortable doing things with it, she/he should be:
A. Discouraged
B. Made to write with left hand
C. Allowed his preference
D. Sent to seek medical help

64. Which of the following statements is true about "Learning"?
A. Errors made by children indicate that no learning has taken place
B. Learning is effective in an environment that is emotionally positive and satisfying for learners
C. Learning is not affected by emotional factors at any stage of learning
D. Learning is fundamentally a mental activity

65. It is advantage of giving home work that students:
A. Remain busy at home
B. Study at home
C. May be checked for their progress
D. May develop habit of self study

66. A field trip is arranged for:
A. Making an excursion
B. See other people doing things
C. Note the meaning of action
D. All of the above

67. Students are passive in:
A. Project method B. Discovery method
C. Lecture method D. Inquiry method

68. Demonstration effect means:
A. Effect of advertisement
B. Imitating effect of consumption
C. Effect of entertainment
D. Effect of an experiment

69. Dyslexia is a:
A. Physical disability in which the ability to write is affected by dysfunctional fingers
B. Form of reading disability linked with weak vision
C. Learning difficulty to read fluently and with accurate comprehension despite average intelligence
D. Language based learning difficulty associated with impaired hearing

70. If you find a student wearing some odd dress in your class, you will:
A. Ask the student not to attend the class
B. Make a joke on him
C. Counsel him not to wear such clothes in a class
D. Not pay any attention

71. Some students are backward in studies. What will be your attitude towards, them:
A. Harsh B. Sympathetic
C. Liberal D. Lovable

72. Play therapy is adopted in the study of children in order to:
A. Make the educational process joyful
B. To understand the inner motives and complexes of children
C. Make education more activity centred
D. Highlight the importance of play activities in education

73. The best remedy of the student's problems related with learning is:
A. Suggestion for hard work
B. Supervised study in library
C. Suggestion for private tuition
D. Diagnostic teaching

74. In a democratic country like India, schools should concentrate on:
A. Development of traits to face the hurdles of daily life
B. Development of traits of a good citizenship
C. Preparation for academic excellence
D. Inculcation of values cherished by country

75. It can safely be assumed that a student understands a principle when He/She can:
A. Give more examples of it
B. Use it in solving problems to which it applies
C. Recognise it again when He/She encounters it again
D. Recall the principles as and when asked

76. Despite of your requests as an incharge of time table in the school, A teacher always comes late. In this situation, you will:
A. Insult him in the presence of other teachers
B. Advise him to come in time
C. Report to the principal
D. Remain indifferent to it

77. Every learner is unique means that:
A. No two learners are alike in their abilities, interests and talents
B. Learners do not have any common qualities, nor do they share common goals
C. A common curriculum for all learners is not possible
D. It is impossible to develop the potentials of learners in a heterogeneous class

78. The in-service teacher training can be made more effective by:
A. Using training package which is well prepared in advance
B. Making it residential programme
C. Using co-operative approach
D. Practicing training follow-up procedures

79. In NCTE - the B.Ed. curriculum framework-2014 which of the following is emphasised ______ in education.
A. IT (Information Technology)
B. ICT (Information and Communication Technology)
C. ET (Educational Technology)
D. CT (Communication Technology)

80. How many senses a person uses while watching a film?
A. 1 B. 2
C. 3 D. 4

PART-B

Section-V : (i) Science

81. According to laws of refracation (i = Angle of incidence, r = Angle of refraction):

A. $\frac{i}{r}$ = constant

B. $\frac{\sin i}{\sin r}$ = constant

C. $\sin i = \sin r$

D. i and r are not related

82. For photosynthesis, the green plant needs:

A. CO_2 B. light
C. chlorophyll D. All of these

83. In aquatic plant Hydrilla, stomata are:

A. Present on leaves B. Present on stem
C. Present on roots D. Absent

84. Convex mirror can form:

A. Only real image
B. Only virtual image
C. Both real as well as virtual images
D. Only magnified images

85. The unit of Pressure is:

A. Newton B. Newton per sq.m
C. Per sq.m D. Joule

86. Polio is:

A. Food borne disease B. Water borne disease
C. Air borne disease D. None of the above

87. Two wires A and B are made of the same metal and are of equal lengths but their diameters are in the ratio 1 : 2. Their resistances R_A and R_B have the ratio:

A. 1 : 4 B. 1 : 2
C. 2 : 1 D. 4 : 1

88. According to Einstein the Energy (E), Mass (M) and Velocity of light (C) are related by the equation:

A. $E = M \times C$ B. $E = MC^2$
C. $E = M + C^2$ D. $E + M = C$

89. Plant cell can do:

A. Breathing and Respiration
B. Respiration and Photosynthesis
C. Breathing and Photosynthesis
D. All of these

90. The wave length of X-rays is smaller than that of visible light and:

A. Its speed is more than that of visible light
B. Its frequency is more than that of visible light
C. Its speed is less than that of visible light
D. Its frequency is less than that of visible light

91. The two colours seen at the extreme ends of the pH chart are:

A. Red and Blue B. Red and Green
C. Green and Blue D. Yellow and Green

92. HIV is a:

A. Disease B. Vaccine
C. Virus D. Injection

93. A body is weighed in several liquids of relative densities 1.1, 1.2, 1.3 and 1.4. Its weight will be the least in the liquid of relative density:

A. 1.1 B. 1.2
C. 1.3 D. 1.4

94. A concave lens produces:

A. Virtual image B. Diminished image
C. Erect image D. All of these

95. When two wires of resistances 2 Ohms and 1 Ohm respectively are joined in parallel, their equivalent resistance is:

A. < 1 Ohm B. 1 Ohm
C. 2 Ohm D. > 2 Ohm

96. If red litmus is added to acetic acid solution:

A. It changes to green
B. It becomes blue
C. It remains red
D. It becomes colourless

97. Ultimate main source of energy on the earth is:
A. Coal B. Fossil oil
C. Sun D. Air

98. The Commercial unit of electric energy is:
A. Horse Power B. Kilo Watt Hour
C. Joule D. Watt hour

99. Destruction of forests has resulted in:
A. Shortage of Rain
B. Shortage of Natural Resources
C. Danger to the lives of wild animals and birds
D. All of the above

100. Use of Chlorofluorocarbons:
A. Strengthens Ozone layer in the atmosphere
B. Depletes Ozone layer
C. Does not affect Ozone layer
D. Is not a harmful

Section-V : (ii) Mathematics

101. The Value of sin 60° cos 30° + sin 30° cos 60° is:
A. $\frac{1}{2}$ B. 1
C. –1 D. 2

102. The value of $9 \sec^2 A - 9 \tan^2 A$ is:
A. 0 B. 1
C. 8 D. 9

103. From the top of a 7 m high building, the angle of elevation of the top of a cable tower is 60° and angle of depression of its foot is 45°. The height of tower is:
A. $5(\sqrt{3}+1)$m B. $5(\sqrt{3}-1)$m
C. $7(\sqrt{3}-1)$m D. $7(\sqrt{3}+1)$m

104. The sum of odd numbers between 0 and 50 is:
A. 425 B. 525
C. 625 D. 725

105. The value of $\frac{\sqrt{441}}{3} \times \frac{\sqrt{225}}{5} \times \frac{64}{\sqrt{256}}$ is:
A. 21 B. 28
C. 48 D. 84

106. The value of $\frac{6^{2/3} \times \sqrt[3]{6^7}}{\sqrt[3]{6^6}}$ is:
A. 6 B. 36
C. 216 D. 18

107. A jar contains 24 marbles, some are green and others are blue. If a marble is drawn at random from the jar, then the probability that it is green is $\frac{2}{3}$. The number of blue marbles in the jar is:
A. 4 B. 6
C. 8 D. 10

108. A die is thrown twice. The probability that 5 will come up at least one would be ______.
A. $\frac{25}{36}$ B. $\frac{11}{36}$
C. $\frac{5}{36}$ D. $\frac{10}{36}$

109. Sides of two similar triangles are in the ratio 4 : 9. Areas of these triangles would be in the ratio ______ .
A. 2 : 3 B. 4 : 9
C. 81 : 16 D. 16 : 81

110. The wheels of a car are of diameter 80 cm each. The car runs at a speed of 66 km per hour for 10 minutes. The number of complete revolutions made by each wheel is ______.
A. 2640 B. 3960
C. 4375 D. 4875

111. Metallic spheres of radii 6 cm, 8 cm and 10 cm, respectively, are melted to form a single solid sphere, the radius of this sphere would be ______ .
A. 8 cm B. 12 cm
C. 14 cm D. 16 cm

112. The curved surface area of a right circular cylinder of height 14 cm is 88 cm^2. The diameter of the base of cylinder is:
A. 4 cm B. 3 cm
C. 2 cm D. 1 cm

113. A train which is 500 meter long crosses a 800 meter long platform in one minute five seconds. The speed of the train is ______ .
A. 55 km/hr B. 65 km/hr
C. 70 km/hr D. 72 km/hr

114. The ratio of father's age to his son's age is 7 : 3. The product of their ages is 756. The ratio of their ages after 6 years will be _____.
A. 2 : 1 B. 5 : 2
C. 11 : 7 D. 13 : 9

115. Two numbers are in the ratio of 7 : 4. If 12 is added to the smaller number, then ratio becomes 7 : 5, the bigger number is _____.
A. 77 B. 84
C. 91 D. 98

116. In order to pass an examination, a minimum of 33% marks are required. A candidate obtaining 210 marks fails by 21 marks. The total marks for examination was _____ .
A. 700 B. 600
C. 550 D. 500

117. A shopkeeper has marked selling price 20% above the cost price and allows some discount to the customers, the profit he earns is 8%. The rate of discount is ______.
A. 5% B. 6%
C. 10% D. 12%

118. A conical tent 14 meter in diameter and 4.5 meter high is to be eracted with lateral side 6 meter in length, the cloth required will be _____.
A. 108 m^2 B. 132 m^2
C. 224 m^2 D. 264 m^2

119. Two sides of triangle are 8 cm and 11 cm and the perimeter is 32 cm. Its area is ______ .
A. $3\sqrt{40}$ cm^2 B. $5\sqrt{48}$ cm^2
C. $8\sqrt{30}$ cm^2 D. 50 cm^2

120. The length of a tangent from a point A at a distance of 5 cm from the center of the circle is 4 cm. The radius of the circle is _____.
A. 2 cm B. 3 cm
C. 4 cm D. 4.5 cm

Section-V : (iii) Social Science

121. Who was the last ruler of the Sayyed Dynasty?
A. Mubarak Shah
B. Mohammad Shah
C. Amir Khusro
D. Alam Shah

122. Which article of the constitution is meant to eradicate untouchability?
A. Article 16 B. Article 22
C. Article 29 D. Article 17

123. Which point of the earth is the deepest?
A. Java Trench B. Puerto Rico
C. Mariana Trench D. Lipke Island

124. What is the currency of Malaysia?
A. Dollar B. Pesco
C. Ringgit D. Baht

125. Who wrote the drama '*Malvikagnimitra*'?
A. Vishakhadutta B. Kalidas
C. Kanishka D. Harisena

126. Who founded the regional party 'Shiv Sena'?
A. Devendra Fadnavis
B. Bal Thakre
C. Sharad Yadav
D. Sushil Kumar Modi

127. Which country was affected by the cyclone Hudhud?
A. Indonesia B. Singapore
C. Malaysia D. India

128. Who is the chairman of the NITI Aayog in India?
A. President B. Vice President
C. Prime Minister D. Finance Minister

129. Which of the following is Value-added Tax?
A. Income Tax B. Custom Tax
C. Sales Tax D. Capital Gain Tax

130. What is the currency of Bhutan?
A. Rupee B. Dinar
C. Taka D. Ngultrum

131. Who wrote the famous Tamil literary work Kalingattuparani?
A. Kalladanar B. Amarbhujanga
C. Gangaikanda D. Jayagondan

132. Who wrote the famous work Surya Siddhanta?
A. Varahamihira
B. Aryabhatta
C. Vriddha – Vagabhatta
D. Meghaduta

133. How much is the security deposit for Lok Sabha election?
A. ₹ 25,000 B. ₹ 50,000
C. ₹ 10,000 D. ₹ 5,000

134. Who was the First Female President of Indian National Congress?
A. Sarojini Naidu
B. Indira Gandhi
C. Pratibha Patil
D. Rajkumari Amrit Kaur

135. Who is the present governor of the Reserve Bank of India?
A. Raghuram Rajan B. Manmohan Singh
C. Arun Jetly D. None of these

136. Which gas was released during the Bhopal Gas Tragedy?
A. Methane B. Methyl Isocyanate
C. Acetylene D. Ammonia

137. When was IGNOU established?
A. 1971 B. 1977
C. 1985 D. 1989

138. Through which ocean is most of the world trade carried out?
A. Pacific Ocean B. Arctic Ocean
C. Atlantic Ocean D. Indian Ocean

139. Which is the third largest country in the world?
A. Canada
B. United States of America
C. China
D. Brazil

140. Which certificate indicates a guarantee of quality for agricultural food products like ghee, honey, etc.?
A. ISI B. Agmark
C. BIS D. DPT

Section-V : (iv) English

Directions (Q. Nos. 141-145): *Choose the word that is nearest in meaning to the underlined word.*

141. A good dictionary is <u>indispensable</u> for learning a language.
A. Desirable B. Helpful
C. Valuable D. Essential

142. The police have succeeded in arresting Rajiv's <u>assassin.</u>
A. Opponent B. Enemy
C. Murderer D. Rival

143. Grandmother suffers from <u>chronic</u> arthritis.
A. Of long duration B. Painful
C. Occasional D. Symptomatic

144. Radha is an able lent <u>diffident</u> student.
A. Difficult B. Shy and meek
C. Confused D. Confident

145. His <u>judicious</u> handling of the matter saved the situation from going out of control.
A. Reasonable B. Amicable
C. Cautious D. Nervous

Directions (Q. Nos. 146-150): *In each of the following group of words, only one word is correctly spelt. Select the word with the correct spelling.*

146. A. Reminesent B. Reminescent
C. Reminisent D. Reminiscent

147. A. Hygeine B. Higeine
C. Hygiene D. Hygien

148. A. Harrassment B. Harasment
C. Harrasment D. Harassment

149. A. Spontanity B. Spontaneity
C. Spontaniety D. Sponteneity

150. A. Museam B. Muzeum
C. Museum D. Musium

Directions (Q. Nos. 151-154): *Choose the word which is opposite in meaning to the underlined word.*

151. The culprit acknowledged his guilt.
A. Accepted B. Avoided
C. Repulsed D. Denied

152. Though an amateur, he is a first class player.
A. Renowned B. Seasoned
C. Professional D. Mature

153. The initial estimate of the project was very high.
A. Final B. Full
C. Total D. Rough

154. She found his behaviour towards her distinctly hostile.
A. Graceful B. Friendly
C. Cheerful D. Sweet

Directions (Q. Nos. 155 and 156): *Select the word in each group which does not properly belong to it.*

155. A. Conspicuous B. Conscript
C. Clear D. Visible

156. A. Perfection B. Reflection
C. Inspection D. Retrospection

Directions (Q. Nos. 157-160): *Pick out the most appropriate word from the given alternatives to fill in the blank to complete the sentence.*

157. We _______ trouble on our borders.
A. Comprehend B. Apprehend
C. Supplement D. Complement

158. The police _______ the mob.
A. Scattered B. Disbanded
C. Drove D. Dispersed

159. His tutor went _______ endless trouble to prepare him _______ the test.
A. over : before B. over : against
C. through : in D. through : for

160. He went _______ the room and sat down _______ the sofa.
A. to : in B. into : on
C. from : upto D. in : on

Section-V : (v) हिन्दी

निर्देश (प्रश्न संख्या 161 से 165): *निम्नलिखित गद्यांश को ध्यानपूर्वक पढ़कर उसके आधार पर पूछे गए प्रश्नों के उत्तर दीजिए।*

"सुधार जिस अवस्था में हो, उससे अच्छी अवस्थां आने की प्रेरणा हर आदमी में मौजूद रहती है। हममें जो कमजोरियाँ हैं, वह मर्ज की तरह हमसे चिपटी हुई हैं जैसे शारीरिक स्वास्थ्य एक प्राकृतिक बात है और रोग उसका उल्टा, उसी तरह नैतिक और मानसिक स्वास्थ्य भी प्राकृतिक बात है और हम मानसिक तथा नैतिक गिरावट से उसी तरह संतुष्ट नहीं रहते, जैसे कोई रोगी अपने रोग से संतुष्ट नहीं रहता" जैसे वह किसी चिकित्सक की तलाश में रहता है। उसी तरह हम भी इस फिक्र में रहते हैं कि किसी तरह अपनी कमजोरियों को दूर फेंककर अधिक अच्छे मनुष्य बनें। इसीलिए हम साधु-फकीरों की खोज में रहते हैं। पूजा-पाठ करते हैं, बड़े-बूढ़ों के पास बैठते हैं, विद्वानों के व्याख्यान सुनते हैं और साहित्य का अध्ययन करते हैं।

हमारी सारी कमजोरियों की जिम्मेदारी हमारी कुरुचि और प्रेम भाव से वंचित होने पर है। जहाँ सच्चा सौन्दर्य-प्रेम है, जहाँ प्रेम की विस्तृति है, वहाँ कमजोरियाँ कहाँ रह सकती हैं? प्रेम ही तो आध्यात्मिक भोजन है और सारी कमजोरियाँ इसी भोजन के न मिलने अथवा दूषित भोजन के मिलने से पैदा होती हैं। कलाकार हममें सौन्दर्य की अनुभूति उत्पन्न करता है और प्रेम की उष्णता। उसका एक वाक्य, एक शब्द, एक संकेत इस तरह हमारे अन्दर जा बैठता है कि हमारा अंतःकरण प्रकाशित हो जाता है। पर जब तक कलाकार खुद सौन्दर्य-प्रेम से छककर मस्त न हो और उसकी आत्मा स्वयं इस ज्योति से प्रकाशित न हो, वह हमें प्रकाश कैसे दे सकता है?

161. उपर्युक्त गद्यांश के माध्यम से लेखक ने पाठकों को क्या बताया है?

A. प्रत्येक मनुष्य की कमजोरियाँ
B. प्रत्येक मनुष्य की अच्छाइयाँ
C. शारीरिक स्वास्थ्य
D. जीवन में प्रेम का महत्व

162. लेखक के अनुसार सत्संग, पूजा-पाठ करने, व्याख्यान सुनने और साहित्य का अध्ययन करने का प्रमुख उद्देश्य क्या है?

A. निर्वाण प्राप्ति
B. अपनी कमजोरियों को दूर कर अच्छा मनुष्य बनना
C. मनोकामनाएँ पूरी करना
D. धनवान बनना

163. गद्यांश के अनुसार हमारी सारी कमजोरियों का कारण क्या है?

A. काम और क्रोध
B. लोभ और मोह
C. कुरुचि और प्रेमभाव से वंचित होना
D. उपर्युक्त में से कोई नहीं

164. लेखक के अनुसार आध्यात्मिक भोजन क्या है?

A. प्रेम　　B. पूजा और उपवास
C. कठोर तप　　D. प्रवचन सुनना व नाचना

165. लेखक के अनुसार हमें कलाकार से क्या प्राप्त होता है?

A. मनोरंजन
B. उमंग और आनन्द
C. अभिनय कला
D. सौन्दर्य की अनुभूति और प्रेम की उष्णता

निर्देश (प्रश्न संख्या 166 से 180): *निम्नलिखित प्रत्येक प्रश्न के चार-चार विकल्प दिए गए हैं। उनमें से सही विकल्प चुनिए।*

166. आक का तत्सम शब्द है :

A. अकउआ　　B. अर्क
C. अकर्ज　　D. औक

167. प्रतिक्षण में समास है :

A. अव्ययीभाव　　B. कर्मधारय
C. तत्पुरुष　　D. द्वन्द्व

168. चन्द्रोदय में सन्धि है :

A. दीर्घ　　B. गुण
C. यण　　D. वृद्धि

169. धूमिल में प्रत्यय है :

A. ल　　B. लु
C. इल　　D. मिल

170. इनमें से कौन-सा शब्द जंगल का पर्यायवाची है :

A. विटप　　B. द्रुम
C. शून्य　　D. कान्तार

171. गृहीत का विलोम है :

A. त्याज्य　　B. ग्रहण
C. व्यक्त　　D. ग्राह्य

172. *या मुरलीधर की अधरान-धरी अधार न धरौंगी!*
उपरोक्त पद्यांश में अलंकार है :

A. रूपक　　B. यमक
C. उपमा　　D. उत्प्रेक्षा

173. "सखीन सों देत उराहनो नित्य सो चित्त संकोच सने लहिए" में है :

A. बरवै　　B. छप्पय
C. चौपाई　　D. सवैया

174. 'सरस्वती कंठाभरण' के रचयिता हैं :

A. अप्पय दीक्षित　　B. महिमभट्ट
C. भोजराज　　D. राजशेखर

175. अनुपस्थित शब्द में किस उपसर्ग का प्रयोग हुआ है?

A. अनु　　B. अन्
C. अ　　D. अनुप

176. उष्ण वर्ण हैं :

A. ट, ठ, ड, ढ　　B. श, ष, स, ह
C. प, फ, ब, भ　　D. च, छ, ज, झ

177. 'अक्ल के पीछे लट्ठ लिए फिरना' मुहावरे का अर्थ है :

A. मूर्खतापूर्ण कार्य करना　　B. झगड़ालू प्रवृत्ति का होना
C. मनमानी करना　　D. उद्दंडतापूर्ण कार्य करना

178. सदैव में है :

A. दीर्घ संधि　　B. वृद्धि संधि
C. यण संधि　　D. गुण संधि

179. अनारदाना है :

A. अधिकरण तत्पुरुष

B. अपादान तत्पुरुष

C. सम्बन्ध तत्पुरुष

D. संप्रदान तत्पुरुष

180. ''कौआ चला हंस की चाल' कहावत का अर्थ है :

A. किसी दुष्ट व्यक्ति द्वारा अच्छे व्यवहार का प्रदर्शन करना

B. कौआ चालाक होता है

C. सभ्य व्यक्ति द्वारा चालाकी का प्रदर्शन

D. अच्छे-बुरे का भेद न होना

ANSWERS

1	**2**	**3**	**4**	**5**	**6**	**7**	**8**	**9**	**10**
D	B	D	D	C	C	A	B	A	D
11	**12**	**13**	**14**	**15**	**16**	**17**	**18**	**19**	**20**
B	C	A	B	D	A	A	C	D	C
21	**22**	**23**	**24**	**25**	**26**	**27**	**28**	**29**	**30**
D	A	D	B	A	D	A	D	D	C
31	**32**	**33**	**34**	**35**	**36**	**37**	**38**	**39**	**40**
B	*	B	B	D	C	C	A	C	C
41	**42**	**43**	**44**	**45**	**46**	**47**	**48**	**49**	**50**
D	D	B	A	C	A	B	D	C	D
51	**52**	**53**	**54**	**55**	**56**	**57**	**58**	**59**	**60**
A	D	A	C	C	B	D	B	B	C
61	**62**	**63**	**64**	**65**	**66**	**67**	**68**	**69**	**70**
C	D	C	B	D	D	C	B	C	C
71	**72**	**73**	**74**	**75**	**76**	**77**	**78**	**79**	**80**
B	B	D	D	B	C	A	C	B	C
81	**82**	**83**	**84**	**85**	**86**	**87**	**88**	**89**	**90**
B	D	A	B	B	D	D	B	B	A
91	**92**	**93**	**94**	**95**	**96**	**97**	**98**	**99**	**100**
A	C	A	D	A	C	C	B	D	B
101	**102**	**103**	**104**	**105**	**106**	**107**	**108**	**109**	**110**
B	D	D	C	D	A	C	B	D	C
111	**112**	**113**	**114**	**115**	**116**	**117**	**118**	**119**	**120**
B	C	D	A	B	A	C	B	C	B
121	**122**	**123**	**124**	**125**	**126**	**127**	**128**	**129**	**130**
D	D	C	C	B	B	D	C	A	D
131	**132**	**133**	**134**	**135**	**136**	**137**	**138**	**139**	**140**
D	B	C	A	D	B	C	D	B	B
141	**142**	**143**	**144**	**145**	**146**	**147**	**148**	**149**	**150**
D	C	A	B	A	D	C	D	B	C
151	**152**	**153**	**154**	**155**	**156**	**157**	**158**	**159**	**160**
D	C	A	B	B	D	B	D	D	B
161	**162**	**163**	**164**	**165**	**166**	**167**	**168**	**169**	**170**
D	B	C	A	D	C	A	B	C	A
171	**172**	**173**	**174**	**175**	**176**	**177**	**178**	**179**	**180**
A	A	B	C	B	B	A	D	C	A

Explanatory Answers

15. $7 \overset{3}{\boxed{40}} 10 = 10 \times 7 - 10 \times 3 = 40$

$4 \overset{8}{\boxed{24}} 6 = 6 \times 8 - 6 \times 4 = 24$

$5 \overset{9}{\boxed{?}} 4 = 4 \times 9 - 4 \times 5 = 16$

Hence, 16 will come at the place of question mark.

16. 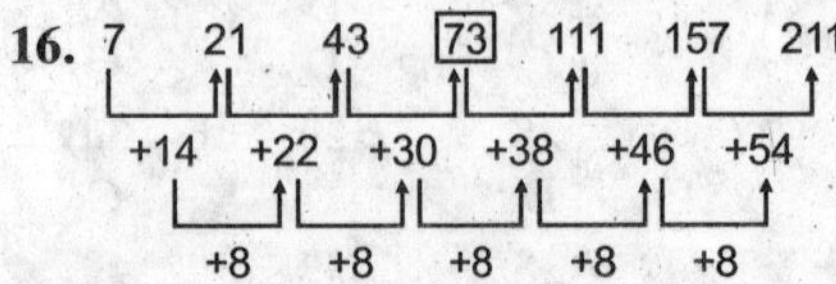

Hence, 73 will come at the place of question mark.

17. 6 24 60 114 186 [276]

+18 +36 +54 +72 +90

+18 +18 +18 +18

Hence, 276 will come at the place of question mark.

18. 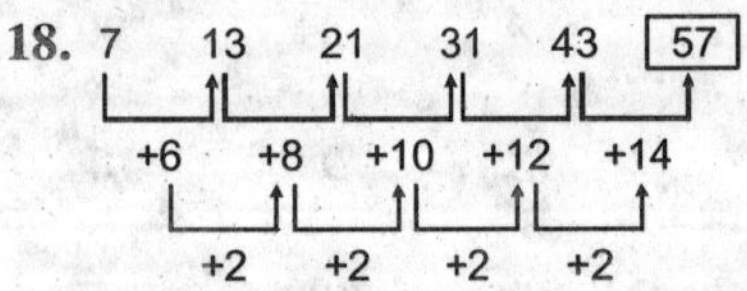

Hence, 57 will come at the place of question mark.

19. 3 15 35 63 [99]

+12 +20 +28 +36

+8 +8 +8

Hence, 99 will come at the place of question mark.

20. ∵ P U Z Z L E is coded as

↓ ↓ ↓ ↓ ↓ ↓

L E P U Z Z

Then, M E N T A L will be coded as

↓ ↓ ↓ ↓ ↓ ↓

A L M E N T

21. C O N F R O N T A T I O N is coded as

↓ ↓ ↓ ↓ ↓ ↓ ↓ ↓ ↓ ↓ ↓ ↓ ↓

5 9 3 1 7 9 3 4 8 4 6 9 3

Then, T O R O N T O will be coded as

↓ ↓ ↓ ↓ ↓ ↓ ↓

4 9 7 9 3 4 9

For Questions 23 to 26.

Geeta	6 – 3 + 3 + 2	8
Sita	6 + 2 – 3	5
Promila	6 + 4 – 4	6
Bhavana	6 – 2 + 4 – 2 – 2	4
Nafisa	6 + 3 – 4 + 2	7

23. Nafisa has 7 balls.

24. Sita has 5 balls.

25. Bhavana has minimum number of balls.

26. Geeta has maximum number of balls.

For Questions 27 to 30.

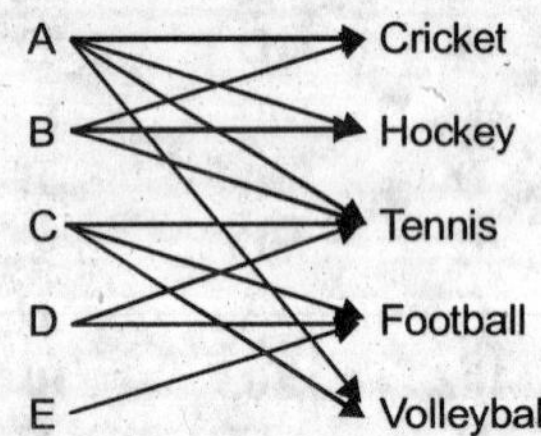

27. A plays Cricket, Hockey and Volleyball.

28. E plays only Football.

29. D plays Tennis and Football.

30. C plays Volleyball and Football.

101. $\sin 60^\circ \, . \, \cos 30^\circ + \sin 30^\circ \, . \, \cos 60^\circ$

$= \sin (60^\circ + 30^\circ)$

$= \sin 90^\circ$

$= 1.$

102. $9 \sec^2 A - 9 \tan^2 A$

$= 9 (\sec^2 A - \tan^2 A)$

$= 9 \times 1 = 9.$

103.

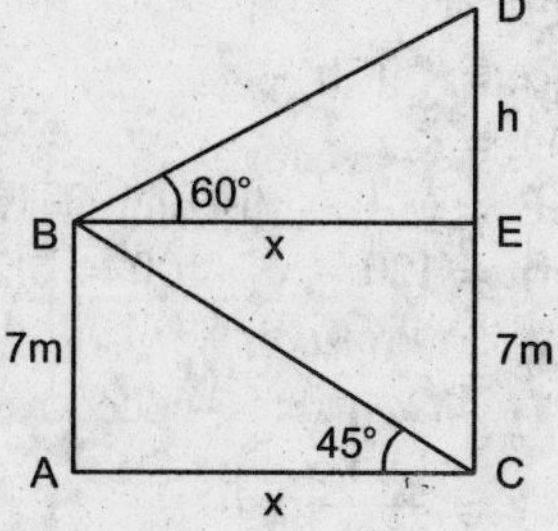

In Δ ABC,

$$\tan 45° = \frac{7}{x} \Rightarrow 1 = \frac{7}{x} \Rightarrow x = 7 \quad ...(i)$$

In Δ BDE,

$$\tan 60° = \frac{h}{x} \Rightarrow \sqrt{3} = \frac{h}{x} \Rightarrow x = \frac{h}{\sqrt{3}} \quad ...(ii)$$

From (*i*) and (*ii*)

$$\frac{h}{\sqrt{3}} = 7 \Rightarrow h = 7\sqrt{3}$$

∴ Height of the tower = $h + 7$

$$= 7\sqrt{3} + 7 = 7\left(\sqrt{3}+1\right) \text{ m.}$$

104. 1, 3, 5, 7, 9, 11, 13 49

$$49 = a + (n - 1)d$$
$$\Rightarrow \quad 49 = 1 + (n - 1) \times 2$$
$$\Rightarrow \quad 49 = 1 + 2n - 2 = 2n - 1$$
$$\Rightarrow \quad 2n = 50 \Rightarrow n = 25$$
$$S_n = \frac{n}{2}\{2a+(n-1)d\}$$
$$S_{25} = \frac{25}{2}\{2\times 1+(25-1)\times 2\}$$
$$= \frac{25}{2}\{2+48\} = \frac{25}{2}\times 50$$
$$= 25 \times 25 = 625.$$

105. $$\frac{\sqrt{441}}{3}\times\frac{\sqrt{225}}{5}\times\frac{64}{\sqrt{256}} = \frac{21}{3}\times\frac{15}{5}\times\frac{64}{16}$$
$$= 7 \times 3 \times 4 = 84.$$

106. $$\frac{6^{2/3}\times\sqrt[3]{6^7}}{\sqrt[3]{6^6}} = \frac{6^{2/3}\times 6^{7/3}}{6^{6/3}} = \frac{6^3}{6^2}$$
$$= 6^{3-2} = 6^1 = 6.$$

107. Let number of green marbles = x

∴ Number of blue marbles = $24 - x$

Probability of green marbles = $\frac{x}{24}$

$$\Rightarrow \quad \frac{2}{3} = \frac{x}{24}$$
$$\Rightarrow \quad 3x = 48 \Rightarrow x = 16$$

∵ Number of green marbles = 16

∴ Number of blue marbles = 24 – 16 = 8.

109. $$\frac{ar\,\Delta ABC}{ar\,\Delta DEF} = \frac{AB^2}{DE^2} = \frac{(4)^2}{(9)^2} = 16:81.$$

110. $C = 2\pi r = 2\times\frac{22}{7}\times 40$ cm

Distance covered in 10 minutes

$$= \frac{10\times 66\times 1000\times 100}{60} = 11 \times 100000 \text{ cm}$$

Number of Complete revolutions

$$= \frac{11\times 100000\times 7}{44\times 40} = \frac{2500\times 7}{4}$$
$$= 625 \times 7 = 4375.$$

111. $$\frac{4}{3}\pi\left(6^3+8^3+10^3\right) = \frac{4}{3}\pi R^3$$
$$\Rightarrow \quad R^3 = 216 + 512 + 1000$$
$$\Rightarrow \quad R^3 = 1728$$
$$\Rightarrow \quad R = \sqrt[3]{1728} = 12 \text{ cm.}$$

112. Curved surface area of cylinder = $2\pi rh$

$$\Rightarrow \quad 88 = 2\times\frac{22}{7}\times r\times 14$$
$$\Rightarrow \quad r = \frac{88\times 7}{44\times 14} = 1 \text{ cm}$$

∴ The diameter = $2r = 2 \times 1 = 2$ cm.

113. $$\text{Speed} = \frac{\text{Distance}}{\text{Time}} = \left(\frac{500+800}{60+5}\right) \text{ m/s}$$
$$= \frac{1300}{65} = 20 \text{ m/s}$$
$$= 20\times\frac{18}{5} \text{ km/hr} = 72 \text{ km/hr}$$

Hence, the speed of the train = 72 km/hr.

114. Let father's age = $7x$ years and son's age = $3x$ years

According to the question,

$$7x \times 3x = 756$$
$$\Rightarrow \quad 21x^2 = 756$$
$$\Rightarrow \quad x^2 = 36$$
$$\Rightarrow \quad x = 6$$

Father's age = $7 \times 6 = 42$ years

Son's age = $3 \times 6 = 18$ years

After 6 years ratio of their ages

$$= \frac{42+6}{18+6} = \frac{48}{24} = 2 : 1.$$

115. Let numbers are x and y.

$$\frac{x}{y} = \frac{7}{4}$$
$$\Rightarrow \quad 4x = 7y \Rightarrow x = \frac{7y}{4}$$
$$\frac{x}{y+12} = \frac{7}{5}$$
$$5x = 7y + 87$$
$$5 \times \frac{7y}{4} = 7(y + 12)$$
$$\Rightarrow \quad 5y = 4y + 48 \Rightarrow y = 48$$
$$x = \frac{7y}{4} = \frac{7 \times 48}{4} = 84$$

Hence, the bigger number = 84.

116. Let, total marks for examination = x

According to the question,

$$33\% \text{ of } x = 210 + 21 = 231$$
$$\Rightarrow \quad \frac{33}{100} \times x = 231$$
$$\Rightarrow \quad x = \frac{231 \times 100}{33}$$
$$= 7 \times 100 = 700$$

Hence, total marks for examination = 700.

117. Let, C.P. = ₹ 100

Marked price = ₹ 120

Let, discount = ₹ x

$$\therefore \quad \text{S.P.} = \text{M.P.} - \text{discount} = 120 - x$$
$$\text{Profit} = 120 - x - 100 = ₹\ 20 - x$$
$$\text{Profit \%} = \frac{\text{Profit}}{\text{C.P.}} \times 100$$
$$\Rightarrow \quad 8 = \frac{20 - x}{100} \times 100$$
$$\Rightarrow \quad 20 - x = 8 \Rightarrow x = 12$$

Hence, rate of discount $= \frac{12}{120} \times 100 = 10\%$.

118. Required length of cloth

$$= \pi rl = \frac{22}{7} \times 7 \times 6 = 132 \text{ m}^2.$$

119.

$$x + 8 + 11 = 32$$
$$\Rightarrow \quad x + 19 = 32$$
$$\Rightarrow \quad x = 13$$
$$\therefore \quad s = \frac{13+8+16}{2} = 16$$
$$\text{Area of } \Delta = \sqrt{s(s-a)(s-b)(s-c)}$$
$$= \sqrt{16(16-11)(16-13)(16-8)}$$
$$= \sqrt{16 \times 5 \times 3 \times 8} = 8\sqrt{30} \text{ cm}^2$$

Hence, area of triangle = $8\sqrt{30}$ cm^2.

120.

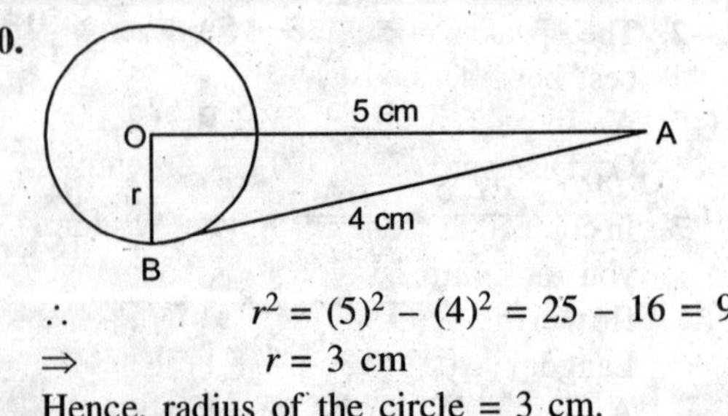

$$\therefore \quad r^2 = (5)^2 - (4)^2 = 25 - 16 = 9$$
$$\Rightarrow \quad r = 3 \text{ cm}$$

Hence, radius of the circle = 3 cm.

Previous Paper (Solved)

IGNOU B.Ed. Entrance Exam 2015*

PART-A

SECTION-I : General English Comprehension

Directions: *Read the following passage carefully and choose the best answer out of the four choices given after each question that follows:*

Donny was a good bowler, and a good man. He was one of us. He was a man who loved the outdoors... and bowling...., and as a surfer he explored the beaches of Southern California, from La Joll to Leo Carrillo and... up to... Pismo. He died, like so many young men of his generation, he died before his time. In your wisdom, Lord, you took him, as you took so many bright flowering young men at Khe Sanh, at Langdok, at Hill 364. These young men gave their lives. And so would Donny. Donny, who loved bowling. And so, Theodore Donald Karabotsos, in accordance with what we think your dying wishes might well have been, we commit your final mortal remains to the bosom of the Pacific Ocean, which you loved so well. Good night, sweet prince.

1. In this passage, the speaker's attitude towards Donny is primarily one of
A. Mournful eulogy
B. Unbiased detachment
C. Clear hostility
D. Elated nostalgia

2. The speaker's attitude towards bowling can best be described as
A. Indifference B. Respect
C. Disregard D. Contempt

3. In context, the tone of "In your wisdom, Lord, you took him, as you took so many bright, flowering young men at Khe Sanh, at Langdok, at Hill 364," is best described as
A. Impatient B. Baffled
C. Resigned D. Ambivalent

4. The speaker's tone in the last two sentences is best described as
A. Irritated B. Confused
C. Curious D. Solemn

5. In "....... as you took so many bright, flowering young men......" *bright* most, nearly mean
A. Light B. Intelligent
C. Vivid D. Dazzling

6. In "to the bosom of the Pacific Ocean," *bosom* most nearly means
A. Chest B. Column
C. Comfort D. Trunk

7. The reference to "Khe Sanh, at Langdok, at Hill 364" suggests
A. Donny will be burried at Hill 364
B. Donny died in combat
C. The speaker misses these places
D. The speaker also lost friends at these places

8. *Lord* refers to
A. The king of Hill 364
B. The Governor of California
C. The God
D. The President of U.S.A.

9. "Donny was a good bowler, and a good man" is a
A. Simple sentence
B. Complex sentence
C. Compound sentence
D. Complex-Compound sentence

10. In "He was a man who loved the outdoors... and bowling....," bowling is
A. A verb B. A noun
C. An adjective D. An adverb

*Held on 20-09-2015

SECTION-II : LOGICAL AND ANALYTICAL REASONING

Directions (Qs. 11 to 14): *Study the following information carefully and answer the questions that follow:*

There are six members M, N, O, P, Q and R in a family, O is the sister of R, N is the brother-in-law of R's mother, P is the father of M and R is the grandson of P. There are two ladies in the family.

11. Who is the mother of R?
A. N B. O
C. Q D. P

12. The members of the family belong to how many generations?
A. Two B. Three
C. Four D. Either two or three

13. The two female members in the family are
A. P, Q B. N, Q
C. R, O D. O, Q

14. Who is the daughter of M and Q?
A. P B. R
C. N D. O

15. Find the missing number.

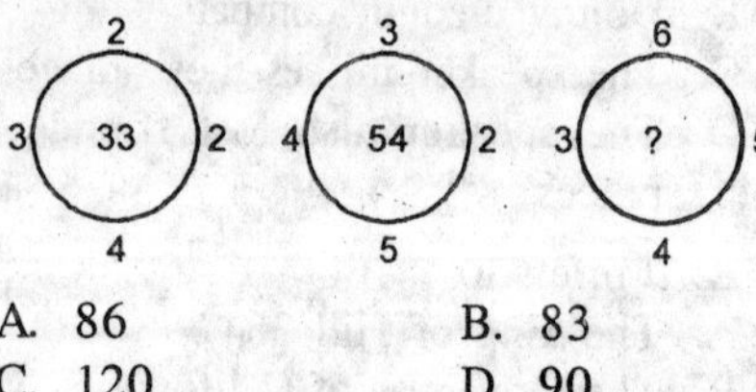

A. 86 B. 83
C. 120 D. 90

Directions (Qs. 16 to 19): *In the following questions a series is being given. Select from the alternatives the correct term to fill in the missing term.*

16. 0, 7, 26, 63, ?, 215
A. 104 B. 124
C. 126 D. 134

17. 3, 16, 42, 81, 133, ?
A. 166 B. 185
C. 198 D. 208

18. 1, 8, 27, ?, 125, 216
A. 54 B. 64
C. 84 D. 100

19. 2, 9, 23, 51, 107, ?
A. 214 B. 216
C. 218 D. 219

20. Which pair is different in some way from the others in the following?
A. Forest – Elephant
B. Sea – Crocodile
C. Passenger – Luggage
D. Class – Student

21. If 'Family' is coded as 316459 and 'Sister' is coded as 747820, then 'Mistress' will be coded as
A. 64870277
B. 64708277
C. 64782077
D. 64780277

22. If 'boy' is coded as AAQQZZ, then 'cat' will be coded as
A. CCBBUU B. BBCCTT
C. BBCCUU D. BBCCSS

Directions (Qs. 23 to 27): *Read the following paragraph to answer questions that follow:*

A and B play Cricket and Tennis, B and E play Hockey, A and C play Volleyball, C and D play Hockey and Tennis and C and E play Football.

23. Who does *not* play Tennis?
A. B B. D
C. E D. C

24. Who plays Cricket, Tennis and Volleyball?
A. C B. D
C. E D. A

25. Who plays Hockey, Cricket and Tennis?
A. A B. B
C. C D. D

26. Who plays only Hockey and Tennis?
A. A B. C
C. D D. E

27. Who plays Volleyball, Hockey, Tennis and Football?
A. A B. C
C. D D. B

Directions (Qs. 28 to 30): *Read the following paragraph to answer the questions that follow:*

A, B, C, D and E have seven balls each. B gives two balls to E, who gives one ball to A. C gives three balls to D, who gives two balls to A. E gives three balls to B, who gives two balls to C. B gives five balls to D.

28. How many balls does A have?
A. 5 B. 6
C. 10 D. 13

29. How many balls does C have?
A. 6 B. 5
C. 1 D. 10

30. Who has got the maximum number of ball now?
A. A B. D
C. C D. E

SECTION-III : EDUCATIONAL AND GENERAL AWARENESS

31. The Speaker of Lok Sabha in India is elected by the
A. Members of Lok Sabha
B. Members of Lok Sabha and Rajya Sabha
C. Council of Ministers
D. Speakers of State Legislative Assemblies

32. The responsibility for framing the Constitution of independent. India was entrusted to the
A. Lok Sabha
B. Rajya Sabha
C. Constituent Assembly
D. Parliament and State Legislative Assemblies

33. The amended Article 45 of our Constitution directs the State to promote
A. Pre-school Education
B. Primary Education
C. Elementary Education
D. Non-formal Education

34. According to NCTE regulations, a senior secondary teacher should possess
A. Post-graduation degree
B. Post-graduation degree with B.Ed.
C. Post-graduation degree with M.Ed.
D. Post-graduation with M.Phil.

35. What does three language formula imply?
A. Three languages should be taught in schools.
B. Examinations should be conducted in three languages.
C. The study of three languages should be made compulsory at the senior stage.
D. Every student should three langauges in schools.

36. What is an Open University?
A University that imparts education through
A. Distance mode
B. Correspondence mode
C. Face-to-face interaction in classrooms
D. Organisation of the open book examinations

37. In India, Education Day is celebrated on the occasion of the birthday of
A. Maulana Abul Kalam Azad
B. Dr. Zakir Husain
C. Dr. S. Radhakrishnan
D. Dr. B.R. Ambedkar

38. The members of Lok Sabha in India are elected by
A. All the citizens of India
B. Citizens above the age of 21 years
C. Registered voters
D. Education citizens of India

39. Green Revolution made India self-sufficient in
A. Milk production
B. Green trees and plants
C. Production of foodgrains
D. Green forests

40. Sarva Shiksha Abhiyan aims at
A. Enrolment of all girls in schools
B. Enrolment of all boys in schools

C. Enrolment of all children in schools
D. Enrolment and completion of Elementary education by all children

41. The Central Universities are established in India by
A. A Resolution of the Union Cabinet
B. A Resolution of the Council of Ministers
C. A Resolution of the Central Advisory Board of Education (CABE)
D. An Act of Parliament

42. Which one of the following authorities has been entrusted with the responsibility for the redressel of grievances under the RTE Act, 2009?
A. CABE B. NCERT
C. NCPCR D. NCHR

43. Juvenile Justice Act applicable for children below the age of 18 years prescribe maximum punishment of
A. Two years B. Three years
C. Five years D. Six years

44. The name of Montessori is associated with
A. Pre-school Education
B. Special Education
C. Secondary Education
D. Primary Education

45. The National University for Educational Planning and Administration (NUEPA) has the responsibility to
A. Set up Universities
B. Administer Schools and Colleges
C. Conduct Research relating to Educational Planning
D. Assessment of Higher Education Institutions

46. The corporal punishment in schools has been prohibited by the
A. RTE Act, 2009
B. Domestic Violence Act, 2005
C. Child Labour Prohibition Act
D. Juvenile Justice Act

47. Acharya Chanakya was a teacher in the Gurukul located at
A. Taxila B. Nalanda
C. Vikramshila D. Vaishali

48. Which one of the following is the major source of Vitamin D?
A. Sun
B. Mineral Water
C. Multigrain Bread
D. Fruits and Vegetables

49. Scientific temperament means
A. Temperament to take decisions on the basis of reasoning
B. Interest in the study of science
C. Ability to undertake scientific experiments
D. Ability to speak on scientific themes

50. Who advocated for craft centred education?
A. Lala Lajpat Rai B. B.R. Ambedkar
C. Mahatma Gandhi D. Mahatma Phule

51. The declaration of the state of internal emergency in India in 1975 was approved by the
A. Prime Minister of India
B. Speaker of Lok Sabha
C. Chief of Army Staff
D. President of India

52. Who became the Prime Minister of India after Rajiv Gandhi in 1989?
A. V.P. Singh B. P.V. Narsimha Rao
C. Charan Singh D. Chandra Shekhar

53. The disease hypertension is also known as
A. Low Blood Pressure
B. High Blood Pressure
C. Migraine
D. Arthritis

54. The T.V. serial 'Bharat Ek Khoj' was based on the book '*Discovery of India*' written by
A. M.N. Roy B. Mahatma Gandhi
C. Lala Lajpat Rai D. Jawaharlal Nehru

55. Comprehensive Evaluation means
A. Evaluation in all school subjects
B. Evaluation of student performance in scholastic and co-scholastic areas
C. Question paper comprising all types of questions
D. Question paper comprising questions from the entire syllabus

SECTION-IV : TEACHING-LEARNING AND THE SCHOOL

56. The major purpose of co-curricular activities in a school is to
A. help students achieve well-adjusted personality
B. provide relief from the usual classroom routine
C. give students an orientation to the world of work
D. provide for the vicarious satisifaction of the needs of students

57. The school curriculum should be planned to agree with
A. the general culture of the school in the past
B. the goals, purposes and interests of the students
C. the training and interests of the teacher
D. the available textbooks in various subjects

58. The effectiveness of the school supervision must be judged in terms of
A. the greater community satisfaction
B. the greater personal satisfaction
C. the reduced classroom misbehaviour
D. the greater pupil progress towards the goals of education

59. The teacher's first duty is towards the
A. community
B. students
C. subject he/she teaches
D. school authorities

60. The most important function of the teacher is to
A. guide students' growth
B. provide remedial help wherever needed
C. impart effective teaching
D. maintain order and discipline in the class

61. The school children are likely to suffer the worst effects educationally from a teacher who
A. is an emotionally immature individual
B. has partial grasp or understanding of his/her subject
C. cannot integrate the subject-matter
D. cannot organize his/her subject logically

62. The major goal in the classroom discipline should be to promote
A. good study conditions
B. good student conduct
C. quiet and order in the classroom
D. self-direction on the part of students

63. As it applies to the classroom, the teacher's role in motivation is essentially a matter of
A. arousing needs in children
B. channelling the energies of live and alert students into constructive activites
C. creating new interests
D. placing attracting incentives with him the reach of students

64. In developing a new topic or a lesson, the teacher should begin with
A. an overview of the subject
B. an explanation of the importance of the subject
C. some interests already possessed by the students
D. the teacher's own interest

65. If the student seems to be fatigued from the mental work, the teacher should
A. decrease the amount of work he/she has to do
B. provide him/her with greater variety of tasks
C. encourage him/her to develop persistence and ask him to continue despite fatigue
D. increase the attractiveness of the rewards to be attained on continuing

66. The classroom discipline should be oriented towards
A. social conformity
B. personal and social adjustment
C. self-direction
D. acceptable classroom behaviour

67. In order for a lesson to be effective, it is necessary for the teacher to
A. relate the material to the child's experience
B. organise the content so that the child can understand it as such

C. plan the lesson systematically
D. explain the lesson giving examples and full details

68. When a child asks a question regarding subject-matter, the teacher should generally
A. give straight answer to satisfy the child's curiosity
B. refer him to textbook or other references
C. refer the question to another child for answer
D. help the child arrive at his/her own answer

69. The rejected child is likely to be
A. aggressive
B. negative
C. truant
D. fearless and adventuresome

70. The crucial aspect of the evaluation of school learning is
A. preparing tests
B. judging adequacy of performance
C. measuring growth
D. assigning grades

71. In the context of school, continuous and comprehensive evaluation (CCE) implies
A. continuous monitoring of teachers' performance
B. assessment of both scholastic and co-scholastic aspects of learning
C. making teacher accountable to the parents and the school
D. assessment not to be spread over the total instructional time

72. A good "Head" of an educational institution is the one who
A. understands what is good educational administration and applies its principles with a strong hand
B. is particularly careful about discipline and does not compromise with misconduct or misbehaviour
C. is flexible in his/her approach and works cooperatively and with a human touch
D. allows freedom to the staff and the students and least interferes in their affairs

73. Freedom in education implies that
A. students should be allowed to do any activity if it facilitates learning
B. students should be allowed to join any course of study that they are interested in
C. students should be allowed to do any activity they like to do or are interested in
D. All the above are implied

74. The political slogan "All human beings are equal," infact means that
A. from a certain angle, all human beings are the same
B. all human beings need to be given fair or equitable treatment
C. all human beings need to be given the same opportunities
D. all human beings need to be given equal treatment

75. Objectives of education are ***not*** helpful in
A. understanding child development
B. selecting instructional material
C. designing learning experiences
D. preparing evaluation tools

76. In which of the following methods is the existing knowledge used to draw conclusions?
A. Inductive reasoning method
B. Deductive reasoning method
C. Survey method
D. Discovery method

77. The respect of the student for the teacher should stem primarily from the teacher's
A. legal authority
B. status as an adult
C. personal integrity and goodwill
D. status as a parent substitute

78. The crucial aspect of scientific process is
A. the problem B. the hypothesis
C. the method D. the result

79. A child who reads the numbers wrongly has the following learning disability:
A. Dyscrasis B. Dyslexia
C. Dyspepsia D. Dyscalculia

80. Which of the following comes first in the sequence of deriving a concept?
A. Abstraction B. Differentiation
C. Experiencing D. Generalization

PART-B*

SECTION-V: SUBJECTIVE COMPETENCE : (i): SCIENCE

81. Large intestine in humans mainly carries out
A. absorption
B. assimilation
C. digestion of fats
D. digestion of carbohydrates

82. The opening and closing of stomatal pores depend upon
A. oxygen
B. temperature
C. water in guard cells
D. concentration of CO_2 in stoma

83. Acid rain happens because the
A. Sun heats up the upper layer of the atmosphere
B. burning of fossil fuels releases oxides of carbon, nitrogen and sulphur in the atmosphere
C. electrical charges are produced due to friction amongst the clouds
D. Earth's atmosphere contains acid

84. Fuel used in thermal power plants is
A. water B. uranium
C. biomass D. fossil fuels

85. The S.I. unit of magnetic field intensity is
A. Gauss B. Torr
C. Tesla D. Newton

86. Autotrophic organisms include
A. bacteria and virus
B. bacteria and fungi
C. green plants and some bacteria
D. green plants and all bacteria

87. A molecule of ammonia (NH_3) has
A. only single bond
B. only double bonds
C. only triple bonds
D. two double bonds and one single bond

88. Solubility of alcohol in water is due to
A. low density of alcohol
B. volatile nature of alcohol
C. ionization
D. hydrogen bonding

89. Which is the following has the most non-metallic character?
A. N B. O
C. C D. F

90. Which is the common method of reproduction in majority of fungi and bacteria?
A. Binary fission B. Spore formation
C. Fertilization D. Multiple fission

91. Which among the following diseases is ***not*** sexually transmitted?
A. Syphils B. Hepatitis
C. HIV-AIDS D. Gonorrhoea

92. The fossil remains of Archaeopteryx is a connecting link between
A. reptiles and mammals
B. reptiles and birds
C. fishes and amphibians
D. amphibians and reptiles

93. The S.I. unit of converging ability of a lens is
A. cm B. mm
C. dioptre D. power

94. The laws of reflection hold good for
A. plane mirror only
B. concave mirror only
C. convex mirror only
D. all mirrors irrespective of their shapes

95. Which one of the following is an example of biotic component of the environment?
A. Water B. Temperature
C. Wind D. Vegetation

96. An ecosystem includes
A. all living organisms
B. all non-living organisms
C. both living and non-living organisms
D. sometimes living and sometimes non-living organisms

* Any one subject is to be attempted from Part 'B'.

97. Select the ***wrong*** statement.
A. Forests provide a variety of products.
B. Forests have greater plant diversity
C. Forests do not conserve soil
D. Forests conserve water

98. Which of the following is acidic in nature?
A. Lime juice B. Human blood
C. Lime water D. Antacid

99. To get 2W resistance using 6W resistors, the number of them required is
A. 2 B. 3
C. 4 D. 6

100. Windmill is used in large scale in
A. Delhi
B. Kanyakumari
C. Denmark
D. Kenya

(ii) : MATHEMATICS

101. If $x + \frac{1}{x} = 4$, then $x^2 + \frac{1}{x^2}$ is
A. 8 B. 12
C. 14 D. 16

102. The value of $\frac{\sqrt{729}+\sqrt{441}}{\sqrt{729}-\sqrt{441}}$ is
A. 8 B. $\frac{1}{8}$
C. 80 D. $\sqrt{\frac{1170}{288}}$

103. Two men on either side of a 75 m high tower observe the top of the tower with angles of elevation of 30° and 60° respectively. The distance between the two men is
A. $25\sqrt{3}$ m B. $50\sqrt{3}$ m
C. $75\sqrt{3}$ m D. $100\sqrt{3}$ m

104. The value of sin 25° cos 65° + cos 25° sin 65° is
A. $\frac{1}{2}$ B. –1
C. 1 D. 2

105. The value of $2 \tan^2 45° + \cos^2 30° - \sin^2 60°$ is
A. 2 B. 1
C. $\frac{1}{2}$ D. –1

106. The first and last terms of an A.P. are 5 and 45 respectively. How many terms, with common difference 4, are there in the A.P.?
A. 11 B. 8
C. 10 D. 12

107. The mean of first 8 observations is 18 and that of last 8 observations is 20. If the mean of all 15 observations is 19, the 8th observations is
A. 17 B. 18
C. 19 D. 20

108. In a hockey match, a player was able to score 6 goals in 30 matches. The probability that the player was able to score a goal is
A. 0.6 B. 0.5
C. 0.3 D. 0.2

109. The sides of a triangle are 5 cm 12 cm and 13 cm respectively. The area of the triangle is
A. 24 cm^2 B. 30 cm^2
C. 36 cm^2 D. 40 cm^2

110. The diameter of a cone is 14 cm and its slant height is 9 cm. The area of its curved surface is
A. 126 cm^2 B. 198 cm^2
C. 296 cm^2 D. 396 cm^2

111. A metallic spherical ball of radius 4.2 cm is melted and recast into the shape of a cylinder of radius 6 cm. The height of the cylinder will be
A. 2.74 cm B. 3.24 cm
C. 3.74 cm D. 4.24 cm

112. The area of a sector of a circle with radius 6 cm and sector angle of 60° is

A. $\frac{99}{7}$ cm² B. $\frac{164}{7}$ cm²

C. $\frac{66}{7}$ cm² D. $\frac{132}{7}$ cm²

113. An express train travels a distance of 420 km at a uniform speed. By increasing its speed by 10 km/hour it takes one hour less for the same journey. The original speed of the train is

A. 45 km/hr B. 50 km/hr
C. 55 km/hr D. 60 km/hr

114. A fater is 25 years older than his son. Ten years back, the ratio between the ages of the father and the son was 2 : 1. The present age of the son is

A. 25 years B. 30 years
C. 35 years D. 40 years

115. Minimum pass marks for an examination are 45%. A student obtains 300 marks but fails by 60 marks. The total marks for the examination are

A. 700 B. 800
C. 900 D. 1000

116. In a mixture weighing 50 kg, the ratio of copper and zinc is 3 : 2. Another 5 kg of zinc is added to the mixture. The new ratio of copper to zinc will be

A. 6 : 5 B. 5 : 6
C. 4 : 3 D. 3 : 4

117. There are 300 people in an old age home. If each one is given 200 gms of ration daily, it is enough for 36 days. If 100 more people join the old age home and the ration is reduced to 180 gms per day, then the ration will be sufficient for

A. 26 days B. 30 days
C. 32 days D. 40 days

118. Mohan buys a pen for ₹ 121. If the wholesaler's cost price is ₹ 100 and the shopkeeper and who-lesaler earn profit at equal rate, then their percentage of profit is

A. 10% B. 11%
C. 9.5% D. 8.5%

119. Given, four distinct points, no three of them are collinear. Then the number of lines that can be drawn through them is

A. 2 B. 4
C. 6 D. 8

120. Circles are said to be concentric if

A. they have same radius
B. they have different radii
C. their centres are collinear
D. they have the same centre

(iii) : SOCIAL SCIENCE

121. Entry for normal loss is recorded in the

A. Balance Sheet
B. Profit and Loss Account
C. Trading Account
D. None of the above

122. New capital issue is placed in the

A. Secondary Market B. Primary Market
C. Black Market D. None of the above

123. Which Article of the Constitution provides the Parliament the power to amend the Constitution?

A. 376 B. 370
C. 368 D. 390

124. Who is generally acknowledged as the pioneer of Local Self-Government in modern India?

A. Rippon B. Mayo
C. Lytton D. Curzen

125. Where was the Arya Samaj set up for the first time in 1875?

A. Amritsar B. Lahore
C. Bombay D. Delhi

126. Alauddin Khilji captured the Delhi throne after securing fabulous wealth from

A. Chanderi B. Gujarat
C. Devagiri D. Madurai

127. The tropical grassland is called
A. Pampas B. Llanos
C. Savannah D. None of the above

128. Which is the largest river system of the Peninsular region?
A. Godavari B. Kaveri
C. Narmada D. Mahanadi

129. Buland Darwaza is associated with
A. Shershah B. Babur
C. Akbar D. Jahangir

130. Malik Kafur was the General of which Sultan?
A. Balban
B. Alauddin Khilji
C. Mohammad Bin Tughlaq
D. Firoz Shah Tughlaq

131. The Indian sub-continent was originally a part of
A. Jurassicland B. Angaraland
C. Aryavarta D. Gondwanaland

132. Suez National Canal links up Mediterranean Sea with the
A. Atlantic Ocean B. Pacific Ocean
C. North Sea D. Red Sea

133. Karl Marx's book *Das Kapital* was published in
A. 1857 B. 1862
C. 1867 D. 1872

134. Who propounded the market law?
A. Adam Smith B. J.B. Say
C. T.R. Malthus D. None of the above

135. The Doctrine of Lapse owed its origin to
A. Lord William Bentinck
B. Lord Dalhousie
C. Lord Rippon
D. Lord Curzon

136. In Economics, the terms 'Utility' and 'Usefulness' have
A. Same meaning
B. Different meaning
C. Opposite meaning
D. None of the above

137. Who among the following was the first female Governor of a State in free India?
A. Mrs. Sarojini Naidu
B. Mrs. Sucheta Kripalani
C. Mrs. Indira Gandhi
D. Mrs. Vijaya Laxmi Pandit

138. Which one of the following represents the lines joining the places of equal rainfall?
A. Isohypes B. Isohalines
C. Isobars D. Isohyets

139. In Faizabad, the Revolt of 1857 was led by
A. Ahmadullah
B. Bakht Khan
C. Khan Bahadur Khan
D. Nana Saheb

140. The relationship between the 'value of money' and the 'price level' in an economy is
A. Direct B. Inverse
C. Proportional D. Stable

(iv) : English

Choose the most appropriate response out of the four choices given after every question. Each question carries one mark.

Directions (Qs. 141 and 142): *In each of the following questions, some alternatives have been suggested for the idioms/phrase. Choose the option which best expresses the meaning.*

141. "By leaps and bounds"
A. Rapidly B. Slowly
C. Peacefully D. Strongly

142. "A bolt from the blue"
A. Something unexpected
B. Something unpleasant
C. Something horrible
D. Something unexpected and unpleasant

143. Out of the four alternatives, choose the one which can be substituted for "One who is good at many things".
A. Versatile B. Universal
C. Cosmopolitan D. Secular

144. Choose the correctly spelt word
A. Manufactre B. Manufacture
C. Monufacture D. Manufactuer

145. Choose the correctly spelt word.
A. Aggregete B. Agrregete
C. Aggregate D. Agregate

146. Choose the indirect form of the following sentence.
Rajan said, "O that I were a child again!"
A. Rajan exclaimed with wonder that he was a child again.
B. Rajan wondered that were he a child again.
C. Rajan wished that he had been a child again.
D. Rajan wished that he were a child again.

147. Choose the indirect form of the following sentence:
The manager said, "Well, what can I do for you?"
A. The manager asked what he could do for him.
B. The manager exclaimed what he could do for you.
C. The manager wanted to know what he could do for you.
D. The manager said that he couldn't do anything for him.

148. The passive voice of "Who is creating this mess?" is
A. Who has created this mess?
B. By whom has this mess been created?
C. By whom this mess is being created?
D. By whom is this mess being created?

149. The active voice of "The clown was laughed at by them." is
A. They were laughing at the clown.
B. The were laughing on the clown.
C. They laughed at the clown.
D. They were laughed at by the clown.

Directions (Qs. 150 to 152): *Choose the most appropriate words to fill in the blanks.*

150. Ramesh .... the business deal without wasting any time.
A. damaged B. facilitated
C. clinched D. expressed

151. I complimented him .... his success in the examination.
A. through B. on
C. about D. for

152. The dramatist must cater .... the taste of the audience.
A. to B. over
C. into D. for

153. Who said "*A thing of beauty is a joy forever*"?
A. Frost B. Shelley
C. Keats D. Coleridge

154. Which one of the following is considered the last play of Shakespeare?
A. Cymbeline B. Pericles
C. The Winter's Tale D. Henry-VIII

155. Which one of the following poems is composed by John Keats?
A. Ode to Duty
B. Ode to the West Wind
C. Ode to a Nightingale
D. Ode on Solitude

156. Who is known as "The Prince of English Essayists"?
A. Lamb B. Addison
C. Eliot D. Steele

157. Shakespeare's "Measure for Measure" is a
A. Romance B. Tragi-Comedy
C. Dumb show D. Mime

158. Who said that "*Hell is a city much like London*"?
A. Shelley B. Frost
C. Keats D. Coleridge

159. In the sentence "I shall write to you when I have time," ***when I have time*** is a
A. Noun clause B. Adverb clause
C. Adjective clause D. None of these

160. In the sentence, "The boy who topped the class is my brother," ***who topped the class*** is a
A. Noun clause B. Adverb clause
C. Adjective clause D. None of these

(v) : हिन्दी

निर्देश (प्रश्न सं. 161-165): *निम्नलिखित गद्यांश को ध्यानपूर्वक पढ़कर उसके आधार पर पूछे गये प्रश्नों के उत्तर दीजिए।*

"आज हम इस असमंजस में पड़ें हैं और यह निश्चय नहीं कर पाए हैं कि हम किस ओर चलेंगे और हमारा ध्येय क्या है? स्वभावतः ऐसी अवस्था में हमारे पैर लड़खड़ाते हैं। हमारे विचार में भारत के लिए और सारे संसार के लिए सुख और शांति का एक ही रास्ता है और वह है अहिंसा और आत्मवाद का। अपनी दुर्बलता के कारण हम उसे ग्रहण न कर सके, पर उसके सिद्धांतों को तो हमें स्वीकार कर ही लेना चाहिए और उसके प्रवर्तन का इंतजाम करना चाहिए। यदि हम सिद्धांत ही न मानेंगे तो उसके प्रवर्तन की आशा कैसे की जा सकती है? जहाँ तक मैंने महात्मा गाँधी के सिद्धांत को समझा है, वह इसी आत्मवाद और अहिंसा के, जिसे वे सत्य भी कहा करते थे, मानने वाले और प्रवर्तक थे। उसे ही कुछ लोग आज गाँधीवाद का नाम भी दे रहे हैं। यद्यपि महात्मा गाँधी ने बार-बार यह कहा था कि 'वे किसी नए सिद्धांत या वाद के प्रवर्तक नहीं हैं और उन्होंने अपने जीवन में प्राचीन सिद्धांतों का अमल कर दिखाने का यत्न किया है।' विचार कर देखा जाए तो जितने सिद्धांत अन्य देशों, अन्य-अन्य कालों और स्थितियों में भिन्न-भिन्न नामों और धर्मों से प्रचलित हुए हैं, सभी अन्तिम और मार्मिक अन्वेषण के बाद इसी तत्त्व या सिद्धांत में समाविष्ट पाए जाते हैं। केवल भौतिकवाद इनसे अलग है। हमें असमंजस की स्थिति से बाहर निकलकर निश्चय कर लेना है कि हम अहिंसावाद, आत्मवाद और गाँधीवाद के अनुयायी और समर्थक हैं न कि भौतिकवाद के। प्रेय और श्रेय में से हमें श्रेय को चुनना है। श्रेय ही हितकर है, भले ही वह कठिन और श्रमसाध्य हो। इसके विपरीत प्रेय आरंभ में भले ही आकर्षक दिखाई दे, उसका अन्तिम परिणाम अहितकर होता है।"

161. हमारे पैर लड़खड़ाते हैं, क्योंकि हम

A. लक्ष्य से अनजान और दिशाहीन हैं

B. अशक्त और दुर्बल हैं

C. भौतिकवाद में आस्था रखते हैं

D. अकर्मण्य हैं

162. लेखक के विचार में विश्व में सुख-समृद्धि और शांति स्थापित हो सकती है, केवल

A. अहिंसा और अनात्मवाद द्वारा

B. अनिश्चय और असमंजस की स्थिति से उबरकर

C. भौतिकवाद और अनात्मवाद को समन्वित करके

D. अहिंसा और आत्मवाद को अपनाकर

163. अहिंसा एवं सत्य के मार्ग में सबसे बड़ी बाधा है

A. असत्य मार्ग का सरल होना

B. सत्य के मार्ग की दुर्गमता

C. हिंसा के प्रति सहज आकर्षण

D. मनुष्य की अपनी दुर्बलता

164. हमें स्वयं को किस दुविधा से मुक्त करना चाहिए?

A. लक्ष्य और दिशा की

B. श्रेय और प्रेय की

C. गाँधीवाद और भौतिकवाद की

D. सिद्धांत और व्यवहार की

165. विश्व की विभिन्न विचारधाराएँ और प्रमुख वाद अंततः किस तत्त्व में समाविष्ट पाए जाते हैं?

A. सत्य में   B. सुख-साधना में

C. धार्मिक-आस्था में   D. शांति-अन्वेषण में

निर्देश (प्रश्न सं. 166-180): *निम्नलिखित प्रत्येक प्रश्न के चार-चार विकल्प दिए गए हैं। उनमें से सही विकल्प चुनिए।*

166. इनमें से किस कवि ने भ्रमरगीत प्रसंग को अपनी रचनाओं में स्थान ***नहीं*** दिया?

A. रसखान   B. सूरदास

C. रत्नाकर   D. नंददास

167. इनमें से किस वाक्य की क्रिया सकर्मक है?

A. रमेश का आचरण अच्छा है।

B. वह रात भर जागता रहा।

C. आकाशवाणी से यह समाचार प्रसारित हुआ।

D. आपसे मिलकर बड़ी प्रसन्नता हुई।

168. इनमें से कौन-सा शब्द विशेषण ***नहीं*** है?

A. दिग्भ्रम   B. दिग्भ्रमित

C. दिग्भ्रांत   D. उद्भ्रांत

169. इनमें से कौन-सा शब्द शेष तीन से भिन्न है?

A. संपृक्त   B. संयुक्त

C. संलीन   D. संश्लिष्ट

170. इनमें से कौन-सा शब्द अरबी-फारसी का ***नहीं*** है?

A. नतीजा   B. भरपूर

C. कायम   D. तहजीब

171. इनमें से किस शब्द में 'अव' उपसर्ग 'हीन' का अर्थ ***नहीं*** देता?

A. अवमूल्यन B. अवनति
C. अवमानना D. अवधान

172. तुम्हारा परीक्षा में प्रथम आना तो ऐसा है जैसे ....।

A. ऊँट के मुँह में जीरा
B. घोड़े की बला तबेले के सिर
C. अंधे के हाथ बटेर लगना
D. अंधा क्या जाने बसंत की बहार

173. 'विजन वन बल्लरी पर, सोती थी सुहाग भरी' में अलंकार हैं

A. अनुप्रास, विरोधाभास
B. अनुप्रास, मानवीकरण
C. पुनरूक्तिप्रकाश, मानवीकरण
D. विरोधाभास, पुनरूक्तिप्रकाश

174. इनमें से कौन-सा शब्द स्त्रीलिंग है?

A. अंबार B. भरमार
C. भंडार D. कोठार

175. इनमें से कौन-सा भाव शेष तीन से भिन्न है?

A. पीड़ा B. वेदना
C. अवसाद D. करुणा

176. इनमें से कौन-सा वाक्य ***अशुद्ध*** है?

A. वे तो वहाँ जाने के लिए तैयार ही नहीं है।
B. मुझे आशा है कि आप मेरे सुझावों पर विचार करेंगे।
C. दो-चार साल बाद ये तो नहीं होंगे, लेकिन ये होगा।
D. इस पुस्तक में ऐसा क्या है कि तुम इसे छोड़ ही नहीं रहे।

177. इनमें में किस वाक्य में भाववाच्य का प्रयोग हुआ है?

A. आज बच्चों को इनाम दिया गया।
B. कल विद्यालय में छुट्टी नहीं है।
C. हवा के झोंके से खिड़की खुल गई।
D. इस गर्मी में सोया नहीं जाएगा।

178. इनमें से किसमें 'अ' उपसर्ग का प्रयोग हुआ है?

A. अरमान B. अम्लान
C. अपमान D. अनुमान

179. इनमें से कौन-सा शब्द प्रत्यय रहित है?

A. मलयानिल B. स्वप्निल
C. उर्मिल D. स्नेहिल

180. इनमें से किसमें बहुव्रीहि समास ***नहीं*** है?

A. वज्रायुध B. दिगंबर
C. वाचस्पति D. श्वेतांबर

ANSWERS

1	2	3	4	5	6	7	8	9	10
A	B	C	D	B	C	D	C	B	B
11	**12**	**13**	**14**	**15**	**16**	**17**	**18**	**19**	**20**
C	B	D	D	A	B	C	B	D	C
21	**22**	**23**	**24**	**25**	**26**	**27**	**28**	**29**	**30**
D	C	C	D	B	C	B	C	A	B
31	**32**	**33**	**34**	**35**	**36**	**37**	**38**	**39**	**40**
A	C	B	B	A	A	A	B	C	D
41	**42**	**43**	**44**	**45**	**46**	**47**	**48**	**49**	**50**
D	C	B	D	C	A	A	A	A	C
51	**52**	**53**	**54**	**55**	**56**	**57**	**58**	**59**	**60**
D	A	B	D	B	A	B	D	B	A
61	**62**	**63**	**64**	**65**	**66**	**67**	**68**	**69**	**70**
A	D	B	C	B	C	C	D	A	C
71	**72**	**73**	**74**	**75**	**76**	**77**	**78**	**79**	**80**
B	A	A	B	A	B	C	C	D	C
81	**82**	**83**	**84**	**85**	**86**	**87**	**88**	**89**	**90**
A	C	B	D	C	C	A	D	D	B

91	92	93	94	95	96	97	98	99	100
B	B	C	D	D	C	C	A	B	B
101	102	103	104	105	106	107	108	109	110
C	A	D	C	A	A	C	D	B	B
111	112	113	114	115	116	117	118	119	120
A	D	D	C	B	A	B	A	C	D
121	122	123	124	125	126	127	128	129	130
C	B	C	A	C	C	C	A	C	B
131	132	133	134	135	136	137	138	139	140
D	D	C	B	B	B	A	D	A	B
141	142	143	144	145	146	147	148	149	150
A	A	A	B	C	C	A	D	C	C
151	152	153	154	155	156	157	158	159	160
B	A	C	D	C	A	B	A	B	C
161	162	163	164	165	166	167	168	169	170
A	D	D	B	A	A	C	A	A	B
171	172	173	174	175	176	177	178	179	180
D	C	B	B	D	C	D	B	C	C

SOME SELECTED EXPLANATORY ANSWERS

11-14. Based on given data the family tree are like this:

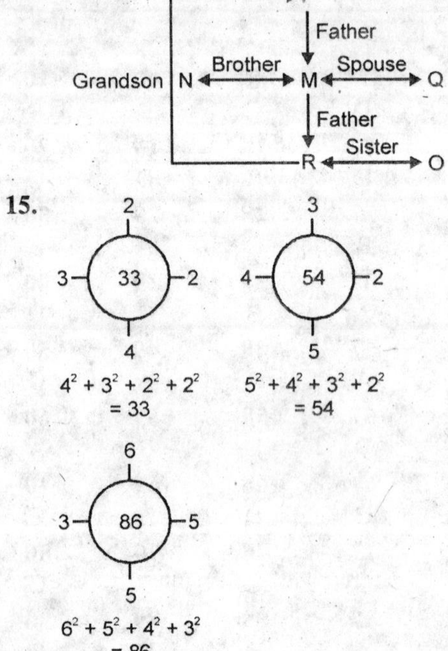

16.

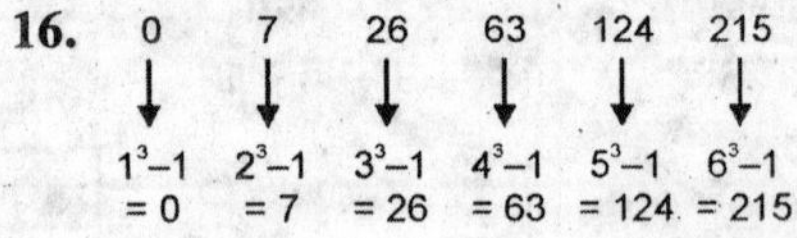

17.

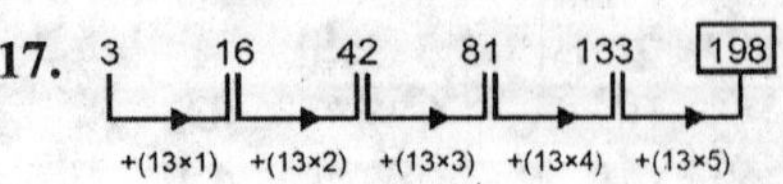

18.

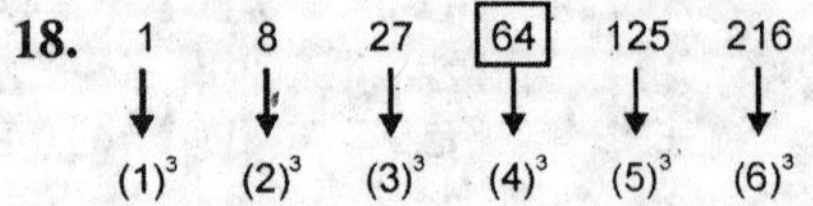

19. 2 9 23 51 107 219

$+(7\times2^0)$ $+(7\times2^1)$ $+(7\times2^2)$ $+(7\times2^3)$ $+(7\times2^4)$

21. From given information:

Letter	F	A	M	I	L	Y	S	T	E	R
Code	3	1	6	4	5	9	7	8	2	0

Hence, code of the word is '64780277'.

22.

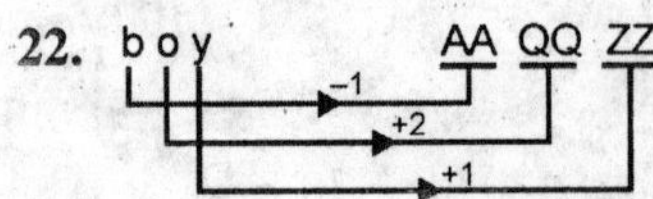

Similarly,

cat → BB CC UU (c −1 → BB, a +2 → CC, t +1 → UU)

23-27.

	A	B	C	D	E
Cricket	✓	✓			
Tennis	✓	✓	✓	✓	
Hockey		✓	✓	✓	✓
Volleyball	✓		✓		
Football			✓		✓

101. $\because \; x - \dfrac{1}{x} = 4$

$\therefore \; x^2 + \dfrac{1}{x^2} = \left(x - \dfrac{1}{x}\right)^2 - 2(x)\left(\dfrac{1}{x}\right)$

$= (4)^2 - 2 = 14$

102. $\dfrac{\sqrt{729}+\sqrt{441}}{\sqrt{729}-\sqrt{441}} = \dfrac{27+21}{27-21} = \dfrac{48}{6} = 8$

103.

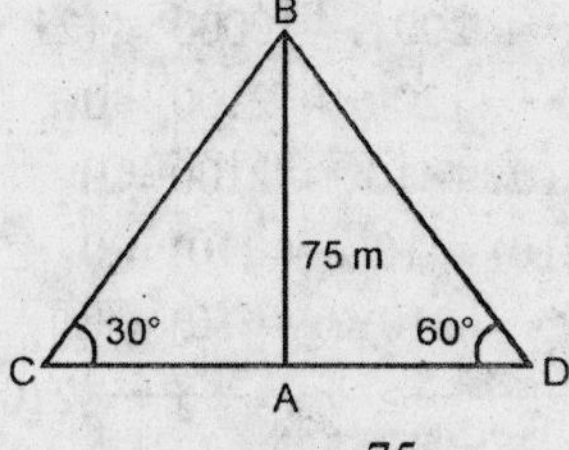

$\tan 30° = \dfrac{75}{x}$

$\Rightarrow \quad \dfrac{1}{\sqrt{3}} = \dfrac{75}{x}$

$\Rightarrow \quad x = 75\sqrt{3}$ m

$\tan 60° = \dfrac{75}{y} \Rightarrow \sqrt{3} = \dfrac{75}{y}$

$\Rightarrow \quad y = \dfrac{75}{\sqrt{3}} \times \dfrac{\sqrt{3}}{\sqrt{3}} = 25\sqrt{3}$

$\therefore \quad x + y = 75\sqrt{3} + 25\sqrt{3} = 100\sqrt{3}$ m.

Hence, the distance between the two men $= 100\sqrt{3}$ m.

104. $\sin 25° \times \cos 65° + \cos 25° \times \sin 65°$
$= \sin(25° + 65°) = \sin 90° = 1$

105. $2\tan^2 45° + \cos^2 30 - \sin^2 60°$

$= 2 \times (1)^2 + \left(\dfrac{\sqrt{3}}{2}\right)^2 - \left(\dfrac{\sqrt{3}}{2}\right)^2 = 2$

106. nth term of A.P. $= a + (n-1)d$

$\Rightarrow 45 = 5 + (n-1)4 \Rightarrow 45 - 5 = 4n - 4$

$\Rightarrow 40 + 4 = 4n \Rightarrow 4n = 44 \Rightarrow n = 11$

107. Total of first 8 observations $= 8 \times 18 = 144$
Total of least 8 observations $= 20 \times 8 = 160$
Total of 15 observations $= 15 \times 19 = 285$
Hence, the 8th observation
$= (144 + 160) - (285) = 304 - 285 = 19$

108. Required probability $= \dfrac{6}{30} = \dfrac{1}{5} = 0.2$

109. $S = \dfrac{a+b+c}{2} = \dfrac{5+12+13}{2} = \dfrac{30}{2} = 15$

Area of triangle

$= \sqrt{S(S-a)(S-b)(S-c)}$

$= \sqrt{15(15-5)(15-12)(15-13)}$

$= \sqrt{15 \times 10 \times 3 \times 2} = \sqrt{900} = 30 \text{ cm}^2$

110. Curved surface area of cone

$= \pi r l = \dfrac{22}{7} \times 7 \times 9 = 198 \text{ cm}^2$

111. Volume of cylinder = Volume of sphere

$\Rightarrow \pi \times r^2 \times h = \dfrac{4}{3}\pi r^3$

$\Rightarrow 6 \times 6 \times h = \dfrac{4}{3} \times 4.2 \times 4.2 \times 4.2$

$\Rightarrow h = \dfrac{4 \times 42 \times 42 \times 42}{3 \times 6 \times 6 \times 1000}$

$= \dfrac{4 \times 14 \times 7 \times 7}{1000} = \dfrac{56 \times 49}{1000} = \dfrac{2744}{1000}$

$= 2.744$ cm $= 2.74$ cm

112. Area of sector $= \dfrac{\theta}{360°} \times \pi r^2$

$= \dfrac{60}{360} \times \dfrac{22}{7} \times 6 \times 6 = \dfrac{132}{7} \text{ cm}^2$

113. Let, the original speed of the train = x km/hr

According to the question,

$$\frac{420}{x} - \frac{420}{x+10} = 1$$

$\Rightarrow 420(x + 10 - x) = x^2 + 10x$

$\Rightarrow \quad x^2 + 10x - 4200 = 0$

$$x = \frac{-10 \pm \sqrt{100 + 4 \times 4200}}{2} = \frac{-10 \pm \sqrt{16900}}{2}$$

$$= \frac{-10 \pm 130}{2} = 60 \text{ km/hr.}$$

114. Let, present age of son = x years

Father's age = $(x + 25)$ years

According to the question,

$$\frac{x+25-10}{x-10} = \frac{2}{1}$$

$\Rightarrow \quad \frac{x+15}{x-10} = \frac{2}{1}$

$\Rightarrow \quad 2x - 20 = x + 15$

$\Rightarrow \quad x = 35$

Hence, the present age of son = 35 years.

115. Let, total marks for the examination = x

According to the question,

45% of x = 300 + 60

$\Rightarrow \quad \frac{45}{100} \times x = 360$

$\Rightarrow \quad x = \frac{360 \times 100}{45} = 800$

116. Amount of copper in 50 kg mixture

$= \frac{3}{5} \times 50 = 30$ kg

Amount of zinc = $\frac{2}{5} \times 50 = 20$ kg

According to the questions,

Amount of copper = 30 kg

and amount of zinc

= 20 + 5 = 25 kg

$\therefore$ Required ratio = $\frac{30}{25}$ = 6 : 5.

117. Required no. of days

$$= \frac{300 \times 200 \times 36}{400 \times 180} = 30 \text{ days.}$$

118. Let, profit percent of wholesaler = x%

Profit = $\frac{x}{100} \times 100$ = ₹ x

S.P. of wholesaler

= CP + profit

= 100 + x = ₹ (100 + x)

C.P. of shopkeeper = ₹ (100 + x)

Profit = $\frac{x}{100} \times (100 + x) = \frac{x(100+x)}{100}$

S.P. = $(100 + x) + \frac{x(100+x)}{100}$

$= \frac{10000 + 100x + 100x + x^2}{100}$

$= \frac{x^2 + 200x + 10000}{100}$

According to the question,

$x^2 + 200x + 10000 = 121 \times 100$

$\Rightarrow \quad x^2 + 200x - 2100 = 0$

$\Rightarrow x^2 + 210x - 10x - 2100 = 0$

$\Rightarrow x(x + 210) - 10(x + 210) = 0$

$\Rightarrow \quad (x + 210)(x - 10) = 0$

$\Rightarrow \quad x = -210$

or $\quad x = 10$

Hence, profit % = 10%

119.

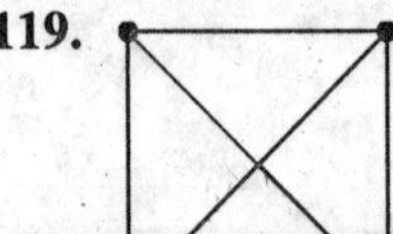

Required number of lines = 6

120.

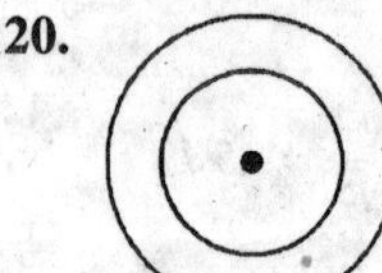

Circles having the same centre but with different radii are said to be concentric circles.

Previous Paper (Solved)

IGNOU B.Ed. Entrance Test 2014

PART-A

SECTION-I : General English Comprehension

Directions (Qs. 1 to 10): *Read the following passage carefully and choose the best answer out of the four choices given after each question that follows:*

Among the most important themes in the Disney movie *The Little Mermaid* are those of questioning conventional thinking, and pursuing a dream. Not only is Ariel, the little mermaid, demonstrating original thought (something that many seem to think she is lacking), but also she is rebelling against her speciesist father. When Ariel expresses her love for the human prince, King Trident is furious. When Ariel points out angrily that he does not understand her, or even know the man whom she loves, Trident retorts, "Know him? I don't need to know him! He's a human!" In a very real way Disney is encouraging children to question preconceived ideas that we may have against a certain group.

Disney also teaches children to pursue what they love. We see that Ariel's love for Prince Eric is more important than all else. In turning to the Sea Witch, Ursula, for help, Ariel makes a mistake, but no true hero or heroine is flawless. Ariel puts herself, her family, and all merfolk in danger, but we see that with the help of her prince, she is able to put everything right.

At the end of the film, when Ursula has forced King Trident to sacrifice his kingdom for his daughter's soul, the Sea Witch rises out of the water, gigantic and terrifying, wearing the king's crown and holding his magic trident. She laughs evilly and declares that she is the ruler of all mermen and women. "So much for true love!" she screams victoriously. Eric, however, succeeds in piloting the prow of his ship straight through her belly, vanquishing her. The moral here is that while we all make mistakes, what is truly important is how we right the wrongs we may do to others.

1. The author's main point in the passage is that
- A. Ariel should not have been allowed to marry Prince Eric
- B. Only Prince Eric truly understood Ariel
- C. Ariel demonstrated original thought
- D. *The Little Mermaid* teaches children to follow their hearts

2. Why does the author use parentheses around the comment (Something that many seem to think she is lacking)?
- A. To indicate a side comment to the reader
- B. To indicate that it is unimportant
- C. To indicate a humorous tone
- D. To indicate a shift in meaning

3. Ariel's father is called a 'speciesist' because he
- A. Does not know Eric
- B. Oppose Ariel's love based only on Eric being human
- C. Does not understand Ariel
- D. Is furious

4. Which of the following would best illustrate the assertion made in the lines "Disney is encouraging children to question preconceived ideas that we may have against a certain group"?
- A. A movie about the development of the iPod

B. A movie that details the horrors of war
C. A movie about a girl who overcomes her fear of snakes
D. A movie that documents the travels of a rock band

5. Ursula's quote "So much for true love" primarily suggests that
A. The marriage was unacceptable to her
B. She is mocking true love
C. She is speciesist
D. Trident was her true love

6. "Vanquishing" most nearly means
A. Loving B. Succeeding
C. Vanishing D. Defeating

7. The author's attitude towards *"The Little Mermaid"* is primarily one of
A. Appreciation B. Frustration
C. Stoicism D. Ambivalence

8. Among the most important themes in the Disney movie *The Little Mermaid* are those of questioning conventional thinking, and pursuing a dream. In this sentence, what part of speech is 'thinking'?
A. Verb B. Noun
C. Adjective D. Adverb

9. In the sentence in Q. No. 8, what part of speech is 'questioning'?
A. Verb B. Noun
C. Adjective D. Adverb

10. When Ariel expresses her love for the human prince, King Trident is furious. This is a
A. Simple sentence
B. Complex sentence
C. Compound sentence
D. Complex-Compound sentence

SECTION-II : Logical and Analytical Reasoning

Directions (Qs. 11 to 15): *Six persons A, B, C, D, E and F participated in a debate. Out of the six persons two were ladies; E and his unmarried sister were new entrants this year in the debate; husband of D was winner of last year and participated in this year's debate; A and C were runner-up last year; this year's winner was neither a new entrant nor winner of last year; B left the debate in the middle for some unavoidable reason; at the end of the debate, C secured more points than A but less than E and F.*

On the basis of above information answer the following questions:

11. Who is the husband of D?
A. A B. B
C. E D. C

12. Who was the winner last year?
A. A B. B
C. D D. E

13. Who is the sister of E?
A. C B. D
C. F D. A

14. Who was the winner in the debate this year?
A. B B. C
C. D D. A

15. Find the missing number.

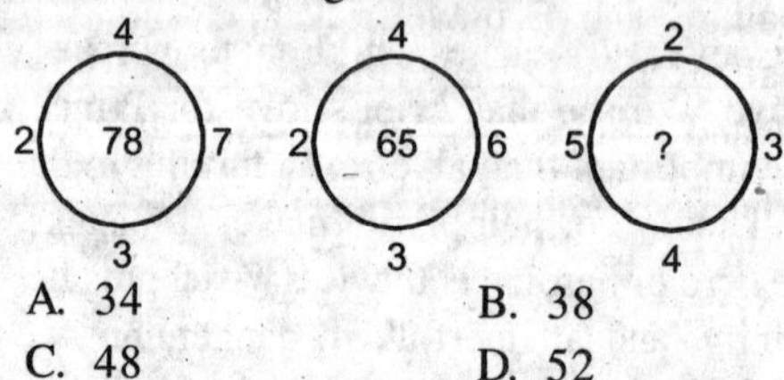

A. 34 B. 38
C. 48 D. 52

Directions (Qs. 16 to 19): *In each of the following questions an incomplete series of numbers with one blank is given. Identify the missing number from the given alternatives.*

16. 1, 8, 27, 64, ?, 216
A. 85 B. 125
C. 155 D. 205

17. 2, 11, 38, 119, ?
A. 357 B. 380
C. 362 D. 418

18. 4, 15, 37, 70, ?, 169
A. 103 B. 106
C. 117 D. 114

19. 29, 54, 103, 200, 393, ?
A. 586 B. 490
C. 678 D. 778

20. Which pair is different in some way from others in the following?
A. Milk – Butter
B. Inkpot – Ink
C. Sugarcane – Sugar
D. Coconut – Oil

21. If 'Family' is coded as 316459 and 'Sister' is coded as 747820, then 'Mystery' will be coded as
A. 6987209 B. 6798209
C. 6978209 D. 6972809

22. If GIRL is coded as HHJJQQNN, then FOND will be coded as
A. GGPPMMEE B. GGPPMMFF
C. GGNNMMFF D. GGPPNNFF

Directions (Qs. 23 to 27): *Read the following paragraph to answer questions that follow:*

A and B play Football and Hockey. C and E play Tennis and Cricket. A and D play Tennis and Volleyball. B and E play Cricket. C and E play Volleyball. C and D play Hockey. D and E play Football and Cricket.

23. Who does *not* play Cricket?
A. A B. B
C. C D. E

24. Who plays Football, Hockey and Tennis?
A. D B. C
C. B D. E

25. Who plays only Tennis, Cricket, Volleyball and Hockey?
A. A B. B
C. C D. D

26. Who plays only Football, Hockey and Cricket?
A. A B. B
C. C D. D

27. Who plays all these games except Hockey?
A. B B. E
C. D D. C

Directions (Qs. 28 to 30): *Read the following paragraph to answer the questions that follow:*

A, B, C, D, E all have six balls. B gives two balls to E who gives one ball to D. A gives four balls to C who gives two balls to B. B gives three balls to D, who gives one ball to A.

28. How many balls does B have?
A. 2 B. 8
C. 7 D. 3

29. How many balls does C have?
A. 3 B. 7
C. 8 D. 9

30. Now, who has got the maximum number of balls?
A. B B. C
C. D D. E

SECTION-III : EDUCATIONAL AND GENERAL AWARENESS

31. RTE Act 2009 grants Right to Free and Compulsory Education to the children between
A. 3–11 years B. 6–14 years
C. 6–11 years D. 3–14 years

32. The members of Rajya Sabha in India are elected by the members of
A. Municipal Committee and Corporations
B. District Councils
C. State Legislative Assemblies
D. Panchayats

33. School Education is presently included in which of the following lists in our Constitution specifying functions of various governments?
A. State List B. Union List
C. Concurrent list D. None of these

34. To create a new State in India, a bill is to be passed by
A. State Assembly
B. Lok Sabha
C. Rajya Sabha
D. Both Lok Sabha and Rajya Sabha

35. District Institutes of Education and Training (DIETs) have been set up for improving the quality of
A. Elementary Education
B. Secondary Education
C. Primary Education
D. Pre-School Education

36. Who presided over the Constituent Assembly that framed the Constitution of independent India?
A. B.R. Ambedkar
B. Rajendra Prasad
C. Jawahar Lal Nehru
D. Sarojini Naidu

37. The 10 + 2 + 3 pattern of education was recommended by
A. Education Commission 1964–1966
B. Secondary Education Commission 1952–1953
C. University Education Commission 1948–1949
D. National Commission on Teachers 1983–1984

38. Which organisation prepares National Curriculum Framework (NCF) for School Education?
A. NCERT B. CBSE
C. NUEPA D. NCTE

39. In our Constitution, Right to Free and Compulsory Elementary Education is included in the Section on
A. Fundamental Rights of Citizens
B. Directive Principles of State Policy
C. Human Rights
D. Rights of Children

40. Who was the Prime Minister of India at the time of the creation of independent Bangladesh?
A. V.P. Singh
B. Indira Gandhi
C. Morarji Desai
D. I.K. Gujral

41. What was the major objective of the Quit India Movement?
A. To gain complete independence
B. To win dominion status
C. To get more representation in the central legislative assembly
D. To ensure employment of more Indians in the Government

42. Article 51 of the Constitution of India lists
A. Fundamental Rights of Citizens
B. Duties of Citizens
C. Rights of Children
D. Human Rights

43. Who gave the slogan 'Back to the Vedas'?
A. Swami Vivekanand
B. Swami Dayanand
C. Raja Ram Mohan Rai
D. Sri Aurobindo

44. Which of the following organisations does *not* deal with school education?
A. CBSE B. SCERT
C. AICTE D. DIET

45. Why have Navodaya Vidyalayas been set up?
A. To provide residential facilities to children
B. To provide quality education to ST students
C. To provide quality education to minorities
D. To provide quality education to talented students in residential settings

46. Which one of the following is the highest civilian award given to eminent persons?
A. Padma Vibhushan
B. Param Vir Chakra
C. Bharat Ratna
D. Maha Vir Chakra

47. Which organisation is responsible for granting recognition to Teacher Education Institutes?
A. NCTE B. NCERT
C. SCERT D. UGC

48. The film *'Guide'* was based on the novel of the same title written by

A. R.K. Narayan B. Chetan Bhagat

C. Mulk Raj Anand D. Jhumpa Lahiri

49. According to Mahatma Gandhi, what should be the medium of instruction at the primary stage?

A. Regional Language of the state

B. Hindi

C. English

D. Child's mother-tongue

50. Which one of the following is *not* a part of North-Eastern India?

A. Mizoram

B. Tripura

C. Andaman and Nicobar Islands

D. Nagaland

51. Which one of the following was passed in the last session of the 15th Lok Sabha?

A. Right to Information Bill

B. Right to Education Bill

C. Street Vendors Bill

D. Right to Employment Bill

52. Teacher's Day in India is celebrated on the occasion of the birthday of

A. Dr. Zakir Husain

B. Dr. Radhakrishnan

C. Jawahar Lal Nehru

D. Sri Aurobindo

53. Which country is *not* a member of SAARC?

A. Nepal B. Pakistan

C. Bhutan D. China

54. India is a Republic because

A. Head of the State is elected by the people

B. Prime Minister is elected by the people

C. Prime Minister is appointed by the Head of the State

D. Prime Minister is supported by the majority of Parliamențarians

55. Which of the following States in India did *not* become independent in 1947?

A. Gujarat

B. Goa

C. Himachal Pradesh

D. West Bengal

SECTION-IV : TEACHING-LEARNING AND THE SCHOOL

56. The function of a teacher in a democratic classroom is to

A. allow students completely free choice without any interference or suggestions

B. tell students what are intelligent choices among various alternatives

C. help students become more capable of making intelligent choices among increasingly significant alternatives

D. make the choices for the student himself/herself

57. For learning to be effective a goal must be meaningful in terms of

A. curricular objectives

B. intellectual ideas involved

C. learners needs and purposes

D. the standard of the school

58. The key to motivation in the classroom is

A. an interest inherent in the subject-matter

B. the teacher's personality

C. the emotional climate of the classroom

D. the suitability of the curricular experiences

59. The chief function of work experience programme in schools is to provide

A. youth with work experience

B. business and industry with better workers

C. freedom for teachers to handle more students

D. a better basis for giving vocational guidance

60. A student has a problem. He/She asks the teacher "What shall I do?" The teacher should

A. tell the student the course of action to take after considering his/her abilities

B. tell the student what he/she would do is he/she were in the student's place
C. ask the student questions which will develop the information needed for an intelligent decision
D. tell the student to figure out for himself/herself, since he/she would develop the ability to find solutions to problems

61. The best informed opinion of ability grouping is that
A. it encourages individual initiative and leadership
B. it eliminates the problem of individual differences
C. it encourages students to make maximum use of their potential
D. it needs to be explored further before it is accepted or rejected

62. According to modern educators, discipline refers to
A. rules affecting conduct of action
B. a way of promoting constructive and positive behaviour
C. controlling the class by enforcing obedience and conformity
D. curbing of students' misbehaviour

63. Social development is essentially a matter of
A. conformity to the demands of social order
B. achievement of social security and acceptance
C. the integration of one's purposes with those of social order
D. the development of social skills

64. Two boys have an I.Q. of 120 each. It can be concluded that
A. both will be successful in high school and college
B. the parents of both are above average in intelligence
C. both would have the same aptitude to the same degree
D. none of the above is necessarily true

65. Which of the following is *not* a product of learning?
A. Attitudes B. Concepts
C. Growth D. Skills

66. It can be safely assumed that a student understands a principle when he/she can
A. answer specific objective type questions
B. give appropriate examples of it
C. repeat it verbally
D. use it in solving unfamiliar problems to which it applies

67. A dominated over-protected child is likely to be
A. aggressive B. delinquent
C. quarrelsome D. withdrawn

68. Perhaps the greatest satisfaction in teaching is
A. sense of service to the society
B. sense of contribution to the pupil's growth
C. a feeling of love for and by children
D. a sense of status and power as a teacher

69. Awarding 'grades' in place of marks is recommended because
A. it will improve the overall quality of education
B. teaching and learning will be facilitated
C. differentiation among students based on marks will be eliminated
D. 'grades' are easier to give than marks

70. Which of the following is *not* true about teaching?
A. As a result of teaching a student must learn
B. Teaching involves intention that someone must learn something
C. Teaching is characterised by a special relationship between the teacher and the taught
D. Teaching is a necessary but not a sufficient condition of learning

71. Choose the most appropriate answer.
Regarding acquisition of knowledge, people say that
A. sense perception is the only valid source of knowledge

B. it is reason alone which can provide us true knowledge
C. it is through reason and perception that we can get the true knowledge of the world
D. we never get knowledge because it does not lie out there; we construct knowledge on our own

72. Child-centred education means
A. designing curriculum by consulting the child
B. planning educational experiences as the child wants them
C. organising teaching with maximum involvement of student(s)
D. leaving the child free to plan his/her learning without the aid of the teacher

73. Which of the following is the most important single factor underlying the success of a beginning teacher?
A. His/Her attitude or outlook
B. His/her personality and ability to relate to the class
C. His/Her communication and organisational ability
D. His/Her scholarship and intellectual capacity

74. Teachers' main responsibility lies in
A. planning educational experiences
B. promoting human relations with parents
C. experimenting with teaching techniques
D. implementing administrative policies

75. When school children become mischievous, explosive, rebellious or apathetic, the teacher should first look into
A. the atmosphere of the home from which they come
B. the appropriateness of the work assigned and the demands made upon them
C. the undermining influences of the home and the community
D. the sociometric structure of the class

76. Generally the most effective approach to dealing with the child's aggressive behaviour is
A. to give him/her due punishment when he/she shows aggressive tendencies
B. to channel his/her aggression into legitimate areas of competition
C. to reward him/her for friendly behaviour and to ignore his/her aggressive behaviour
D. to insist that he/she apologises for his/her undesirable behaviour

77. Which of the following describes the extent of the effect of heredity upon development?
A. Heredity determines how far we will go
B. Heredity determines how far we can go
C. Heredity is the primary determinant of how far we will go
D. Heredity is the primary determinant of how far we can go

78. The greatest deterrent to creativity on the part of the child is
A. the adult insists on perfection and conformity to adult standards
B. the failure on the part of adults to provide the needed inspiration
C. his/her unwillingness to put in the effort required for perfection
D. his/her easy discouragement and his short span of attention

79. A child who uses a wheelchair
A. should not be in a regular school
B. should study only in a special school meant for physically challenged
C. should be given education along with non-disabled students in a regular school
D. should be given education in a regular school but in a separate section

80. The chief point of distinction between a teacher-made test and standardised test lies in the area of
A. objectivity
B. norms
C. marketability
D. overall quality

PART-B

SECTION-V (i): SCIENCE

81. Which of the following is *not* a physical change?
A. Boiling of water to give water vapour
B. Melting of ice to give liquid water
C. Dissolution of salt in water
D. Combustion of Liquefied Petroleum Gas (LPG)

82. Which of the following gives the correct increasing order or acidic strength?
A. Water < Acetic acid < Hydrochloric acid
B. Water < Hydrochloric acid < Acetic acid
C. Acetic acid < Water < Hydrochloric acid
D. Hydrochloric acid < Water < Acetic acid

83. The ability of metals to be drawn into thin wires is known as
A. ductility B. malleability
C. sonorosity D. conductivity

84. Gunmetal contains
A. Cu = 60%, Sn = 40%
B. Cu = 80%, Sn = 20%
C. Cu = 70%, Sn = 30%
D. Cu = 90%, Sn = 10%

85. MRI stands for
A. Magnets Resonant Imaging
B. Magnetic Resonance Imaging
C. Magnetic Radar Imaging
D. Magnet Radial Imaging

86. What is the maximum resistance which can be made using five resistors each of $\frac{1}{5}\Omega$?
A. $\frac{1}{5}\Omega$ B. $10\ \Omega$
C. $5\ \Omega$ D. $1\ \Omega$

87. Which of the following is *not* associated with growth of plants?
A. Auxins B. Gibberellins
C. Cytokinins D. Abscisic acid

88. In a neuron, conversion of electrical signal to a chemical signal occurs at/in
A. cell body B. axonal end
C. dendritic end D. axon

89. Drinking alcohol is very harmful and it ruins the health. 'Drinking alcohol' stands for
A. drinking methyl alcohol
B. drinking ethyl alcohol
C. drinking propyl alcohol
D. drinking isopropyl alcohol

90. Which of the following elements does *not* lose an electron easily?
A. Mg B. Na
C. K D. Ca

91. Length of pollen tube depends on the distance between
A. pollen grain and upper surface of stigma
B. pollen grain on upper surface of stigma and ovule
C. pollen grain in anther and upper surface of stigma
D. upper surface of stigma and lower part of style

92. Gonorrhoea is caused by a bacterium called
A. *Neisseria gonorrhoeae*
B. *Treponema pallidum*
C. *Lactobacillus*
D. *Streptococcus*

93. Which of the following is *not* a natural resource?
A. Soil B. Water
C. Electricity D. Air

94. Which of the following is a 'biodiversity hot spot'?
A. Rivers B. Forests
C. Deserts D. Oceans

95. Depletion of ozone is mainly due to
A. chlorofluorocarbon
B. carbon monoxide
C. methane
D. pesticides

96. Which group of organisms are *not* constituents of a food chain?

A. Grass, lion, rabbit
B. Plankton, man, fish, grasshopper
C. Wolf, grass, snake, tiger
D. Frog, snake, eagle, grass, grasshopper

97. Red light is used for danger signal as

A. it has higher wavelength
B. it can travel large distance
C. it scatters the least
D. it scatters the longest

98. Twinkling of stars is due to atmospheric

A. dispersion of light by water droplets
B. refraction of light by different layers of varying refractive indices
C. scattering of light by dust particles
D. internal reflection of light by clouds

99. The chief function of lymph nodes in the body is to

A. produce red blood cells
B. collect and destroy pathogens
C. produce a hormone
D. destroy the old and worn out red blood cells

100. Which is the first enzyme to mix food in the digestive tract?

A. Pepsin B. Cellulase
C. Amylase D. Trypsin

(ii) : Mathematics

101. If $x-\frac{1}{x}=9$, then $x^2+\frac{1}{x^2}$ is

A. 83 B. 81
C. 79 D. 72

102. The value of $\frac{\sqrt{32}+\sqrt{48}}{\sqrt{8}+\sqrt{12}}$ is

A. 2 B. $\sqrt{2}$
C. 4 D. 8

103. A 15 m high, vertical straight tree gets broken by the wind in such a way that its top touches the ground making an angle of 60° from the ground. At what height did the tree break?

A. 5.96 m B. 5.19 m
C. 6.96 m D. 6.19 m

104. The value of sec A (1 – sin A) (sec A + tan A) is

A. –1 B. 1
C. 2 D. $\frac{1}{2}$

105. The value of $\frac{5\cos^2 60° + 4\sec^2 30° - \tan^2 45°}{\sin^2 30° + \cos^2 30°}$ is

A. $\frac{37}{12}$ B. $\frac{47}{12}$
C. $\frac{57}{12}$ D. $\frac{67}{12}$

106. Second and third terms of an A.P. are 14 and 18 respectively. The sum of its first 51 terms is

A. 5610 B. 5614
C. 5606 D. 5618

107. The mean of first 8 prime numbers is

A. 7.425 B. 8.625
C. 9.625 D. 10.425

108. A fair coin is tossed 100 times and head occurs 58 times and tail occurs 42 times. The experimental probability of getting a head is

A. $\frac{50}{100}$ B. $\frac{42}{100}$
C. $\frac{58}{100}$ D. $\frac{42}{58}$

109. The sides of a triangle are 13 cm, 14 cm and 15 cm. The area is

A. 42 cm^2 B. 21 cm^2
C. 63 cm^2 D. 84 cm^2

110. A toy is in the form of a cone of radius 3.5 cm mounted on a hemisphere of same radius. The total height of the toy is 15.5 cm. Total surface area of the toy is

A. 214.5 cm^2 B. 146.5 cm^2
C. 324.5 cm^2 D. 114.5 cm^2

111. Three metallic spheres of radii 6 cm, 8 cm and 10 cm respectively, are melted and recast to form a solid sphere. The radius of this sphere is

A. 8 cm B. 10 cm
C. 12 cm D. 14 cm

112. Area of a quadrant of a circle whose circumference is 22 cm is

A. $\frac{77}{4}$ cm^2 B. $\frac{77}{8}$ cm^2
C. $\frac{154}{3}$ cm^2 D. $\frac{154}{6}$ cm^2

113. A train travels 360 km at a uniform speed. By increasing its speed by 5 km/hr it takes one hour less for the same journey. The original speed of the train is

A. 45 km/hr B. 40 km/hr
C. 50 km/hr D. 60 km/hr

114. Ratio of the ages of a father and son at present 2 : 1. Fifteen years back it was 3 : 1. The present age of the father is

A. 70 years B. 65 years
C. 55 years D. 60 years

115. Passing marks in an examination are 40%. A student obtains 200 marks and fails by 40 marks. The total marks for the examination are

A. 600 B. 550
C. 500 D. 450

116. In a mixture of 60 kg, the ratio of cement and sand is 3 : 1. Another 15 kg of cement is added to the mixture. The ratio of cement and sand now is

A. 1 : 4 B. 3 : 2
C. 4 : 1 D. 2 : 3

117. There are 400 children in a children's home. If each one is given 200 gm of ration daily, it is enough for 30 days. 100 more children join the home and ration intake is reduced to 150 gm per day. The ration will be sufficient for

A. 30 days B. 32 days
C. 35 days D. 40 days

118. Abdul has purchased a cycle for ₹ 4,176. The manufacturer earns a profit of 16 per cent and both wholesaler and retailer earn profit at the rate of 20 per cent each. The manufacturer's cost price is

A. ₹ 3,200 B. ₹ 3,000
C. ₹ 2,700 D. ₹ 2,500

119. Given three distinct non-collinear points. The maximum number of lines that can be drawn through them is

A. 2 B. 3
C. 4 D. 5

120. The number of diameters of a circle is

A. one B. two
C. ten D. infinite

(iii) : Social Science

121. Which unit of valuation is known as 'Paper Gold'?

A. Petrodollar B. SDR
C. Eurodollar D. GDR

122. The coastline that borders the state of Kerala, is known as

A. Konkan Coast
B. Malabar Coast
C. Coromandel Coast
D. Canara Coast

123. Who is the founder of World Economic Forum?

A. Klaus Schwab
B. John Kenneth Galbraith
C. Robert Zoellick
D. Paul Krugman

124. The concept of sustainable development relates to
A. Consumption levels
B. Exhaustible levels
C. Social equity
D. None of these

125. Article-17 of the Constitution provides for
A. Equality before law
B. Equality of opportunity in matters of public employment
C. Abolition of titles
D. Abolition of untouchability

126. Where did the practice of 'Shadow Cabinet' originate?
A. USA
B. Great Britain
C. Italy
D. France

127. The Indian Citizenship Act was passed in
A. 1950 B. 1952
C. 1955 D. 1960

128. Saka Era which starts from 78 AD represents
A. Kanishka's reign
B. Prosperity of Harsha
C. Shivaji's reign
D. Chandragupta's reign

129. The foundation stone of the Gateway of India was laid in
A. 1911 B. 1927
C. 1857 D. 1947

130. Almatti Dam is located on which of the following rivers?
A. Godavari
B. Kaveri
C. Krishna
D. Mahanadi

131. Which of the following are the youngest mountains of India?
A. Aravallis
B. Himalayas
C. Nilgiris
D. Vindhyachal

132. Gresham's law in Economics relates to
A. Supply and demand
B. Circulation of currency
C. Consumption of supply
D. Distribution of goods and services

133. Revealed Preference Theory was propounded by
A. Adam Smith
B. Marshall
C. P.A. Samuelson
D. J.S. Mill

134. The Indian Independence League was set up by
A. Rash Behari Bose
B. S.M. Joshi
C. Aruna Asaf Ali
D. Jai Prakash Narayan

135. The description of Caste System is found in
A. Rig Veda
B. Sam Veda
C. Yajur Veda
D. None of these

136. The capital of Pallavas was
A. Arcot
B. Kanchi
C. Malkhed
D. Banaras

137. In early medieval India, what did the term 'Jital' refer to?
A. Weight B. Diet
C. Coin D. Game

138. Which of the following is *not* a Kharif crop?
A. Rice B. Groundnut
C. Maize D. Barley

139. Which one of the following is a landlocked sea?
A. Timor Sea
B. Arafura Sea
C. Greenland Sea
D. Aral Sea

140. Which of the following straits separates Europe from Africa?
A. Bering B. Dover
C. Gibraltar D. Malacca

(iv) : English

Choose the most appropriate response out of the four choices given after every question. Each question carries one mark.

Directions (Qs. 141 to 142): *In each of the following questions, some alternatives have been suggested for the idioms/phrase. Choose the option which best expresses the meaning.*

141. "Pay through the nose"
A. Pay huge loans
B. Pay a reasonable price
C. Pay an extremely high price
D. Make a quick buck

142. "Rest on one's laurels"
A. To be unhappy
B. To be motivated
C. To be impatient
D. To be complacent

143. Out of the four alternatives, choose the one which can be substituted for "To talk much without coming to the point".
A. Verbosity B. Garrulousness
C. Loquacity D. Circumlocution

144. Choose the correctly spelt word
A. Ancestry B. Ancastry
C. Encestry D. Encastry

145. Choose the correctly spelt word
A. Haritage B. Heritage
C. Heritege D. Haritege

146. Choose the indirect form of the following sentence:
Mary said to Robert, "Let him come, then we shall see him."
A. Mary said to Robert that if he came, then we would see him.
B. Mary asked Robert if he come, we will see him.
C. Mary told Robert if he comes, we will see him.
D. Mary said to Robert if he comes, we would see him.

147. Choose the indirect form of the following sentence:
He said, "I have often told you not to waste your time."
A. He said that he had often told him not to waste your time.
B. He said that he had often told him not to waste his time.
C. He said that he had often suggested to him not to waste my time.
D. He told that he had often told him not to waste my time.

148. The passive voice of "One should keep one's promise" is
A. One's promise should be kept by us.
B. One's promise should be kept.
C. A promise should be keeping.
D. A promise should be kept by us.

149. The active voice of "A lion may be helped even by a little mouse" is
A. A little mouse may even help a lion.
B. Even a little mouse may help a lion.
C. A little mouse can even help a lion.
D. Even a little mouse ought to help a lion.

Directions (Qs. 150 to 152): *Choose the most appropriate words to fill in the blanks.*

150. If I had worked hard, I .... very high marks in the examination.
A. scored
B. would score
C. could score
D. would have scored

151. Suitable steps are taken to bring .... the cost of living.
A. in B. over
C. on D. down

152. When I saw her after many years .... thoughts filled my mind.
A. galaxy B. feeling
C. numerous D. multitude

153. Who said "If winter comes, can spring be far behind"?
A. Frost B. Shelley
C. Keats D. Coleridge

154. Which one of the following considered the last tragedy of Shakespeare?
A. Othello B. Macbeth
C. Hamlet D. Coriolanus

155. Which one of the following poems is composed by William Wordsworth?
A. Ode to Duty
B. Ode to the West Wind
C. Ode to a Nightingale
D. Ode on Solitude

156. Who is known as "The Prince of English Essayists"?
A. Lamb B. Addison
C. Eliot D. Steele

157. At the end of the play "Measure for Measure" who was married to Angelo?
A. Julietta B. Isabella
C. A whore D. Mariana

158. Who said that "Child is the father of the man"?
A. Wordsworth B. Pope
C. Milton D. Shakespeare

159. In the sentence "Indira Gandhi, who was killed in 1984, was the first woman Prime Minister in India."
who was killed in 1984 is a:
A. Noun clause B. Adverb clause
C. Adjective clause D. None of these

160. In the sentence "This is the town where that great man was born."
where that great man was born is a:
A. Noun clause B. Adverb clause
C. Adjective clause D. None of these

ANSWERS

1	2	3	4	5	6	7	8	9	10
D	A	B	D	B	D	A	B	A	B
11	12	13	14	15	16	17	18	19	20
B	B	C	C	D	B	C	D	D	B
21	22	23	24	25	26	27	28	29	30
C	B	A	A	C	B	B	D	C	C
31	32	33	34	35	36	37	38	39	40
B	C	C	D	A	B	A	A	A	B
41	42	43	44	45	46	47	48	49	50
A	B	B	C	D	C	A	A	D	C
51	52	53	54	55	56	57	58	59	60
C	B	D	A	B	C	C	D	D	C
61	62	63	64	65	66	67	68	69	70
D	B	C	D	C	D	D	B	C	A
71	72	73	74	75	76	77	78	79	80
C	C	C	A	C	B	D	A	C	B
81	82	83	84	85	86	87	88	89	90
D	A	A	D	B	D	D	B	B	A
91	92	93	94	95	96	97	98	99	100
C	A	C	B	A	C	C	B	B	C
101	102	103	104	105	106	107	108	109	110
A	A	C	B	D	A	C	C	D	A
111	112	113	114	115	116	117	118	119	120
C	B	B	D	A	C	B	D	B	D

121	122	123	124	125	126	127	128	129	130
B	B	A	B	D	B	C	A	A	C
131	132	133	134	135	136	137	138	139	140
B	B	C	A	A	B	C	D	D	C
141	142	143	144	145	146	147	148	149	150
C	D	D	A	B	D	B	B	B	D
151	152	153	154	155	156	157	158	159	160
D	C	B	D	A	A	D	A	A	A

SOME SELECTED EXPLANATORY ANSWERS

11-14. From given Datas:

F is E's sister and B is D's husband and as new entrant are not winner, so D is winner.

16. 1, 8, 27, 64, 125, 216

$\downarrow$ $\downarrow$ $\downarrow$ $\downarrow$ $\downarrow$ $\downarrow$

$(1)^3$, $(2)^3$, $(3)^3$, $(4)^3$, $(5)^3$, $(6)^3$,

17. 2, 11, 38, 119, 362,

$+3^2$ $+3^3$ $+3^4$ $+3^5$

18. 4, 15, 37, 70, 114, 169,

+11 +22 +33 +44 +55

19. 29, 54, 103, 200, 393, 778,

× 2 – 4 × 2 – 5 × 2 – 6 × 2 – 7 × 2 – 8

21. From given information:

Word	F	A	M	I	L	Y	S	I	S	T	E	R
Code	3	1	6	4	5	9	7	4	7	8	2	0

Hence, code for word Mystery is '6978209'.

23-27.

Football	Hockey	Tennis	Cricket	Volleyball
A, B, D, E	A, B, C, D	C, E, A, D	B, C, D, E	A, C, D, E

101. $\because\ x - \frac{1}{x} = 9$

squaring both sides,

$$x^2 + \frac{1}{x^2} - 2 = (9)^2$$

$$\therefore \quad x^2 + \frac{1}{x^2} = 81 + 2 = 83.$$

102. $$\frac{\sqrt{32}+\sqrt{48}}{\sqrt{8}+\sqrt{12}} = \frac{4\sqrt{2}+4\sqrt{3}}{2\sqrt{2}+2\sqrt{3}}$$

$$= \frac{4\left(\sqrt{2}+\sqrt{3}\right)}{2\left(\sqrt{2}+\sqrt{3}\right)} = 2$$

103.

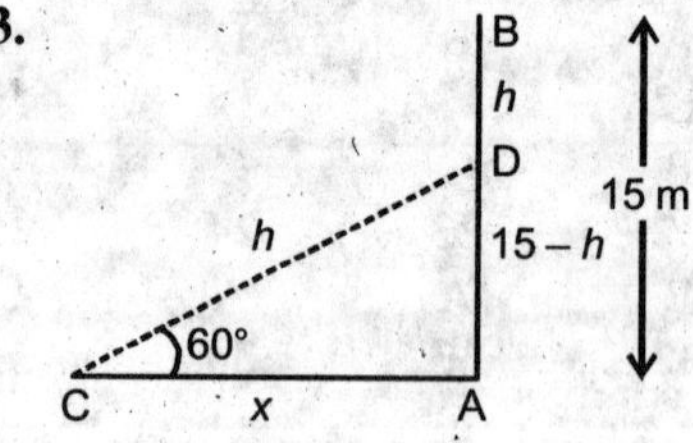

$$\cos 60° = \frac{x}{h}$$

$$\Rightarrow \quad \frac{1}{2} = \frac{x}{h}$$

$$\Rightarrow \quad h = 2x$$

$$\Rightarrow \quad x = \frac{h}{2}$$

$$\tan 60° = \frac{15-h}{x}$$

$$\Rightarrow \quad \sqrt{3} = \frac{15-h}{x}$$

$$\Rightarrow \quad \sqrt{3}x = 15 - h$$

$\Rightarrow \quad \sqrt{3}\times\frac{h}{2} = 15 - h$

$\Rightarrow \quad \sqrt{3}h = 30 - 2h$

$2h+\sqrt{3}h = 30$

$h\left(2+\sqrt{3}\right) = 30$

$\Rightarrow \quad h = \frac{30}{2+\sqrt{3}}$

$\Rightarrow \quad h = \frac{30}{2+\sqrt{3}}\times\frac{2-\sqrt{3}}{2-\sqrt{3}}$

$= \frac{30(2-1.732)}{4-3}$

$= 30\times\frac{268}{1000} = \frac{804}{100} = 8.04$

$\therefore$ 15 – h = 15 – 8.04 = 6.96 m.

104. sec A (1 – sin A) (sec A + tan A)
$\Rightarrow$ (sec A – sec A . sin A) (sec A + tan A)
= (sec A – tan A) (sec A + tan A)
= $\sec^2 - \tan^2 A = 1$.

105. $\dfrac{5\times\left(\frac{1}{2}\right)^2+4\left(\frac{2}{\sqrt{3}}\right)^2-1}{1}$

$[\because \sin^2\theta+\cos^2\theta=1]$

$= 5\times\frac{1}{4}+4\times\frac{4}{3}-1$

$= \frac{5}{4}+\frac{16}{3}-1 = \frac{15+64-12}{12}$

$= \frac{64+3}{12} = \frac{67}{12}$.

106. Let first term of AP is a and common difference = d

$a + d = 14$ ...(*i*)
$a + 2d = 18$ ...(*ii*)

Subtract (*i*) from (*ii*) we get

$d = 4$ and $a = 10$

$\because \quad S_n = \frac{n}{2}\{2a+(n-1)d\}$

$\therefore \quad S_{51} = \frac{51}{2}\{2\times10+(50)\times4\}$

$= \frac{51}{2}\{20+200\}$

= 51 × 110 = 5610

107. First 8 prime numbers are
2, 3, 5, 7, 11, 13, 17, 19

$\text{Mean} = \frac{2+3+5+7+11+13+17+19}{8}$

$= \frac{77}{8} = 9.625$.

109. $S = \frac{a+b+c}{2} = \frac{13+14+15}{2} = \frac{42}{2} = 21$

Area of $\Delta = \sqrt{s(s-a)(s-b)(s-c)}$

$= \sqrt{21\times8\times7\times6}$

$= \sqrt{3\times7\times2\times2\times2\times7\times3\times2}$

= 3 × 7 × 2 × 2 = 84 cm^2.

110. Height of cone = 15.5 – 3.5 = 12 cm

Slant height $= \sqrt{\left(\frac{7}{2}\right)^2+(12)^2} = \sqrt{\frac{625}{4}}$

$= \frac{25}{2}$ cm

C.S.A of cone $= \pi rl = \frac{22}{7}\times\frac{7}{2}\times\frac{25}{2} = \frac{275}{2}$ cm^2

C.S.A of hemisphere $= 2\pi r^2$

$= 2\times\frac{22}{7}\times\frac{7}{2}\times\frac{7}{2} = 77$ cm^2

$\therefore$ Total surface area of toy
= 137.5 + 77 = 214.5 cm^2.

111. According to the question,

$\frac{4}{3}\pi R^3 = \frac{4}{3}\pi(6^3+8^3+10^3)$

$\Rightarrow \quad R^3 = 216 + 512 + 1000$

$\Rightarrow \quad R^3 = 1728$

$\therefore \quad R = \sqrt[3]{1728} = 12$ cm.

112. $C = 2\pi r$

$\Rightarrow \quad 22 = 2\times\frac{22}{7}\times r$

$\Rightarrow \quad r = \frac{7}{2}$ cm

Area of quadrant of a circle $= \frac{1}{4}\pi r^2$

$= \frac{1}{4}\times\frac{22}{7}\times\frac{7}{2}\times\frac{7}{2} = \frac{77}{8}$ cm^2.

113. Let the original speed = x km/hr

According to the question,

$$\frac{360}{x} - \frac{360}{x+5} = 1$$

$$\Rightarrow \quad \frac{360(x+5-x)}{x(x+5)} = 1$$

$\Rightarrow \quad x^2 + 5x - 1800 = 0$

$\Rightarrow \quad (x - 40)(x + 45) = 0$

$\Rightarrow x = 40$ or $x = -45$

$\therefore$ Required speed = 40 km/hr.

114. Let present age of father = $2x$ years

son's age = x years

According to the question,

$$\frac{2x-15}{x-15} = \frac{3}{1}$$

$\Rightarrow \quad 3x - 45 = 2x - 15$

$\Rightarrow \quad x = 30$

$\therefore$ Father's present age $= 2x = 2 \times 30$

$= 60$ years.

115. Let total marks for the examination = x

40% of $x = 200 + 40$

$\Rightarrow \quad \frac{40}{100}\times x = 240$

$\Rightarrow \quad x = \frac{240\times 100}{40} = 600.$

116. Amount of cement $= \frac{3}{4}\times 60 = 45$ kg

Amount of sand $= \frac{1}{4}\times 60 = 15$ kg

Now amount of cement = 45 + 15 = 60 kg

$\therefore$ Required ratio $= \frac{60}{15} = \frac{4}{1} = 4 : 1.$

117. Required days $= \frac{400\times 30\times 200}{500\times 150} = 32$

Hence, the ration will be sufficient = 32 days.

118. C.P. of retailer $= \frac{4176\times 100}{120} =$ ₹ 3480

C.P. of whole saler $= \frac{3480\times 100}{120} =$ ₹ 2900

$\therefore$ C.P. of manufacturer $= \frac{2900\times 100}{116} =$ ₹ 2500

Previous Paper (Solved)

IGNOU B.Ed. Entrance Test 2013

PART-A

SECTION-I : General English Comprehension

Directions (Qs. 1 to 10): *Read the following passage carefully and choose the best answer out of the four choices given after each question that follows:*

"The Tower" is a poem written by Yeats. It has three parts that correspond to three stages of life, or three modes of relating to the world, but not in a scheme as simple as youth, adulthood and old age. Rather, the first and third parts or the first and third poems in a three poem sequence chart the internal experiences of an accelerating mind within a decelerating body. The second part is a more external reminiscence, passing elegiacally over the lore of the land. The dying poet is taking a nostalgic survey of this works. The first and third parts take place within a dreaming mind, while the second takes place within the dream.

If we think of this poem as a ceremony, the first part senses that the end is near, but is not ready to face it; the second part is a preparation ritual, and the third arrives at readiness and passes into nothing. If this passing is to have any meaning, the poet must propel himself enthusiastically into the next world rather than fall, withered and bedraggled, out of this one. To do so, he must find the memories in which he was most alive, may be ones that still hurt the most. These moments were truly his, and so are truly his to leave behind.

1. The "three stages of life" refers to:
A. youth, adulthood and old age
B. body, teenager, adult
C. the life cycle of a poem
D. three ways of being in the world

2. "The first and third poems" differ from the second in that:
A. they are nostalgic
B. they give an account of the poet's inner experience
C. they are part of a cremation ceremony
D. they are enthusiastic

3. The phrase "passing elegiacally over the lore of the land indicates that the poet was:
A. a slow runner
B. speaking at a funeral
C. narrating ancient tales
D. taking stock of his life's work

4. The poet must "find the memories in which he was most alive" in order to:
A. keep away death
B. become a poet
C. regain memories
D. leave this world with significance

5. The author compares the poem as a whole to:
A. folklore
B. a dying person
C. a ceremony
D. a memory

6. "The Tower" is a poem written by Yeats. This is a:
A. simple sentence
B. complex sentence
C. compound sentence
D. complex-compound sentence

7. 'The second part is a more external reminiscence passing elegiacally over the lore of the land.' This is a:
A. complex sentence

B. compound sentence
C. complex-compound sentence
D. simple sentence

8. 'Passing' in the sentence in question 7 is a:
A. Gerund
B. Present participle
C. Past participle
D. None of the above

9. "Passing" in 'If this passing is to have any meaning' is a:
A. noun B. finite verb
C. non-finite verb D. none of the above

10. "The next world" refers to:
A. the world of youth
B. the world of adulthood
C. the world of old age
D. the world of death

SECTION-II : LOGICAL AND ANALYTICAL REASONING

Directions (Qs. 11 to 15): *A and B play Hockey and Football. B and C play Cricket and Football. C and E play Cricket and Volleyball. D and E play tennis. A and C play Volleyball and Football. A and D play Hockey and Football.*

On the basis of above information answer the following questions:

11. Who does not play football?
A. B B. C
C. D D. E

12. Who plays Hockey, Football and Tennis?
A. E B. D
C. C D. A

13. Who plays Cricket, Hockey and Football?
A. A B. C
C. B D. E

14. Who plays Cricket, Volleyball and Tennis?
A. E B. D
C. C D. A

15. Who plays Hockey, Volleyball and Football?
A. A B. B
C. C D. E

16. If 'clock' is coded as 36938 and 'leave' is coded as 12452, then 'cave' should be coded as:
A. 4325 B. 3451
C. 3453 D. 3452

17. If 'sky' is coded as TTMMXX, then 'Lie' will be coded as:
A. MMLLDD B. MMKKDD
C. MNOOCC D. NNKKFF

18. If 'case' is coded as ECUG and 'Burn' is coded as CWTR. How 'earn' is encoded?
A. GDTP B. HCTP
C. GCTR D. GDPT

19. For every correct answer, a student scores one mark but for every incorrect answer she/he loses $\frac{1}{3}$ mark. She/He answered 108 questions but scored zero (0). How many questions she/he answered incorrectly?
A. 81 B. 78
C. 87 D. 72

Directions (Qs. 20 to 23): *Read the following paragraph to answer questions that follow:*

A, B, C, D, E all have nine marbles. B gives two marbles to D, who gives one marble to E. C gives 5 marbles to E who gives two marbles to A. C gives two marbles to B who gives three marble to E. D gives three marbles to A who gives two marbles to B.

20. How many marbles A has?
A. 7 B. 9
C. 10 D. 12

21. How many marbles B has?
A. 6 B. 7
C. 8 D. 10

22. How many marbles C has?
A. 3 B. 2
C. 6 D. 7

23. Now, who has got the maximum number of marbles?
A. B B. C
C. D D. E

Directions (Qs. 24 to 27): *A series of numbers is given, where one term is missing. Select the missing term from the given alternatives.*

24. 0, 3, 8, 15, 24, 35, ?
A. 48 B. 46
C. 49 D. none of the above

25. 2, 9, 30, 93, 282, ?
A. 746 B. 846
C. 849 D. 843

26. 24, 39, 416, 525, 636, ?
A. 736 B. 749
C. 864 D. 849

27. 40, 29, ?, 13, 8
A. 20 B. 18
C. 22 D. 17

Directions (Qs. 28 to 30): *In the following questions, Three words are given. First word is related to the second word. You have to select from the given alternatives, the fourth word which would be related to the third word in similar way.*

28. Advocate : Law : : Cook : ?
A. Cooking B. Kitchen
C. Food D. Recipes

29. Frame : Picture : : Water : ?
A. Lake B. Island
C. Bay D. Boundaries

30. Psychology : Mind : : Trigonometry : ?
A. Mathematics B. Mensuration
C. Geometry D. Triangles

SECTION-III : EDUCATIONAL AND GENERAL AWARENESS

31. We cannot see during a fog because of:
A. Reflection of light B. Internal reflection
C. Refraction D. Scattering of light

32. An orange is a rich source of:
A. Proteins B. Carbohydrates
C. Vitamin C D. Iodine

33. Which one of the following rights was described by B.R. Ambedkar as 'the heart and soul of the constitution'?
A. Right of freedom of religion
B. Right of property
C. Right of equality
D. Right of constitutional remedies

34. In 1888 Sir Syed Ahmed founded the:
A. Patriotic Association
B. Upper India Mohammadan Association
C. National Conference
D. Muslim League

35. What is the main purpose of Panchayati Raj?
A. To increase agricultural production
B. To create employment
C. To make people politically conscious
D. To make people participate in developmental administration

36. Aurobindo Ghosh was defended in the Alipur bomb case by:
A. B.C. Pal B. Motilal Nehru
C. Bhulabhai Desai D. C.R. Das

37. 'Give me blood and I promise you freedom' was uttered by:
A. Bhagat Singh
B. Chandra Shekhar Azad
C. Sardar Patel
D. Subhash Chandra Bose

38. Which of the following states has the least literacy rate?
A. Himachal Pradesh B. Rajasthan
C. Uttar Pradesh D. Madhya Pradesh

39. Tea will cool most easily in a:
A. Glass cup B. Clay cup
C. Metal cup D. Porcelain cup

40. Two shirts are warmer than one of the same material but of double thickness because:
A. Intervening air between two shirts prevents flow of heat from body to outsides

B. Specific heat of single shirt is more than that of two shirts
C. Specific heat of two shirts is more than that of one shirt
D. Air has large specific heat

41. The disease with high levels of uric acid in the blood is the characteristic of ....
A. Arthritis B. Rheumatism
C. Gout D. Rheumatic heart

42. The most important uranium ore deposits occur in:
A. Canada B. Pakistan
C. China D. Zaire

43. Where is the greatest variety of flowers found?
A. Sikkim B. Assam
C. Uttarakhand hills D. Kerala

44. Education commission (1964-66) had focussed on:
A. Elementary Education
B. Secondary Education
C. Higher Education
D. All the above

45. A committee headed by Ishwar Bhai Patil looked into various aspects of:
A. Higher Education
B. Technical Education
C. Medical Education
D. General Education

46. Which of the following is the characteristic feature of the National Curriculum Framework (NCF 2005)?
A. Learning while earning
B. Learning without burden
C. Learning with memorisation
D. Learning for competition

47. Jawahar Navodaya Vidyalayas were recommended by:
A. Mudaliar Commission 1952-53
B. National Policy on Education 1968
C. National Policy on Education 1986
D. National Knowledge Commission (2006-2009)

48. Continuous and Comprehensive Evaluation (CCE) is:
A. Formative in nature
B. Summative in nature
C. Creative in nature
D. Both Formative and Summative in nature

49. As per Right to Free and Compulsory Education Act 2009, private schools will have to admit:
A. 25% children of Economically weaker section
B. 25% children of SC/ST category
C. 15% children of Economically weaker section
D. 15% children of SC/ST category

50. Identification of learning gaps of children and plugging them is done through:
A. Reflective teaching
B. Remedial teaching
C. Team teaching
D. Reteaching

51. Graphical representation of very high quality accomplishment happens to be ....
A. Positively skewed
B. Laptokurtic
C. Negatively skewed
D. Platykurtic

52. Monitoring the working of Elementary Schools is the responsibility of:
A. Gram Panchayat
B. Mother Teacher Association
C. School Management Committee
D. Parent Teachers Association

53. General Intelligence is:
A. An innate capacity
B. Acquired ability
C. A common attribute for all
D. A specific talent

54. Detailed recommendations about women education are available in the report of:
A. Triguna Sen Committee
B. Harsha Mehta Committee
C. Ram Murti Committee
D. Tara Chand Committee

55. Education Cess is being levied for supporting:
A. Elementary Education
B. Secondary Education
C. Both Elementary and Secondary Education
D. All levels of education

SECTION-IV : TEACHING-LEARNING AND THE SCHOOL

56. Which of the following functions of schools justifies the statement that a school should be pioneer of social upliftment?
A. Normal function of school
B. Progressive function of school
C. Conservative function of school
D. Reactionary function of school

57. Which of the following statements can't be accepted?
A. Schools are necessarily affected by changes in society.
B. School can be powerful agents of social change.
C. Schools are potential agents of disintegration.
D. Schools are social agencies of cultural transmission

58. Which of the following goes against the spirit of equality of educational opportunity?
A. Public schools
B. Government aided schools
C. Ashram schools
D. Navodaya Vidyalayas

59. Which of the following sequence is an appropriate order of learning a language?
L → Listening; R → Reading; S → Speaking; W → Writing.
A. LSWR B. SLWR
C. SLRW D. LSRW

60. The school through its programmes helps student:
A. assimilate culture
B. ignore other cultures
C. protest culture
D. make them cultured

61. The main aim of class room teaching should be:
A. to develop self confidence among learners.
B. to train learners for some vocation.
C. to prepare them for higher classes.
D. to facilitate learning.

62. Right to Education Act 2009 has banned:
A. Corporal punishment
B. Mental Harassment
C. Both corporal punishment and Mental harassment
D. Extra classes

63. Teaching environment in the school can be adversely affected if:
A. Corporal punishment is always given.
B. Learner is motivated to write for wall magazine.
C. Teacher is given freedom to use innovative methods.
D. There are frequent PTA meetings.

64. In your view play / activities in schools is:
A. necessary for psycho-motor development
B. a simple waste of time
C. not required because of heavy academic schedule
D. all the above

65. A good class room discipline implies:
A. total silence with attention to teacher
B. students to remain active in learning activities
C. students do not ask any question
D. students to be busy in self study

66. Effective learning depends on:
A. interest of the child
B. difficulty level of the learning
C. either A or B
D. Both A and B

67. A teacher would become more effective if:
A. students score high marks
B. teacher uses good instructional aids
C. she/he helps learners to achieve mastery in learning
D. she/he helps students to ask questions

68. In order to elicit the response "year 269 BC" while concluding a lesson on 'Ashoka', which of the following questions would be the best?
A. When did Ashoka succeed the throne?

B. After whom did Ashoka succeed the throne?
C. In which year did Ashoka's coronation take place?
D. Any of the above questions

69. The best way to handle a wrong response of a student would be
A. to explain the subject matter in detail again
B. to tell the student that your answer is wrong
C. to ask another student to give the correct answer
D. to explain and give another chance to give answer

70. For developing an objective type class room test, which one of the following types would be most suited?
A. multiple choice type
B. true-false type
C. select the correct reason
D. fill in the blank

71. A teacher in the class should keep his / her speech:
A. intonated
B. low volume
C. high volume
D. moderate volume

72. Developing 'Scientific attitude' among learners can be best accomplished through:
A. teaching of sciences
B. telling them to accept
C. accepting what elders speak
D. accepting facts only after examining and verifying

73. Which one of the following sequence to the process of the classroom teaching?

[D-Delivery; E-Evaluation; F-Feedback; K-Knowing the target learner; P-Planning]

A. PKDFE B. KPDFE
C. KPDEF D. PKDEF

74. In order to avoid unnecessary psychological problems arising out of annual examination system we should use:
A. periodical tests only
B. periodical tests with corrective measures
C. tests by teachers of other schools
D. no testing at all

75. Mid-day Meal programme in Govt. schools meets which need of the child?
A. Safety
B. Physiological
C. Love/belongingness
D. Self actualization

76. While asking a probing question in a class which of the following can effect the response adversely?
A. clear intent
B. having no previous material to refer to
C. use of double negatives
D. questions with one correct answer

77. A mentally challenged child:
A. can't attain mastery in tasks at all
B. can attain mastery with alternative suitable environment and method
C. can attain but would need more time
D. can attain mastery like any other child

78. Aptitude tests are used to:
A. measure achievement
B. measure proficiency
C. predict one's success in a profession
D. measure potentiality

79. Awarding grades in place of numerical marks is recommended because:
A. grades are easier to award
B. teaching-learning will be facilitated
C. it will improve quality of education
D. it will reduce errors in judgement

80. Communication in the classroom would be more effective if:
A. sender uses the same coding system as his/her receiver decodes
B. sender proceeds slowly but systematically
C. receiver is willing to receive
D. being done in congenial environment

PART-B

SECTION-V (i): SCIENCE

81. What happens, when zinc metal is dipped in copper sulphate solution?

A. the solution becomes colourless and reddish brown copper metal gets deposited

B. no reaction takes place

C. the solution becomes green and copper metal gets deposited

D. the solution remains blue and copper metal gets deposited

82. In binary fission of a cell:

A. Cytoplasm and nucleus divide at the same time.

B. The division of nucleus is followed by the division of cytoplasm.

C. The division of cytoplasm is followed by the division of nucleus.

D. The cytoplasm and nucleus do not divide.

83. When a cell is kept in a hypotonic solution then water moves:

A. into the cell

B. out of the cell

C. no movement of water takes place

D. none of these is correct

84. The isomers of C_6H_{14} are:

A. 4 B. 5

C. 6 D. 3

85. Which among the following diseases is ***not*** sexually transmitted?

A. Syphillis B. Hepatitis

C. HIV-AIDS D. Gonorrhoea

86. A full length image of a distant tall building can definitely be seen by using:

A. a concave mirror

B. a convex mirror

C. a plane mirror

D. both concave as well as plane mirror

87. The human eye forms the image of an object at its:

A. cornea B. iris

C. pupil D. retina

88. Which one of the following is an artificial ecosystem?

A. Pond B. Crop field

C. Lake D. Forest

89. Extensive plantation of trees to increase forest cover is known as:

A. Agro-forestry B. Social forestry

C. Afforestation D. Deforestation

90. Which of the following is an exothermic process?

A. Reaction of water with quicklime

B. Dilution of an acid

C. Evaporation of water

D. Sublimation of Camphor

91. Which among the following is ***not*** a base?

A. NaOH B. KOH

C. NH_4OH D. C_2H_5OH

92. Blood bank of the body is:

A. spleen B. heart

C. liver D. bone marrow

93. Electrical resistivity of a given metallic wire depends upon:

A. its length

B. its thickness

C. its shape

D. nature of material

94. Growth of the plant or plant parts towards the earth is called:

A. phototropism B. hydrotropism

C. thigmotropism D. geotropism

95. The unit of electric power may also be expressed as:

A. Volt ampere B. Kilowatt hour

C. Watt second D. Joule second

96. Biogas is a better fuel as it has:

A. 75% methane

B. higher calorific value

C. residual manure

D. all of these

97. Which of the following is different from the other three?
A. petroleum B. coal
C. natural gas D. geothermal

98. The centre for controlling body temperature is:
A. Hypothalamus
B. Cerebellum
C. Central nervous system
D. Cerebrum

99. The ability of metals to be drawn into thin wire is known as:
A. ductility
B. malleability
C. sonorousity
D. conductivity

100. Galvanisation is a method of protecting iron from rusting by coating with a thin layer of:
A. Galium B. Aluminium
C. Zinc D. Silver

(ii) : MATHEMATICS

101. The value of $(a^{x-y})^{x+y} . (a^{y-z})^{y+z} . (a^{z-x})^{z+x}$ is:
A. 0 B. 1
C. –1 D. $x + y + z$

102. The fifteenth part, the twelfth part and seventh part of a certain number when added together give 1353, the number is:
A. 6150 B. 6420
C. 6240 D. 4620

103. The value of $\frac{(0.035)^2 - (.0045)^2}{.0395}$ is:
A. 0.0305 B. 0.0395
C. 0.0345 D. 0.0354

104. An article which costs A ₹ 50 is sold to B at a profit of 20%; B sells it to C at a profit of 25%; C sells it to D at a profit of 40%. The price D paid for the article is:
A. ₹ 147 B. ₹ 105
C. ₹ 85 D. ₹ 95

105. The number which must be subtracted from 11, 15, 21 each so that the middle number so obtained is the mean proportional of the other two, is:
A. 6 B. 5
C. 4 D. 3

106. A sum of money put at compound interest amounts in 2 years to ₹ 3380 and in 3 years to ₹ 3515.20. The money invested is:
A. ₹ 3125 B. ₹ 3215
C. ₹ 3512 D. ₹ 3152

107. A pen is sold at ₹ 60.00 cash or ₹ 20.00 cash down payment and ₹ 8 per month for six months. The rate of interest is:
A. 80% B. 100%
C. 110% D. 120%

108. In an examination 77% candidates passed in English and 66% passed in Mathematics and 13% failed in both subjects. If 392 passed in both subjects the total number of candidates is:
A. 500 B. 600
C. 700 D. 800

109. A can do as much work in 2 days as B can do in 3 days, and B as much in 4 days as C in 5 days. If A, B and C together can do a piece of work in 5 days then A alone will do it in:
A. 15 days B. 12 days
C. 11 days D. 10 days

110. The value of (1 + cotθ – cosecθ) (1 + tanθ + secθ) is:
A. 1 B. –1
C. 2 D. –2

111. The value of sec70° sin20° + cos20° cosec70° is:
A. 1 B. –1
C. 2 D. –2

112. The angles of elevation of the top of tower from two points *a* and *b* from the base and in the same straight line with it are complementary. The height of the tower is:

A. $\sqrt{ab}$ B. $\sqrt{\frac{a}{b}}$

C. ab D. $\frac{a}{b}$

113. The difference between the sides at right angles in a right angled triangle is 14 cm. The area of the triangle is 120 cm². The perimeter of the triangle is:

A. 26 cm B. 36 cm
C. 54 cm D. 60 cm

114. The area of a square is the same as the area of a circle. Their perimeters are in the ratio:

A. 1 : 1 B. 2 : π
C. π : 2 D. $\sqrt{\pi}:2$

115. The radii of two cylinders are in the ratio 2 : 3 and their heights are in the ratio 5 : 3. The ratio of their volumes is:

A. 27 : 20 B. 20 : 27
C. 4 : 9 D. 9 : 4

116. The circular ends of a bucket are of radii 35 cm and 14 cm and the height of the bucket is 40 cm. Its volume is:

A. 60060 cm² B. 80080 cm²
C. 70040 cm² D. 80160 cm²

117. The height (in cm) of 15 students of a class are

141, 151, 146, 155, 148, 150, 158, 147, 159, 152, 153, 149, 150, 160, 161.

The mean height is:

A. 152 B. 153
C. 152.5 D. 151

118. A bag contains 3 white, 4 red and 5 black balls. One ball is drawn at random. The probability that the ball drawn is neither black nor white is:

A. $\frac{1}{4}$ B. $\frac{1}{2}$

C. $\frac{1}{3}$ D. $\frac{2}{3}$

119. Two vertices of a ΔABC are A(–1, 4) and B(5, 2) and its centroid is G(0, –3). The coordinate of C are:

A. (4, 3) B. (4, 15)
C. (–4, –15) D. (–15, –4)

120. The sum of all two digit odd positive integers is:

A. 2475 B. 2574
C. 2745 D. 2457

(iii) : SOCIAL SCIENCE

Directions (Qs. 121 to 140): *Choose the correct answer out of the four for each of the following question:*

121. Who was the Viceroy of India when Rowlatt Act passed?

A. Hardings II
B. Chelmsford
C. Simon
D. Minto II

122. The Vindhyan System of Rocks is important for the production of:

A. precious stones and building material
B. iron ore and managanese
C. bauxite and mica
D. copper and uranium

123. Which of the following acts gave representation to Indians for the first time in the legislature?

A. Indian Council Act 1909
B. Indian Council Act 1919
C. Govt. of India Act 1935
D. Govt. of India Act 1942

124. Which document was developed mentioning Samudragupta's Achievements?

A. Kalinga Edict
B. Hathigumpha Edict
C. Indica
D. Allahabad Prasasti

125. Which of the following Articles of the Directive Principles of State Policy deals with

the promotion of International Peace and Security?
A. Article 51
B. Article 48A
C. Article 43A
D. Article 41

126. In which of the following matters does Lok Sabha has supremacy?
A. Railway Budget
B. Defence Budget
C. Foreign Affairs
D. Financial Bill

127. As per existing law what is the minimum per day wages paid to a worker from unorganised sector in India?
A. ₹ 50 B. ₹ 75
C. ₹ 100 D. ₹ 125

128. Who is the first law officer of the Govt. of India?
A. The Chief Justice of India
B. Union Law Minister
C. Attorney General of India
D. Law Secretary

129. Many a times we see in financial Journals / Bulletins a term M_3, what does the term M_3 mean?
A. Currency in circulation on a particular day
B. Total value of the foreign Exchange on a particular day
C. Total value of Export Credit on a given date
D. Total value of the tax collected in a year

130. Many a times we read in the newspapers that RBI has changed or revised a particular ratio / rate by a few base points. What is meant by base point?
A. Ten per cent of one hundredth point
B. One hundred of 1%
C. One hundred of 10%
D. Ten per cent of 1000

131. Nagarjuna Sagar Dam is built across the river:
A. Cauvery B. Krishna
C. Narmada D. Godavari

132. Firoz Shah founded many cities, which of the following was not built by him?
A. Jaunpur
B. Fatehpur Sikri
C. Hisar
D. Fatehabad

133. The Red Sea is an example of a:
A. folded structure
B. faulted structure
C. lava structure
D. residual structure

134. Isochrones are lines joining places with equal:
A. longitude
B. travelling time from a point
C. rainfall
D. frost

135. The pepper plant is a:
A. tree B. vine
C. shrub D. small herb

136. Which kind of power accounts for the largest share of power generation in India?
A. Hydro Electricity
B. Thermal
C. Nuclear
D. Solar

137. An image of dancing girl on the coins was found from:
A. Kalibangan B. Harappa
C. Mohenjodara D. Ropar

138. The Italian traveller who gave a very praise worthy account of the Vijaynagar Empire was:
A. Barbosa
B. Marco Polo
C. Nicolo Conti
D. Tome Pires

139. Iqtas were:
A. hereditary assignments
B. the personal property of the nobles
C. generally transferable revenue assignments
D. orders passed by kings and queens

140. The number of languages listed in 8th schedule of the Constitution of India is:
A. 15 B. 18
C. 22 D. 14

(iv) : ENGLISH

Directions (Qs. 141 to 149): *Choose the most appropriate response out of the four choices given after every question. Each question carries one mark.*

141. The phrase 'widow's walk' means:
A. railed walkway atop a seaside house
B. an unsteady gait
C. wreath - laying ceremony
D. none of the above

142. The phrase 'deadman's hand' means:
A. a poker hand with two pairs
B. an unseen force
C. weakened leader
D. none of the above

143. A doctor who specialises in the treatment of the heart is called:
A. neurologist B. cardiologist
C. opthalmologist D. orthopaedist

144. Choose the correctly spelt word:
A. Sykosis B. Psykosis
C. Psychosis D. Sychosis

145. Choose the correctly spelt word:
A. ellegory B. allegory
C. alegory D. elegory

146. The indirect form of the sentence:
Aftabh asked his wife, "Where is my book?" is:
A. Aftabh asked his wife where is my book.
B. Aftabh asked his wife where his book was.
C. Aftabh asked his wife where his book is.
D. Aftabh asked his wife where is his book.

147. The indirect form of the sentence:
Anita said, "I went to Australia last year" is:
A. Anita said that I went to Australia last year.
B. Anita said that she went to Australia last year.
C. Anita said that she had gone to Australia last year.
D. Anita said that I had gone to Australia last year.

148. The passive voice of "Labourers are making the road" is:
A. The road is being made by labourers.
B. The road is made by labourers.
C. The road has been made by labourers.
D. The road was being made by labourers.

149. The active voice of "Anil was fined by the police for not stopping at the red light".
A. Anil fined the police for not stopping at the red light.
B. Anil not stopping at the red light was fined by the police.
C. The police fined Anil for not stopping at the red light.
D. The police fined Anil not stopping at the red light.

Directions (Qs. 150 to 152): *Choose the most appropriate words to fill in the blanks.*

150. Charles ______ go to Paris next month.
A. have B. will
C. had D. has

151. My son has been living in Paris ______ ten years.
A. since B. from
C. for D. till

152. Friends often seek out Asha's ______ as she is known for her ability to listen carefully and offer unbiased advice.
A. concern B. trouble
C. empathy D. counsel

153. In which of the following plays of Shakespeare Bertrice was the heroine?
A. Merchant of Venice
B. Much ado about nothing
C. Othello
D. Midsummer Night's Dream

154. Who wrote the poem 'Ode to the West Wind'?
A. Keats B. Coleridge
C. Wordsworth D. Shelley

155. Who wrote the novel 'Return of the Native'?
A. George Eliot B. Thomas Hardy
C. Emily Bronte D. Jane Austen

156. Who wrote the play 'End Game'?
A. Samuel Beckett
B. George Bernard Shaw

C. Eugene O'Neil
D. Shakespeare

157. Who is the heroine in the novel 'Return of the Native'?

A. Ursula B. Eustacia
C. Catharine D. Tess

158. Which of the following is ***not*** a poet of the Victorian Age?

A. Browning B. Tennyson
C. Shelley D. Arnold

159. In the sentence 'I have read that book which is lying on the table'.
Which is lying on the table is a:

A. Noun clause B. Adverb clause
C. Adjective clause D. None of the above

160. In the sentence 'Rashmi is the girl who has won the first prize'.
Who has won the first prize is a:

A. Noun clause B. Adverb clause
C. Adjective clause D. None of the above

(V) हिन्दी

निर्देशः (प्रश्न 161 से 165 तक): *दिए गए गद्यांश को ध्यान पूर्वक पढ़कर पूछे गए प्रश्नों के उत्तर दीजिए।*

हमारा मन हजारों निरुद्देश्य प्रश्न लिए वैज्ञानिक खोजों में उलझकर अशान्त बन रहा है। मन की दुनिया में प्रश्नों के सिवाय और क्या है? हृदय के संसार में केवल उत्तर-ही-उत्तर है। प्रेम है, करुणा है, विश्वास है, प्रतीक्षा है, समर्पण है और जिज्ञासा की शान्ति है, व्याकुलता की इतिश्री है। मन बहुरूपिया है। गिरगिट की तरह रंग बदलता रहता है। कभी वह दार्शनिक, कभी तार्किक, कभी वैज्ञानिक, राजनेता, तो कभी चिन्तक बनकर स्वयं को धोखे में डाल देता है। मन में प्रश्नों का उत्पन्न होना वैसा ही है, जैसाकि वृक्ष की शाखाओं पर नूतन पल्लवों का अंकुरण।

मन की तुलना एक मरुस्थल से की जा सकती है जहाँ रेत और मृगमरीचिका के सिवाय ऐसा कुछ भी नहीं होता जिससे जीवन में सुख-शान्ति, आनन्द और विश्राम का एहसास हो सके, परन्तु फिर भी ऐसा लगता है कि मन ही सब कुछ कर रहा है। मन ने आपको अपना गुलाम बना लिया है। आपके व्यक्तित्व का वह मालिक बन बैठा है।

मन ने हमारे हृदय के प्रेम और करुणा को भी पादाक्रान्त कर दिया है। पश्चिमी दर्शन और बुद्धिजीवी मन को ही बुद्धि का स्वामी मानकर मन को रिझाने के उपायों की वकालत करते देखे जाते हैं।

हृदय सब कुछ सुन लेता है, समझ लेता है और सारी जिज्ञासाओं का समाधान करने की क्षमता भी रखता है तथा जिसका सीधा सम्बन्ध उस दिव्य चेतना से है जिसे आत्मा कहा जाता है, उसे मन की तानाशाही ने इतना अशान्त बना दिया है कि वह दर-दर का भिखारी बना नजर आता है। हृदय में परमशान्ति का अक्षय कोश है, दिव्यता का भण्डार है, प्रेम और करुणा का अजस्त्र-निर्झर है। वही आज संवेदनाहीन, निष्करुण और निष्ठुर होता जा रहा है। मानवता मरती जा रही है; मनमानापन फल-फूल रहा है।

हृदय की आत्मा-परमात्मा का सेतु है। वही संसार में प्रेम से रहना और किसी के काम आना तथा मधुर संगीत निकालना सिखाता है। हृदय से ही आनन्द की वर्षा होती है। ध्यान भी हृदय गुफा की ही देन है। हमें हृदय का साथ करना होगा। मन को वश में करने का झंझट क्यों पाला जाए? वश में करने के चक्कर में पड़कर जीवन में संघर्ष क्यों करना? मन को अपने अनुकूल बना सको तो ठीक, नहीं तो उसकी उपेक्षा कर दो। मन को दृष्टा बनकर देखो। उसे महत्व देना छोड़कर भावजगत का आश्रय लेकर हृदय में आनन्द, शान्ति विश्वास और प्रेम का सदा अनुभव करो। यही अपना वास्तविक स्वरूप है।

161. इस गद्यांश का उपयुक्त शीर्षक क्या होगा?

A. मन की तानाशाही B. विज्ञान की भूल
C. शान्ति का उपाय D. हृदय की सुरक्षा

162. 'व्याकुलता' की इतिश्री'—का क्या तात्पर्य होगा?

A. मन के अनुसार कार्य करना
B. प्रश्नों का समाधान हृदय की अनुभूति से स्वतः होना
C. वैज्ञानिक खोज में सफलता मिलना
D. आत्मशान्ति की अनुभूति

163. मन में उठने वाले निरुद्देश्य प्रश्नों की तुलना किससे की गई है?

A. वैज्ञानिक खोजों से

B. मृगमरीचिका से

C. मरुस्थल के वृक्षों की हरियाली से

D. तानाशाही से

164. हृदय में निम्नलिखित गुणों में से कौन-सा गुण नहीं है?

A. करुणा B. प्रेम

C. तर्क D. आनन्द

165. हमारा वास्तविक स्वरूप क्या है?

A. संघर्षमय जीवन

B. मन की प्रसन्नता

C. भावजगत का सुख

D. संवेदन हीनता

निर्देशः (प्रश्न 166 से 180 तक): *निम्नलिखित प्रत्येक प्रश्न के साथ चार विकल्प दिये गये हैं। उनमें से सही विकल्प चुनिए।*

166. रवीनद्रनाथ ठाकुर द्वारा रचित हमार राष्ट्रगान किस भाषा में है?

A. खड़ीबोली B. बाँग्ला

C. मराठी D. गुजराती

167. इनमें से कौन-सी रचना 'वीरगाथाकाल' की है?

A. शिवा वावनी B. पृथ्वीराज रासो

C. पंचवटी D. हल्दीघाटी

168. 'मधुशाला' किसकी कृति है?

A. उमर खैयाम

B. शेखसादी

C. गोपालदास नीरज

D. हरिवंशराय बच्चन

169. उत्तर भारत की हिन्दी कृतियों में किस लिपि का सर्वाधिक व्यवहार होता है?

A. पाण्डुलिपि B. देवनागरी

C. रोमन D. गुरुमुखी

170. 'सूरसागर' की रचना किस विधा में है?

A. पद B. छंद

C. चौपाई D. कवित्त

171. निम्नलिखित में से कौन-सी वर्तनी अशुद्ध नहीं है?

A. आर्शिवाद B. आर्शीवाद

C. आशिर्वाद D. आशीर्वाद

172. निम्नलिखित में से 'रत्नगर्भा' किसका अर्थ होगा?

A. मेदिनी B. धरा

C. वसुधा D. अवनि

173. निम्नलिखित में से कौन-सा प्रयोग संधि नियमों के अनुसार अशुद्ध है?

A. मनोमय B. मनोकामना

C. मनोहर D. मनोरोग

174. पुरातन का विलोम शब्द कौन-सा है?

A. नूतन B. सनातन

C. अधुनातन D. वर्तमानकालीन

175. यदि 'पञ्चानन' का अर्थ शिव हो, तो इसमें कौन-सा समास होगा?

A. द्विगु B. अव्ययीभाव

C. द्वन्द्व D. बहुव्रीहि

176. "जीतने की इच्छा करने वाला" इस कथन के लिए कौन-सा एक शब्द उचित है?

A. जिज्ञासु B. जिगीषु

C. जिजीविषु D. विविदिषु

177. कनक कनक ते सौगुनी, मादकता अधिकाय।
या पाए बौराय जग, वा खाए बौराय।।
उपर्युक्त दोहे में कौन-सा अलंकार है?

A. यमक B. श्लेष

C. दृष्टान्त D. अतिशयोक्ति

178. 'प्रणम्य' की तरह 'क्षमा' से कौन-सा शब्द ठीक है?

A. क्षमाशील B. क्षम्य

C. क्षमी D. क्षाम्य

179. 'व्यावहारिक' की तरह 'प्रमाण' का कौन-सा विशेषण शब्द ठीक है?

A. प्रामाण्य B. प्रामाणिक

C. प्रमाणिक D. प्रामाणीक

180. निम्नलिखित वाक्यों में कौन-सा वाक्य शुद्ध है?

A. उसने न खुद करा है, न किसी से कराया है

B. तुमको हमारे से क्या बैर है

C. हम आपकी कुशल-क्षेम के आकांक्षी हैं

D. कृप्या फूल तोड़ना मना है

ANSWERS

1	2	3	4	5	6	7	8	9	10
D	B	B	D	B	A	A	A	A	D
11	12	13	14	15	16	17	18	19	20
D	B	C	A	A	D	B	C	A	D
21	22	23	24	25	26	27	28	29	30
C	B	D	A	C	B	A	D	D	D
31	32	33	34	35	36	37	38	39	40
D	C	C	A	D	D	D	C	D	D
41	42	43	44	45	46	47	48	49	50
C	A	C	D	A	B	C	C	A	B
51	52	53	54	55	56	57	58	59	60
B	C	C	C	A	B	C	A	D	D
61	62	63	64	65	66	67	68	69	70
A	C	A	A	B	A	B	C	D	C
71	72	73	74	75	76	77	78	79	80
A	D	D	B	A	A	B	D	A	D
81	82	83	84	85	86	87	88	89	90
A	A	B	B	B	B	D	A	C	A
91	92	93	94	95	96	97	98	99	100
D	A	D	D	B	D	D	A	A	C
101	102	103	104	105	106	107	108	109	110
B	D	A	B	D	A	D	C	C	C
111	112	113	114	115	116	117	118	119	120
C	A	D	D	B	B	A	C	C	A
121	122	123	124	125	126	127	128	129	130
B	A	C	D	A	D	C	A	A	A
131	132	133	134	135	136	137	138	139	140
B	B	C	B	B	D	B	C	C	B
141	142	143	144	145	146	147	148	149	150
B	B	B	C	B	B	C	A	C	B
151	152	153	154	155	156	157	158	159	160
C	D	B	D	B	A	B	C	C	C
161	162	163	164	165	166	167	168	169	170
A	D	C	C	C	B	B	D	B	A
171	172	173	174	175	176	177	178	179	180
D	C	A	A	D	B	A	B	B	C

SOME SELECTED EXPLANATORY ANSWERS

16. 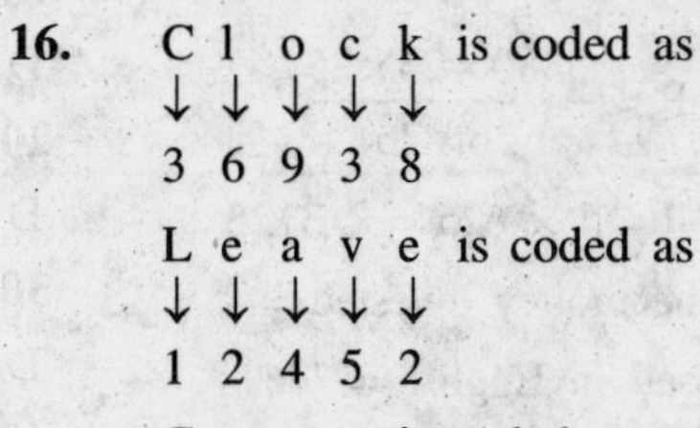
C l o c k is coded as
↓ ↓ ↓ ↓ ↓
3 6 9 3 8

L e a v e is coded as
↓ ↓ ↓ ↓ ↓
1 2 4 5 2

∴ C a v e is coded as
↓ ↓ ↓ ↓
3 4 5 2

17. S k y is coded as
↓ ↓ ↓
TT MM XX

∴ L i e is coded as
↓ ↓ ↓
MM KK DD

19. Let number of incorrect answers = x

∴ number of correct answers = 180 – x

According to the question,

$$(108 - x) \times 1 + (x)\left(-\frac{1}{3}\right) = 0$$

$$\Rightarrow \quad 108 - x - \frac{x}{3} = 0$$

$$\Rightarrow \quad x + \frac{x}{3} = 108$$

$$\Rightarrow \quad \frac{4x}{3} = 108$$

$$\Rightarrow \quad x = \frac{108 \times 3}{4} = 81$$

Hence, number of incorrect answers = 81

20. A has (9 + 2 + 3 – 2) = 12 marbles

21. B has (9 – 2 + 2 – 3 + 2) = 13 – 5 = 8 marbles

22. C has (9 – 5 – 2) = 9 – 7 = 2 marbles

23. D has (9 + 2 – 1 – 3) = 11 – 4 = 7 marbles

E has (9 + 1 + 5 – 2 + 3) = 18 – 2 = 16 marbles

Hence, E has got maximum no. of marbles.

24. 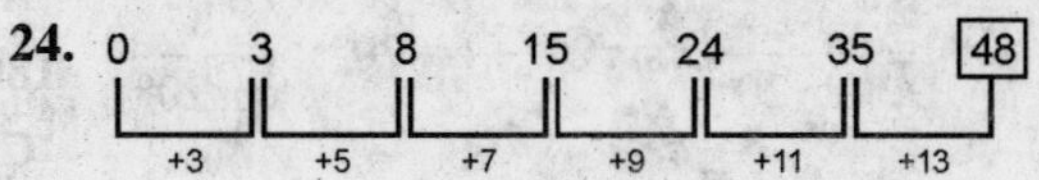

25. 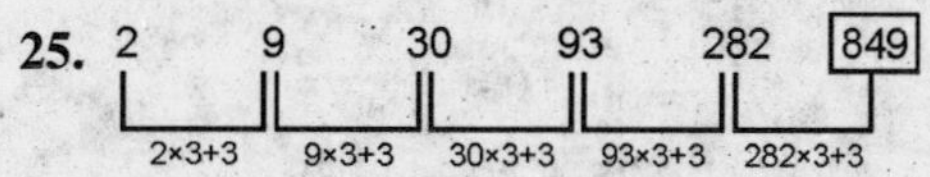

26. 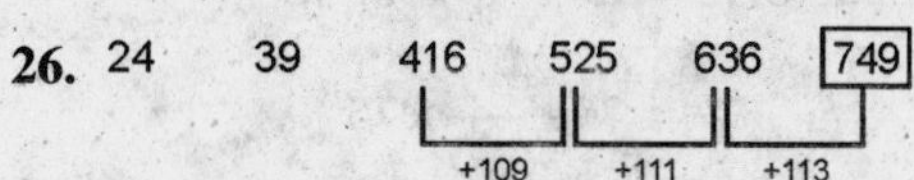

27. 40 29 [20] 13 8

11 9 7 5

101. $(a^{x-y})^{x+y} . (a^{y-z})^{y+z} . (a^{z-x})^{z+x}$

$= a^{x^2-y^2} \times a^{y^2-z^2} \times a^{z^2-x^2}$

$= a^{x^2-y^2+y^2-z^2+z^2-x^2}$

$= a^0 = 1$

102. Let the number = x

According to the question,

$$\frac{x}{15} + \frac{x}{12} + \frac{x}{7} = 1353$$

$$\Rightarrow \quad \frac{28x + 35x + 60x}{420} = 1353$$

$$\Rightarrow \quad 123x = 1353 \times 420$$

$$\Rightarrow \quad x = \frac{1353 \times 420}{123}$$

$$= 11 \times 420 = 4620$$

103. $\dfrac{(0.035)^2 - (0.0045)^2}{0.0395}$

$= \dfrac{(0.035 + 0.0045)(0.035 - 0.0045)}{0.0395}$

$= \dfrac{0.0395 \times (0.0305)}{0.0395}$

$= 0.0305$

104. SP of A = 20% of 50 + ₹ 50

$= \dfrac{20}{100} \times 50 + 50$

= 10 + 50 = ₹ 60

SP of B = ₹ 60 + 25% of 60

$= 60+\frac{25}{100}\times 60$

= 60 + 15 = ₹ 75

SP of C = 75 + 40% of 75

$= 75+\frac{40}{100}\times 75$

= 75 + 30 = ₹ 105

Hence, the price D paid for the article = ₹ 105

105. Let the required number = x

According to the question,

$11 - x,\ 15 - x,\ 21 - x$

$(15 - x)^2 = (11 - x)(21 - x)$

$\Rightarrow 225 + x^2 - 30x = 231 - 11x - 21x + x^2$

$\Rightarrow x^2 - 30x + 225 = x^2 - 32x + 231$

$\Rightarrow \quad 2x = 6$

$\Rightarrow \quad x = 3$

Hence, the required number = 3

106. $A = P\left(1+\frac{r}{100}\right)^t$

$\Rightarrow 3515.20 = P\left(1+\frac{r}{100}\right)^3 \quad ...(i)$

and $\quad 3380 = P\left(1+\frac{r}{100}\right)^2 \quad ...(ii)$

Dividing (*i*) by (*ii*)

$\frac{3515.20}{3380} = \left(1+\frac{r}{100}\right)$

$\Rightarrow 1+\frac{r}{100} = \frac{26}{25}$

$\Rightarrow \frac{r}{100} = \frac{26}{25}-1 = \frac{1}{25}$

$\Rightarrow \quad r = 4\%$

Putting the value of r in (*ii*)

$\Rightarrow \quad 3380 = P\left(1+\frac{4}{100}\right)^2$

$\Rightarrow \quad 3380 = P\left(\frac{26}{25}\times\frac{26}{25}\right)$

$\Rightarrow \quad P = \frac{3380\times 25\times 25}{26\times 26}$

$\Rightarrow \quad P = 5 \times 625 = ₹\ 3125$

Hence, the money invested = ₹ 3125

108. Passed in English = 77%

Passed in Mathematics = 66%

Passed in both subjects = (100 – 13)

= 87%

Total passed % = 77 + 66 – 87

= 56%

∴ Total number of candidates

$= \frac{100}{56}\times 392 = 700$

110. $(1 + \cot\theta - \operatorname{cosec}\theta)(1 + \tan\theta + \sec\theta)$

$= \left(1+\frac{\cos\theta}{\sin\theta}-\frac{1}{\sin\theta}\right)\left(1+\frac{\sin\theta}{\cos\theta}+\frac{1}{\cos\theta}\right)$

$= \left(\frac{\sin\theta+\cos\theta-1}{\sin\theta}\right)\left(\frac{\cos\theta+\sin\theta+1}{\cos\theta}\right)$

$= \frac{(\sin\theta+\cos\theta)^2-(1)^2}{\sin\theta\cdot\cos\theta}$

$= \frac{\sin^2\theta+\cos^2\theta+2\sin\theta\cdot\cos\theta-1}{\sin\theta\cdot\cos\theta}$

$= \frac{1+2\sin\theta\cdot\cos\theta-1}{\sin\theta\cdot\cos\theta}$

$= \frac{2\sin\theta\cdot\cos\theta}{\sin\theta\cdot\cos\theta} = 2$

111. sec 70° . sin 20° + cos 20° . cosec 70°

= sec (90° – 20°) · sin 20° + cos 20° · cosec (90° – 20°)

= cosec 20° · sin 20° + cos 20° · sec 20°

$= \frac{1}{\sin 20^\circ}\times\sin 20^\circ+\cos 20^\circ\times\frac{1}{\cos 20^\circ}$

= 1 + 1 = 2

112.

In ΔABD,

$$\tan(90° - \theta) = \frac{h}{b}$$

$$\cot\theta = \frac{h}{b} \quad ...(i)$$

In ΔABC,

$$\tan\theta = \frac{h}{a} \quad ...(ii)$$

Multiplying (*i*) and (*ii*)

$$\cot\theta \times \tan\theta = \frac{h}{b} \times \frac{h}{a}$$

$$\Rightarrow \quad 1 = \frac{h^2}{ab}$$

$$\Rightarrow \quad h^2 = ab \Rightarrow h = \sqrt{ab}$$

Hence, the height of the tower = $\sqrt{ab}$

113. 

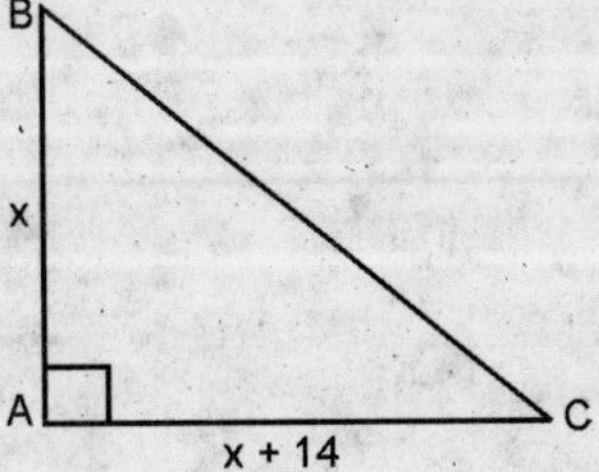

$$\text{Area of } \Delta ABC = \frac{1}{2} \times x \times (x + 14)$$

$$\Rightarrow \quad 120 = \frac{1}{2} \times (x^2 + 14x)$$

$$\Rightarrow \quad x^2 + 14x - 240 = 0$$

$$\Rightarrow \quad x^2 + 24x - 10x - 240 = 0$$

$$\Rightarrow x(x + 24) - 10(x + 24) = 0$$

$$(x + 24)(x - 10) = 0$$

either $x = -24$ or $x = 10$

but $x \neq -24$

$$\therefore \quad x = 10,$$

$$x + 14 = 10 + 14 = 24$$

Now, $BC^2 = (10)^2 + (24)^2$

$$= 100 + 576 = 676$$

$$\therefore \quad BC = \sqrt{676} = 26 \text{ cm}$$

$\therefore$ Perimeter of $\Delta ABC = 10 + 24 + 26 = 60$ cm

114. Area of square = x^2

Area of circle = πr^2

$$\pi r^2 = x^2$$

$$\therefore \quad r^2 = \frac{x^2}{\pi}$$

$$r = \frac{x}{\sqrt{\pi}}$$

$$\frac{2\pi r}{4x} = \frac{2\pi \times x}{4 \times x \times \sqrt{\pi}} = \frac{\sqrt{\pi}}{2}$$

$\therefore$ Required ratio = $\sqrt{\pi} : 2$

115. $$\frac{V_1}{V_2} = \frac{\pi \times (2x)^2 \times 5x}{\pi (3x)^2 \times 3x} = \frac{4 \times 5}{9 \times 3} = \frac{20}{27}$$

$\therefore$ Required ratio = 20 : 27

116.

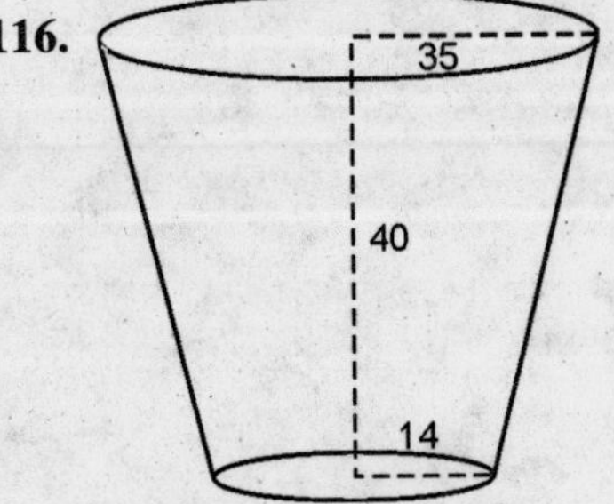

Volume of bucket

$$= \frac{1}{3} \times \pi(R^2 + r^2 + R \cdot r) \cdot h$$

$$= \frac{1}{3} \times \frac{22}{7}(35^2 + 14^2 + 35 \times 14) \times 40$$

$$= \frac{1}{3} \times \frac{22}{7}(1225 + 196 + 490) \times 40$$

$= \frac{22}{21} \times 1911 \times 40$

$= 880 \times 91 = 80080 \text{ cm}^3$

117. $\text{Mean} = \frac{141+151+146+155+148+150+158+147+159+152+153+149+150+160+161}{15}$

$= \frac{2280}{15} = 152$

$\therefore$ Mean height = 152 cm

118. Total ball = 3 + 4 + 5 = 12

Required probability $= \frac{4}{12} = \frac{1}{3}$

119.

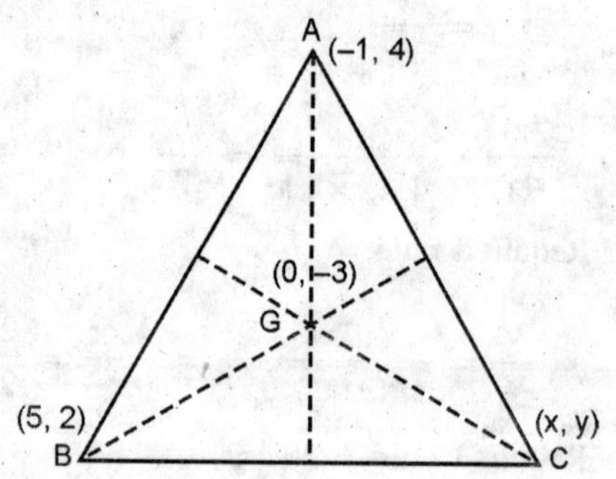

According to the question,

$0 = \frac{-1+5+x}{3} \Rightarrow x + 4 = 0 \Rightarrow x = -4$

$-3 = \frac{4+2+y}{3} \Rightarrow y + 6 = -9 \Rightarrow y = -15$

Hence, co-ordinate of C are (–4, –15).

120. Odd numbers of two digit numbers are 11, 13, 15, 17, ..., 99.

nth term $= a + (n - 1)d$

$\Rightarrow \quad 99 = 11 + (n - 1) \times 2$

$\Rightarrow \quad 99 = 11 + 2n - 2 = 2n + 9$

$\Rightarrow \quad 2n = 99 - 9 = 90$

$\Rightarrow \quad n = 45$

$S_n = \frac{n}{2}\{2a+(n-1)d\}$

$S_{45} = \frac{45}{2}\{2\times11+(45-1)2\}$

$= \frac{45}{2}\{22+88\} = \frac{45}{2}\times110$

$= 45 \times 55 = 2475$

Previous Paper (Solved)

IGNOU B.Ed. Entrance Test 2012

PART-A

SECTION-I : General English Comprehension

Directions (Qs. 1 to 10): *Read the passage carefully and answer the questions chosen from the 4 choices given against each.*

Educational planning should aim at meeting the educational needs of the entire population of all age groups. While the traditional structure of education has a three layer hierarchy from the primary stage to the university represents the core, we should not overlook the periphery which is equally important. Under modern conditions, workers need to rewind or renew, their enthusiasm, or strike out in a new direction, or improve their skills as much as any University professor. The retired and the aged have their own needs as well. Educational planning in other words, should take care of the needs of everyone.

Our structure of education have been built-up on the assumption that there is a terminal point to education. This basic defect has become all the more harmful today. A UNESCO report certified 'Learning to Be' prepared by Edgar Faure and others in 1973 asserts that the education of children must prepare future adult for various forms of self learning. A viable education system of the future should consist of modules with different kinds of functions serving a diversity of constituents. And performance not the period of study should be the basis for credentials.

In view of the fact that the significance of a commitment to lifelong learning and lifetime education is being discussed only in recent years even in educationally advanced countries, the possibility of idea becoming an integral part of educational thinking seems to be a far cry. To move in the direction means much more than some simple rearrangements of the present organization of education. But a good beginning can be made by developing open university programmes for older learners of different categories and introducing extension services in the conventional colleges and schools. These institutions should also learn to cooperate with community organizations such as libraries, health services etc.

1. Educational planning should aim at meeting the education needs of:
- A. Early childhood age group
- B. Teenagers
- C. All age groups
- D. None of the above

2. The traditional structure of education has a:
- A. Two layer hierarchy
- B. Three layer hierarchy
- C. Four tier system
- D. All of the above

3. According to the passage, the present education structure assumes that:
- A. All people can be educated as per need
- B. Educational planning at present is practical
- C. Education is one time process
- D. None of the above

4. The basis for credentials for viable education system should be:
- A. Performance
- B. Period of study
- C. Study hours
- D. All of the above

5. Our structure of education have been built up on the assumption that:
- A. There are many faces of education
- B. There is no system of education

C. There is terminal point to education
D. None of the above

6. In the context of the passage, the meaning of "A far cry" is:
   A. A cry coming from a far place
   B. A cry going to a far place
   C. A cry heard at a far place
   D. Having a little possibility

7. Which of the following is closest in meaning to the word 'meeting' as used in the passage?
   A. Contacting B. Approaching
   C. Introducing D. Satisfying

8. Which of the following is opposite to the word 'integral' as used in the passage?
   A. Essential B. Independent
   C. Major D. Minor

9. Integrating the concept of life long education with the educational structure would imply:
   A. Close down conventional schools/colleges
   B. Longer duration of formal courses
   C. Simple rearrangement of present educational organization
   D. None of the above

10. Which of the following is not true in the context of the given passage?
   A. Life long learning is a recent concept
   B. Worker's knowledge and skills also need to be updated constantly
   C. 'Learning to Be' subscribes to the view that there is a terminal point to education
   D. School and college should also start extension services

SECTION-II : Logical and Analytical Reasoning

11. Which of the following would be the next number in the series 8, 15, 29, 57?
   A. 99 B. 113
   C. 103 D. 101

12. Which of the following numbers will be inserted in place of the (?) mark?
   35 (78) 40 45 (97) 35 25 (?) 30
   A. 66 B. 56
   C. 67 D. 71

13. Find the missing term in the following:
   ACEG : DFHJ : : QSUV : ?
   A. TVXY B. MNPR
   C. OQST D. KMNP

14. Find the odd man out from the following words:
   A. Gun B. Rifle
   C. Sabers D. Revolver

15. Find the odd man out.
   A. Glaucoma B. Cataract
   C. Eczema D. Trachoma

16. Which of the following number will be placed in place of the (?) mark in the number series?
   3, 5, 6, ? , 9, 15
   A. 10 B. 12
   C. 15 D. 22

17. If 'BEARING' is coded as 1234567. 'PARE' will be coded as:
   A. 4234 B. 4321
   C. 4345 D. 4342

18. If RADIO is coded as 'UDGLR', PHOTO will be coded as:
   A. OIPWR B. OTOPT
   C. SKRWR D. SKPWR

19. 10 women can harvest a field in 3 days. How many women can harvest the same field in 2 days?
   A. 29 B. 15
   C. 30 D. 35

20. In an examination, 360 students passed out of 450. Find the percentage of pass students.
   A. 80% B. 60%
   C. 20% D. 70%

21. What percentage of 85 is 17?
   A. 25% B. 30%
   C. 5% D. 20%

22. If the price of sugar is 25% more than price of Gur, then price of Gur is how much per cent less than sugar?
   A. 25% B. 20%
   C. 80% D. 30%

23. A truck covers a distance of 51 km in 8.5 litres of diesel. How much diesel is required to cover a distance of 165 km?
A. 27.5 litres B. 2.5 litres
C. 30 litres D. 21.5 litres

24. If 23 : 23 : : 23 : x. Then value of x is:
A. 23 B. 47
C. 69 D. 70

25. If 'friend' bears relation to 'friendly' which word in the options given below bear the same relation with opponent?
A. Enemy B. Hostile
C. Defeat D. Contest

26. The cost of 16 cm of cloth is ₹ 60, calculate the cost of 6 cm.
A. ₹ 22.5 B. ₹ 26
C. ₹ 56 D. ₹ 62

27. The difference between 20% of 172 and 272 is:
A. 40 B. 20
C. 35 D. 30

28. Find the largest number which can divide 124 and 93 exactly.
A. 24 B. 31
C. 26 D. 27

29. A man completes a work in 15 days, working 4 hours daily. In how many days he will complete the work, working 6 hours daily?
A. 10 days B. 60 days
C. 34 days D. 30 days

30. Karan walks 90 metres in 2 minutes. How much distance, he will cover in 5 minutes?
A. 225 m B. 180 m
C. 340 m D. 50 m

SECTION-III : EDUCATIONAL AND GENERAL AWARENESS

31. The Kathakali dance belongs to the state:
A. Kerala B. Tamil Nadu
C. Andhra Pradesh D. Assam

32. The first women speaker of the Lok Sabha is:
A. Nazma Heptullah B. Mayawati
C. Meera Kumar D. Maneka Gandhi

33. The food factory of the cell is:
A. Cell membrane B. Mitochondria
C. DNA D. Stem cell

34. Iodine is used in the treatment of:
A. Beri Beri B. Goitre
C. Night blindness D. Rickets

35. Normal temperature of human body is:
A. 46.8°C B. 94.8°F
C. 98.6°F D. 49.8°C

36. Transfer of genetic information from one generation to the other is accomplished by:
A. DNA
B. Transfer RNA
C. Messenger RNA
D. Messenger and Transfer RNA

37. Which tax is not levied by the Central Government?
A. Wealth Tax B. Profession Tax
C. Income Tax D. Excise Tax

38. Chanakya was known in his childhood as:
A. Ajaya B. Chanakya
C. Vishnugupta D. Deogupta

39. Highest Literacy rate is in the state of:
A. Bihar B. Kerala
C. Rajasthan D. Uttar Pradesh

40. Which state in the country has the largest number of districts?
A. Madhya Pradesh B. Maharashtra
C. Tamil Nadu D. Uttar Pradesh

41. The first President of India was:
A. Jawaharlal Nehru
B. Sardar Patel
C. Dr. Rajendra Prasad
D. Mahatma Gandhi

42. The movie 'Chak De India' is based on which sport?
A. Cricket B. Football
C. Hockey D. Badminton

43. Who is the President of USA?
A. Bill Clinton B. George W. Bush
C. Hillary Clinton D. Barack Obama

44. Which state is known for its folk dance 'Garba'?
A. Punjab B. Gujarat
C. Rajasthan D. Haryana

45. The capital of Arunachal Pradesh is:
A. Shillong B. Dimapur
C. Dispur D. Itanagar

46. The national bird of India is:
A. Peacock B. Dove
C. Pigeon D. Eagle

47. Who was the first woman ruler in India?
A. Noorjahan B. Razia Sultana
C. Chandbibi D. Mumtaj Mahal

48. The Vice-President presides over the:
A. Lok Sabha
B. Rajya Sabha
C. Union Council of Ministers
D. Planning Commission

49. When water is heated from 0°C to 100°C, its volume:
A. Increases
B. Decreases
C. Does not change
D. First decreases and then increases

50. Who among the following conquered a large part of China?
A. Ashoka B. Harshavardhan
C. Kanishka D. Samudra Gupta

51. Cloudy nights are warmer compared to clear cloudless nights, because clouds:
A. prevent cold waves from the sky from descending on earth
B. reflect back the heat given off by earth
C. produce heat and radiate it towards earth
D. absorb heat from the atmosphere and send it towards earth

52. 'Bharat Ratna' award was first given in the year:
A. 1956 B. 1954
C. 1952 D. 1957

53. The first Indian to win a gold medal in Olympics was:
A. Bijender Kumar B. Milkha Singh
C. P.T. Usha D. Abhinav Bindra

54. National flag of India was designed by:
A. Mahatma Gandhi
B. Subhas Chandra Bose
C. Pingali Venkaiyya
D. Jawaharlal Nehru

55. Good Friday is celebrated on:
A. The Martyrdom Day of Jesus Christ
B. Birthday of Jesus Christ
C. Christmas Day
D. None of the above

SECTION-IV : TEACHING-LEARNING AND THE SCHOOL

56. The true objective of education is:
A. Making students able so that they can earn a living
B. Preparing students for jobs
C. Helping students to acquire knowledge
D. Facilitating the all round development of the students

57. The job of teacher is to:
A. Help students in self study
B. Motivate students to study
C. Create a good environment for studies
D. Tell students about the mistakes committed by them

58. It is important for the teachers to have:
A. Complete knowledge of the subject
B. Complete knowledge of the teaching methods
C. Knowledge about the students
D. All of the above

59. Maladjustment in children is:
A. A result of frustration
B. A reason of frustration
C. Another name of frustration
D. None of the above

60. In your view the profession of a teacher is:
A. A stop-gap arrangement
B. Profitable
C. Full of fun and frolic
D. The best

61. The use of different methods during the course of teaching:

A. Keeps attention of students focused
B. Makes classroom teaching quite interesting
C. Help students understand concepts and topics
D. All of the above

62. Memory is a part of:
A. Aptitude B. Attitude
C. Intelligence D. All of these

63. Looking grown up, but behaving like a child is termed as:
A. Locomotor disability
B. Visual disability
C. Hearing disability
D. Mental disability

64. Poor language development leads to:
A. Poor memory
B. Short attention span
C. Difficulty in communication
D. Poor economic condition

65. Piaget was a:
A. Singer B. Special educator
C. Psychologist D. Pediatrician

66. Education of children with disabilities ensures better acceptance of disability and potential of children with disability for:
A. Education B. Employment
C. Social activities D. All of these

67. Finding hidden toy is an example of:
A. Language development
B. Social development
C. Motor development
D. Cognitive development

68. Special school is a typical example of:
A. Integrated setting B. Inclusive setting
C. Mainstreaming D. Segregation

69. The children who perform much below their potential are known as:
A. Mentally retarded
B. Under achiever
C. Gifted children
D. Physically Handicapped

70. Mental Retardation is referred as:
A. Mental illness
B. Mental ailment
C. Intellectual disability
D. Pervasive developmental disorder

71. Disability may occur:
A. Only among the highly educated
B. Only among the rich
C. Only among the poor
D. Across all social economic group

72. IQ score of _____ indicates mental retardation.
A. below 70 B. below 90
C. below 80 D. below 100

73. PWD Act, 1995 states ______ job reservations for persons with disabilities.
A. 3% B. 2%
C. 4% D. 5%

74. Total communication involves:
A. Single modality B. Dual modality
C. All modalities D. No modalities

75. Inclusive education is related to:
A. Pre school special education
B. Resource room and resource teacher
C. Integrated set up
D. None of the above

76. Stuttering is a:
A. Voice disorder
B. Fluency disorder
C. Articulation disorder
D. Language disorder

77. NIVH is situated at:
A. Mumbai B. Delhi
C. Dehradun D. Ahmedabad

78. Rehabilitation Council of India does the registration of:
A. Teachers
B. Rehabilitation professionals
C. Both A and B
D. None of the above

79. Abacus is used by:
A. Visually impaired persons
B. Hearing impaired persons
C. All the persons with disabilities
D. None of the above

80. If the age of mother is ___ there in higher risk for the birth of child with mental retardation.
A. below 18 years
B. above 35 years
C. below 18 and above 35 years
D. None of the above

PART-B

SECTION-V (I): SCIENCE

81. Which of the following represents a chemical change?
A. Evaporation of alcohol
B. Sublimation of iodine
C. Heating of a platinum wire in a bunsen flame
D. Heating of mercuric oxide powder

82. The chemical used as a 'fixer' in photography is:
A. Sodium sulphate
B. Sodium thiosulphate
C. Ammonium persulphate
D. Borax

83. Which of the following in solid state is known as dry ice?
A. Ammonia B. Nitrogen
C. Carbon dioxide D. Hydrogen

84. The tape of tape recorder is coated with:
A. Copper sulphate
B. Mercury
C. Ferromagnetic powder
D. Zinc oxide

85. During dehydration, what is slightly lost actually?
A. Sodium Chloride
B. Potassium Chloride
C. Calcium Chloride
D. Calcium Sulphate

86. Rayon is chemically a:
A. cellulose B. amylase
C. glucose D. pectin

87. The process of obtaining salt from sea water is called:
A. Evaporation B. Sublimation
C. Crystallization D. Distillation

88. The silver surface of thermos flask prevents the transfer of heat by:
A. Convection B. Conduction
C. Radiation D. Reflection

89. The hardness of water can be removed by:
A. Zeeolite B. Sodium Silicate
C. Boiling D. None of these

90. The most common acid found in the nature is:
A. Citric acid
B. Lactic acid
C. Acetic acid
D. Hydrochloric acid

91. The speed of light will be minimum, while passing through:
A. Vacuum B. Glass
C. Air D. Water

92. The final image produced by a simple microscope is:
A. Virtual and erect B. Erect and real
C. Real and inverted D. Virtual and real

93. The change of ice into water is a/an:
A. Chemical change
B. Physical change
C. Atomic change
D. Electrical change

94. An air bubble in water will act like a:
A. Convex lens B. Convex mirror
C. Concave lens D. Concave mirror

95. Plants absorb water from the soil by:
A. Gravitational process
B. Capillary process
C. Hygroscopic process
D. None of these

96. The main endocrine gland present in human body is:
A. Pituitary gland B. Adrenal gland
C. Thyroid gland D. Pancreas gland

97. In human body, the water quantity is about:
A. 20% B. 100%
C. 80% D. 65%

98. Which of the following chemicals is used for preserving fruit juices in India?
A. Sodium hydroxide
B. Potassium nitrate
C. Ammonium sulphate
D. Sodium benzoate

99. The atmospheric layer nearest to earth is :

A. Stratosphere B. Troposphere
C. Ionosphere D. Mesosphere

100. Which of the following gases does not pollute air?

A. Sulphur dioxide
B. Nitrogen oxide
C. Carbon dioxide
D. Carbon monoxide

(II) : MATHEMATICS

101. The mean of reciprocal of x and y is equal to:

A. $\frac{2(x+y)}{xy}$ B. $\frac{x+y}{x-y}$
C. $\frac{2x}{x+y}$ D. $\frac{x+y}{2xy}$

102. The fractions given below are in their lowest terms. Supply the missing figures:

$$5\frac{1}{x} \times y\frac{3}{4} = 20$$

A. 3, 1 B. 3, 3
C. 1, 5 D. 4, 1

103. Complete the series : 1, 2, 4, 7, 13, 24, 44, ?

A. 80 B. 64
C. 81 D. 66

104. Find the sum of all numbers up to 1000 which are divisible by 19.

A. 26182 B. 21588
C. 13262 D. 33868

105. The average of three numbers is 135. The largest number is 180 and the difference of other two is 25. The smallest number is:

A. 130 B. 100
C. 125 D. 120

106. Ten per cent of twenty plus twenty per cent of ten equals:

A. 2 per cent of 200 B. 1 per cent of 200
C. 10 per cent of 20 D. 20 per cent of 10

107. If 70% of P is equal to 40% of Q. The ratio of P to Q is:

A. 4 : 7 B. 7 : 4
C. 4 ; 11 D. 7 : 11

108. If a clock strikes 12 times in 22 seconds. In how much time it will strike 6 times?

A. 10 seconds B. 11 seconds
C. 15 seconds D. 8 seconds

109. HCF of two numbers is 24 and LCM is 5304. If one of the number is 408 then other number is:

A. 1146 B. 312
C. 32 D. 302

110. Sohan is three times older than Gopal. Five years back, he was four times older than Gopal. Find the present age of Gopal.

A. 15 years B. 18 years
C. 20 years D. 12 years

111. If all the triangles on the same base and within the same parallels, the perimeter is least if the triangle is:

A. Equilateral B. Isosceles
C. Right angled D. Obtuse angled

112. tan 30° cos 60° sin 60° = ?

A. $\frac{1}{\sqrt{3}}$ B. $\frac{1}{2}$
C. 1 D. $\frac{1}{4}$

113. The value of $\frac{\sin 39°}{\cos 51°}$ is:

A. 0 B. $\frac{1}{2}$
C. ∞ D. 1

114. 70% of 280 is same as:

A. 40% of 49 B. 35% of 140
C. 7% of 28 D. None of these

115. The average of 7 consecutive numbers is 33. The highest of these numbers is:

A. 30 B. 33
C. 36 D. 35

116. What is the number in the series in place of the question mark?

0, 2, 6, ?, 30, 62

A. 18 B. 24
C. 14 D. 10

117. Find the value of $5\frac{6}{7} \times 3\frac{1}{4} + 40\%$ of 35 = ?

A. $17\frac{17}{28}$ B. $16\frac{17}{28}$

C. $16\frac{9}{14}$ D. $33\frac{1}{28}$

118. Which of the following values are equal?

(i) 1^4 (ii) 4°

(iii)0^4 (iv) 4^1

A. (i) and (iv) B. (i) and (iii)
C. (i) and (ii) D. (ii) and (iii)

119. Which of the following is not a prime number?

A. 157 B. 2
C. 131 D. 1

120. Find the greatest number out of the following:

(i) $3.\sqrt{1.728}$ (ii) $\frac{\sqrt{3}-1}{\sqrt{3}+1}$

(iii) $\left(\frac{1}{2}\right)^{-2}$ (iv) $\frac{17}{8}$

A. (iii) B. (ii)
C. (iv) D. (i)

(III) : Social Science

Directions (Qs. 121 to 140): *Choose the correct answer out of the four:*

121. Mohen-jo-daro is situated at:

A. Punjab B. Gujarat
C. Sindh D. Uttar Pradesh

122. The first governor general of the independent India was:

A. C. Rajagopalachari
B. Dr. Rajendra Prasad
C. Lord Mountbatten
D. Dr. B.R. Ambedkar

123. Grand Trunk road was made by:

A. Chandragupta Maurya
B. Shahjahan
C. Shershah Suri
D. Lord Dalhousi

124. Large production of jute is at the delta of river:

A. Damodar B. Sindh
C. Ganga D. Satluj

125. Which state of India is largest in area?

A. Uttar Pradesh B. Madhya Pradesh
C. Assam D. West Bengal

126. The highest mountain peak in India is:

A. Kanchenjunga B. Mount Everest
C. Nanda Devi D. Annapurna

127. Largest river in India is:

A. Ganga B. Kaveri
C. Brahmaputra D. Godavari

128. Father of local self governance is:

A. Lord Ripen B. Lord Curzon
C. Lord Minto D. Lord Dalhousi

129. Section 370 of constitution of India gives special status to which state?

A. Sikkim
B. Nagaland
C. Arunachal Pradesh
D. Jammu and Kashmir

130. The members of Rajya Sabha are elected:

A. Directly by people
B. By members of parliament
C. By members of legislative assembly
D. By the president of India

131. Who constitutes the Finance Commission?

A. Lok Sabha
B. President
C. Rajya Sabha
D. Finance Minister

132. Who is the Chairperson of Planning Commission?

A. Prime Minister
B. Home Minister
C. President
D. Finance Minister

133. Panchayati Raj system was first introduced in the state of:

A. Bihar B. West Bengal
C. Andhra Pradesh D. Rajasthan

134. The capital of Sikkim is:
A. Gangtok B. Shillong
C. Imphal D. Dispur

135. The state with highest population density is:
A. Uttar Pradesh
B. Arunachal Pradesh
C. West Bengal
D. Bihar

136. The smallest state of India is:
A. Haryana B. Punjab
C. Bihar D. Goa

137. The state with highest number of tribes is:
A. West Bengal B. Bihar
C. Jharkhand D. Madhya Pradesh

138. Who said 'Go back to Vedas'?
A. Dayanand Saraswati
B. Vivekananda
C. Swami Shradhananda
D. Ram Krishna Paramhansa

139. Who initiated 'Deen-e-elahi?
A. Jahangir B. Shershah
C. Aurangzeb D. Akbar

140. Coal production is highest in the state of:
A. Jharkhand B. Odisha
C. Bihar D. Madhya Pradesh

(IV) : ENGLISH

Directions (Qs. 141 to 145): *Fill in the blanks.*

141. The habit of working has been growing ____ the factory workers.
A. upon B. over
C. to D. with

142. He could not put up ___ the master's rudeness.
A. for B. in
C. at D. with

143. India is committed ___ a policy of peaceful co-existence.
A. in B. to
C. for D. with

144. He backed away stumbling _____ the door.
A. for B. through
C. at D. with

145. He has made all his efforts _____ passing the medical entrance examination.
A. against B. on
C. with D. in

Directions (Qs. 146 to 150): *Complete the sentence by adding correct sentence from the options.*

146. Though he was the best player :
A. moreover he was never chosen for the team
B. but he was never chosen for the team
C. on the other hand, he was never chosen for the team
D. he was never chosen for the team

147. I hope you ________.
A. are enjoying your meal
B. have been liking your meal
C. have enjoying your meal
D. are liking your meal

148. He went to the market after he
A. had completed his work
B. was completing his work
C. was completed with his work
D. had been completed his work

149. Please open the window : I wish
A. that I hear the band
B. for hearing the band
C. that I will hear the band
D. to hear the band

150. He ordered his servent
A. that go home
B. that he go to home
C. to go home
D. that he should go home

Directions (Qs. 151 to 155): *Choose the correct analogous word from the options.*

151. Temperature-Summer/<u>Humidity</u>- ?
A. Volcano B. Ocean
C. River D. Rain

152. Bulb-Light /Chimney?
A. Smoke B. Watch
C. Night D. Stone

153. Physician-Patient/Leader-?

A. Chair B. Public
C. Voter D. Self

154. Writer-Book/Lyricist-?

A. Music B. Song
C. Poet D. Poem

155. Tiger-Forest/Man-?

A. Society B. Herd
C. Attic D. House

Directions (Qs. 156 to 160): *Choose the incorrect word or phrase from underlined words not needed in the sentence.*

156. (A) Is there any more/(B) reasons/(C) that you can give for/(D) this defeat?

157. (A) However, jogging/(B) nor dieting/(C) carried to/(D) the extreme can be harmful.

158. (A) He is/(B) so/(C) clever/(D) as his brother.

159. (A) Although he is blind,/(B) but he /(C) can play chess/(D) skillfully.

160. (A) What will happen/ (B) suppose /(C) if we do not meet him /(D) there?

(V) हिन्दी

निर्देशः (प्रश्न 161 से 165 तक): *दिए गए गद्यांश को ध्यान पूर्वक पढ़कर पूछे गए प्रश्नों के उत्तर दीजिए।*

भारत की नारियों ने स्वतंत्रता संग्राम के समय अपनी शक्ति, त्याग और बलिदान का परिचय दिया। उन्होंने शिक्षा, विज्ञान और राजनीति के क्षेत्र में भी अपना अमूल्य योगदान देकर यह सिद्ध कर दिखाया है कि नारी में भवानी जैसी शक्ति भी विद्यमान है। समाज में नारी के अनेक रूप देखने को मिलते हैं। वह जहाँ माता का दायित्व निभाती है, वहीं वह पत्नी, बहन और बेटी के कर्त्तव्य का भी निर्वाह करती है। नारी गृहिणी के रूप में सम्पूर्ण परिवार की व्यवस्था को देखती है और पूरे घर का संचालन भी करती है। नारी विवेक सम्पन्न होती है, तभी तो उसका परिवार सुखमय और शान्तिपूर्वक जीवन व्यतीत करता है। नारी पत्नी के रूप में पति की मार्गदर्शिका, जीवन संगिनी, सहधर्मिणी मानी गई है। शिक्षित नारी अन्धविश्वासों और कुप्रथाओं के जाल में नहीं फँसती। यदि आज के वातावरण में देखा जाए, तो समाज का गौरव और स्वाभिमान नारी के बल पर ही टिका है। हमारा प्रयास नारी को प्रत्येक क्षेत्र में अग्रणी बनाने का होना चाहिए।

161. नारी देश और समाज के लिए क्या करती है?

A. नारी समाज में शिक्षिका बनती है।
B. नारी देश और समाज में अनेक कर्त्तव्यों का पालन करती है।
C. नारी का समाज में योगदान नगण्य है।
D. नारी समाज का एक हिस्सा बनती है।

162. स्वतंत्रता संग्राम के समय नारी ने अपनी किन-किन शक्तियों का परिचय दिया?

A. अपने ज्ञान एवं कुशल व्यवहार का।
B. अपने विवेक एवं बुद्धि का।
C. अपनी संचालन शक्ति का।
D. अपनी शक्ति, त्याग और बलिदान का।

163. नारी विवेक सम्पन्न होती है, तभी तो उसका परिवार .... ।

A. सम्पन्न होता है
B. सभ्य कहलाता है
C. ज्ञानवान बनता है
D. सुखमय और शांतिपूर्वक जीवन व्यतीत करता है।

164. समाज में नारी कितने रूपों में जानी जाती है?

A. माँ एवं बहन
B. पत्नी एवं प्रेयसी
C. मार्गदर्शिका
D. माता, पत्नी, बहन एवं बेटी

165. हमारा प्रयास नारी को प्रत्येक क्षेत्र में .... बनाने का होना चाहिए।

A. सम्पन्न B. सुदृढ़
C. शक्तिशाली D. अग्रणी

निर्देशः (प्रश्न 166 से 180 तक): *निम्नलिखित प्रत्येक प्रश्न के साथ चार विकल्प दिये गये हैं। उनमें से सही विकल्प चुनिए।*

166. निम्नलिखित में से कौन-सा 'पुष्प' का पर्यायवाची नहीं है?

A. फूल B. कुसुम
C. वारण D. सुमन

167. 'पद्मावत' किस भाषा में रचित है?

A. ब्रज B. मगही
C. अवधी D. संस्कृत

168. निम्नलिखित में से हिन्दी भाषा का पहला समाचार-पत्र कौन-सा था?

A. बंगदूत
B. उदंत-मार्तण्ड
C. दैनिक भास्कर
D. युगांतर

169. 'तुषार' का अर्थ है:

A. पाला
B. हिमकण
C. हिम
D. कपूर

170. 'सिनेमा' किस प्रकार का शब्द है?

A. देशज़
B. विदेशज
C. तत्सम
D. तद्भव

171. 'स्वयं सत्ता में आ जाने वाला' कहलाता है:

A. जारज
B. स्वयंभू
C. स्वेदज
D. मानव

172. 'धनंजय' में कौन-सा समास है?

A. अव्ययीभाव
B. बहुव्रीहि
C. कर्मधारय
D. तत्पुरुष

173. 'अभिषेक' का सन्धि विच्छेद है:

A. अभि + सेक
B. अभिः + सेक
C. अभि + षेक
D. अभिः + षेक

174. 'विद्यालय' किस प्रकार की संज्ञा का उदाहरण है?

A. भाववाचक संज्ञा
B. व्यक्तिवाचक संज्ञा
C. जातिवाचक संज्ञा
D. द्रव्यवाचक संज्ञा

175. 'हँसना' कौन-सी क्रिया है?

A. सकर्मक
B. अकर्मक
C. प्रेरणार्थक
D. अपूर्ण

176. 'उत्तम' का विलोम शब्द है:

A. अधम
B. बुरा
C. अत्युत्तम
D. अनुपम

177. 'यथासंभव' में कौन-सा समास है?

A. अव्ययीभाव
B. द्वन्द्व
C. कर्मधारय
D. द्विगु

178. 'रबीन्द्र नाथ ठाकुर' को उनकी किस रचना के लिए नोबेल पुरस्कार मिला था?

A. कादम्बरी
B. गीतांजलि
C. नील दर्पण
D. राष्ट्रीय गीत

179. 'निम्नलिखित में से कौन-सा वाक्य शुद्ध है?

A. राम ने आज आना है।
B. हमें बड़ों की बात माननी चाहिए।
C. आज जोरों का वर्षा हो रही है।
D. उसकी आँखों में आँसू बह रहा है।

180. 'राजनीति' शब्द का विशेषण है:

A. राजनीतिक
B. राजनीतिज्ञ
C. राजनैतिक
D. राजनेतिक

ANSWERS

1	2	3	4	5	6	7	8	9	10
C	B	D	A	C	B	D	B	D	C
11	**12**	**13**	**14**	**15**	**16**	**17**	**18**	**19**	**20**
B	B	A	C	C	A	D	C	B	A
21	**22**	**23**	**24**	**25**	**26**	**27**	**28**	**29**	**30**
D	B	A	A	B	A	B	B	A	A
31	**32**	**33**	**34**	**35**	**36**	**37**	**38**	**39**	**40**
A	C	B	B	C	A	B	C	B	D
41	**42**	**43**	**44**	**45**	**46**	**47**	**48**	**49**	**50**
C	C	D	B	D	A	B	B	D	C
51	**52**	**53**	**54**	**55**	**56**	**57**	**58**	**59**	**60**
B	B	D	C	A	D	C	D	A	D
61	**62**	**63**	**64**	**65**	**66**	**67**	**68**	**69**	**70**
D	C	D	C	C	D	D	C	A	D

71	72	73	74	75	76	77	78	79	80
D	A	A	C	C	B	C	D	D	C
81	**82**	**83**	**84**	**85**	**86**	**87**	**88**	**89**	**90**
D	B	C	C	A	A	A	B	C	A
91	**92**	**93**	**94**	**95**	**96**	**97**	**98**	**99**	**100**
A	D	B	C	B	D	D	D	B	C
101	**102**	**103**	**104**	**105**	**106**	**107**	**108**	**109**	**110**
D	B	C	A	B	A	A	A	B	A
111	**112**	**113**	**114**	**115**	**116**	**117**	**118**	**119**	**120**
D	D	D	D	C	C	D	C	D	A
121	**122**	**123**	**124**	**125**	**126**	**127**	**128**	**129**	**130**
C	C	C	C	B	A	A	A	D	C
131	**132**	**133**	**134**	**135**	**136**	**137**	**138**	**139**	**140**
B	A	D	A	D	D	D	A	D	A
141	**142**	**143**	**144**	**145**	**146**	**147**	**148**	**149**	**150**
B	D	B	C	B	D	A	A	D	C
151	**152**	**153**	**154**	**155**	**156**	**157**	**158**	**159**	**160**
D	A	B	B	A	A	B	B	A	B
161	**162**	**163**	**164**	**165**	**166**	**167**	**168**	**169**	**170**
B	D	D	D	D	C	C	B	A	B
171	**172**	**173**	**174**	**175**	**176**	**177**	**178**	**179**	**180**
B	C	C	C	A	A	A	B	B	B

SOME SELECTED EXPLANATORY ANSWERS

11. 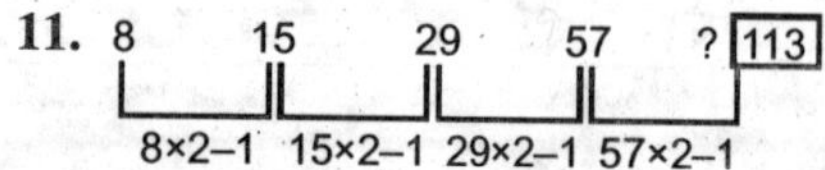

Hence, required number = 113.

13. 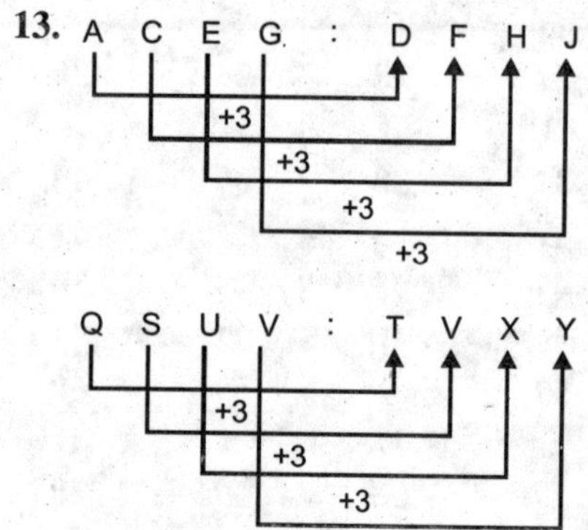

14. Gun, rifle and revolver are weapons used for firing bullets whereas saber is a heavy sword with curved blade used in the sport of fencing.

15. Glaucoma, cataract and trachoma are diseases related to eye whereas eczema is a medical condition in which patches of skin become rough.

16. 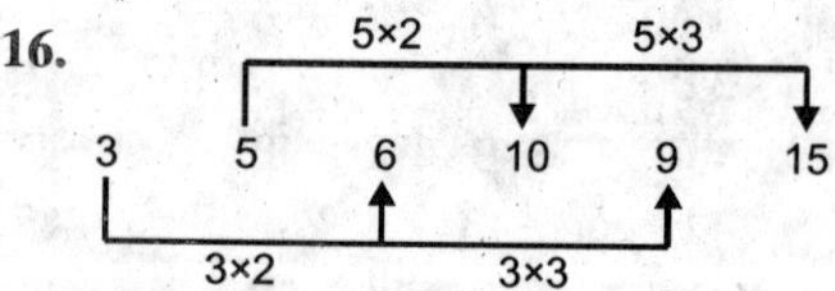

Hence, number 10 will be placed in place of the (?) mark in the number series.

17. 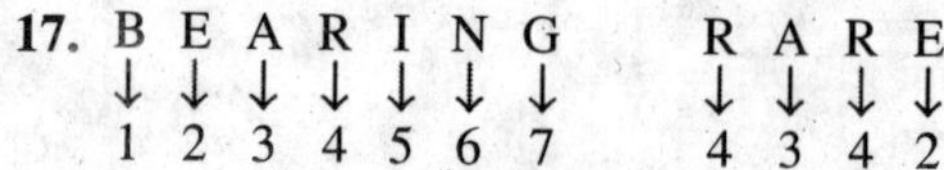

19. No. of women harvest the field in 3 days = 10

In 2 days = $\frac{10 \times 3}{2}$ = 15 women

Hence, required number of women = 15

20. Out of 450 students 360 students passed.

Required percentage = $\frac{360}{450} \times 100 = 80\%$

21. $x\%$ of 85 = 17

$\Rightarrow \frac{x}{100} \times 85 = 17 \quad \Rightarrow x = \frac{17 \times 100}{85} = 20\%$

Hence, 20% of 85 = 17.

22. Required percentage = $\left(\frac{25}{100+25} \times 100\right)$

$= \frac{25}{125} \times 100 = 20\%$

23. 51 km distance covers in 8.5 litres of diesel.

165 km distance covers in $\frac{8.5}{51} \times 165$ litrees

$= .5 \times 55 = 27.5$ litres

24. $\frac{23}{23} = \frac{23}{x}$

$\Rightarrow 1 = \frac{23}{x} \quad \Rightarrow x = 23.$

25. As friend behaves in a kind or friendly way. Opponent behaves in unfriendly or hostile way.

26. Cost of 16 cm of cloth = ₹ 60

Cost of 6 cm of cloth = ₹ $\frac{60}{16} \times 6$ = ₹ 22.5.

27. (272 – 172) of 20% $= 100 \times \frac{20}{100} = 20.$

28. HCF of 124 and 93 = 31

Hence, largest number = 31.

29. Required days = $\frac{15 \times 4}{6}$ = 10 days.

30. Required distance = $\frac{90}{2} \times 5 = 45 \times 5 = 225$ m.

101. Reciprocal of $x = \frac{1}{x}$

and reciprocal of $y = \frac{1}{y}$

Mean = $\frac{\frac{1}{x}+\frac{1}{y}}{2} = \frac{\frac{y+x}{xy}}{2} = \frac{x+y}{2xy}.$

102. $5\frac{1}{x} \times y\frac{3}{4} = 20$

$\Rightarrow \frac{5x+1}{x} \times \frac{4y+3}{4} = 20$

$\Rightarrow (5x+1)(4y+3) = 80x$

By putting $x = y = 3$ we get the required result.

Hence, $x = 3, y = 3$.

103. 1, 2, 4, 7, 13, 24, 44, ?

$1 + 2 + 4 = 7$

$2 + 4 + 7 = 13$

$4 + 7 + 13 = 24$

$7 + 13 + 24 = 44$

$13 + 24 + 44 = 81$

Hence, next number is 81.

104. 19, 38, 57, ... 988

$988 = a + (n-1)d = 19 + (n-1)19 = 19 + 19n - 19$

$\Rightarrow 19n = 988 \quad \Rightarrow n = 52$

$S_{52} = \frac{52}{2}\{2 \times 19 + (52-1)19\}$

$= 26\{38 + 51 \times 19\} = 26\{38 + 969\}$

$= 26 \times 1007 = 26182$

105. Let numbers are A, B and C.

A + B + C = 135 × 3 = 405

Let C = 180

∴ A + B = 405 – 180 = 225

B – A = 25

∴ 2B = 225 + 25 = 250

B = 125

A + B = 225 ⇒ A = 225 – 125 = 100

∴ Smallest number = 100.

106. 10% of 20 + 20% of 10

$= \frac{10}{100} \times 20 + \frac{20}{100} \times 10$

$= 2 + 2 = 4$

2% of $200 = \frac{2}{100} \times 200 = 4$

107. 70% of P = 40% of Q

$\Rightarrow \frac{70}{100} \times P = \frac{40}{100} \times Q$

$\frac{7P}{10} = \frac{4Q}{10} \quad \Rightarrow 7P = 4Q \quad \Rightarrow \frac{P}{Q} = \frac{4}{7}$

Hence, ratio of P : Q = 4 : 7.

108. In order to hear 12 strikes, there are 11 intervals (12 – 1) and time of each interval is uniform. Hence, time to hear each strike is $22 \div 11$ = 2 seconds.

Now to hear 6 strikes, there are (6 – 1) *i.e.*, 5 intervals for which the time taken is 5×2 = 10 seconds.

Hence, it will take 10 seconds for a clock to strike 6.

109. Other number $= \frac{HCF \times LCM}{\text{One number}}$

$= \frac{24 \times 5304}{408} = 312$.

110. Let present age of Gopal be x years

$\therefore$ Sohan's age = $3x$ years

5 years ago, Gopal's age = $(x - 5)$ years

5 years ago, Sohan's age = $(3x - 5)$ years

According to the question,

$3x - 5 = 4(x - 5)$

$\Rightarrow 3x - 5 = 4x - 20$

$\Rightarrow \quad x = 15$

Hence, Gopal's present age = 15 years.

112. $\tan 30° \times \cos 60° \times \sin 60°$

$= \frac{1}{\sqrt{3}} \times \frac{1}{2} \times \frac{\sqrt{3}}{2} = \frac{1}{4}$.

113. $\frac{\sin 39°}{\cos 51°} = \frac{\sin 39°}{\cos(90 - 39°)} = \frac{\sin 39°}{\sin 39°} = 1$.

114. 70% of $280 = \frac{70}{100} \times 280 = 196$

40% of $49 = \frac{40}{100} \times 49 \neq 196$

35% of $140 = \frac{35}{100} \times 140 = 49 \neq 196$

7% of $28 = \frac{7}{100} \times 28 = \frac{196}{100} \neq 196$

Hence, correct answer is D.

115. $x + (x + 1) + (x + 2) + (x + 3) + (x + 4) + (x + 5) + (x + 6) = 33 \times 7$

$7x + 21 = 231$

$\Rightarrow \quad 7x = 210$

$\Rightarrow \quad x = 30$

$\therefore$ The highest number = $x + 6 = 30 + 6 = 36$.

116. 0, 2, 6, ?, 30, 62

↓ ↓ ↓ ↓ ↓ ↓

0×2+2 2×2+2 6×2+2 14×2+2 30×2+2

Hence, the number in place of question mark = 14.

117. $5\frac{6}{7} \times 3\frac{1}{4} + 40\%$ of 35

$= \frac{41}{7} \times \frac{13}{4} + \frac{40}{100} \times 35$

$= \frac{533}{28} + 14 = \frac{533 + 392}{28}$

$= \frac{925}{28} = 33\frac{1}{28}$.

118. $1^4 = 1 \times 1 \times 1 \times 1 = 1$

$4^0 = 1 \quad (\because x^0 = 1)$

Hence, both are equal.

119. 1 is not a prime number.

120. $3 \times \sqrt{1.728} = 3 \times 1.31 = 3.93$

$\frac{\sqrt{3} - 1}{\sqrt{3} + 1} \times \frac{\sqrt{3} - 1}{\sqrt{3} - 1} = \frac{3 + 1 - 2\sqrt{3}}{3 - 1} = \frac{4 - 2\sqrt{3}}{2}$

$= \frac{2(2 - \sqrt{3})}{2} = 2 - \sqrt{3}$

$\left(\frac{1}{2}\right)^{-2} = \left(\frac{2}{1}\right)^{2} = \frac{2 \times 2}{1 \times 1} = \frac{4}{1} = 4$

$\frac{17}{8} = 2.125$

Hence, greatest number $= \left(\frac{1}{2}\right)^{-2}$.

Previous Paper (Solved)

IGNOU B.Ed. Entrance Test 2011

PART-A

SECTION-I : GENERAL ENGLISH COMPREHENSION

Directions: *Read the following passage carefully and choose the best answer out of the four choices given after each question that follow:*

According to Albert Einstein, the non-mathematician is seized by a mysterious shuddering when he hears of 'four - dimensional' things; he is seized by a feeling, which is very familiar to the thoughts awakened by the occult. And at the same time the statement that the world in which we live is a four-dimensional space-time continuum is quite a common - place statement.

This might lead to an argument regarding the use of the term "common place" by Einstein. Yet the difficulty lies more in the wording than the ideas. Einstein's concept of the universe as a four - dimensional space - time continuum becomes plain and clear, when what he means by continuum becomes clear. A continuum is something that is continuous; a ruler, for example, is a one - dimensional space continuum. Most rulers are divided into inches and fractions, scaled down to one - sixteenth of an inch. Will it be possible to conceive of a ruler, which is calibrated to a millionth or billionth of an inch. In theory there is no reason why the steps from point to point should not be even smaller. What distinguishes a continuum is the fact that the space between any two points can be sub-divided into an infinite number of small divisions.

A rail road track is one - dimensional space continuum and on it the engineer of a train can describe his position at any time by citing a single co-ordinate point, i.e. a station or a milestone. A sea captain, however, has to worry about two dimensions. The surface of the sea is two - dimensional continuum and the co-ordinate points by which a sailor fixes his positions in his two dimensional continuum are latitude and longitude. An airplane pilot guides his plane through a three - dimensional continuum, hence he has to consider not only latitude and longitude, but also his height above the ground. The continuum of an airplane pilot constitutes space as we perceive it. In other words, the space of our world is a three - dimensional continuum. Just indicating its position in space is not enough while describing any physical event, which involves motion. How position changes in time also needs to be mentioned. Thus to give an accurate picture of the operation of a New York-Chicago Express, one must mention not only that it goes from New York to Albany to Syracuse to Cleveland to Toledo to Chicago, but also the times at which it touches each of these points. This can be done either by means of a time table or a visual chart. If the miles between New York and Chicago are plotted horizontally on a piece of paper and the hours and minutes are plotted vertically, then a diagonal line properly drawn across the page illustrates the progress of the train in two - dimensional space-time continuum. This type of graphic representation is familiar to most newspaper readers, a stockmarket chart, for example, pictures financial events in a two dimensional dollar-time continuum. Similarly for the best picturization of the flight of an airplane from New York to Los Angeles, a four-dimensional space-time continuum is essential. The latitude, longitude and altitude will only make sense to the traffic manager of the airline if the time co-ordinate is mentioned. Therefore, time is the fourth dimension. If a flight has to be looked at, perceived as a whole, it wouldn't work if it is broken down into a series of disconnected takeoff, climbs, glides, and landing; it needs to be looked at and perceived as a continuous four-dimensional space-time continuum curve.

1. In order to explain a difficult topic, the author uses—
A. simply phrased definitions
B. a quotation from Einstein
C. an incessant metaphor
4. familiar images

2. The significant feature of a continuum, according to the passage, revolves around—
A. the divisibility of the interval between any two points
B an ordinary ruler's caliber for marking
C. its unending curve
D. its variety of co-ordinates

3. The purpose of this passage is to highlight the point that :
A. pilots and sea captains have something in common
B. stockmarket charts may be helpful to physicists
C. the fourth dimension is time
D non-mathematicians are often afraid of the common place

4. According to the passage, an airline's traffic manager depends upon all the following except—
A. latitude and longitude
B. altitude
C. the time co-ordinate
D. the continuous curve in co-ordinate four

5. The underlying tone of this passage is—
A. persuasive B. differential
C. candid D. instructive

6. According to the author, if one wishes to portray a physical event in which motion plays a role, one has to—
A make use of a time table
B. indicate how position changes in time
C. describe it graphically
D. be aware of altitude, latitude and longitude

7. The sea captain's example has been cited in order to—
A. help understand a two dimensional continuum
B. set up a logical progression
C. mitigate the gap between the engineer and pilot
D. to sustain our interest in the reading of the passage

8. 'Feeling' in the first paragraph is—
A. a noun B. a verb
C. a gerund D. an adjective

9. In the first paragraph, 'mysterious' is—
A. a noun B. a verb
C. an adjective D. none of these

10. In the first paragraph, the word 'Occult' has been used. Which of the following does not come under occult ?
A. Physics B. Mathematics
C. Chemistry D. All of these

SECTION - II : LOGICAL AND ANALYTICAL REASONING

Direction (*Q.11-14*): *Each of the following two statements are followed by two conclusions. Assuming that the given statements are true, you have to decide which conclusion follows strictly from the given statements. Select your answer from the alternatives.*

11. Statement:

All boys are not students.
Some students are not employed.

Conclusions :

I. These boys are not employed.
II. Some employed one are not boys.

A. Only I follows
B. Only II follows
C. Both I and II follow
D. Neither I nor II follows

12. Statements:
All furnitures are pens.
All pens are pencils.

Conclusions :
I. Some furnitures are pencils.
II. All pencils are furnitures.

A. Only I follows
B. Only II follows
C. Both I and II follow
D. Neither I nor II follows

13. Statements:
No dog is animal.
No animal is living being.

Conclusions:
I. No animal is dog.
II. Some living beings are dogs.

A. Only I follows
B. Only II follows
C. Both I and II follow
D. Neither I nor II follows

14. Statements:
No bird has wings.
All birds are rational.

Conclusions :
I. Wingless beings are birds.
II. Some rationals are birds.

A. Only I follows
B. Only II follows
C. Both I and II follow
D. Neither I nor II follows

Direction ***(Q.15-18)***: *In the following questions a series is being given. Select from the alternatives the correct term to fill in the missing term.*

15. 5, 7, 10, 11, 15, 15, 20,..........

A. 22 B. 19
C. 20 D. 21

16. $\frac{2}{\sqrt{5}}, \frac{3}{5}, \frac{4}{5\sqrt{5}}, \frac{5}{25}, ...$

A. $\frac{6}{25}$ B. $\frac{7}{25}$
C. $\frac{6}{25\sqrt{5}}$ D. $\frac{7}{25\sqrt{5}}$

17. 3, 15, 39, 75,......,

A. 93 B. 101
C. 99 D. 123

18. 25, 25, 27, 22, 30, 19, 34, 16,.......

A. 39 B. 35
C. 32 D. 13

Directions ***(Q.19-22)***: *The following questions are based on the following diagrams. Circles (irrespectives of the size or location) represent objects. You have to identify which of the following diagrams would represent best the relationship between given terms.*

(A) (B) (C) (D) (E)

19. Which of the above five diagrams would best represent - Musicians, Instrumentalists, Violinists?

A. (A) B. (B)
C. (C) D. (E)

20. Which of the above five diagrams would best represent - People, Painters, Boys?

A. (E) B. (D)
C. (A) D. (B)

21. Which of the above five diagrams would best represent - Mothers, Fathers and Teachers?

A. (A) B. (B)
C. (D) D. (E)

22. Which of the above five diagrams would best represent - Men, Women and Children?

A. (A) B. (C)
C. (E) D. None

Direction ***(Q.23-26)***: *In the following questions, there are two sets of figures. You have to find a figure from the answer figures which can best suit the question figure series.*

23. Problem Figure

Answer Figures

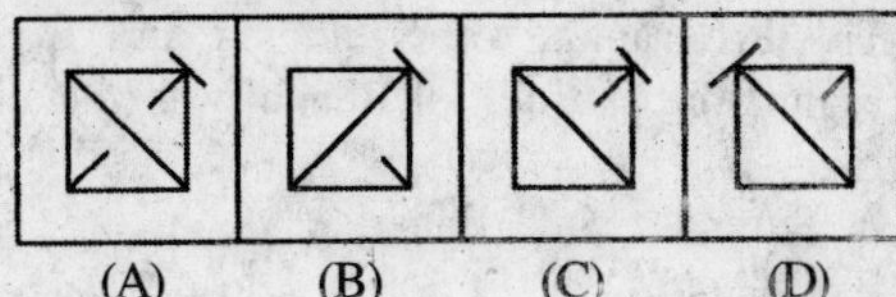

24. Problem Figure

Answer Figures

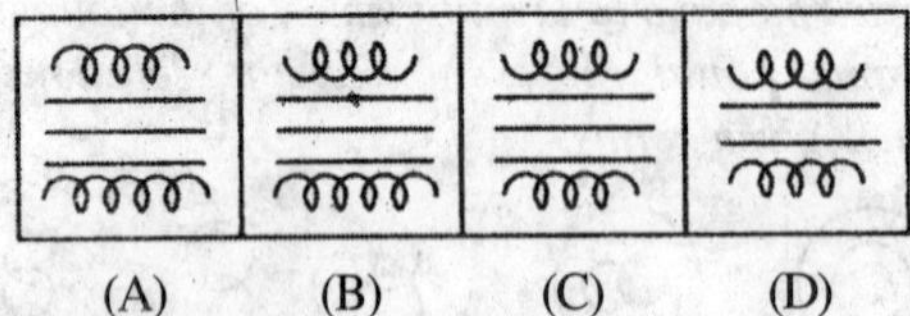

25. Problem Figure

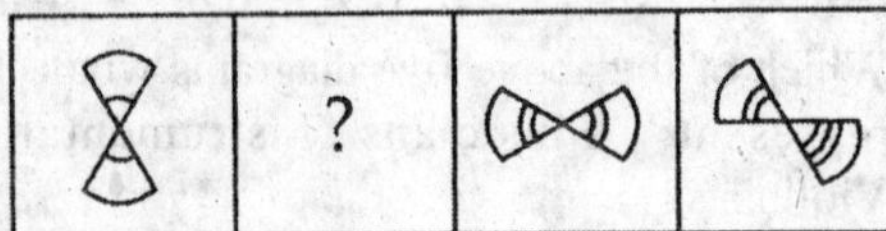

Answer Figures

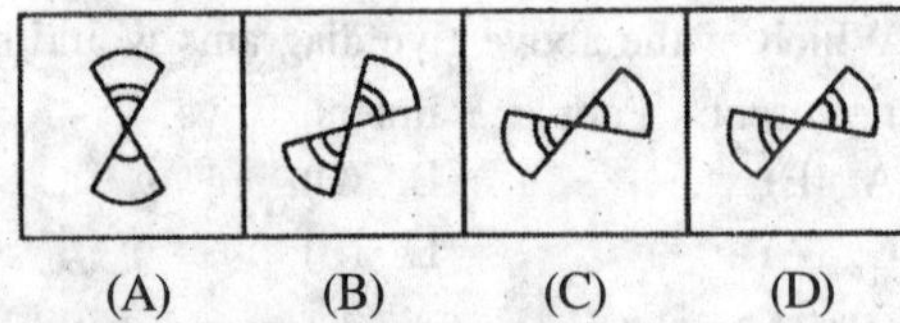

26. Problem Figure

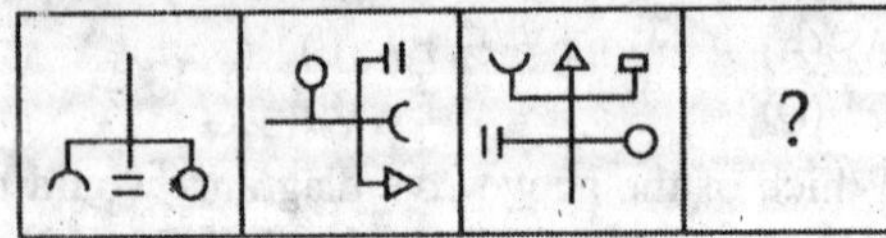

Answer Figures

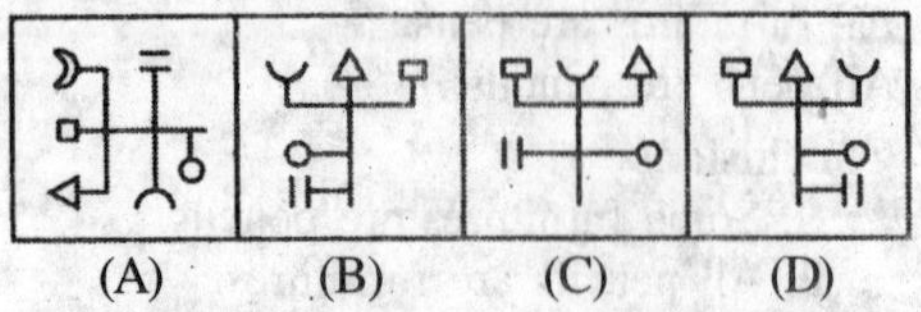

27. A student gets one mark for every correct answer but 1/3 mark is deducted for every wrong answer he gives. In 108 questions his total score is zero. How many questions has he answered wrong?

A. 27 B. 30
C. 81 D. 54

28. Identify the odd member of this group?

A. 13 B. 61
C. 73 D. 69

29. In the following arrangement of numbers how many times 5 is preceded by 4 but not followed by 7 ?

4 5 7 1 2 5 4 6 4 5 4 7 5 4 5 6 5 7 4

A. ....1 B. 2
C. ....3 D. 4

30. If

SHAPE is BURST
BORE is XLKT
CLIME is YAPCT

then BISHOP can be coded as :

A. XPBULS B. XEPLST
C. XPALUE D. XPBVLT

SECTION-III : EDUCATION AND GENERAL AWARENESS

Direction: *Each question is followed by four alternative responses. Choose the best answer and write its serial number.*

31. Gandhiji's 'Champaran Movement' was for—

A. The security rights of Harijans
B. Civil disobedience movement
C. Maintaining the unity of Hindu Society
D. Solving the problems of indigo workers

32. The Programme of Swadeshi and Boycot against the partition of Bengal was visualized by—

A. Surendra Nath Banerjee
B. B.C.Pal
C. Aurobindo Ghosh
D. Rash Behari Ghosh

33. Right to Education 2009 provides for : —

A. Free and Compulsory Elementary Education to all children up to the age of 14 years
B. Free and Compulsory Elementary Education to all children upto the age of 18 years
C. Free and Compulsory Elementary Education to all children in the age group of 6-14 years
D. Free and Compulsory Elementary Education to all children in the age group of 6 - 18 years

34. The soft smooth feel of the skin with "after shave lotion" is due to the presence of :

A. Alcohol B. Glycerol
C. Menthol D. Perfume

35. The fourth dimension in Physics was introduced by—

A. Isaac Newton B. Albert Einstein
C. Galileo D. Neil Bohr

36. Which of the following is rich in Carbohydrates, Proteins and Fats ?

A. Rice grains B. Soyabean seeds
C. Mango fruit D. Cabbage leaves

37. The main purpose of Panchayat Raj is—

A. to create employment
B. to make people politically conscious
C. to increase agriculture production
D. to make people participate in developmental administration

38. The longest sea shore line is along the state of—

A. Gujarat B. Maharashtra
C. Orissa D. Kerala

39. In India, Diamonds are found at—

A. Panna (M.P.)
B. Golconda (A.P.)
C. Khetri (Rajasthan)
D. Mayurbhanj (Orissa)

40. The most malleable metal is—

A. Platinum B. Silver
C. Iron D. Gold

41. Soda water contains—

A. Carbonic Acid B. Sulphuric Acid
C. Nitric Acid D. Carboxylic Acid

42. Who said, "The Principles (Directive Principles) should be made the basis of all the future legislation"?

A. Pt. Nehru B. Dr. B.R. Ambedkar
C. Dr. B.N. Rao D. Dr. Zakir Hussain

43. Indian National Congress was born during the Governor Generalship of—

A. Lord Ripon
B. Lord William Bentick
C. Lord Dufferin
D. Lord Curzon

44. Chanakya was also known as—

A. Bhattasvamin B. Vishnu Gupta
C. Rajasekhara D. Visakhadutta

45. Which one of the following is NOT an astronomical object ?

A. Pulsar B. Brittle star
C. Black hole D. Quasar

46. Who among the following Gurus introduced the Gurumukhi script for the spoken language of Punjabis ?

A. Guru Nanak B. Guru Angad
C. Guru Amardas D. Guru Ramdas

47. Mudaliar Commission had focussed on—

A. Elementary Education
B. Secondary Education
C. Higher Secondary Education
D. Higher Education

48. Rashtriya Madhyamik Shiksha Abhiyan (RMSA) is—

A. a programme run by NGOs and supported by the government.
B. a programme sponsored by donor agencies from abroad.
C. a programme run on "no profit no loss" basis.
D. a programme of the Government of India for Universalization of Secondary Education.

49. A committee in the post independence era that looked into various aspects of vocational education was headed by—

A. Ishwar Bhai Patel
B. Triguna Sen
C. Malcom Adisheshaiyah
D. M.G. Chhagla

50. The concept of Neighbourhood schools was given by—

A. Radhakrishnan Commission
B. Mudaliar Commission
C. Kothari Commission
D. All the above

51. Basic Education was conceptualized by—

A. Dr. Rajendra Prasad
B. Dr. Zakir Hussain
C. Mahatma Gandhi
D. Rabindra Nath Tagore

52. The World Conference on Education For All (EFA) was held on Jomtien (Thailand) in the year :

A. 1986 B. 1990'

C. 1992 D. 2000

53. District Institutes of Education and Training came into existence owing to :

A. Recommendations of Kothari Commission.

B. Recommendations of the NCERT.

C. Recommendations of National Policy on Education (1986).

D. Recommendations of Rama Murthy Committee.

54. Quality of school education can be improved by—

A. providing more trained teachers.

B. improving text books.

C. improving classroom processes.

D. All of the above.

55. Education for values cannot be imparted formally because—

A values are disputable

B. there is dearth of teachers

C. these are acquired by grown ups

D. these are caught and not taught

SECTION-IV : TEACHING-LEARNING AND SCHOOL

56. A school curriculum can best be defined as—

A. sum total of knowledge to be provided to learners

B. the sum total of organised pupil experiences under the patronage of the school

C. the complete array of the courses of study

D. all the materials used to further pupil's activities

57. The chief objective of organising work experiences in school is—

A. preparing youths for future vocations

B. establishing relationship between school and workplace

C. providing free time to teachers after engaging students

D. co-ordinated development of learners besides cognitive development

58. Who should select the Instructional Materials—

A. The teacher

B. Head of the Department

C. Principal of the Institute

D. A committee of experts

59. Why should classroom furniture be movable ?

A. it is easier to maintain

B. it helps maintain discipline

C. it suits to the different instructional needs

D. it is economical in cost

60. What should be the primary function of a school as an agent of society ?

A. To maintain social norms.

B. To prepare the child for social life.

C. To provide students understanding of their environment.

D. To develop vocational competence among students.

61. What should be the main goal of the school learning process ?

A. Development of potentialities of the learner

B. Assimilation of knowledge

C. Development of learners in both cognitive and non-cognitive areas

A. Development of values and attitudes

62. A teacher should be well versed with the theories of learning because—

A. it helps the teacher to know the needs of the learners

B. it helps the teacher to understand the attitudes and interests of the learners

C. it helps the teacher to know the ways different students learn

D. it ensures discipline in the classroom

63. What should be the basic determinant of a good discussion in a class ?

A. Skills of the teacher

B. Knowledge of the teacher and students

C. The unity of purpose and interest of the class
D. Mastery over the topic

64. Which one of the following can not be related to identity need of adolescents ?
A. Need to get higher achievement
B. Need to be recognised
C. Need to belong
D. None of the above

65. 'MLL' is basically an approach which assumes—
A. all students can learn a task
B. every learning task can't be learnt
C. objectives can be achieved if defined well
D. none of the above

66. The modern concept of Education is based on the belief that—
A. it rely only on concrete experiences as the medium.
B. child should adapt to the needs and goals of the society.
C. education should synchronize with child's motives, needs and interests.
D. academic competence should play a supreme role.

67. Probably the greatest satisfaction in teaching is—
A. a feeling of love for and by children
B. a sense of service to mankind
C. a secured monetary gain
D. a sense of contribution to pupils growth

68. Who would be the worst sufferer in common school in terms of scholastic achievement ?
A. Backward child B. Girl child
C. Normal child D. Gifted child

69. Readiness of a child for a specific school subject would depend upon—
A. his physiological maturity
B. his previous academic achievements
C. his motivational level and self-concept
D. None of the above

70. The best rationale for the use of A-V aids lies in the fact that—
A. it facilitates teaching - learning process
B. it makes learning concrete
C. it activates our two senses
D. it is just other way of doing the thing

71. 'Epidiascope' equipment can be used for—
A. seeing things clearly
B. projecting an opaque object on screen
C. copying an object
D. enlarging an object

72. Which of the following can not be a part of a test to measure intellectual ability of a learner?
A. To meet the demand of a situation
B. To learn and use past learning
C. To solve the problems which a learner confronts
D. To make sound ethical judgements and moral decisions

73. In which area of the following maximum transfer of training is possible ?
A. Memorization B. Generalization
C. Perception D. Habit formation

74. Which of the following is likely to be the greatest threat to an emotionally insecure child?
A. No discipline at all
B. Over-indulgent discipline
C. Adult - imposed discipline
D. Self - regulated discipline

75. What should a teacher do, in order to promote long-term retention ?
A. Avoid occurrence of mistakes
B. Encourage remembering the material accurately
C. Use the material during discussion and provide some more advanced material
D. Reinforce the learning with the introduction of similar material immediately

76. The art and science of teaching to adolescent learners is termed as :
A. Andragogy
B. Pedagogy
C. Teaching Technology
D. Behaviour Modification

77. Which one of the following is the right sequence of the process of teaching ?
[D $\rightarrow$ delivery; E $\rightarrow$ Evaluation; F $\rightarrow$ Feedback
K $\rightarrow$ Knowing the target learner; P $\rightarrow$ Planning]

A. PKDEF B. KPDFE
C. PKDFE D. KPDEF

78. What is the basic difference between Teaching and Learning ?
A. Teaching is mediated behaviour, learning, is not.
B. Learning is mediated behaviour, teaching is not.
C. Both are mediated behaviour.
D. There is no difference.

79. On a particular rainy day, your students are not in a mood to study. What would you prefer to do ?
A. ask them to go to the library
B. revise a lesson
C. organise a quiz programme on a topic
D. give dictation

80. Which of the following would be the best way to inculcate value - co-operation among your students ?
A. Organise a lecture on the topic
B. Organise cultural programme
C. Organise a camp for one
D. Playing a role model

PART-B

SECTION-V (I): SCIENCE

81. Refractive index of a medium—
A. has no unit
B. has an unit
C. has a value equal to 1 or less than one
D. has a value less than one

82. Three primary colours are—
A. red, green and yellow
B. red, green and blue
C. green, yellow and orange
D. violet, yellow and red

83. Which physical quantity is represented by Coulomb per second ?
A. charge B. electric current
C. potential difference D. resistance

84. A wire of resistance 2 ohms is bent in the form of a closed circle. The effective resistance between the two points at the end of any diameter of the circle is ;
A. 0.5 ohm B. 1 ohms
C. 2 ohms D. 4 ohms

85. The frequency of an alternating current whose direction changes after every 0.01 second is :
A. 1 Hz B. 2 Hz
C. 50 Hz D. 100 Hz

86. How much solar energy will be received by 1 m^2 area in one hour ? (Solar constant = 1.4 kW/m^2)—
A. 1400 × 1 J B. 1400 × 60 J
C. 1.40 × 60 × 60 J D. 1400 × 60 × 60 J

87. Speed of light is maximum in the following (out of 4 given media)—
A. water B. glass
C. diamond D. air

88. Average age of red blood cells (RBC) is approximately :
A. one day B. 30 days
C. 60 days D. 120 days

89. On adding lime juice to distilled water its pH—
A. remains unchanged
B. becomes 7
C. becomes less than 7
D. becomes more than 7

90. The valency shown by an element having atomic number 12 is—
A. 1 B. 2
C. 4 D. 6

91. Chemical formula for baking soda is—
A. NaOH B. $NaHCO_3$
C. $Ca(OH)_2$ D. Na_2CO_3

92. Pure gold is :
A. 1 carat gold B. 18 carat gold
C. 22 carat gold D. 24 carat gold

93. The agency responsible for running space research programmes in India is—
A. IRS B. UGC
C. ISRO D. IARI

94. The first Indian satellite sent to space was named—

A. Rohini B. Dhruv

C. Aryabhatt D. Sputnik

95. In Hydrilla plant stomata are present—

A. On stem

B. On leaves

C. On both stem and leaves

D. No where as they are absent in Hydrilla

96. The excretory unit of kidney is—

A. neuron B. hormone

C. photon D. nephron

97. The author of the book 'The origin of species' is—

A. Charles Darwin B. Lamarck

C. J.D. Watson D. Weismann

98. The time period of geosynchronous satellite is—

A. One hour

B. Twelve Hours

C. Twenty-four hours

D. One year

99. If we draw a V-I graph for a conductor (V = P.D. across the conductor and I = current flowing through it) it will be as shown in figure.

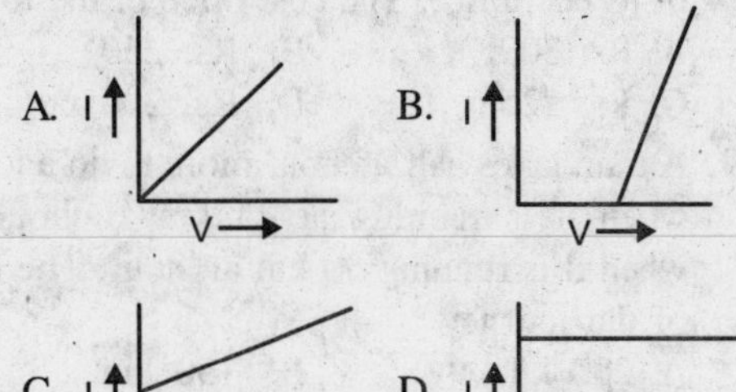

100. AIDS is caused by—

A. Fungus B. Virus

C. Bacterium D. Malnutrition

(II) : MATHEMATICS

101. The value of $\frac{1}{1+\sqrt{2}}+\frac{1}{\sqrt{2}+\sqrt{3}}+\frac{1}{\sqrt{3}+\sqrt{4}}$ $+.........+\frac{1}{\sqrt{8}+\sqrt{9}}$ is :

A. 1 B. –1

C. 2 D. –2

102. The smallest number which is a perfect square and contains 7936 as a factor is :

A. 264016 B. 241606

C. 246160 D. 246016

103. The value of

$$\left(\frac{1}{x^{a-b}}\right)^{\frac{1}{a-c}}\times\left(\frac{1}{x^{b-c}}\right)^{\frac{1}{b-a}}\times\left(\frac{1}{x^{c-a}}\right)^{\frac{1}{c-b}}$$ is—

A. 0

B. –1

C. 1

D. 2

104. A sum of Rs. 1200 is lent partly at 6% and partly at 4%. If the total interest for $3\frac{1}{2}$ years be Rs. 224, the amount lent at 6% is—

A. Rs. 800 B. Rs. 252

C. Rs. 224 D. Rs. 168

105. A's share is to B's share as 3 : 4 and B's share is to C's share as 6 : 7. The ratio of the shares of A to C is—

A. 12 : 14 B. 9 : 12

C. 9 : 14 D. 4 : 6

106. The price of sugar increased by 25%. How much per cent should a man decrease his consumption so that there is no increase in his expenditure ?

A. 25% B. 20%

C. 15% D. 10%

107. The list price of a pen is Rs. 160. A customer buys it for Rs. 122.40. He gets two successive discounts - one 10% and the other unknown. The rate of second discount is—

A. 4% B. 15%
C. 6% D. 8%

108. A man sells a toy for Rs. 80 more than he paid for it and realizes a profit equal to two-fifths of its cost price. The cost price of the toy is—

A. Rs. 300 B. Rs. 250
C. Rs. 225 D. Rs. 200

109. A train takes half an hour more to do a journey when it is running at 25 km an hour than when it is running 30 km an hour. The length of the journey is—

A. 200 km B. 150 km
C. 100 km D. 75 km

110. The value of

$$\left(\frac{\sin 27°}{\cos 63°}\right)^2 + \left(\frac{\cos 63°}{\cos 27°}\right)^2 - 2 \sin 30° \text{ is :}$$

A. 2 B. –2
C. 1 D. –1

111. The value of 0 less than 90° which satisfy the equation $3 \tan \theta + \cot \theta = 5 \operatorname{cosec} \theta$ is :

A. 30° B. 45°
C. 60° D. 15°

112. From the top of a building 60 metres high the angles of depression of the top and bottom of a tower are observed to be 30° and 60°. The height of the tower is :

A. 40 m B. $40\sqrt{3}$ m
C. 20 m D. $20\sqrt{3}$ m

113. The ages of 12 persons are given below :
48, 42, 47, 43, 48, 56, 50, 56, 65, 56, 65, 60
The modal age is :

A. 65 B. 56
C. 50 D. 60

114. A room 5 m long and 4 m wide is surrounded by a Verandah which occupies 22 sq m. The width of the Verandah is :

A. 1 m B. 1.5 m
C. 2 m D. 2.5 m

115. A cone and a cylinder are of the same height. Their radii of the bases are in the ratio of 2 : 1. The ratio of their volumes is :

A. 2 : 3 B. 3 : 2
C. 3 : 4 D. 4 : 3

116. A right circular cone is 8 cm high and the radius of the base is 2 cm. The cone is melted and recast into a sphere. The diameter of the sphere is :

A. 8 cm B. 6 cm
C. 4 cm D. 2 cm

117. The mean of the following data is 20.6.

x :	10	15	20	25	35
f :	3	10	x	7	5

The missing frequency (x) is

A. 25 B. 15
C. 10 D. 8

118. If two coins are tossed once, the probability of getting at least one head is :

A. $\frac{1}{2}$ B. $\frac{1}{4}$
C. $\frac{2}{3}$ D. $\frac{3}{4}$

119. If two of the vertices of a ΔABC are (1, 2), (4, 5) and (5, 3) is the centroids then the third vertex of the triangle is :

A. (10, 2) B. (15, 9)
C. (5, 9) D. (15, 3)

120. The sum to n terms of an A.P is given by $3n^2 + 3n$. The 5th term of the A.P is :

A. 42 B. 36
C. 30 D. 24

(III) : SOCIAL SCIENCE

Directions: *Choose the correct answer out of the four :*

121. The most important kingdom in Deccan and Central India after the Maurya has that of the :

A. Satvahans B. Cholas
C. Pallavas D. Pandyan

122. Alberuni came to India in :

A. 9th Century AD
B. 10th Century AD

C. 11th Century AD
D. 12th Century AD

123. The planning commission was set up in :
A. March 1950 B. March 1951
C. April 1951 D. April 1952

124. What is the consequence of the writ of Habeas Corpus?
A. The person under detention is set free
B. The public servant is restrained from taking any action
C. The officer not competent to take certain action is told not to go ahead with the action
D. More information is sought from the lower court

125. Which of the following river is called 'Biological Desert' due to heavy population?
A. Brahmaputra B. Ganga
C. Damodar D. Yamuna

126. Which of the following foreign kings was not a contemporary of Ashoka?
A. Antiochos Theos
B. Magas
C. Ptolemy Philadelphos
D. Daurius II

127. Who is remembered as the pioneer of Economic Nationalism?
A. Bipin Chandar Pal
B. Gokhale
C. R.C. Dutt
D. Madan Mohan Malviya

128. Lapps inhabit—
A. East Africa
B. European Steppes
C. South American grasslands
D. European Tundra

129. India's national game is :
A. Football B. Cricket
C. Tennis D. Hockey

130. Who is one of the propounders of the binary star theories?
A. Laplace B. Kant
C. La-Pichon D. Jeffreys

131. In which state was Panchayat Raj first introduced?
A. Gujarat B. Rajasthan
C. Bihar D. Andhra Pradesh

132. The electoral system of India is largely based on the pattern of :
A. Britain B. France
C. USA D. None of these

133. Monoculture is a typical characteristic of :
A. Shifting cultivation
B. Subsistence farming
C. Specialized horticulture
D. Commercial grain farming

134. Horse latitudes is the term applied to the :
A. 0° – 5° N and S latitudes
B. Polar circles
C. 30° – 40° N and S latitudes
D. 40° – 60° N and S latitudes

135. In the vedic period goghna refers to :
A. One who gifts cattle
B. One who slaughters cattle
C. A guest
D. The bridegroom

136. 'Half an hour discussion' can be raised in the house of parliament after giving notice to the :
A. Presiding officer of the house
B. The Secretary - General of the house
C. The Secretary of the department of parliamentary affairs
D. Concerned minister

137. Fiscal policy is connected with :
A. Exports and imports
B. Public revenue and Expenditure
C. Issue of currency
D. Population control

138. Who of the following was the first speaker of Lok Sabha?
A. Hukum Singh
B. G.S. Dhilon
C. G.V. Mavalankar
D. Ananthaswayanam Ayenger

139. Who amongst the following was impeached in England for Acts Committed as Governor General of India?
A. Wellesley B. Cavendish Bentick
C. Cornwallis D. Warren Hastings

140. Which year is known as 'Year of the Great divide' with regard to population growth in India?
A. 1921 B. 1947
C. 1951 D. None of these

(IV) : English

Directions: *Choose the most appropriate response out of the four choices given after every question. Each question carries one mark.*

141. Which of the following words means the same as 'desultory?

A. purposeful B. planned
C. stray D. connected

142. The antonym of 'Abstemious' is :

A. festive B. hedonistic
C. boisterous D. frigid

143. The antonym of 'iota' is :

A. falsehood B. scrap
C. molecule D. plethora

144. A doctor who specialises in the treatment of the brain is called :

A. ophthalmologist B. cardiologist
C. neurologist D. pulmonologist

145. Choose the correctly spelt word :

A. procide B. proceed
C. procid D. procede

146. Choose the correctly spelt word :

A. pronunciation B. pronounciation
C. pronuncation D. pronouncation

147. The indirect form of the sentence :
She said, "I have finished my work" is :

A. She said I have finished my work.
B. She said she have finished my work.
C. She said that she had finished her work.
D. She said she has finished my work.

148. Choose the correctly spelt word :

A. inocuous B. inocous
C. innocuous D. innocous

149. The indirect form of the sentence : She asked her student "Have you done your homework?" is :

A. She asked her student have you done your homework
B. She asked her student if she has done your homework
C. She asked her student if she have done her homework
D. She asked her student whether she had done her homework

150. The passive voice of 'someone stole her purse' is :

A. A thief stole her purse.
B. Her purse has been stolen by someone.
C. Her purse has been stolen by a thief.
D. Her purse got stolen.

151. The active voice of 'He has been sent to Canada by his company for training' is :

A. He has gone to Canada for training.
B. His company sent him to Canada for training.
C. His company has sent him to Canada for training.
D. His company went to Canada for training.

152. The most appropriate word to fill in the blank in 'They __ come here next week'.

A. have B. will
C. had D. has

153. The most appropriate word to fill in the blank is 'I have not seen her __ ages'.

A. since B. for
C. till D. from

154. Desdemone was the heroine in which play of Shakespeare?

A. Hamlet
B. King Lear
C. Merchant of Venice
D. Othello

155. Who wrote the poem 'Ode on intimations of Immortality'?

A. Keats B. Byron
C. Wordsworth D. Shelly

156. In which novel is Gabriel Oak the hero?

A. Far from the Madding crowd
B. Emma
C. Mayor of Casterbridge
D. Return of the Nature

157. Who wrote the novel 'Wuthering Heights' ?

A. George Eliot B. Emily Bronte
C. Charlotte Bronte D. Jane Austen

158. The play 'Desire under the Elino' was written by :

A. Bernard Shaw B. Samuel Beckett
C. Eugene O'Neil D. Shakespeare

159. In the sentence 'Denmark is a country which is in Europe'—
which is in Europe is a :
A. Noun clause B. Adjective clause
C. Adverb clause D. None of the above

160. 'Ram, as well as Shyam, is an Engineer' is a :
A. Simple sentence
B. Compound sentence
C. Complex sentence
D. Complex - Compound sentence

(V) हिन्दी

निर्देश (प्रश्न 161 से 165 तक): *दिये गये गद्यांश को ध्यानपूर्वक पढ़िये और उसके आधार पर पूछे गये प्रश्नों के यथोचित उत्तर दीजिये:*

जिसके अन्दर जितनी पवित्र भावनाएं प्रवाहित होती हैं उतना ही आत्मा का तेज बढ़ता जाता है, आभामण्डल-विस्तृत होता जाता है। जहाँ अहंकार है, अशुद्ध भावनाएं हैं, उन सम्बन्धों में कभी भी निःस्वार्थ प्रेम पनप नहीं सकता है। आज हर एक प्राणी क्या चाहता है – प्रेम चाहिए। एक शिशु को भी प्यार चाहिए तो वयोवृद्ध भी प्रत्येक से प्रेमपूर्ण और आदर पूर्वक व्यवहार की अपेक्षा रखता है। ऐसा नहीं है कि बुजुर्ग ने सारे जीवन प्रेम और सम्मान पाया है तो अब बुढ़ापे मे उसे प्यार और सम्मान न भी मिले तो चलेगा। नहीं। हर इंसान को प्यार चाहिए और वह भी निःस्वार्थ, सहज और आत्मीय भाव से भरा हुआ। यह तभी सम्भव है जब परस्पर पवित्र भावनायें हों सामन्जस्यपूर्ण व्यवहार हो और निःस्वार्थ प्रेम प्रवाहित होता हो।

आज के तनावपूर्ण वातावरण में हर व्यक्ति सहानुभूति, सद्भाव और सौहार्द तो चाहता है किन्तु कैसी विडम्बना है कि यदि कोई प्यार से बात करता है तो व्यक्ति संशयग्रस्त होने लगता है कि यह व्यक्ति मुझसे इतने प्यार से क्यों व्यवहार कर रहा है? मुझसे इसकी क्या अपेक्षा है? लेकिन जहाँ समझदारी है वहाँ व्यक्ति प्रेमपूर्ण व्यवहार पाकर कृतज्ञता का अनुभव कर तनाव मुक्त हो जाता है। उसे मन में शान्ति और जीवन में सच्चे सुख की तत्काल अनुभूति होने लगती है।

प्रत्येक व्यक्ति जीवन में आनन्द की उपलब्धि चाहता है पर उसके जीवन में आनन्द और खुशी नहीं है। क्योंकि वह आत्मशक्ति जाग्रत करने के बारे में बेखबर है। आत्मा का निज गुण शान्ति और आनन्द है और यही उसकी शक्ति है। दूसरे शब्दों में यही आत्मा का स्वधर्म है। आत्मा में ज्ञान की शक्ति, पवित्रता, प्रेम और शान्ति की शक्ति है। प्रत्येक वस्तु का अपना गुणधर्म होता है। जैसे पानी का गुणधर्म है– शीतलता, अग्नि का गुणधर्म है– उष्णता। पानी को कितना ही उबालो किन्तु वह पुनः अपने शीतल स्वरूप में लौट आता है।

हम प्रार्थना के माध्यम से ईश्वर से सुख-शान्ति, शक्ति, ज्ञान और सद्भाव की ही तो मांग करते हैं। हम कहते हैं –'असतो मा सद् गमय।' 'तमसो मा ज्योतिर्गमय।' ऐसी प्रार्थना इसीलिए करते हैं कि हमारा स्वभाव 'असत' नहीं सत है, 'अन्धकार' नहीं ज्योतिर्मय है। हमें अपने स्वधर्म में स्थित होने पर ही सुख और शान्ति मिल सकती है। स्वधर्म में ही हमारे अन्दर पवित्र भाव जागते हैं। गीता में भी भगवान श्री कृष्ण अर्जुन को यही प्रेरणा देते हैं कि स्वधर्म को जाग्रत कर उसमें स्थित होकर युद्ध कर। मनुष्य अपने स्वधर्म से दूर हो गया है और परधर्म के अधीन हो गया है। ज्ञान के विपरीत अज्ञान और प्रेम के विपरीत अहंकार के वश में हो गया है। अहंकार और अज्ञान तो परधर्म है। मन में पवित्रता और शुद्धि के स्थान पर दुर्भावना और अपवित्रता आ गयी है। अपवित्रता तो परधर्म है। प्रेम के बदले नफरत आ गई है। ये नफरत परधर्म है। शान्ति के बदले जीवन में क्रोध आ गया है। ये क्रोध परधर्म है। परधर्म के अधीन होने पर ही व्यक्ति स्वयं में सहजता अनुभव नहीं करता है। गुणों के स्थान पर व्यक्ति के जीवन में काम, क्रोध, लोभ, मोह, ईर्ष्या, अहंकार और द्वेष का दबदबा है।

161. इस गद्यांश का उपयुक्त शीर्षक क्या होगा?
A. आभामण्डल B. निःस्वार्थ प्रेम
C. आत्मा का स्वधर्म D. शान्ति की प्राप्ति

162. किस प्रकार के प्रेम से जीवन में सहजता आती है?
A. अपेक्षापूर्ण B. उपेक्षापूर्ण
C. निःस्वार्थपूर्ण D. अपवित्रता रहित

163. गीता का प्रेरक संदेश क्या है?
A. परधर्म के अधीन न हों।
B. कर्म निःस्वार्थ भाव से करें।
C. आत्मस्थ होकर शान्तिलाभ करें।
D. युद्ध के बिना शान्ति और सुख नहीं मिलता।

164. व्यक्ति के आभामण्डल का विकास कब होता है?
A. अहंकार और अधिकार भावना से।
B. तनावमुक्त जीवन जीने की कला से।
C. आत्मशक्ति के विकास से।
D. निःस्वार्थ सेवा करने से।

165. स्वधर्म में स्थित होने का क्या तात्पर्य है?
A. अपने धर्म के अनुसार ही पूजा पाठ करें।
B. आत्मा के आध्यात्मिक गुणों का विकास करना।
C. ईर्ष्या, द्वेष, अहंकार और पाखण्ड छोड़ देना।
D. शान्ति और आनन्द का अनुभव करना।

निर्देश (प्रश्न 166 से 180 तक): *निम्नलिखित प्रत्येक प्रश्न के साथ-साथ चार-चार विकल्प दिये गये हैं। उनमें से सही विकल्प चुनिए।*

166. जायसी की 'पद्मावत' किस भाषा में रची गई है?
A. हिन्दी B. उर्दू
C. मराठी D. अवधी

167. रामचन्द्रिका किस कवि की कृति है?
A. मतिराम B. केशव
C. वृन्दकवि D. नरहरिदास

168. निम्नलिखित में से नरोत्तमदास की कृति कौन-सी है?
A. सुदामा चरिता B. कृष्णप्रिया
C. गोपी गीत D. उद्धव-संवाद

169. 'मृगनयनी' उपन्यास के लेखक कौन हैं?
A. भगवती चरण वर्मा B. हजारी प्रसाद द्विवेदी
C. वृन्दावनलाल वर्मा D. मन्नू भण्डारी

170. निम्नलिखित में से कौन-सी रचना गोस्वामी तुलसीदास की नहीं है?
A. हनुमान चालीसा B. हनुमान बाहुक
C. रामायण D. रामलला नहछू

171. निम्नलिखित में से किसकी वर्तनी अशुद्ध है?
A. प्रार्थ्य B. क्रतज्ञता
C. आनन्द D. आशीर्वाद

172. 'निरपेक्ष' शब्द का सन्धि विच्छेद होगा :
A. निर् + पेक्ष B. नि + पेंक्ष
C. निर + पेक्ष D. निः + अपेक्ष

173. निम्नलिखित में किस शब्द की वर्तनी शुद्ध है?
A. कृप्या B. उपरोक्त
C. आदर्णीय D. उज्ज्वल

174. प्राच्य का विलोम शब्द कौन-सा है?
A. उदीच्य B. प्रतीच्य
C. पाश्चात्य D. अर्वाचीन

175. 'दबदबा होना' इसका अर्थ क्या है?
A. दबकर रहना B. प्रभाव होना
C. हीन अनुभव करना D. भयभीत होना

176. व्यावहार्य की तरह 'उदार' से कौन-सा शब्द ठीक है?
A. औदार्य B. अनुदार्य
C. उदारता D. औदर्य

177. 'सौहार्द' शब्द किस शब्द से बना है?
A. सुहार्द B. सुहृद
C. सुहर्द D. सोहृद

178. 'जिसका कोई शत्रु न हो' इस कथन के लिए कौन-सा एक शब्द उचित है?
A. शत्रुन्जय B. रिपुसूदन
C. अजातशत्रु D. अरहन्त

179. 'तीरे हिये मेरे पीर रघुवीर के।' इस पद्यांश में कौन-सा अलंकार है?
A. विभावना B. असंगति
C. प्रतीप D. विशेषोक्ति

180. निम्नलिखित वाक्यों में कौन-सा वाक्य शुद्ध है?
A. हम तुम्हें बुलाये थे।
B. मैंने जो सोचा था वही हुआ।
C. कृप्या मुझे छुट्टी प्रदान करें।
D. मैंने आज ही घर जाना होगा।

ANSWERS

1	2	3	4	5	6	7	8	9	10
B	A	C	D	B	B	B	A	C	D
11	**12**	**13**	**14**	**15**	**16**	**17**	**18**	**19**	**20**
B	A	A	B	C	C	D	A	A	D
21	**22**	**23**	**24**	**25**	**26**	**27**	**28**	**29**	**30**
D	D	C	B	A	A	C	D	B	A
31	**32**	**33**	**34**	**35**	**36**	**37**	**38**	**39**	**40**
D	C	C	B	B	B	D	A	A	D
41	**42**	**43**	**44**	**45**	**46**	**47**	**48**	**49**	**50**
A	B	C	B	B	B	B	D	C	C
51	**52**	**53**	**54**	**55**	**56**	**57**	**58**	**59**	**60**
C	B	C	D	D	B	D	D	C	B
61	**62**	**63**	**64**	**65**	**66**	**67**	**68**	**69**	**70**
A	B	B	C	A	C	D	D	C	C
71	**72**	**73**	**74**	**75**	**76**	**77**	**78**	**79**	**80**
B	D	C	B	D	B	B	B	C	C
81	**82**	**83**	**84**	**85**	**86**	**87**	**88**	**89**	**90**
C	B	A	B	C	C	D	D	C	B
91	**92**	**93**	**94**	**95**	**96**	**97**	**98**	**99**	**100**
B	D	C	C	D	D	A	C	A	B
101	**102**	**103**	**104**	**105**	**106**	**107**	**108**	**109**	**110**
C	D	C	A	C	B	B	D	D	C
111	**112**	**113**	**114**	**115**	**116**	**117**	**118**	**119**	**120**
C	A	B	A	D	C	A	D	A	C
121	**122**	**123**	**124**	**125**	**126**	**127**	**128**	**129**	**130**
A	C	A	A	D	D	C	D	D	B
131	**132**	**133**	**134**	**135**	**136**	**137**	**138**	**139**	**140**
B	A	B	C	C	B	B	C	D	A
141	**142**	**143**	**144**	**145**	**146**	**147**	**148**	**149**	**150**
C	B	D	C	B	A	C	C	D	B
151	**152**	**153**	**154**	**155**	**156**	**157**	**158**	**159**	**160**
C	B	B	D	C	A	B	C	B	C
161	**162**	**163**	**164**	**165**	**166**	**167**	**168**	**169**	**170**
C	C	A	C	D	D	B	A	C	C
171	**172**	**173**	**174**	**175**	**176**	**177**	**178**	**179**	**180**
B	A	D	B	B	A	B	C	B	B

SOME SELECTED EXPLANATORY ANSWERS

11. All boys are not students
i.e., Some boys are students.
Some students are not employed
i.e., Some students are employed.

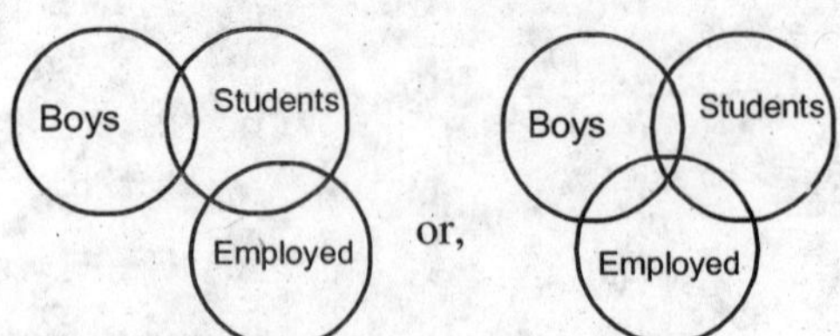

12.

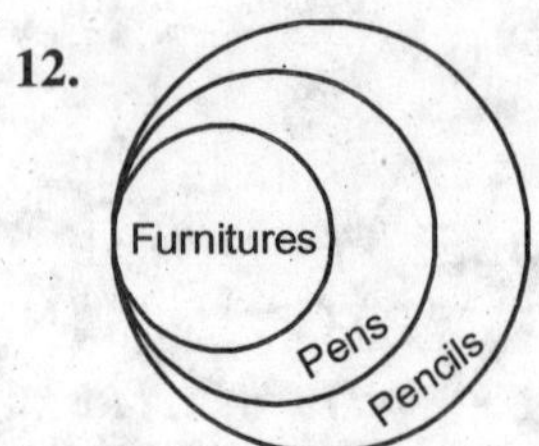

13.

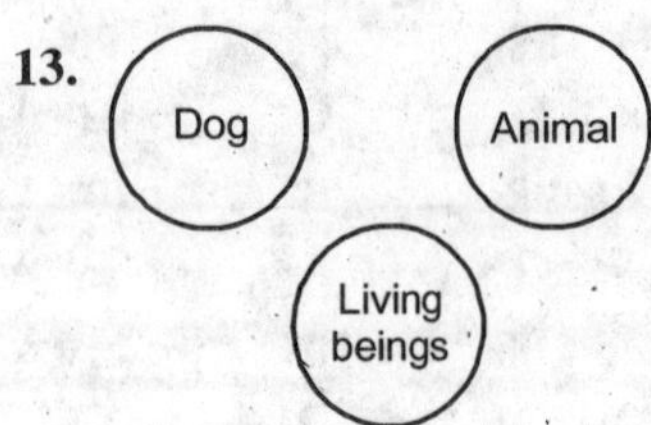

or,

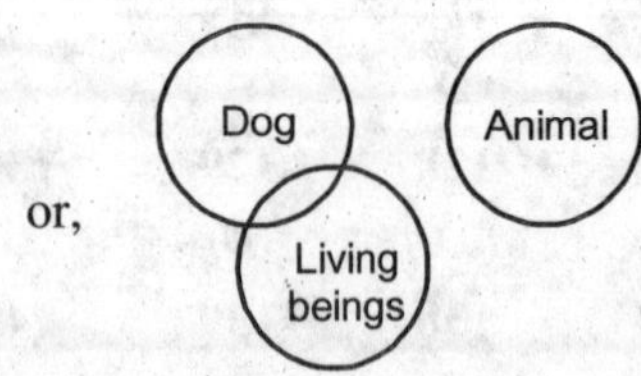

14. In the statement it has not said that only bird has not wings. Hence, we can not say that wingless beings are bird.

In the second statement it has said that all birds are rational, *i.e.,* some rationals are birds.

Hence, only conclusion (II) follows.

15. 5 7 10 15 15 20 [20]

+5 +5 +5

+8 +5

16. $\frac{2+1}{\sqrt{5}\times\sqrt{5}}=\frac{3}{5}$

$$\frac{3+1}{5\times\sqrt{5}}=\frac{4}{5\sqrt{5}},\ \frac{4+1}{5\sqrt{5}\times\sqrt{5}}=\frac{5}{25},$$

$$\frac{5+1}{25\times\sqrt{5}}=\frac{6}{25\sqrt{5}},$$

17. 3 15 39 75 [123]

+12 +24 +36 +48

18. 25 25 27 22 30 19 34 16 [39]

+2 +3 +4 +5

–3 –3 –3

19. All violinists are instrumentalist and all instrumentalists are Musician.

20. Some painters may be boys and some boys may be painters. But all painters and boys are people.

21. Some mothers and some fathers may be teachers but a father can not be a mother and vice-versa.

22. No diagram can represent the given words.

23. A line segment revolves round the square clockwise and second line segment appears at lower left corner after every two question figures.

24. Sum of line segment and rings of spring like design is in decreasing order as 14, 13, 12, 11 and 10.

25. Number of arcs in the both sides of intersection point of the question figure increases as 2, 3, 4, 5 ....

26. Number of designs in question figure increases as 3, 4, 5, 6 ....

27. Let the student answered x questions.

From question, $x-\frac{108-x}{3}=0$

$\Rightarrow\ 3x-108+x=0$

$\Rightarrow\ 4x=108$

$\therefore\ x=27$

Hence, required number of questions

$= 108 - 27 = 81.$

28. Rest are prime numbers.

101. $\frac{1}{1+\sqrt{2}} \times \frac{\sqrt{2}-1}{\sqrt{2}-1} = \frac{\sqrt{2}-1}{2-1} = \sqrt{2}-1$

$\frac{1}{\sqrt{3}+\sqrt{2}} \times \frac{\sqrt{3}-\sqrt{2}}{\sqrt{3}-\sqrt{2}} = \frac{\sqrt{3}-\sqrt{2}}{3-2} = \sqrt{3}-\sqrt{2}$

$\frac{1}{\sqrt{4}+\sqrt{3}} \times \frac{\sqrt{4}-\sqrt{3}}{\sqrt{4}-\sqrt{3}} = \frac{\sqrt{4}-\sqrt{3}}{4-3} = \sqrt{4}-\sqrt{3}$

....

$\frac{1}{\sqrt{9}+\sqrt{8}} \times \frac{\sqrt{9}-\sqrt{8}}{\sqrt{9}-\sqrt{8}} = \frac{\sqrt{9}-\sqrt{8}}{9-8} = \sqrt{9}-\sqrt{8}$

$\sqrt{2}-1+\sqrt{3}-\sqrt{2}+\sqrt{4}-\sqrt{3}+....+\sqrt{9}-\sqrt{8}$

$= -1+3 = 2.$

102. $246016 = 7936 \times 31 + 0.$

103. $x^{\circ} = 1.$

104. $SI = \frac{x \times 6 \times 7}{2 \times 100} = \frac{21x}{100}$

$SI = \frac{(1200-x) \times 4 \times 7}{2 \times 100} = \frac{14(1200-x)}{100}$

According to the question,

$\frac{21x}{100} + \frac{14(1200-x)}{100} = 224$

$21x + 16800 - 14x = 224 \times 100$

$\Rightarrow \quad 7x = 5600$

$x = 800$

$\therefore$ Amount lent at 6% = Rs 800.

105. $\frac{A}{B} = \frac{3}{4}$

$3B = 4A$

$B = \frac{4A}{3} \quad ...(i)$

Again $\frac{B}{C} = \frac{6}{7}$

$7B = 6C$

$B = \frac{6C}{7} \quad ...(ii)$

from (*i*) and (*ii*)

$\frac{4A}{3} = \frac{6C}{7}$

$28A = 18C$

$\frac{A}{C} = \frac{18}{28} = \frac{9}{14}$

$\therefore \quad A : C = 9 ; 14$

106. $\frac{25}{125} \times 100 = 20\%.$

107. $\because$ List Price = Rs 160

first dis = 10%

$Dis = 160 \times \frac{10}{100} = Rs\ 16$

S.P. of article after 10% dis = 160 – 16

= Rs 144.

Let second discount = x%

$Dis = 144 \times \frac{x}{100} = \frac{144x}{100}$

According to the question,

$144 - \frac{144x}{100} = 122.40$

$\frac{14400 - 144x}{100} = \frac{12240}{100}$

$144x = 2160$

$x = \frac{2160}{144} = 15$

$\therefore$ Second discount = 15%.

108. Let CP = Rs x

$\therefore \quad SP = x + 80$

Profit = $x + 80 - x$ = Rs 80

According to the question,

$80 = \frac{2}{5}$ of x

$\therefore \quad x = \frac{80 \times 5}{2} = 200$

The cost price of the toy = Rs 200.

109. Let distance = x km

time taken at speed 25 km/hr = $\frac{x}{25}$ hrs.

time taken at speed 30 km/hr = $\frac{x}{30}$ hrs.

According to the question,

$$\frac{x}{25} - \frac{x}{30} = \frac{1}{2} \Rightarrow \frac{6x - 5x}{150} = \frac{1}{2}$$

$\Rightarrow x = 75$

$\therefore$ The length of the Journey = 75 km.

110. $$\left[\frac{\sin 27°}{\cos(90 - 27°)}\right]^2 + \left[\frac{\sin(90 - 27°)}{\cos 27°}\right]^2 - 2 \times \frac{1}{2}$$

$$= \left(\frac{\sin 27°}{\sin 27°}\right)^2 + \left(\frac{\cos 27°}{\cos 27°}\right)^2 - 1$$

$= 1 + 1 - 1 = 1.$

111. $$\frac{3\sin\theta}{\cos\theta} + \frac{\cos\theta}{\sin\theta} = \frac{5}{\sin\theta}$$

$$\frac{3\sin^2\theta + \cos^2\theta}{\cos\theta \cdot \sin\theta} = \frac{5}{\sin\theta}$$

$$3(1 - \cos^2\theta) + \cos^2\theta = 5\cos\theta$$

$$2\cos^2\theta + 5\cos\theta - 3 = 0$$

$$2\cos^2\theta + 6\cos\theta - \cos\theta - 3 = 0$$

$$2\cos\theta(\cos\theta + 3) - 1(\cos\theta + 3) = 0$$

$$(2\cos\theta - 1)(\cos\theta + 3) = 0$$

either $\cos\theta = \frac{1}{2}$ or $\cos\theta = -3$ not possible.

$\cos\theta = \cos 60°$

$\Rightarrow \quad \theta = 60°.$

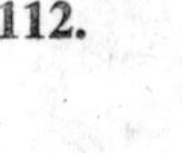

112.

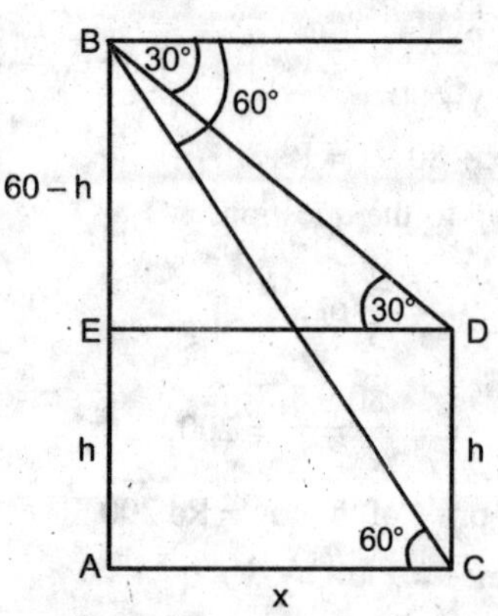

Let AB is building and CD is tower.

In ΔABC,

$$\tan 60° = \frac{60}{x}$$

$$\sqrt{3} = \frac{60}{x}$$

$$x = \frac{60}{\sqrt{3}} \times \frac{\sqrt{3}}{\sqrt{3}} = 20\sqrt{3} \quad ...(i)$$

In ΔBED,

$$\tan 30° = \frac{60 - h}{x}$$

$$\frac{1}{\sqrt{3}} = \frac{60 - h}{x}$$

$$x = \sqrt{3}(60 - h) \quad ...(ii)$$

from (*i*) and (*ii*)

$$\sqrt{3}(60 - h) = 20\sqrt{3}$$

$$h = 60 - 20$$

$$h = 40$$

$\therefore$ Height of the tower = 40 m.

113. The number 56 is used 3 times.

$\therefore$ mode = 56.

114. Let width of the verandah = x m.

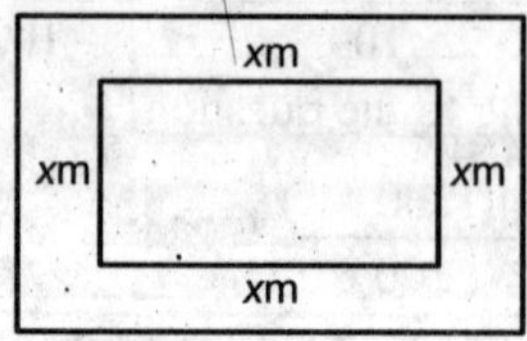

Area without verandah = $5 \times 4 = 20$ m^2

Area with verandah = $(5 + x + x)(4 + x + x)$ m^2

According to the question,

$$(5 + 2x)(4 + 2x) = 20 + 22 = 42$$

$$20 + 10x + 8x + 4x^2 = 42$$

$$4x^2 + 18x - 22 = 0$$

$$2x^2 + 9x - 11 = 0$$

$$2x^2 + 11x - 2x - 11 = 0$$

$$x(2x + 11) - 1(2x + 11) = 0$$

$$(2x + 11)(x - 1) = 0$$

$x = 1$ or $x = \frac{-11}{2}$ not possible.

$\therefore$ The width of the verandah = 1m.

115.

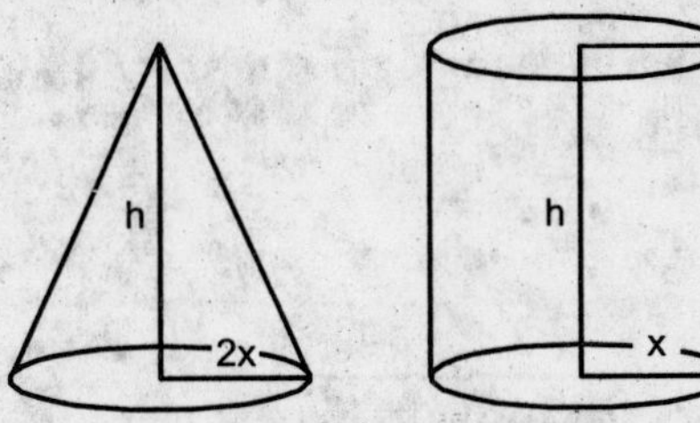

$$\frac{\text{Volume of cone}}{\text{Volume of cylinder}} = \frac{1}{3}\frac{\pi(2x)^2 \times h}{\pi x^2 \times h} = 4:3.$$

116. Volume of the cone = Volume of sphere

$$\frac{1}{3}\pi(2)^2 \times 8 = \frac{4}{3}\pi r^3$$

$$32 = 4r^3$$

$$r = 2$$

$\therefore$ The diameter of the sphere = 4 cm.

117.

x	f	fx
10	3	30
15	10	150
20	x	$20x$
25	7	175
35	5	175
	$x+25$	$20x+530$

$$\text{Mean} = \frac{20x+530}{x+25}$$

$$20.6 = \frac{20x+530}{x+25}$$

$$20.6x + 515 = 20x + 530$$

$$x = \frac{15 \times 10}{6} = 25.$$

118. At least one head = {HH, HT, TH}
Number of favourable ways = 3

$\therefore$ Required probability = $\frac{3}{4}$.

119. Let third vertex = x_3, y_3, centreoid = (5, 3)
According to the question,

$$5 = \frac{x_1 + x_2 + x_3}{3}$$

$$5 = \frac{1+4+x_3}{3} \Rightarrow x_3 = 15 - 5 = 10$$

$$3 = \frac{y_1 + y_2 + y_3}{3}$$

$$3 = \frac{2+5+y_3}{3} \Rightarrow y_3 = 9 - 7 = 2$$

$\therefore$ The third vertex of the triangle = (10, 2).

120. $S_n = 3n^2 + 3n$

$S_1 = 3(1)^2 + 3(1) = 6$

$S_2 = 3(2)^2 + 3(2) = 18$

$S_3 = 3(3)^2 + 3(3) = 36$

$S_1 = a_1 = 6$

$a_2 = S_2 - S_1 = 18 - 6 = 12$

$a_3 = S_3 - S_2 = 36 - 18 = 18$

$\therefore$ 6, 12, 18, 24, 30 are in A.P.

$\therefore$ 5th term of AP = 30.

Previous Paper (Solved)

IGNOU B.Ed. Entrance Test 2010

PART-A

SECTION-I : GENERAL ENGLISH COMPREHENSION

Directions: *Read the following passage carefully and pick out the best answer out of the four choices given in each question:*

Adventure is the spirit that motivates persons to undertake difficult tasks. However the spirit of adventure tends to be restrained by caution. Sometimes this caution gives warning of the potential dangers, when our foremost thoughts are of safety first. Yet in some men the urge for adventure may be so strong that it overwhelms the primary instinct of self preservation and inspires them to attempt the impossible.

Adventure may not always be successful. It is enough if adventure is impelled by courage. Indeed the failure of a gallant enterprise often touches our heart deeply even more than if it were a success.

There has never been a person, who knew no fear, but the finer the courage of the person, the lesser will one betray fear. When we think of persons who go after adventure with a complete disregard for danger. We should remember that their bodies are as sensible to agony as ours, and thier mind suffers from same anxieties.

1. According to the writer, the spirt of adventure is to—
A. take all work
B. undertake difficult tasks
C. readiness to take risk
D. None of the above

2. Sometimes the caution acts as warning to—
A. nature of task
B. not to go for the task
C. potential dangers
D. All of the above

3. In some person; the urge for adventure is so strong that—
A. it discourages the person
B. it overwhelms the primary instinct
C. it gives the time to think
D. it always shows the danger

4. According to this passage, a courageous person—
A. doesn't care for any danger
B. doesn't easily express fear
C. cannot express fear
D. None of the above

5. According to this text the adventure is impelled by—
A. Success B. Courage
C. Danger D. All of the above

6. A truely courageous persons are also—
A. Sensitive to their body
B. Sensitive to their mind
C. Gain control over their body and mind
D. Sensitive to their mind and body

7. Adventurous persons always—
A. prefer to live happy life
B. inspires to attempt the impossible
C. love to live together
D. None of the above

8. Adventure is a—
A. Characteristics of a person
B. Courage of a person
C. Both A and B
D. None of the above

9. According to this text, the adventure and courage have a—

A. negative correlation
B. positive correlation
C. zero correlation
D. Both A and B

10. The passage expressed that—
A. Adventure is always successful
B. Adventure cannot be unsuccessful
C. Adventure may not always be successful
D. Adventure will never be successful

SECTION - II : LOGICAL AND ANALYTICAL REASONING

Direction (*Q.11-15*): *Find the best suited missing number from the given alternatives.*

11. 1, 4, 8, 11, 15, _?_, 22
A. 19 B. 18
C. 20 D. 17

12. 1, 4, 9, 16, _?_
A. 23 B. 24
C. 25 D. 30

13. 1, 2, 6, 24, _?_
A. 120 B. 144
C. 30 D. 140

14. 1, 3, 9, _?_, 81
A. 12 B. 15
C. 27 D. 25

15. A, E, _?_, O, U
A. F B. I
C. G D. L

Direction (*Q.16-20*): *Three words are given, first two words are related. Find the appropriate word from the given options for third word.*

16. Taka : Bangladesh : : Rupiah : ?
A. Spain B. Denmark
C. Indonesia D. Malaysia

17. Ghalib : Poetry : : Picasso : ?
A. Drama B. Literature
C. Sculpture D. Painting

18. Tarlatan : Muslin : : Poplin : ?
A. Jute B. Wool
C. Cotton D. Rayon

19. Ottawa : Canada : : Canberra : ?
A. Argentina B. Switzerland
C. Austria D. Australia

20. King : Throne : : Rider : ?
A. Seat B. Saddle
C. Horse D. Chair

21. If UMESH is coded as 'FNVHS', POT will be coded as—
A. JLG B. KMG
C. KLG D. LKG

22. If BEAT is coded as YVZG, MILD will be coded as—
A. NORW B. ONRW
C. WORN D. NROW

23. If NUMBER is coded as UNBMRE, GHOST will be coded as—
A. HOGTS B. HGOTS
C. HGDST D. HGSOT

24. If RADIO is coded as UDGLR; PHOTO will be coded as—
A. OIPWR B. OTOPT
C. SKRWR D. SKPWR

25. If WORLD is coded as ASVPH; GLOBE will be coded as—
A. OJSH B. KPSFI
C. KPSIF D. KPSHE

26. If it was Saturday on day before yesterday, which day will it be two days after day after tomorrow.
A. Monday B. Tuesday
C. Sunday D. Friday

27. Out of the following words, which word will cover at serial no. 2 in the dictionary.
A. Practice B. Practical
C. Practicable D. Practise

28. Seven men eat 28 fruits in 4 minutes. How much will one man take to eat one fruit?
A. 4 minutes B. 3 minutes
C. 20 seconds D. 1 minute

29. If order of English alphabet is reversed, which will be letter no. 11 from the left?
A. P B. Q
C. N D. M

30. Mohan said Beena, "Your father is the son of my mother's sister". What is Beena's relation with Mohan?
A. Brother
B. Niece
C. Cousin sister
D. Niece (sister's daughter)

SECTION-III : EDUCATION AND GENERAL AWARENESS

31. Right to education to all children between the age of 6 to 14 years is related to the article—
A. Article 20 B. Article 21
C. Article 22 D. Article 23

32. The state of India where female literacy is lowest—
A. Bihar B. Uttar Pradesh
C. Rajasthan D. Madhya Pradesh

33. Vishwanathan Anand is a champion of—
A. Chess B. Billiards
C. Snooker D. Archery

34. Who accompanied Edmund Hilary on Mount Everst?
A. Tenzing Norgay B. Sherpa Lepzing
C. Chirstopher D. Dilip Sardesai

35. BIHU is the festival of ....
A. Bihar B. Asom
C. Uttarakhand D. Meghalaya

36. First May is observed as—
A. International Women's Day
B. International Workers Day
C. World Environment Day
D. World Health Day

37. Whose signatures are found on one rupee note?
A. Finance Secretary
B. Governor of RBI
C. Finance Minister
D. Deputy Finance Minister

38. World famous Rock Garden is situated at—
A. Kolkata B. Jaipur
C. Chandigarh D. Bengaluru

39. The nuclear test site Pokharan is situated in the state of—
A. Haryana B. Rajasthan
C. Madhya Pradesh D. Jammu & Kashmir

40. 97th Constitutional Amendment deals with—
A. Elementary Education
B. Power of Vice President
C. Power of the Election Commission
D. Anti Defection Bill

41. Which of the following is not included in four Vedas?
A. Rigveda B. Samaveda
C. Atharvveda D. Ayurveda

42. Which one of the following is the sacred book of Sikhs?
A. Adi Granth Sahib
B. Guru Granth Sahib
C. Govind Granth Sahib
D. Maha Granth Sahib

43. The Mauryan Capital city was—
A. Prayag B. Pataliputra
C. Vaishali D. Ujjaini

44. Fatehpur Sikri was built by—
A. Babur B. Jahangir
C. Humayun D. None of these

45. In the eye donation, which part of the eye is transplanted from the donor?
A. Cornea B. Lens
C. Retina D. The whole eye

46. The full form of ISRO is—
A. Indian Space Research Organisation
B. International Satellite Research Organisation
C. Indian Satellite Research Organisation
D. International Space Research Organisation

47. Zero as a numeral was discovered by the—
A. Arabs B. Egyptians
C. Greeks D. Indians

48. The stupa at Sanchi was built by—
A. Kanishka B. Harshavardhan
C. Ashoka D. Samudragupta

49. Akbar tried to found a new religion because—
A. He wanted to become famous as a religious hero
B. He had a vision telling him to do so
C. He wanted to unite the people of many religious who lived in his empire under one religion
D. He did not believe in the old religion

50. Hiuen Tsang, the famous Chinese pilgrim visited India during the reign of—
A. Ashoka B. Chandragupta II
C. Kanishka D. Harshvardhan

51. The construction of Qutub Minar was initiated by Qutab-Uddin-Aibak and completed by—
A. Balban B. Firoj Tuglak
C. Iltutmish D. Alauddin Khilji

52. The universal blood donour group is—
A. A B. O
C. B D. AB

53. Jim Corbett National Park is in—
A. Uttarakhand B. Assam
C. Maharashtra D. Madhya Pradesh

54. The language spoken by the largest number of people in the world is—
A. English B. Hindi
C. Chinese D. French

55. NSSO means—
A. National Sample Survey Organisation
B. National Survey of Survivors Organisation
C. National Simple Survey Organisation
D. National Study on Surgical Operation

SECTION-IV : TEACHING-LEARNING AND SCHOOL

56. By which method the students learn to the maximum extent?
A. By seeing B. By reading
C. By listening D. By doing themselves

57. Which quality of the teacher is liked the most by the students?
A. Punctuality
B. Impartiality
C. Love for discipline
D. Dominance

58. What should the teacher do to maintain the interest of students in class teaching?
A. Maximum use of blackboard
B. Extensive use of examples from the practical life
C. Extensive use of teaching materials/aids
D. Giving ample opportunity to students for discussion/delibrations

59. You think that the surprise tests is justified because—
A. Students remain frightened due to these
B. You do not need to prepare yourself at home
C. You can escape the teaching session
D. The abilities and knowledge levels of students can be truely judged through such tests

60. A teacher should work according to—
A. His own liking
B. The need of the time
C. His capacity to work
D. His needs

61. Children with disabilities must get education because—
A. They are vulnerable
B. They have special needs
C. It is a basic constitutional right
D. They are poor

62. Which of the following is a sensory disorder?
A. Hearing Impairment
B. Mental Retardation
C. Cerebral Palsy
D. Neuro muscular Disorder

63. International Disability Day is—
A. 1st December B. 3rd December
C. 6th January D. 4th December

64. Rehabilitation Council of India was established in—
A. 1992 B. 1980
C. 1994 D. 1986

65. PWD Act was enacted in—
A. 1996 B. 1997
C. 1995 D. 1996

66. CBR is short form of—
A. Custom Based Rehabilitation
B. Community Based Rehabilitation
C. Committee Based Rehabilitation
D. Cost Based Rehabilitation

67. Itinerant teacher is—
A. Another name for resource teacher
B. Serves only one school
C. Serves more than one school
D. Both A and C

68. Congenital Disability means disability which occurs—
A. By birth B. After one year
C. After birth D. None of the above

69. Multiple disability means—
A. Cerebral Palsy
B. Low vision
C. Mental Retardation
D. More than one disability

70. How many categories of professionals are covered under RCI Act?
A. 12 B. 16
C. 15 D. 3

71. How many disabilities are recognised by PWD Act 1995?
A. 3 B. 7
C. 6 D. 10

72. The National Institute for Mentally Handicapped is located at—
A. Delhi B. Kolkata
C. Srinagar D. Secunderabad

73. The most recent International legal Instrument in the field of disability is—
A. Biwako Millenium Frame Work
B. Beijing Declaration
C. UN Standard Rules
D. UN convention for the Rights of Persons with Disabilities

74. Braille is based on—
A. Dots B. Lines
C. Raised D. None of the above

75. Decible is the unit for measuring—
A. Visual acquity B. Hearing level
C. Mental level D. All of the above

76. Registration of rehabilitation professional is the work of—
A. MCI B. AICTE
C. RCI D. NCTE

77. Accident may result in—
A. Orthopaedic Impairment
B. Visual Impairment
C. Hearing Impairment
D. All of the above

78. Mental Retardation is—
A. A disease
B. Absence of brain
C. Slow function of brain
D. A condition

79. Learning depends on—
A. Intelligence B. Parental attitude
C. Peer attitude D. None of these

80. Blindness and Deafness are—
A. Sensory deficits B. Mental deficits
C. Motor deficits D. Neuro deficits

PART-B

SECTION-V (I): SCIENCE

81. Lime water contains—
A. Calcium carbonate
B. Calcium hydroxide
C. Calcium bicarbonate
D. Sodium sulphate

82. Which of the following represents a chemical change?
A. Evaporation of alcohol
B. Sublimation of iodine
C. Heating of a platinum wire in bunsen flame
D. Heating of mercuric oxide powder

83. Pencillin is obtained from—
A. Algae fungi B. Fungi
C. Synthetics D. None of these

84. Isotopes differ in—
A. Number of electrons
B. Number of protons
C. Number of neutrons
D. Protons and neutrons

85. The drug most widely used to relieve pain is—
A. Paracetamol B. Aspirin
C. Morphine D. Nimusulide

86. A person climbing a hill bends forward in order to—
A. Avoid slipping B. Increase speed
C. Reduce fatigue D. Increase stability

87. The technique used to transmit audio signals in television broadcast is—
A. Amplitude modulation
B. Frequency modulation
C. Pulse code modulation
D. Time division multiplexing

88. Which of the following is the most elastic?
A. carbon B. rubber
C. glass D. paper

89. Energy is measured in the same unit as that of—
A. Work B. Power
C. Momentum D. Inertia

90. A device used in converting a.c. current into d.c. is called—
A. Transformer B. Rectifier
C. Induction coil D. Dynamo

91. Which of the following blood group is universal recipient?
A. A B. B
C. AB D. O

92. Which of the following is most important for digestion?
A. Proteins B. Milk
C. Fat D. Vitamins

93. The human skull consists of—
A. 22 bones B. 14 bones
C. 8 bones D. None of these

94. The first life of earth came—
A. In water B. On land
C. In air D. On mountains

95. DNA is concentrated in the—
A. Microsome B. Nucleus
C. Protoplasm D. Chromatin

96. Why is 28th February is observed as National Science Day?
A. Birth of Dr. Bhabha
B. First Indian atomic explosion
C. The world came to know about Raman Effect
D. A SLVD-1 launched

97. Which of the following is neither an element nor a compound?
A. Air B. Water
C. Glucose D. Gold

98. Which of the following gas does not pollute air?
A. Carbon dioxide
B. Carbon monoxide
C. Nitrogen oxide
D. Sulphur dioxide

99. The main atmospheric gas responsible for green house effect is—
A. Nitrogen B. Oxygen
C. Ozone D. Carbon dioxide

100. The atmospheric layer nearest to earth is—
A. Stratosphere B. Troposphere
C. Ionosphere D. Mesosphere

(II) : MATHEMATICS

101. Which of the following is not a prime number—
A. 1 B. 2
C. 131 D. 157

102. Express 36 as a product of prime number—
A. $2 \times 3 \times 6$
B. 6×6
C. $2 \times 2 \times 3 \times 3$
D. 4×9

103. Complete the series—
1, 2, 4, 7, 13, 24, 44, ?
A. 81 B. 80
C. 64 D. 66

104. The value of $(4^2)^3$ is—
A. $4 \times 2 \times 3$ B. 16×3
C. 4^3 D. 4^6

105. One of the factors of $6x^2 - 19x - 36$ is $(3x + 4)$. State the other factor—
A. $(2x - 9)$ B. $(6x - 19)$
C. $(6x - 9)$ D. $(2x - 19)$

106. If $3x^2 + 5x - 2 = 0$, find the value of x—
A. $\frac{1}{3}$ or -2 B. $\frac{1}{3}$ or 2
C. $-\frac{1}{3}$ or 2 D. $-\frac{1}{3}$ or -2

107. The mean of reciprocals of x and y is equal to—
A. $\frac{2(x+y)}{xy}$ B. $\frac{2x}{x+y}$
C. $\frac{x+y}{2xy}$ D. $\frac{x+y}{x-y}$

108. If $(2x)^x = 512$, then x is equal to—
A. 2 B. 3
C. 4 D. 5

109. Find the sum of all numbers upto 100—
A. 4950 B. 5100
C. 5000 D. 5050

110. Log $\frac{1}{2} = ?$
A. $-\frac{1}{3}$ B. $\frac{1}{2}$
C. $-\frac{1}{2}$ D. $\frac{1}{3}$

111. $\sqrt{41-\sqrt{21+\sqrt{19-\sqrt{9}}}} = ?$
A. 3 B. 5
C. 6 D. 6.4

112. The value of $\frac{\sqrt{3}+\sqrt{2}}{\sqrt{3}-\sqrt{2}}$ is—
A. $5+2\sqrt{6}$ B. $5-2\sqrt{6}$
C. $3+\sqrt[2]{5}$ D. $3-\sqrt[2]{5}$

113. What is the 20% of 30% of 40%?
A. 2.4% B. 3.0%
C. 24% D. 30%

114. A book publisher sold 250 books and had a gain equal to selling price of 50 books. Find profit per cent of the publisher.
A. 25 B. 20
C. 50 D. 10

115. 20 boys finish a work in 30 days, then 40 boys can finish in—
A. 20 days B. 10 days
C. 25 days D. 15 days

116. Which is correct?
A. $\log_1$ (Mn) = log a M + log a n
B. log a (M + n) = log a M + log a n
C. log a (M – n) = log a M – log a n
D. $\log a \left(\frac{M}{n}\right) = \log a M + \log a n$

117. The ratio of 1 hour and 15 minutes to 5 hours is—
A. 2:5 B. 4:15
C. 3:8 D. 1:4

118. If $\sin\theta = \frac{5}{13}$, then $\cot\theta$ is equal to—
A. $\frac{12}{5}$ B. $\frac{13}{12}$
C. $\frac{13}{5}$ D. $\frac{12}{13}$

119. The value of $\frac{\sin 39°}{\cos 51°}$ is—
A. 0 B. $\frac{1}{2}$
C. ∞ D. 1

120. If the volume of a sphere is divided by its surface area, the result is 27 cm. Find the radius of the sphere.
A. 9 cm B. 27 cm
C. 81 cm D. 63 cm

(III) : Social Science

121. The planet nearest to sun is—
A. Mars B. Mercury
C. Venus D. Neptune

122. Thimpu is the capital of—
A. Sikkim B. Meghalaya
C. Bhutan D. Mizoram

123. Railways was introduced in India in the year—
A. 1901 B. 1883
C. 1853 D. 1908

124. Kolar gold mines are in the state of—
A. Madhya Pradesh B. Karnataka
C. Tamil Nadu D. Orissa

125. The novel 'Devdas' is written by—
A. Sharatchandra Chatterjee
B. Rabindranath Tagore
C. Prem Chandra
D. Bankimchandra Chattopadhyaya

126. Ballarpur is known for—
A. Writing paper B. Coal mines
C. Fertilizers D. Cement plant

127. India is a 'republic' because—
A. Democratic rule exists here
B. Its head of state (country) is elected
C. Its constitution is written
D. All of the above

128. The duration of 'Zero hour' in Lok Sabha is—
A. 15 minutes B. Half-an-hour
C. One hour D. Not-specified

129. Lakshadweep is a group of .... islands.
A. 22 B. 27
C. 32 D. 35

130. The Sikh Guru who faught against the Mughals was—
A. Guru Nanak Dev
B. Guru Arjun Dev
C. Guru Tegh Bahadur
D. Guru Gobind Singh

131. How many spokes are there in our national emblem 'Ashok Chakra'?
A. 12 B. 15
C. 20 D. 24

132. The first Indian film in colour was—
A. Jhansi ki Rani B. Aan
C. Sairandhri D. Ramrajya

133. British shifted their capital from Calcutta to Delhi in—
A. 1905 B. 1909
C. 1911 D. 1914

134. Who gave the slogan 'Jai Hind'?
A. Mahatma Gandhi
B. Pandit Jawaharlal Nehru
C. Subhash Chandra Bose
D. Bhagat Singh

135. The number of seats allotted to different states in the Lok Sabha is determined on the basis of state's—
A. Population B. Size
C. Resources D. Location

136. The Andes Mountain range is in—
A. Europe B. North America
C. Africa D. South America

137. Konkan Railway runs between—
A. Mumbai-Manglore
B. Mumbai-Goa
C. Manglore-Trivendram
D. Goa-Kanya Kumari

138. The Indus Valley people had trade relations with—
A. Greece B. Egypt
C. Ceylon D. Mesopotamia

139. Which of the following is not an essential elements of the state?
A. Territory B. Society
C. Government D. Population

140. When a bill is referred to a joint meeting of both the houses of the Indian Parliament, it has to be passed by—
A. A simple majority
B. Three-fourth majority
C. Two-third majority
D. Absolute majority of total membership

(IV) : ENGLISH

141. Fill up the blanks—
I tried to give him good advice but he .... to listen.
A. prevented B. avoided
C. refused D. denied

142. I am given to .... that you want to be a doctor.
A. learn B. understand
C. think D. predict

143. Rita always sets her alarm so that she can ...... at 8.00 am.
A. think over B. write down
C. think through D. wake up

144. If you are agitated too much it will .... your judgement.
A. impede B. impair
C. impose D. impel

145. She always insisted on the need to .... between ends and means.
A. analyse B. define
C. distribute D. distinguish

146. Choose the word with correct spellings.
A. Sychology B. Sykology
C. Psychology D. Psykology

147. The synonym of the word 'infinite' is—
A. unique B. indefinite
C. vague D. endless

148. Choose the wrongly spelt word.
A. Believe B. Relieve
C. Grieve D. Decieve

Directions: *Choose the appropriate set from those given below to fill in the blanks.*

149. Hundred students competed .... one another .... a single scholarship.
A. with : over B. with : for
C. among : over D. between : for

150. We went .... the room and sat down .... a sofa.
A. to : in B. into : on
C. from : upon D. in : on

151. Substitute with one word—"events which happened at the same time".
A. Coincidently B. Incidently
C. Simultaneously D. Momentarily

Directions: *Fill up the blanks with correct preposition.*

152. Gopal is born .... poor parents.
A. to B. for
C. of D. froms

153. You are senior .... me.
A. by B. to
C. than D. of

154. Yogesh is certainly stronger .... the two.
A. among B. between
C. of D. than

155. I am not .... sure of its as you are.
A. quite B. so
C. very D. perfectly

156. He was kind enough to accede .... his request.
A. in B. to
C. with D. over

Directions: *Find out the word of same meaning from 4 words for the word given above.*

157. Sentimental
A. over sensitive
B. aroused
C. sensible
D. overwhelmed with emotions

158. Unanimous
A. timely
B. judicious
C. half hearted
D. agreed upon by everyone

159. Ample
A. Sufficient B. Very little
C. Plentiful D. Inadequate

160. Vulgar
A. Uncivilized B. Rough
C. Nauseatic D. Stubborn

(V) हिन्दी

निर्देशः (प्रश्न 161 से 165 तक): *दिये गये गद्यांश को ध्यानपूर्वक पढ़कर पूछे गये प्रश्नों के उत्तर दीजियेः*

राजनीति और विद्या सगी बहने हैं। दोनों का अलग रहना कठिन हैं। दोनों के स्वभाव भिन्न हैं, किन्तु लक्ष्य एक है। दोनों का लक्ष्य है कि व्यक्ति और समाज़ को अधिक सुख पहुँचे। इतिहास इस बात का साक्षी है कि जब भी किसी राष्ट्र में क्रान्ति का बिगुल बजा तो वहाँ के छात्र मात्र दृष्टा नहीं रहे अपितु उन्होंने क्रान्ति की बागडोर संभाली। परतन्त्रता काल में स्वतंत्रता के लिये और वर्तमान काल में भ्रष्टाचारी सरकारों के उन्मूलन के लिये भारत में छात्रशक्ति ने अग्रसर होकर क्रान्ति का आह्वान किया। इंडोनेशिया और ईरान में छात्रों ने सरकार का तख़्ता ही पलट दिया। बांग्लादेश को अस्तित्व में लाने में ढाका विश्वविद्यालय के छात्रों के बलिदान को भुलाया नहीं जा सकता।

गद्यांश के आधार पर निम्नलिखित प्रश्न (161 से 165) संभावित उत्तर विकल्पों के साथ दिये गये हैं। सही विकल्प को चुनिए।

161. निम्नलिखित में कौन-सा कथन सही नहीं है?
A. विद्या और राजनीति सहोदरा है।
B. दोनों की प्रकृति समान है।
C. दोनों का उद्देश्य एक है।
D. दोनो परस्पर सहयोगी हैं।

162. संसार का इतिहास साक्षी है कि छात्र—
A. राष्ट्र में क्रान्ति के दर्शक रहे हैं।
B. क्रान्ति के कारण बनें।
C. क्रान्ति में खड़े हो गये।
D. क्रान्ति में अग्रणी रहे।

163. छात्रों के संघर्ष के उद्देश्यों में क्या शामिल नहीं था?
A. परतन्त्रता के लिये
B. स्वतन्त्रता के लिये
C. भ्रष्टाचार मिटाने के लिये
D. सरकार गिराने के लिये

164. कई देशों में क्रान्ति का श्रेय किसको जाता है?
A. विद्यार्थियों को B. सामान्य जनता को
C. उद्योगपतियों को D. राजनीतिज्ञों को

165. छात्रों ने आहवान किया—
A. शान्ति का B. शक्ति का
C. अहिंसा का D. क्रान्ति का

निर्देश (प्रश्न 166 से 180 तक): *निम्नलिखित में से प्रत्येक प्रश्न के साथ चार-चार विकल्प दिये गये हैं। सही विकल्प को चुनिए।*

166. 'सुगम' का विलोम शब्द है—
A. सुलभ B. दुर्गम
C. सुदूर D. नरक

167. 'जो किसी का पक्ष न ले'—कहलाता है—
A. न्यायाधीश B. निस्वार्थी
C. निर्भर D. निष्पक्ष

168. 'सादर' में कौन-सा उपसर्ग है?
A. सा B. दर
C. स D. अर

169. हिन्दी वर्णमाला में कुल कितने अक्षर हैं?
A. 44 B. 33
C. 46 D. 43

170. निम्नलिखित में तत्सम शब्द हैः
A. पानी B. बाजार
C. दूरदर्शन D. दुग्ध

171. महादेवी वर्मा की किस रचना के लिये उन्हें ज्ञानपीठ पुरस्कार मिला?
A. यामिनी B. दामिनी
C. यामा D. कामिनी

172. 'पुष्पलता' में कौन-सा समास है?
A. कर्मधारय B. तत्पुरुष
C. अव्ययीभाव D. द्वन्द

173. भारतीय संविधान के किस अनुच्छेद में हिन्दी को राजभाषा के रूप में स्वीकार किया गया है?
A. अनुच्छेद 343 B. अनुच्छेद 344
C. अनुच्छेद 342 D. अनुच्छेद 24

174. 'विच्छेद' का सन्धि विच्छेद क्या है?
A. वि + छेद B. विच्छ + एद
C. विः + छेद D. विस् + छेद

175. निम्नलिखित भाषाओं में किस भाषा की लिपि देवनागरी नहीं है?
A. हिन्दी B. मराठी
C. संस्कृत D. पंजाबी

176. "हे राम! रक्षा करो!" 'हे राम!' पद में कौन-सा कारक है?
A. सम्बोधन B. कर्ता
C. सम्बन्ध D. अधिकरण

177. निम्नलिखित में से कौन-सी रचना 'भक्तिकाल' की है?
A. महाभारत B. रामचरितमानस
C. रामायण D. मेघदूतम्

178. 'अंक में लेना' मुहावरे का अर्थ है—
A. गले लगाना
B. वात्सल्य प्रेम प्रदर्शित करना
C. प्रेम प्रदर्शित करना
D. गोद में बिठाना

179. निम्नलिखित में से अशुद्ध वाक्य कौन-सा है?
A. मैंने थोड़ी देर बाद जाना है।
B. आप सपरिवार आमन्त्रित हैं।
C. कृपया हमारे घर आइए।
D. जब भी आप आये, मुझसे मिलें।

180. "चरण कमल बन्दौ हरि राई" में कौन-सा अलंकार है?
A. यमक B. रूपक
C. उत्प्रेक्षा D. अनुप्रास

ANSWERS

1	2	3	4	5	6	7	8	9	10
B	B	B	A	B	D	D	C	B	C
11	**12**	**13**	**14**	**15**	**16**	**17**	**18**	**19**	**20**
B	C	A	C	B	C	D	C	D	B
21	**22**	**23**	**24**	**25**	**26**	**27**	**28**	**29**	**30**
C	D	D	C	B	D	B	D	A	B
31	**32**	**33**	**34**	**35**	**36**	**37**	**38**	**39**	**40**
B	A	A	A	B	B	A	C	B	A
41	**42**	**43**	**44**	**45**	**46**	**47**	**48**	**49**	**50**
D	A	B	D	A	A	D	C	B	D
51	**52**	**53**	**54**	**55**	**56**	**57**	**58**	**59**	**60**
C	B	A	C	A	D	B	C	D	B
61	**62**	**63**	**64**	**65**	**66**	**67**	**68**	**69**	**70**
C	D	B	D	C	B	D	A	D	B
71	**72**	**73**	**74**	**75**	**76**	**77**	**78**	**79**	**80**
B	D	D	C	B	C	D	C	A	C
81	**82**	**83**	**84**	**85**	**86**	**87**	**88**	**89**	**90**
A	C	B	C	B	D	B	A	A	D
91	**92**	**93**	**94**	**95**	**96**	**97**	**98**	**99**	**100**
B	D	B	A	B	C	A	C	D	B
101	**102**	**103**	**104**	**105**	**106**	**107**	**108**	**109**	**110**
A	C	A	D	A	A	C	B	D	B
111	**112**	**113**	**114**	**115**	**116**	**117**	**118**	**119**	**120**
C	A	A	B	D	A	D	A	D	C
121	**122**	**123**	**124**	**125**	**126**	**127**	**128**	**129**	**130**
B	C	C	B	A	A	D	C	D	C
131	**132**	**133**	**134**	**135**	**136**	**137**	**138**	**139**	**140**
D	C	C	C	A	D	C	D	B	A
141	**142**	**143**	**144**	**145**	**146**	**147**	**148**	**149**	**150**
C	C	D	B	D	C	D	D	B	B
151	**152**	**153**	**154**	**155**	**156**	**157**	**158**	**159**	**160**
C	A	B	C	B	B	D	D	A	A
161	**162**	**163**	**164**	**165**	**166**	**167**	**168**	**169**	**170**
B	D	A	A	D	B	D	A	B	D
171	**172**	**173**	**174**	**175**	**176**	**177**	**178**	**179**	**180**
C	B	A	C	D	A	B	D	A	B

SOME SELECTED EXPLANATORY ANSWERS

11. $1 + 3 = 4, 4 + 4 = 8, 8 + 3 = 11, 11 + 4 = 15$
$15 + 3 = \boxed{18}, 28 + 4 = 22$

12. $1^2 = 1, 2^2 = 4, 3^2 = 9, 4^2 = 16, 5^2 = \boxed{25}$

13. $1 \times 2 = 2, 2 \times 3 = 4, 6 \times 4 = 24, 24 \times 5 = \boxed{120}$

21.

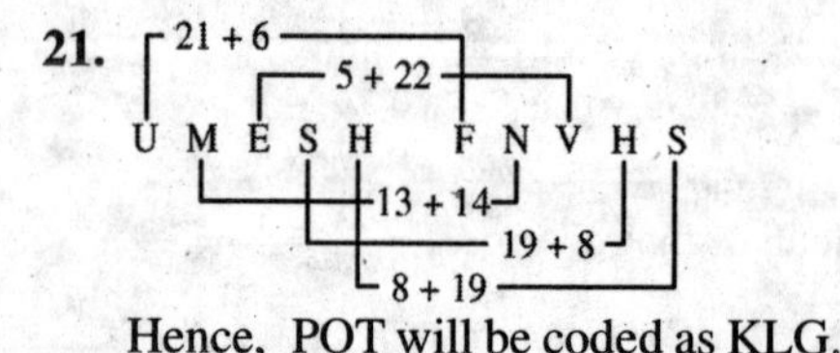

Hence, POT will be coded as KLG.

22. 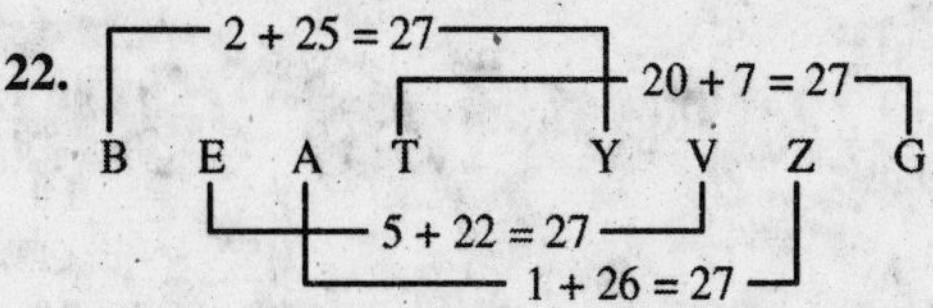

Hence, MILD will be coded as NROW.

23. N U M B E R → U N B M R E

Hence, GHOST will be coded as HGSOT.

26.

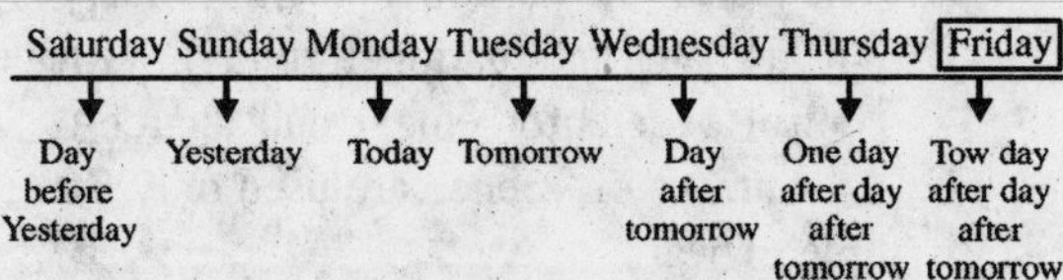

28. Required time = $\frac{4\times7}{28}$ = 1 minute.

29. ZYXWVUTSRQ [P] ONMLKJIHGFE DCBA

101. 1 is neither prime nor composit.

102. 2 and 3 are prime numbers.

104. $(4^2)^3 = (4)^{2\times3} = 4^6$

105. Dividing $6x^2 - 19x - 36$ by $(3x + 4)$

$$3x+4\overline{)6x^2-19x-36}(2x-9$$
$$\underline{\underset{-}{}6x^2 \underset{-}{+} 8x}$$
$$-27x-36$$
$$\underline{\underset{+}{-}27x \underset{+}{-} 36}$$
$$\times \quad \times$$

So, other factor will be $2x - 9$.

106. $3x^2 + 5x - 2 = 0$

$\Rightarrow \quad 3x^2 + 6x - x - 2 = 0$

$\Rightarrow \quad 3x(x+2) - 1(x+2) = 0$

$\Rightarrow \quad (3x-1)(x+2) = 0$

$\Rightarrow \quad x = \frac{1}{3}, -2$

107. Reciprocal of x and y = $\frac{1}{x}$ and $\frac{1}{y}$

$\therefore$ Mean of the reciprocal = $\frac{\frac{1}{x}+\frac{1}{y}}{2} = \frac{x+y}{2xy}$

108. Since $(2^x)^x = 512$

$\Rightarrow \quad (2^x)^x = 2^9 = (2^3)^3 \quad \Rightarrow \quad x = 3$

109. Sum of all numbers upto 100 = $\frac{n(n+1)}{2}$

$= \frac{100\times101}{2} = 5050$

111. $\sqrt{41-\sqrt{21+\sqrt{19-\sqrt{9}}}}$

$= \sqrt{41-\sqrt{21+\sqrt{19-3}}} = \sqrt{41-\sqrt{21+\sqrt{16}}}$

$= \sqrt{41-\sqrt{25}} = \sqrt{41-5} = \sqrt{36} = 6$

112. $\frac{\sqrt{3}+\sqrt{2}}{\sqrt{3}-\sqrt{2}} = \frac{\sqrt{3}+\sqrt{2}}{\sqrt{3}-\sqrt{2}}\times\frac{\sqrt{3}+\sqrt{2}}{\sqrt{3}+\sqrt{2}}$

$= \frac{(\sqrt{3})^2+(\sqrt{2})^2+2\sqrt{6}}{3-2}$

$= 5+2\sqrt{6}$

114. On selling 250 books their is a gain of 50 books

$\therefore$ On selling 1 books their is a gain of $\frac{50}{250}$

$\therefore$ On selling 100 books their is a gain of

$\frac{50}{250}\times100 = 20\%$

118. Given $\sin\theta = \frac{5}{13}$

$\cos\theta = \sqrt{1-\left(\frac{5}{13}\right)^2} = \sqrt{1-\frac{25}{169}} = \sqrt{\frac{144}{169}}$

$\therefore \quad \cot\theta = \frac{\cos\theta}{\sin\theta} = \frac{\frac{12}{13}}{\frac{5}{13}} = \frac{12}{5}$

120. $\frac{\text{Volume of sphere}}{\text{Surface area of sphere}} = 27$

$\Rightarrow \quad \frac{\frac{4}{3}\pi r^3}{4\pi r^2} = 27 \quad \Rightarrow \quad \frac{r}{3} = 27 \Rightarrow r = 81$

Previous Paper (Solved)

IGNOU B.Ed. Entrance Test 2009

PART-A

SECTION-I : GENERAL ENGLISH COMPREHENSION

Direction: *Read the following passage carefully and answer these questions from the given options.*

It is known that science is not a great opponent to humanity but war. Science only reflects social powers. Obviously, Science is creative in the age of peace but at the time of war it changes into destruction. Generally, scientific weapons are not responsible for war but make the war horrible. Till now, these weapons brought us to the edge of ruins. Instead of ban science, main problem to us is, stop war. We have to establish a global government, who makes relations better among the nations and ensures no use of power. In this effort people's participation is must, including scientists. Hiroshima bombing warns us to take effective measures soon. More time have passed but no action has been taken. Now, the big question to us is— Can education and tolerance, intimacy and creative thinking win over our destructive ability? Necessarily, it must be answer. Science would help us, but we have to develop our decisive capacity, too.

1. According to author real enemy of humanity is not science but war. Why—
A. Science only invents weapons, by which war is made
B. At the time of war, science becomes destructive
C. Scientific weapons are real cause of war
D. Only scientific weapons not caused the war but it make the war horrible

2. War can be stopped if—
A. Science is not permitted to ruin all
B. By law and international ruling, we can control over enforcement and anarchy
C. Advantages of science are used only at the time of war
D. Scientific weapons may not be used for announcement of war

3. According to author, our problem is—
A. To stop the science making the real image of social powers
B. To ban the scientific activity everywhere
C. To ensure stoping war
D. To stop scientist from destructive scientific activity

4. To control destructive attitude—
A. Social strength is encouraged
B. Education and enlarged view
C. Inner approach and constructive thinking
D. (B) and (C) both

5. Brought us to the edge of ruins, means—
A. Brought near the death and ruin
B. Brought on the new door of future
C. To evolve in destructive activity
D. To indicate mystric fate

6. Which of the followings is not included in the passage—
A. People blame science without any reason for war
B. Uses of science for destructive motive
C. There is no contribution of science and its invented weapons to show the war fear

D. For the establishment of World Peace, the role of science comes after man

7. World peace is established by—

A. Use of power

B. Communal harmony

C. National government

D. None of these

8. Meaning of— "Our work is likely begun" is—

A. It is not begun yet

B. Recently it is begun

C. Half it is completed

D. It is begun, but not completed till now

9. What is the meaning of 'Tolerance' in the passage—

A. make distance

B. make equality

C. make challange

D. Communal intimacy

10. Which of the following is appropriate title?

A. Science and social powers

B. Science and dreadful sights of war

C. Science and world peace

D. Science and new generation

SECTION II : LOGICAL AND ANALYTICAL REASONING

Direction: *(Q.11-14) Select the right answer in the following series?*

11. 5, 10, 30, ..., 600

A. 50 B. 60

C. 120 D. 200

12. 42, 24, 53, 35, 64, ...

A. 46 B. 48

C. 75 D. None of these

13. 0, 7, 26, 63, ...

A. 93 B. 103

C. 121 D. 124

14. B, ..., J, P, V

A. C B. F

C. G D. H

Direction: *(Q.15-18) There is a code for each english word. Choose the right option on the basis of code, from the given options.*

15. Code 'CZMBD' is for 'DANCE', then what will be for 'ENGLISH'?

A. FMHMJTI B. DMFKHRG

C. CLFKHRG D. DOHKHRG

16. Code 'WVZI' is for 'DEAR' then what will be for 'PALE'?

A. KZOV B. KAOU

C. VZOV D. KZOU

17. Code 'UVTKMG' is for 'STRIKE' then the code 'KMLMBW' will be for which word?

A. MONDAY B. IONOZU

C. MONODY D. IKJKZU

18. Code 'IDHEL' is for 'DELHI' then what will be for 'TUFAN'?

A. TNAUF B. NATUF

C. NTAUF D. NTUAF

19. If 14 February comes 4 days prior to Monday in a superannuation, then which day will be on 17 March?

A. Monday B. Tuesday

C. Wednesday D. Sunday

20. First E is as far as second E in the word 'PRECIPITATE', give the name of that letter which is situated at the same distance from the third letter in the English alphabet.

A. J B. K

C. L D. M

Direction: *(Q.21-24) Read the following passage.*

When Varun born, his father Tarun was 30. Paternal aunt of Varun, Urvashi is 3 year younger than her brother Tarun and 5 year younger than her husband Yogesh. There are three children of Yogesh and Urvashi–Kamal, Jalaj and Vaishali. Kamal born on his father's 28th birthday. After 10 year his brother Jalaj is of less than 7 years of half of his father and his sister Vaishali will be of 1/3 of her mother's age. Kamal was born 12 years earlier.

21. Which one is correct in descending order, according to age?
A. Yogesh, Kamal, Varun, Vaishali
B. Tarun, Yogesh, Vaishali, Varun
C. Urvashi, Yogesh, Varun, Vaishali
D. Jalaj, Vaishali, Kamal, Varun.

22. Which one is correct in ascending order according to age?
A. Varun, Vaishali, Jalaj, Kamal
B. Varun, Tarun, Urvashi, Vaishali
C. Vaishali, Jalaj, Kamal, Urvashi
D. Vaishali, Kamal, Jalaj, Varun

23. Elder sister of Varun, Sarita can be younger than—
A. Vaishali
B. Kamal and Vaishali
C. Jalaj
D. Urvashi

24. Who among the family is younger than as many people, as he is elder?
A. Vaishali B. Kamal
C. Varun D. Jalaj

Direction: *(Q.25-27) There are some problematic figures and after that four options are given. There is one figure which is in order of problematic figure. Choose the figure.*

25. **26.**

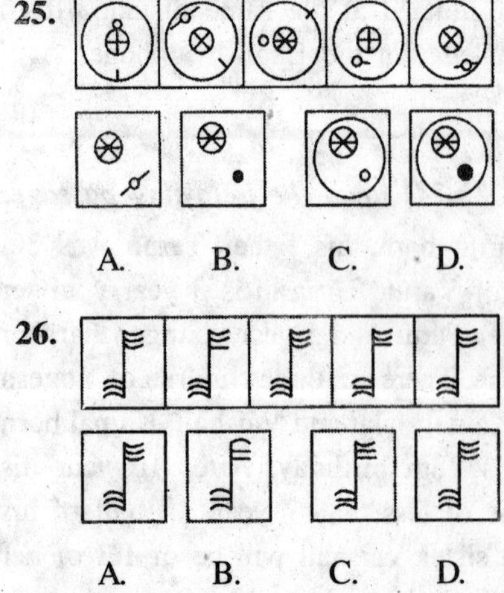

A. B. C. D.

A. B. C. D.

27.

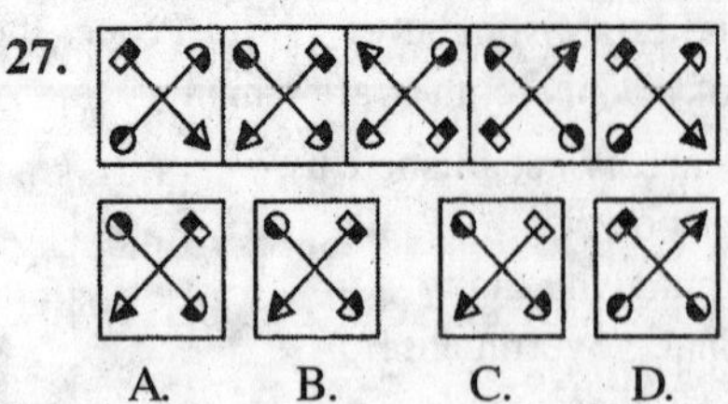

A. B. C. D.

Direction: *(Q. 28-30) Two conclusion I and II are given in the following question which are derived from first two statement. Assume that both statement are true and decide whether the conclusions are correct or not. Choose the right option.*

28. Statement:
No one human is animal.
Some animals are intelligent.
Conclusion:
I. Some human are intelligent.
II. Some intelligent are human.
A. Only I is true
B. Only II is true
C. I and II both are true
D. No one is true

29. Statement:
All chairs are pen.
All pens are also pencils.
Conclusion:
I. Some pencils are chairs.
II. All pencils are chairs.
A. Only I is true
B. Only II is true
C. I and II both are true
D. No one is true

30. Statement:
All children are not students.
Some students are not appointed.
Conclusion:
I. Some children are not appointed.
II. Some are appointed but they are not children.
A. Only I is true
B. Only II is true
C. I and II both are true
D. No one is true

SECTION III : EDUCATIONAL AND GENERAL AWARENESS

31. Who is the first Satyagrahi, selected by Mahatma Gandhi to lead the Personal Civil Disobedience Movement in October 1940?

A. Vinoba Bhave

B. Jawahar Lal Nehru

C. C. Rajgopalachari

D. Dr. Rajendra Prasad

32. India is the leading producer and consumer of which crop—

A. Rice B. Tea

C. Pulses D. Oil seeds

33. Who is awarded by Nobel prize for Economics?

A. Pope John Paul-II B. Condiliza Rice

C. John Maikken D. Paul Krugman

34. Which of the following is the movement path of stars/plants around the Sun?

A. Elliptical B. Circular

C. Parabolic D. Linear

35. Who is awarded by Booker Prize for the novel 'The White Tiger'?

A. Amitabh Ghosh

B. Arundhati Roy

C. Arvind Adiga

D. Mahashweta Devi

36. Which river makes 'Shiva Samundram' waterfall in South India?

A. Narmada B. Kaveri

C. Krishna D. Godavari

37. If the President of India has to resign, to which person he/she will write?

A. Chief Election Commissioner

B. Speaker of the Lok-Sabha

C. Prime Minister

D. Vice-President

38. Who established India's first Women University?

A. M.G. Ranade

B. Dhondho Keshav Karve

C. R.G. Bhandarkar

D. Gopal Krishna Gokhale

39. Which Sikh Guru was hanged by the order of Badshah (ruler) Jahangir?

A. Guru Arjun Deo

B. Guru Teg Bahadur

C. Guru Govind Singh

D. Guru Ramdas

40. Aga Khan Palace is situated in—

A. Ahmedabad B. Mumbai

C. Chennai D. Pune

41. The number of Chromosomes in the human body are—

A. 42 B. 44

C. 46 D. 48

42. Which pair is false among the followings—

A. Venus—the brightest planet

B. Jupitor—the biggest planet

C. Murcury—the fastest planet

D. Mars—Closest planet to the earth

43. 'World Ozone Day' is celeberated on—

A. 14 July B. 5 September

C. 16 September D. 10 November

44. Which language is not mentioned in the eighth schedule of Indian constitution?

A. Urdu B. Sanskrit

C. English D. Nepali

45. Most of the active volcanoes are situated around—

A. Indian Ocean B. Atlantic Ocean

C. Pacific Ocean D. Arctic Ocean

46. Jawahar Navodya Vidyalaya was established on the recommendation of—

A. National Education Policy (1986)

B. Programme of Action (amendment 1992)

C. Indian Education Commission (1966)

D. Review Committee of the National Education Policy (1986)

47. Who was the Chairman of the committee constituted for the investigation related to giving moral education during 1958-59.

A. Dr. Sampurna Nand
B. Dr. M.C. Changla
C. Sri Svaran Singh
D. Sri Sriprakash

48. Who recommended work experience in the school syllabus, as its integral part?
A. Melcom Adisheshaiya Committee
B. Ishwar Bhai Patel Committee
C. Tarachand Committee
D. Abaut-Vud-Committee

49. As a constitutional body N.C.T.E (National Council of Teachers Education) was established on—
A. 1985 B. 1986
C. 1992 D. 1995

50. By the reluctant of National Education Policy (1986), 'Operation Blackboard' was Commenced on—
A. 1988 B. 1990
C. 1992 D. 1995

51. "Kahne ko kuch bhi kaho, Parantu Desi swabhawik shashan hi sarvottam hota hai" (Anything can be said, but pure own swadeshi rule is the best). It is the statement of—
A. Dayanand Saraswati
B. Lala Lajpat Rai
C. Bal Gangadhar Tilak
D. Mahatma Gandhi

52. Which was the first committee, established to evaluate the problem of expenditure and obstruction in growth?
A. Jakir Husain Committee
B. Rammurthy Committee
C. Hunting Committee
D. Sri Prakash Committee

53. Which age group of children are included in 'Sarvashikhsha Abhiyaan'?
A. 0 – 14 years
B. 6 – 14 years
C. 3 – 18 years
D. 6 – 18 years

54. Which Indian political party was established in Tashkent?
A. Indian National Congress
B. Farmers and Labours Party
C. Gadar Party
D. Indian Communist Party

55. Who was the chairman of Secondary Education Commission (1952-53)?
A. Dr. S. Radha Krishnan
B. Dr. Lakshmiswami Mudalier
C. Dr. Ligun Sen
D. Dr. D.S. Kothari

SECTION IV : TEACHING-LEARNING AND THE SCHOOL

56. A Student had made you fool prior to one day. What will be your reaction when the same student gives you a good suggestion.
A. You expect it
B. You will say another student to evaluate it
C. You will accept it happily
D. You will evaluate it yourself

57. Which can not be the reason of discipline—
A. To accept the importance of obey the rules
B. To accept the personal right and dignity
C. To accept the value of freedom, equality and Justice.
D. To accept its good role to achieve the aim.

58. Which is the best medium of broadcasting for a scholar?
A. Teacher
B. Media
C. Communication
D. Excellence conversation

59. When a student gives wrong answer to any question, then what is the appropriate treatment for him?
A. Snapped not for learning the Chapter.
B. To re-struct the question so that right answer can be given
C. To re-struct the question, giving the clue
D. To give the right answer with explanation

60. From the following which can make a teacher effective?
A. If he uses instruction supportive materials

B. If he helps in motive search of readable chapter

C. If he gives examples and asks questions from the lesson

D. If he helps students to know the answer

61. Which technic is not suitable to learn science?

A. Observation method

B. Equipment method

C. Conclusion method

D. Listening method

62. Many specialists advocate the system of "Open Book Exam System". On this—
(Give the appropriate answer)

A. Large number of books will be needed for Board

B. More potential will be needed to make question papers

C. Student's participation will be needed

D. Special examiners/evaluaters will be needed to examine answer sheets

63. If students did not understand the lesson taught by you, what should you do?

A. Prior knowledge of students will be re-examined

B. Lesson will be taught again

C. Lesson will be taught again with more examples.

D. It will be left at present to teach in future.

64. 'Pedagogy' is called—

A. Teaching science

B. Art of learning

C. Teaching-excellence-Science and Art both

D. Communication (Presentation) Science

65. Which order will be most suited?
[If M → Motivation, I → Clarification, P → Presentation and R→ Conclusion]

A. MIPR B. PMIR

C. PMRI D. MPRI

66. What does not come in the newly proposed concept 'CCE' (Continuous and Comprehensive Evaluation)

A. Soft planning of evaluation

B. To keep the teachers busy in the evaluation work

C. Determination of teaching and non-teaching aspects of learner

D. Evaluation through Portfolio / documentation

67. Why is it necessary to participate the community in school education?

A. Supervision of teacher's work

B. To improve the school-environment

C. To collect extra resources

D. For the growth of best human resources

68. Which is not the meaning of Alternative school?

A. Charwaha School

B. Education to not the school going children

C. Education of neighbour child in that surroundings

D. Child education near the construction sites

69. A best teacher is, who....... (exact option)

A. inspires the students

B. provides all necessary help to students

C. helps to score good marks

D. maintains discipline in the class

70. In making time-table what should be cared most?

A. Principle of Justice

B. Principle of case of tiredness

C. Principle of differentiation

D. Principle of flexibility

71. What will be the best mode for development of Co-operate-value?

A. To make an arrangement of lectures on this subject

B. To organise cultural programmes

C. Arrangement of a camp for one month

D. To play an ideal role

72. Which of the followings can increase the quality of education?

A. To extend one hour time-period

B. Service period teacher training

C. Solution and treatment teaching

D. By help-books

73. What is the main difference between formal schools and open schools?

A. First are organised
B. Second use less facial factor in their education system
C. Second use modern equipments
D. None of these

74. In the view of social agency, school can be called a .... agent.

A. Primary
B. Secondary
C. Complementary
D. Tertiary

75. Various types of competitions should be organised in schools, because—

(*i*) sufficient fund is available for this.
(*ii*) It helps to develop mutual understanding among different groups.

A. Only (i) is relevant
B. Only (ii) is relevant
C. Both (i) & (ii) are relevant
D. Both (i) & (ii) are irrelevant

76. Which can not be the stage of learning?

A. Procedure
B. Difference-perception
C. Exercise
D. Imagination

77. Which of the following is decisive for teaching work?

A. To make effective the excellence
B. To educate
C. True management of classes
D. Communication with students

78. What will be the indication when a group of students gets more marks in the question-paper made by any teacher?

A. It is a group of high achiever
B. Teacher has taught well
C. Question-paper is good
D. None of these

79. Conclusion of any communication is perceivable senses based on our sensible organ which—

A. sends direct code information to the brain
B. explains received information
C. works by selected process on received information
D. processes only the information.

80. Which of the following is not the quality of questions to know the answer of asked questions to the children?

A. clear meaning
B. not necessary of references
C. use of two negative words in a sentence
D. to be specific answers.

PART-B

SECTION V : (I) SCIENCE

81. Jaundice is due to the infection of—

A. Brain
B. Liver
C. Kidney
D. Spleen

82. In a normal person average rate of heart beat is—

A. 82 B. 92
C. 72 D. 98

83. EEG is used for the observation of which part of the body?

A. Heart B. Lungs
C. Brain D. Muscles

84. Colour of cows milk is light yellow due to—

A. Zenthophil
B. Riboflevin
C. Ribulos
D. Kerotin

85. Which of the following is infectious—

A. Diabetes B. Diphtheria
C. Arthritis D. Cancer

86. Which of the following is less in Anaemia?
A. Haemoglobin B. Collagen
C. Highoglobin D. Myosin

87. Which of the following disease spreads through air?
A. Plague B. Typhoid
C. Tuberculosis D. Cholera

88. Cereals are rich sources of—
A. Starch B. Glucose
C. Fructose D. Maltose

89. Aspirin is the ordinary name of—
A. Salicylic Acid
B. Salicylate
C. Methyl Salicylate
D. Acetylsalicylic Acid

90. Reason of small Pox is—
A. Rubiola Virus B. Variola Virus
C. Varicela D. Mixovirus

91. Carbon Monoxide is an inflammable gas. Which of the following is also an inflammable gas—
A. Helium B. Nitrogen
C. Oxygen D. Hydrogen

92. In the Aerobic Respiration which of the following is needed—
A. Heat B. Water
C. Oxygen D. Sunlight

93. Which of the following does not produce Hydrogen in reaction with water—
A. Potassium B. Cadmium
C. Sodium D. Lithium

94. Ozone contains—
A. Only Oxygen
B. Oxygen and Nitrogen
C. Hydrogen and Carbon
D. Oxygen and Carbon

95. Which of the following liquid is of low density—
A. Fresh water
B. Salt water
C. Petrol
D. Mercury

96. Which of the following theory is used to produce low-temperature—
A. Super conductivity
B. Joule-Kelvin effect
C. Thermoelectric effect
D. Adiabatic demagnetisation

97. Photoelectric cell transforms—
A. Mechanical energy into electrical energy
B. Heat energy into mechanical energy
C. Light energy into chemical energy
D. Light energy into electrical energy

98. Two stones of different masses if fallen down from the peak of the building—
A. small stone reaches before on the ground
B. big stone reaches before on the ground
C. both stones reach together on the ground
D. it depends on the construction of stones

99. Pulsar are—
A. stars moving towards earth
B. stars moving far away to earth
C. fastest moving stars
D. stars having high temperature

100. Ozone hole in the atmosphere is situated at—
A. Above the Arctic ocean
B. Above the Antarctica
C. Above the India
D. Above the Alaska

(II) Mathematics

101. Find the value of

$$\frac{a^2-b^2}{a-b} - \frac{a^3-b^3}{a^2-b^2}$$

A. $\frac{a+b}{ab}$ B. $\frac{a-b}{ab}$
C. $\frac{ab}{a+b}$ D. $\frac{ab}{a-b}$

102. Some people collected 72 rupees by giving equal amount. If three persons were less then each had to give 4 rupees more. How many people were there?
A. 8 B. 9
C. 12 D. 24

103. If $25^{n-1} = 5^{2n-1} - 100$, then what is the value of n?

A. 0 B. 1
C. 2 D. –1

104. The difference of simple interest and recurring interest of any amount in 3 years by the rate of 10% is 31 rupees. What will be the principal amount?

A. 1331 B. 1200
C. 1000 D. 800

105. There are 5 : 2 ratio of milk and water in any mixture of 35 litre. If 5 litre more milk is mixed in it then what will be the ratio of milk and water in the new?

A. 3 : 1 B. 25 : 10
C. 30 : 25 D. 2 : 7

106. If the speed of a passenger train is enhanced with 10 km per hour, then it takes 3 hours less time to cover a distance of 360 km. Find the average speed of the train.

A. 25 km/hour B. 30 km/hour
C. 40 km/hour D. 60 km/hour

107. If 25 people finished one project in 15 days doing 8 hours job, then how many days will be taken by 20 people for doing two-times more job?

A. 50 days B. 40 days
C. 30 days D. 25 days

108. Monthly average income of a person (January, February, and March) was 1500 rupees, and monthly average income of February, March and April was 1800 rupees. If his income of April is 1600 then what was his January's income?

A. Rs. 700 B. Rs. 800
C. Rs. 1000 D. Rs. 1200

109. A person buys two pen in 150 rupees, he sells one of them at 12% profit and the other at 12% loss. He realises that he has sold both of them at same price, then what will be the ratio of buying price of both pen?

A. 1 : 2 B. 3 : 2
C. 4 : 5 D. 11 : 14

110. If $\sec\theta = \frac{5}{4}$, then what will be the value of $\frac{\sec\theta - 2\cos\theta}{\tan\theta - \cot\theta}$.

A. $\frac{7}{12}$ B. $\frac{3}{5}$
C. $\frac{1}{12}$ D. $\frac{1}{7}$

111. What will be the value of tan 5° tan 10° tan 45° tan 80° tan 85°?

A. 0 B. 1
C. –1 D. 2

112. Angle of elevation of top of a high building and a helicopter flying right above the building are 30° and 60° respectively from a point 'P' on the ground. Find out the height of helicopter from ground.

A. 30 metre B. 45 metre
C. 60 metre D. 70 metre

113. Mean of 11 numbers is 35. If the mean of first 6 number and the mean of last 6 numbers are gradually 32 and 37 then what will be the 6th number?

A. 27 B. 28
C. 29 D. 30

114. If the length of any rectangle is increased by 50% and the breadth decreased by 50%, a new rectangle is formed, what will be the area of a new rectangle?

A. 50% less than first rectangle
B. 50% more than first rectangle
C. 25% more than first rectangle
D. 25% less than first rectangle

115. If the radius of any circle is increased by two times then what will increase in its surface area?

A. 400% B. 300%
C. 200% D. 100%

116. Ratio of radius and height of a right circular cone is 5 : 12. If volume of the cone is 314 cm^3 then find the slant height of the cone?

A. 13 cm B. 12 cm
C. 8 cm D. 5 cm

117. Sixth and seventh observations of twelve observations which are arranged in an increasing order are 14 and 15, then what is the median of all the twelve observations?

A. 14.5 B. 14
C. 15 D. 15.5

118. What is the distance of a pt (1, 2) from the mid pt of a line segment joining (6, 8) and (2, 4)?

A. 4 B. 5
C. 6 D. 8

119. What is the common difference of an A.P. if mth term of the A.P. is $\frac{1}{m}$ and nth term is $\frac{1}{n}$?

A. $\frac{1}{mn}$ B. $-\frac{1}{mn}$
C. $\frac{m}{n}$ D. $\frac{n}{m}$

120. If two coins are tossed simultaneously then what will be the probability of getting at least one head?

A. $\frac{1}{4}$ B. $\frac{1}{3}$
C. $\frac{3}{4}$ D. $\frac{4}{3}$

(III) Social Science

121. Three bigha corridor combines—

A. India and Pakistan
B. India and China
C. Bangladesh and Pakistan
D. Bangladesh and India

122. Who built the Vijay Stambh in Chittor?

A. Maharana Pratap
B. Rana Sangram Singh
C. Rana Kumbha
D. Rana Ratan Singh

123. Which religious book was called as 'mother' by Gandhiji?

A. Ramayana
B. The New Testament
C. Bhagvatgeeta
D. Kuran Sharif

124. Tihari water electrical complex is situated on the bank of river—

A. Alaknanda B. Mandakini
C. Dhauli Ganga D. Bhagirathi

125. The person who had made the design of Rashtrapati Bhawan was—

A. Adward Stone B. Le Kaburje
C. Advin Lutians D. Tarun Dutta

126. 'Quit India' movement 1942 was commenced in the month of—

A. January B. March
C. August D. December

127. Match the following—

Group-I
(a) Keshav Chandra Sen
(b) Dayanand Saraswati
(c) Atmaram Pandurang
(d) Syed Ahmed Khan

Group-II
1. Prarthana Samaj
2. Brahma Samaj
3. Aligarh Movement
4. Arya Samaj

	(a)	(b)	(c)	(d)
A.	4	1	3	2
B.	1	4	2	3
C.	2	4	1	3
D.	3	2	4	1

128. Who was the first British President of Indian National Congress?

A. George Yule
B. William Vederbern
C. A.O. Hume
D. Henery Coton

129. Which person is known as 'Grand old man of India'?

A. Bal Gangadhar Tilak
B. Dada Bhai Nauroji
C. Moti Lal Nehru
D. Lala Lajpat Rai

130. Who wrote the 'Akbarnama'?
A. Akbar B. Birbal
C. Abul Fajal D. Bhagwan Das

131. In India, Panchayati Raj System was introduced—
A. In 1950 B. In 1945
C. In 1959 D. In 1962

132. The person who was elected twice as the Vice-President was—
A. Dr. S. Radhakrishnan
B. Shri R. Venkat Raman
C. Dr. Shankar Dayal Sharma
D. Shri V. V. Giri

133. By which amendment of Indian constitution two words - Socialist and Secular was added in the Preamble?
A. 28 B. 40
C. 42 D. 52

134. Indian constitution adhered to—
A. 26 January, 1950
B. 26 January, 1952
C. 15 August, 1948
D. 26 November, 1949

135. Who was the first lady governor of a state in free India?
A. Smt. Sarojini Naidu
B. Smt. Sucheta Kriplani
C. Smt. Indira Gandhi
D. Smt. Vijaya Luxmi Pandit

136. Name the parliamentary committee which scrutinizes the report of Comptroller and Auditor General.
A. Estimates Committee
B. Select Committee
C. Public Accounts Committee
D. None of these

137. Which of the following shows the joining line of the places where rainfall are equal?
A. Iisohips B. Iisohelienj
C. Isobar D. Isohytes

138. Equator line is—
A. the line which joins the North and South pole
B. the imaginary line which moves exactly in the centre of the earth of North and South Pole
C. A girdle around Saturn (planet)
D. An axis of rotation of earth

139. Which is not correct when the interest rate is high in the economic system?
A. saving increases
B. process of lend decreases
C. cost of production increases
D. resultant of capital increases

140. Labour Intensive Technique will be selected in—
A. In labour surplus economy
B. In capital surplus economy
C. In developed economy
D. In developing economy

(IV) ENGLISH

Directions: *(Q.141-142) Choose the one which best expresses the meaning of the given word.*

141. CONDONE
A. Grieve B. Endure
C. Forgive D. Ignore

142. VALIDATE
A. Absolve B. Respect
C. Estimate D. Confirm

Directions: *(Q.143-144) Choose the one which is most opposite in meaning.*

143. MALIGN
A. Protect B. Promote
C. Pacify D. Praise

144. BARBAROUS
A. Civil B. Cool
C. Calm D. Civilized

145. Change the following active voice into passive one—
Does the noise disturb you?
A. You are disturb by the noise
B. Are you disturbed by the noise

C. You are disturbing by the noise
D. Are you disturbing by the noise

146. Change the Narration—
He said, 'where is the book?'
A. He asked me where the book is
B. He asked me where the book was
C. he asked me where was the book
D. he asked me where is the book

Directions: *(Q.147-148) Give one word for the following expressions—*

147. One who is honourably discharged from service.
A. Retired B. Emeritus
C. Relieved D. Emancipated

148. A statement that can have a double meaning.
A. Verbose B. Ambivalent
C. Epigraph D. Ambiguous

Directions: *(Q.149-151) The Italic part of the sentence may have an error. Make the given sentence meaningful and correct by replacing from the given alternatives.*

149. Are you *more cleverer than us*?
A. more cleverer to us
B. cleverer to us
C. cleverer than us
D. No improvement

150. If *I were him* I would have not accepted the offer.
A. If I was him
B. If I were he
C. If I had he
D. No improvement

151. You can buy almost anything in this store, *can you*?
A. Isn't it?
B. Do you?
C. Can't you?
D. No improvement

152. We thought that she... the job.
A. gets B. is getting
C. will get D. would get

153. I shall not be late for dinner ......
A. unless the train will be late
B. unless the train will not be late
C. unless the train will not be late
D. unless the train is late

Directions: *(Q.154-155) Choose the word/ phrase nearest better/correct in meaning to the Italic part of the given sentence.*

154. There are people who always *eulogize* the achievements of others—
A. exaggerate B. appreciate
C. approve D. encourage

155. When I went to see my friend, I found that he *was gone out*—
A. Had gone
B. Has gone
C. Had been going
D. No improvement

156. *Caesar* and *Cleopatra* is a play written by—
A. Shakesperare
B. Marlowe
C. George Bernard Shaw
D. Dryden

157. Who holdes the view that "Poetry divorced from morality is value-less"?
A. Wordsworth B. Arnold
C. T.S. Eliot D. Milton

158. Who said "I admire Jonson, but love Shakespeare"?
A. Dryden B. Dr. Johnson
C. Arnold D. Pope

159. Who is the author of the *Decline and Fall of the Roman Empire*?
A. Ruskin
B. Edmund Burke
C. Edward Gibbon
D. William Robertson

160. Which is the first regular tragedy in English?
A. Roister Doister
B. Gorboduc
C. Morte de Arthur
D. Troylus and Cryseyde

(V) हिन्दी

निर्देश (प्रश्न 161 से 165 तक): *नीचे दिए गए गद्यांश को ध्यान से पढ़िए तथा उसके आधार पर पूछे गए प्रश्नों के उत्तर दीजिए—*

जीवन का उद्देश्य एक रहस्य है। वह कठिन जरूर है फिर भी ऐसा नहीं है कि उसे जाना ही न जा सके। लगातार उस पर सोचते रहने से इसके भेदों से पर्दा उठा भी है। आधुनिक युग में अत्यंत सूक्ष्म तथा वैज्ञानिक आकलन से बने उपकरण सचमुच विलक्षण हैं। भौतिकशास्त्र के प्रचुर आविष्कार हमें उन विश्वसनीय उपायों का स्पष्ट आभास दे रहे हैं, जिनसे जीवन को उन्नत बनाया जा सकता है, लेकिन सारे उपकरणों, रणनीतियों तथा खोजों के बावजूद ऐसा लगता है कि हम अभी भी नियति के हाथ का खिलौना ही हैं। हम अपनी नियति तय नहीं कर पाते। प्रकृति हम पर हावी है। हम उसके आगे असहाय महसूस करते हैं। हमें प्रकृति के प्रभुत्व से मुक्ति पानी ही चाहए। उसे पाने के लिए हमें एक लम्बी यात्रा तय करनी होगी।

हम प्रकृति की दया पर जीते हैं। उसकी दया पर ही बने रहना सचमुच मुक्ति नहीं कही जा सकती है। हमारे उत्साही मन को उस समय बेरुख बेबसी जकड़ लेती है जब हम प्रकृति की मार को सहते हैं। बाढ़-तूफान या भूकम्प इत्यादि का शिकार हो जाते हैं। कभी-कभी महसूस करते हैं कि बिना किसी सीधी वजह के हमारे प्रियजन हमसे छिन जाते हैं। कभी कोई बीमारी या दुर्घटना हमें समय से पहले उठा लेती है। अक्सर हमें कोई प्रत्यक्ष तर्क और कारण समझ में नहीं आता तब हमें अहसास होता है कि हमने बहुत कुछ हासिल किया है, लेकिन हमने वास्तविक विजय नहीं पाई है। जीवन को हम जैसा जीना चाहते हैं वैसा जी नहीं पा रहे हैं। हम उसे अपने अनुरूप ढालने की तमाम कोशिशें करते हैं, लेकिन ढाल नहीं पाते हैं। हम गेहूँ के आटे की बनी रोटी खाते हैं क्या हम जानते हैं कि गेहूँ को किसने बनाया? रोटी का पाचन होकर आत्मसात कराने का कार्य कौन करता है?

जीवन के हर पक्ष में तमाम निश्चितताओं के साथ हमें एक अनिश्चित सत्ता स्वीकारनी होगी, एक अपरिहार्य निर्भरता दिखाई देगी। हम नहीं जानते कि दिल धड़कना कब बन्द कर देगा? यहाँ हमें अपने सच्चे अमर आत्म की जरूरत महसूस होती है जिसके विश्वास से हम बिना किसी परेशानी के निर्बाध रूप से आगे जा सकें। उस उच्चतर सत्ता के सामने परम निर्भयता और समर्पण का अभ्यास किए बिना जीवन का परम रहस्य उद्घाटित नहीं होगा।

161. इस गद्यांश का उपयुक्त शीर्षक क्या होगा?
A. जीवन का रहस्यमय उद्देश्य
B. जीवन का परम रहस्य
C. जीवन की बाध्यताएं
D. निर्भयता और समर्पण का अभ्यास

162. जीवन को समुन्नत कैसे बनाया जा सकता है?
A. वैज्ञानिक उपकरणों की उपलब्धि से
B. प्रकृति पर विजय प्राप्त करके
C. आत्मसत्ता की उपस्थिति का अभ्यास करके
D. प्रकृति की दया पर निर्भर रहने से

163. 'नियति के हाथ का खिलौना' इस कथन का क्या तात्पर्य है?
A. प्रकृति के साथ आनंदित रहना
B. प्रकृति के आगे असहाय महसूस करना
C. प्रकृति के अनुसार ढल जाना
D. प्रकृति की सत्ता स्वीकार करना

164. 'हम अपनी नियति तय नहीं कर पाते' इस कथन का क्या अभिप्राय है?
A. जीवन लक्ष्य निर्धारित नहीं कर पाते
B. लम्बी यात्रा तय नहीं कर पाते
C. जीवन जीना नहीं आता
D. जीवन का परम रहस्य उद्घाटित नहीं होता

165. हमारी अपरिहार्य निर्भरता किस पर होगी?
A. प्रकृति पर
B. अमर आत्मा पर
C. भौतिकशास्त्र के उपकरणों पर
D. प्रकृति के प्रभुत्व से मुक्ति पर

166. 'पृथ्वीराज रासो' किस भाषा में रचित है?
A. अवधी B. ब्रजभाषा
C. भोजपुरी D. राजस्थानी

167. पहेली की तरह ही 'मुकरियाँ' किस कवि की प्रसिद्ध रचना है?
A. अमृता प्रीतम B. अमीर खुसरो
C. चन्दवरदाई D. नंददास

168. निम्नलिखित में से 'भगवतीचरण वर्मा' की रचना कौन-सी है?
A. अशोक के फूल
B. अब मैं नाच्यौ बहुत गोपाल
C. कहि न जाय का कहिए
D. रश्मिरथी

169. 'मैला आँचल' किसका उपन्यास है?
A. अशोक बाजपेयी
B. फणीश्वरनाथ रेणु
C. गोपाल प्रसाद नीरज
D. हीरानंद वात्स्यायन

170. निम्नलिखित में से कौन-सी प्रेमचंद की रचना नहीं है—
A. गबन
B. वरदान
C. शतरंज के खिलाड़ी
D. टेड़े-मेड़े रास्ते

171. निम्नलिखित में से किसकी वर्तनी शुद्ध है?
A. प्राथ्र्य B. चर्ण
C. अनुगृहीत D. पूज्यनीय

172. 'उपरि-उक्त' के जुड़ने से कौन-सा शब्द बनेगा?
A. उपरोक्त B. उपर्युक्त
C. उपर्योक्त D. उपरुक्त

173. इनमें से किस शब्द की वर्तनी अशुद्ध है?
A. मनोकामना B. मनोयोग
C. मनोदशा D. मनोरथ

174. 'औदार्य' की तरह 'व्यवहार' शब्द से कौन-सा शब्द ठीक है?
A. व्यवहार्य B. व्यावहार्य
C. व्यवहारी D. व्यावहारिक

175. 'जाया और पति' के स्थान पर समस्त पद कौन-सा ठीक है?
A. जायापति B. जयापति
C. दम्पती D. दम्पत्ति

176. 'दोहावली' किसकी कृति है?
A. मतिराम B. बिहारी
C. घनानंद D. तुलसी

177. 'तोता-चश्म' का इनमें से कौन-सा अर्थ सही है?
A. मिठ बोला B. अविश्वसनीय
C. कृतघ्न D. हितैषी

178. "जिसे मनोवांछित की प्राप्ति हो गई है" इस कथन के लिए एक शब्द कौन-सा उचित है?
A. आप्तकाम B. संतुष्ट
C. पूर्णकाम D. निष्काम

179. पत्रा ही तिथि पाइए, वा घर के चहुँ पास।
निशि दिन पूनौ ही रहत, आनन ओप उजास।।
इस दोहे में कौन-सा रस है?
A. अद्भुत B. हास्य
C. शृंगार D. वात्सल्य

180. निम्नलिखित वाक्यों में से कौन-सा वाक्य शुद्ध है?
A. मेरे को कल छुट्टी पर जाना होगा
B. आप ही तो मना किये थे
C. मुझको लौटने में विलम्ब हो गया
D. कपड़े डालकर तुमने मेरे साथ क्या करा?

ANSWERS

1	2	3	4	5	6	7	8	9	10
D	B	C	D	A	C	A	A	C	B
11	**12**	**13**	**14**	**15**	**16**	**17**	**18**	**19**	**20**
C	A	D	D	B	A	C	C	B	B

21	22	23	24	25	26	27	28	29	30
A	C	B	B	C	C	A	D	A	D
31	32	33	34	35	36	37	38	39	40
A	B	D	C	C	B	D	A	A	D
41	42	43	44	45	46	47	48	49	50
C	D	C	D	C	D	A	B	D	A
51	52	53	54	55	56	57	58	59	60
A	C	B	D	B	D	B	D	D	C
61	62	63	64	65	66	67	68	69	70
D	B	C	C	B	A	B	A	B	B
71	72	73	74	75	76	77	78	79	80
D	B	B	C	C	A	A	B	D	D
81	82	83	84	85	86	87	88	89	90
B	C	C	D	B	A	A	A	D	B
91	92	93	94	95	96	97	98	99	100
D	C	B	A	C	A	D	C	C	B
101	102	103	104	105	106	107	108	109	110
C	B	C	C	A	B	C	A	D	B
111	112	113	114	115	116	117	118	119	120
B	A	C	D	B	A	A	B	B	C
121	122	123	124	125	126	127	128	129	130
D	C	C	D	C	C	C	A	B	C
131	132	133	134	135	136	137	138	139	140
C	A	C	A	A	C	D	B	D	A
141	142	143	144	145	146	147	148	149	150
B	D	D	D	B	B	B	D	C	B
151	152	153	154	155	156	157	158	159	160
C	D	C	B	A	C	A	A	C	B
161	162	163	164	165	166	167	168	169	170
B	C	B	D	B	A	A	A	B	D
171	172	173	174	175	176	177	178	179	180
D	B	B	B	D	D	A	B	A	C

SOME SELECTED EXPLANATORY ANSWERS

101. $\dfrac{a^2-b^2}{a-b}-\dfrac{a^3-b^3}{a^2-b^2}$

$$=\frac{(a+b)(a-b)}{a-b}-\frac{\left[(a-b)(a^2+ab+b^2)\right]}{(a+b)(a-b)}$$

$$=a+b-\frac{(a^2+ab+b^2)}{a+b}$$

$$=\frac{a^2+2ab+b^2-a^2-ab-b^2}{a+b}=\frac{ab}{a+b}.$$

102. Let no. people = x

According to the question

$$x\times y=72 \quad ...(i)$$

$$\Rightarrow \quad y=\frac{72}{x}$$

Now, $(x-3)(y+4)=72$

$\Rightarrow xy+4x-3y-12=72 \quad ...(ii)$

From (i) and (ii)

$$xy=xy+4x-3y-12$$

$\Rightarrow \quad 4x - 3y = 12$

$$4x - 3\left(\frac{72}{x}\right) = 12$$

$\Rightarrow \quad 4x^2 - 216 = 12x$

$\Rightarrow \quad 4x^2 - 12x - 216 = 0$

$\Rightarrow \quad x^2 - 3x - 54 = 0$

$\Rightarrow \quad x^2 - 9x + 6x - 54 = 0$

$\Rightarrow \quad x(x-9) + 6(x-9) = 0$

$\Rightarrow \quad (x-9)(x+6) = 0$

either $x = 9$ or $x = -6$ (not possible)

$\therefore$ Required no. of people = 9.

103. $25^{n-1} = 5^{2n-1} - 100$

$\Rightarrow \quad 5^{2n-1} - 25^{n-1} = 100$

$\Rightarrow \quad \frac{5^{2n}}{5} - (5^2)^{(n-1)} = 100$

$\Rightarrow \quad \frac{5^{2n}}{5} - 5^{2n-1} = 100$

$\Rightarrow \quad \frac{5^{2n}}{5} - \frac{5^{2n}}{25} = 100$

$\Rightarrow \quad \frac{5 \times 5^{2n} - 5^{2n}}{25} = 100$

$\Rightarrow \quad 5^{2n}[5 - 1] = 2500$

$\Rightarrow \quad 5^{2n} = \frac{2500}{4} = 625$

$\Rightarrow \quad 5^{2n} = (5)^4$

$\Rightarrow \quad 2n = 4$

$\Rightarrow \quad n = 2$

104. Let principal = Rs 100

$$SI = \frac{100 \times 10 \times 3}{100} = \text{Rs } 30$$

$$A = P\left(1 + \frac{r}{100}\right)^t$$

$$= 100\left(1 + \frac{10}{100}\right)^3 = 100 \times \left(\frac{11}{10}\right)^3$$

$$= \frac{1331}{10}$$

$$C.I. = A - P = \frac{1331}{10} - 100$$

$$= \frac{331}{10} = 33.1$$

C.I. – S.I. = 33.1 – 30 = 3.1

when diff. is Rs 3.1 then P = Rs 100

when diff. is Rs 31 then P = $\frac{100}{3.1} \times 31$

$$= \frac{100}{31} \times 31 \times 10$$

$\therefore \quad$ P = Rs 1000.

105. Amount of milk = $\frac{5}{7} \times 35 = 25$ litre

Amount of water = $\frac{2}{7} \times 35 = 10$ litre

Now,

Amount of milk = 25 + 5 = 30 litre

Amount of water = 10 litre

$\therefore$ Ratio of milk and water in the new mixture

= 30 : 10

= 3 : 1.

106. Let the average speed of the train = x km/hr

According to the question,

$$\frac{360}{x} - \frac{360}{x+10} = 3$$

$\Rightarrow \quad \frac{360(x+10-x)}{x(x+10)} = 3$

$\Rightarrow x^2 + 10x - 1200 = 0$

$\Rightarrow \quad (x+40)(x-30) = 0$

$\Rightarrow x = -40$ or $x = 30$

$\therefore$ Required speed = 30 km/hr.

108. Jan. + Feb. + March = 1500 × 3 = 4500

Feb. + March + April = 1800 × 3 = 5400

Feb. + March = 5400 – 1600 = 3800

$\therefore$ January's income = 4500 – 3800 = Rs 700.

110. $\because \sec\theta = \frac{5}{4} = \frac{h}{b} \quad \therefore p = 3$

$\cos\theta = \frac{b}{h} = \frac{4}{5}$

$\tan\theta = \frac{p}{b} = \frac{3}{4}$, $\cot\theta = \frac{b}{p} = \frac{4}{3}$

Now, $\frac{\sec\theta - 2\cos\theta}{\tan\theta - \cot\theta} = \frac{\frac{5}{4} - 2 \times \frac{4}{5}}{\frac{3}{4} - \frac{4}{3}}$

$$= \frac{\frac{5}{4}-\frac{8}{5}}{\frac{9-16}{12}} = \frac{\frac{25-32}{20}}{-\frac{7}{12}} = -\frac{7}{20}\times-\frac{12}{7} = \frac{12}{20} = \frac{3}{5}.$$

111. tan 5° . tan 10° . tan 45° . tan 80° . tan 85°
= tan 5° × tan (90 – 5)° × tan 10° . tan (90 – 10)° × tan 45°
= tan 5° × cot 5° × tan 10° × cot 10° × tan 45°
= 1 × 1 × 1 = 1.

113. Required 6th number = (32 × 6 + 37 × 6) – (35 × 11)
= 6(32 + 37) – 385
= 6 × 69 – 385
= 414 – 385 = 29.

114. Tricky Method

Percentage increase in the length of rectangle = 50%
and percentage decrease in the breadth of rectangle = 50%

∴ Percentage increase or decrease in the area

of the rectangle = $\left[50-50+\frac{50\times(-50)}{100}\right]\%$

$= -\frac{2500}{100}\% = -25\%$

Since negative (–) sign indicate decrease.
Hence, the area will decrease by 25%.

115. Area of circle = πr^2
Now, area of circle = $\pi(2r)^2 = 4\pi r^2$
Area increased = $4\pi r^2 - \pi r^2 = 3\pi r^2$

Percentage increased area = $\frac{3\pi r^2}{\pi r^2}\times 100 = 300\%$.

116. Let radius of cone = $5x$ cm
and height of cone = $12\,x$ cm

volume of cone = $\frac{1}{3}\pi(5x)^2\times 12x$

$\Rightarrow \frac{1}{3}\times\frac{22}{7}\times 25x^2\times 12x = 314$

$\Rightarrow\quad 3.14\times 100\,x^3 = 314$

$\Rightarrow\quad 314\,x^3 = 314$

$\Rightarrow\quad x^3 = 1$

$\Rightarrow\quad x = 1$

∴ Radius = $5x = 5\times 1 = 5$ cm
height = $12x = 12\times 1 = 12$ cm

slant height = $\sqrt{(5)^2+(12)^2} = \sqrt{169} = 13$ cm.

117. Here $n = 12$ which is even number

$$\therefore \text{median} = \left[\frac{\frac{n}{2}\text{th term + next term}}{2}\right]$$

$$= \left[\frac{\text{6th term + 7th term}}{2}\right]$$

$$= \frac{14+15}{2} = \frac{29}{2} = 14.5.$$

119. Let first term of A.P. = a and common difference = d

$\frac{1}{m} = m\text{th term} = a\,(m-1)d$ ...(*i*)

$\frac{1}{n} = n\text{th term} = a\,(n-1)d$ ...(*ii*)

Subtract (*ii*) from (*i*)

$$\frac{1}{m}-\frac{1}{n} = (m-1)d-(n-1)d$$

$$\Rightarrow \frac{n-m}{mn} = d[m-1-n+1]$$

$$\Rightarrow \frac{-(m-n)}{mn} = d(m-n)$$

$$\Rightarrow d = \frac{-(m-n)}{mn\times(m-n)} = -\frac{1}{mn}.$$

120. Required probability = $\frac{3}{4}$.

Previous Paper (Solved)

IGNOU B.Ed. Entrance Test 2008

PART-A

SECTION-I : GENERAL ENGLISH COMPREHENSION

Directions (Qs. 1 to 10): *Read the following passage carefully and pick out the best answer out of the four choices given in the questions that follow.*

A duty is an obligation. It is something we owe to others as social beings when we live together. We must let others live with us. My right of living implies my duty to my fellow beings to allow them the same conditions of life. In fact, rights and duties are correlated. What is a right in regard to one may be a duty in regard to others. Rights and duties are two sides of the same coin. We should always observe from the standpoint of others. Moral duty is more effective than legal rights. A moral duty is that which is binding upon the people on moral grounds. It is my moral duty to help the poor because of being a member of the society.

I must try to create conditions that contribute to the welfare of humanity. Similarly, I owe a duty to my parents—to be obedient and respectful to them. This duty originates from the sense of responsibility which is directly related to our conscience. So this is concerned with a moral duty which any person owes without a legal bondage.

A sense of duty is paramount for the proper development of civilization. Hypocrisy is quite reverse to the sense of duty. It involves wickedness, while duty involves sincerity and faithfulness.

1. According to the passage, rights and duties are—
A. Two sides of the same coin
B. Correlated
C. Both (A) and (B)
D. Neither (A) nor (B)

2. According to the passage legal duty is—
A. More important than moral duty
B. Less important than moral duty
C. More effective than moral duty
D. Less effective than moral duty

3. Duty comes from—
A. Responsibility
B. Legal bondage
C. Hypocrisy
D. None of the above

4. Which of the following statements is **not** correct according to the passage?
A. Hypocrisy involves wickedness
B. Hypocrisy is opposed to duty
C. Duty involves sincerity
D. Sense of duty is not important for the development of civilization

5. Which of the following moral duties has **not** been mentioned in the passage?
A. Moral duty towards our motherland
B. Moral duty towards our parents
C. Moral duty towards the poor
D. Moral duty to contribute to the welfare of humanity

6. Which of the following is **not** related to moral duty?
A. Sense of responsibility
B. Conscience
C. Hypocrisy
D. Sincerity

7. Why is it a duty to help the poor?
A. Because I am poor
B. Because I am rich

C. Because I belong to the society
D. Because God wants this

8. Why should I be obedient and respectful to my parents?
A. Because of my sense of responsibility
B. Because of legal bonding
C. Because of civilization
D. Because of hypocrisy

9. "We should always observe from the standpoint of others." This is a—
A. Simple sentence
B. Complex sentence
C. Compound sentence
D. Phrase

10. The word 'always' in "We should always observe from the standpoint of others" is a/an—
A. Adverb B. Adjective
C. Noun D. Verb

SECTION II : LOGICAL AND ANALYTICAL REASONING

Directions (Qs. 11 to 14): *In each of the following questions an incomplete series of numbers, with one blank is given, identify the missing member from the given alternatives.*

11. 1, 27, 125, ...?..... 729
A. 242 B. 314
C. 307 D. 343

12. 2, 5, 10, 50, 500, ...?.....
A. 25000 B. 560
C. 550 D. 540

13. 3, 14, 47, ...?..... 443, 1334
A. 61 B. 89
C. 146 D. 445

14. 2, 9, 30, 93, 282, ...?.....
A. 849 B. 846
C. 649 D. 746

Directions (Qs. 15 to 18): *In each of the following questions there are five groups of letters. First is the primary one, followed by four; out of which one is different from the rest. Identify this odd member.*

15. IIJL
A. QQSV B. EEFH
C. AABD D. MMNP

16. ABAC
A. BCBD B. PRPQ
C. CDCE D. STSU

17. BXTP
A. OKGC B. DZVR
C. XTOK D. EAWS

18. DINS
A. HMSX B. FKPU
C. JOTY D. NSXC

19. Which pair is different in some way from others in the following pairs?
A. Bottle and ink
B. Can and oil
C. Bag and clothes
D. Boat and ship

Directions (Qs. 20 to 24): *In each of the following questions there are five figures. First is a reference figure. Among the answer figures one figure does not belong to the class to which the first figure belongs. Identify this odd figure.*

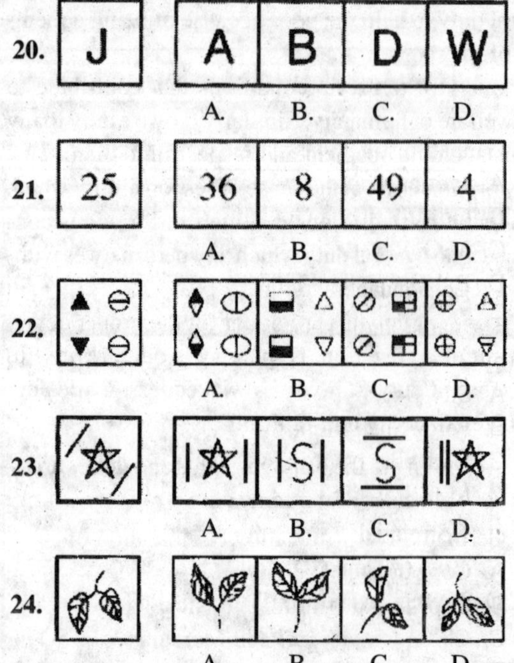

Directions (Qs. 25 to 28): *In each of the following questions two statements are followed by two conclusions. Assuming that the two given statements are true (however absurd they may be) decide which of the two conclusions follows strictly from the given statements. Select the most appropriate alternative.*

25. All men are chairs.
All animals are chairs.
Conclusions:
I. All men are animals.
II. No animal is a man.
A. Only I follows
B. Only II follows
C. Both I and II follow
D. Neither I nor II follows

26. Buckets are means of transport.
Stairs are means of transport.
Conclusions:
I. Buckets are stairs.
II. Some stairs are buckets.
A. Only I follows
B. Only II follows
C. Both I and II follow
D. Neither I nor II follows

27. No bird has wings.
All birds are rational.
Conclusions:
I. Some rationals have wings.
II. Wingless are birds.
A. Only I follows
B. Only II follows
C. Both I and II follow
D. Neither I nor II follows

28. All philosophers are rational people.
Some rational people are happy.
Conclusions:
I. Some happy people are philosophers.
II. Some happy people are rational.
A. Only I follows
B. Only II follows
C. Both I and II follow
D. Neither I nor II follows

29. Which is the fourth letter to the left of the letter that is mid-way between 'O' and 'P' in 'CARDIOGRAPH'?
A. D B. I
C. O D. R

30. Which is the odd term in the following list?
A. January B. May
C. April D. August

SECTION III : EDUCATIONAL AND GENERAL AWARENESS

31. Ganpati festival was started by—
A. Jyotiba Phule
B. Gopal Krishna Gokhale
C. M.G. Ranade
D. Bal Gangadhar Tilak

32. The name 'Indian National Congress' was given by—
A. S.N. Banerjee
B. Feroz Shah Mehta
C. Dadabhai Naoroji
D. M.G. Ranade

33. German Silver is the alloy combination of—
A. Copper, Zinc and Nickel
B. Copper, Aluminium and Nickel
C. Chromium, Nickel and Mercury
D. Copper, Lead and Chromium

34. Who is considered the 'Guardian of public purse'?
A. President
B. Parliament
C. Comptroller and Auditor General
D. Public Accounts Committee

35. Where is Nandapa Wildlife Sanctuary?
A. Andhra Pradesh
B. Arunachal Pradesh
C. Himachal Pradesh
D. Madhya Pradesh

36. Which of the following committees on education is considered as the Magna Carta of English Education in India?
A. Wood's Despatch
B. Raleigh Commission
C. Saddler Commission
D. Hunter Commission

37. Who said— "Patriotisim is religion and religion is love for India"?
A. Swami Vivekananda
B. Raj Narain Bose
C. Bal Gangadhar Tilak
D. Bankim Chandra Chatterjee

38. The famous 'Kirtistambha' at Chittor was built by—
A. Rana Pratap B. Rana Kumbha
C. Rana Hammir D. Rana Sangram Singh

39. Gold coins in India were first introduced by—
A. Sakas B. Parthians
C. Indo-Greeks D. Kushans

40. Light year is the unit of—
A. Time B. Distance
C. Light D. Intensity of light

41. Which of the following is known as 'morning star'?
A. Venus B. Mars
C. Jupiter D. Saturn

42. All the following foods lack vitamin C, except—
A. Rice B. Meat
C. Cheese D. Milk

43. The fourth state of matter is—
A. Super fluids
B. Small particles suspended in the gas
C. Liquid crystals
D. Plasma

44. The leading producer of coffee in the world is—
A. Turkey B. Brazil
C. Venezuela D. Cuba

45. The Bhutia group of languages does **not** include—
A. Ladakhi B. Tibetan
C. Lepcha D. Sherpa

46. The largest producer of sugarcane in India is—
A. Andhra Pradesh B. Gujarat
C. Punjab D. Uttar Pradesh

47. Which of the following matchings is **wrong**?
A. Vijayawada – Narmada
B. Lucknow – Gomti
C. Badrinath – Alaknanda
D. Ayodhya – Saryu

48. The first nuclear reactor of India was named as—
A. Urvashi B. Rohini
C. Kamini D. Apsara

49. Fundamental right to education has been brought through—
A. 83rd Constitution (Amendment) Act
B. 86th Constitution (Amendment) Act
C. 93rd Constitution (Amendment) Act
D. 96th Constitution (Amendment) Act

50. Integrated Child Development Scheme (ICDS) caters to—
A. Early Child care and Education alone
B. Early Child care and Education with five other components
C. Early Child care and Education with four other components
D. Early Child care and three other components

51. Education Commission in independent India which focused on Secondary Education was chaired by—
A. Dr. D.S. Kothari
B. A. Lakshmiswami Mudaliar
C. Dr. S. Radhakrishnan
D. Triguna Sen

52. Education Commission in pre-independence India which comprehensively covered all aspects of education is known as—
A. Saddler Commission
B. Hunter Commission
C. Sargent Plan
D. Abbot-Wood Report

53. Tarachand Committee provided recommendations on—
A. Student's Unrest
B. Religious and Moral Education
C. Vocationalisation of Education
D. Secondary Education

54. State expenditure of 6 per cent of G.D.P. was recommended by—
A. Kothari Commission (1966)
B. National Education Policy (1968)
C. National Policy on Education (1986)
D. Review Committee on NPE (1986)

55. The latest National Curriculum Framework by NCERT came into existence in—
A. 2000 B. 2004
C. 2005 D. 2006

SECTION IV : TEACHING-LEARNING AND THE SCHOOL

56. What would be your approach if a student interrupts in your class?
A. You will ask him to leave the class
B. You will ask him to behave properly
C. You will assess his reasons to do the same
D. You will give him extra home-work

57. How would you prefer to address a student who has not completed his home-work?
A. When you are going to complete it?
B. You did not do it. Try it
C. Why did you not complete it?
D. You better ignore it now

58. Schools should be concerned with the development of child, which should include—
A. Acquisition of knowledge by the child
B. Acquisition of life-skills by the child
C. Acquisition of skills required by the nation
D. Acquisition of skills required by a healthy person

59. The main reason for non-achievement of full literacy in India is—
A. Lack of funds
B. Incapability of utilization of funds
C. Lack of suitable facilities
D. Lack of will to achieve the goal

60. The main purpose of 'Parent-Teacher-Association (PTA)' in any school is to—
A. Keep students in check/control
B. Collect additional funds for remedial teaching
C. Share understanding of the problems faced by school
D. Involve parents for improvement of school functioning

61. A student gives a partially correct respond to your question. Then you will—
A. Seek further information
B. Provide reinforcement
C. Reframe your question
D. Tell the correct information

62. School can be called a social agent if—
A. It transmits knowledge
B. It educates about rights and duties
C. It imparts knowledge about traditions and values
D. It organises various activities

63. One basic difference between traditional schools and open learning schools is that—
A. The former are systematic
B. The latter do not cultivate cultural values
C. The latter use modern gadgets
D. The former carry personal touch

64. School can be considered a ..... group as far as socialising agency is concerned.
A. Primary
B. Secondary
C. Supplementary
D. Tertiary

65. Which of the following statements is not true?
A. Acquisition of 'life-skills' is part of maturation
B. Acquisition of 'life-skills' is part of social process
C. 'Life-skills' are directly moulded
D. 'Life-skills' are learnt

66. A student wants to share his problem with his teacher and visits the teacher for the same at his home. In such a situation, the teacher should—
A. Suggest to him to escape from his home
B. Contact the student's parents and provide help
C. Extend reasonable help and boost his morale
D. Warn him to never visit his home

67. If a student alleges against you for showing favouritism in evaluation of scripts, how would you deal with him?
A. Reject his allegations
B. Adopt punitive measure
C. Make efforts to reveal his position
D. Show his answer book and few more

68. The major responsibility with which school personnel have been entrusted is that of—
A. Adjusting social demands to the needs of the child
B. Adjusting the child to conform to the demands of society

C. Changing human nature to conform to social expectations
D. Preparing the child to change the society

69. In order to develop a good rapport with students, a teacher should (select the most important activity)—
A. Love his students
B. Be friendly with all
C. Pay individual attention
D. Communicate well

70. The best reason because of which a teacher can command respect from his students is if—
A. He follows innovative practices in the class
B. He dictates notes to the class
C. He reads and explains the textbook
D. He does not give home assignment

71. Development of moral values among students is very important. What would you do to develop the same?
A. Encourage moral value related works
B. Organise lectures
C. Display stories based on moral values
D. Present yourself as a role model

72. Teaching aids are useful because they—
A. Help teacher's work
B. Activate all senses
C. Help students to be attentive
D. Make learning more meaningful

73. Teacher's class-room behaviour should be good because—
A. It will set an example
B. Students will be more attentive
C. Environment would be conducive to learning
D. Students will appreciate it

74. You have a class which is very heterogeneous in height. You should allow a seating arrangement—
A. Which is random
B. Where smaller students are allowed to sit in such a way that they can see and participate easily in class activities
C. Which is purely based on height
D. That has taller students on one side of the class

75. Which one of the following may not be the best reason for cheating in the class-room examination?
A. Too lazy to study
B. Parental pressure for good marks
C. Fear of failure
D. Self-prestige

76. In this age of academic excellence demand, inclusion of games and sports in schools is—
A. A wastage of time
B. Taking away a lot of time from academic work
C. Giving time for leisure or relaxation
D. Necessary for the co-ordinated development of the individual

77. Which one of the following pairs is odd (or not properly associated)?
A. Froebel – Playway
B. Maria Montessori – Divergent thinking
C. Keller – Co-operative learning
D. Gandhiji – Soiled hands

78. While teaching the concept of a 'circle', which one of the following would be the best way to do it?
A. Present a picture of a circle
B. Present pictures of circles of various sizes
C. Present pictures of circles and ellipses
D. Present pictures of circles and polygons

79. Teaching would be more effective if the teacher—
A. Makes his intent purposeful
B. Is master of the subject
C. Uses various instructional aids
D. Declares his objectives in the beginning

80. In a democratic country like India, schools should concentrate on—
A. Development of traits to face hurdles of daily life
B. Inculcation of values cherised by the community
C. Preparation for academic excellence
D. Development of traits of good citizenship

PART-B

SECTION V : (I) SCIENCE

81. Clothes do not dry quickly on a rainy day because on a rainy day—
A. Humidity is high
B. Humidity is low
C. Temperature becomes high
D. Atmospheric pressure rises

82. Joule is the unit of—
A. Force
B. Power
C. Energy
D. Pressure

83. The audible range of hearing for average human beings is—
A. 20 Hz to 20 KHz
B. 2 Hz to 20 Hz
C. 2 Hz to 20 KHz
D. 2 KHz to 20 KHz

84. Tritium is an—
A. Isobar of Hydrogen
B. Isotope of Hydrogen
C. Isobar of Helium
D. Isotope of Helium

85. Which of the following ions helps in the opening and closing of stomata?
A. Na^+
B. K^+
C. Ca^{++}
D. None of the above

86. Which of the following does not have plus (+) or minus (–) signs marked on it?
A. Resistor
B. Ammeter
C. Voltmeter
D. Battery

87. Photosynthesis is a—
A. Catabolic process
B. Anabolic process
C. Amphibolic process
D. All of these

88. If a mirror forms an erect but diminished image of an object placed anywhere in front of it, is a—
A. Concave Mirror
B. Plane Mirror
C. Convex Mirror
D. Concave and Convex Mirror (both)

89. The instrument to measure atmospheric pressure is called—
A. Pyrometer
B. Thermopile
C. Barometer
D. Manometer

90. Orange colour of the setting sun is due to—
A. Reflection of light
B. Diffusion of light
C. Scattering of light
D. Polarisation of light

91. What is the final colour of blue litmus when a dilute solution of NaOH is added to it?
A. Red
B. Pink
C. Orange
D. Blue

92. Pick the odd one out—
A. Fermentation
B. Aerobic Respiration
C. Anaerobic Respiration
D. Breathing

93. Hypotonic solution as compared to Hypertonic solution has—
A. More solute
B. Less solute
C. Same solute
D. Nothing can be said about the amount of solute

94. Volt is the unit of—
A. Charge
B. Current
C. Resistance
D. Potential difference

95. Two resistors having resistances of 1 ohm and 2 ohms respectively are connected in series with a battery. The current through the 2 ohms resistor is 2 amperes. The current through the 1 ohm resistor will be—

A. 0.5 amp B. 1 amp
C. 2 amp D. 4 amp

96. The addition of which one of the following will decrease the pH value of water?
A. Caustic Soda
B. Baking soda
C. Salt
D. Hydrochloric acid

97. The branch of science that deals with tumours is—
A. Osteology B. Anatomy
C. Oncology D. Urology

98. Pneumonia is a disease associated with—
A. Liver B. Lungs
C. Gums D. Kidney

99. 'Decibel' is a measure of—
A. Time B. Distance
C. Intensity of sound D. Energy

100. Which of the following have the highest frequency?
A. Heat waves
B. Sound waves
C. Ultraviolet rays
D. Gamma rays

(II) Mathematics

101. The value of

$$\frac{a\sqrt{a}+b\sqrt{b}}{\left(\sqrt{a}+\sqrt{b}\right)(a-b)}+\frac{2\sqrt{b}}{\sqrt{a}+\sqrt{b}}-\frac{\sqrt{ab}}{a-b} \text{ is—}$$

A. 0 B. 1
C. $\sqrt{ab}$ D. $\left(\sqrt{a}+\sqrt{b}\right)$

102. In a mixture of 35 litres, the ratio of milk and water is 5 : 2. Another 5 litres of milk is added to the mixture. The ratio of milk and water in the new mixture is—
A. 3 : 1
B. 1 : 3
C. 2 : 3
D. 3 : 2

103. Walking at 4 km an hour, a peon reaches his office 5 minutes late. If he walks at 5 km an hour, he will be 4 minutes too early. The distance of his office from the residence is—
A. 5 km B. 4 km
C. 3 km D. 2 km

104. If $5^{x-2} . 3^{2x-3} = 135$, then the value of x is—
A. 0 B. 1
C. 2 D. 3

105. The simple interest on a certain amount at 4% p.a. for 4 years is Rs. 80 more than the interest on the same sum for 3 years at 5% p.a. The sum is—
A. Rs. 6000 B. Rs. 7200
C. Rs. 7500 D. Rs. 8000

106. A trader marks an article at 30% more than the cost price. He gives 10% discount to his customers and gains Rs. 25.50 per article. The cost price of the article is—
A. Rs. 150 B. Rs. 200
C. Rs. 175 D. Rs. 250

107. The price of sugar is increased by 25%. How much per cent should a man decrease his consumption so that there is no increase in his expenditure?
A. 10% B. 20%
C. 5% D. 15%

108. Rs. 6500 were divided equally among a certain number of persons. Had there been 15 more persons each would have got Rs. 30 less. The original number of persons was—
A. 65 B. 60
C. 50 D. 40

109. 2 men and 6 boys can do in 4 days a piece of work which would be done again in 4 days by 4 men and 3 boys. One man will do it in—
A. 36 days B. 24 days
C. 16 days D. 12 days

110. If $\sin A = 24/25$, the value of $\tan A + \sec A$, where $0° < A < 90°$ is—

A. 49 B. 25

C. 24 D. 7

111. If $\tan A = n \sin B$ and $\sin A = m \sin B$, then the value of $\cos^2 A$ is—

A. m^2/n^2 B. $m^2 \times n^2$

C. $m^2 - n^2$ D. $m^2 + n^2$

112. The angle of elevation of the top of a hill at the foot of a tower is 60° and the angle of elevation of the top of the tower from the foot of the hill is 30°. If the tower is 50 m high, the height of the hill is—

A. 100 m B. 125 m

C. 150 m D. 200 m

113. A steel wire when bent in the form of a square encloses an area of 121 sq. cm. If the same wire is bent into the form of a circle, the area of the circle is—

A. 88 sq. cm B. 142 sq. cm

C. 154 sq. cm D. 212 sq. cm

114. The number of spherical bullets that can be made out of a solid cube of lead whose edge measures 44 cm, if the diameter of each bullet be 4 cm, is—

A. 2541 B. 847

C. 1270 D. 363

115. The ratio between the radius of the base and the height of a cylinder is 2 : 3. If its volume is 1617 cm^3, the total surface area of the cylinder is—

A. 575 cm^2 B. 770 cm^2

C. 1205 cm^2 D. 1500 cm^2

116. The median of the following data is—
25, 34, 31, 23, 22, 26, 35, 26, 20, 32

A. 25.5 B. 26

C. 26.5 D. 25

117. The average weight of 10 men is decreased by 3 kg when one of them whose weight is 80 kg is replaced by a new person. The weight of the new person is—

A. 70 kg B. 60 kg

C. 50 kg D. 73 kg

118. The value of k so that the points A $(k, 1)$, B $(2, 1)$ and C $(5, -1)$ are collinear is—

A. 4 B. 3

C. 2 D. 1

119. The common difference of the A.P. a, $a + d$, $a + 2d$, ... for which the 20th term is 10 more than the 18th term, is—

A. 4 B. –4

C. –5 D. 5

120. Two dice are thrown simultaneously. The probability of getting a total of atleast 10 is—

A. 5/12 B. 1/6

C. 5/6 D. 1/12

(III) Social Science

121. The Treaty of Sreerangapattanam was between Tipu Sultan and—

A. Cornwallis

B. Clive

C. Warren Hastings

D. Wellesley

122. The famous Besnagar Pillar Inscription of century 150 BC refers to the great theistic cult of—

A. Panchika and Hariti

B. Pashupatis

C. Krishna-Vasudeva

D. Shakti

123. What is the water hyacinth?

A. A weed

B. A medicinal plant

C. A decorative plant

D. A highly sought after plant

124. To which of the following bills must the President accord his sanction without sending it back for recommendations?

A. Ordinary bills

B. Finance bills

C. Bills passed by both the houses of Parliament

D. Bills seeking amendment to the Constitution

125. The amendment procedure of the Indian Constitution has been modelled on the constitutional pattern of—
A. Canada B. USA
C. Switzerland D. South Africa

126. Indian Railways tied up with which of the following to launch a co-branded card and traveller loyalty card to tap the huge railway passengers market?
A. BoB cards B. Citibank card
C. SBI card D. None of these

127. Which bank advertises itself as the world's local bank?
A. Citibank B. HSBC
C. ICICI Bank D. ABN Amro

128. In which state is Silent Valley located?
A. Tamil Nadu
B. Kerala
C. Assam (Asom)
D. Arunachal Pradesh

129. Which of the following is not a promotional and motivational measure suggested in the National Population Policy 2000?
A. Reward Panchayat and Zila Parishad for promoting small family norm
B. Incentive to adopt two child norm
C. Couples below poverty line will be given health insurance plans
D. Banning abortion facilities (looking at female infanticides)

130. Who said, "HANOZ DELHI DOOR AST"?
A. Nizamuddin Aulia B. Farid
C. Nasiruddin D. None of these

131. In which of the following constitutional documents did the British Government for the first time, officially lay down as the goal of constitutional development in India, not only dominion status, but also responsible Government?
A. Indian Council Act, 1892
B. Indian Council Act, 1909
C. Government of India Act, 1919
D. Government of India Act, 1935

132. In which state is chromite abundantly found?
A. Maharashtra B. Madhya Pradesh
C. Orissa D. Karnataka

133. For what is the Manas Sanctuary in Assam known?
A. Bear B. Tiger
C. Wild ass D. Birds

134. The Rajya Sabha can take initiative in—
A. Censuring a Central Minister
B. Creating a new All India Service
C. Considering Money Bills
D. Appointing Judges

135. Which of the following provides the largest part of the demand for loanable funds in India?
A. Hire purchase borrowers
B. Private house purchasers
C. Corporate businesses
D. Farmers

136. Who amongst the following was impeached in England for acts committed as Governor General of India?
A. Wellesley
B. Cavendish Bentinck
C. Cornwallis
D. Warren Hastings

137. The National Stock Exchange of India (NSEI) was inaugurated in—
A. July 1992 B. July 1993
C. July 1994 D. July 1995

138. One of the major towns of the Godavari region in the Satavahana kingdom was—
A. Pratishthana B. Arikamedu
C. Kokkhai D. Maski

139. In the Islamic (Mughal) buildings that came up in India, the elements of decoration did not include—
A. Calligraphy
B. Depiction of living beings
C. Geometry
D. Foliage

140. Jaya is the name of a high yielding variety of—
A. Wheat B. Rice
C. Bajra D. Cotton

(IV) English

141. Choose the word opposite in meaning to 'Dormant' —
A. Inert B. Deaf
C. Indulgence D. Active

142. Choose the word opposite in meaning to 'Malignant'—
A. Virulent B. Benign
C. Prudent D. Swallow

143. The word 'Tacit' means—
A. Formal B. Fear
C. Silent D. Celestial

144. The word 'Enunciate' means—
A. Matter B. Express
C. Evil D. Detest

145. 'One who is well-versed in the science of languages is called a—
A. Philosopher B. Theologist
C. Philologist D. Zoologist

146. 'A person who abstains from all kinds of alcoholic drinks' is called a—
A. Drunkard B. Angler
C. Teetotaller D. Heretic

147. Choose the correctly spelt word—
A. Coloqial B. Coloquial
C. Colloqial D. Colloquial

148. Choose the misspelt word—
A. Perceive B. Believe
C. Relieve D. Receive

149. Choose what expresses the meaning of the phrase 'a black sheep'—
A. Stranger
B. Convict
C. Gentleman
D. A family member one disapproves of

150. Choose what expresses the meaning of 'pull the wool over one's eye'—
A. Delay B. Encourage
C. Suppress D. Deceive

151. Choose the passive voice of—'Who ate my cheese?'
A. By whom is my cheese being eaten?
B. By whom was my cheese eaten?
C. By whom will my cheese be eaten?
D. By whom was my cheese been eaten?

152. Choose the indirect speech of—My father said, 'Study hard'—
A. My father scolded me to study hard
B. My father asked me to study hard
C. My father requested me to study hard
D. My father said that I must study hard

153. Choose the most appropriate word to fill in the blank in the sentence—
My father is angry ..... me.
A. On B. With
C. In D. None of these

154. Choose the most appropriate word to fill in the blank in the sentence—
Trust ..... God, and do your duty.
A. Of B. With
C. In D. On

155. Who wrote the poem 'Tintern Abbey'?
A. Keats B. Shelley
C. Wordsworth D. Byron

156. Who wrote the novel 'A Tale of Two Cities'?
A. Austen B. Dickens
C. Hardy D. Bronte

157. Who wrote the play 'All's well that ends well'?
A. Brecht
B. Eugene O'Neill
C. Shaw
D. William Shakespeare

158. Farmer Boldwood and Sergeant Troy are characters in the novel—
A. The Mayor of Casterbridge
B. Far from the Madding Crowd
C. The Return of the Native
D. Tess of the d' Urbervilles

159. Robert Browning was a poet of which period in literature?
A. Age of Reason B. Romantic Period
C. Victorian Period D. Modern Period

160. Which of the following is not a language skill?
A. Reading B. Writing
C. Thinking D. Speaking

(V) हिन्दी

निर्देश (प्रश्न 161 से 165): *नीचे दिए गए गद्यांश को ध्यान से पढ़िए और बाद में पूछे गए प्रश्नों के उत्तर दीजिए।*

अंग्रेजों के पदार्पण के पश्चात् भारत की शिक्षा-पद्धति में आमूल-चूल परिवर्तन आया। उसका उद्देश्य शासन-व्यवस्था को चलाने के लिए कम खर्च पर क्लर्क पैदा करना था। मैकाले का कहना था– ''हमें भारतीय लोगों के एक ऐसे वर्ग के निर्माण का भरसक प्रयत्न करना है जो हमारे और उन करोड़ों लोगों के बीच, जिन पर हम शासन करते हैं, दुभाषिये का काम कर सकें। हम ऐसे वर्ग का निर्माण करें जो रंग और रक्त में भले ही भारतीय हों, किन्तु रुचियों, विचारों, नैतिक मूल्यों और बौद्धिक दृष्टिकोण आदि में पूर्णरूपेण अंग्रेज हों।'' मैकाले का स्वप्न साकार हो गया। प्रचलित शिक्षा-पद्धति लॉर्ड मैकाले द्वारा मुखरित उद्देश्य की पूर्ति में शत-प्रतिशत सफल रही है किन्तु अंग्रेजों की राजनैतिक कूटनीति का रोना रोने से भारत का कल्याण नहीं होगा। हमें स्वतंत्र भारत की परिस्थितियों और आवश्यकताओं के अनुरूप शिक्षा-प्रणाली को ढाल लेना चाहिए।

शिक्षा का वास्तविक उद्देश्य चरित्र को उन्नत करके जीवन को उच्च आदर्शों से प्रेरित करना तथा व्यक्तित्व का सन्तुलित और समन्वित विकास करना है। विद्यार्थियों में निरन्तर बढ़ती हुई अनुशासनहीनता, उद्दण्डता, उच्छृंखलता और प्रशासनिक भ्रष्टाचार इस बात का प्रत्यक्ष प्रमाण है कि वर्तमान शिक्षा चरित्र-निर्माण और व्यक्तित्व के संतुलित और समन्वित विकास में असफल रही है आज की खर्चीली शिक्षा जनसामान्य के पहुंच से दूर होती जा रही है। मुंशी प्रेमचन्द ने कहा था – खर्चीली शिक्षा कभी चरित्रवान् व्यक्ति पैदा नहीं कर सकती। कितना अच्छा हो कि 'पढ़ो और कमाओ' की योजनाएं प्रचलन में आएं।

161. मैकाले का कौन-सा स्वप्न साकार हुआ–
A. ब्रिटिश साम्राज्य की स्थापना का
B. अंग्रेज-भक्त क्लर्कों को पैदा करना
C. अंग्रेजी पढ़ाकर विचारशील युवक तैयार करना
D. भारतीयों को अपनी प्राचीन महत्ता और गौरव का विस्मरण कराना

162. आमूल-चूल परिवर्तन का अर्थ क्या है?
A. आंशिक घटा-बढ़ी करना
B. रसोई के चूल्हों में परिवर्तन
C. प्रारम्भ से अन्त तक बदलाव लाना
D. शासन-पद्धति में परिवर्तन लाना

163. स्वतंत्र भारत में शिक्षा का उद्देश्य निम्नलिखित में से सर्वाधिक महत्त्वपूर्ण कौन-सा है?
A. नेतृत्व की शिक्षा देना
B. व्यक्तित्व का समन्वित विकास करना
C. बेरोजगारी दूर करना
D. भ्रष्टाचार-उन्मूलन करना

164. किन लोगों को 'काले अंग्रेज' कहा जाता है?
A. ऐसे भारतीय जो बौद्धिक दृष्टिकोण में अंग्रेजों जैसे हैं
B. अफ्रीका के निवासी लोग
C. दक्षिण भारतीय लोग
D. अनुशासनहीन उच्छ्रंखल नवयुवक

165. जीवन को प्रेरित करने वाले उच्च आदर्श कौन-से हैं?
A. रुचियों, विचारों और नैतिक मूल्यों में अंग्रेजों की तरह बनें
B. देश-प्रेम और नैतिकता को जीवन में अपनाएं
C. शिक्षा को कम खर्चीला बनाएं
D. धर्मनिरपेक्ष शिक्षा-व्यवस्था अपनाएं

निर्देश (प्रश्न 166 से 180): *निम्न में से प्रत्येक प्रश्न के साथ-साथ चार-चार विकल्प दिए गए हैं। उनमें से सही विकल्प चुनिए।*

166. ब्रज और अवधी किस काल में काव्य की प्रमुख भाषाएं थीं?
A. वीरगाथा काल　B. रीतिकाल
C. छायावादी युग　D. भक्तिकाल

167. 'कबीर' किस भाषा के कवि माने जाते हैं?
A. पूर्वी हिन्दी　B. मागधी
C. सधुक्कड़ी　D. भोजपुरी

168. 'जिसके बिना काम न चले' इस अर्थ में कौन-सा शब्द उपयुक्त है?
A. अनिवार्य　B. अविकल
C. अनिर्धार्य　D. अपरिहार्य

169. कौन-सी वर्तनी शुद्ध है?
A. सुश्रूषा　B. शुश्रूषा
C. शुस्रूषा　D. षुश्रूसा

170. सौप्रस्थानिक-कार्यक्रम कौन-सा होता है?

A. विदाई समारोह B. स्वागत समारोह
C. अलंकरण समारोह D. श्रद्धाञ्जलि कार्यक्रम

171. इनमें से कौन-सा शब्द शुद्ध नहीं है?

A. उज्ज्वल B. महात्म्य
C. स्वास्थ्य D. उपलक्ष्य

172. अति + अधिक मिलकर बनता है

A. अत्याधिक B. अतीधिक
C. अत्यधिक D. अत्यधीक

173. 'आर्जव' किस मूल शब्द से बना है?

A. अर्जन B. आरजू
C. अर्ज D. ऋजु

174. 'खाला जी का घर' इस मुहावरे का अर्थ है

A. आसान काम B. कठिन काम
C. व्यर्थ की जगह D. आराम करने का स्थान

175. 'मूर्धा' का विशेषण कौन-सा शब्द है?

A. मूर्ध्नि B. मूर्धन्य
C. मूर्धण्य D. मूर्धेय

176. निम्नलिखित में से अव्ययीभाव समास का उदाहरण कौन-सा पद है?

A. राजभाषा B. पशु-पक्षी
C. गांव-गांव D. देहलता

177. राम नाम मणि दीप धरि, जीह देहरी द्वार।
तुलसी भीतर-बाहिरौ, जो चाहसि उजियार॥
इस दोहे में कौन-सा अलंकार है?

A. रूपक B. उपमा
C. उत्प्रेक्षा D. श्लेष

178. निम्नलिखित वाक्यों में से कौन-सा वाक्य शुद्ध है?

A. आपके एक-एक शब्द प्रभावशाली हैं।
B. मैंने उसकी पुस्तक सधन्यवाद लौटा दी।
C. घर पर सब कुशल है।
D. मैंने आज जाना है।

179. 'आज के पाथे आज नहीं जलाए जाते' इस लोकोक्ति का क्या भाव है?

A. हाथ पर सरसों नहीं जमती
B. हर कार्य में धैर्य चाहिए
C. आज बोया बीज भविष्य में वृक्ष बनकर फल देता है
D. जल्दी का काम शैतान का होता है।

180. 'हनुमान-चालीसा' किसकी रचना है?

A. हनुमान प्रसाद पोद्दार B. महाकवि भूषण
C. महावीर प्रसाद D. तुलसीदास

ANSWERS

1	2	3	4	5	6	7	8	9	10
C	D	A	D	A	C	C	A	A	A
11	**12**	**13**	**14**	**15**	**16**	**17**	**18**	**19**	**20**
D	A	C	A	A	B	C	A	D	A
21	**22**	**23**	**24**	**25**	**26**	**27**	**28**	**29**	**30**
B	B	D	B	D	D	B	B	A	C
31	**32**	**33**	**34**	**35**	**36**	**37**	**38**	**39**	**40**
D	C	A	C	B	A	A	B	C	B
41	**42**	**43**	**44**	**45**	**46**	**47**	**48**	**49**	**50**
A	D	D	B	A	D	A	D	B	B
51	**52**	**53**	**54**	**55**	**56**	**57**	**58**	**59**	**60**
B	B	D	C	C	C	C	B	D	D
61	**62**	**63**	**64**	**65**	**66**	**67**	**68**	**69**	**70**
B	D	D	B	A	C	D	B	C	A
71	**72**	**73**	**74**	**75**	**76**	**77**	**78**	**79**	**80**
D	D	C	B	D	D	D	B	C	D

81	82	83	84	85	86	87	88	89	90
A	C	A	B	B	A	C	C	C	C
91	92	93	94	95	96	97	98	99	100
D	A	B	D	C	D	C	B	C	D
101	102	103	104	105	106	107	108	109	110
B	A	C	D	D	A	B	C	B	D
111	112	113	114	115	116	117	118	119	120
A	C	C	A	B	B	C	C	D	D
121	122	123	124	125	126	127	128	129	130
A	A	A	B	D	C	B	B	D	A
131	132	133	134	135	136	137	138	139	140
C	C	B	B	C	D	A	A	B	B
141	142	143	144	145	146	147	148	149	150
D	B	C	B	C	C	D	A	D	D
151	152	153	154	155	156	157	158	159	160
B	B	B	C	C	B	D	B	C	C
161	162	163	164	165	166	167	168	169	170
B	C	B	A	B	D	C	D	A	A
171	172	173	174	175	176	177	178	179	180
B	C	A	D	B	C	A	B	C	D

SOME SELECTED EXPLANATORY ANSWERS

12. $2 \times 5 = 10$, $10 \times 5 = 50$,
$50 \times 10 = 500$, $500 \times 50 = 25000$

19. In all the rest the first is used to fill the second.

20. All the rest are consonants alike 'J' while 'A' is vowel.

21. All the rest are perfect squares.

22. In all the rest, the lower designs are the mirror image of the upper designs.

23. In all the rest, the straight lines are both sides of the middle design.

24. In all the rest both the leaves are not joined at one place.

30. All the rest have thirty days each.

92. Fermentation is an enzymatic transformation of organic substracts. Rest three do not need enzymatic transformation.

95. In series connection same current flows through all the resistances.

102. Milk in 35 litres of mixture

$$= 35 \times \frac{5}{7} = 25 \text{ litres}$$

Water in the original mixture

$$= 35 - 25 = 10 \text{ litres}$$

Milk in new mixture = 25 + 5 = 30 litres and water in new mixture = 10 litres

∴ Ratio of milk and water in new mixture

$$= \frac{30}{10} = \frac{3}{1}.$$

103. Let distance be x km.

Then, $\frac{x}{4} - \frac{x}{5} = \frac{9}{60}$

$\Rightarrow \frac{5x - 4x}{20} = \frac{9}{60}$

$\Rightarrow 5x - 4x = \frac{9 \times 20}{60}$

$\Rightarrow x = 3$ km.

105. Let the sum be Rs. x

Then,

$$\frac{x \times 4 \times 4}{100} - \frac{x \times 3 \times 5}{100} = 80$$

$$\Rightarrow \quad \frac{4x}{25} - \frac{3x}{20} = 80$$

$$\Rightarrow \quad \frac{16x - 15x}{100} = 80$$

$$\Rightarrow \quad x = \text{Rs. } 8000$$

106. Let C.P. = Rs. 100

then, marked price = 130

and S.P. $= 130 \times \frac{90}{100}$

$= 117$

Gain = 117 – 100 = 17

If gain is Rs. 17 then c.p. 100

and if gain is 25.50 then

$$\frac{25.50 \times 100}{17} = \text{Rs. } 150.$$

107. Reduction in consumption

$$= \left(\frac{25}{125} \times 100\right)\%$$

$= 20\%.$

113. Let side of square = x cm

then area of the square = $x^2 = 121$

$x = 11$ cm

From Question

Perimeter of the square

= Circumference of the circle

$$\Rightarrow \quad 4 \times x = 2\,\pi\,r$$

(r = radius of the circle)

$$\Rightarrow \quad 4 \times 11 = 2 \times \frac{22}{7} \times r$$

$$\Rightarrow \quad r = 7$$

$\therefore$ Area of the circle $= \pi \times r^2$

$$= \frac{22}{7} \times 7^2 = 154 \text{ sq. cm.}$$

Previous Paper (Solved)

IGNOU B.Ed. Entrance Test 2007

PART-A

SECTION-I : General English Comprehension

Directions: *Read the following passage carefully and pick out the best answer out of the four choices given in the questions that follow.*

Motivations for ruralism in underdeveloped countries are understandably different from those in developed countries. There, it is a sheer physical necessity for the very act of human survival. In the Third World countries, which are predominantly rural, the only lever that can lift human life above its present subhuman level, is rural development. Rural life in such countries has been stagnating for centuries. Nothing worthwhile has been done to ameliorate the conditions of the rural population which is only slightly different from that of their quadruped counterparts. Ignorance, ill-health and poverty have become synonyms of rural life in the undeveloped and underdeveloped countries. But the worst tragedy is that the concerned human populations have taken this state of affairs for granted, as something unalterable, something for which there is no remedy. Every ray of hope has gone out of their lives. In such countries, rural development is the inevitable conditon of any material or non-material advancement. As such, enlightened sections of all such countries have been taking an ever growing interest in the question of rural development.

This was also a part of the legacy of their freedom struggle. In countries like India, it is well known that attempts at rural development were an inseparable part of the independence movement. Leaders like Gandhiji realised quite well that Real India lived in her stagnating villages. Cities, which were mostly the products of Western colonialism, were just artificial showpieces. Even then, there were two worlds. The posh areas, where the affluent few, mostly the products and custodians of imperial interest lived, were little islands engulfed by the vast ocean of dirt, represented by the vast majority of people.

Cities were by no means unknown to India. In ancient India, they were integral parts, organically related to the rest of the country and society. Cities in ancient India were the flowers of the cultural and artistic excellence of the nation, modern cities are just parasites, preying on and debilitating the country.

Hence, Gandhiji started the 'Go to Village Movement' which alone, according to him could bring freedom to India and sustain it. Rural development had the place of pride in his strategy for the nations's freedom. Thus, it had its origin in the freedom struggle.

1. People are taking greater interest in rural development because:

A. they have realised the indispensability of it

B. they have been suffering from severe health problems

C. nothing worthwhile can be done in the near future

D. they have now become optimistic about it

2. Which of the following is the 'lever' according to the passage?

A. Non-material advancement

B. Stagnation of rural life

C. Upliftment of the rural masses

D. Enlightenment of certain sections of the society

3. Which of the following is the worst tragedy according to the author?
A. The subhuman condition of the people in villages
B. The pessimism of the rural people about their own condition
C. Lack of realisation of the importance of rural development
D. Exploitation of rural people by city dwellers

4. Which of the following statements is *not* true in the context of the passage?
A. Rural folk in the Third World countries feel that their subhuman condition cannot be changed.
B. Only rural development can raise the standard of living of the people in Third World countries.
C. Most of the rich people living in modern cities are genuinely concerned about rural development.
D. Rural development is a prerequisite for any other advancement and progress.

5. Rural development was considered as a part of India's freedom movement because:
A. Imperial interest lived only in villages
B. The country comprised of mainly villages
C. Gandhiji was against Western colonialism
D. Real India was then under the British rule

6. The Standard of living of human beings in Third World countries is:
A. improving very rapidly
B. immune to any improvement
C. subhuman despite best efforts for improvement
D. not far better than that of animals

7. Which of the following, best describes the two divergent worlds of modern cities?
A. A few rich people and many poor people
B. Posh area and affluent people
C. Commercial and industrial exploitation
D. Patrons of Western products and custodians of imperial interests.

8. Which of the following statements is true in the context of the passage?
A. Most Third World countries are undergoing fast urbanisation
B. India's struggle for freedom has been considered as a part of rural development.
C. Rural folk are very optimistic about improvement in their condition.
D. In the present context, ignorance, poverty and ill-health are inseparable parts of rural life.

9. Choose the expression which is closest in meaning to 'Predominantly' as used in the passage.
A. weakly
B. undoubtedly
C. scarcely
D. in a greatly visible way

10. Choose the word that is opposite in meaning to 'Ameliorate' as used in the passage.
A. worsen B. lessen
C. expedite D. hasten

SECTION II : LOGICAL AND ANALYTICAL REASONING

Directions (11-14): *Read the passage to answer the questions that follow.*
There is a cube with six surfaces painted Red, White, Blue, Yellow, Black and Green in such an order that Black is at the top face, Green is bottom and the other four colours are arranged in the order given in an anticlockwise direction of the surfaces. Now answer the following questions (11-14), if Red is towards you.

11. If the cube is rotated horizontally first by 180°, then rotated downwardly by 180°, then which colour would be facing downward?
A. White B. Blue
C. Yellow D. Black

12. If the cube is rotated clockwise (right to left) horizontally by 180° from initial position and then rotated upwardly by 90°, then which colour of the cube would be facing you?

A. Green B. Red
C. Blue D. Black

13. In the above question (12) which colour would be facing on the left side of you?
A. Red B. Green
C. White D. Yellow

14. Which colour(s) would be bounded by Yellow, Green and White?
A. Red B. Blue
C. Red and Blue D. Red and Yellow

Directions (15-18) : *In the following diagram, square stands for those who take tea, triangle stands for those who take coffee, circle stands for those who take cold drinks. Study the diagram carefully to answer the questions (15-18) that follow.*

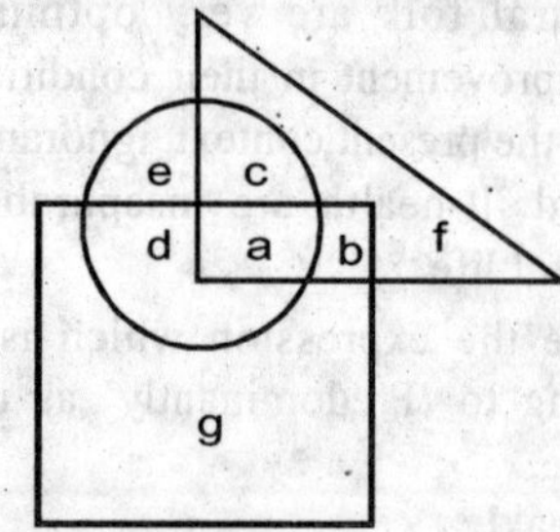

15. The persons who take tea and coffee but do not take cold drinks are represented by which letter?
A. a B. b
C. c D. d

16. The persons who take tea and cold drinks but do not take coffee are represented by which letter?
A. a B. b
C. c D. d

17. The persons who take tea, coffee and cold drinks are represented by which letter?
A. a B. b
C. c D. d

18. The persons who take cold drinks and coffee but do not take tea are represented by which letter?
A. a B. b
C. c D. d

Directions (19-22) : *In the following questions an incomplete series with one blank is given. Find out the best suited missing number from the given alternatives.*

19. 1, 4, 8, 11, 15, ?, 22
A. 19 B. 18
C. 17 D. 20

20. 1, 4, 9, 16, ?
A. 23 B. 24
C. 25 D. 30

21. 1, 3, 7, 15, 31, ?
A. 62 B. 63
C. 61 D. 71

22. 1, 2, 6, 24, ?
A. 120 B. 144
C. 30 D. 140

Directions (23-26) : *In each of the following questions there are five figures. First is a reference figure. Among the rest four figures one figure does not belong to a class to which first figure belongs. Identify this odd figure.*

Reference Figure **Answer Figures**

23.

A. B. C. D.

24.

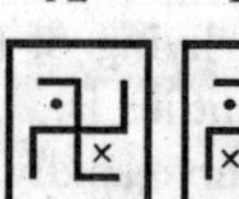
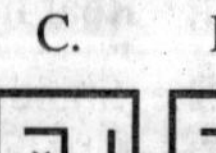
A. B. C. D.

25.
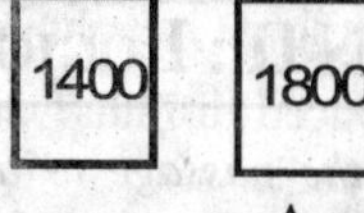

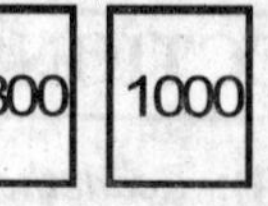

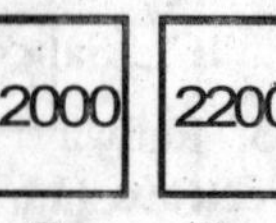

A. B. C. D.

26.
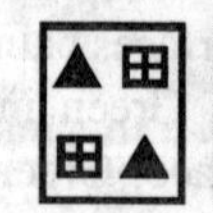

A. B. C. D.

Directions (27-30): *In each of the following questions, two statements are followed by two conclusions. Assuming the first two statements to* *be true (however absurd they may be), decide which of the two follows logically from the given statements. Select the most appropriate alternative from the ones given.*

27. All boys are not students.
Some students are not employed.
Conclusions:
I. Some boys are not employed.
II. Some employed ones are not boys.
A. Only I follows
B. Only II follows
C. Both I and II follow
D. Neither I nor II follows

28. All animals are dogs.
All cats are animals.
Conclusions:
I. All cats are dogs.
II. All dogs are cats.
A. Only I follows
B. Only II follows
C. Both I and II follow
D. Neither I nor II follows

29. All chairs are pens.
All pens are pencils.
Conclusions:
I. Some pencils are chairs.
II. All chairs are pencils.
A. Only I follows
B. Only II follows
C. Both I and II follow
D. Neither I nor II follows

30. No men are animals.
Some animals are intelligent.
Conclusions:
I. Some men are not intelligent.
II. Some intelligent beings are men.
A. Only I follows
B. Only II follows
C. Both I and II follow
D. Neither I nor II follows

SECTION III : EDUCATIONAL AND GENERAL AWARENESS

31. The first woman president of the Indian National Congress was:
A. Sucheta Kriplani
B. Rajkumari Amrit Kaur
C. Annie Besant
D. Sarojini Naidu

32. The earliest inscriptions on stone in India were in which language?
A. Prakrit B. Pali
C. Sanskrit D. Brahmi

33. Railways were introduced in India when the Governor General of India was:
A. Curzon B. Dalhousie
C. Hardinge D. Ripon

34. What should be given to an athlete for instant energy?
A. Carbohydrates B. Protein
C. Fat D. Vitamins

35. The place in India receiving the lowest rainfall is:
A. Leh B. Jaisalmer
C. Bikaner D. Jodhpur

36. Cow's milk is a rich source of:
A. Vitamin A B. Vitamin B
C. Vitamin C D. Vitamin D

37. Earthquake is measured by using:
A. Barometer B. Laser rays
C. Seismograph D. Altimeter

38. Mudaliar Commission (1952-53) had recommended opening of:
A. Kendriya Vidyalayas
B. Multipurpose Secondary Schools
C. Navodaya Vidyalayas
D. Vocational Institutes

39. Emphasis on Common School System was first laid by:
A. Radhakrishnan Commission (1949)
B. Mudaliar Commission (1953)
C. Kothari Commission (1966)
D. National Policy on Education (1986)

40. The first committee which looked into the problem of wastage and stagnation at primary stage was:
A. Hartog Committee
B. Sri Prakash Committee
C. Zakir Hussain Committee
D. Ram Murti Committee

41. "Give me blood and I promise you freedom" was uttered by:
A. Bhagat Singh
B. Chandrashekhar Azad
C. Sardar Patel
D. Subhash Chandra Bose

42. Which of the following is *not* the principle of Panchsheel?
A. Non-alignment
B. Peaceful co-existence
C. Non interference in each others international affairs
D. Mutual respect for each others territory and sovereignty

43. In India, diamonds are found at:
A. Panna (Madhya Pradesh)
B. Golkunda (Andhra Pradesh)
C. Khetri (Rajasthan)
D. Gulbarga (Karnataka)

44. The first free and private university in India, completely independent of Government and receiving no grant from it, was:
A. Banaras Hindu University
B. Aligarh Muslim University
C. Women's University, Pune
D. Vishwa Bharati, Shantiniketan

45. '*Pakistan Papers*' has been authored by:
A. Brig. H.S. Sodhi
B. K.K. Bhargava
C. Dr. Sadiq Hussain
D. Mani Shankar Aiyar

46. Which city will host 2010 Commonwealth Games?
A. London B. New Delhi
C. Paris D. Melbourne

47. Mr. Harita Kaur has the distinction of being first Indian woman:
A. Doctor to create a test tube baby
B. Pilot to fly an aircraft solo
C. Induced in Indian Navy
D. Employed in a petrol pump

48. Silver is most abundantly found in the state of:
A. Bihar B. Tamil Nadu
C. Rajasthan D. Karnataka

49. Which of the following is *wrongly* matched?
A. Television – Baird
B. Transistor – Shockley
C. Typewriter – Sholes
D. Thermometer – Celsius

50. The Chief Election Commissioner of India is:
A. elected by the Parliament
B. nominated by the Prime Minister
C. appointed by the President of India
D. appointed by the Ministry of Parliamentary Affairs

Directions : *Indicate the correct answer.*

51. Agha Khan Palace, where Kasturba Gandhi died while under detention along with Mahatma Gandhi is at:
A. Bombay B. Pune
C. Ahmedabad D. Bangalore

52. Wular Lake is in the state of :
A. Orissa
B. Gujarat
C. Jammu & Kashmir
D. Madhya Pradesh

53. Mandal Panchayats were recommended by:
A. Ashok Mehta Committee
B. Balwant Rai Mehta Committee
C. Narsimhan Committee
D. Sarkaria Commission

54. The Indian constitution is divided into how many parts?
A. 22 B. 20
C. 18 D. 16

55. According to U.N. Convention on the 'Rights of the Child' which of the following is *not* correct?
A. Safe drinking water
B. Adequate standard of living
C. Employment
D. Protection from exploitation

SECTION IV : TEACHING-LEARNING AND THE SCHOOL

Directions: *Indicate the correct answer.*

56. The concept of Basic Education was given by:
A. Dr. Zakir Hussain
B. Dr. Rajendra Prasad
C. Mahatma Gandhi
D. Rabindranath Tagore

57. The most important indicator of the quality of school education is:
A. infrastructure facilities in schools
B. textbooks and teaching-learning material
C. classroom processes
D. attainment level of children

58. Student's learning difficulties can be best addressed by:
A. advising them to work hard
B. suggesting private tuitions
C. supervised study in the library
D. remedial teaching

59. 'Inservice teachers' training can be made effective by:
A. using training package developed in advance
B. making it residential
C. using participatory approach
D. putting follow up mechanism in practice

60. Anti-child labour law (1986):
A. prohibits all forms of child labour until the age of 14 years
B. prohibits child labour in hazardous occupations only
C. prohibits child labour during school hours
D. prohibits child labour by putting responsibility on the employers about their education.

61. For being successful in life, students should be encouraged to:
A. selective study
B. casual study
C. intensive study
D. learning by rote memorisation

62. Students' absenteeism should:
A. be the concern of headmaster and parents
B. be dealt with by school authorities as per the rules
C. be taken up seriously by the teachers
D. be accorded less priority as against those present in the class

63. Organisation of co-curriclar activities should be the responsbility of:
A. the headmaster
B. the teacher appointed for this purpose
C. teachers interested in it
D. all the teachers

64. Students who bring out alternative solutions and cite the books not prescribed by the teacher should be:
A. discouraged
B. encouraged
C. advised to talk to the teacher outside the class
D. advised to follow the class notes to score better in the examinations

65. Experienced teachers don't require detailed planning for a lesson because:
A. they can teach better without it
B. inquisitive students are only few
C. they don't face any challenge even if some mistakes are committed
D. they can manage with brief outline using their expertise gained so far

66. Education should aim at:
A. developing vocational skills among students
B. developing social awareness among students
C. preparing students for examinations
D. preparing students for life

67. Best way of homework checking is:
A. getting it done through bright students
B. getting the answers checked collectively in the class

C. getting it checked on sample basis
D. getting it checked by teacher her/himself regularly

68. Periodic tests be given to students to:
A. inform students progress to their guardians
B. undertake the exercise as required under rules
C. train students for final examinations
D. take corrective measures on the basis of feedback from the results

69. Student's failure should be considered as:
A. failure of the system
B. failure of the teacher
C. failure of textbooks
D. failure of individual student

70. Training needs of teachers can be identified realistically by:
A. asking teachers about it
B. asking the supervisors of teachers
C. analysing teacher profiles
D. analysing pupil achievement data

71. Problem of school dropouts can be effectively tackled by:
A. reducing curriculum load
B. teachers empathy
C. attractive school environment
D. providing incentives

72. An ideal teacher is one who:
A. covers the full course
B. helps students in learning
C. is a friend, philosopher and guide
D. likes discipline

73. Public Examination System should continue because:
A. it is good for comparison
B. it has greater acceptability
C. it promotes teaching-learning in schools
D. teachers are not trustworthy

74. A committee to review the National Policy on Education (1986) was headed by:
A. Ramamurti
B. P.C. Alexander
C. Chitra Naik
D. P.C. Chunder

75. Teacher motivation and commitment can be enhanced by:
A. offering them high salaries
B. providing inservice training
C. allowing them private tuitions
D. providing them professional support on the basis of monitoring results

76. An essential component in the curriculum for out of school children should be:
A. literacy skills
B. life skills
C. numeracy skills
D. vocational skills

77. Tax payers are contributing towards Elementary Education by paying:
A. income tax
B. tuition fees
C. for private tuitions
D. education cess

78. Education of girls needs to be given priority because:
A. girls happen to be more intelligent than boys
B. girls are less in number than boys
C. girls have been discriminated against boys in the past
D. girls only can lead social change

79. Success of inclusive education depends on:
A. community support
B. high quality teaching-learning materials
C. high quality textbooks
D. attitudinal change among teachers

80. Quality of school education depends heavily on:
A. Infrastructure facilities
B. Financial provisions
C. International support
D. Quality of teacher education

PART-B

SECTION V : (I) SCIENCE

81. Which of the following colours has the shortest wavelength?
A. Red B. Orange
C. Yellow D. Violet

82. In a diesel engine, the fuel is ignited by:
A. a spark plug
B. liquid oxygen
C. the heat generated when air is compressed in the cylinder
D. vaporization under partial vacuum

83. How many moons does the Pluto have?
A. None B. One
C. Two D. Six

84. The weight of a body on the moon is:
A. 1/5th of its weight on earth
B. 1/6th of its weight on earth
C. 1/7th of its weight on earth
D. 1/100th of its weight on earth

85. The scientific study of the action of chemicals upon living beings is called:
A. Pharmacy
B. Pharmacognosy
C. Pharmacology
D. Biochemistry

86. In the manufacturing of match stick, which of the following is used?
A. Potassium
B. Sodium
C. White phosphorous
D. Red phosphorous

87. What did Fleming discover?
A. Vitamin A B. Vaccines
C. Sulphonamides D. Penicillin

88. The substance present inside a fluorescent tube which emits light is:
A. Nitrogen B. Mercury vapour
C. Sodium cyanide D. Air

89. The biological process by which changes occur in genes is known as:
A. Adaptation B. Evolution
C. Natural selection D. Mutation

90. Agronomy is the study of:
A. behaviour of agricultural animals
B. field crop production and soils
C. names of agricultural plants
D. all of these

91. Cold-blooded animals are those animals whose:
A. blood is cold
B. blood is blue, not red
C. body temperature varies with that of the surroundings
D. body temperature is always constant

92. What is the technical term for fish farming?
A. Aviculture B. Sericulture
C. Pisciculture D. Zooculutre

93. The vision defect of eyes as a result of which a person is unable to see distant objects clearly, is called:
A. Hypermetropia
B. Long sightedness
C. Astigmatism
D. Myopia

94. Which of the following diseases is caused by amoeba?
A. Paralysis B. Cholera
C. Dysentery D. Typhoid fever

95. The wind blowing from the land towards the sea during the night is known as:
A. Ordinary breeze B. Sea breeze
C. Land breeze D. Cold breeze

96. Dots are placed on dice in such a fashion that the sum of dots on any two opposite sides is always:
A. 9 B. 7
C. 6 D. 8

97. If the earth did not spin:
A. we would have no seasons
B. half of earth would always be in sunlight
C. there would be no summer in the northern hemisphere
D. all of the above

98. The most abundant element in the earth's crust is:
A. Oxygen
B. Silicon
C. Aluminium
D. Iron

99. The term Green Revolution refers to:
A. increase in milk production
B. increase in vegetable production
C. involvement of Dr. Green in agriculture
D. increase in crop production

100. When a person donates blood, approximately how much of his/her blood is taken?
A. 250 – 300 ml
B. 1000 ml
C. 1 – 2 litre
D. 50 ml

(II) MATHEMATICS

101. The value of:
$$\frac{\sqrt{\frac{1+a}{1-a}}+\sqrt{\frac{1-a}{1+a}}}{\sqrt{\frac{1+a}{1-a}}-\sqrt{\frac{1-a}{1+a}}}-\frac{1}{a} \text{ is}$$
A. 0
B. 1
C. a
D. $2 + a$

102. If $p = x + y$ and $q = x - y$, then the expression $\frac{p+q}{p-q}-\frac{p-q}{p+q}$ has a value:
A. $\frac{x^2-y^2}{4xy}$
B. $\frac{x^2-y^2}{xy}$
C. $\frac{x^2+y^2}{2xy}$
D. 0

103. One-third of a number is greater than one-fourth of its successor by one. The number is:
A. 27
B. 39
C. 15
D. 18

104. When the repeating decimal 0.363636 .... is written in simplest fractional form, the sum of numerator and denominator is:
A. 135
B. 114
C. 45
D. 15

105. A number of persons paid equal amounts and collected Rs. 72. If there were 3 persons less, then each would have to contribute Rs. 4 more. The number of people was:
A. 12
B. 9
C. 36
D. 6

106. A sum of Rs. 61 is divided among A, B, and C. A gets twice as much as B and C gets Rs. 5 less than A and B together. The amount that C gets is:
A. Rs. 22
B. Rs. 33
C. Rs. 28
D. Rs. 11

107. 6.4% of 2.5 is:
A. 16
B. 1.6
C. 0.6
D. 0.16

108. The ratio of incomes of A and B is 9 : 7. The ratio of their expenditures is 4 : 3. If each of them saves Rs. 200 per month, then the monthly income of A is:
A. Rs. 3,600
B. Rs. 1,400
C. Rs. 2,700
D. Rs. 1,800

109. The sum of the series 2+ 4 + 6 ... + 98 + 100 is:
A. 2601
B. 2550
C. 2499
D. 1545

110. If $\sin A = \frac{24}{25}$, the value of tan A + sec A, where $\theta° < A < 90°$ is:
A. 7
B. 5
C. 1
D. $\frac{24}{7}$

111. If the H.C.F. of the polynomials $x^3 - 3x^2 + px + 24$ and $x^2 - 7x + q$ is $(x - 2)$, the value of $(p + q)$ is:
A. 0
B. 20
C. –20
D. 40

112. The value of $\frac{3\sin 62°}{\cos 28°}-\frac{\sec 42°}{\operatorname{cosec} 48°}$ is:
A. 0
B. 1
C. –1
D. 2

113. Each edge of a cube is increased by 50%, the percentage increase in the surface area of the cube is:
A. 50 B. 100
C. 125 D. 200

114. The outer diameter of a spherical shell is 10 cm and the inner diameter is 8 cm. The volume of the metal contained in the shell is (Use $\pi = \frac{22}{7}$):
A. 255.6 cm^3 B. 2044.9 cm^3
C. 265.3 cm^3 D. 523.8 cm^3

115. Two poles of heights 7 metres and 12 metres stand on a plane ground. If the distance between their feet is 12 metres, the distance between their tops is:
A. 5 m B. 13 m
C. 15 m D. 20 m

116. The lengths of the diagonals of a rhombus are 24 cm and 10 cm. The side of the rhombus is:
A. 14 cm B. 17 cm
C. 13 cm D. 12 cm

117. The mean of 25 observations is 36. If the mean of first 13 observations is 32 and the mean of last 13 observations is 39, the 13th observation is:
A. 26 B. 25
C. 24 D. 23

118. The mid-points of the sides of a triangle ABC are (1, 1), (3, –3) and (4, 5). The coordinates of the centroid of Δ ABC are:
A. $\left(\frac{8}{3}, 1\right)$ B. $\left(\frac{8}{3}, 3\right)$
C. $\left(3, \frac{8}{3}\right)$ D. $\left(1, \frac{8}{3}\right)$

119. Two coins are tossed simultaneously. The probability of getting at least one head is:
A. $\frac{1}{4}$ B. $\frac{3}{4}$
C. $\frac{1}{2}$ D. 1

120. There are 600 men in a fort. If each of them is given 180 g of ration daily, there is ration enough for 25 days. If 300 men are increased and the ration is decreased to 150 g daily, the number of days for which the ration will be sufficient now is:
A. 20 days B. 16 days
C. 28 days D. 30 days

(III) Social Science

Directions: Choose one out of the given from options.

121. What is the rank of India in the 2004 Index of Economic Freedom, published by the Heritage Foundation and the Wall Street Journal?
A. 84 B. 71
C. 121 D. 90

122. Who was the Governor-General when the 1857 revolt broke out?
A. Dalhousie B. Canning
C. Curzon D. Lawrence

123. The Twelfth Finance Commission has recommended to bring down the revenue deficit of the Centre and the State to zero by
A. 2005-2006 B. 2006-2007
C. 2007-2008 D. 2008-2009

124. In Union Budget 2005, the finance minister introduced a new tax called FBT. What is the full name of the term FBT?
A. Fiscal Benefit Tax
B. Fringe Benefit Tax
C. Fixed Benefit Tax
D. None of these

125. Fawazil was
A. extra payment made to the nobles
B. excess amount paid to the Exchequer by the Iqtedar
C. revenue assigned in lieu of salary
D. none of these

126. Which one of the following is *not* a statutory body?
A. The Election Commission

B. The Union Public Service Commission
C. The Planning Commission
D. The Finance Commission

127. Which of the following countries is *not* a member of Mercosur?
A. Brazil B. Paraguay
C. Peru D. Chile

128. Which theory makes the use of Jigsaw fit in its support?
A. Tidal Hypothesis
B. Tetrahydral Hypothesis
C. Cycle of Erosion
D. Continental Drift Theory

129. Where is the famous Tuscarora dweep located?
A. Near USA
B. Off Japan
C. Off Lakshadweep
D. Near the Australian coast

130. In which of the following countries has there been the highest rise in overall level of skilled unemployed during 2000-2002?
A. India B. China
C. France D. USA

131. The Rigveda consists of
A. 1028 hymns B. 1000 hymns
C. 2028 hymns D. 1038 hymns

132. Blizzards are characteristic of .... region.
A. Equatorial B. Tropical
C. Antarctic D. Temperate

133. Which of the following Harappan sites are located in Uttar Pradesh?
A. Kalibangan B. Banawali
C. Alamgirpur D. Sutkagen-dor

134. The Prime Minister Manmohan Singh has constituted a task force to prepare a long term plan for the social and economic development of:
A. Tamil Nadu
B. Manipur
C. Jammu and Kashmir
D. Uttarakhand

135. How many islands make up Hong Kong?
A. 235 B. 245
C. 205 D. 206

136. Commonwealth Bank belongs to which country?
A. Australia B. New Zealand
C. United Kingdom D. Philippines

137. What does NIFE refer to?
A. A crop
B. An instrument
C. A marine organism
D. A type of rock

138. Who started the Madras Labour Union in 1918?
A. Kanji Dwarkadas and Umar Sobhani
B. G. Ramanjulu Naidu and G.C. Chetti
C. T.K. Murlidhar and H.B. Mahaduvle
D. C.K. Annadurai and K.T. Ramchandar

139. Which of the following rivers is called Biological Desert due to heavy population?
A. Brahmaputra B. Ganga
C. Damodar D. Yamuna

140. Where do Bhagirathi and Alaknanda join to form Ganga?
A. Karna Prayag B. Dev Prayag
C. Rudra Prayag D. Gangotri

(IV) ENGLISH

141. Choose the word which is opposite in meaning to the word 'Tentative'.
A. Developed B. Final
C. Immediate D. Urgent

142. Which word is opposite in meaning to the underlined word in the sentence – 'His <u>meanness</u> is proverbial'?
A. Timidity B. Kindness
C. Generosity D. Pragmatism

143. Choose the synonym of 'Voracious'.
A. Hungry B. Wild
C. Quick D. Angry

144. Choose the synonym of the underlined word in the sentence – 'Reading of poetry is not congenial to his taste.'

A. Helpful B. Preferable
C. Suited D. Beneficial

145. Choose the appropriate word that can substitute – 'Animals that can live on land as well as water.'

A. Amorphous B. Ambivalent
C. Ambiguous D. Amphibian

146. One who cannot be corrected' may be substituted by the word:

A. Incurable B. Incorrigible
C. Invulnerable D. Hardened

147. Choose the correctly spelt word.

A. Surveillance B. Survaillance
C. Surveilance D. Survellance

148. Choose the misspelt word.

A. Commend B. Appraise
C. Behaviour D. Mentenance

149. Choose what best expresses the meaning of the idiom "To meet one's Waterloo'.

A. To die fighting
B. To meet one's final defeat
C. To die an ignobale death
D. To meet a strong adversary

150. Choose the best expresses the meaning of the underlined phrase in the sentence. 'It is high time that India did something about its population problem?

A. Appropriate time
B. Already late
C. Auspicious moment
D. Desired occasion

151. Choose the Passive Voice of 'Who teaches you English?'

A. English is taught by whom?
B. By whom will you be taught English?
C. By whom were you taught English?
D. By whom are you being taught English?

152. Choose the corret Indirect speech of — I said to my brother, "Let us got to some hill station for a change."

A. I permitted my brother to got to some hill station for a change.
B. I suggested to my brother that we should go to some hill station for a change.
C. I asked my brother to go to some hill station for a change.
D. I asked my brother if he would go to some hill station for a change.

153. Pick out the most appropriate word to fill in the blank in the sentence. "There is no doubt that one has to keep .... with the changing times."

A. pace B. himself
C. aside D. oneself

154. Choose the correct preposition to complete the sentence.

"I shall not desert you .... all the world."

A. by B. for
C. with D. from

155. Who wrote the poem *"Rape of the Lock"*?

A. Chaucer B. Pope
C. Dryden D. Shakespeare

156. Who wrote the novel *"Sons and Lovers"* ?

A. Lawrence B. Austen
C. Bronte D. Hardy

157. Who wrote the play *"Man and the Superman"*?

A. Shakespeare B. Eliot
C. Shaw D. Yeats

158. The communicative approach to Language Teaching – Learning lays stress on:

A. translation B. language use
C. grammar D. usage of structures

159. Bathsheba Everdene was the heroine in the novel.

A. *Return of the Native*
B. *Tess of d'Urberviues*
C. *Far from the Madding Crowd*
D. *Mayer of Casterbridge*

160. Wordsworth was a poet of which period in literature?

A. Age of Reason
B. Romantic Period
C. Victorian Period
D. Modern Period

(V) हिन्दी

निर्देश (161-165) : *नीचे दिए गए गद्यांश को ध्यान से पढ़िए और बाद में पूछे गए प्रश्नों के उत्तर दीजिए।*

शिष्टजनों द्वारा अनुष्ठित आचरण मात्र कल्पना-उद्भूत सामाजिक शिष्टाचार नहीं है अपितु गंभीर वैज्ञानिक रहस्यों से ओत-प्रोत ऐसा संस्कार है जो मानव जीवन में गुणाधान प्रक्रिया को प्रशस्त करता है। भारतीय संस्कृति में शिष्टाचार का श्रीगणेश सामाजिक व्यवहार के सिंहद्वार – अभिवादन से होता है। ईश्वराभिवादन, पूज्यजनों को प्रणाम, नमस्कार, प्राञ्जलि, अञ्जलिपुट, प्रणिपात, नामोच्चारणपूर्वक नमन, प्रदक्षिणापूर्वक सम्मान तथा साष्टांग प्रणाम पर्यायभेद से अभिवादन के ही विविध रूप हैं। प्रतिदिन या विशिष्ट अवसरों पर कर्म में सफलता और दीर्घायुष्य-प्राप्ति हेतु माता-पिता तथा गुरुजनों को अभिवादन करना केवल भारतीय संस्कृति में ही विद्यमान है। अध्यात्म-विज्ञान की मान्यता है कि किसी वरेण्य व्यक्ति के आगमन पर प्राणस्पन्दन की गति ऊर्ध्वमुखी होकर ऊर्जस्वित हो जाती है। उनका आशीर्वाद प्राप्त कर प्राण ऊर्जावान् बन जाते हैं। आज अन्य क्षेत्रों की भाँति शिष्टाचार के विधि-विधान में प्रदूषण और अवमूल्यन निर्बाध गति से हो रहा है। 'हाय', 'ही', 'हलो' करने वालों को भला हाथ जोड़कर मस्तक झुकाना कैसे रास आ सकता है? त्याग-वैराग्यसम्पन्न अल्पवयस्क या वयोवृद्धों को अभिवादन करना हमारी पुरातन आचार-पद्धति है।

गद्यांश के आधार पर निम्नलिखित प्रश्न (161 से 165), संभावित उत्तर विकल्पों के साथ दिए गए हैं। सही विकल्प को चुनिए।

161. शिष्टाचार का प्रथम सोपान क्या है?
A. कुशलक्षेम पूछना
B. मुस्कराते हुए बात करना
C. अभिवादन करना
D. भेंट देना

162. गुरुजनों को अभिवादन करने का कौन-सा कृत्य विधिसम्मत **नहीं** है?
A. चरण स्पर्श करना
B. हाथ जोड़कर सिर झुकाना
C. साष्टांग प्रणाम करना
D. हाथ मिलाना

163. आशीर्वाद ग्रहण करने का वैज्ञानिक रहस्य क्या है?
A. मन प्रसन्न हो जाता है
B. प्राण ऊर्जस्वित हो जाते हैं
C. असम्भव कार्य सम्भव हो जाता है
D. हमारा आत्मविश्वास बढ़ता है

164. सामाजिक कुशलता प्राप्त करने का सिंहद्वार क्या है?
A. श्रीगणेश का पूजन
B. सहभोज का आयोजन
C. प्रत्येक व्यक्ति को अपना गुरु मानना
D. विधिपूर्वक यथायोग्य अभिवादन

165. 'सबहिं मानप्रद आप अमानी' का अभिप्राय है–
A. स्वयं सम्मान की चाह न कर सबको सम्मान देना
B. सबके मान की परवाह करने से पहले अपनी चिन्ता करना
C. मान पाकर आपा न खोना
D. अपने सम्मान के समान दूसरों का भी सम्मान करना

निर्देश (166-180) : *निम्नलिखित प्रत्येक प्रश्न के साथ चार-चार विकल्प दिए गए हैं। सही विकल्प चुनिए।*

166. मलिक मोहम्मद जायसी की 'पद्मावत' किस भाषा में है?
A. उर्दू B. फारसी
C. अवधी D. मगधी

167. संस्कृत भाषा की इनमें से कौन-सी लिपि है?
A. देवनागरी B. ब्राह्मी
C. गुरुमुखी D. शारदा

168. 'छायावाद' किस काल की प्रवृत्ति है?
A. आदिकाल
B. भक्तिकाल
C. आधुनिक काल
D. किसी काल की नहीं

169. कौन-सी वर्तनी शुद्ध है?
A. श्रीहरी B. पूज्यनीय
C. मनःकामना D. कवित्री

170. इनमें अशुद्ध वाक्य कौन-सा है?
A. मैंने थोड़ी देर बाद जाना है।
B. आप सपरिवार आमंत्रित हैं।

C. कृपया हमारे घर आइए।

D. आप जब भी आयें, मुझसे मिलें।

171. 'अभिमुख होने' के अर्थ में किस मुहावरे का प्रयोग है?

A. छत्तीस का आँकड़ा होना

B. एक और एक ग्यारह होना

C. निन्यानवे का चक्कर

D. तिरेसठ की तरह होना

172. उपरि + उक्त मिलकर सन्धिष्ठ पद क्या होगा?

A. उपरुक्त B. उपर्युक्त

C. उपरोक्त D. उप्रयुक्त

173. 'रसोईघर' का समास-विग्रह है–

A. रसोई का घर B. रसोई और घर

C. रसोई के लिए घर D. घर की रसोई

174. निविदा किसे कहते हैं?

A. अपील करना B. टेण्डर

C. विदाई-समारोह D. प्रार्थना-पत्र

175. 'वह मेरी बात <u>चुपचाप सुन रहा था</u>।'
इस वाक्य में रेखांकित पद क्या है?

A. क्रिया-विशेषण B. विशेषण

C. संज्ञा D. अव्यय

176. 'कण्ठ' का विशेषण होगा–

A. कण्ठी B. काठी

C. कण्ठक D. कण्ठ्य

177. तो पर वारौं उरबसी, सुनि राधिके सुजान।
तू मोहन के उरबसी, ह्वै उरबसी-समान।।
इस दोहे में यमक अलंकार किस शब्द के कारण है?

A. वारौं B. सुजान

C. समान D. उरबसी

178. 'विनयपत्रिका' किसकी रचना है?

A. केशवदेव B. तुलसीदास

C. बिहारीलाल D. मैथिलीशरण गुप्त

179. 'जिसने प्रणय पाथेय माना जीत उसकी ही रही' इस काव्य-पंक्ति में क्या भाव है?

A. जीवन-संघर्ष में कायर की हार होती है

B. निरन्तर संघर्षरत रहने वाला जीतता है

C. प्रेमयुक्त जीवन सदा विजयी होता है

D. प्रेम ही संघर्षपूर्ण जीवन का विरामस्थल है

180. 'यथाशक्ति' शब्द में कौन-सा समास है?

A. अव्ययीभाव B. तत्पुरुष

C. कर्मधारय D. बहुव्रीहि

ANSWERS

1	2	3	4	5	6	7	8	9	10
A	C	B	C	B	D	A	D	D	A
11	**12**	**13**	**14**	**15**	**16**	**17**	**18**	**19**	**20**
D	A	C	C	B	D	A	C	B	C
21	**22**	**23**	**24**	**25**	**26**	**27**	**28**	**29**	**30**
B	A	D	B	C	C	A	A	B	A
31	**32**	**33**	**34**	**35**	**36**	**37**	**38**	**39**	**40**
C	D	B	A	B	A	C	A	D	D
41	**42**	**43**	**44**	**45**	**46**	**47**	**48**	**49**	**50**
D	A	A	D	D	B	A	C	D	C
51	**52**	**53**	**54**	**55**	**56**	**57**	**58**	**59**	**60**
B	C	B	A	A	C	D	D	D	A
61	**62**	**63**	**64**	**65**	**66**	**67**	**68**	**69**	**70**
C	C	D	B	D	D	D	D	A	D
71	**72**	**73**	**74**	**75**	**76**	**77**	**78**	**79**	**80**
D	B	C	A	B	D	D	C	A	A

81	82	83	84	85	86	87	88	89	90
D	A	A	B	C	D	D	A	D	B
91	**92**	**93**	**94**	**95**	**96**	**97**	**98**	**99**	**100**
C	C	D	C	C	B	D	C	D	A
101	**102**	**103**	**104**	**105**	**106**	**107**	**108**	**109**	**110**
A	B	C	D	B	C	D	D	B	A
111	**112**	**113**	**114**	**115**	**116**	**117**	**118**	**119**	**120**
A	D	C	A	B	C	D	A	B	A
121	**122**	**123**	**124**	**125**	**126**	**127**	**128**	**129**	**130**
C	D	D	D	B	C	B	A	B	A
131	**132**	**133**	**134**	**135**	**136**	**137**	**138**	**139**	**140**
A	A	C	B	A	A	A	C	B	A
141	**142**	**143**	**144**	**145**	**146**	**147**	**148**	**149**	**150**
B	B	A	C	D	B	A	D	B	A
151	**152**	**153**	**154**	**155**	**156**	**157**	**158**	**159**	**160**
A	B	A	D	B	A	C	B	C	B
161	**162**	**163**	**164**	**165**	**166**	**167**	**168**	**169**	**170**
C	D	B	D	A	C	A	C	B	A
171	**172**	**173**	**174**	**175**	**176**	**177**	**178**	**179**	**180**
D	B	A	B	A	D	D	B	B	A

SOME SELECTED EXPLANATORY ANSWERS

101. $\dfrac{\sqrt{\dfrac{1+a}{1-a}}+\sqrt{\dfrac{1-a}{1+a}}}{\sqrt{\dfrac{1+a}{1-a}}-\sqrt{\dfrac{1-a}{1+a}}}-\dfrac{1}{a}$

$=\dfrac{1+a+1-a}{1+a-1+a}-\dfrac{1}{a}$

$=\dfrac{2}{2a}-\dfrac{1}{a}$

$=0$

102. $\because p = x + y$ and $q = x - y$

$\therefore \dfrac{p+q}{p-q}-\dfrac{p-q}{p+q}$

$=\dfrac{(p^2+2pq+q^2)-(p^2-2pq+q^2)}{p^2-q^2}$

$=\dfrac{4pq}{p^2-q^2}$

$=\dfrac{4(x+y)(x-y)}{(x+y)^2-(x-y)^2}$

$=\dfrac{4(x^2-y^2)}{x^2+2xy+y^2-x^2+2xy-y^2}$

$=\dfrac{x^2-y^2}{xy}$

103. Let the number be x and the successor is $x + 1$

ATQ, $\dfrac{1}{3}x-\dfrac{1}{4}(x+1)=1$

$\Rightarrow 4x - 3x - 3 = 12$

$\Rightarrow x = 15$

104. Suppose $x = 0.363636$ ....(*i*)

Multiplying both sides of (*i*) by 100,

$100\,x = 36.363636$.... ...(*ii*)

Subtracting (*i*) from (*ii*), we get
$99x = 36$

$$\therefore x = \frac{36}{99} = \frac{4}{11}$$

Thus, the sum of numerator and denominator of $\frac{4}{11}$ is 15.

105. Let the number of people be x.
As per the given condition,

$$\frac{72}{x-3} - \frac{72}{x} = 4$$

$$\Rightarrow \frac{72[x - x + 3]}{x(x-3)} = 4$$

$$\Rightarrow 4(x^2 - 3x) = 72 \times 3$$

$$\Rightarrow x^2 - 3x - 54 = 0$$

$$\Rightarrow x(x-9) + 6(x-9) = 0$$

Either $x + 6 = 0$ or $x - 9 = 0$
$x = -6$ (not possible) $x = 9$

106. Let the amount of B be Rs. x
so that the amount of A = Rs. $2x$
The amount of C = Rs. $(3x - 5)$
ATQ,
$x + 2x + (3x - 5) = 61$
$\Rightarrow 6x = 66$
$\therefore x = 11$
Thus, the amount that "C" gets
$= 3 \times 11 - 5$
= Rs. 28

107. 6.4% of $2.5 = \frac{6.4}{100} \times 2.5$

$$= \frac{64}{1000} \times \frac{25}{10}$$

$= 0.16$

108. Let the income of A = Rs. $9x$
and the income of B = Rs. $7x$
Also, the expenditure of A = Rs. $4y$
and the expenditure of B = Rs. $3y$
As per the condition,
$9x - 4y = 200$ ...(*i*)
And $7x - 3y = 200$ ...(*ii*)
Solving eqn. (*i*) and (*ii*) we get
$x = 200$
So, income of A = 9×200
= Rs. 1800

109. Here, $a = 2$

$$d = 4 - 2 = 2$$

$$t_n = a + (n-1)d$$

$$\Rightarrow 100 = 2 + (n-1) \times 2$$

$$\Rightarrow 100 = 2 + 2n - 2$$

$$\therefore n = \frac{100}{2} = 50$$

$$\therefore S_n = \frac{n}{2}\{2a + (n-1) \times d\}$$

$$S_{50} = \frac{50}{2}\{2 \times 2 + (50-1) \times 2\}$$

$$= 25(4 + 49 \times 2)$$

$$= 25 \times 102$$

$$= 2550$$

110. $\because \sin A = \frac{24}{25}$

$$\cos A = \sqrt{1 - \sin^2 A} = \sqrt{1 - \left(\frac{24}{25}\right)^2}$$

$$= \sqrt{1 - \frac{576}{625}} = \sqrt{\frac{625 - 576}{625}}$$

$$= \sqrt{\frac{49}{625}} = \frac{7}{25}$$

$\therefore$ The value of tan A + sec A

$$= \frac{\sin A}{\cos A} + \frac{1}{\cos A}$$

$$= \frac{1 + \sin A}{\cos A}$$

$$= \frac{1 + \frac{24}{25}}{\frac{7}{25}}$$

$$= \frac{\frac{49}{25}}{\frac{7}{25}} = \frac{49}{7} = 7$$

111. Since, HCF of the polynomials $x^3 - 3x^2 + px + 24$ and $x^2 - 7x + q$ is $x - 2$

Here we put $x = 2$ in the given polynomials, we have

$(2)^3 - 3 \times 2^2 + p \times 2 + 24 = 0$

$\Rightarrow 8 - 12 + 2p + 24 = 0$

$2p = -20$

$\therefore p = -10$

Again, $(2)^2 - 7 \times 2 + q = 0$

$\Rightarrow 4 - 14 + q = 0$

$\Rightarrow -10 + q = 0$

$\therefore q = 10$

$\therefore p + q = -10 + 10 = 0$

112. $\dfrac{3 \sin 62°}{\cos 28°} - \dfrac{\sec 42°}{\cos 48°}$

$$= \frac{3\sin(90° - 28°)}{\cos 28°} - \frac{\sec 42°}{\operatorname{cosec}(90 - 42°)}$$

$$= \frac{3 \cos 28°}{\cos 28°} - \frac{\sec 42°}{\sec 42°}$$

$= 3 - 1$

$= 2$

113. Suppose each edge of the cube be x, on increasing 50% of each edge,

New edge $= x + \frac{1}{2}x = \frac{3x}{2}$

Original surface area of the cube $= 6l^2$

$= 6x^2$

New surface area of the cube

$$= 6\left(\frac{3x}{2}\right)^2$$

$$= 6 \times \frac{9x^2}{4}$$

$$= \frac{27}{2}x^2$$

Increase in surface area

$$= \frac{27}{2}x^2 - 6x^2$$

$$= \frac{27x^2 - 12x^2}{2}$$

$$= \frac{15x^2}{2}$$

$\therefore$ % increase

$$= \frac{\frac{15x^2}{2}}{6x^2} \times 100 = 125$$

114. The volume of the metal contained in the shell

$$= \frac{4}{3}\pi(R^3 - r^3)$$

Here $R = 5$, $r = 4$

$$\therefore V = \frac{4}{3}\pi\left[(5)^3 - (4)^3\right]$$

$$= \frac{4}{3} \times \frac{22}{7}[125 - 64]$$

$$= \frac{4}{3} \times \frac{22}{7} \times 61$$

$= 255.619 \approx 255.62 \text{ cm}^3$

115.

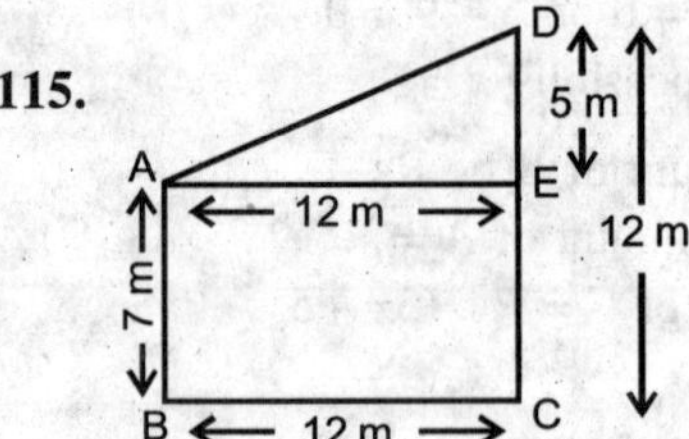

AB = 7 m

CD = 12 m

BC = AE = 12 m

DE = CD – CE

= CD – AB

= 12 – 7 = 5 m

$AD^2 = AE^2 + DE^2$

$= (12)^2 + (5)^2$

$= 144 + 25 = 169$

$\therefore AD = \sqrt{169} = 13$ m

116. $d_1 = 24$ cm

$d_2 = 10$ cm

Sides of the rhombus

$$= \frac{1}{2}\sqrt{d_1^2 + d_2^2}$$

$= \frac{1}{2}\sqrt{(24)^2 + (10)^2}$

$= \frac{1}{2}\sqrt{576 + 100}$

$= \frac{1}{2}\sqrt{676}$

$= \frac{1}{2} \times 26 = 13$ cm

117. Sum of 25 observations = 25 × 36 = 900
Sum of first 13 observations = 13 × 32 = 416
Sum of last 13 observations = 13 × 39 = 507
Thus, the 13th observation
= 416 + 507 – 900
= 923 – 900
= 23

118. $\frac{x_1 + x_2}{2} = 1$

$\Rightarrow x_1 + x_2 = 2$ ...(*i*)

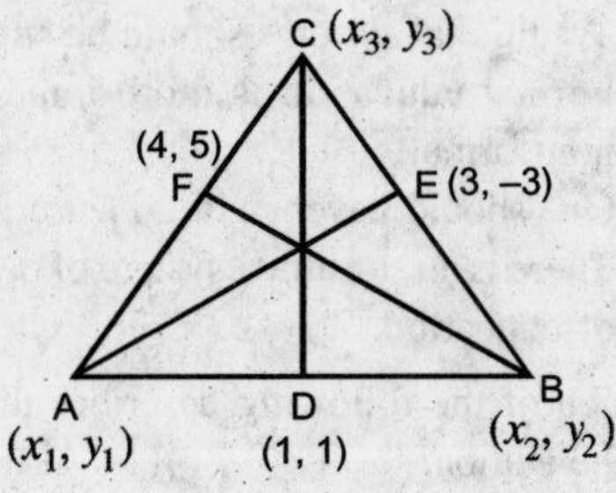

$\frac{y_1 + y_2}{2} = 1$

$\Rightarrow y_1 + y_2 = 2$ ...(*ii*)

$\frac{x_2 + x_3}{2} = 3$

$\Rightarrow x_2 + x_3 = 6$ ...(*iii*)

$\frac{y_2 + y_3}{2} = -3$

$\Rightarrow y_2 + y_3 = -6$ ...(*iv*)

$\frac{x_3 + x_1}{2} = 4$

$\Rightarrow x_1 + x_3 = 8$ ...(*v*)

$\frac{y_3 + y_1}{2} = 5$

$\Rightarrow y_1 + y_3 = 10$ ...(*vi*)

Adding (*i*), (*iii*), (*v*), we get

$2(x_1 + x_2 + x_3) = 16$

$\therefore x_1 + x_2 + x_3 = 8$

$\therefore \frac{x_1 + x_2 + x_3}{3} = \frac{8}{3}$

Similarly, adding (*ii*), (*iv*) and (*vi*)

$2(y_1 + y_2 + y_3) = 6$

$\therefore y_1 + y_2 + y_3 = 3$

$\therefore \frac{y_1 + y_2 + y_3}{3} = \frac{3}{3} = 1$

Hence, the co-ordinates of centroid is $\left(\frac{8}{3}, 1\right)$.

119. S = (H, H) (HT), (TH) (TT)
n(S) = 4
E = (HT) (TH) (HH)
n(E) = 3

$\therefore$ Probablity, $P = \frac{n(E)}{n(S)} = \frac{3}{4}$

120. Each of man get his daily ration = 180 g
Daily consumption of 600 men
= 600 × 180 g = 108000 g
= 108 kg
∴ Ration for 25 days
= 108 × 25 kg
= 2700 kg
Now, after increasing 300 men and decreasing the ration upto 150 g, we have
Total no. of men = 600 + 300
= 900
Total quantity of ration
= 900 × 150g
= 135000 g
= 135 kg

No. of days = $\frac{2700}{135} = 20$.

Previous Paper (Solved)

IGNOU B.Ed. Entrance Test 2006

PART-A

SECTION-I : GENERAL ENGLISH COMPREHENSION

Directions : *Read the following passage carefully and pick out the best answer out of the four choices given in the questions that follow.*

Educational planning should aim at meeting the educational needs of the entire population of all age groups. While the traditional structure of education as a three layer hierarchy from the primary stage to the university represents the core, we should not overlook the periphery which is equally important. Under modern conditions, workers need to rewind or renew, their enthusiasm, or strike out in a new direction, or improve their skills as much as any university professor. The retired and the aged have their own needs as well. Educational planning, in other words, should take care of the needs of everyone.

Our structures of education have been built up on the assumption that there is a terminal point to education. This basic defect has become all the more harmful today. A UNESCO report entitled 'Learning to Be' prepared by Edgar Faure and others in 1973 asserts that the education of children must prepare future adults for various forms of self-learning. A viable education system of the future should consist of modules with different kinds of functions serving a diversity of constituents. And performance, not the period of study, should be the basis for credentials. The writing is already on the wall.

In view of the fact that the significance of a commitment to lifelong learning and lifetime education is being discussed only in recent years even in educationally advanced countries, the possibility of the idea becoming an integral part of educational thinking seems to be a far cry. For, to move in that direction means much more than some simple rearrangement of the present organization of education. But a good beginning can be made by developing open university programmes for older learners of different categories and introducing extension services in the conventional colleges and schools. These institutions should also learn to cooperate with the numerous community organizations such as libraries, museums, municipal recreation programmes, health services, etc.

1. What is the main thrust of the author?

A. Traditional systems should be strengthened

B. Formal education is more important than non-formal

C. One should never cease to learn

D. There is no substitute system of open system of education.

2. Which of the following describes the purpose of the author?

A. To criticise the present educational system

B. To strengthen the present educational practices

C. To support non-conventional educational organizations

D. None of these

3. According to the passage, the present education structures assume which of the following?

A. All people can be educated as per their needs

B. Education planning at present is very much practical

C. Education is a one time process

D. Discussions on lifelong learning should continue

4. Which of the following is not true in the context of the given passage?
A. Lifelong learning is a recent concept
B. Workers' knowledge and skills also need to be updated constantly
C. 'Learning to Be' subscribes to the view that there is a terminal point to education
D. Schools and colleges should also start extension services

5. According to the author, the concept of 'lifetime education' is
A. as old as traditional education
B. still in formative stages
C. in vogue in advanced countries
D. not practical or desirable

6. Integrating the concepts of lifelong education with the educational structure would imply
A. closing down conventional schools and colleges
B. longer durations for all formal courses
C. simple rearrangement of present educational organizations
D. None of these

7. In the context of the passage, what is the meaning of the sentence "The writing is already on the wall"?
A. Everything is uncertain now-a-days
B. Changes have already taken place
C. The signs of change are already visible
D. You cannot change the future

8. Which of the following is closest in meaning to the word 'meeting' as used in the passage?
A. Approaching B. Contacting
C. Introducing D. Satisfying

9. Which of the following is opposite to the word 'integral' as used in the passage?
A. Essential B. Independent
C. Major D. Minor

10. Which of the following is opposite in meaning to the phrase 'a far cry' as used in the passage?
A. A reality
B. A theoretical suggestion
C. Very funny
D. Next to impossible

SECTION II : LOGICAL AND ANALYTICAL REASONING

Directions : *In the following questions (11-15) a series of numbers or alphabets (of English language) is being given. You have to identify the missing number or alphabet which bears the same relation with others.*

11. 1, 3, 9, ?, 81
A. 12 B. 15
C. 27 D. 25

12. A, E, ?, O, U
A. F B. I
C. G D. L

13. 1, 2, 6, 24, 120, ?
A. 144 B. 480
C. 600 D. 720

14. 37, 47, 58, ?, 79, 89
A. 67 B. 68
C. 69 D. 71

15. 1221, 2442, 3663, 4884, ?
A. 5885 B. 6105
C. 6006 D. 8448

Directions : *In the following questions (16-20), find the term from the given alternatives for the missing place marked?*

16. LUNCH : OWQEK : DINNER : ?
A. HJPOIS B. HKPPIT
C. GKQPHT D. GKPOHT

17. AUTHENTIC : AVTIEOTJC : : GENUINE : ?
A. GFNUIPE B. GFNVIOE
C. GFNVJOE D. GFVNOJE

18. ODOUR : ? : : SMELL :PPBOI
A. LGLXO B. LGKXP
C. LALIO D. LGMYP

19. COMMERCE : FSRSLZLO : : BEGIN : ?
A. EHKNU B. EIMOV
C. EIKNU D. EILOU

20. TREASON : ?: : REWARD : UHZDUG

A. WUGCURQ
B. WUHDWRQ
C. WUHDVRQ
D. WGHDVRQ

Directions : *In each of the following questions (21-25), two statements are followed by two conclusions. Assuming the first two statements to be true, (however absurd it may be) decide which of the two logically follows strictly from the given statements. Select the most appropriate alternative from the ones given.*

21. All apples are fruits.
No fruit is vegetable.
Conclusions:
I. All apples are vegetables.
II. All fruits are apples.
A. Only I follows
B. Only II follows
C. Both I and II follow
D. Neither I nor II follows

22. All watches are machines.
All machines are living beings.
Conclusions:
I. All machines are watches.
II. All watches are living beings.
A. Only I follows
B. Only II follows
C. Both I and II follow
D. Neither I nor II follows

23. Some birds are dolls.
All animals are dolls.
Conclusions:
I. All birds are dolls.
II. Some animals are dolls.
A. Only I follows
B. Only II follows
C. Both I and II follow
D. Neither I nor II follows

24. All lenses are mirrors.
All mirrors are brushes.
Conclusions:
I. All lenses are brushes.
II. All brushes are lenses.
A. Only I follows
B. Only II follows
C. Both I and II follow
D. Neither I nor II follows

25. All animals are not birds.
Some animals are vertebrates.
Conclusions:
I. All birds are vertebrates.
II. Some birds are animals.
A. Only I follows
B. Only II follows
C. Both I and II follow
D. Neither I nor II follows

Directions : *In the following questions (26-30) three figures resemble each other, you have to identify the odd one.*

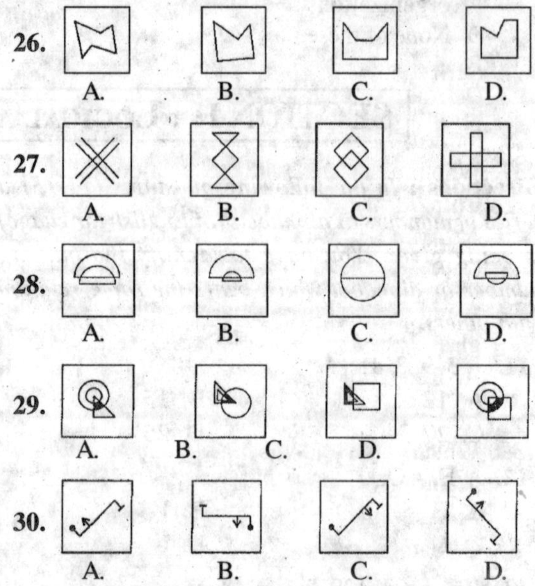

SECTION III : EDUCATIONAL AND GENERAL AWARENESS

Directions : *Indicate the correct answer.*

31. Who among the following attended all the three Round Table Conferences?

A. Madan Mohan Malviya
B. Mahatma Gandhi
C. Mohammad Ali Jinnah
D. Dr. B.R. Ambedkar

32. The script of Indus Valley Civilisation was
A. Brahmi B. Tamil
C. Kharosthi D. Undeciphered

33. The book *'Wings of Fire'* has been authored by
A. Arundhati Roy
B. A.B. Vajpayee
C. A.P.J. Abdul Kalam
D. V.S. Naipaul

34. 'Lugano Trophy' is awarded to the best men team for
A. Badminton B. Road Walking
C. Hockey D. Cricket

35. Fundamental Right to education for children in the age group six to fourteen years has been conferred by
A. 73rd Constitution Amendment Act
B. 76th Constitution Amendment Act
C. 86th Constitution Amendment Act
D. 93rd Constitution Amendment Act

36. Committee to review the National Policy on Education (1986) was chaired by
A. Triguna Sen
B. Acharya Narendra Dev
C. Acharya Ram Murti
D. K.C. Pant

37. Who is associated with the creation of Pentium Chip?
A. Arun Netravali B. C. Kumar Patel
C. Vinod Dham D. Sabeer Bhatia

38. A red object, when seen through a thick blue glass, appears
A. Red B. Violet
C. Green D. Black

39. Which of the following mountains are the oldest according to geological history?
A. Aravalli B. Nilgiris
C. Satpura range D. Vindhyas

40. Who presides over the joint sittings of the two houses of Parliament?
A. President
B. Vice President or a nominee of the President
C. Prime Minister
D. Speaker of the Lok Sabha

41. India is the largest producer and consumer of
A. Rice B. Tea
C. Pulses D. Oilseeds

42. Languages of Austric family are spoken by
A. Mundas B. Khasis and Kols
C. Nicobarese D. All of these

43. Which is the earliest engineering educational institution in India?
A. IIT Kharagpur
B. BHU (IT) Varanasi
C. Roorkee Engineering College (IIT) Roorkee
D. Birla Institute of Technology and Science, Pilani

44. What is 'funny bone'?
A. A nerve B. A muscle
C. A blood vessel D. A bone

45. Which organisation is actively involved in school education and teacher education at the national level?
A. NIEPA B. NCERT
C. NCTE D. NDRI

46. Where is the poem written by Abul Fazl, inscribed?
A. Fathepur Sikri
B. On the Ibadat Khana
C. On the tomb of Amir Khusro
D. On the tomb of Salim Chishti

47. Who said "Say what you will, the indigenous native rule is by far the best"?
A. Mahatma Gandhi
B. Gopal Krishna Gokhale
C. Bal Gangadhar Tilak
D. Dayanand Saraswati

48. Who is the living legend of *Shahnai?*
A. Bismillah Khan
B. Bade Gulam Ali Khan
C. Pandit Bhim Sen Joshi
D. Pandit Jasraj

49. National Science Day is celebrated every year on
A. February 24 B. February 28
C. March 8 D. May 1

50. Who is the director of the movie, Phoolan Devi– Bandit Queen?

A. Ismail Merchant
B. Seema Biswas
C. Vinod Chopra
D. Shekhar Kapoor

51. When a person enters a dark room from bright light he/she cannot see anything clearly for sometime and starts seeing slowly because

A. the iris contracts
B. the iris expands
C. the length of lense increases
D. the distance between the lense and retina increases

52. Branch of Science concerned with the study of relationship of plants to their environment is

A. Cytology
B. Physiology
C. Ecology
D. Morphology

53. When milk is converted into curd, the sour taste is due to

A. Acetic acid
B. Citric acid
C. Lactic acid
D. Tartaric acid

54. According to Buddha, the sorrow of life can be ended by

A. Walking on the path of Tathagata
B. Practising severe penance
C. Following the rituals of Tripitaka
D. Eliminating all desires

55. TRYSEM is

A. a training programme for young entrepreneurs for self employment
B. a training programme for rural youth for self employment
C. a training programme for urban youth for self employment
D. a training programme for women for self employment

SECTION IV : TEACHING-LEARNING AND THE SCHOOL

Directions : *Indicate the correct answer.*

56. Good education is characterised by

A. good schooling facilities
B. good teachers and good school environment
C. good human relationships
D. good classroom processes and good learning by children

57. Burden on children is due to

A. heavy school bags
B. parental apathy
C. non comprehension
D. poor facilities

58. Main aim of teaching should be

A. to develop self confidence among children
B. to train them in vocational activities
C. to facilitate learning
D. to promote them to next class

59. On finding a child putting too many questions in the class, you would like to

A. ignore the child
B. ask him to keep quiet and not to disturb
C. satisfy the queries in and outside the class
D. ask the child to call his parents to meet the teacher

60. Problems in language learning arise due to lack of

A. methodology of teaching
B. availability of materials
C. teaching of mother tongue
D. teacher's competence

61. Co-curricular activities are necessary to

A. entertain children
B. promote harmonius development of personality
C. ensure inter-personal relationships
D. identify a team of children for cultural programmes

62. You are taking a class and children are requesting you to allow them to watch the snake charmer conducting a show nearby, you would like to

A. counsel the children and involve them into classroom activity making it interesting

B. allow them for 5–10 minutes as they would not take interest in the lesson otherwise
C. leave the class and ask the snake charmer to go away
D. rebuke them to behave properly

63. Private tuitions should be
A. acceptable as these are required by weak children
B. acceptable as these supplement teacher's income
C. banned as these affect classroom teaching
D. banned as these encourage malpractices

64. Concept of *"Neighbourhood School System"* was highlighted by
A. Radhakrishnan Commission
B. Mudalier Commission
C. Kothari Commission
D. National Policy on Education, 1986

65. Corporal Punishment should be permitted
A. to maintain discipline
B. to reinforce positive behaviour
C. to develop respect for teachers
D. under no circumstances

66. Usual teaching-learning processes can be supplemented by the following to improve the quality:
A. Extra coaching
B. Diagnostic and remedial teaching
C. Enrichment programmes
D. Inservice teacher education

67. School based evaluation can solve the problem of
A. Mass copying
B. Students' indiscipline
C. Unrealistic assessment
D. Teacher's social reputation

68. A true teacher is one who
A. teaches the subject well
B. inspires the students
C. behaves friendly with the students
D. is a disciplinarian

69. Level of teacher motivation depends on
A. high salaries
B. officer like status
C. professional training
D. commitment towards pupils and profession

70. Main aim of schooling should be
A. high pass percentage
B. completion of course in time
C. disciplined life of children
D. acquisition of competencies among children

71. School curriculum should *not* include the following in a secular democratic country:
A. religious education
B. education for values
C. education about religions
D. moral education

72. Insistence about admission of twenty per cent children from weaker sections of society into fee charging institutions is
A. justified
B. confusing
C. superfluous
D. unjustified

73. Parents should
A. monitor teachers' work
B. arrange for tuitions
C. periodically discuss the progress of their child
D. not interfere in school activities

74. Privately managed schools generally are preferred by people because
A. they are English medium schools
B. they have better qualified teachers
C. they have no corruption
D. they ensure quality through proper monitoring

75. Rabindranath Tagore emphasized the following in education:
A. purposiveness
B. organic linkages with the environment
C. perfection
D. relevance

76. Alternative schooling does *not* cater to the
A. street children
B. migrant children
C. out of school children
D. children in school

77. The term inclusive education refers to
A. education of SC/ST children

B. education of children of minority groups
C. education of children with disabilities alongwith normal ones.
D. education in multigrade settings

78. Failing of students is mainly a reflection on
A. students' intelligence
B. parental carelessness
C. the system of education
D. examination pattern

79. Success of students in education mainly depends upon
A. quality instructional time
B. money spent
C. quality home facilities
D. tuitions

80. As a teacher you do *not* agree to the statement that
A. teachers should be given due place in the society
B. teachers should be given immunity about children's failure
C. teachers should be given recurrent training
D. teachers should be given awards for excellent performance

PART-B

SECTION V : (I) SCIENCE

81. Which of the following are *not* electromagnetic waves?
A. Infra-red waves
B. Laser waves
C. Ultrasonic waves
D. Microwaves

82. Domestic electric meters record the consumption of electricity in
A. Volts B. Amperes
C. Watts D. Ohms

83. Which of the following is used for time keeping in an atomic clock?
A. Cesium B. Helium
C. Plutonium D. Nitrogen

84. When an aeroplane takes off, air pressure on the
A. top surface of its wings is less than the air pressure on the bottom surface
B. top surface of its wings is more than the air pressure on the bottom surface
C. top and bottom surfaces of its wings is exactly equal
D. wings is zero

85. The pH value of pure water is
A. 7 B. 0
C. 14 D. –1.0

86. The substance which readily hardens, when mixed with water is
A. Plaster of Paris
B. Granite
C. Lime
D. Silica

87. The gas commonly used for cooling in a domestic refrigerator is
A. Carbon monoxide
B. Propane and butane mixture
C. Helium
D. Neon

88. Stainless steel is basically formed by the combination of iron and
A. Chromium B. Carbon
C. Manganese D. Cobalt

89. The tube which connects the mouth to the stomach is known as
A. oesophagus B. trachea
C. larynx D. intestine

90. DNA molecules have the shape of
A. a string of beads
B. a double helix
C. a cylindrical mass
D. None of the above

91. Which portion of the egg contains cholesterol?
A. Egg white B. Shell of the egg
C. Egg yolk D. All parts equally

92. Aspirin is the common name of
A. salicylic acid
B. salicylate
C. acetyl salicylic acid
D. methyl salicylate

93. During galvanization, the substance which is coated on the surface of iron to protect it from rusting is
A. galium B. aluminium
C. tin D. zinc

94. The intensity of earthquakes is measured by
A. Algal scale B. Crescograph
C. Ritcher scale D. Cryptograph

95. Solar eclipse occurs when
A. earth comes between sun and moon
B. moon is at right angle to the earth
C. moon comes between sun and earth
D. sun comes between moon and earth

96. Which of the following are fossil fuels?
A. Coal and biogas
B. Petroleum and biogas
C. Biogas and coal gas
D. Coal, petroleum and natural gas

97. Clouds of interstellar matter found in space is known as
A. galaxies B. constellations
C. quasars D. nebula

98. The mass of a material divided by its volume is its
A. gravity B. relative density
C. specific gravity D. density

99. The removal of a piece of tissue from a living person for examination is known as
A. autopsy B. necropsy
C. biopsy D. histology

100. If a red coloured rose is examined in green light, it will appear
A. white B. black
C. grey D. brown

(II) MATHEMATICS

101. The value of

$$\left(a^{x-y}\right)^{x+y} \cdot \left(a^{y-z}\right)^{y+z} \cdot \left(a^{z-x}\right)^{z+x} \text{ is}$$

A. 0 B. 1
C. – 1 D. x + y + z

102. If $A = x - \frac{1}{x}$ then the value of $A - \frac{1}{A}$ is

A. $\frac{2}{x}$ B. $\frac{2x^2-1}{x}$

C. $\frac{x^4+1-x^2}{x\left(x^2-1\right)}$ D. $\frac{x^4-3x^2+1}{x\left(x^2-1\right)}$

103. Two numbers are in the ratio 3 : 4. If the sum of their squares is 900, the smaller number is
A. 18 B. 24
C. 16 D. 27

104. If 4 men or 6 boys can do a piece of work in 20 days then 12 men and 2 boys will do the same work in
A. 10 days B. 8 days
C. 6 days D. 5 days

105. The difference between simple interest and compound interest on a sum at 5% in 2 years is Rs. 2.50. The sum is
A. Rs. 2,500 B. Rs. 2,000
C. Rs. 1,000 D. Rs. 1,500

106. The value of sin 60° cos 30° + cos 60° sin 30° is
A. 0 B. 1

C. $\frac{1}{2}$ D. $\frac{\sqrt{3}}{2}$

107. If I had walked 1km/hour faster I would have taken 10 minutes less to walk a distance of 2 km. The rate of my walking is
A. 4 km/hour B. 3 km/hour
C. 6 km/hour D. 3.5 km/hour

108. The radius of a semicircular disc is 10.5 cm. The perimeter of the disc is

A. 33 cm B. 21 cm
C. 44 cm D. 54 cm

109. Three consecutive vertices of a parallelogram are A (1, 2), B(1, 0) and C (4, 0). The fourth vertex D is

A. $\left(\frac{5}{2}, 1\right)$ B. (2, 1)
C. (4, 2) D. (2, 4)

110. One year ago, a man was 8 times as old as his son. Now his age is equal to the square of his son's age. The present age of the son is

A. 5 years B. 6 years
C. 7 years D. 8 years

111. PT is a tangent to a circle from an exterior point P and PAB is a secant intersecting the circle at A and B such that PA = 3 cm and PT = 6 cm. The measure of PB is

A. 9 cm B. 10 cm
C. 12 cm D. 8 cm

112. A bag contains 4 red, 5 black and 6 white balls. A ball is drawn at random. The probability that the ball drawn is red or white is

A. $\frac{2}{5}$ B. $\frac{4}{15}$
C. $\frac{1}{3}$ D. $\frac{2}{3}$

113. If 4 times the fourth term of an AP is equal to 7 times the 1st term, then the ratio of 1st term to the common difference is

A. 4 : 1 B. 1 : 4
C. 2 : 3 D. 3 : 2

114. The circumference of the base of a 9 m high cone is 44 m. The volume of the cone is

A. 1386 m^3 B. 198 m^3
C. 154 m^3 D. 462 m^3

115. The mode for the series 2, 3, 2, 5, 6, 3, 4, 7, 4, 9 is

A. 4.5 B. 4
C. 3 D. 3.5

116. The HCF of $x^2 + x - (2k + 2)$ and $2x^2 + kx - 12$ is $x + 4$. The value of k is

A. 0 B. 1
C. 2 D. 4

117. If $\sec\theta + \tan\theta = a$ then $\frac{a^2 - 1}{a^2 + 1}$ is equal to

A. $\sin\theta$ B. $\cos\theta$
C. $\operatorname{cosec}\theta$ D. $\cot\theta$

118. The area of a square that can be inscribed in a circle of radius r is

A. πr^2 B. $\sqrt{2}\, r^2$
C. $4r^2$ D. $2r^2$

119. Two isosceles triangles have equal vertical angles and their areas are in the ratio 4 : 25. The ratio of their corresponding heights is

A. 2 : 5 B. 1 : 5
C. 2 : 1 D. 1 : 4

120. A rectangular piece of paper is 22 cm long and 12 cm wide. A cylinder is formed by rolling the paper along its length. The volume of the cylinder is

A. 66 cm^3 B. 31 cm^3
C. 132 cm^3 D. 462 cm^3

(III) SOCIAL SCIENCE

Note : *Choose one out of the given four options.*

121. What is the name of the man who discovered that the Monsoon winds blow regularly across the Arabian Sea in summer?

A. Ptolemy B. Hippalus
C. Pliny D. Megasthenes

122. Who is remembered as the pioneer of Economic Nationalism?

A. Bipin Chandar Paul
B. Gokhale
C. R.C. Dutt
D. Madan Mohan Malviya

123. In the Allahabad district in 1929, at a time of the world-wide economic depression, 'no tax' campaign on behalf of peasants was led by

A. Jawahar Lal Nehru
B. Sahajanand Saraswati
C. M.N. Roy
D. P.C. Joshi

124. 'My own belief is that the Congress is tottering, and one of my great ambition is to assist it to a peaceful death.' Who said it?

A. Winston Churchill
B. Lord Canning
C. Lord Curzon
D. Mohammad Ali Jinnah

125. Aurangzeb was a scholar of

A. Poetry
B. Muslim theology and jurisprudence
C. Persian literature
D. Persian warfare

126. Who is connected with the 'Blue Water' Policy?

A. Albuquerque B. Dupleix
C. De Almeida D. Robert Clive

127. Who was called the 'Rapheal of the East'?

A. Bihzad of Herat
B. Sayyad Ali
C. Khwaja Abdus Samad
D. Farrukh Beg

128. Fiscal policy is connected with

A. Exports and imports
B. Public revenue and expenditure
C. Issue of currency
D. Population control

129. The expression 'The Union of States' used in the Constitution has been taken from the Constitution of

A. Canada B. USA
C. USSR D. Germany

130. Which one of the following statements correctly describes 'a hung Parliament'?

A. A Parliament in which no party has a clear majority
B. The Prime Minister has resigned but the Parliament is not dissolved
C. The Parliament lacks the quorum to conduct business
D. A lame duck Parliament

131. For what is Philadelphia well known?

A. Ship building B. Dairy industries
C. Locomotives D. Silk textiles

132. Which state is the leading producer of thorium?

A. Kerala B. Bihar
C. Orissa D. Madhya Pradesh

133. Who are believed to be the oldest inhabitants of India?

A. Mediterraneans B. Negritoes
C. Nordics D. Mongoloids

134. Most of the precipitation in India is

A. Cyclonic B. Convectional
C. Orographic D. Stormy

135. Who put forth the nebular hypothesis explaining the origin of the earth?

A. Wegener
B. Laplace
C. Kant
D. Jeans and Jeffreys

136. Leeds is well known for

A. Cotton textiles B. Iron smelting
C. Films D. Woollen textiles

137. The plan holiday refers to the period

A. 1965-68 B. 1966-69
C. 1967-70 D. 1978-80

138. Which of the following is the Indian contribution to Parliamentary procedures?

A. Zero session
B. Cut-motion
C. Adjournment motion
D. Guillotine

139. The only European country which did *not* prohibit or impose heavy duties on the import of Indian cotton goods was

A. Germany B. France
C. Holland D. Italy

140. Regarding the earliest surviving Buddhist art, what *cannot* be said to have particularly appealed to the Europeans is that it was

A. Non-symbolic B. Anecdotal
C. Iconographic D. Narrative

(IV) ENGLISH

141. The synonym of the word 'infinite' is

A. unique
B. indefinite
C. vague
D. endless

142. The word 'enjoined' in the sentence, 'Dinesh's mother enjoined him to change his ways' can be replaced by

A. asked
B. pleaded
C. urged
D. threatened

143. The antonym of 'audacious' is

A. timid
B. vulgar
C. low
D. incredible

144. The one-word substitute for 'A person who hates women' is

A. Misanthropist
B. Masochist
C. Misogynist
D. Misogamist

145. Which word can fill in the blank in the sentence: The prolonged illness left him totally ________

A. enervated
B. invalid
C. indisposed
D. healthy

146. Pick out the most appropriate pair of words to fill in the blanks in the sentence:
We must prevent endangered wild animal species from becoming ________ in order that our future generations may ________ the great diversity of human life.

A. rare _____escape
B. extinct _____ enjoy
C. outdated _____ know
D. powerful _____notice

147. Choose the correct meaning of the idiom: Hobson's choice

A. feeling of insecurity
B. accept or leave the offer
C. excellent choice
D. no choice at all

148. Choose the correct meaning of the idiom underlined in the sentence:
In almost every meeting, Rakesh tries to <u>rule the roost</u>.

A. to make friends
B. to remain aloof
C. to become popular
D. to dominate

149. Choose the meaning of the underlined phrase in the sentence:
He has been working <u>on and off</u> for several years on this project.

A. at intervals
B. rarely
C. painstakingly
D. continuously

150. Pick out the meaning of the underlined phrase in the sentence:
I must <u>take exception</u> to your remark.

A. accept gladly
B. consider carefully
C. object to
D. ignore

151. Pick out the most appropriate phrase to fill in the blank in the sentence: He managed to ____ in the examination.

A. get out
B. get up
C. get through
D. get on

152. The sentence, 'You must look into this matter.' is in Active voice. Pick out the correct sentence in Passive voice.

A. This matter has been looked into by you.
B. This matter may be looked into by you.
C. This matter should be looked into by you.
D. This matter will be looked into by you.

153. The sentence, 'Do you communicate with others?' is in Active voice. Pick out the correct sentence in Passive voice.

A. Are others communicated with by you?
B. Are others being communicated with by you?
C. Were others being communicated with by you?
D. Have others been communicated with by you?

154. She asked the teacher, "Is tomorrow a holiday?" is in Direct speech. Choose the correct sentence in Indirect speech.

A. She asked the teacher whether it was a holiday the next day.
B. She asked the teacher whether it is a holiday the next day.
C. She asked the teacher whether it was a holiday tomorrow.
D. She asked the teacher whether it is a holiday tomorrow.

155. Rashmi told Amit, "I bought a car yesterday," is in Direct speech. Choose the correct sentence in Indirect speech.
A. Rashmi said to Amit that I have bought a car the previous day.
B. Rashmi told Amit that she had bought a car the previous day.
C. Rashmi said to Amit that she had bought a car the previous day.
D. Rashmi told Amit that she had bought a car yesterday.

156. Choose the correctly spelt word:
A. Embarasment B. Embarassment
C. Embarrasment D. Embarrassment

157. Choose the wrongly spelt word:
A. Believe B. Relieve
C. Grieve D. Decieve

158. The poem '*Ode on Intimations of Immortality*' was written by
A. William Wordsworth
B. Thomas Grey
C. Lord Byron
D. Alfred Tennyson

159. The novel '*Woothering Heights*' was written by
A. Thomas Hardy
B. Charlotte Bronte
C. Emily Bronte
D. Joseph Conrad

160. The play '*Desire under the Elms*' was written by
A. William Shakespeare
B. Hendrick Ibsen
C. Bernard Shaw
D. Eugene O'Neill

(V) हिन्दी

प्रश्न संख्या 161 से 165 के लिए निर्देशः *दिए गए गद्यांश को ध्यान से पढ़िए और बाद में पूछे गए प्रश्नों के उत्तर दीजिए। गद्यांश के आधार पर निम्नलिखित प्रश्न (161 से 165), संभावित उत्तर विकल्पों के साथ दिए गए हैं। सही विकल्प को चुनिए।*

मानव-जीवन के सौ वर्षों को चार भागों में बाँटा गया है। वास्तव में सम्पूर्ण जीवन सतत् प्रयत्न करते हुए व्यक्तित्व का विकास करने के लिए है। व्यक्तित्व के विकास की दिशा अवस्था के अनुसार बदलती है। विशेष प्रकार की योग्यताओं को विकसित करने के लिए अनुकूल वातावरण की आवश्यकता पड़ती है। आश्रम-व्यवस्था के अनुसार जीवन-भर श्रम करते हुए मानव अधिकाधिक सफलता प्राप्त कर सकता है। जीवन का प्रथम आश्रम ब्रह्मचर्य अधिक से अधिक ज्ञान करने के लिए था। ब्रह्मचर्याश्रम में जो ज्ञान प्राप्त किया जाता है उसी की मात्रा के अनुरूप जीवन की सफलता होती है। इसी के बल पर गृहस्थाश्रम में वह अधिक से अधिक धन कमा कर लोक-कल्याण कर सकता है। मनुष्य की आध्यात्मिक प्रवृत्तियाँ स्वान्तः सुखाय होती हैं। इनके द्वारा वह वानप्रस्थ और संन्यास में शान्ति प्राप्त करता है।

161. वास्तव में सम्पूर्ण जीवन किस लिए है?
A. सतत् प्रयत्न करते हुए व्यक्तित्व के विकास के लिए
B. श्रम करते हुए सफलता प्राप्त करने के लिए
C. अधिक से अधिक धन कमाने के लिए
D. अधिक से अधिक ज्ञान प्राप्त करने के लिए

162. व्यक्तित्व के विकास की दिशा कैसे बदलती है?
A. योग्यताओं के विकास के अनुसार
B. अनुकूल वातावरण के अनुसार
C. अवस्था के अनुसार
D. सतत् प्रयत्नों के अनुसार

163. प्राप्त ज्ञान की मात्रा के अनुरूप क्या होता है?
A. जीवन की सफलता B. सुख की प्राप्ति
C. धन की प्राप्ति D. शान्ति की प्राप्ति

164. लोक-कल्याण कब अधिक किया जा सकता है?

A. ब्रह्मचर्याश्रम में B. वानप्रस्थ में
C. गृहस्थाश्रम में D. संन्यास में

165. मनुष्य शान्ति किसके द्वारा प्राप्त करता है?

A. ज्ञान के द्वारा
B. धन के द्वारा
C. लोक-कल्याण के द्वारा
D. आध्यात्मिक प्रवृत्तियों के द्वारा

प्रश्न संख्या 166 से 180 के लिए निर्देशः *निम्नलिखित प्रत्येक प्रश्न के साथ चार-चार विकल्प दिए गए हैं। सही विकल्प चुनिए।*

166. अवधी किस क्षेत्र के आसपास बोली जाती है?

A. मथुरा B. लखनऊ
C. जयपुर D. भरतपुर

167. हिन्दी साहित्य के आदि काल का दूसरा नाम क्या है?

A. वीरगाथा काल B. भक्ति काल
C. सूफी काल D. रीति काल

168. कौन-सी वर्तनी शुद्ध है?

A. अभियुत्त B. अबियुक्त
C. अभियुक्त D. अभियूत्त

169. इनमें सही वाक्य क्या है?

A. सभी विद्यार्थियों की इच्छा होती है कि अधिक अंक प्राप्त करें।
B. अधिक अंक प्राप्त करने की इच्छा सभी विद्यार्थियों में होती है।
C. सभी विद्यार्थियों की इच्छा अधिक अंक प्राप्त करने की होती है।
D. सभी विद्यार्थी अधिक अंक प्राप्त करने की इच्छा करते हैं।

170. ''एक थैली के चट्टे-बट्टे होना'' का क्या अर्थ है?

A. चट्टे-बट्टे एक थैली में होना
B. सभी का एक जैसा होना
C. एक वर्ग के लोगों की हानि होना
D. सबको मिल कर काम करना

171. पीताम्बर शब्द का अर्थ है

A. पीला आम B. पीले मुख वाला
C. पीला रंग D. पीले कपड़े वाला

172. लिपिक किसे कहते हैं?

A. जो टंकण कार्य करता है
B. जो क्लर्क है
C. जो रंग-रोगन करता है
D. जो लीपने का कार्य करता है

173. ''सम्प्रदान'' कारक का चिह्न है

A. में, पै, पर B. के लिए
C. को D. का, के, की

174. निम्नलिखित शब्दों में कौन-सा शब्द 'नृपति' का पर्यायवाची नहीं है?

A. भूपति B. महीपति
C. कुलपति D. राजा

175. ''लम्बोदर'' में कौन-सा समास है?

A. अव्ययीभाव B. बहुव्रीहि
C. कार्मधारय D. द्वन्द्व

176. ''पावक'' शब्द का सन्धि-विच्छेद है

A. पा + वक B. पाव् + अक
C. पौ + अक D. पा + आवक

177. ''कमर टूट जाना'' का अर्थ है

A. कमर की हड्डी टूटना
B. घबरा जाना
C. असफल होना
D. शक्ति या साहस न रहना

178. ''कामायनी'' किस लेखक की कृति है?

A. सुमित्रानन्दन पंत B. महादेवी वर्मा
C. जयशंकर प्रसाद D. हरिवंश राय बच्चन

179. ''भारत की प्राचीनतम लिपि ब्राह्मी मानी जाती है''– यह किस प्रकार का वाक्य है?

A. संयुक्त B. सरल
C. साधारण D. मिश्र

180. बतरस लालच लाल की मुरली धरी लुकाई।
सौंह करैं, भौंहनि हंसैं, देन कहैं नट जाँई।।
यहाँ "नट" शब्द का क्या अर्थ है?

A. नाटक करना B. छिप जाना
C. मना करना D. झगड़ा करना

ANSWERS

1	2	3	4	5	6	7	8	9	10
C	B	A	C	B	D	C	D	B	A
11	**12**	**13**	**14**	**15**	**16**	**17**	**18**	**19**	**20**
C	B	D	B	B	C	B	A	D	C
21	**22**	**23**	**24**	**25**	**26**	**27**	**28**	**29**	**30**
D	B	D	A	B	B	A	C	C	C
31	**32**	**33**	**34**	**35**	**36**	**37**	**38**	**39**	**40**
D	D	C	B	D	C	B	D	A	D
41	**42**	**43**	**44**	**45**	**46**	**47**	**48**	**49**	**50**
B	D	A	A	B	B	C	A	B	D
51	**52**	**53**	**54**	**55**	**56**	**57**	**58**	**59**	**60**
B	C	C	D	B	C	C	C	C	D
61	**62**	**63**	**64**	**65**	**66**	**67**	**68**	**69**	**70**
B	A	C	D	D	D	C	B	D	D
71	**72**	**73**	**74**	**75**	**76**	**77**	**78**	**79**	**80**
A	A	C	D	A	D	C	C	A	B
81	**82**	**83**	**84**	**85**	**86**	**87**	**88**	**89**	**90**
C	C	A	A	A	A	D	A	A	B
91	**92**	**93**	**94**	**95**	**96**	**97**	**98**	**99**	**100**
C	C	D	C	C	D	D	D	C	B
101	**102**	**103**	**104**	**105**	**106**	**107**	**108**	**109**	**110**
B	D	A	C	C	B	B	D	C	C
111	**112**	**113**	**114**	**115**	**116**	**117**	**118**	**119**	**120**
C	A	A	D	A	B	A	D	A	D
121	**122**	**123**	**124**	**125**	**126**	**127**	**128**	**129**	**130**
B	C	B	C	B	A	A	B	A	A
131	**132**	**133**	**134**	**135**	**136**	**137**	**138**	**139**	**140**
A	B	B	C	B	D	B	A	C	C
141	**142**	**143**	**144**	**145**	**146**	**147**	**148**	**149**	**150**
D	D	A	C	A	B	D	D	A	C
151	**152**	**153**	**154**	**155**	**156**	**157**	**158**	**159**	**160**
C	C	A	A	B	D	D	A	C	B
161	**162**	**163**	**164**	**165**	**166**	**167**	**168**	**169**	**170**
A	C	A	C	D	B	A	C	B	B
171	**172**	**173**	**174**	**175**	**176**	**177**	**178**	**179**	**180**
D	B	B	C	B	C	D	C	B	C

SOME SELECTED EXPLANATORY ANSWERS

11. $1 \times 3 = 3$

$3 \times 3 = 9$

$9 \times 3 = \boxed{27}$

$27 \times 3 = 81$

12. All are vowels.

13. 1, 2, 6, 24, 120, $\boxed{720,}$

$\times 2$ $\times 3$ $\times 4$ $\times 5$ $\times 6$

14. 37, 47, 58, $\boxed{68,}$ 79, 89,

+10 +11 +10 +11 +10

15. 1221, 2442, 3663, 4884, 6105,

×2, ×3, ×4, ×5

16. L U N C H → O W Q E K (+3, +2, +3, +2, +3)

D I N N E R → G K Q P H T (+3, +2, +3, +2, +3, +2)

17. AUTHENTIC → AVTIEOTJC (+1)

GENUINE → GFNVIOE (+1)

18. S M E L L → P P B O I (+3)

O D O U R → L G L X O (+3)

19. C O M M E R C E → F S R S L Z L O (+3, +4, +5, +6, +7, +8, +9, +10)

B E G I N → E I L O U (+3, +4, +5, +6, +7)

20. R E W A R D → U H Z D U G (+3)

T R E A S O N → W U H D V R Q (+3)

21. 

A = Apple, F = Fruit, V = Vegetable

22.
W
M
LB

W = Watches, M = Machines,
LB = Living Beings

23. 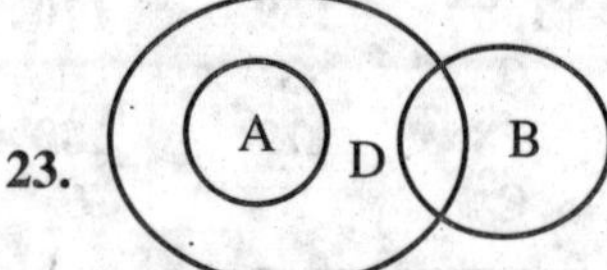

A = Animal, D = Dolls, B = Bird

24. 

L = Lense, M = Mirror, B = Brush

25. 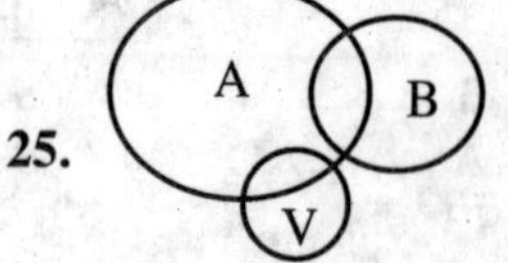

A = Animal, B = Bird,
V = Vertebrates

26. It has only five faces.

28. There is no overlapping.

29. Outer part is coloured.

101. $a^{(x-y)(x+y)} \cdot a^{(y-z)(y+z)} \cdot a^{(z-x)(z+x)}$

$a^{x^2-y^2} \cdot a^{y^2-z^2} \cdot a^{z^2-x^2}$

$a^{(x^2-y^2)+(y^2-z^2)+(z^2-x^2)}$

$a^0 = 1$

102. $A = x - \frac{1}{x}$

$$A - \frac{1}{A} = \left(x - \frac{1}{x}\right) - \frac{1}{\left(x - \frac{1}{x}\right)}$$

$$= \frac{\left(x - \frac{1}{x}\right)^2 - 1}{x - \frac{1}{x}} = \frac{\left(x^2 - 2 + \frac{1}{x^2}\right) - 1}{x - \frac{1}{x}}$$

$$= \frac{x^2 + \frac{1}{x^2} - 3}{\frac{x^2 - 1}{x}} = \frac{\frac{x^4 + 1 - 3x^2}{x^2}}{\frac{x^2 - 1}{x}}$$

$$= \frac{x^4 + 1 - 3x^2}{x^2} \cdot \frac{x}{x^2 - 1}$$

$$= \frac{x^4 - 3x^2 + 1}{x\left(x^2 - 1\right)}$$

103. $\frac{x}{y} = \frac{3}{4} \quad \therefore \quad x = \frac{3y}{4}$

$x^2 + y^2 = 900$

$$\left(\frac{3y}{4}\right)^2 + y^2 = 900$$

$\frac{9y^2}{16} + y^2 = 900$

$25y^2 = 900 \times 16$

or $y^2 = \frac{900 \times 16}{25}$

or $y = \sqrt{\frac{900 \times 16}{25}}$

$= \frac{30 \times 4}{5} = 24$

$x = \frac{3 \times 24}{4} = 18$

104. $4M = 6B$

$1M = \frac{6}{4}B$

$12M = \frac{6}{4} \times 12 = 18B$

12 Men + 2 Boys = 18 Boys + 2 Boys
= 20 Boys

$\because$ 6 Boys are doing a work in 20 days

$\therefore$ 1 Boy is doing a work in 20 × 6 days

$\therefore$ 20 Boys are doing a work in $\frac{20 \times 6}{20} = 6$ days

105. $\left[x\left(1+\frac{5}{100}\right)^2 - x\right] - \frac{x \cdot 5 \cdot 2}{100} = 2.50$

$\Rightarrow \left[x\left(\frac{21}{20}\right)^2 - x\right] - \frac{x}{10} = 2.50$

$\Rightarrow \left[\frac{441x}{400} - x\right] - \frac{x}{10} = 2.50$

$\Rightarrow \frac{441x - 400x}{400} - \frac{x}{10} = 2.50$

$\Rightarrow \frac{41x}{400} - \frac{x}{10} = 2.50$

$\Rightarrow \frac{41x - 40x}{400} = 2.50$

or $x = 2.50 \times 400 =$ Rs. 1000

106. Sin 60° Cos 30° + Cos60° Sin 30°

$\frac{\sqrt{3}}{2} \cdot \frac{\sqrt{3}}{2} + \frac{1}{2} \cdot \frac{1}{2}$

$= \frac{3}{4} + \frac{1}{4}$

$= \frac{3+1}{4} = \frac{4}{4} = 1$

107. Suppose Speed = x km/h

time taken, $t_1 = \frac{\text{distance}}{\text{speed}} = \frac{2}{x} h$

if Speed = $(x + 1)$ km/h

then time $= t_2 = \frac{2}{x+1}$ h ...(*i*)

but according to question,

time, $t_2 = \left(\frac{2}{x} - \frac{10}{60}\right)$h ...(*ii*)

From eq. (*i*) and (*ii*)

$\frac{2}{x+1} = \frac{2}{x} - \frac{1}{6}$

$\frac{2}{x} - \frac{2}{x+1} = \frac{1}{6}$

$\frac{2x+2-2x}{x(x+1)} = \frac{1}{6}$

or $\frac{2}{x(x+1)} = \frac{1}{6}$

or $x^2 + x = 12$

or $x^2 + x - 12 = 0$

or $x^2 + 4x - 3x - 12 = 0$

or $x(x + 4) - 3(x + 4) = 0$

$(x - 3)(x + 4) = 0$

$\therefore$ $x = 3$ km/h

108. $r = 10.5$ cm

perimeter of semicircular disc
$= (\pi r + 2r)$

$= \frac{22}{7} \cdot 10.5 + 2 \times 10.5$

$= 33 + 21 = 54$ cm

109. 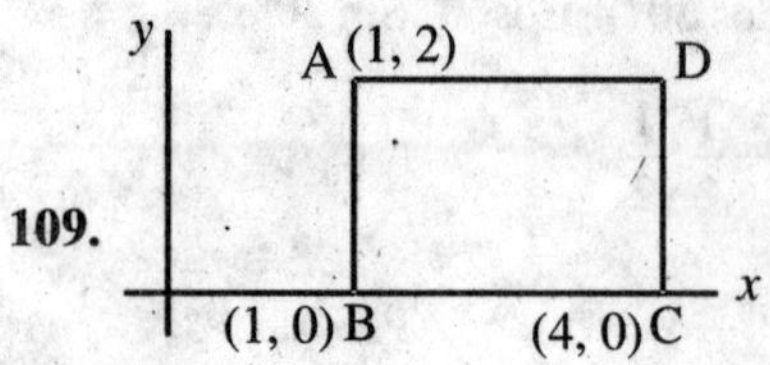

$\therefore$ D $\rightarrow$ (4, 2)

110. $(F-1) = 8(s-1)$

$\therefore$ $F - 1 = 8s - 8$

$\therefore$ $8s - F = 7$ ...(*i*)

Now, $F = s^2$, putting this value in eq. (*i*)

$8s - s^2 = 7$

or $s^2 - 8s + 7 = 0$

or $s^2 - s - 7s + 7 = 0$

or $s(s-1) - 7(s-1) = 0$

or $(s-7)(s-1) = 0$

$\therefore$ $s = 7$ or 1

But it could not be 1 yr because then it will not fulfill the conditions.

$\therefore$ $s = 7$

111. 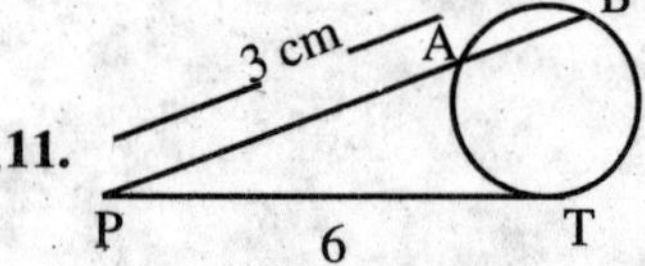

$PA \cdot PB = PT^2$

$\Rightarrow$ $3(3 + x) = 36$

$\Rightarrow$ $x = 9$

$\therefore$ $PB = 3 + 9 = 12$ cm.

112. Total no. of Red & White ball = 10

Total no. of ball = 15

Probability of extracting Red or white ball =

$\frac{10}{15} = \frac{2}{5}$

113. *n*th term of A.P. is given by

$a_n = a + (n-1)d$ where,

a is first term and *d* is comm. diff.

$a_4 = a + (4-1)d$

$\therefore$ $a_4 = a + 3d$

from question,

$4(a + 3d) = 7a$

or $4a + 12d = 7a$

or $3a = 12d$

$a = 4d$

$\therefore$ ratio of Ist term to comm. diff.

$\frac{a}{d} = \frac{4d}{d} = 4:1$

114. Vol. of cone = $\frac{1}{3}\pi r^2 h$

$2\pi r = 44$

$\therefore$ $r = \frac{44}{2} \cdot \frac{7}{22} = 7$

$\therefore$ Vol = $\frac{1}{3} \cdot \frac{22}{7} \times 7 \times 7 \times 9$

$= 462$ m^3

118. 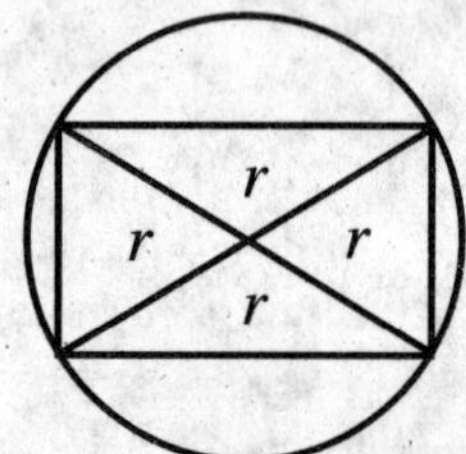

area of square = $\frac{1}{2}$ diagonal^2

$= \frac{1}{2}(2r)^2 = \frac{1}{2} \cdot 4r^2 = 2r^2$

119. 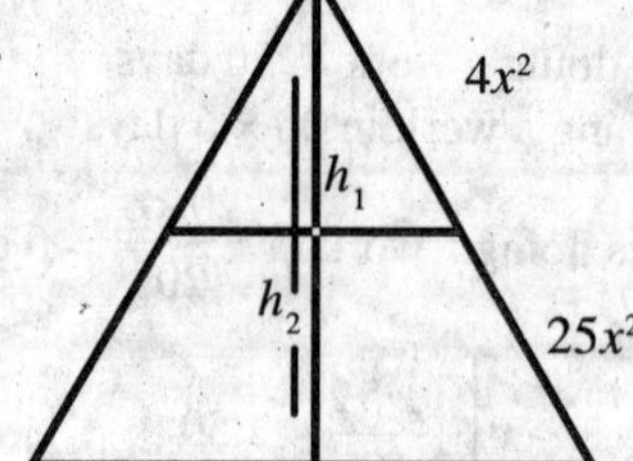

$\frac{a_1}{a_2} = \frac{4x^2}{25x^2} = \left(\frac{h_1}{h_2}\right)^2$

$\frac{h_1}{h_2} = \sqrt{\frac{4x^2}{25x^2}} = \frac{2x}{5x} = \frac{2}{5}$

120. Vol. of cylinder = $\pi r^2 h$

$2\pi r = 22$

$\therefore$ $r = 22 \cdot \frac{7}{22} \cdot \frac{1}{2} = \frac{7}{2}$

$\therefore$ $\pi r^2 h = \frac{22}{7} \times \frac{7 \cdot 7}{2 \times 2} \times 12$

$= 462$ cm^3

Previous Paper (Solved)

IGNOU B.Ed. Entrance Test 2005

PART-A

SECTION-I : GENERAL ENGLISH COMPREHENSION

Directions : *Read the following passage carefully and pick out the best answer out of the four choices given in each question.*

Philately, the hobby of collecting and studying postage stamps, can indeed lead to a bright future full of possibilities. Even the beginner can improve his general knowledge, his geography and his power of observation by collecting stamps. He begins to notice other countries and becomes inquisitive. To satisfy his curiosity, he starts asking his classmates, teachers and even parents questions about those countries. Soon he will discover the different currencies used throughout the world and will be amused by some of the things that appear on the stamps.

For example, British stamps never have the name of the country on them, but sometimes, include, as an occasional part of their design, the emblems of England, Scotland, Northern Ireland and Wales which make up the United Kingdom. Some stamps show maps which include lands claimed by others. The philatelist will notice that the stamps of some countries are far more interesting than those of others. Stamps of France, Brazil, Vietnam and India, for example, are both beautiful and informative. Some philatelists specialise in collecting stamps of one country or continent only; others collect stamps which deal with one subject only, like flowers, animals, landscapes, or famous men. Whether you are a specialist, a novice, or just collecting anything you can lay your hands on, there is much to be learnt from this hobby.

Sometimes some sheets of stamps are printed wrongly and sold out before the error is detected. Such stamps become oddities and are highly prized. A philatelist with some luck may have a windfall.

1. The nearest meaning of "inquisitive" in para 1 is

   A. curious B. cautious
   C. concerned D. organised

2. Which one of the following has ***not*** been mentioned as a benefit of philately in this text?

   A. One improves one's power of observation
   B. If lucky, one may become rich
   C. One learns about different countries
   D. One becomes fond of oddities

3. A philatelist soon learns about the currencies of other countries because

   A. he is curious
   B. the denomination of the stamp is printed on it
   C. he asks questions
   D. every stamp carries the name of its country

4. A "novice" according to this text is a person who

   A. has recently taken to philately
   B. is fond of collecting all types of postage stamps
   C. asks many questions about stamps
   D. is thinking of becoming a philatelist

5. A philatelist may find stamps from some countries relatively more interesting because they

   A. differ in their design
   B. tell more and are attractive
   C. use a different printing process
   D. can become oddities

6. Postage stamps from which one of the following countries are quite unlike others?

   A. India B. Brazil
   C. France D. Britain

7. Some stamps become 'oddities' because they
A. are highly sought after
B. have been wrongly priced
C. are defective
D. have an odd design

8. British stamps _____ carry the emblems of England, Scotland, Northern Ireland and Wales as a part of their design.
A. always B. seldom
C. occasionally D. never

9. Postage stamps of ____, ____ and _____ are relatively more popular with philatelists.
A. France, Monaco, Brazil
B. England, Vietnam, India
C. India, France, Monaco
D. France, Brazil, India

10. Philatelists who want to specialise usually ***do not*** collect stamps of
A. one denomination only
B. one country only
C. one continent only
D. flowers only

SECTION II : LOGICAL AND ANALYTICAL REASONING

11. Which would be the next number in the series?
8, 15, 29, 57, ?
A. 99 B. 113
C. 103 D. 101

12. Insert the missing number.

35	(78)	40
45	(97)	35
25	(?)	30

A. 66 B. 56
C. 67 D. 71

13. If $8 \div 5 = 6425$, $9 \div 6 = 8136$ then $4 \div 3 = ?$
A. 4421 B. 1690
C. 1609 D. 4381

14. If MOZART = 30, PICASSO = 35; then REMBRANDT = ?
A. 40 B. 45
C. 50 D. 65

15. If the word HYDERABAD is written as IZEFSBCBE in code, then AMRITSAR could be written as
A. BNTHUTBS B. BNSJUTBS
C. BLQHSRBT D. CNSFUTBS

16. Hemant is older than Chittaranjan. Vikas is older than Shridhar. Mallika is not as old as Vikas but is older than Chittaranjan. Shridhar is not as old as Chittaranjan. Who is the youngest?
A. Hemant B. Chittaranjan
C. Shridhar D. Mallika

17. Find the missing in the following.
ACEG : DFHJ : : QSUV : ?
A. TVXY B. MNPR
C. OQST D. KMNP

Directions (Qs. 18–19): *Read the following statements carefully.*
(1) All P and X are N.
(2) All N except P are X.
(3) No P are M.
(4) No R and N.
(5) All M are either X or R.
(6) No Q are X.

18. Which of the following statements must be true if the above six statements are true?
(i) No R are P
(ii) Some X and P
(iii) Some X are M
A. (i) only
B. (i) and (ii) only
C. (i) and (iii) only
D. (i), (ii) and (iii), all the three

19. Which of the following must be *false* given the conditions as stated?
A. No Q are P
B. Some Q are neither N nor R
C. Some R are X
D. All R are M

20. The pair of words given here has a definite relationship. Find out from the given options the pair with the similar relationship.

Ecstasy : Gloom
A. congratulation : occasion
B. diligent : successful
C. measure : scale
D. humiliation : exaltation

21. Find the odd one out.
A. ANW B. DPU
C. GRT D. JTQ

22.
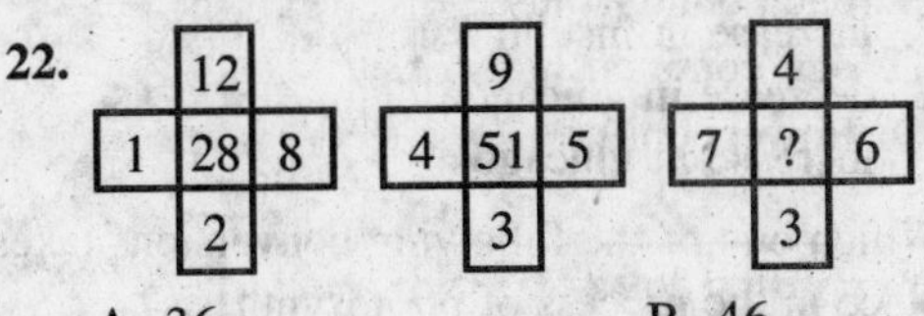

A. 36 B. 46
C. 38 D. 26

23.
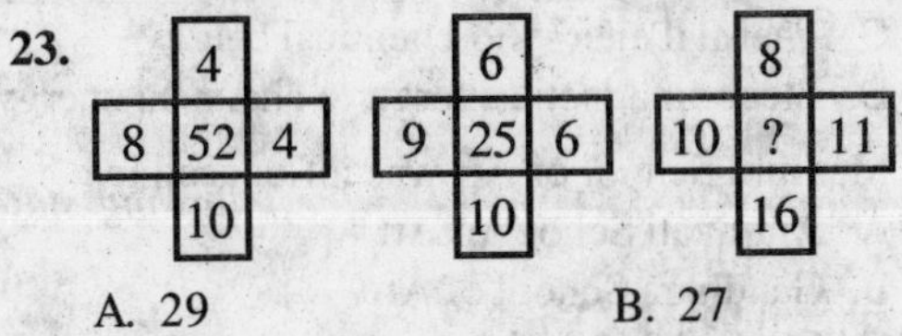

A. 29 B. 27
C. 31 D. 35

24. A motor cycle costs Rs. 40,000 when its is brand new. At the end of each year it is worth 4/5 of what it was at the beginning of the year. What is the motor cycle worth when it is 3 years old?
A. Rs. 16,000 B. Rs. 25,600
C. Rs. 20,480 D. Rs. 24,820

25. Which of the following represents a meaningful order of the given words?
1. elected 2. nomination
3. voting 4. oath-taking
5. canvassing
A. 5 2 1 3 4 B. 5 2 3 1 4
C. 2 5 3 1 4 D. 2 3 1 5 4

Directions (Qs. 26–30): *Which figure will follow next in the sequence?*

26.
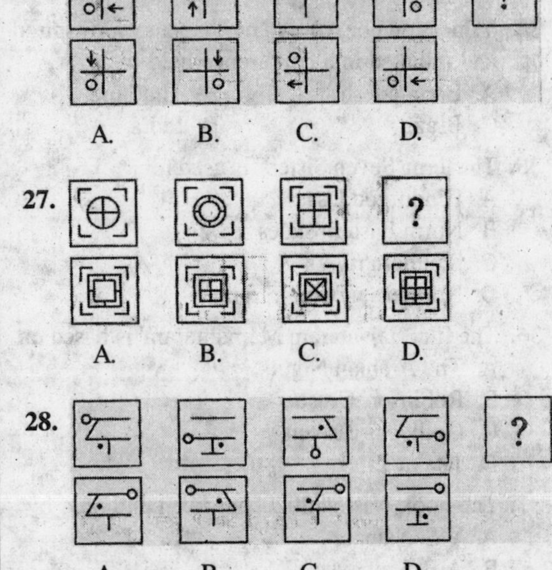

29.
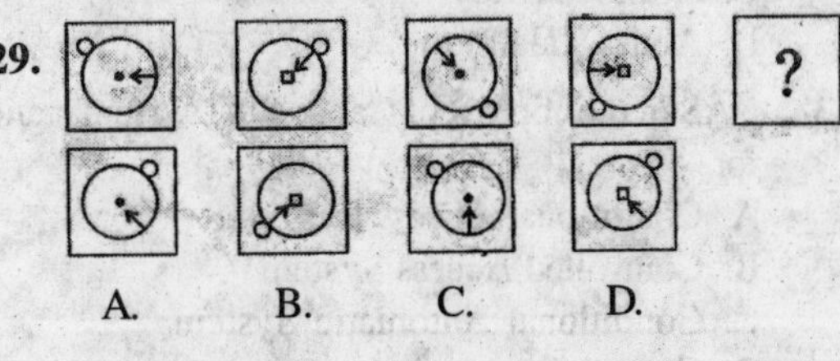

30.
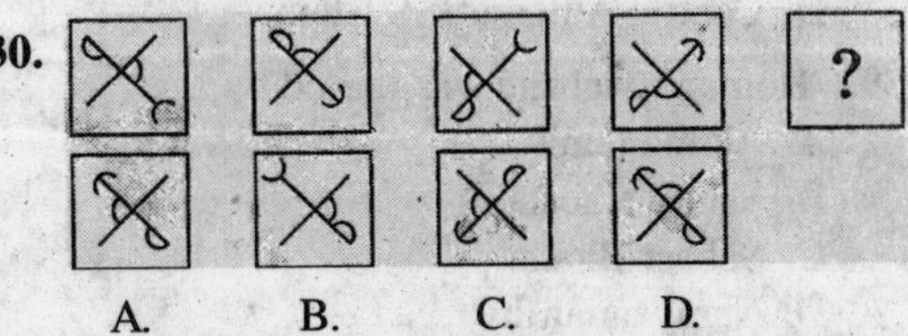

SECTION III : EDUCATIONAL AND GENERAL AWARENESS

Directions : *Indicate the correct answer.*

31. Multimedia is a combination of
A. Video, audio and graphic presentations
B. Text, movies and sound presentations
C. Desktop, animation and graphic presentations
D. None of these

32. Twinkling of the stars is caused by
A. Tyndall effect
B. Brownian movements
C. Refraction
D. Reflection

33. The first education commission of post independence India was known as

A. National Education Commission
B. Secondary Education Commission
C. Acharya Narendra Dev Committee
D. University Education Commission

34. 'Education For All' as a movement was inspired and initiated in a conference held in
A. Bangladesh B. Thailand
C. Brazil D. India

35. The term 'Seven Sisters' is used for
A. Hindu goddesses
B. North Eastern states
C. Southern rivers
D. Northern mountain ranges

36. The film 'Jajantaram Mamantaram' is based on
A. The Arabian Nights
B. Robinson Crusoe
C. Gulliver's Travels
D. Jataka Tales

37. The book 'Vision 2020' has been authored by
A. V.S. Naipaul
B. A.B. Vajpayee
C. Arundhati Roy
D. Abdul Kalam

38. CAS in the context of Cable T.V. system stands for
A. Conditional Access System
B. Controlled Access System
C. Conditional Automatic System
D. Central Automatic System

39. 'Hotmail' website was started by
A. Azim Premji
B. Vinod Khosla
C. Sabeer Bhatia
D. Narayanmurthy

40. Wisden's Indian Cricketer of the Century Award was given to
A. Sunil Gavaskar
B. G. Vishwanath
C. Kapil Dev
D. Sachin Tendulkar

41. The state which has the highest literacy rate among the following is
A. Mizoram
B. Assam
C. Meghalaya
D. Maharashtra

42. Rupee is ***not*** the national currency of
A. Nepal B. Pakistan
C. Sri Lanka D. Bangladesh

43. Diabetes Mellitus is caused by
A. decrease in insulin
B. increase in insulin
C. decrease in glucagon
D. increase in glucagon

44. Which one of the following conversions takes place in the process of photosynthesis?
A. Heat energy to kinetic energy
B. Thermal energy to electro-magnetic energy
C. Thermal energy to chemical energy
D. Electromagnetic energy to chemical energy

45. Mathura School of Art was influenced by
A. Amravati School of Art
B. Gandhara School of Art
C. Chola School of Art
D. Nathdwara School of Art

46. The most common blood group found among the Indians is
A. B^+ B. AB^-
C. O^+ D. AB^+

47. The oldest era amongst the following is
A. Christian B. Saka
C. Hijri D. Vikrami

48. Height of a building is measured by
A. Fathometer
B. Seismograph
C. Sextant
D. None of the above

49. The correct sequence of the following historical figures is
A. Shivaji → Shershah Suri → Tipu Sultan → Maharaja Ranjit Singh
B. Shershah Suri → Shivaji → Tipu Sultan → Maharaja Ranjit Singh
C. Shershah Suri → Shivaji → Maharaja Ranjit Singh → Tipu Sultan
D. Shivaji → Shershah Suri → Maharaja Ranjit Singh → Tipu Sultan

50. The body responsible for prescribing norms and standards for teacher education courses in the country is commonly known as

A. N.C.E.R.T. B. U.G.C.
C. N.C.T.E. D. N.I.E.P.A.

51. Which of the following is not one of the pillars of education prescribed by the UNESCO's Commission on Education for the Twenty-first Century?

A. Learning to earn
B. Learning to know
C. Learning to live together
D. Learning to be

52. Kishori Amonkar is known for her contribution to

A. Painting B. Films
C. Dancing D. Singing

53. English as a medium of education was introduced in India in

A. 1838 B. 1853
C. 1835 D. 1883

54. The Speaker of the Lok Sabha is elected by

A. the people directly
B. all the members of the Lok Sabha
C. all the members of Parliament
D. the members of the majority party in the Parliament

55. What is Fifth June known for the world over?

A. Human Rights Day
B. World Disability Day
C. World Teacher's Day
D. World Environment Day

SECTION IV : TEACHING-LEARNING AND THE SCHOOL

56. A good teacher is one

A. who gives shape to the personality of the child like a potter does to a vessel
B. who fills the mind of the child with knowledge
C. who looks after the child like a gardener taking care of the plants
D. who keeps the child under control and observation

57. The view that 'educational institutions should be substantially, if not fully, self-supporting was held by

A. Sri Aurobindo
B. Swami Vivekananda
C. Mahatma Gandhi
D. Swami Dayananda

58. Organising special programmes of education for children of construction labourers comes under

A. Formal education
B. Non-formal education
C. Informal education
D. Special education

59. Which is the most appropriate description of learning given here?

A. It is a process of habit formation
B. It is the skill to meet new situations
C. It is the skill to affect economy of effort and time to solve a problem
D. It is the consciousness one acquires after solving a problem

60. Schools are concerned with human development which includes choices related to

A. leading long and healthy life
B. acquisition of knowledge
C. having access to resources needed for a decent life
D. All the above

61. Pedagogy is considered to be the

A. Science of teaching
B. Art of learning
C. Science of communication
D. Art of assimilation

62. The most important task for a teacher is

A. to put students in possession of truth
B. to remove their difficulties
C. to put them (students) in search of truth
D. to constantly demand higher standards of achievement

63. Which is the most effective combination of ways to promote value-based behaviour?

A. Instructions and reading of selected text
B. Putting up ideals, examples and freedom to reflect
C. Examples and conducive atmosphere
D. Examples, conducive atmosphere and self-reflection

64. The purpose of co-curricular activities in the schools in
A. to boost self-confidence of students
B. to enhance their competitive spirit
C. to enrich learning experience of students
D. to provide relief from the rigour of academic work

65. The most acceptable image of a teacher is that of
A. an authoritarian
B. a democratic functionary
C. indulgent
D. learned but indifferent

66. On finding a normal child behaving in an erratic manner in the class, you would like to
A. pull up the child there and then
B. talk to the child after the class
C. ask the child to leave the class
D. ignore the child

67. The most acceptable order of steps in the process of teaching in a class is
A. Motivation – Presentation – Illustration – Recapitulation
B. Motivation – Presentation – Recapitulation – Illustration
C. Presentation – Motivation – Recapitulation – Illustration
D. Presentation – Motivation – Illustration – Recapitulation

68. A common, modern school is ***not*** expected to look after the
A. mental health of the child
B. academic achievements of the child
C. religious aspects of the child
D. physical health of the learner

69. 'In learning, the child should be allowed to follow his/her own mind' was advocated by
A. Rabindranath Tagore
B. Mahatma Gandhi
C. Swami Vivekananda
D. Sri Aurobindo

70. Sports and physical activities in a school curriculum are primarily meant for
A. break from the monotony of classwork
B. promoting health consciousness amongst all
C. winning name and fame for the school
D. nurturing talent for competition in sports

71. There is a noisy disturbance outside your classroom. Which of the following would you like to do?
A. Raise the pitch of your voice
B. Ask students to strictly follow a given assignment rather silently
C. Stop work and allow the students to relax till the noise reduces
D. Close doors and windows of the classroom and dictate useful tips

72. Inductive approach in teaching means
A. initiating the child to new subject
B. teaching through specific instruction
C. group learning as opposed to individualised learning
D. arriving at generalisations with the help of examples

73. The main purpose of 'Parent-Teacher Associaton' (P.T.A.) in a school is to
A. keep the students in check and control
B. collect additional funds for providing facilities to the learners
C. share understanding of the problems faced by the school
D. modify curriculum in accordance with the wishes of parents

74. Comparing positive (natural) sciences with social sciences, which of the following statements is ***not*** acceptable?
A. The ideational fields of the two types of disciplines are different
B. The judgements of positive sciences cannot be doubted

C. Positive sciences carry more predictability about heir data than social sciences
D. Positive sciences are deterministic whereas social sciences are directional

75. Which of the following is an appropriate order for learning of a language?
A. Listening – Speaking – Writing – Reading
B. Speaking – Listening – Writing – Reading
C. Listening – Speaking – Reading – Writing
D. Listening – Reading – Speaking – Writing

76. 10 + 2 system of school education was accepted after the recommendations of
A. Mudaliar Commission
B. Kothari Commission
C. Radhakrishnan Commission
D. National Policy on Education, 1966

77. 'That new learning should be correlated to the acquired knowledge and other subjects' was emphasized by
A. Rabindranath Tagore (Shanti Niketan)
B. J. Krishnamurthi (Rishi Valley)
C. Mahatma Gandhi (Basic education)
D. Annie Besant

78. The main purpose of punishment ought to be
A. to scare the student from repeating the mistake
B. to scare others from repeating it
C. to vindicate law or a rule
D. to reform the erring student

79. As a teacher you do ***not*** agree with the statement that
A. School should be an extension of the family in some respects
B. School should be like a miniature community
C. School should be well protected from the social influences
D. School should be a place for developing students' potential

80. The best way to reform our examination system is to
A. have no examination at all
B. have internal evaluation only
C. have external assessment only
D. have internal evaluation and external assessment supplementing each other

PART-B

SECTION V : (I) SCIENCE

81. The carriers of genetic information are
A. Proteins
B. Lipids and Minerals
C. Nucleic acids
D. Carbohydrates

82. Wind velocity is measured by
A. Anemometer
B. Hydrometer
C. Barometer
D. Hygrometer

83. The causative organism of rabies disease is
A. Bacterium
B. Virus
C. Fungus
D. Algae

84. Which of the following is ***not*** a plant product?
A. Cotton B. Lac
C. Jute D. Sugar

85. Which vitamin in blood plays an important role in clotting?
A. Vitamin A B. Vitamin D
C. Vitamin E D. Vitamin K

86. The digestion of starch in the diet starts in the
A. Liver B. Stomach
C. Intestine D. Mouth

87. Vitamin C is chemically known as
A. Ascorbic acid
B. Aspartic acid
C. Citric acid
D. Tartaric acid

88. Which one of the following radiations is most penetrating?
A. X-rays B. Alpha rays
C. Beta rays D. Gamma rays

89. An atom with an electronic configuration 2, 8, 8 has a valency of
A. – 1 B. Zero
C. + 1 D. + 8

90. Which of the following elements forms the largest number of compounds?
A. Hydrogen B. Oxygen
C. Silicon D. Carbon

91. Which of the following gases has lowest density?
A. Argon B. Helium
C. Oxygen D. Nitrogen

92. In the formation of Ni^{++}, nickel
A. gains two electrons
B. loses two electrons
C. loses two protons
D. gains two protons

93. If 8.0 g of a metallic oxide on decomposition gives 1-6 g oxygen, what is the equivalent weight of the metal?
A. 8 B. 16
C. 32 D. 64

94. Sphere A attracts Sphere B as well as Sphere C. Sphere B repels Sphere C. If Sphere C is negatively charged it can be concluded that
A. Sphere A is positively charged
B. Sphere A is netagively charged
C. Sphere A is either positively charged or is uncharged
D. Sphere A is either negatively charged or is uncharged

95. The domestic consumption of electricity is calculated in
A. Joules B. Watts
C. Kilowatt/hour D. Kilowatt hours

96. The apparent depth of a pond full of water whose real depth is 8 metres will be
A. 2 metres B. 3 metres
C. 6 metres D. 8 metres

97. The rays which are ***not*** deflected by electric or magnetic field are
A. Alpha rays B. Beta rays
C. Gamma rays D. Positive rays

98. A metal surface ejects electrons when hit by green light but no electron is ejected when hit by yellow light. The electrons will be ejected when the surface is hit by
A. Blue light B. Red light
C. Infra-red light D. Heat rays

99. Two coils have a combined resistance of 12 ohms when connected in series and 3 ohms when connected in parallel. The respective resistances are
A. 4 ohms, 8 ohms B. 6 ohms, 6 ohms
C. 9 ohms, 3 ohms D. 10 ohms, 2 ohms

100. A hole is drilled through the earth along its diameter and a stone is dropped into it. At the centre of the earth, the stone possesses
A. Acceleration B. Kinetic energy
C. Potential energy D. no energy

(II) MATHEMATICS

101. If $4x^3 + 3x^2 + 2x + 4$ is divided by $x + 1$, the remainder will be
A. 13 B. 1
C. – 1 D. – 13

102. 20% of 150 is the same as
A. 10% of 75 B. 40% of 300
C. 40% of 75 D. 30% of 225

103. Two successive discounts of 10% and 20% on a commodity are equal to a total discount of
A. 30% B. 32%
C. 25% D. 28%

104. $x : y :: m : n$ is the same as
A. $x : n :: y : m$ B. $x : n :: m : y$
C. $x : m :: y : n$ D. $x : m :: n : y$

105. The LCM of $(a^4 – b^4)$ and $(a^2 – b^2)^2$ is
A. $(a^2 – b^2)$ B. $(a^2 – b^2)^2$
C. $(a^2 – b^2)^2 (a^4 – b^4)$ D. $(a^2 – b^2)^2 (a^2 + b^2)$

106. The equation whose roots are half the roots of the equation $x^2 + 3x + 2 = 0$ is

A. $2x^2 + 3x + 1 = 0$ B. $2x^2 + 3x - 1 = 0$
C. $x^2 + 6x + 8 = 0$ D. $x^2 + 6x - 8 = 0$

107. The distance between the points (1, 2) and (1, –1) is

A. $\sqrt{13}$ B. 3
C. 1 D. $\sqrt{5}$

108. A sequence is in Arithmetic Progression. If the first term of the sequence is 5 and the common difference is 4, then the 10th term is

A. 45 B. 41
C. 35 D. 31

109. Peter's annual income from salary in the year 2002–2003 is Rs. 3,20,000. He makes a saving of Rs. 50,000 in specified forms. The rebate in income tax on account of savings will be

A. Rs. 10,500 B. Rs. 10,000
C. Rs. 7,500 D. Nil

110. If P is the principal and r is the rate of interest per annum compounded after every x months, then the amount at the end of y years will be

A. $P\left(1+\frac{r.x}{100}\right)^{xy}$

B. $P\left(1+\frac{r.x/12}{100}\right)^{12y/x}$

C. $P\left(1+\frac{x/12}{r.100}\right)^{12y/x}$

D. $P\left(1+\frac{r.x}{100}\right)^{12x/y}$

111. Mohan's age is 3 times that of Sohan and Ram is 6 years older than Sohan. If the age of Ram is 24 years, Mohan's age is

A. 6 years B. 10 years
C. 54 years D. 90 years

112. The sides of a triangle are 3 cm, 4 cm and 5 cm. The area of the triangle is

A. 6 cm^2 B. 12 cm^2
C. 15 cm^2 D. 20 cm^2

113. If two isosceles triangles have equal vertical angles and their areas are in the ratio 9 : 16, then their heights are in the ratio

A. 4 : 3 B. 3 : 4
C. 16 : 9 D. 9 : 16

114. The sum of the opposite angles of a cyclic quadrilateral would be

A. 360° B. 90°
C. 180° D. not definite

115. A circle is inscribed in a square of side 5 cm. The ratio of the perimeter of the square and the circumference of the circle is

A. 10 : 10 π B. 4 : π
C. 5 : π D. 120 : 6.25 π

116. $\frac{\text{cosec A}}{\text{cosec A} - 1} ++ \frac{\text{cosec A}}{\text{cosec A} + 1}$ is equal to

A. 1 B. $\sec^2 A$
C. $\text{cosec}^2 A$ D. $2 \sec^2 A$

117. The median of the following distribution is

x	0	1	2	3	4	5	6	7	8
f	1	9	26	59	72	52	29	7	1

A. 3 B. 4
C. 59 D. 72

118. Three iron cubes, the lengths of whose sides are 3 cm, 4 cm and 5 cm respectively, are moulded and a new cube is formed. The length of the side of the new cube would be

A. 4 cm B. 6 cm
C. 12 cm D. 20 cm

119. A cone of height 10 cm and base radius 4 cm, is divided by a plane parallel to the base and 5 cm above it. The ratio of the volumes of the smaller cone and the original cone is

A. 1 : 2 B. 1 : 4
C. 1 : 8 D. 3 : 4

120. The radius of a solid sphere is r cm. If it is divided into two equal halves, the total surface area of both the parts is

A. $8 \pi r^2$ sq. cm B. $5 \pi r^2$ sq. cm
C. $4 \pi r^2$ sq. cm D. $6 \pi r^2$ sq. cm

(III) Social Science

121. Budha preached his first sermon at
A. Lumbini B. Sarnath
C. Varanasi D. Gaya

122. Meghasthenes visited India during the reign of
A. Harsha
B. Ashoka
C. Chandra Gupta Maurya
D. Kanishka

123. The *Ain-e-Akbari* was written by
A. Farishta B. Badauni
C. Birbal D. Abul Fazal

124. Ibn Batuta visited India during the reign of
A. Balban
B. Ala-uddin Khilji
C. Razia
D. Muhammad Bin Tughlaq

125. The Third Battle of Panipat was fought between
A. Britishers and Marathas
B. Marathas and Rajputs
C. Afghans and Sikhs
D. Marathas and Afghans

126. The Quit India Movement was launched in
A. 1930 B. 1940
C. 1942 D. 1946

127. The Partition of Bengal in 1905 was done by
A. Lord Curzon B. Lord Wellesley
C. Hastings D. Ripon

128. Which of the following is ***not*** a Himalayan river?
A. Saryu B. Alakananda
C. Mandakini D. Narmada

129. Which is known as the home of the Asiatic lions?
A. Gir National Park
B. Dudhwa National Park
C. Kanha National Park
D. Corbett National Park

130. One of the states through which the Tropic of Cancer passes is
A. Jammu and Kashmir
B. Bihar
C. Himachal Pradesh
D. Jharkhand

131. Which river forms its delta in Orissa?
A. Krishna B. Mahanadi
C. Godavari D. Kaveri

132. Which state is the leading producer of red chillies?
A. Punjab B. Karnataka
C. West Bengal D. Andhra Pradesh

133. What is Raniganj famous for?
A. Iron ore B. Coal
C. Manganese D. Mica

134. The ideals of Liberty, Equality and Fraternity enshrined in the Preamble of the Constitution of India were adopted under inspiration from
A. The Russian Revolution
B. The American Declaration of Independence
C. The U.N. Charter
D. The French Revolution

135. The President of India is
A. the Head of the State
B. the Head of the Government
C. the Head of the Government as well as the State
D. None of the above

136. The Vice President of India is
A. directly elected by the people
B. elected by the same electoral college which elects the President
C. elected by the members of Lok Sabha and Rajya Sabha at a joint meeting
D. elected by the members of Rajya Sabha alone

137. Which one of the following did ***not*** occupy the office of the Prime Minister?
A. Jagjivan Ram B. Morarji Desai
C. Chandra Shekhar D. Both (A) and (C)

138. The Official Language of India is
A. English B. Hindi
C. Tamil D. Urdu

139. The 42nd Amendment to the Constitution
A. introduced Fundamental Duties for the first time
B. made the Directive Principles justiciable

C. made elementary education as a Fundamental Right

D. did none of the above

140. Who was the first Speaker of the Lok Sabha?

A. Hukum Singh

B. G.S. Dhillon

C. Ananthaswayanam Ayengar

D. G.V. Mavalankar

(IV) English

Directions (Qs. 141-142): *Fill in the blanks in the following sentences by selecting the most appropriate alternative from amongst the four choices given.*

141. If you drink too much it will..... your judgement.

A. impede B. impair
C. impose D. impel

142. She always insisted on the need to..... between ends and means.

A. analyse B. define
C. distribute D. distinguish

Directions (Qs. 143-144): *In the following groups of words only one is spelt correctly. Select the correct one.*

143. A. Gratutious B. Gratutous
C. Gratuitous D. Greatutous

144. A. Sychology B. Sykology
C. Psychology D. Psykology

Directions (Qs. 145-146): *In the following questions, out of four alternatives, choose the one which can be substituted for the given sentence.*

145. Study of the relations of living things to environment

A. Biology B. Physiology
C. Geology D. Ecology

146. A person who believes that everything happens is for the good

A. Pessimist B. Optimist
C. Sadist D. Masochist

Directions (Qs. 147-148): *Given below are the four parts of a complete sentence. Mark the part which contains an error.*

147. A. The number of people

B. applying were so large

C. that the college had to

D. stop issuing application forms.

148. A. Drawing water from the well

B. is preferable

C. than depending on

D. the erratic water supply

Directions (Qs. 149-150): *Choose the appropriate set from those given below to fill in the blanks in the following sentences.*

149. Hundreds students competed ..... one another..... a single scholarship.

A. with : over B. with : for
C. among : over D. between : for

150. We went.....the room and sat down ..... a sofa.

A. to : in B. into : on
C. from : upon D. in : on

151. Choose the correct direct form of the given indirect sentence.

The teacher told me that if I did not work, I would fail.

A. The teacher told me that, "If I do not work I will fail."

B. The teacher said to me, "If you do not work you will fail."

C. The teacher warned me, "If you do not work you will be failed."

D. The teacher told me, "If you will not work you will fail."

152. Choose the word from the words given below which can substitute the underlined words in both the given sentences:

I. His understanding of the subject was really good.

II. Mohan had to hold on to the handle of the door with all his strength.

A. make B. pull
C. seize D. grasp

Directions (Qs. 153-154): *In the following items. Choose the correct meaning of the given phrase/idiom from the given alternatives.*

153. Make hay while the sun shines
A. Do your work during the day time
B. Make the best use of an opportunity
C. Make money while in power
D. Take advantage of your position

154. A left handed compliment
A. Insincere praise
B. Genuine praise
C. Well deserved praise
D. Approval

Directions (Qs. 155-156): *Choose the word that is opposite in meaning to the underlined word in the given sentences.*

155. The culprit <u>accepted</u> his crime.
A. refused B. challenged
C. denied D. repulsed

156. Anirudh drove to the place through a <u>circuitous</u> route.
A. short B. roundabout
C. obvious D. direct

Directions (Qs. 157-158): *Choose the word which is nearest in meaning to the bold word from the words given below.*

157. He is **deluding** himself with false hopes.
A. satisfying B. entertaining
C. misleading D. assuring

158. He cast a **cursory** glance over the papers before signing them.
A. short B. eager
C. hurried D. inquisitive

159. Given below is an active sentence. Choose the passive form of the sentence from the alternatives given below :
The Constituent Assembly's Drafting Committee prepared the Constitution.
A. The Constitution was prepared by the Constituent Assembly's Drafting Committee
B. The Constitution prepared by the Constituent Assembly's Drafting Committee
C. The Constituent Assembly's Drafting Committee was prepared by Constitution
D. The Constituent Assembly's Drafting Committee was prepared by the Consitution

160. Choose the correct tense of the verb in the given sentence from the options given below:
Our beloved India had become independent in 1947.
A. Simple Past
B. Past Continuous
C. Past Perfect
D. Past Perfect Continuous

(V) हिन्दी

निर्देश: *दिए गए गद्यांश को ध्यान से पढ़िए और बाद में पूछे गए प्रश्नों (161 से 165) के उत्तर दीजिए।*

विद्या और राजनीति सगी बहनें हैं। दोनों का पृथक् रहना कठिन है। दोनों के स्वभाव भिन्न हैं, किन्तु लक्ष्य एक है। व्यक्ति और समाज को अधिक से अधिक सुख पहुँचाना दोनों का लक्ष्य है। संसार का इतिहास इस बात का साक्षी है कि जब भी किसी राष्ट्र में क्रांति का बिगुल बजा तो वहाँ के छात्र मात्र द्रष्टा नहीं रहे अपितु उन्होंने क्रांति की बागडोर संभाली। परतंत्रता काल में स्वातंत्र्य के लिए और वर्तमान काल में भ्रष्टाचारी सरकारों के उन्मूलन के लिए भारत में छात्रशक्ति ने अग्रसर होकर क्रांति का आह्वान किया। इण्डोनेशिया और ईरान में छात्रों ने सरकार का तख़्ता ही पलट दिया। बांग्लादेश को अस्तित्व में लाने में ढाका विश्वविद्यालय के विद्यार्थियों का योगदान भुलाया नहीं जा सकता।

गद्यांश के आधार पर निम्नलिखित प्रश्न (161 से 165), उत्तर विकल्पों के साथ दिए गए हैं। सही विकल्प को चुनिए।

161. निम्नलिखित में कौन-सा कथन सही **नहीं** है?
A. विद्या और राजनीति सहोदरा है
B. दोनों की प्रकृति समान है
C. दोनों का उद्देश्य एक है
D. दोनों परस्पर सहयोगी हैं

162. संसार का इतिहास साक्षी है कि छात्र
A. राष्ट्र में क्रांति के दर्शक रहे
B. क्रांति के कारण बने

C. क्रांति में खड़े हो गए
D. क्रांति में अग्रणी रहे

163. छात्रों ने संघर्ष किया
A. परतंत्रता के लिए
B. स्वतंत्रता के लिए
C. भ्रष्टाचार मिटाने के लिए
D. सरकारें गिराने के लिए

164. कई देशों में क्रांति का श्रेय किसको जाता है
A. विद्यार्थियों को
B. सामान्य जनता को
C. उद्योगपतियों को
D. राजनीतिज्ञों को

165. छात्रों ने आह्वान किया
A. शान्ति का
B. शक्ति का
C. अहिंसा का
D. क्रांति का

निर्देश (प्रश्न 166 से 180): *प्रत्येक प्रश्न के उत्तर के रूप में चार-चार विकल्प दिए गए हैं। सही विकल्प को चुनिए।*

166. खड़ी बोली किस क्षेत्र के आसपास बोली जाती है?
A. लखनऊ
B. दिल्ली
C. पटना
D. नागपुर

167. तुलसीदास ने किस भाषा में लेखन किया था?
A. अवधी
B. ब्रज
C. भोजपुरी
D. मैथिली

168. कौन-सी वर्तनी शुद्ध है?
A. चर्तुवेदी
B. चतुरवेदी
C. चतुर्वेदी
D. चुतुर्वेदि

169. इनमें सही वाक्य क्या है?
A. अपना पत्र के नीचे नाम लिख दो
B. नीचे पत्र के अपने नाम लिख दो
C. नीचे अपना पत्र के नाम लिख दो
D. पत्र के नीचे अपना नाम लिख दो

170. अपने मुँह मियाँ मिट्ठू बनने का क्या अर्थ है?
A. मीठी-मीठी बात करना
B. अपनी प्रशंसा करना
C. अपने तोते की प्रशंसा करना
D. मीठी वस्तुएं एकत्रित करना

171. केसरी शब्द का अर्थ है
A. शेर
B. केसर का तेल
C. पगड़ी
D. शिखर

172. जो मुकदमा करता है उसे कहते हैं
A. अभियुक्त
B. प्रतिवादी
C. वादी
D. नियोगी

173. अधिकरण कारक का चिह्न है?
A. का, के, की
B. को
C. के लिए
D. में, पर

174. मधुकर का समानार्थक क्या है?
A. शहद
B. भ्रमर
C. रीछ
D. रोटी

175. यथाशक्ति में कौन-सा समास है?
A. अव्ययीभाव
B. बहुव्रीहि
C. कर्मधारय
D. द्वन्द्व

176. नीरव में कौन-सी सन्धि है?
A. स्वर सन्धि
B. व्यंजन सन्धि
C. विसर्ग सन्धि
D. दीर्घ सन्धि

177. 'हथेली पर सरसों जमाना' का अर्थ क्या है?
A. जादू दिखाना
B. काम झटपट कर लेना
C. अच्छी खेती करना
D. असंभव कार्य कर लेना

178. "भारत-भारती" के लेखक कौन हैं?
A. सुब्रह्मण्यम भारती
B. मैथिलीशरण गुप्त
C. अयोध्यासिंह उपाध्याय
D. जय शंकर प्रसाद

179. "हमारे जीवन का उद्देश्य है कि दूसरों की सहायता करें।" यह किस प्रकार का वाक्य है?
A. संयुक्त
B. सरल
C. साधारण
D. मिश्र

180. "लाली मेरे लाल की....." यहाँ लाल से क्या अभिप्राय है?
A. बेटा
B. कीमती पत्थर
C. ईश्वर
D. मनुष्य

ANSWERS

1	2	3	4	5	6	7	8	9	10
A	D	B	C	B	D	D	C	D	A
11	**12**	**13**	**14**	**15**	**16**	**17**	**18**	**19**	**20**
B	B	C	B	B	C	A	A	C	D
21	**22**	**23**	**24**	**25**	**26**	**27**	**28**	**29**	**30**
D	B	A	C	C	D	A	D	C	B
31	**32**	**33**	**34**	**35**	**36**	**37**	**38**	**39**	**40**
A	C	D	D	B	C	D	A	C	C
41	**42**	**43**	**44**	**45**	**46**	**47**	**48**	**49**	**50**
A	D	A	C	B	A	D	D	B	C
51	**52**	**53**	**54**	**55**	**56**	**57**	**58**	**59**	**60**
C	D	C	B	D	D	C	C	C	B
61	**62**	**63**	**64**	**65**	**66**	**67**	**68**	**69**	**70**
A	C	B	C	B	B	A	C	A	B
71	**72**	**73**	**74**	**75**	**76**	**77**	**78**	**79**	**80**
D	D	C	B	B	D	C	D	C	D
81	**82**	**83**	**84**	**85**	**86**	**87**	**88**	**89**	**90**
C	A	A	B	D	D	A	D	B	D
91	**92**	**93**	**94**	**95**	**96**	**97**	**98**	**99**	**100**
B	B	B	A	C	A	C	A	C	D
101	**102**	**103**	**104**	**105**	**106**	**107**	**108**	**109**	**110**
B	C	D	C	D	A	B	B	D	B
111	**112**	**113**	**114**	**115**	**116**	**117**	**118**	**119**	**120**
C	A	B	C	B	D	B	B	C	D
121	**122**	**123**	**124**	**125**	**126**	**127**	**128**	**129**	**130**
B	C	D	D	D	C	A	D	A	D
131	**132**	**133**	**134**	**135**	**136**	**137**	**138**	**139**	**140**
B	D	B	D	C	C	A	B	A	D
141	**142**	**143**	**144**	**145**	**146**	**147**	**148**	**149**	**150**
B	D	C	C	D	B	B	C	B	D
151	**152**	**153**	**154**	**155**	**156**	**157**	**158**	**159**	**160**
B	D	B	A	C	D	C	C	A	C
161	**162**	**163**	**164**	**165**	**166**	**167**	**168**	**169**	**170**
A	D	B	A	D	B	A	C	D	B
171	**172**	**173**	**174**	**175**	**176**	**177**	**178**	**179**	**180**
C	C	D	B	A	C	D	A	A	A

SOME SELECTED EXPLANATORY ANSWERS

11. 8 → 15 → 29 → 57 → [113]

+7, +14, +28, +56

12. $\because$ $35 \div 5 = 7$ $\quad 40 \div 5 = 8$ $\quad$ 78

$45 \div 5 = 9$ $\quad 35 \div 5 = 7$ $\quad$ 97

$\therefore$ $25 \div 5 = 5$ $\quad 30 \div 5 = 6$ $\quad$ 56

13. $8 \div 5 = 8^2 + 5^2 = 6425$

$9 \div 6 = 9^2 + 6^2 = 8136$

$4 \div 3 = 4^2 + 3^2 = 1609$

14. MOZART = 30

$\Rightarrow$ number of letter in this word $\times 5 = 6 \times 5 = 30$

PICASSO = 35

$\Rightarrow$ number of letter in this word $\times 5 = 7 \times 5 = 35$

REMBRANDT

$\Rightarrow$ number of letter in this word $\times 5 = 9 \times 5 = 45$

15. Since

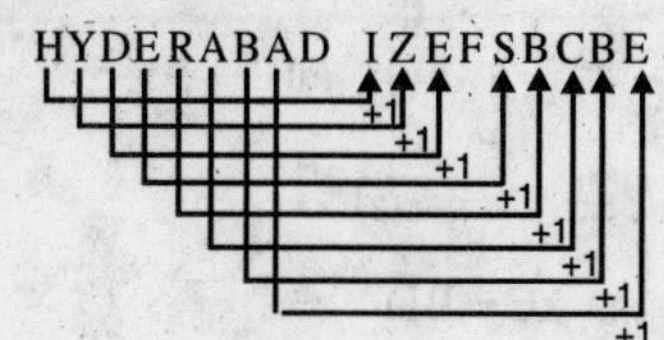

Thus,

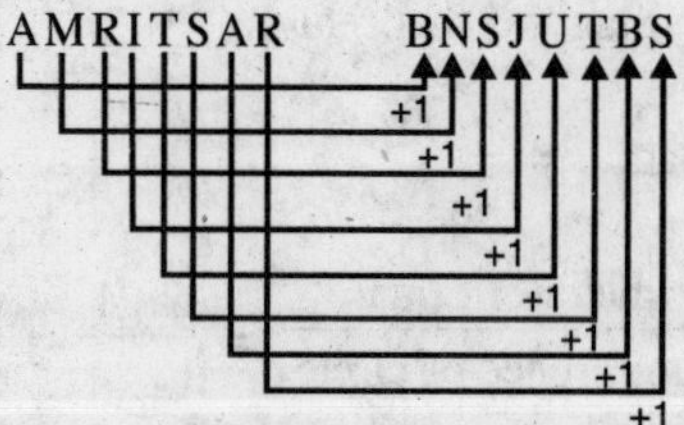

16. Hemant > Chittranjan I

Vikas > Shridhar II

Vikas>Mallika>Chittranjan III

Chittranjan > Shridhar IV

from all the equations

Hemant > Vikas > Mallika > Chittranjan > Shridhar

Thus, Shridhar is youngest.

17. A C E G D F H J

+3 +3 +3 +3

Thus

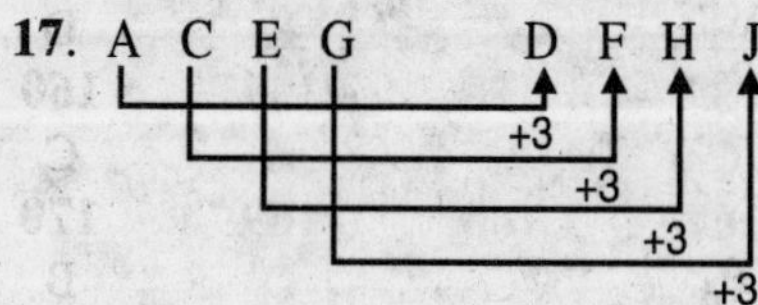

22. $1 \times 12 + 8 \times 2 = 12 + 16 = 28$

$9 \times 4 + 5 \times 3 = 36 + 15 = 51$

$7 \times 4 + 6 \times 3 = 28 + 18 = 46$

24. Price at the end of 1st year

$= 40000 \times \frac{4}{5} = 32000$

Price at the end of 2nd year

$= 32000 \times \frac{4}{5} = 25600$

$\therefore$ Price at the end of 3rd year

$= 25600 \times \frac{4}{5} = 20480$

25. Only option 3 represent the meaningful order.

26. "O" figure moves one step clockwise, "↑" figure follows it and "↑" also moves 90° clockwise in itself. So only option D is satisfying this rule.

101. Let $x + 1 = 0$

$\therefore x = -1$

now put the value of x in the given equation

$4x^3 + 3x^2 + 2x + 4$

$= 4(-1)^3 + 3(-1)^2 + 2(-1) + 4$

$= -4 + 3 - 2 + 4 = 1$

102. 20 % of 150 = 40% of 75

$\frac{20}{100} \times 150 = \frac{40}{100} \times 75$

$30 = 30$

103. Let the price be Rs. 100

now the first discount

$= 100 \times \frac{90}{100} = \text{Rs. } 90$

2nd discount $= 90 \times \frac{80}{100}$

= Rs. 72

total discount = 100 – 72

= 28%

105. Let $P(x) = a^4 - b^4$

$= (a^2)^2 - (b^2)^2$

$= (a^2 + b^2)(a^2 - b^2)$

and $z(x) = (a^2 - b^2)^2$

H.C.F. of $P(x)$ and $Z(x) = a^2 - b^2$

$\therefore$ L.C.M. P (x) and Z (x)

$$= \frac{P(x) \times Z(x)}{H.C.F. of P(x) \text{ and } Z(x)}$$

$$= \frac{(a^2+b^2)\,(a^2-b^2)\,(a^2-b^2)^2}{a^2-b^2}$$

$= (a^2 + b^2)\ (a^2 - b^2)^2$

107. Distance between the points

$= \sqrt{(1-1)^2 + (2-(-1)^2}$

$= \sqrt{0^2+3^2}$

$= 3$

108. nth term $= a + (n-1)\,d$

$= 5 + (10-1)\,4$

$= 5 + 36 = 41$

111. $\because$ Age of Ram = 24 years

$\therefore$ Age of Sohan = 18 years

Since Mohan's age is 3 times that of Sohan

Thus, the age of Mohan

$= 18 \times 3$

$= 54$ years

112. As per data the triangle is right angle triangle $(3^2 + 4^2 = 5^2)$

$\therefore$ Area of right triangle $= \frac{1}{2} \times$ base $\times$ height

$= \frac{1}{2} \times 3 \times 4 = 6 \text{ cm}^2$

115. ABCD is a square with side 5 cm.

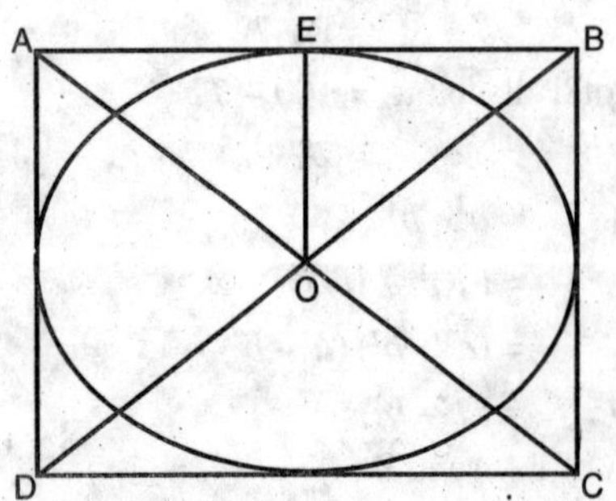

BD = AC = diagonal of the square

$\therefore$ Area of the square

$= \frac{1}{2}$ (diagonal)^2 = (side)^2

$\Rightarrow \frac{1}{2}$ (diagonal)$^2 = 5 \times 5$

$\Rightarrow$ diagonal $= \sqrt{50}$

$\because$ AC = BD $= \sqrt{50}$

$\therefore$ OB $= \frac{\sqrt{50}}{2}$

$\therefore$ By Pythagoras theorem

O E = Radius $= \frac{5}{2}$

$$\therefore \frac{\text{Perimeter of Square}}{\text{Circumference of circle}} = \frac{5 \times 4}{2.\pi.\frac{5}{2}} = \frac{4}{\pi}$$

116. $\frac{\text{cosec A}}{\text{cosec A} - 1} + \frac{\text{cosec A}}{\text{cosec A} + 1}$

$$\Rightarrow \frac{\text{cosec A(cosecA} + 1) + \text{cosec A(cosec A} - 1)}{\text{cosec}^2 \text{ A} - 1}$$

$$\Rightarrow \frac{\text{cosec}^2\text{A} + \text{cosec A} + \text{cosec}^2\text{A} - \text{cosecA}}{\text{cosec}^2 \text{ A} - 1}$$

$$\Rightarrow \frac{2 \text{ cosec}^2 \text{A}}{\text{cosec}^2 \text{ A} - 1} \Rightarrow \frac{2 \text{ cosec}^2 \text{A}}{\cot^2 \text{A}}$$

$$\Rightarrow \frac{2 \text{ cosec}^2 \text{A}}{\frac{\cos^2 \text{A}}{\sin^2 \text{A}}}$$

$$\Rightarrow \frac{2 \text{ cosec}^2 \text{A}. \sin^2 \text{A}}{\cos^2 \text{ A}}$$

$$\Rightarrow \frac{2 \text{ cosec}^2 \text{A}. \frac{1}{\text{cosec}^2 \text{A}}}{\cos^2 \text{ A}}$$

$$= \frac{2}{\cos^2 \text{ A}} = 2 \sec^2 \text{A}$$

117.

x	f	$c.f.$
0	1	0
1	9	10
2	26	36
3	59	95
<u>4</u>	72	167
5	52	219
6	29	248
7	7	255
8	1	256

N = 256

Median=Value of $\left(\frac{N+1}{2}\right)$ th item

$$= \frac{256+1}{2} = 128.5 \text{ the item}$$

Hence, the median of group is 4.

118. Total volume of smaller cube

$= 3^3 + 4^3 + 5^3 = 27 + 64 + 125$

$= 216$

$\therefore$ Volume of larger cube = 216

$\therefore$ Side of larger cube $= (216)^{1/3} = 6$ c.m.

119. Volume of larger cone $= \frac{1}{3}\pi r^2 h$

$$= \frac{1}{3}\pi .4^2 .10$$

and volume of smaller cone

$$= \frac{1}{3}\pi r^2 h$$

$$= \frac{1}{3}\pi 2^2 .5$$

$$\therefore \frac{\text{volume of smaller cone}}{\text{volume of larger cone}}$$

$$= \frac{\frac{1}{3}\pi .2^2 .5}{\frac{1}{3}\pi .4^2 .10}$$

$= 1 : 8$

120. Total surface area of two hemisphere

$= 2 \times 3\ \pi r^2$

$= 6\ \pi r^2$

Previous Paper (Solved)

IGNOU B.Ed. Entrance Test 2004

PART-A

SECTION-I : GENERAL ENGLISH COMPREHENSION

Directions : *Read the following passages carefully and pick out the best answer out of the four choices given in each question.*

Adventure is the spirit that urges men to undertake hazardous tasks, for adventure implies readiness to embark on a course of action that involves risk. However the spirit of adventure tends to be restrained by caution. More often that not, this caution gives warning of the potential dangers when our foremost thoughts are of safety first. Yet in some men the urge for adventure may be so strong that it overwhelms the primary instinct of self-preservation and inspires them to attempt the impossible.

Adventure need not always be successful. It is enough if the adventure is impelled by courage. Indeed, the failure of a gallant enterprise often touches our heart deeply even more than if it were a success. The vision of Mallory and Irvine toiling indomitably through the mists towards the summit of Mount Everest, never to return, inspires us for more than if they had attained their objective. Success in dangerous enterprises often brings material rewards, but a glorious failure brings greater honour and admiration.

There has never been a person who knew no fear, but the finer the courage of the person, the lesser will one betray fear. When we think of persons who go after adventure with a complete disregard for danger, we should remember that their bodies are as sensible to agony as ours and that their minds suffer from same anxieties. If we wish to pursue real adventure, we must fight gigantic battles within ourselves and overcome hunger, love of life, the pull of home and even the love of our beloved ones.

1. According to the writer, the spirit of adventure is characterised by

A. ever readiness
B. eagerness to take risks
C. a concern for safety
D. potential dangers

2. According to this text,

A. some men pursue adventure even at grave risk to their life
B. some men needlessly attempt the impossible
C. some men are so strong that they feel nothing is impossible
D. only the foolhardy attempt the impossible

3. The contextual meaning of "a gallant enterprise" in para 2 is

A. a brave-hearted project
B. a difficult adventure that requires lot of courage
C. a brave adventure that is bound to fail
D. an adventure that has a strong appeal for the really brave

4. The word "vision" in para 2 can be replaced with

A. dream B. image
C. apparition D. vivid picture

5. ... Mallory and Irvine **toiling indomitably** .... The closest meaning of the bold words here is

A. struggling hopelessly
B. struggling ceaselessly and reaching the top
C. working hard without rest
D. working hard for long and not giving up

6. The author wants the reader to understand that

A. Mallory and Irvine reached the top but only after a valiant effort

B. Mallory and Irvine, though brave, were doomed to fail
C. Mallory and Irvine died but their attempt was indeed grand
D. Mallory and Irvine should have given up the attempt because of bad weather and returned to the base camp

7. The author maintains that "a glorious failure brings greater honour and admiration" because it
A. shows human spirit at its best even against heavy odds
B. inspires the young and the old
C. reveals that failure too contributes to success
D. establishes that even in their finest hour human beings remain vulnerable

8. According to this text, a really courageous person
A. doesn't care for any danger
B. doesn't easily express fear
C. cannot express fear
D. did not and does not exist

9. According to the author, the truly courageous
A. are sensitive to their body and spirit
B. feel like everyone else
C. become superhuman
D. gain control over their body and mind

10. The author advocates that in order to pursue real adventure, we must first
A. wage a fight within ourselves
B. conquer our sensations and feelings
C. rise above everyone else
D. become really brave

SECTION II : LOGICAL AND ANALYTICAL REASONING

11. What number should replace the question mark?
68, 64, 32, 28, 14, 10, 5, ?
A. 1 B. 2
C. 3 D. 4

12. Which number comes next in the following series?
5, 10, 20, 40, 80, ?
A. 100 B. 120
C. 140 D. 160

13. What would be 50% of 10% of 25% of 40% of 60% of 2000?
A. 100 B. 50
C. 10 D. 6

14. Complete the last number of the series
3, 6, 9, 12, 15, 18, 21, 24, 2_
A. 7 B. 3
C. 6 D. 8

15. Multiply all the integers from – 4 to + 4. The product obtained is
A. – 576 B. + 576
C. 0 D. +144

16. When the temperature in Celsius is 0° and 100°, it is 32° and 212° respectively in Fahrenheit. What is the temperature in Celsius, when it is 104° in Fahrenheit?
A. 38° B. 40°
C. 42° D. 39°

17. The petrol tank of my scooter was $\frac{4}{5}$th full when I left home. After I used 2 litres of petrol, the tank was only $\frac{2}{3}$rd full. What is the capacity of the scooter?
A. 15 litres B. 10 litres
C. 12 litres D. 8 litres

18. 4 monkeys take 4 minutes to eat 4 bananas each. How many minutes will 8 monkeys take to eat 4 bananas each?
A. 8 minutes B. 6 minutes
C. 4 minutes D. 2 minutes

19. There are some shirts in my bag. Six have half sleeves, eight have buttons, three are without collars and two are blue. What is the minimum number of shirts in my bag?
A. 19 B. 8
C. 14 D. 10

20. What does the following coded message convey?
TCHLI USEIC SLAUS EECCL RUEET
A. CLUE is clear B. This is a secret
C. Lies are classic D. Use lesser chilli

21. SOAP : TPBQ : : FOAM : ?

A. GPBN
B. HARD
C. DROP
D. ENAL

22. Select the pair of words that expresses the relationship that is most similar to that of the following pair : WATER : THIRST

A. Juice : Fruit
B. Food : Hunger
C. Cake : Oven
D. Milk : Cow

23. SCHOOL is coded as LOOHCS, TEACHER will be coded as

A. CHEATER
B. RECHEAT
C. RETEACH
D. REHCAET

24. UJH is decoded as THE. What word would be decoded as QQVM YOVV?

A. ADVANCED
B. POSITION
C. QUESTION
D. GOODNESS

25. In a pack of playing cards, what is the total value of the number cards?

A. 55
B. 52
C. 204
D. 220

26. One brother says to his younger brother "Two years ago, I was three times as old as my brother was. In three years time, I will be twice as old as my brother." How old are they each now?

A. 21 years, 9 years
B. 24 years, 10 years
C. 17 years, 7 years
D. 8 years, 4 years

27. A man was born on February 29, 1944 and so was 55 in 2000. How many birthdays has he had?

A. 14
B. 15
C. 55
D. 56

28. Ravi, Shashi, Suraj and Tara pick up shells from the seaside. Ravi picked up 7 more than Shashi; Tara picked up 9 less than Suraj; Suraj has picked up one more than Ravi. Who has picked up the least number of shells?

A. Ravi
B. Shashi
C. Suraj
D. Tara

29. I have Rs 135 in my wallet and still do not have the exact change for a Rs. 100 note. To make this possible, I must have one more

A. 20-rupee note
B. 1-rupee note
C. 10-rupee note
D. hundred rupee note

30. Most children living in slums are poor in health. Therefore Bittoo and Chhoti, two slum children, cannot be healthy. The conclusion is

A. absolutely true
B. absolutely false
C. probably true
D. probably false

SECTION III : EDUCATIONAL AND GENERAL AWARENESS

31. The campaign 'Education For All' is a programme of

A. World Bank
B. NCERT
C. Ministry of Human Resource Development, Government of India
D. UNICEF

32. Acharya Rammurthi Committee reviewed recommendations of

A. Kothari Commission, 1964-66
B. Radhakrishnan Commission, 1948
C. National Education Policy, 1986
D. Mudaliar Commission, 1952

33. Yashpal Committee is known for its recommendations on

A. teaching of science
B. teaching of values
C. reducing the curriculum load on children
D. teaching Indian history and culture

34. According to the Constitution of India, no citizen shall be denied admission into any educational institution maintained by the state or receiving aid out of state funds on grounds of

A. religion
B. caste
C. language
D. religion, race, caste, language or any of these

35. The phrase 'A Beautiful Tree' was used for the indigenous education system that prevailed in India when Britishers came, by

A. Rabindra Nath Tagore
B. Mahatma Gandhi
C. Annie Besant
D. Aurobindo

36. The Constitution of India was recently amended to provide for
A. making elementary education a Fundamental Right
B. punishment for children if they do not go to school
C. allowing opening of private schools for children
D. making school education compulsory for girls only

37. Girls should be educated in order to
A. give them economic independence
B. prepare them to bring up their children better
C. assist their husbands to advance in society
D. help them develop their individuality and personality to the fullest

38. Polio drops are meant for children
A. between 5 and 10 years of age
B. below 5 years of age
C. living in villages and slums
D. suffering from polio

39. Ex-President of India, Dr. A.P.J. Kalam is the author of a book entitled
A. *River of Fire*
B. *Discovery of India*
C. *My Experiments with Missiles*
D. *Wings of Fire*

40. Satyajit Ray is known mainly for his
A. Films B. Stories
C. Poems D. Dramas

41. Vijay Tendulkar is a famous
A. Novelist
B. Cricket Player
C. Playwright
D. Hockey Player

42. 'Operation Sarp Vinash' was meant to
A. kill poisonous snakes in forests
B. prepare medicines to cure from snake bite
C. organise surgery for cancer
D. flush out terrorists in Jammu and Kashmir

43. 'Anne Frank — The Diary of a Young Girl' is a book that records
A. the life of Jews under the Nazi, Adolf Hitler
B. the life of Russians transported to Siberia by Stalin
C. the story of the rule in Italy under Mussolini
D. the life in the Victorian age in England

44. 'Black Gold' is
A. Coal B. Petrol
C. A precious stone D. Pepper

45. Modern numerals known as 'Arabic' numerals were invented by
A. Arabs B. Greeks
C. Indians D. Persians

46. The Captain of the Indian Hockey Team which won the Cup in the Triangular Tournament against Australia and Pakistan in June, 2003 was
A. Dhanraj Pillay
B. Baljit Singh Dhillon
C. Gagan Ajit Singh
D. Jugran Singh

47. Salman Rushdie had a *fatwa* against him for his book entitled
A. *Midnight's Children*
B. *The Satanic Verses*
C. *Shame*
D. *The Moor's Last Sigh*

48. David Beckham is a famous
A. Tennis Champion
B. Hollywood Actor
C. Computer Engineer
D. Football Player

49. Which highly infectious disease was declared in 1979 to have been completely eradicated?
A. Malaria B. Plague
C. Small pox D. Chicken pox

50. The name of the spaceship in which Kalpana Chawla performed her last journey is
A. Columbia B. Voyager
C. Discoverer D. Soyuz

51. Which country is bounded by Iran, Afghanistan, China and India?
A. Iraq B. Pakistan
C. Nepal D. Kazakhstan

52. When did Tenzing and Hillary reach the summit of Everest?

A. May 29, 1947
B. May 29, 1953
C. May 29, 1959
D. May 29, 1973

53. M.F. Hussain is a well known

A. Writer B. Painter
C. Sculptor D. Film Director

54. The currency of the European Union is known as

A. Mark B. Kroner
C. Euro D. Rouble

55. The film 'Devdas' is based on a novel written by

A. Sarat Chandra Chatterji
B. Bankim Chandra
C. Mahashweta Devi
D. Rabindra Nath Tagore

SECTION IV : TEACHING-LEARNING AND THE SCHOOL

56. A good teacher is one

A. who answers all questions asked by pupils
B. who tells the pupils where to find the answers
C. whose pupils do not need to ask any questions
D. who wants children to learn only what he is teaching

57. IGNOU has been established by

A. the University Grants Commission
B. Indira Gandhi
C. An Act of Parliament
D. Association of Indian Universities

58. Complete silence in a class is a necessary indication of

A. good teaching
B. classroom management
C. fear of punishment by the teacher
D. lack of interest among students

59. Children learn better when they are

A. always punished for mistakes
B. praised for good performance
C. unsure of punishment and rewards
D. left entirely to themselves

60. 'Joyful learning' is a movement based on the theory that

A. students should find joy in school learning
B. entertainment should be the main aim of education
C. all teaching should be based on playway method
D. children should be free to do whatever they like

61. School should

A. follow what the society wants it to do
B. strictly follow the rules of the government
C. always do what pleases the parents
D. give a lead to the society in the right direction

62. A teacher should proceed further in his teaching in a class only when the following have understood what he was teaching:

A. all students
B. the best students
C. the average students
D. the weak students

63. A teacher can effectively discourage students from cheating in an examination by

A. strict invigilation
B. strong punishment for cheating
C. inculcating 'honesty' as an important virtue
D. forcing social boycott of those who cheat

64. The terms *Shiksha Mitra* or *Saraswati Putra* are used for

A. persons with high general and teacher education qualifications
B. non-government organisations working for spreading education among the poor
C. members of parent-teacher associations
D. persons employed by the community to teach in primary schools, mainly in rural areas

65. Nursery schools should

A. prepare children for entrance to prestigious schools
B. provide regular instruction in the three Rs
C. somehow keep the children engaged and out of mischief
D. provide for all round natural development of children

66. 'Teacher Empowerment' essentially means
- A. authority of the teacher to decide what to teach and how
- B. complete authority for student discipline
- C. freedom to administer schools
- D. high salaries to teachers

67. From the point of view of environment, children's school bags should be made of
- A. Leather
- B. Plastic
- C. Canvas
- D. Fur

68. Mid-day meals in primary schools should be provided to
- A. all children
- B. children below the poverty line
- C. children poor in health
- D. only girls

69. A new subject for primary classes recently introduced by the NCERT is
- A. Moral Education
- B. Social Studies
- C. Art of Healthy and Productive Life
- D. Environmental Studies

70. The main objective of "Work Experience" in schools is to
- A. build strong muscles
- B. pass time usefully
- C. create respect for manual labour
- D. prepare for vocation for livelihood

71. Computer Literacy means
- A. knowledge about the origin and use of computers
- B. competence to prepare computer programme
- C. knowledge about repairing a computer
- D. elementary skills in simple use of computers

72. Non-formal education has been used in India for literacy of
- A. adults above 35 years of age
- B. age-group 15–35 years only
- C. age-group 6–14 years only
- D. age-groups 6–14 years and 15–35 years

73. If a student talks rudely to a teacher, the teacher should
- A. talk back more rudely to him
- B. complain to the Principal
- C. stop talking to him
- D. be cool and counsel him quietly later

74. Handicapped children should be
- A. kept away from normal schools and children
- B. given opportunity just like normal children
- C. treated as a liability and helped out of pity
- D. integrated in normal schools with special facilities

75. The merit of a school is best measured by
- A. the results of its students in public examinations
- B. the success of its students in the job market
- C. the emphasis on its turning out good human beings
- D. the achievements of its students in higher studies

76. Scientific Temper can be developed among children only by
- A. study of science subjects
- B. use of technological aids
- C. stimulating curiosity and inquiring mind while teaching any subject
- D. conducting practicals in a routine manner

77. A spirit of competition among students
- A. makes them perform better
- B. creates jealousy
- C. creates mental tensions
- D. develops an unhealthy personality

78. If a colleague praises a teacher to his face but talks ill of him at his back, the teacher should
- A. talk ill of him
- B. quarrel with him
- C. ignore what he says and avoid him
- D. continue keeping normal relations with him

79. Activity-centred school is one in which
- A. theory is always followed by practice
- B. practical activity forms the basis of all learning
- C. children are not passive listeners
- D. children do manual work

80. Private tuitions are ***not*** desirable because
- A. the teachers lose respect among parents
- B. they affect classroom teaching adversely
- C. they give teachers undeserved income
- D. they make children dependent and careless about self-study

PART-B

SECTION V : (I) SCIENCE

81. Which one of the following is a mixture?
A. Sugar
B. Air
C. Common salt (sodium chloride)
D. Liquid oxygen

82. One litre of oxygen at N.T.P. contains
A. $22.4 \times 6.02 \times 10^{23}$ molecules
B. 6.02×10^{23} molecules
C. 0.602×10^{23} molecules
D. $\frac{6.02 \times 10^{23}}{22.4}$ molecules

83. If 9 grams of a trivalent metal are combined with 8 grams oxygen, the atomic weight of the metal will be
A. 9 B. 18
C. 27 D. 36

84. Insulin is a
A. Vitamin B. Antibiotic
C. Hormone D. Antiseptic

85. Diamond and graphite are two forms of carbon. These are
A. Isomers B. Allotropes
C. Isotopes D. Isobars

86. Beta rays are
A. high speed electrons
B. high speed neutrons
C. high speed protons
D. doubly ionised helium atoms

87. Composition of heavy water is
A. H_2O B. D_2O
C. $(H_2O)_2$ D. $2H_2O$

88. Genetic information is stored in
A. DNA
B. RNA
C. Ribosomes
D. Endoplasmic reticulum

89. Proteins are made of
A. Fatty acids B. Sugars
C. Nucleic acids D. Amino acids

90. Parasites are characterized by the presence of
A. Root system
B. Leaves without chlorophyll
C. Velamen roots
D. Haustoria

91. Which of the following substances is produced during photosynthesis?
A. Carbohydrate B. Protein
C. Fat D. Amino acid

92. Earthworm lacks
A. Reproductive system
B. Alimentary canal
C. Excretory system
D. Distinct head

93. The term pH refers to
A. NaCl concentration in a solution
B. Hydrogen ion concentration
C. H_2O concentration in a solution
D. Sugar concentration in a solution

94. Which of the following is ***not*** related to 'distance' or 'its measurement'?
A. Micrometer B. Light year
C. Angstrom D. Hertz

95. When a constant force is applied to a body, it moves with uniform
A. Speed B. Velocity
C. Acceleration D. Momentum

96. If two equal forces have a resultant equal to the force itself, the angle between them will be
A. 0° B. 60°
C. 90° D. 120°

97. When a body is moving up, the acceleration due to gravity acting on it will be
A. Directed upwards
B. Directed downwards
C. Nil
D. Directed horizontally

98. An ice cube floats in a glass of water. When the ice cube melts, the water level will
A. Rise
B. Fall
C. Remain unchanged
D. First fall and then rise

99. If there are no scattering particles in the earth's atmosphere, the colour of the sky will be
A. Blue B. Black
C. White D. Green

100. If the length of a wire is doubled and its cross-sectional area is also doubled, the new resistance will
A. Be halved
B. Become double
C. Remain the same
D. Become four times

(II) MATHEMATICS

101. If a and b are any two consecutive integers such that $ab \neq 0$, then $a + b$ is a number which is
A. even
B. zero
C. odd
D. None of the above

102. 72% of which number is 8% of 36?
A. 324 B. 50
C. 16 D. 4

103. $\frac{3}{\sqrt{8}+\sqrt{5}}$ is equal to
A. $\sqrt{8}-\sqrt{5}$
B. $3(\sqrt{8}-\sqrt{5})$
C. $\frac{3(\sqrt{8}-\sqrt{5})}{13}$
D. $\frac{\sqrt{8}-\sqrt{5}}{13}$

104. The ratio $m : n$ is the same as
A. $m+x : n+x$ B. $m^2 : n^2$
C. $mp : nq$ D. $mx : nx$

105. The HCF of $12\,(x^3y^3)^4$, $16\,(x^4y^4)^2$ and $24\,(x^3y^3)^3$ is
A. $12\,x^3y^3$ B. $4\,x^8y^8$
C. $24\,x^{12}y^{12}$ D. $48\,x^{12}y^{12}$

106. The quadratic equation whose roots are double and opposite in sign of the roots of $x^2 + 5x + 6 = 0$ is
A. $x^2 - 10x - 24 = 0$
B. $x^2 + 10x + 24 = 0$
C. $x^2 - 10x + 24 = 0$
D. $x^2 + 10x - 24 = 0$

107. If each of the dimensions of a rectangle is increased by 100%, the area is increased by
A. 100% B. 200%
C. 300% D. 400%

108. A die is thrown once. The probability of getting a multiple of 2 or 3 is
A. 1/2 B. 1/3
C. 2/3 D. 5/6

109. A sum of money becomes double in 8 years at compound interest. In how much time will it become 8 times?
A. 16 years B. 24 years
C. 32 years D. 64 years

110. A briefcase is available for Rs. 1000 cash or for Rs. 600 cash down payment and Rs. 420 to be paid after 6 months. The excess amount of Rs. 20 is the interest charged on
A. Rs. 1000 for 6 months
B. Rs. 600 for 6 months
C. Rs. 420 for 6 months
D. Rs. 400 for 6 months

111. Two years ago a man was six times as old as his own son. In 18 years he will be twice as old as his son. Their present ages are
A. 32 years, 7 years
B. 34 years, 9 years
C. 36 years, 11 years
D. 38 years, 13 years

112. The equation $(a-b)\,x^2 + 2\,(a+b)\,x + q\,(a-b)^{-1} = 0$ has equal roots if q is
A. $a^2 + b^2$ B. $(a+b)^2$
C. $a^2 - b^2$ D. $(a-b)^2$

113. ABC is an equilateral triangle of side 4 cm, D, E, F are the mid points of BC, CA and AB. Thus DEF is a triangle. If P, Q, R are the mid points of the three sides of Δ DEF, then triangle PQR is a/an

A. isosceles triangle
B. right angled triangle
C. equilateral triangle
D. None of the above

114. The number of diagonals in a regular hexagon is

A. 6 B. 2
C. 12 D. 9

115. AOB and COD are two perpendicular diameters of a circle. P is a point on OA. If CP produced meets the circle at X then which of the following is/are correct?

A. $\angle CPO = \frac{1}{2} \angle ODX$
B. $\angle CPO = \angle ODX$
C. $\angle CPO = 2\angle ODX$
D. None of the above

116. If $\cos\theta = \frac{2a}{1+a^2}$ and θ is an acute angle, then cosec θ is

A. $\frac{1-a^2}{1+a^2}$ B. $\frac{1+a^2}{2a}$
C. $\frac{2a}{1-a^2}$ D. $\frac{1+a^2}{1-a^2}$

117. An observer, 1.5 m tall is standing $30\sqrt{3}$ m away from a tower 31.5 m high. The angle of elevation of the top of the tower from his head will be

A. 30° B. 45°
C. 60° D. 90°

118. The mean of the following distribution is:

x	10	15	20	25
Frequency	2	3	3	2

A. 225 B. 22.5
C. 175 D. 17.5

119. The length, breadth and height of a godown are in the ratio of 6 : 5 : 4. If the total surface area of the godown is 592 m^2, then its breadth is

A. 10 m B. 12 m
C. 20 m D. 8 m

120. The radius of a circular cone is halved and its height is increased 4 times. The new volume with respect to the previous one will be

A. half B. double
C. four times D. unchanged

(III) SOCIAL SCIENCE

121. Kautilya's *Arthashastra* is a book on

A. Religion
B. Principles and Practice of Statecraft
C. Duties of the king
D. Foreign Policy

122. The famous singer at Akbar's Court was

A. Birbal B. Todarmal
C. Tulsidas D. Tansen

123. Shivaji was imprisoned by Aurangzeb at

A. Agra B. Poona
C. Delhi D. Lahore

124. The Doctrine of Lapse was introduced by

A. Hastings B. Canning
C. Dalhousie D. Wellesley

125. Who was the author of *Anandmath?*

A. Sharat Chandra
B. Bankim Chandra Chattopadhyaya
C. Rabindra Nath Tagore
D. Ishwar Chandra Vidyasagar

126. Who gave us the slogan "Do or Die" during India's Struggle for Independence?

A. Mahatma Gandhi
B. Jawahar Lal Nehru
C. Bal Gangadhar Tilak
D. Subhash Chandra Bose

127. Arya Samaj was founded by

A. Gopal Krishna Gokhale
B. Bal Gangadhar Tilak
C. Swami Shraddhanand
D. Swami Dayanand Saraswati

128. Which planet is closest to the Sun?
A. Earth B. Mercury
C. Pluto D. Saturn

129. Which of the following has the oldest rocks in our country?
A. The Himalayas
B. The Shivaliks
C. The Indo-Gangetic Plains
D. The Aravallis

130. Through which states does the river Chambal flow?
A. U.P., M.P., Rajasthan
B. M.P., Gujarat, U.P.
C. Rajasthan, M.P., Bihar
D. M.P., Andhra Pradesh, U.P.

131. Which of the following rivers of India flow towards the west?
A. Godavari B. Kaveri
C. Narmada D. Krishna

132. Latitude of $23\frac{1}{2}°$ N is called
A. Tropic of Cancer
B. Tropic of Capricorn
C. Equator
D. None of the above

133. Which one is ***not*** a major port on the West Coast?
A. Cochin B. Haldia
C. New Mangalore D. Mumbai

134. The Constitution of India came into force on
A. 26th January 1952
B. 15th August 1947
C. 26th November 1949
D. 26th January 1950

135. To be eligible for election as President of India, a candidate must be
A. over 35 years of age
B. over 60 years of age
C. over 55 years of age
D. no age limit prescribed by the Constitution

136. Who is the Supreme Commander of the armed forces in India?
A. The Prime Minister
B. The Union Defence Minister
C. The Chief of the Army Staff
D. The President

137. Who of the following is considered the custodian of the Lok Sabha?
A. The Prime Minister
B. The Speaker
C. The Leader of the Opposition
D. The Chief Whip of the Ruling Party

138. The Money Bill can originate
A. only in Rajya Sabha
B. only in Lok Sabha
C. both in Rajya Sabha and Lok Sabha
D. None of the above

139. The Supreme Court of India was set up
A. by the Constitution
B. under the Indian Independence Act, 1947
C. through an Act of Parliament in 1950
D. under the Government of India Act, 1935

140. The Governor of a State in India is
A. elected by the State Legislature
B. nominated by the Prime Minister
C. appointed by the President
D. elected by the Parliament

(IV) ENGLISH

Directions (Qs. 141-142): *Fill in the blanks in the following sentences by selecting the most appropriate alternative from amongst the four choices given.*

141. I tried to give him good advice, but he ..... to listen.
A. prevented B. avoided
C. refused D. denied

142. I am given to ..... that you want to be a doctor
A. learn B. understand
C. think D. predict

Directions (Qs. 143-144): *In the following groups of words only one is spelt correctly. Select the correct one.*

143. A. Tentamount B. Tantemount
C. Tantamount D. Tentemount

144. A. Reminescent B. Riminescent
C. Reminiscent D. Riminisent

Directions: *In the following questions (145-146), out of four alternatives, choose the one which can be substituted for the given phrase.*

145. To examine one's own thoughts and feelings
A. Meditation B. Introspection
C. Retrospection D. Reflection

146. A child of unusual or remarkable talent
A. Prodigy B. Diligent
C. Freak D. Scholar

Directions (Qs. 147-148): *Given below are the four parts of a complete sentence. Mark the part which contains an error.*

147. A. The tallest
B. of the two trees
C. fell during
D. the storm yesterday

148. A. Two solutions to the traffic problem
B. have been put forward
C. but neither
D. have been tried

Directions (Qs. 149-150): *Choose the appropriate set of prepositions from those given below to fill in the blanks in the following sentences.*

149. He took advantage ..... my ignorance but gained nothing ..... the end.
A. with; in B. against; at
C. of; in D. from; for

150. His teacher went ..... endless troubles to prepare him ..... the test.
A. over; before B. over; against
C. through; in D. through; for

151. Choose the correct direct form of the given indirect sentence.
Radha asked me why I was late.
A. Radha said to me, "Why are you late?"
B. Radha said to me, "Why was I late?"
C. Radha said to me, "Why am I late?"
D. Radha said to me, "Why were you late?"

152. Choose the word from the words given below which can substitute the underlined words in both the given sentences:
I. Some of the edible oils <u>have</u> a high cholesterol content.
II. The forest authorities have failed to <u>control</u> poaching in that area.
A. contain B. suppress
C. restrain D. possess

Directions (Qs. 153-154): *In the following items choose the correct meaning of the given phrase/idiom.*

153. To bury the hatchet
A. to quarrel over small things
B. to destroy
C. to make up a quarrel
D. to repair costly furniture

154. A bolt from the blue
A. a great calamity
B. a strange event
C. a painful event
D. an unexpected and unwelcome event

Directions (Qs. 155-156): *Choose the word that is opposite in meaning to the bold word in the given sentences.*

155. Now-a-days the market is full of **spurious** drugs
A. costly B. powerful
C. effective D. genuine

156. We have to fight against **dog-matism** and fanaticism.
A. open-mindedness B. clarity
C. freedom D. tolerance

Directions (Qs. 157-158): *Choose the word which is nearest in meaning to the bold word from the words given below.*

157. A **conscientious** worker is always admired by everyone.
A. obedient B. sincere
C. skilful D. careful

158. Dr. S. Radhakrishnan has written and **erudite** commentary on the Bhagwad Gita.
A. scholarly B. inspiring
C. effective D. perfect

159. Given below is an active sentence. Choose the passive form of the sentence from the alternatives given below:
Subhash Chandra Bose formed the Indian National Army for the liberation of his beloved motherland, India.

A. The Indian National Army was formed by Subhash Chandra Bose for the liberation of his beloved motherland, India
B. The Indian National Army formed Subhash Chandra Bose for the liberation of his beloved motherland, India
C. Subhash Chandra Bose was formed the Indian National Army for the liberation of his motherland, India
D. The Indian National Army for the liberation of his motherland, India formed by Subhash Chandra Bose

160. Choose the correct tense of the verb in the given sentence from the options given below: The Constitution of India had come into force from 26th January, 1950.
A. Simple Past
B. Past Continuous
C. Past Perfect
D. Past Perfect Continuous

(V) हिन्दी

निर्देशः *दिए गए गद्यांश को ध्यान से पढ़िए और बाद में पूछे गए प्रश्नों (161 से 165) के उत्तर दीजिए।*

मनुष्य जीवन में अधिकतर समय और शक्ति पैसा अर्जित करने में ख़र्च हो जाते हैं। आख़िर मनुष्य द्रव्यार्जन के लिए इतनी दौड़ धूप क्यों करता है? इस प्रश्न का सीधा उत्तर है कि जीवन के लगभग सभी भौतिक सुख सम्पत्ति की सहायता से ही प्राप्त होते हैं। इसमें कोई संदेह नहीं कि मनुष्य की भौतिक आवश्यकताओं को पूरा किया जाना आवश्यक है। भौतिक आवश्यकताओं की पूर्ति और जीवन के सर्वांगीण विकास में बहुत घनिष्ठ संबंध है। न केवल मनुष्य के सर्वोमुखी विकास के लिए अपितु उसके जीवन-धारण के लिए भी न्यूनतम अर्थ की आवश्यकता होती है। इस न्यूनतम अर्थ का भी अभाव हो तो मनुष्य को रोटी और कपड़े की चिन्ता सताती है। उसका अधिकतर समय और शक्ति इनकी व्यवस्था करने में समाप्त हो जाएंगे। जीवन का सुख और सन्तोष उसके लिए दुर्लभ हो जाएंगे।

गद्यांश के आधार पर निम्नलिखित प्रश्न (161 से 165), उत्तर के विकल्पों के साथ दिए गए हैं। सही विकल्प को चुनिए।

161. व्यक्ति अपना अधिकतर समय व्यतीत करता है
A. सर्वतोमुखी विकास में
B. द्रव्यार्जन में
C. भौतिक सुख-प्राप्ति में
D. पैसा खर्च करने में

162. मनुष्य धन कमाता है ताकि
A. सम्पत्ति जुड़ सके
B. भौतिक सुख मिल सके
C. सुख और सन्तोष मिले
D. सर्वांगीण विकास हो

163. भौतिक आवश्यकताओं की पूर्ति का घनिष्ठ संबंध है
A. पैसा कमाने से
B. जीवन-धारण से
C. सर्वांगीण विकास से
D. रोटी और कपड़ा से

164. मनुष्य की शक्ति प्रायः व्यय होती है
A. मौलिक आवश्यकताओं की पूर्ति में
B. दौड़-धूप में
C. जीवन-धारण में
D. सुख-सम्पत्ति कमाने में

165. इस गद्यांश का उपयुक्त शीर्षक है
A. जीवन का उद्देश्य
B. धनार्जन का महत्त्व
C. सर्वांगीण विकास
D. भौतिक सुख

निर्देश (प्रश्न 166 से 180)ः *प्रत्येक प्रश्न के उत्तर के रूप में चार-चार विकल्प दिए गए हैं। सही विकल्प को चुनिए।*

166. ब्रज भाषा का विकास किस भाषा से हुआ?
A. अर्धमागधी
B. शौरसेनी
C. पालि
D. पैशाची

167. तुलसीदास ने किस ग्रंथ की रचना की?
A. उत्तर रामचरित
B. बालचरित
C. तुलसी रामायण
D. रामचरितमानस

168. कौन-सी वर्तनी शुद्ध है?
A. आर्शीवाद
B. आशिर्वाद
C. आशीर्वाद
D. आर्शिवाद

169. "सीता हँसती है।" वाक्य में कौन-सी क्रिया है?
A. अकर्मक
B. द्विकर्मक
C. विकर्मक
D. सकर्मक

170. "नौ दो ग्यारह होना" का अर्थ है
A. सही गणित करना

B. नौ जमा दो ग्यारह होना
C. जल्दी-जल्दी करना
D. भाग जाना

171. करण कारक के लिए प्रयोग होता है
A. से (पृथक् होना) B. के लिए
C. से (द्वारा) D. का, के, की

172. "यामा" किस लेखक की कृति है?
A. सुभद्रा कुमारी चौहान
B. महादेवी वर्मा
C. हरिवंश राय बच्चन
D. सूर्यकान्त त्रिपाठी निराला

173. तत्पुरुष समास में कौन-सा पद प्रधान होता है?
A. पूर्वपद B. अन्यपद
C. उभयपद D. उत्तरपद

174. सही वाक्य क्या है?
A. लड़कियों को रस्सी से बांधकर लकड़ियों को दे दो।
B. रस्सी से बांधकर लड़कियों को लकड़ियाँ दे दो।
C. लकड़ियों को रस्सी से बांधकर लड़कियों को दे दो।
D. लकड़ियाँ लड़कियों को रस्सी से बांधकर दे दो।

175. माता-पिता में किस समास का प्रयोग है?
A. बहुव्रीहि B. द्वन्द्व
C. द्विगु D. कर्मधारय

176. यदि + अपि = यद्यपि में कौन-सी सन्धि है?
A. यण् B. गुण
C. वृद्धि D. दीर्घ

177. तीव्र का विलोम क्या है?
A. तेज़ B. धीमा
C. मन्द D. जल्दी

178. उर्मिला उपन्यास के लेखक कौन हैं?
A. जयशंकर प्रसाद B. इलाचन्द्र जोशी
C. सुदर्शन D. प्रेमचन्द

179. "जैसे उड़ि जहाज को पंछी फिरि जहाज पर आवै" यहां पंछी का अर्थ है
A. पक्षी B. यात्री
C. मन D. नाविक

180. "राम से बैठा न गया" यहाँ कौन-सा वाच्य है?
A. भाववाच्य B. कर्मवाच्य
C. कर्तृवाच्य D. मिश्रवाच्य

ANSWERS

1	2	3	4	5	6	7	8	9	10
B	C	B	C	B	C	A	A	D	B
11	**12**	**13**	**14**	**15**	**16**	**17**	**18**	**19**	**20**
A	D	D	A	C	B	A	C	B	C
21	**22**	**23**	**24**	**25**	**26**	**27**	**28**	**29**	**30**
A	B	D	B	D	C	A	D	B	C
31	**32**	**33**	**34**	**35**	**36**	**37**	**38**	**39**	**40**
D	C	C	D	C	A	D	B	D	A
41	**42**	**43**	**44**	**45**	**46**	**47**	**48**	**49**	**50**
A	D	A	A	C	A	B	D	B	A
51	**52**	**53**	**54**	**55**	**56**	**57**	**58**	**59**	**60**
B	B	B	C	A	B	C	A	C	A
61	**62**	**63**	**64**	**65**	**66**	**67**	**68**	**69**	**70**
D	A	C	D	D	A	C	A	D	B
71	**72**	**73**	**74**	**75**	**76**	**77**	**78**	**79**	**80**
D	B	D	D	C	C	A	D	B	D
81	**82**	**83**	**84**	**85**	**86**	**87**	**88**	**89**	**90**
B	B	C	C	B	A	B	A	D	D
91	**92**	**93**	**94**	**95**	**96**	**97**	**98**	**99**	**100**
A	D	B	D	C	D	B	B	B	C

101	102	103	104	105	106	107	108	109	110
C	D	A	D	B	C	C	C	B	D
111	112	113	114	115	116	117	118	119	120
A	B	C	D	B	D	A	D	A	D
121	122	123	124	125	126	127	128	129	130
B	D	A	C	B	A	D	B	D	A
131	132	133	134	135	136	137	138	139	140
C	A	B	D	A	D	B	B	D	C
141	142	143	144	145	146	147	148	149	150
C	A	C	C	B	A	A	D	C	D
151	152	153	154	155	156	157	158	159	160
A	A	C	D	D	A	B	A	A	C
161	162	163	164	165	166	167	168	169	170
B	B	C	A	B	B	D	C	A	D
171	172	173	174	175	176	177	178	179	180
C	B	D	C	B	A	C	B	C	B

SOME SELECTED EXPLANATORY ANSWERS

11. 68 64 32 28 14 10 5 1
(−4, ÷2, −4, ÷2, −4, ÷2, −4)

12. 5 10 20 40 80 160
(×2, ×2, ×2, ×2, ×2)

13. $$\frac{50}{100}\times\frac{10}{100}\times\frac{25}{100}\times\frac{40}{100}\times\frac{60}{100}\times 2000 = 6$$

14. 3 6 9 12 15 18 21 24 27
(3×1, 3×2, 3×3, 3×4, 3×5, 3×6, 3×7, 3×8, 3×9)

15. The multiplication of all the integers from –4 to +4 = 0

$-4\times-3\times-2\times-1\times0\times1\times2\times3\times4=0$

16. $\frac{C}{100}=\frac{F-32}{180}$ or, $\frac{C}{100}=\frac{104-32}{180}$ or,

$$\frac{C}{100}=\frac{72}{180}$$

or, $C=\frac{72\times100}{180}=40°$

17. According to problem 2 litres petrol was used

Now $\frac{4}{5}-\frac{2}{3}=\frac{2}{15}$ parts

$\therefore$ $\frac{2}{15}$ parts = 2 litres

$\therefore$ 1 or full = $\frac{2\times15}{2}$ = 15 litres

18. According to the question, the time taken by 4 monkeys will be same by 8 monkeys in eating the bananas.

22. As water is related to thirst
So food is related to hunger.

23. As the word SCHOOL is reversed as LOOHCS.
In the same way TEACHER will be REHCAET.

24. U J H → T H E In the same way
(−1, −2, −3)

Q Q V M Y O V V
↓ ↓ ↓ ↓ ↓ ↓ ↓ ↓
P O S I T I O N

25. According to the question,
The number cards are = 1, 2, 3, 4, 5, 6, 7, 8, 9 and 10, 1 + 2 + 3 + 4 + 5 + 6 + 7 + 8 + 9 + 10 = 55
There are four categories of cards
$\therefore$ Total value of the number cards = 55 × 4 = 220

26. Let the age of younger brother = x years and the age of elder brother = y years
According to the question

$$3(x-2) = y-2$$

$$3x-6 = y-2$$
$$3x-y = -2+6$$
$$3x-y = 4 \quad ...(i)$$

According to second condition

$$(x+3)\times 2 = y+3$$
$$2x+6 = y+3$$
$$2x-y = -6+3$$

After transposal

$$2x-y = -3 \quad ...(ii)$$

After solving the equations (*i*) and (*ii*),

we get $x = 7$ and $y = 17$

27. The man was born in Leap year. Therefore, his birthday will be in only in Leap year. There are 14 leap years from 1944 to 2000.

$\therefore$ The man had 14 times of his birthday.

28. Ravi — Shashi — Suraj — Tara

According to the question,

Let Shashi picked A shells

then Ravi picked = (A + 7)

and Suraj picked = {(A + 7) + 1}

Tara picked = {(A + 7) + 1} – 9

= (A – 1) shells

$\therefore$ Answer is Tara.

101. If a and b are two consecutive integers

$\therefore$ If $a = 2x$

then $b = 2x+1$

$\therefore$ $a+b = 2x+2x+1 = 4x+1$

$\therefore$ + 1 shows the number will be odd.

102. Let the number be = x

$\therefore$ 8% of 36 = 72% of x

$$\therefore \frac{8}{100} \text{ of } 36 = \frac{72}{100} \text{ of } x$$

$$\frac{8}{100}\times 36 = x\times\frac{72}{100}$$

$$x = \frac{8\times 36\times 100}{100\times 72} = 4$$

103. $\dfrac{3}{\sqrt{8}+\sqrt{5}}$

Multiply $\sqrt{8}-\sqrt{5}$ in numerator and denominator.

$$= \frac{3}{\sqrt{8}+\sqrt{5}}\times\frac{\sqrt{8}-\sqrt{5}}{\sqrt{8}-\sqrt{5}}$$

$$= \frac{3\left(\sqrt{8}-\sqrt{5}\right)}{\left(\sqrt{8}\right)^2-\left(\sqrt{5}\right)^2} = \frac{3\left(\sqrt{8}-\sqrt{5}\right)}{8-5}$$

$$\because (a+b)(a-b) = a^2-b^2$$

$$= \frac{3\left(\sqrt{8}-\sqrt{5}\right)}{3} = \sqrt{8}-\sqrt{5}$$

104. $m:n = \dfrac{m}{n}$.

If numerator and denominator are multiplied by same number there will be no difference.

$\therefore$ The answer is $\dfrac{mx}{nx}$ or $mx : nx$

105.

$$12\,(x^3y^3)^2 = 12.x^{12}.y^{12}$$
$$16\,(x^4y^4)^2 = 16.x^8.y^8$$
$$24\,(x^3y^3)^3 = 24.x^9\,y^9$$

H.C.F. of 12, 16 and 24 = 4

H.C.F. of $x^{12}y^{12}$, x^8y^8 and $x^9y^9 = x^8y^8$

$\therefore$ H.C.F. = $4\,x^8y^8$

106. Let the roots be α and β of equation

$x^2+5x+6=0$

$$\therefore \quad x = \frac{-b\pm\sqrt{b^2-4ac}}{2a}$$

$$= \frac{-5\pm\sqrt{5^2-4\times 1\times 6}}{2\times 1}$$

$$= \frac{-5\pm\sqrt{25-24}}{2}$$

$$\alpha = \frac{-5+1}{2} = \frac{-4}{2} = -2$$

$$\beta = \frac{-5-1}{2} = -\frac{6}{2} = -3$$

According to question, now

$\alpha = 4$

$\beta = 6$

$\therefore$ Required equation

$$= x^2-(\alpha+\beta)\,x+\alpha\beta$$
$$= x^2-(4+6)\,x+4\times 6$$
$$= x^2-10x+24$$

107. (rectangle with sides x and y)

Let the length of rectangle = x metres and breadth of rectangle = y metre

$\therefore$ Area = xy m^2

According to question, length and breadth are increased by 100%

$\therefore$ Length = $2x$ metres

Breadth = $2y$ metres

Area = $2x \times 2y = 4xy$ m^2

Difference in area = $4xy - xy = 3xy\ m^2$

$\therefore$ % increase = $\dfrac{3xy \times 100}{xy} = 300\%$

108. The multiple of 2 or 3 in the die = 2, 3, 4, 6

$\therefore$ Probability = 4

$\therefore$ Priority of probability = $\dfrac{4}{6} = \dfrac{2}{3}$

109. Amount = Principal $\left(1 + \dfrac{R}{100}\right)^T$

where R = Rate of interest

T = Time

According to question,

Let P be Principal

$$\therefore \quad 2P = P\left(1 + \frac{R}{100}\right)^8$$

$$2 = \left(1 + \frac{R}{100}\right)^8$$

It shows that principal becomes double in 8 years

$\therefore$ It will be 8 times

$$= 2^3 = \left\{\left(1 + \frac{R}{100}\right)^8\right\}^3$$

$$= 8 = \left(1 + \frac{R}{100}\right)^{24}$$

= 24 years

110. The cost price of the briefcase = Rs 1000

Cash payment = Rs 600

Remaining amount = 1000 – 600 = Rs 400

Time = 6 months

Payment after 6 months = Rs 420

Interest = 420 – 400 = Rs 20

$\therefore$ Rs. 20 is the interest charged on Rs. 400 for 6 months

111. Let the age of the son = x years

And the age of the father = y years

2 years ago, the age of the son = $(x - 2)$ years

2 years ago, the age of the father = $(y - 2)$ years

According to the question –

$$6(x-2) = (y-2)$$
$$6x - 12 = y - 2$$
$$6x - y = 12 - 2$$
$$6x - y = 10 \qquad ...(i)$$

After 18 years,

The age of the son = $(x + 18)$ years

The age of the father = $(y + 18)$ years

According to second condition–

$$2(x + 18) = y + 18$$
$$2x + 36 = y + 18$$
$$2x - y = -36 + 18$$
$$2x - y = -18 \qquad ...(ii)$$

from eqns. (i) and (ii)

$$\begin{array}{rcr} 6x - y &=& 10 \\ 2x - y &=& -18 \\ - \quad + && + \\ \hline 4x &=& 28 \\ \hline \end{array}$$

$x = 7$

Put the value of x in eqn. (1)

$$6x - y = 10$$
$$6 \times 7 - y = 10$$
$$42 - y = 10$$
$$y = 32$$

112. $(a-b)x^2 + 2(a+b)x + q(a-b)^{-1} = 0$

Roots are equal, if

$$b^2 - 4ac = 0$$

$\Rightarrow \quad b^2 = 4ac$

$\Rightarrow [2(a+b)]^2 = 4 \times (a-b).\ [q(a-b)^{-1}]$

$\Rightarrow 4(a+b)^2 = 4(a-b)q.\ \dfrac{1}{(a-b)}$

$q = (a+b)^2$

113. 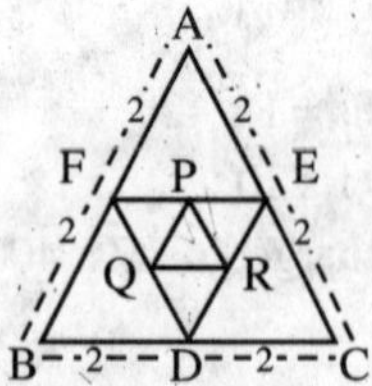

AB = AC = BC = 4 cm

$$\frac{AB}{2} = \frac{AC}{2} = \frac{BC}{2} = \frac{4}{2} = 2 \text{ cm}$$

AF = BF = AE = EC = BD = DC = 2 cm

AC || FD

BC || FE

and AB || ED

∴ FD = DE = EF = 2 cm

In the same way PQ = QR = PR = 1 cm

∴ The triangle is equilateral triangle.

114. 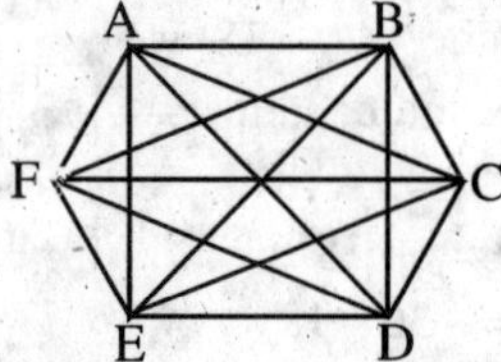

The number of diagonals in a regular hexagon = 9 (AE, AD, AC, BF, BE, BD, FC, EC, FD)

115. 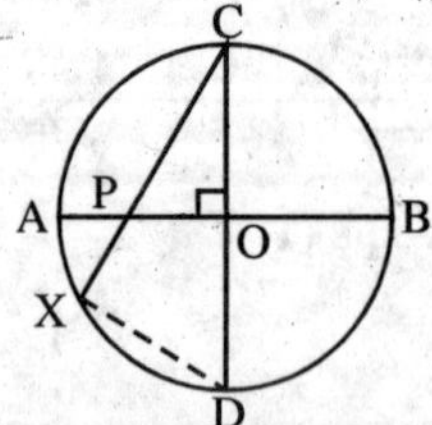

In Δ CPO and Δ CXD

∠COP = ∠CXD = 90°

Because angle formed by diameter at circumference = 90°

∠PCO = ∠XCD

∴ Third angle ∠CPO = ∠CDX

(∵ sum of three angles of a triangle = 180°)

∴ ∠CPO = ∠CDX = ∠ODX

117. 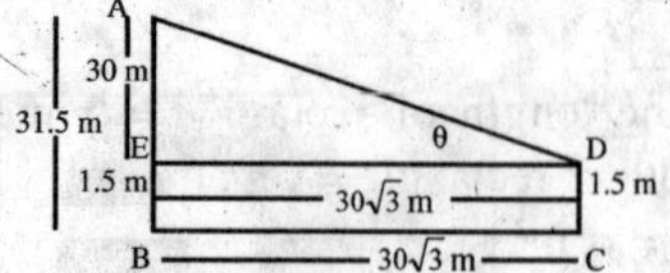

$$\tan\theta = \frac{AE}{DE}$$

$$\tan\theta = \frac{30}{30\sqrt{3}} = \frac{1}{\sqrt{3}}$$

$$\tan\theta = \frac{1}{\sqrt{3}} \text{ \& } \tan 30° = \frac{1}{\sqrt{3}}$$

$$\therefore \theta = 30°$$

119. 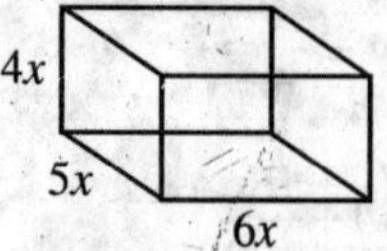

Length : Breadth : Height = 6 : 5 : 4

Length = $6x$

Breadth = $5x$

Height = $4x$

The total surface area of the godown = 2 (Length × Breadth + Length× Height + Breadth × Height)

$592 = 2(6x.5x + 6x.4x + 5x.4x)$

$592 = 148x^2$

$\Rightarrow x^2 = 4 \quad \Rightarrow x = 2$

∴ Breadth = $5x = 5 \times 2 = 10$ m

120. According to question

$$\frac{\text{Volume of first cone}}{\text{Volume of new cone}}$$

$$= \frac{\frac{1}{3}\pi r^2 h}{\frac{1}{3}\pi\left(\frac{r}{2}\right)^2 4h} = \frac{r^2 h}{\frac{r^2}{4}.4h} = \frac{1}{1} = \text{unchanged}$$